T0270500

Explorer

The Life of **Richard E. Byrd**

Lisle A. Rose

UNIVERSITY OF MISSOURI PRESS

COLUMBIA

Copyright © 2008 by
The Curators of the University of Missouri
University of Missouri Press, Columbia, Missouri 65211
Printed and bound in the United States of America
All rights reserved
First paperback printing, 2024

Library of Congress Cataloging-in-Publication Data

Rose, Lisle A., 1936–
    Explorer : the life of Richard E. Byrd / Lisle A. Rose.
        p.   cm.
    Summary: "Rose presents the first complete biography of this popular
yet controversial explorer, including his first adventure in Greenland in
1925, his flights to the North and South Poles and across the Atlantic,
his soul-shattering ordeal in Antartica at Advance Base in 1934, and the
decline of his later years"—Provided by pubisher.
    Includes bibliographical references and index.
    ISBN 978-0-8262-1782-0 (hardcover alk. paper) | 978-0-8262-2324-1 (paperback alk. paper)
    1. Byrd, Richard Evelyn, 1888–1957.   2. Explorers—United States—
Biography.   I. Title.
    G585.B8R68 2008
    919.8'904—dc22
    [B]

                                                    2007035754

⊚™ This paper meets the requirements of the
American National Standard for Permanence of Paper
for Printed Library Materials, Z39.48, 1984.

Designer: Kristie Lee
Typesetter: The Composing Room of Michigan, Inc.
Typefaces: Adobe Garamond, Stone Sans, and Rockwell

The University of Missouri Press offers its grateful acknowledgment to
an anonymous donor whose generous grant in support of the publication
of outstanding manuscripts has assisted us with this volume.

For Lt. Lyle Philip ("Phil") Tonne, USN, and
Col. Quenten Wilkes, USAF: Absent friends

Contents

List of Maps ix

Acknowledgments xi

Introduction 1

Chapter 1   "Danger Was All That Thrilled Him" 7

Chapter 2   Reaching for the Skies 30

Chapter 3   Breakthrough 60

Chapter 4   Triumph 101

Chapter 5   Hero 144

Chapter 6   Celebrity 169

Chapter 7   The Secret Land 181

Chapter 8   Southward 215

Chapter 9   Zenith 249

Chapter 10 Politico 284

Chapter 11 Jeopardy 313

Chapter 12 Breakdown 343

Chapter 13 Stumbling 384

Chapter 14 Recovery 405

Chapter 15 "Ever a Fighter So" 431

Notes 463

Selected Bibliography 515

Index 521

Maps

North Polar Region xiii

Route Flown by Byrd, May 9, 1926 xiv

Antarctic Continent xv

Aerial Flights during the First Byrd Antarctic Expedition xvi

Official Map of the Second Byrd Antarctic Expedition xvii

Summer Field Explorations of 1934 xviii

Flight Tracks of Air Operations, Operation Highjump xix

Acknowledgments

Any book is a collaboration among many people, and *Explorer* is no exception. The manuscript has been read and greatly strengthened by Raimond Goerler, John Behrendt, and my wife, Harriet Dashiell Schwar. Professor Behrendt in particular saved me from a number of embarrassing errors of fact and interpretation regarding Antarctic science. Navy navigator John Rose read the chapter on the North Polar flight and provided several maps. Professor Goerler, Laura Kissel, and the staff of the Byrd Polar Archives at The Ohio State University in Columbus have been unfailingly helpful and pleasant through the more than half-dozen years I have worked on the project, pointing me to important materials I might have otherwise missed, and discussing various aspects of Richard Byrd's life and times. Their professionalism is impressive, their unflagging enthusiasm and support deeply appreciated.

The good people of Winchester, Virginia, particularly Senator Harry F. Byrd, Professor Warren Hofstra of Shenandoah University, the Winchester-Frederick County Historical Society, and the staff of the Handley Regional Library, were unfailingly hospitable and helpful during my brief stays there. Senator Byrd devoted a morning to discussing his famous uncle with me, while Professor Hofstra rather ignited this entire project when he kindly invited me to speak at the centenary of Richard Byrd's birth so many years ago.

Liz Safly and her colleagues in the manuscript division of the Harry S. Truman Library, Independence, Missouri, provided me with key materials on Admiral Byrd's steadily deteriorating relations with President Truman and the unhappy results, while the staffs of the National Archives and Records Service Center in Suitland, Maryland, and the Library of Congress facilitated my research into the papers of Byrd's polar colleagues.

Bolling Byrd Clarke answered a number of key questions I had as the manuscript developed. Wendell Summers, Elgin Long, William Molett, and Thomas J. Poulter Jr. readily granted permission to quote from critically important unpublished materials, while Bryan Shoemaker, Colin Bull, Merlyn D. Paine, Dian Olson Belanger, and Sheldon Mark provided encouragement along the way. Mr. Summers also provided a fascinating character portrait of the Admiral of the Antarctic. Jon and Kathy Campbell provided great kindness—and several important sources—at a dark moment.

Finally, I owe special gratitude to Beverly Jarrett, Jane Lago, Clair Willcox, Annette Wenda, and the rest of the staff at the University of Missouri Press who have once again, much to my joy, taken on a major project. No writer anywhere can find a finer group of professionals with whom to work.

With such impressive backing, it hardly needs to be said that all errors of fact and interpretation that may remain are solely my responsibility.

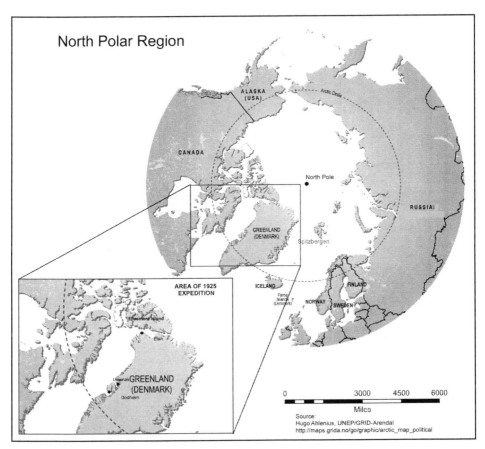

North Polar Region

AREA OF 1925 EXPEDITION

Source:
Hugo Ahlenius, UNEP/GRID-Arendal
http://maps.grida.no/go/graphic/arctic_map_political

Created by John M. Rose, 2007.

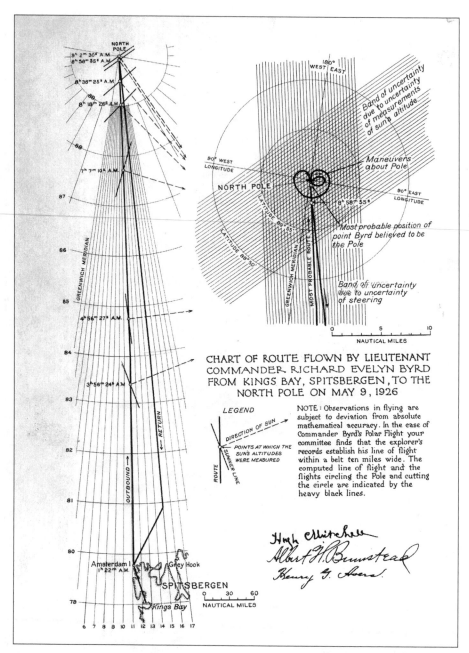

CHART OF ROUTE FLOWN BY LIEUTENANT COMMANDER RICHARD EVELYN BYRD FROM KINGS BAY, SPITSBERGEN, TO THE NORTH POLE ON MAY 9, 1926

LEGEND

NOTE: Observations in flying are subject to deviation from absolute mathematical accuracy. In the case of Commander Byrd's Polar Flight your committee finds that the explorer's records establish his line of flight within a belt ten miles wide. The computed line of flight and the flights circling the Pole and cutting the circle are indicated by the heavy black lines.

Courtesy Byrd Polar Research Center Archives, The Ohio State University, Columbus.

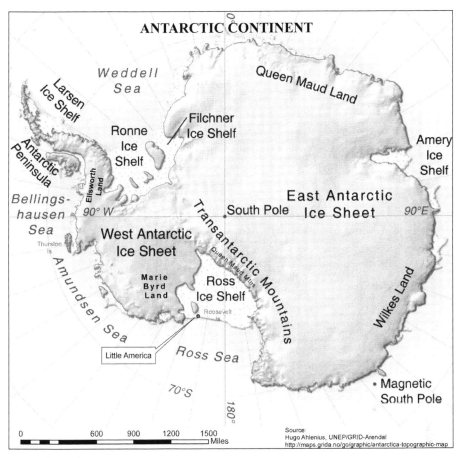

Created by John M. Rose, 2007.

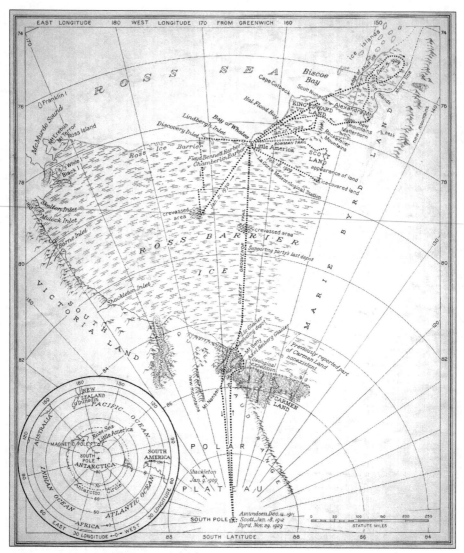

Contemporary map of aerial flights (including the South Pole) during the First Byrd
Antarctic Expedition, 1928–1930. Courtesy Byrd Polar Research Center Archives,
The Ohio State University, Columbus.

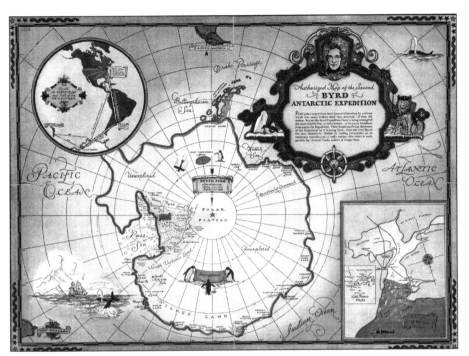

Official map of the Second Byrd Antarctic Expedition, 1933–1935, with inset map of the Bay of Whales. Courtesy Byrd Polar Research Center Archives, The Ohio State University, Columbus.

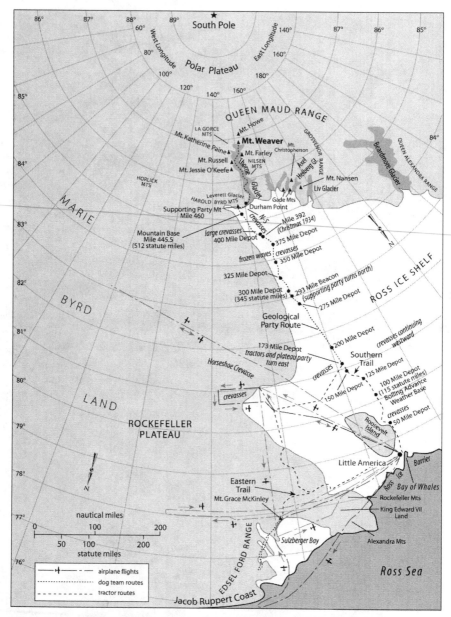

The summer field explorations of 1934 included operations for aircraft and the three main surface parties. To Mile 173, the routes for the tractors and Supporting, Plateau, and Geological parties overlapped; to Mile 293, only the Supporting and Geological parties overlapped. From Mile 293, the Geological Party continued south alone. (Some map information derived from "Operations Map," *National Geographic,* 1935, by Commander Harold E. Saunders, USN, Rawson and Darley, archived at the Byrd Polar Research Center, Papers of Admiral Richard E. Byrd, 9267.) Courtesy of M. L. Paine

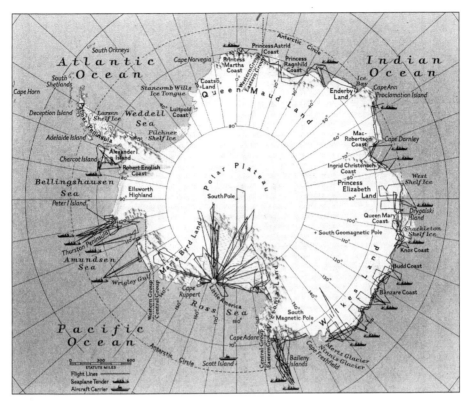

Flight tracks of air operations, Operation Highjump, December 1946–March 1947.
Courtesy Byrd Polar Research Center Archives, The Ohio State University, Columbus.

Explorer

Introduction

There are no heroes now. Our cynical, mistrustful age has no use for them, nor for adventuring, which all too often seems contrived and, in the case of amateurs on Everest, foolhardy as well. The world's last legitimate explorers, NASA's lunar astronauts, might have been the high priests of the Right Stuff, but they were also Spam in a can. As long as they performed for the space agency, their free spirits were subordinated and sanitized to conform to an image of bloodless competence. They played not many roles but just one: interchangeable cogs in a drama that exalted technology above humanity. Not even the *Challenger* and *Columbia* disasters could efface the image or change the reality.

But in the years between the world wars, when the twentieth century was still young and the Western public grasped at the last fragile tendrils of belief and hope left from the physical and moral wreckage of the western front, great men performing valiant deeds in far-off, exotic places could still set popular pulses pounding. For many years, Richard Evelyn Byrd stood above all the rest—even Lindbergh.

In the drab Depression years of the midthirties, a newspaper editor gushed, "'Dickey' Byrd is going south again! What romance is wrapped in those few words!" What a relief for readers and radio listeners, tired of the deadly squabbles between Europe's dictators and democrats and ground down by the daily effort to make or find a living in the midst of constant privation, to imaginatively follow the admiral back down to that remote, frozen land at the bottom of the earth where courageous men accomplished great things in the bleak polar wastes. "Romance again! As in the days of Lindbergh," when a lone eagle had winged his way across a vast, stormy ocean to Paris and into the hearts of the world. Byrd himself, "with several companions," had followed Lucky Lindy across the Atlantic "and made history by such daring." But where Lindbergh had retreated into a stubborn privacy, then fled the country following the kidnap-murder of his infant son, Byrd kept himself before the public with a series of adventures that comprised "the whole-

1

some things of modern days which lifts the spirit out of the rut of depression and puts us once again into the realms of romantic life."[1]

There has been no one quite like him in American life. Born a little less than a quarter century after the Civil War in a quiet agricultural corner of a defeated southern state, Byrd left Dixie to become in the 1920s and '30s a Boston gentleman and the emblem of American industrial enterprise on the far frontiers of global exploration. He became a decisive figure whose achievements helped shape the last hundred years into the American century. Few men live their dreams. Richard Byrd did. And he tasted all the joys, triumphs, disappointments, animosities, and loneliness that the experience inevitably conveys.

At the beginning of World War II, journalist and publicist Charlie Murphy, who probably knew Byrd as well as anyone, observed that despite its continued dash and glamour, exploring was not only a "backward profession" but a dying one. Personal, derring-do exploration had become a way of life in the nineteenth century as eager Europeans pushed into darkest Africa, the remotest mountain and desert areas of Asia, and the Far North, seeking river sources, maritime passages, exotic flora and fauna, and hitherto unknown peoples and tribes, all in the name and service of Knowledge. After 1900 the polar regions had become the world's last frontier, and epic races to reach the top and bottom of the earth had thrilled publics from Moscow to Manchester to Modesto. Newspapers and book publishers paid lavishly for exclusive rights to tales of discoveries on the far fringes of the known world. But with much of the globe apparently known and sketched in by 1918, the professional explorer became "an anachronistic fragment, caught like the kangaroo, behind the evolutionary eight ball," his innate romanticism "suspect in a materialistic world." The enormous sums paid to the greatest twentieth-century adventurers fell far short of their needs, and most lived and perished on the edge of penury. Wealthy dilettantes such as Lincoln Ellsworth or "museum explorers" dedicated to writing monographs or filling specimen cases might justify their escapist motives. But the old-time professional explorer who determinedly plied his trade was "doomed by a shrinking geography to comb comparatively worthless vacancies" and may even have been "ashamed to justify exploring for exploring's sake."

Not Dick Byrd. When Roald Amundsen disappeared forever into the Arctic mists in 1928, Byrd caught the Norwegian's falling torch to become "the world's No. 1 explorer." From the outset, he was dependent on the rich and famous for handouts to buy ships, planes, and supplies, "and upon lectures and books for a wage." Yet somehow he pulled it off. While others fell by the wayside or cut back sensational plans, finding that all their "endurance and resourcefulness developed by their Spartan travels are inadequate to solve the problem of earning a living between times at home," Byrd had become "the financial genius of the ice caps . . . still plying his trade on the grand scale." As he himself remarked, "I've put exploration into Big Business." His achievements strengthened an already striking "pride of family" and gave to his character and to features that were "feminine in their delicacy" a "latent imperiousness."[2]

Byrd loved not only heroic adventure but also politics, power, and influence, and he played the game of public policy with relish and some success from the twenties to the end of his life. Early in his career the ambitious young naval officer became friends with Franklin Roosevelt, while his always affectionate and caring brother Harry became the dominant political force in Virginia and then a major conservative influence on the national scene. Richard plotted and maneuvered behind the scenes of Democratic Party politics in the twenties. He worked to elect FDR in 1932 and to launch the New Deal the following year. As the European dictators rose to power he became a prominent spokesman for international peace. When war divided the nation between isolationists and interventionists in 1940 and 1941, Byrd abandoned his peace crusade and spoke out on behalf of his old friend in the White House. In World War II he made significant contributions to victory through airpower. In the early fifties, as a cold war strategist, he helped persuade foreign and military policy makers of the critical importance of the Arctic and especially Greenland in any future air war with the Soviet Union before turning to international refugee work. One of his last correspondents was South Vietnam's Ngo Dinh Diem.

He enjoyed the good life onto whose lower rungs he had been born as a certifiable Virginia gentleman, and he came to revere business and those businessmen who so materially aided him over the years as the exemplifications of American greatness and can-do progress. Among his closest friends were the titans of American enterprise Edsel Ford, John D. Rockefeller Jr., John and Rodman Wanamaker, and Thomas Watson of IBM. They, in turn, revered him for his organizational skills and fiscal integrity in mounting his great South Polar expeditions and his almost puppylike willingness to place his glory and prestige at their call.

As his ceaselessly busy and adventurous life unfolded, he helped shape the notion, function, and role of celebrity in popular culture. The documentaries that Hollywood faithfully turned out about his South Polar adventures were filled with tension and drama, much of it contrived or exaggerated; his many well-written books and articles celebrated heroic striving, with himself always leading a bracing band of adventurers; and his appearance at every town and city on his interminable lecture tours was always the occasion for luncheons, dinners, meetings with schoolchildren, and adulatory editorials in the local press. He became for several generations of Americans the personification of adventure.

Yet even in the midst of an exciting and demanding public life, Dick Byrd never forgot those who helped him to the top. The successes that many of those who wintered over in Antarctica later enjoyed were due in varying measure to Byrd's continuing interest in and friendly concern for their welfare, "repaying his perceived moral debt to them by support in their career moves. In extremely few cases did a man fail in gratitude for all that being a 'Byrdman' meant to his subsequent career."3 Byrd's private papers fully support biologist Alton Lindsey's grateful memory. Literally folder upon folder is crammed with congratulatory or supportive correspondence between Byrd and one or more of his "boys." Other folders are full of letters from Byrd to one or more of his friends or agents around the country, pleading the cause of this or that former expedition member who had fallen on hard times. Could not something be done for him?

Most of his men responded with affection and respect, if not outright adoration. Edward Goodale, himself no slouch when it came to courage out on a distant Antarctic trail, wrote that Byrd "was as brave a man as I ever knew." Years later the dog team driver marveled "to see how the man could go out and plan these major expeditions and accomplishments, knowing full well that he would have to face dangerous situations where his life could be threatened."4

Byrd was remarkably fortunate in all his endeavors. In the two privately sponsored Antarctic expeditions that he commanded he never lost a man, despite a number of potentially disastrous situations. South Polar weather and the Antarctic terrain "are treacherous and unpredictable," Lindsey observed, and most of Byrd's young men had had no contact with them. (Exploring in those days was a young man's game, and the average age of the fifty-three people wintering over on the second Byrd Antarctic expedition was twenty-six.) "We were, especially during the field season, scattered widely in small groups, over a vast landscape, or alone as I usually was when working on animal life." Lindsey quoted British polar authority Brian Roberts's observation that in hindsight it is impossible not to wonder in looking back on those Byrd expeditions "at the extraordinary risks which were constantly taken without fatal consequences." The men of the expeditions "became aware of this as the time in Antarctica wore on, and we referred to the phenomenon as 'Byrd luck.'"5

Much of that luck derived from Byrd's approach to exploring. He could be hard—very hard—not only on slackers, shirkers, and failures but even on those he believed were slipping on the job. His acolyte Paul Siple, who proved a brilliant polar scientist from the start, warned novice Alton Lindsey at the beginning of the second Antarctic expedition that "it was a most uncomfortable experience to be called on the carpet by Byrd for some inadequacy or failure, as Byrd was not tolerant of major errors. His cold eye and short treatment could effectively skewer a transgressor." Siple, comfortable in his own skin, had no problem with this approach; others, like Finn Ronne, clearly wilted under the pressure.[6]

Ultimately, Dick Byrd oversold himself and his always uncertain profession. From the beginning a growing number of critics, including the influential Frederick Lewis Allen, accused him of overpublicizing his achievements: "Heroism, however gallant, lost something of its spontaneous charm when it was subjected to scientific management and syndicated in daily dispatches," Allen grumped.[7] As the century turned dark with economic depression and global war, adventuring, however exalted the purpose, seemed ever more frivolous and irrelevant. In the slow, steady decline of Dick Byrd's influence during the last two decades of his life we can trace a fundamental shift in human affairs away from the man of action and accomplishment and toward a more collectivist and impersonal approach to adventure and knowledge—progress, if you will, by committee.

To those who grew up in the 1950s and afterward Byrd will, I suspect, always remain unknowable. The persona he projected is too rational, too disciplined, too contained, too "uptight" for the sensualists of the early twenty-first century. There was a good bit of the metallic in the man. There is no evidence that in his many lecture tours he allowed groupies to gather about him; there were no scandals attached to him, no recorded affairs with adoring members of either sex. Throughout his life he remained almost inhumanly blameless. At six he fell in love with a summer playmate, married her two decades later, and remained utterly devoted to her—as she was to him—for the next forty-two years.

His chief vices were jealousy and pettiness, which made enemies who gossiped and speculated against him. He could also, as we shall see, play shamelessly to the media in order to advertise forthcoming ventures. But beneath it all, the man possessed a genuine nobility and seriousness of purpose. "The flight made by Captain Lindbergh has challenged the admiration of the world," Byrd wrote to his patron in the summer of 1927 after the Lone Eagle had beaten him in the race to fly nonstop to Paris. "It stands as a masterpiece of aviation." In commenting about his own, earlier, North Polar flight, Byrd observed:

> We revealed no startling information to the world. We made no aeronautical records of altitude or duration. We did not even suffer any extraordinary hardships that might have made an enthralling tale of hairbreadth escape, nor can we so much as claim any great personal achievement. We simply took advantage of the knowledge gained by three centuries of arctic heroes and applied our Navy training to Aviation—that great science born in this country; and so added a short paragraph to the story of man's conquest of the globe on which we live.[8]

There were frequent assertions of alcoholism, but in contexts and under conditions that leave room for question, if not doubt. In any case, heavy drinking is a rather recent entry in the catalog of public vices. Byrd's generation chose to interpret boozing as a positive gesture against a capricious, often cruel, world. Byrd also made many friends who spoke of him with great warmth a quarter century ago when I first researched his life. Twenty-five years later as I prepared this account, those who remained spoke warmly of him still and expressed bewilderment that anyone could doubt his word. Of course, the admiral was a showman, they said, but he was an honest one. Down on the ice in Antarctica, the worst vice attributed to him and his men was overindulgence in alcohol; in the end he and they all exhibited remarkable restraint and even a measure of good nature in the claustrophobic all-male atmosphere of a polar camp buried for months on end beneath Antarctica's icy winter night. And in the process, they laid many of the foundations of contemporary science.

Perhaps the post–September 11 generation with its heightened awareness of the fragility of life and society, of the consequent need for sacrifice and for a sense of boundaries and communal commitment, will find Dick Byrd more knowable and congenial. Whatever one's posture and perspective, his remarkable contributions to twentieth-century life and science are undeniable. It is time—well past time—to familiarize ourselves with him.

Chapter 1

"Danger Was All That Thrilled Him"

They left him alone in fifty-degrees-below-zero temperature, 123 miles beyond the last outpost of civilization. It was March 28, 1934, and all around his solitary little hut dug painstakingly into the South Polar snow, the Ross Ice Barrier stretched "flat as the Kansas Plains," rolling on "forever to meet the sky in a round of unbroken horizon." The collection of tractors, dogs, and men who had finished setting the scene of his coming ordeal were "just a pinprick in infinity," anxious to be off home to the comparative warmth, safety, and limited society of Little America base camp. Paul Siple and Bud Waite, two of his most trusted lieutenants, lingered for a moment behind their jaunty little red-hooded Citroen snow tractor, wanting to say a last word, but someone snapped out an impatient, "For Christ's sake, get going," and first Siple and then Waite, after mumbling something unintelligible, hurried off. The tractor party had intended to drive back the previous day, but four miles out a radiator in one of the two vehicles froze, and Pete Demas, in unscrewing the cap, had badly burned both hands. The men had returned to spend the night crammed in the warmth of the tiny dwelling. Now, as they hurriedly drove away against a huge noon sun burning up the northern sky so close to the horizon that it might have been a sunset, Richard Evelyn Byrd, self-styled Virginia gentleman, naval officer, and explorer who had crowded a lifetime of adventure into the previous decade, suddenly felt "utterly at loose ends" for the first time in his life. Ahead, he hoped, lay six months of creative solitude. As the sun slipped away and the long polar night clamped down on the vast shelf of ice, he would man the world's most remote weather station, making careful daily observations of wind, temperature, and moisture. Some snickered that he had been put out to pasture by his fellow explorers who could not stand his ways, or that he had gone to do "some serious drinking." Whatever the case, Dick Byrd, a slim but robust forty-five year old with a gift for self-promotion and the visionary's driving desire to do good in the world, had set himself a daunting task.

It began badly. Unable to tear his eyes away from his departing comrades clattering away across the purple and orange ice scape, Byrd waited "until the receding specks had dropped for good behind a roll" on the barrier. "Only the vanishing exhalations" of their vapor trail remained. Turning reluctantly to the little hut carefully set in a deep depression in the ice, Byrd slid down the ladder, only to discover that the shoulder he had wrenched helping the tractor men stow the sledges suddenly "hurt like the devil."[1]

Few men or women can sustain the kind of pace Dick Byrd had set by the time of his self-imposed isolation at "Advance Base." Fatally susceptible to hubris and to overreach, America's last explorer began a devastating ordeal that frigid polar day seventy-odd years ago that would leave him more broken in body and wounded in spirit than he would ever admit.

He was born into a late-nineteenth-century Virginia family avid to regain lost status. Mother Eleanor was "the beautiful and accomplished daughter" of Joel W. Flood of Appomattox Court House, Virginia, and granddaughter of the late Charles J. Faulkner of West Virginia. Both men had enjoyed long political careers in the Virginia and West Virginia legislatures; Charles had been appointed minister to France by President Buchanan. Eleanor's maternal uncle Charles James Faulkner Jr. had been a member of the U.S. Senate from West Virginia, and her brother Henry Delaware Flood was starting a brilliant political career that would take him from the Virginia Senate to a twenty-year career in Congress, crowned by chairmanship of the House Foreign Affairs Committee during World War I.[2]

Father Richard carried the name of one of the most distinguished "First Families of Virginia." The first Byrd to enter Virginia had been William Byrd, later known as William the First, who came to the "wild and thriving" James River country in the late seventeenth century to claim his maternal uncle's modest estate, including slaves.[3] Young Byrd "came of an old stock of quiet, well-to-do English gentry, who, so far as is known, never had been especially distinguished or enterprising." The energetic young colonist quickly broke the mold. By 1680, only six years away from England, the twenty-eight year old obtained a grant of ownership over the Falls of the James River. He had already laid out a crude path or trail four hundred miles long, extending into the wilderness from a point on the river just below present-day Richmond. "On this his traders traveled and trafficked with the Indians and settlers far into what is now North Carolina." His couriers sold slaves, rum, molasses, and anything else that could be marketed. In 1683, young Byrd proposed to Governor Culpeper a bold plan to explore and occupy the country west of the Alleghenies, thereby solidifying relations with the Native American tribes while checking the French coming down from Canada. The governor rejected the proposal. The colony was still relatively new and fragile, and London would not commit the necessary men and resources for westward expansion. His Majesty's Government would soon have good cause to rue its refusal, as Virginia eventually became embroiled in wars with the French and Indians that lasted for seventy-five years.[4]

With his profit margin constantly expanding, Byrd bought huge tracts of land, establishing his son, William Byrd II, of Westover Plantation as a gentleman farmer of the first rank. Visiting Englishmen might sneer at Virginia's frontier slave planters as at best bourgeois aristocrats, comparable to the simple yeoman farmers one encountered back home, but William II proved to be more than that. Among other achievements he built a great house, amassed a large library, read the classics, wrote the perceptive *Essay upon the Government of the English Plantations* that complained of the mother country's neglect and ignorance of the colonies, patronized the local church, and generally enjoyed "good health, good thoughts and good humor, thank God Almighty." He also enjoyed a flaming sex life that embarrassed his successors no end when it was revealed in the late 1930s in the pages of William's diary unearthed by diligent scholars. At one point, Richard, now a famous explorer, exploded in anger, venting his spleen to various members of the far-flung clan. "I am very much incensed over the fact (or what appears to be a fact) that the people that found William Byrd's diary are publishing it without asking our permission. Personally, I think it is outrageous that certain parts of it are not deleted." The diary segment found by the Virginia Historical Society "is far spicier than any parts of the diary already published. William Byrd never meant for anyone to read his diary. Are we going to sit back and let these things be done without any objection?" For Byrds to become public laughingstocks was simply insupportable. "I think it is outrageous," Richard told his older brother, U.S. senator Harry Byrd, "that fellow Southerners would not consult us about matters such as this." Harry agreed and hoped to suppress publication. But the diary segments duly appeared, and after several futile months of fulmination, Richard dropped the matter, but his bitterness remained.[5]

William II's son proved just as licentious but utterly lacking in responsibility, as third children of founding families occasionally prove to be, and thereafter the family fortunes entered a prolonged state of decline. While the Byrds of Westover clung to enough of their land, wealth, and standing (despite steadily falling agricultural prospects) to be considered prominent throughout the eighteenth century, Thomas Byrd decided early in the following century to move out of the Tidewater country and into the comparatively raw frontier of the Shenandoah Valley, settling in the little town of Winchester. Thomas's son, the first Richard Evelyn Byrd, represented Winchester in the antebellum Virginia Assembly, as did Richard's son, William, who moved to the Texas frontier shortly before the Civil War to establish a law practice in Austin. William became adjutant general of the state before heading back north to join his father in the Rebel cause. Both men served in the Confederate army, and William was captured and imprisoned for a time. After the war, he brought his Texas wife, Jennie River Byrd, and their young Austin-born son, Richard Evelyn II, back to Winchester. He moved his family into his father's three-story house on Washington Street and prepared to practice law.

The following years were good to William and to Richard Evelyn. "Conservative old Winchester," then a town of five or six thousand people, lay some seventy-five miles west and a bit south of Washington, D.C. It was, according to one northern writer of the 1920s, "complacent but proud of its wealth of Colonial and Civil War romance." At one time or another George Washington, Daniel Morgan, Stonewall Jackson, and Jubal Early had headquartered there. So had the Yankee cavalryman Phil Sheridan, but Winchester folk did not and do not talk much about that. Yanks and Rebs fought over the town on dozens of occasions. No Winchesterian ever forgot the War, or the Cause that defined and sustained it. Eleanor Byrd was a proud and patriotic American lady who just before and during World War II would cry in movie theaters whenever the flag was shown before a film. But at the end of her long and active life when she was a reclusive invalid, Eleanor insisted that only books on Lee and his lieutenants be read to her. After a fourth book on Lee, her devoted caretaker, Maude Ludwig, wrote Richard that his mother had grown somewhat tired of the general, "so I have changed to Stonewall Jackson." At the end of the twentieth century Winchester's proud Confederate heritage could still be felt at the local historical library with its numerous portraits of Jackson leading his troops and bidding farewell to a lovely young woman amid the Christmas snows of 1861.[6]

The townspeople refused to let the defeat of the Cause defeat them. In the 1870s and early '80s they embraced the ideal of the New South, pursuing modest industrial and railroad development. They brought electricity and the telephone to main street and expanded their local orchards to the point where Winchester apples were to be found in urban food markets throughout much of the East and Upper South. Eventually, Winchester apples found their way into the English and European markets. Prosperity swelled William's law practice sufficiently to permit son Richard to matriculate at the University of Virginia and later to earn his degree at the University of Maryland School of Law in Baltimore. By the time of his marriage to Eleanor, young Richard was clearly making his own mark in the world.

With their background and connections Richard and his bride could have lived anywhere in Virginia, but they clearly preferred to be associated with the doughty folk of the Shenandoah Valley rather than the snobs of the Tidewater. Years later, an unidentifiable but sympathetic editor explained their choice. Both the valley and the Tidewater region were "authentic Virginia." But valley people were mainly "Scotch-Irish pioneers, while the other was peopled by slave-owning landlords living on large plantations." Valley folk were "hard-bitten worshipers of facts, practical people who have received from their forebears the lessons of hard experience in subduing a new country. The Tidewater people are more elegant, more interested in theories and in cultural matters and more addicted to eloquence and persuasion."[7]

Like his father, young Richard Evelyn II threw himself into the modest renaissance of his town as lawyer, judge, and state representative. By all accounts he could be a prickly, feisty man. But he was approachable—insisting that everyone call him "Dick"—and many saw greatness in him. Douglas Southall Freeman, a prominent Richmond editor of the early twentieth century and chronicler of the Army of Northern Virginia, once remarked that Richard Evelyn "had the most acute intellect possessed by any Virginian of my lifetime, and with it he had absolute unhesitating courage and . . . the most complete candor in dealing with press and public that ever I had the privilege of observing. I never knew him to balk at any question put to him concerning any public issue." A newsman on the *Richmond Times-Dispatch* remembered talking alone for hours with Richard Evelyn, who was "always willing to spend time with young men."[8]

He could be at once hotheaded and cool, "the most fearless man I ever saw," according to Shenandoah National Bank president R. Gray Williams.[9] Once in court he threw an inkwell at an opposing lawyer and hit him badly enough to draw blood and calls for his arrest. On another occasion he ignored the pleas of his wife and friends, and rode alone into the mountains west of town to deal with some murderous rascals who had been terrorizing the area. He went in for a day, heard evidence, dealt sentences, got the miscreants incarcerated, and left before the dim-witted families of the killers could react.

It was said that Richard Evelyn was not fond of politics or politicians, but he entered the public arena out of a sense of duty. Some thought him "the greatest speaker the Virginia House of Delegates has had in two generations." A rabid defender of states' rights and an uncompromising white supremacist whose fear of "miscegenation" was implicit but unmistakable, he wrote a brief against Virginia's ratification of the federal income tax amendment that conservatives hailed as classic.[10] He resisted several calls to run for governor and stayed aloof from the Virginia political machine that his brother-in-law Henry Delaware Flood constructed over in Richmond. But Richard Evelyn was smitten with Woodrow Wilson, whose second wife, Edith Bolling Galt, was a distant relation to Eleanor Bolling Byrd, and in 1912 he successfully fought the Flood people to carry the state for the Virginia son turned Princeton president and New Jersey governor. When Wilson reached the White House he insisted that Richard Evelyn accept the posts of assistant attorney general and then attorney general for southwestern Virginia.[11] Thus, despite himself, a reluctant Byrd wielded substantial political power.

This quirky, imposing, attractive, combative man, stocky and of average height, with high forehead and determined chin, had a love of the bottle. "Occasionally he would retreat to a little cabin in the Blue Ridge Mountains named Byrd's Nest for periodic binges."[12] Eleanor was not amused, and the marriage was often tense, reflecting a clash of strong wills. But both parents were united in a determination to see that their children got the love, discipline, and freedom needed to succeed. Harry came first, on June 10, 1887; Richard arrived fifteen months later, on October 25, 1888, and Tom a year after that.

The boys revered Richard Evelyn—"I never expect to meet a man with the scintillating brilliance my father possessed," Dick would confide years later. But he was a hard man, impatient of weakness and frailty. He never quite understood his middle son, and according to Eleanor this man of politics and the law remained skeptical of Richard's life of professional adventure.[13] She was the opposite. The boys adored her. "Just yesterday," Richard wrote her in the summer of 1950, "Harry and I were talking about the fact that because you were so wonderful yourself and so wonderful to us when we were youngsters, you made things so much easier for us throughout our whole lives." In another letter he applauded Eleanor for being "a person to want your sons and grandsons to do what they ought to do." Franklin D. Roosevelt complimented both Richard and Harry on their mother, comparing Eleanor to Sara Delano Roosevelt. But whereas both women possessed formidable personalities, Sara Delano forever sought to ensnare "my boy Franklin" in her clutches, to keep him close to Hyde Park and to her, especially after his polio attack. Eleanor Byrd was the opposite. She wanted her boys to fly, in some cases literally. She "never kicked" when Richard went into aviation during World War I. And when Tom, already a well-established businessman in Winchester, volunteered for action in 1917, she "cheered him on and told him that he was doing what was right." She gave similar encouragement to her nephews and grandchildren in 1942. "That is the kind of American citizen you are," her middle son gushed, "and we are very, very proud of you." Once he confided to his mother that he kept her picture on his bedroom dresser, surrounded by fresh white roses. In his many letters he addressed her as "Sweetheart."[14]

Eleanor was as formidable as her husband. Richard remembered her "full of pep," and one of his friends who knew her well wrote in 1939 that even in her seventies she remained "one of the great ladies of Virginia, with a debutante's energy and a mind as sharp as a steel trap, the terror of the horsey Northern women who invade the Shenandoah Valley during the hunting season." The horse defined the vigorous outdoor life of the northern valley, and Eleanor excelled as a horsewoman. She rode often and was "a wonderful rider." A century ago, every woman rode sidesaddle, and Richard professed bafflement that anyone could ride that way with the elegance and grace that his mother displayed.[15]

Eleanor never wanted daughters (though the Byrds took in and raised a little girl named Margaret, whose mother had died in childbirth), and she and her husband brought their boys up with a striking combination of discipline and indulgence. "I don't know of any boys who had a happier home life than we did," Dick told her. Theirs was "a happy and normal and unafraid childhood."[16]

The family had settled in at 326 Amherst Street, a half mile from downtown Winchester. The lot is now occupied by an automobile dealership, but in those days it contained a substantial house with a large barn in the rear. Across the street, now also long gone, was the "beautiful spacious mansion" that General Daniel Morgan built with the help of Hessian soldiers following the Revolutionary War. Close by was the Cumberland Valley Railroad Depot where trains came and went down and up the valley from Staunton to Martinsburg and beyond to distant Hagerstown.[17]

Richard would recall ducking for apples in the side yard under Eleanor's benign gaze and dressing near the stove on a winter morning because Richard, like his mother, disliked the cold ("I think you still hate the cold," Richard wrote Eleanor in later years, whereas "I have grown to like it and dislike the heat"). But the household was often in an uproar caused by three exuberant, irrepressible boys. Richard recalled his parents, "without too much kick," letting their sons "tear the house to pieces" with pillow fights, but when he broke a hall window for the third time batting a tennis ball, "Pop gave me a good spanking." The mortified boy decided to run away, but changed his mind before anyone realized he was gone. Home, after all, looked better than West Virginia up the road.[18]

From his earliest days, young Richard suffered from an affliction well known to another famous American, Teddy Roosevelt: he was a frail youngster who grew up short and "puny." Winchester folk recalled that the lad's father was not happy about this and that his brothers early on took advantage of it and would beat on him on occasion. Young Dick, who aspired in his early years to be both a frontiersman and a football player, decided to do something about it. With single-minded devotion he began to build up his body through vigorous exercise. He climbed trees and drain spouts: "there are very few houses in Winchester over the roofs of which he has not roamed." Soon Harry and Tom learned to leave their brother alone, and his father made no more complaints about his son's frailty. Years later, young Harry, recently elected governor of the commonwealth, would tell a reporter of his brother's remarkable will. "I have never known a boy nor a young man as determined as Dick. He would let nothing stop him in doing what he set out to accomplish." His course of physical development "was one of the most persistent, determined things I ever saw," and once in a fight, "He never knew how to let go. . . . [H]e would stick to the scrap until physical exhaustion forced him to the point of collapse." All his life Dick Byrd would exercise daily, maintaining a wiry, powerful physique that doubtless prolonged his stressful life by several if not many years. According to Winchester friends, his regimen taught him something else—thoroughness. Several remarked on the connection between young Dick's determined pursuit of a powerful body and his single-minded planning and preparation for the successful North Polar flight years later. "After he had determined upon a course of physical exercise he hewed to the line every day," one of them remembered. "He never missed. . . . He has always been thorough. This was shown by the way he had everything ready for his flight to the pole."[19]

The father encouraged his boys to band together, to walk the streets of town looking for fun and adventure; they should not pick fights, but they were not to avoid them. "I believe that Tom, Dick and Harry became quite well known in Winchester on account of the sequence of names and because we always stuck together," Dick would recall. He was right. The lads were taunters and teasers, operating at the edge of acceptable behavior. But they were not considered bad because they were polite. Winchester folk maintained that "with all his mischievous ways," little Dick Byrd "was a born gentleman. He was courteous and had an affable, friendly manner that quickly made him friends." All the boys displayed a streak of temper or cheek. "No one could lick any one of the three without accounting to the others." Tom was the most peaceable, always going to extremes to avoid trouble. "But when he found he could not avoid it, he was a terror." Dick remembered the seven year old, "mad as hell," chasing him into the bathroom with a carving knife. Dick locked himself in, then climbed down the nearby lightning rod, leaving Tom "carving on the bathroom door." Harry was not far behind, once receiving "a dramatic spanking on the porch in front of a lot of people when he made a bonfire in the barn." (This was Dick's story; townsfolk recalled that it was he, not Harry, who had set fire to the barn and that Richard Evelyn had been burned about the arms when he rushed in, fearing one or more of his boys were inside.)

But Dick proved the most rambunctious. Eleanor later told grandson Harry Flood Byrd that she saw early on that Dick had an adventurous nature. She remembered him "always doing dangerous things. He was always on top of a house or tree. Danger was all that thrilled him." She told an interviewer that her middle son had been "born an adventurer and explorer, absolutely without fear." He also possessed a fierce sense of loyalty. On one occasion, visiting their mother's family near Appomattox, Harry, Dick, and Tom, styling themselves the Western Gang, began a rock fight with the rival Potato Hill Gang. Harry got hit in the head, which infuriated Dick, who "was ready to kill the whole lot." Poor Harry, his head dripping blood, just wanted to get to a doctor, and Dick had to give way. The clumsy physician stitched up the future governor of the commonwealth so crudely that he was left with a permanent scar.

Claude Swanson, a longtime Virginia senator, secretary of the navy under Franklin Roosevelt, and lifelong friend of the family, recalled that as a boy young Dick "got into rather more than his fair share of mischief, and what his exasperated father used to call 'reckless deviltry.'" For several years the youngster led a gang of schoolboys, though at a time when gangs in polite, conservative American towns like Winchester were more informal social clubs formed by middle-class youngsters than fighting units composed of toughs and urchins. Still, young Dick led his charges into "new and hitherto unheard-of . . . escapade[s]," retaining his leadership "because no matter what was the physical risk or the still more dreaded danger of parental wrath, he was always ready to 'go first' when the challenge came."[20]

Richard loved the woods and meadows of the upper Shenandoah Valley. A large farm in nearby Clarke County had been in the family for nearly a century, and Richard later wrote that the happiest hours of his adolescence were tramping through its hundred acres of untouched oak timber alone with his gun and fox terrier Judy. The dog did most of the hunting, Richard recalled, while he "roamed and let my thoughts run wild. They carried me beyond the valley" and around the world. They also carried him into his father's formidable library (typical for a Byrd) where he later claimed to have devoured every book dealing with ancient history, mathematics, and philosophy by age sixteen and to have completed "a most involved essay" on time and space based largely on his reading of Immanuel Kant. "Like most of the higher thoughts he has placed on paper," friend and biographer Charles J. V. Murphy wrote, Dick preserved the essay "as a secret."[21]

From his experiences alone in the woods and the library, Richard began to conceive himself as a pioneer and philosopher, a muscular thinker and doer constantly "struggling" to master life. In the unpublished portion of the preface for his first book, *Skyward,* some of which reached print via Charles J. V. Murphy's simultaneously published biography, Richard wrote of ancestors who got a "kick . . . out of trying to make first, in everything worthwhile, this wonderful country they settled. The Byrd family of Virginia is just one of the millions of families that has given its members this heritage. They struggled for mobility on the ground. Some of us now struggle for it in the air." At the turn of the twentieth century, that national "yearning for mobility" focused most strongly on the polar regions and, thanks to skillful publicity, most particularly on the race to reach the North Pole. A cluster of Arctic pioneers, led by the navy's Robert Peary, strained for the prize, even as they explored wide swaths of northern Greenland and Arctic Canada. It was said that Dick Byrd devoured tales of such exploration and that in 1900 he recorded in a boyhood diary that he would be the first man to reach the top of the world. He was only twenty when, in 1909, Peary ostensibly snatched the victory from him.[22]

By then aviation had claimed him. Because of the rapidly developing airplane, he later wrote, man could now "move and fly faster than the birds, and as he soars above the earth he catches glimpses of" a future in which "he may gain mastery of his fate."[23] Richard could never precisely formulate a philosophy about man's search for destiny through aviation, but in later years his thought attracted both wealthy patrons and a public still hopeful that science and technology could lead the world into broad sunlit uplands of peace and plenty.

Intelligent, ambitious, disciplined, pugnacious, and restless beneath a formidable veneer of charm, Dick was also driven to restore the family's fortune. Sitting around the fireplace at night after supper and talking, "Pop would tell us things." Grandfather Flood had been "the wealthiest man in Virginia" and Grandfather Byrd "very successful and well off." The war had ruined them. Richard and Eleanor had made a start in reviving the Byrd solvency and reputation, but the boys should carry on. In later years, Richard would write to his mother that what he had heard around the family fireplace all those years before had helped him "to fight the battle of life and win it, and to achieve happiness." When Richard's son married one of the formidable Saltonstall girls of Massachusetts shortly after World War II, Richard was "kind of proud of the Byrd clan when they met" their Yankee in-laws. On another occasion he wrote to Eleanor that "you and Pop started a clan that will go down through the ages."[24]

It was Harry who led the way to renewed family fame and influence. Years before his father had bought the *Winchester Star,* but the paper had never made money. When Richard Evelyn decided to sell it, Harry, then all of sixteen years old, "jumped at the chance" to leave the Shenandoah Academy and assume its operation. The indulgent father let him have his way. But the *Star* was broke, and its supplier, the Antietam Paper Company up in Hagerstown, Maryland, refused to advance either credit or supplies. Harry promptly got on the train and went north. Send me newsprint one day at a time, COD, he told the skeptical company owners, and I'll see that you don't lose a cent. The company grudgingly agreed, and Harry set to work. He became "everything from [printer's] 'Devil' to 'Managing Editor'" of the *Star,* raising money and subscriptions to keep the newsprint coming and the presses rolling. Soon the newspaper was thriving, and Harry quickly bought out the other two papers in town, at one point setting brother Dick to work selling advertisements. The monopoly ensured Harry's career, and he soon purchased the first of several large apple orchards nearby. Richard Evelyn was delighted. "Harry is going places!" he told acquaintances, and so he was. Harry quickly became a leader in local agriculture as he steadily expanded his valuable apple acreage. But his eye was already on broader horizons. Harry brought Tom into both the newspaper and the apple businesses, entrusting his capable younger brother with more and more responsibilities while he laid the foundations of a remarkable political career. In 1915, age twenty-eight, Harry entered the Virginia state senate. Two years later, he began to take over the Flood political machine. For decades thereafter, Virginia was largely his, as he pursued an increasingly influential career in national politics. He also maintained his identification with the family apple business so that by the time he reached the governorship in 1926, he could advertise himself as "one of the largest apple growers east of the Mississippi."[25]

Tom, the least well known of the three, was by temper and inclination in many ways the steadiest. With Harry he guided the apple business through good years and bad, weathering hard times during the Great Depression that virtually destroyed the vital English apple market. Tom also kept the *Star* solvent until he turned it over to Harry's son, Harry Flood Byrd, just before World War II. Dick was always proud of Tom, once telling his mother that popular belief in the Winchester area was that no Byrd since William II "had the wit and sense of humor that Tom has." The youngest Byrd "was the most popular man in Virginia among the F.F.V.'s [that is, First Families of Virginia] and their friends."[26]

All three men were defined not only by genes and family but also by the ethos of the Old South that surrounded them in provincial Winchester. Notions of honor ran deep in their veins. According to Bertram Wyatt-Brown, its keenest student, southern honor was grounded in an unshakable conviction of self-worth. From this perspective, the individual strove to correctly evaluate those around him and how he should approach the general public. A second aspect of southern honor was the claim to self-assessment before the public. But self-assessment did not necessarily mean self-revelation. Throughout his life Richard Byrd spoke and wrote copiously about himself, his ideals, and his adventures. He bared his feelings in countless speeches and in nearly every book, especially *Alone,* that remarkable account of his personal ordeal in 1934 far out on the Ross Ice Shelf. Yet the inner man remained, always, something of an enigma to those who knew him and perhaps to Byrd himself. There was always a stop point, a self-imposed governor, in Richard Byrd that permitted him to approach the very edge of meaningful revelation without, except in the most extreme cases, moving beyond. For all his good humor and charm Byrd was an intensely private individual. The last element of southern honor was the public's assessment of the individual's claim to possess it, based on the behavior of the claimant. "In other words," Wyatt-Brown maintains, "honor is reputation. Honor resides in the individual as his understanding of who he is and where he belongs in the ordered ranks of society." Honor is thus "self-regarding in character. One's neighbors serve as mirrors that return the image of oneself." This "submission to public evaluation," if genuine, prevents "outrageous haughtiness" and encourages affability. Self-confidence, self-understanding, a carefully measured element of self-revelation, and a high degree of amiability were the collective elements of southern honor, and they were what Dick Byrd consistently exhibited to the world. On one level they were what allowed him to manipulate and exploit the public for many years. But he consistently exhibited such traits even at times and places where they were not needed to advance his interests. Once in Wellington, New Zealand, returning from Operation Highjump in 1947, he was standing at a urinal trough with one of his young pilots. A sailor staggered in, "with a bottle of rot-gut whiskey in one hand and you-know-what in the other. The sailor glanced our way, did a double-take and in slurred speech said to the admiral, 'Admiral! Would you have a drink with me?' 'I'm honored to have a drink with you or any of my men,'" Byrd replied, taking the bottle and swigging one down. The pilot, "Windy" Summers, wrote years later that "it was a humbling experience" seeing the admiral "holding himself with one hand and holding that whiskey bottle with the other."[27]

Yet at a young age, Byrd began to display another aspect of his personality that was far from attractive, and one that, at least in youth, his family actively aided and abetted: he could be deceitful. He did not lie invariably, or very often, but enough to disturb colleagues and excite critics. Ultimately, the debunkers would charge him with sins he never committed.

In 1902, as he and his family would first tell it, the adventurous lad, all of eleven years old, traveled around the world alone. His journey took him from Winchester to the Philippines at the invitation of his godfather, Judge Adam C. ("Kit") Carson, who had once worked in Richard Evelyn's law firm and had become a powerful political figure in adjacent Warren County before heading out to the Pacific.

After some months in the archipelago Dick returned home, still on his own, via Ceylon (Sri Lanka), India, Egypt, Europe, and Boston. During a time when only a few adults and their children ever journeyed to the nearest city, and only the wealthiest had the means and leisure to take the "grand tour" to Europe, Dick was lionized. He later wrote privately that he was "met in Boston by a dozen newspaper reporters, and was acclaimed as the youngest globetrotter on record." His parents were praised and faintly damned for allowing such a vulnerable youth to experience life. It was a wonderful story, and Richard Byrd and his family continued to tell it for years with but one change: he had been twelve, not eleven, when he had set off. In the spring of 1950 Dick wrote his mother how impressed a Richmond reporter had been to learn "that when I was 12 years old you agreed to my going around the world by myself and to my staying long enough away from home to do a thorough job of traveling around the world."[28] Unfortunately, the story was inaccurate.

Dick was not twelve—and certainly not eleven—when he left for the Far East, as he claimed and as his family would accept and confirm. He left for the Philippines on August 9, 1902—eleven weeks before his fourteenth birthday—returning to Winchester early the following year. In short, he was not a young, vulnerable boy sent out into a cruel and predatory world by apprehensive parents but an adolescent on the verge of manhood who skipped around the world very quickly for those days. The nation's greatest war had occurred less than forty years before, and a handful of fourteen- and even thirteen-year-old lads had fought and a few died for both the Union and the Confederacy. The great western frontier that had just closed demanded adult responsibilities of boys Dick's age. His brother Harry would become a newspaperman when he was just two years older than Dick was when he returned from abroad.

Moreover, Dick did not travel by himself. According to the *Winchester Star,* "His mother went as far as Washington with him . . . where he will meet Mrs. Wendall who will accompany him on the trip as far as Manila." The woman had obtained "a government position" in the islands, and, therefore, "Master Dick" would "leave her at Manila and complete his tour of the world alone." Byrd did allude vaguely to Mrs. "Wendell" in the unpublished portion of his preface to *Skyward,* saying merely that she was "the only person I knew on board . . . who was a friend of my uncle's." Thereafter, she was never again mentioned. Remarkably venturesome as Dick's globe-trotting undeniably was, he could not avoid embellishing an already striking tale to make himself look even more dramatic and accomplished.[29]

During his journey, Dick wrote a few letters to his family that naturally found their way into the pages of the *Star.* For the first and only time, the clan stated that their lad was fourteen. Three of these letters remain. Each was written in a clear, economical style, the prose straight and direct. In the first Dick described attending a Catholic mass on the Philippine island of Masbate, closing casually with the remark that he was awaiting a boat to Samar, "the place where 50 of our troops were massacred." His second letter from that island mentioned in passing that most of the fighting was over and that he was enjoying swimming and hunting adventures with two young soldiers who hailed from a village near home. He killed a monkey with his first shot, but failed to bring down any thereafter. Only his third letter described an out-of-the-ordinary incident. Back in Manila, Judge Carson, sitting in the room next to where Dick was laboriously typing his letter, sentenced two Filipinos to be hanged. The men "take it just as if nothing else was going on," the boy related. "They do not even change their expression. There is a scaffold which you can see from my window on which six men were hung last year." A fourth communication, which the *Star* published on March 27, 1903, contained young Dick's commission as deputy sheriff, "appointed in the service of Gov. Monreal of Sorenson Province, P.I."[30]

Byrd would later claim much more. Off Japan, he wrote, his ship ran into the worst hurricane the captain had seen in fifty years, and Dick spent the crisis in the grand salon ministering to hysterical ladies. Once young Richard arrived in the disease-ridden archipelago, Judge Carson took him into the field, a .45 strapped to his belt, to fight the insurrectionists ("Ladrones") under Emilio Aguinaldo. Richard and his mates once fell into an ambush out of which they fought, and he escorted prisoners to Manila, where he saw some hanged. Persistent cholera and other diseases induced Carson to "sneak" his charge aboard a freighter for Europe. Before he did so, Richard claimed he had "played doctor" to a cholera victim and promptly fell ill himself. He went to bed thinking he would be dead before morning, only to awaken in the best of health.

Since the Philippine insurrection has been likened to the war in Vietnam, we are entitled to wonder whether Carson cavalierly hazarded the life of a fourteen year old to ambush and death. Nonetheless, a quarter century later Byrd and his then worshipful publicist, Charles Murphy, dutifully recorded the stories in two biographies of the budding explorer.[31] Claude Swanson was doubtless closer to the truth when he later asserted that Dick's Philippine adventures had come when the boy ducked out of Judge Carson's sight to join a sheriff's posse and a constabulary detachment riding out to round up bandits who had broken out of the provincial jail. Still, Swanson did not dispute or modify Byrd's other tales of his Philippine sojourn, quoting a supposed admission by Carson to friends back in Virginia that his supply of gray hairs had notably increased during the boy's visit.[32]

Might some or even most of Dick's tales nonetheless have been true? Off Greenland in 1925, Lieutenant Commander Byrd recorded in his diary (which did not come to public attention for another seventy years) a storm in which "nine or ten Danes . . . came within an ace" of losing their lives. "A very dramatic moment," he wrote. "I have only once before experienced such a wind—a typhoon in the China Sea."[33] As he had not then been back to Asia since his boyhood trip, perhaps the typhoon and some of the other stories he wrote home were true after all. Either that or he was able to maintain a remarkable continuity to his storytelling in which wish became fulfillment and life a perpetual pageant.

Whatever happened or might have happened in the Far East, Dick was strikingly reticent about his trip homeward, which he did by himself. Was it routine, devoid of thrills and romance? Or did the lad suffer adventures he wished no one to know? Byrd's only serious biographer states simply that it "was as exciting as the trip out—around Malaya, through the Indian Ocean, the Gulf of Aden, the Red Sea, the Mediterranean, and the Atlantic Ocean aboard a British tramp steamer." Biographer Edwin Hoyt provides no further details, though it is clear that he may well have enjoyed at least limited access to Dick's family history.[34] An eleven or twelve year old might have been sheltered by his age from the rocks and shoals of the world society on his homeward passage; an almost fifteen-year-old youth would have been more exposed. International travel a century ago involved far more vice, folly, and danger than today. Thugs, sharpers, con artists, hucksters, and harlots abounded who might have been expected to prey on a lone adolescent. Did young Byrd prudently remain aboard his steamer as it rode off the foul ports of India, the Middle East, and Egypt? Or did he go ashore? If so, what happened to him there? We shall never know, for he shrouded the whole experience in a determined silence.

We do know that he returned to Winchester incurably restless. He had seen and tasted so much of a world that none of the adults immediately around him and few of his peers would ever know. The petty discipline and narrow confines of the classroom must have been as agonizing to a lad who had seen the temples of Yokohama and the spires of Port Said (even from shipboard) as was the childish prattle of his contemporaries who began calling the physically slight young man "Dickie." He drifted for several years through a number of schools before settling on Annapolis and a naval career. His first stop was the Shenandoah Valley Academy, "up the street" from his home in Winchester. A friend later recalled the youngster taking chemistry under "Prof." Rankin and a "higher math" course under "Professor" Lace. The academy, a semimilitary school, had a Cadet Corps with an Awkward Squad that Dick whipped into shape for various "Parades, Reviews, etc." during the 1906–1907 school year. The friend remembered eighteen-year-old Dick being "very patient while efficient" as a drill master, spending hours on teaching his

clumsy charges, of whom "none had ever handled an Army Rifle or had any smat-
tering even of military training," how to do an impressive right-face. From Shenandoah Dick passed on to Virginia Military Institute and then the University of Virginia. Where he had not seemed afflicted during his earlier world travels, his
yearlong stays in Lexington and Charlottesville left him deeply homesick. He later hinted that intense hazing at VMI was especially upsetting, and that could well
have caused the pain. In any case, Eleanor missed her middle son with equal fervor, and the two wrote each other every day.35

These unhappy years prompted Dick to an occasional rashness that not even
football could overcome. One day in Charlottesville he walked out of his dormi-
tory and onto a nearby trestle over which a trolley car passed in crossing a street.
He wriggled under the trestle and suspended from it with both hands until a car
came along and rumbled over the somewhat shaky bridge. "What did you get out
of that?" his rather disgusted roommate asked. "Oh, I just wanted to know the
sensation of having a street car pass over me," Byrd replied with a grin.36

The navy proved the perfect antidote to Dick's restless nature. From the moment that he stepped through the gates of the Naval Academy's imposing gray
campus on the banks of the Severn, he seldom returned to Winchester, choosing
to spend his life either abroad or in the North. After a time the only sign of his
southern roots was the almost undetectable drawl in his voice and the ingrained
sense of honor.

Byrd was nearly twenty when he came to Annapolis, rather old for a plebe. But
unlike most of his classmates, his adolescence was largely behind him. He quickly became something of a social lion, a determined gymnast, and an equally determined if undersized football player. He was elected chairman of the plebe class;
as a third classman (sophomore) he was an enthusiastic member of the Hop Committee, and he held more offices during his four years at the academy than any
classmate. He won numerals in track and an expert rifleman's badge and was
sophomore welterweight wrestling champion. His class work inevitably suffered,
though he made sure to do well in the two subjects—mathematics and navigation—that defined a naval officer's professionalism. While his daily regimen of vigorous exercise kept his slender body trim as it finished filling out, his devotion to
athletics would prove fatal to a naval career. Indeed, Byrd's health was always precarious during his Annapolis years. Despite his rigorous exercise regimen, he
seemed almost fragile.

In the days when young men were occasionally killed playing the still brutal
sport of football, "Byrd was one of the most reckless players" on the Navy team.
As a third classman he played so rigorously against Penn that he collapsed, and the
team doctor refused to let him suit up against Army. The following year he got

aration right now after all that you have been through and not knowing if possibly you may be injured is simply agonizing." Yet "I know I can't come until you let me know for it might embarrass you, neither do I want to appear ridiculous on your account." Later that day she wrote again. "If you want me or need me just let me know. I am pretty good where it comes to avoiding people & publicity & I can come over absolutely incognito so that no one will know."

Marie's instinctive reticence was so great that even her daughter Bolling "was not really sure where my mother was born or grew up. Possibly Baltimore or Boston." In fact, it was Boston, though Marie's mother was a Baltimore girl, Helen Andrews. The Ames family claimed to be older in its Americanism than even the Byrds, tracing its lineage back to the *Mayflower.* Family lore had it that Dick and Marie met in Winchester when both were six and were inseparable thereafter. Joseph Blanchard Ames came down to Winchester from Massachusetts each year with his wife and daughter to spend the summer months at a house on Washington Street. Ames had money, and he, his wife, and daughter were doubtless part of that "northern horsey set" intimidated if not terrorized by Eleanor Byrd.

But Marie was spunky in her own right, a gentle, endearing personality with a hard edge when necessary. Some years after Dick's death she received a letter out of the blue from a childhood friend who held "quite a clear memory" of her, both as a little girl "in Boston during the pre–Brimmer Street years" with curls, a violin, and "an extreme sensitiveness" and later as a young woman whose "sympathy was very sweet." The woman also recalled Marie's sister, "a very blond little Catherine in braids," and "your lovely vivid mother whom we all adored." Well educated, Marie became an accomplished violinist, and, somewhat to Winchester's dismay had actually appeared on the wicked stage where no polite girl in those years should ever be found. According to the *Winchester Star,* she was an excellent dancer "and has appeared frequently at semi-professional entertainments for charity benefits, receiving unstinted praise from the press critics." Lest the town think that young Dick was marrying a lady of questionable repute, the *Star* hastened to add that "withal," Marie "is an entirely unaffected, sweet-mannered girl." She had already demonstrated an independent spirit, bringing "new ideas" to the fusty valley town, not the least of which was horseback riding astride rather than sidesaddle. Years later her amused husband would remind his mother that such behavior "was considered in those days down in Virginia to be a very fast thing for a girl to do." Not only was Marie's riding a subject of gossip, but so was her clothing. She wore pleated skirts before the days of jodhpurs.[45]

It was her innate shyness and quietness reflecting great dignity that endeared her to the people of the upper valley, and perhaps to Dick Byrd as well, for their marriage, however split and divided by time and space, would be a love match from beginning to end. She understood him in ways no one else did, and her loyalty and devotion were total. Very probably, what she saw and loved in him was a reflection of her own great virtue: courage. Her own father captured it perfectly in a letter to a family member when Marie was only nine. She had just "made her debut upon the stage and rendered her first little solo on the violin before an audience of at least 300 people at Price Hall," Joseph Ames reported. "I am sure you will say it is impossible that such a timid child as she is could have done it, but she surely did, and got through the ordeal in great form. Poor little dear she looked so small and timid, a little pale of cheek, but still undaunted."[46] That was Marie Ames Byrd.

Richard told her of his love in ways that offered real insights into his mind and soul. "As much as I adored you then," he wrote on their twelfth anniversary when his fame was arcing toward its apex, "I didn't dream that you were going to be so wonderful. Without you I believe I should have lost all faith in goodness and purity. The good Lord and I are the only ones who know what a great little cavalier you have been. You have played the game and fought your battles like a sport and a chivalrous hero at every engagement and you have never once turned the white feather. No one could have been as brave as you, darling." To those who knew the couple, Marie was the heart and soul of the marriage. Several months after Dick's death former chief of naval operations William D. Leahy, an old friend and confidant to both Franklin Roosevelt and Harry Truman, asked young Richard Byrd to "please tell your lovely mother that I shall always consider her largely responsible for your father's success."[47] Dick Byrd would have been the first to agree.

Of course, the wedding, which took place on Wednesday evening, January 20, 1915, was a notable event. The union of prominent Boston and Virginia families, the former quite well off financially, the latter of more modest means, was preceded by luncheons, suppers, parties, and dances. Brother Harry was Dick's best man; the rest of his groomsmen were naval officers in full dress uniforms. The church was full of flowers, and the bride wore ivory satin with a long train. A reception and dance followed, catered by Rauscher of Washington with music by the Louis Flascher orchestra.[48] Then the groom, still an ensign after nearly four years, took his bride on a brief honeymoon before going on to Washington to find an apartment.

Dick finished service on *Dolphin*, then served a year aboard *Mayflower*, where he was in frequent contact with the president as well as senior officers and civilian officials within the Navy Department. It was at this time that he and his bride met another young charmer and rising star in the Democratic Party named Franklin D. Roosevelt, who had just become assistant secretary of the navy. Soon young Roosevelt would be going on Canadian hunting trips with Dick and Harry. Shortly after FDR's death, Byrd told his secretary that Roosevelt "was my closest friend from 1920 up until he became president." When in 1921 the vigorous New Yorker contracted polio, he wrote determinedly to Dick, "By next Autumn I will be able to chase the nimble Moose with you!" It was not to be, of course, but Richard and Marie Byrd were among the many who maintained close ties with Franklin and Eleanor as FDR battled back into the political career that would take him to the White House.[49]

In 1916, however, Byrd's precarious naval career crashed. With a war raging in Europe, President Wilson demanded a navy "second to none." Such a service could not afford to indulge anyone, no matter how promising, who was not 100 percent fit. In his late twenties, his Annapolis classmates racing by him both on the promotion list and in competition for important billets, Dick had nowhere to go. He might have remained a staff man aboard the presidential yacht or somewhere in the Navy Department, the kind of bureaucratic courtier with which Washington has always been filled, men who attach themselves to senior people, then make themselves charmingly indispensable. He would never make flag rank this way, nor, probably, acquire the four stripes of a naval captain. But it was an option for someone who had just married and needed money to keep a bride with a substantial trust fund of her own in the style to which she was accustomed. It was, however, no prospect for a man who had started life always up on the roof or in a tree and had gone around the world at fourteen. Byrd requested the retirement list because of disability. His request granted, he abruptly found himself in limbo.

Chapter 2

Reaching for the Skies

World War I "did a lot of things for a lot of men," Richard would later write. "In a sense it saved me." A "willing cripple suddenly became to a mad world as valuable as a whole man who might be unwilling." Within weeks of his retirement, Richard was back in uniform as a reserve officer tasked with whipping the rapidly forming Rhode Island Naval Militia into shape for possible deployment to European seas and battlefields. His new friend, Assistant Secretary Franklin Roosevelt, applauded his grit. "Good for you. I wish everybody had come right back in as you did." After the inevitable administrative tangles were unsnarled, Byrd reported for duty in June 1916.[1]

It was not an easy job. The militia belonged to Rhode Island, not the United States. Local officials acknowledged Byrd's de facto command status but expected him to work closely with them. Byrd fulfilled his varied assignments admirably. Not only did he transform his charges into acceptable sailors, marines, and aviators, but he also won their hearts. An enlisted man wrote that he would "never be able to pay back all I owe you for your kindness and patience with me." The handful of militia aviators forged tight bonds and begged to be sent to advanced training and overseas as a unit. Byrd wrote strong letters to Washington on their behalf and fought just as hard for those who wanted to go to sea as soon as war was declared. Both interventions were successful, and a grateful flier told Byrd how deeply the entire militia, which by this time included men from Massachusetts, Maine, and Connecticut as well as Rhode Island, appreciated "the loyalty you have shown us in trouble." Richard Byrd would "always be our commander where-ever we go."[2] But once war came, the young Virginian was determined to be part of it.

Two days after Wilson went before Congress, Rhode Island's adjutant general wrote to his old friend Admiral William Sims that young Byrd "is most anxious to serve under you in the event of war or any emergency." Sims, about to embark on a critical, top-secret mission to England, ignored the message, but Byrd was soon summoned to Washington, carrying with him a glowing commendation from Governor Beekman.[3]

As he cooled his heels in the Bureau of Aeronautics, the impatient young man conceived the idea of establishing "a board of naval officers" that would go to France and acquaint itself with "the subject of expeditionary fighting and trench warfare." Such knowledge would be invaluable to the navy, not only during the present war but in years to come as well. For the first but not last time, Richard came across as the quintessential eager beaver: "I could help to do this work because I am intensely and profoundly interested in the matter and am prepared and anxious to go into the trenches for the necessary knowledge." Only one with a total ignorance of the Great War could make such a statement. Claude Swanson came down to the Navy Department from Capitol Hill to press his fellow Virginian's case, but Admiral Palmer, head of navigation, would have none of it. Richard Byrd could not be spared for a ninety-day trip to the European front; America was gearing up rapidly for war, and everyone was needed at home to push mobilization over the top. Secretary Daniels was out of town, and Chief of Naval Operations Benson was unavailable.[4]

When Daniels returned, he personally assigned the rather obstreperous young lieutenant as executive secretary of the navy's Commission on Training Camps. Byrd later dismissed the position as simply a "swivel chair job," moving thousands of enlisted sailors from one training camp or naval base to another.[5] But the position involved more than that. According to the Navy Department's memorandum "Commission on Training Camp Activities," the problem of "supplying the normalities of life" to thousands of boys in training camps "loomed large." The country had not engaged in a major war in a half century. The youngsters, wholly innocent of the world, had left sheltered homes, families, friends, clubs, churches, and colleges and had entered "a strange new life" in which everything was subordinate to the fashioning of an efficient military machine. The task of the naval commission, like that of its army counterpart, was to coordinate the various organizations that might help in reestablishing "as far as possible" old social ties by meeting "the recreational and relaxational needs of young men." The second problem, obviously intertwined with the first, was "the MENACE FROM IMMORALITY— a menace always accentuated in war time, and very grave because of its effect upon the physical health of the men."

The naval commission was to organize recreational activities inside the camps and in the surrounding communities in addition to its work in "the suppression of vice." With its army counterpart, the commission quickly enlisted the aid of such national organizations as the YMCA, YWCA, Knights of Columbus, American Library Association, and American Bureau of Social Hygiene. Within their ranks, the commissions established divisions of law enforcement, social hygiene instruction, athletics, music and song, theatrical entertainments, and the Division of Protective Work for Girls. Raymond Fosdick, a prominent businessman-turned-bureaucrat, was head of the naval commission. Walter Camp, the great Yale football coach who had already established his annual All-American football team, was head of the Division of Athletics. Byrd's later dismissal of his job was doubtless sincere, but he never could do anything halfway, and he again impressed colleagues and superiors with his striking competence and infectious enthusiasm.

Soon after he left the commission, a newly won friend wrote, "Of course I miss you greatly. I suppose I shall always do this." The chaplain of the New York Navy Yard expressed his appreciation "for the work you have done and so well done for the men of the service" and for the navy's Chaplain Corps as well. W. G. Isaacs added that Byrd had been a friend of the chaplains "almost from the time you left the Academy" and had consistently supported and encouraged the corps. His work would not be forgotten. Walter Camp waxed even more eloquent: "Nothing" in connection with his work had "been such a bitter disappointment" as learning that Dick Byrd was leaving the ranks. "I had hardly realized how much your enthusiasm and assistance in every possible direction had meant to me."[6]

But Richard was now determined, as he put it, to "crowd into aviation," and nothing would stop him. He mercilessly pestered both the navy's surgeons and, from a discrete distance, Josephus Daniels himself for a chance to become a pilot. The doctors were adamant. Byrd's assertions to the contrary, flying did involve using one's feet, and Richard Byrd was a semicripple. The young man fell into despair. Over the four-month stretch he spent helping to organize the training camp commission, Byrd claimed to have lost twenty-five pounds, "worrying over the uselessness of what I had become—just a high-class clerk," when what he yearned for and had been trained to do was fight. His health deteriorated so badly that he was summoned once more before the navy board of surgeons and told to take leave. "You're in terrible condition," they told him. Desperate, Byrd begged once more for a chance to fly. Send him to flight training at Pensacola for a month, he said, "and if I don't improve to suit you, I'll do anything you say." At a time when fighting men were needed to fill a multitude of billets, young Byrd's earnestness and dedication won the day. He got his orders to Pensacola and a two months' grace period. It was all the ecstatic man needed. "They were sports, those surgeons," he later observed appreciatively.[7]

The stakes for eager and ambitious young men entering military aviation in those early days were very high. War had stimulated the construction and deployment of countless land-based aircraft, seaplanes, and dirigibles that performed a multitude of tasks, including scouting, strafing, and bombing. Which aircraft type or types would emerge supreme from the crucible of battle, and who should control them? Pilots and bureaucrats engaged in often heated debate over the place and role of airpower in U.S. military policy, and their ongoing conflict drew Richard Byrd and his fellow aviators in both the army and the navy into passionate battles that shaped their lives and careers.

When the young Virginian went to Pensacola in early 1918, however, everyone's immediate goal was simple survival: one's number might come up at any moment flying the tricky, unstable aircraft of the day. Lifesaving parachutes lay in the future. The greatest fliers would prove to be a singular breed. Far from being daredevils, throwing themselves recklessly aloft, they shared an obsession with machinery and an insatiable curiosity about the mysteries and dynamics of flight, and how to master both. Many, like Byrd, had found adult responsibility imposed, bestowed, or earned at a young age. Though each possessed an almost foolhardy sense of self-confidence and, often, a desire to march to his own drummer, they all held an instinctive sense of the limits of risk. They would push those limits, but prudently, carefully, weighing everything they did and anything they demanded of their fragile aircraft. Each knew that there were old pilots, and bold pilots, but no old, bold pilots. Indeed, they coined the adage.

The base itself reflected how far aviation had come in a few short years. An aerial photograph taken shortly after the school's establishment late in 1913 shows a row of tent hangars neatly aligned on a narrow beach next to the scrub and piney woods of the Florida Panhandle. A tongue of wood extends from each hangar to the nearby water; attached to the tip of each tongue are crude one- and two-seat flying machines of various shapes and sizes, as befitted a technology struggling for life and definition.[8]

Four and a half years later when Richard reported for duty at the Naval Aeronautic Station, all had changed. As late as April 1917 the base numbered about 500 officers and men. By Armistice Day 1918, it would grow ten times, to 5,382 personnel. When Byrd arrived, permanent administrative and personnel quarters and hangars for both seaplanes and land-based aircraft were already in existence, soon to be joined by a floating balloon hangar in the "wet basin" next to the permanent observation tower.[9] Aircraft had changed dramatically, too. The crude contraptions of 1914 were giving way to more standardized, aerodynamically efficient, and stable machines with enclosed fuselages supporting integrated tail sections and graceful wings. But aviation remained a grand experiment and flying a risky business.

Richard Byrd saw Pensacola as a blur of white and khaki uniforms, deep blue sky, sparkling waters, and bright sand, everything shimmering in a context of excitement, risk, and death. He apparently thought it no place for a woman and family, for there is no evidence that Marie accompanied him south. Like most men of his generation, Richard maintained stringent views of a woman's place, and that place was not where men conducted strenuous and potentially deadly business. Accepting a young woman's unconventional riding style and "fast" ideas was one thing; exposing her feminine sensibility to engine grease, human sweat, and gruesome death day after day was something that no Virginia gentleman brought up a hundred years ago ever considered. Four decades later, as he sought to organize Operation Deepfreeze to support the International Geophysical Year in Antarctica, Admiral Byrd would express open contempt for the women who volunteered in vain.[10] Some of his Yankee friends did bring their wives and families down to Pensacola, which created further stress and tension as they streamed out of the married officers' housing and enlisted quarters to gather silently on the shoreline after every crash.

Byrd's account of the raw aviation society of Pensacola during World War I is reminiscent of writer Tom Wolfe's description of life at Edwards Air Force Base in the high desert country of southern California thirty years later. In 1917 men still struggled to master the unforgiving laws of physics and nature with cumbersome, poorly designed planes. In 1947 they ruthlessly pushed themselves and their sophisticated, red-hot aircraft far beyond where their grandfathers had gone, up to the very edge of space. The common denominators binding Pensacola and Edwards across the decades were daring and disaster. Strapping even the most up-to-date flying machine to one's bottom and rising to four thousand feet over the blue waters of Pensacola Bay was as potentially deadly as strapping aboard the X-1 and riding it beyond the speed of sound over the dry lake bed at Edwards: one could as easily be killed at sixty miles an hour as six hundred. There was one crucial difference, however: most of the youngsters who flocked to Pensacola in 1917–1918 came from placid and peaceful lives of little challenge where the dynamics of a still-new industrial age were poorly understood. They were innocent chaps, often heartbreakingly ignorant both of their machines and of the limits of their own competence and good fortune. The men of Edwards, war veterans all, took calculated risks, coldly studying and analyzing the missions before them. They were scientific fliers and as such owed much to men like Richard Byrd who had paved the way.

If Byrd is to be believed, he witnessed a fatal crash literally the moment he stepped on the air station. As the plane spun into the bay, killing both men aboard, an old friend he had not seen in years clapped him on the back, told him not to worry, and invited him up for a spin. In those days, Byrd maintained, a man could solo with as little as three hours' flight time; most did it after six. One could also be dead the next day or the next week as he put his plane through some new maneuver. There was a war raging in Europe, and naval aviators expected to be in France and England soon, flying antisubmarine patrols and, in an emergency, missions over the trenches to stop the last great German offensive. But the army boys Over There seemed to get all the glory and publicity. The men of Pensacola were desperate to get into combat with their own planes and show the world what the United States Navy and its flying machines could do in the air.

Yet Byrd somewhat exaggerated the atmosphere. The navy was determined that its pilots be as well trained as possible, and it took the young lieutenant two months to complete his basic training. Not until mid-April 1918 did he become Naval Aviator no. 608. He then took another three weeks to qualify as a seaplane pilot.

Byrd got it right when he wrote that too many cocky young men took deadly risks and too many instructors became the victims of the student pilots they were trying to teach. Nearly all the many accidents and fatalities suffered at Pensacola during Byrd's year there could be attributed to tailspins at higher altitudes and stalls near the ground. One day a pilot beginning to spin down out of control with his tail up accidentally kicked the high side of his rudder, and the plane immediately recovered. From that time on, tailspins should have provoked no panic. But they did. Student fliers often lost their wits when they went into a spin, and their instructors in the other cockpit were helpless to intervene. One student got his foot jammed in the rudder pedal as the aircraft fell to earth. Fortunately, the plane was in a flat spin and pancaked into the water. The student pilot received a cut, his instructor a broken thumb. On another occasion a youngster grabbed the control stick as the plane began to go down and clung to it with a literal death grip. The aircraft augured straight into the water from nearly a mile up. The instructor's body was never found; the student's crushed corpse was recovered from the wreckage, his hands still gripping the stick.

One of Byrd's closest friends was Morgan Draper. "This ensign and his lovely young wife had come to the station filled with enthusiasm for flying and brimming with excitement over the prospect of getting to Europe for active service in the air." Night after night Byrd dined with the happy pair, talking for hours about planes and engines and stunts. Draper became fixated on the idea of shifting seats while aloft. One day he and a colleague went up and disappeared over the horizon. Hours later a clerk in a clothing store in town called the base to say that he had seen a plane hit the water in a straight nosedive. Spray from the crash had gone a hundred feet into the air. The station immediately deployed its array of crash boats and wrecking barges and began searching the spot where the plane had gone in. Richard Byrd was right there. Night fell, and the search continued with huge arc lights. Another seaplane spotted what appeared to be a wingtip and plumped down on the water to investigate. Both pilots left the aircraft and dove to the alleged wreck. They found nothing, but when they surfaced they discovered the wind had pushed their plane far beyond reach. So they, too, had to be rescued. The crash team at last discovered and raised the "pitiful mess" of Draper's plane. The torn body of his copilot was found in the wreckage. Draper had disappeared. His young wife refused to believe he had perished until his corpse washed up several weeks later. It was clear that he had been trying his seat-changing stunt when he lost control of the plane and was pitched out. His copilot could not recover.[11]

Such incidents had a profound effect on Richard Byrd. He had come to Pensacola yearning for the thrill of flying, but aviation soon became an almost holy discipline and experience. One of his first training assignments was to tear down an airplane engine. The vast number of cams, valves, rods, screws, and bolts fascinated the young officer: "They all seemed so *dead,* so unrelated when spread around on the greasy canvas at my feet. . . . To the novice they were as meaningless as so many cobblestones." Then he and an enlisted mechanic were ordered to reassemble the engine. The two worked feverishly, the mechanic huffing and puffing as he labored. When they were done, a small steam crane came panting up and swung the engine into place on an airplane. Byrd suddenly felt a streak of apprehension flash across the back of his neck, "as if I had been touched by a cold finger." Were all the engine parts in place, would it run, would it hold up an aircraft in flight, "would it *live?*" The pilot turned the engine over, and it roared to life. Byrd and the mechanic watched the plane slide across the field, crop the daisies at the end of the runway, and soar safely into the blue. "In watching that plane rise, fly, devour space, I felt that I had helped create something alive; I had contrived a creature that by widening the vista of human life and quickening the processes also thereby lengthened life." Conquering the forces of wind and gravity, he had added to man's triumph over nature.[12] In later years, Byrd seldom flew commercially as he crisscrossed the country on his innumerable lecture tours. He resisted making quick flying trips to see Texas relatives or old friends in California. The train was always his preferred means of travel, and if a train journey would take too long, he would not go. It was as if he reserved flying for the most momentous times of his life; it could never be mundane.

When he soloed in a seaplane he flew carefully and even then "porpoised" his first water landing. One time taking off at sixty miles an hour he crashed into another aircraft spinning down out of control. He was crushed at having lost his plane. Thereafter, he flew not to celebrate himself and his skills but to test the abilities and limits of his aircraft. He quickly concluded that stunt flying had no real purpose unless it was employed to push back the boundaries of aviation science. Byrd wanted to learn all he could about flying; he came to harbor too much respect for both the promise and the scientific aspects of flight to cheapen it with deadly theatrics.

Once again he impressed his superiors. As his own training period approached its close in March 1918, Byrd won assignment as "Aide to the Superintendent for all training of School personnel, other than training in the air and technical mechanical training."[13] His flying skills were modest, but his qualities as a teacher, administrator, and researcher were outstanding. He filled his time outside of classrooms and occasional work on the Crash Evaluation Board, trying to figure out how and why the crude new machines of the air suddenly dove, spun, and turned out of the control of novice pilots. He saw a lot of crushed bodies and broken planes; he never forgot the devil-may-care boys who crashed them, falling two thousand feet in an uncontrollable spin or stalling fifty feet off the ground. So many of them had rich, promising lives before them. Suddenly, they were gone. Byrd concluded that more than half the crashes were caused by pilot error, either bad judgment or inexperience: "Many were caused by disregard of routine orders or carelessness. All these were in the class of 'avoidable crashes.'"[14]

In later years, Byrd would be accused of a fear of flying. If the charge is true—and he embarked on some of the most dangerous adventures in aviation annals—there were ample reasons for his apprehension. During his year at Pensacola he became a voice of sanity and scientific reason in a fledgling profession that attracted more than its share of impulsive fools.

Nonetheless, like most young men of the time, Byrd was rabid to get into the war. How could he get out of the training-and-administration rut? His agile mind quickly found an answer. The navy had ordered several big, new long-range flying boats from legendary pioneer designer Glenn Curtiss. They were deemed perfect for antisubmarine warfare off the coasts of northwestern Europe and the British Isles. Instead of shipping them across the Atlantic, why not fly them over? In later years Byrd would imply that the idea was his, but in fact it belonged to Admiral David W. Taylor, chief constructor of the U.S. Navy, who formally proposed such a flight in August 1917. The idea of flying the Atlantic had actually emerged in the United States three years earlier, when Curtiss and New York department store magnate Rodman Wanamaker, a prominent philanthropist and sportsman, had formally proposed to the Aero Club of America that Curtiss be encouraged to build an aircraft that could cross the Atlantic in a single bound. But Curtiss quickly realized that the requisite technology was simply not available. Nor was it in 1917; no U.S. aircraft then in existence could cross the entire Atlantic. But the admiral's aviation staff concluded that Curtiss now possessed the capability to build aircraft with the range to fly from North America to the Azores and from there to France and England.[15]

Months after Taylor and his men had begun detailed planning of the transatlantic flight, young Lieutenant Byrd erupted onto the scene, committing a cardinal error that may have forever marked him in naval circles as a maverick troublemaker. Without contacting Taylor or apparently anyone else in Washington or even Pensacola, he suggested his independently developed idea of a European flight to a most unlikely civilian, Walter Camp. Byrd naively believed that Camp's "large acquaintance among rich and influential men would make him a keystone in importance if only I could win him over." So the young aviator spent a good part of one night in May 1918 writing a letter proposing "to attempt the hydroaeroplane flight of the Atlantic" if Camp would back him. The five-man flight crew "will all train according to plans laid down by you." In a handwritten note on the margin, Richard begged Camp to "please keep the contents of this letter absolutely and strictly confidential as the flight would be a military operation." In another handwritten note at the bottom of the page, Richard asked Camp if he could raise "some thousands" of dollars from the Aero Club of America "if necessary. The government will probably give the plane or half of it." Byrd was clearly winging a proposal to which no one had as yet given detailed attention. Nonetheless, Camp soon replied with an encouraging cable and, according to Byrd, promptly went to Admiral Peary, the ostensible conqueror of the North Pole, to gain his support. Together, the coach and the admiral approached the Navy Department on Byrd's behalf. "This touched me in a tender spot also," Byrd continued, "because I had long thought a flight across the North Pole was possible."[16]

Byrd next took a friend, Lieutenant Walter Hinton, into his confidence, and together the two men began making long-distance flights from Pensacola out over the Gulf of Mexico, beyond the sight of land. Emboldened by his successes to date, Byrd finally approached the Navy Department itself on July 9, 1918, formally requesting "that I be detailed to make a Trans-Atlantic flight" in one of Glenn Curtiss's NC-1 type of flying boat, "when this boat is completed." Byrd added that it had "long been my ambition to make such a flight" and that he had made an intensive study of the subject. Superintendent F. M. Bennett forwarded Byrd's request with approval, adding that Byrd possessed "the spirit and will to carry this project forward successfully." A transatlantic hop was inevitable in the near future, Bennett wrote, and it would be "appropriate and creditable" for the U.S. Navy to accomplish the feat. Apparently, Byrd was not confident that his proposal would receive favorable attention, though he promised Hinton that if he got orders, Hinton would also. On August 2, three weeks after his formal request to the Navy Department, Richard rented a home in Warrington, near Pensacola, for a year, to begin on September 1 at thirty-five dollars per month. Presumably, Marie would join him. The same day he rented the house, however, Byrd got orders to go to Washington. He departed late that night after a frantic day in which he managed to find a tenant for the Warrington home, packing so hastily that he left his razor and two of his best uniform shirts behind, along with the hapless Walter Hinton. As the Pullman "whirled" him northward, the young Virginian dreamed of flying the Atlantic within a matter of weeks, if not days.[17]

In Washington Byrd cooled his heels for several weeks at the Navy Department. By this time, Captain Noble E. Irwin had been appointed director of naval aeronautics, and on August 12 he gave the eager young flier from Pensacola orders that would get Byrd out of town while providing him an opportunity to participate from afar in the proposed over-ocean flight. Richard was to proceed immediately to Halifax as commander of all U.S. naval aviation in Canada, establishing one or more air stations in Nova Scotia from which antisubmarine operations would be undertaken and perhaps eventually an over-ocean hop to Europe. Irwin soon amplified the orders to include possible creation of a seaplane base on the Newfoundland coast. In the interim, the Nova Scotian facilities would support patrols out into the near Atlantic designed to keep Germany's handful of long-range "cruiser" U-boats clear of the Canadian and northern New England coasts and away from Europe-bound convoys out of North Sydney and Halifax. Byrd's orders emphasized that he was to report directly to Canadian and British officials as well as to the Navy Department. He would have to demonstrate tact and skill as a military diplomat.

Byrd clearly understood the rebuke implied in his orders. Friends in the department had to convince him that commanding an antisubmarine air station in Canada was vital to the war effort. Once he got the station up and running, they quietly assured him, it would be turned over to the Canadians and he and his lads would be sent to France as part of a forthcoming bombing campaign against Germany—the first time aircraft would be used in a strategic role. Buoyed by the promise, still hopeful that a transatlantic flight might be in the works, yet fretful that the war would end before it materialized, he nonetheless carried his orders out promptly and efficiently. Byrd saw to it that Hinton would join him, then headed northward with an advance party of sailors and airmen.

Despite some "hot tussles" with Canadian and U.S. authorities, Byrd and his men got their airplanes and basic supplies from Washington to Halifax and had a crude tent city up and running near the town within three days of their arrival. They floated the wingless fuselages of their planes across the waters of the bay from the city's railroad yards to their new base on the north shore and "transformed our bare plot of ground on the beach to a hustling camp." Unused to explosives, Byrd and his boys had to employ dynamite on several occasions, and Dick later marveled that no one had been blown up in the process.[18]

Within weeks Byrd had another base up and running, pilots, mechanics, and ordnance in place, and was ready to do some serious flying. It proved dangerous from the beginning. The highlands and cliffs of Nova Scotia made the air rough, and frequent fog kept it thick. Piloting the tricky, fragile seaplanes was always risky because "changes were sudden and violent." One morning Byrd was on patrol about twenty miles at sea when he noticed a black cloud to the south. He promptly hauled around, but before he could get back to the station, he was fighting a half gale that whipped the waters of the bay into a running sea. "Just before I landed a wall of fog swept over the lower arm of the harbor. I slipped down not two minutes too soon."[19]

As the summer of 1918 passed into autumn and the winds and fog intensified off Nova Scotia, Byrd and his pilots flew as many antisubmarine patrols as the weather permitted. "Every convoy that came in and went out of Halifax and Sydney was protected by aircraft" from one of the two American naval stations, Richard later wrote with pardonable pride, "and a continual patrol was carried out up and down the coast." In early October, Washington informed its aviation commander in Canada that antisubmarine aerial operations would be expanded the following spring from Nova Scotia to Newfoundland, thus covering ever wider areas of the western Atlantic. He must request permission from Canadian authorities to inspect the Newfoundland coast for a suitable naval aviation station. The Canadians quickly assented, and by the eighteenth Richard was ordered to St. John's to begin his survey. Eight days later he returned to Nova Scotia with a brief but thorough two-page report recommending Cape Broyle harbor on the eastern coast of the Avalon Peninsula as the most suitable base site. The water was deep enough to accommodate a destroyer or seagoing tug as a base ship, headlands and cliffs provided sufficient shelter from wind and storm to ensure safe "maneuvering of the largest type seaplanes," and "telephone, telegraph, dirt road and railroad" lines provided direct connections with St. John's. Washington replied with the welcome news that Byrd had been jumped two full ranks to lieutenant commander on the retired list. He should have been delighted, but there was no word that the big, new flying boats were at last ready to hop north for their transatlantic flight, nor did he hear anything about his most recent application to be part of the flight. Then came word of the armistice, and shortly before Christmas orders came to turn the stations over to the Canadians and return home.[20]

Richard again received fulsome praise for his work. According to British admiral W. T. Grant, he possessed the "power of making friends and of obtaining the spontaneous co-operation of those with whom his work brought him in contact." The U.S. Navy representative at Halifax wrote of Richard's "cordial" cooperation, adding that "by his courtesy and attractive personality," he "has won the hearts of the Canadian people" and had been instrumental in promoting goodwill between the two countries. In a personal response to Grant, Josephus Daniels wrote that Byrd "is a young man to whom I was very closely drawn when I became Secretary of the Navy, and whose character and worth have been proved."[21]

On the way to Washington, Richard learned that the transatlantic flight would be commanded by an old friend, John Towers, with whom Richard had been informally communicating for some time. Shrewd minds in the department realized the threat of peace to naval aviation and were determined to mount a dramatic over-ocean mission that would demonstrate the United States Navy's continuing importance in the new world order. On February 4, 1919, Daniels formally assigned the proposed transatlantic flight a double-A priority.[22] Richard's undoubted elation was quickly dashed when he reached Washington and discovered a second reason for the flight. No one who had served on foreign soil during the late war—and that most definitely included Canada—would be allowed to participate. As well as being a poster event for the seemingly unlimited future of naval aviation, the mission had been continued as a postwar project in part to give employment—and glory—to those senior fliers who had somehow not gotten abroad and into the war. So Byrd would not be going. He suffered another setback when subsequent investigation of the Cape Broyle area revealed that however suitable it might be in the brief weeks of high summer, it was choked with ice floes and bergs during the remainder of the year, including springtime when the navy wanted to mount its transatlantic air mission. Subsequent investigations by others determined that Trepassey Bay on the south coast was best, being in the lee of seasonal ice floes.

The young flier's woes were compounded by illness. For some weeks after his return, he was confined to the Naval Hospital in Washington, victim of the terrible influenza epidemic that raced across Europe and America at the close of the Great War, killing more people than had perished on the recent battlefields. Richard was fortunate. He was confined for only a brief while, winning his release the third week of January 1919. While confined, he learned the navy planned to send him back to Pensacola.[23] Soon wiser minds in the department realized it would be well to keep the brilliant maverick close at hand, for the transatlantic flight was quickly assuming a wholly new cast.

Charles Lindbergh's dramatic solo flight to Paris in 1927 effaced nearly all memory of an earlier, equally dramatic, air race across the Atlantic. It occurred just months into the peace, during the spring of 1919, and involved a half-dozen two-man teams seeking to fly both east to west and west to east across the ocean. Two gallant, long-forgotten Englishmen, John Alcock and Arthur Whitten Brown, became the first ever to fly nonstop from the fringes of the New World (Newfoundland) to the fringes of the Old (Ireland).

Flying over the vast, watery spaces of the earth had long intrigued Western man, and the coming of the internal combustion engine seemed to make it feasible. As early as 1912 and 1913, "air meets" with prizes for various types of flying—racing, stunting, and so on—had become common on both sides of the Atlantic. The powerful British press lord Alfred Harmsworth, Viscount Northcliffe, became the driving force behind much of European aviation development in the immediate prewar years. Northcliffe encouraged all forms and sorts of heavier-than-air flight. Louis Blériot crossed the Channel to claim a five thousand–dollar prize from Northcliffe's *Daily Mail,* and in 1913, far in advance, it would seem, of any possibility of immediate realization, Northcliffe offered a prize of ten thousand pounds—then roughly eighty thousand dollars—to anyone who would fly the Atlantic "from any point in the United States, Canada, or Newfoundland, to any point in Great Britain or Ireland in 72 continuous hours."[24]

Over in the United States, Northcliffe's counterpart was Rodman Wanamaker, heir to the large New York department store fortune, who happily assumed the role of financial angel to a corps of aspiring American aviators. In 1912 Curtiss had easily persuaded Wanamaker to support him in the development of a "flying boat," or seaplane, that theoretically possessed the power and range to hop the Atlantic via the Azores. Two years later, Wanamaker first announced a twenty-five-thousand-dollar prize for a North Atlantic flight, and it was widely assumed that Curtiss's flying boat, to be piloted by an English aviator, would win it.

But the Great War foreclosed any opportunity for airmen to seek the prizes offered by either Wanamaker or Northcliffe. Four years of horrifying industrial warfare, however, did nothing to dampen popular and governmental passions for civil aviation. Just three days after the Armistice, Britain's Aero Club lifted its ban on transatlantic flight. The race was on. Fliers abruptly out of work and casting about for new thrills that could bring them fame and fortune quickly seized the opportunity. The Northcliffe prize dangled before them. Wanamaker did not resume his offer because the U.S. Navy was rumored to be preparing its own flight and, of course, could not compete for civilian prize money of any sort. But newspapers on both sides of the Atlantic, casting about rather frantically for ways to maintain the public excitement of the war years that had sustained artificially high sales, took up the idea of a great Atlantic air race with relish. The U.S. Navy's long-contemplated effort was sucked naturally into the vortex of this latest public excitement.

While languishing in the hospital, Byrd had telephoned Jack Towers. Was he still wanted on the Atlantic flight? "Decidedly so," Towers replied. As soon as he left sick bay, Byrd rushed to Commander Irwin's desk and begged to be given a chance at the Atlantic mission. Irwin, six feet five and not easily intimidated by a man years younger and almost a foot shorter, waffled. Byrd was once again left in limbo, as he had been the previous summer before being ordered to Canada. Richard promptly sat down and wrote a "treatise on the possibility of a trans-Atlantic flight via the Azores that covered matters of operations, navigation, and meteorology."[25] The navy now had a solid planning framework from which to operate. Jack Towers immediately hired his young colleague and eight others to work in the "Trans-Atlantic Flight Section" in the office of the director of aeronautics, selecting and training mechanics and pilots for the proposed flight and preparing the navigational aids that would provide the basis for the Atlantic crossing.

By the spring of 1919, the peat bogs of western Ireland and the remote, rocky coast of eastern Newfoundland had become magnets for fliers eager to cross the eighteen hundred miles of stormy skies and seas between North America and Britain. All were Englishmen, which at once threw the American naval effort into even bolder relief yet raised questions about its "sporting" nature. The Yanks were preparing lavishly, having dispatched a tanker, repair ship, and minelayer to Trepassey Bay to provide maximum support to the four seaplanes scheduled to make the Atlantic hop. They were even preparing to station a line of destroyers only fifty miles apart along the proposed flight route to the Azores and then all the way to Lisbon and Plymouth, England, with several battleships in supporting roles some twenty miles away. No civilian pilot flying from Newfoundland to Ireland (or vice versa) could expect anything remotely like such a safety net. Moreover, the American decision to stage through the Azores rather than directly across the Atlantic seemed to rob their effort of the glory of a single daring jump.

Although the Americans seemed to have much the better of it by going via the Azores, their route created serious navigational problems. As the historian of the American flight observed, it was one thing to take off from Newfoundland and aim a plane at the thirty-six thousand square miles of Ireland, with Scotland and England just a few score miles to the east to count on as a "backstop." The Azores was composed of not quite nine hundred square miles "whose terrain is distributed unevenly among nine specks spread out over an expanse of ocean" as large as Ireland. Miss the Azores, and one's next landfall was nine hundred miles away in the Madeiras.[26] Certainly, the line of destroyers would help *so long as* communications held up. But as late as 1937 when Amelia Earhart disappeared, communications with aircraft aloft remained uncertain. This was particularly the case with aircraft flying over large bodies of water.

Sailors knew how to cross seas, but aviators moving at much more rapid speed far above the horizon in craft that changed position frequently and were often forced to fly through or above clouds and haze demanded dramatically modified instrumentation. Towers made Byrd "solely responsible for all the navigational equipment used in the flight." As usual, the young Virginian was frightfully keen.

He argued that the navy did not need to station destroyers every fifty miles along the flight path between Newfoundland, the Azores, and the coast of western Europe. But he was voted down. In the meantime, he developed an impressive new tool, the aerial sextant, which mounted an artificial horizon bubble in a sturdy, calibrated glass tube filled with a yellow liquid that permitted flight in the absence of a clearly defined horizon. The instrument became standard issue on all cross-water flights for the next twenty years.

Byrd and his mates also helped elaborate a reliable drift indicator that allowed pilots to compensate for winds. The immediate practical success of these two instruments and their widespread adoption truly launched Byrd's aviation career. A decade later he wrote, "I have given many years of time and thought and investigation to the problem of long distance flights, ever since 1918, when I began flying out of sight of land [at Pensacola] to test the possibility of navigating an airplane as a ship is navigated. This is nothing to boast about," Byrd added. "It simply shows that I have had a hobby, just as another man might play golf or shoot clay pigeons." But he was clearly proud of his mastery of this "hobby." The young officer worked tirelessly, "night and day," instructing the command pilots of the four NC seaplanes "in the new science of air navigation," as well as the commanding officer of the dirigible C-5 that might be used as a backup aircraft if the seaplanes for some reason either failed to make the hop or failed to complete it.[27]

There were moments that spring when Richard thought he might become one of the flight members. Towers wanted him. Washington was silent for the time being. The navy had decided on a New York to Europe flight from Rockaway Beach on the southern end of Long Island, adjacent to what is now Kennedy International Airport, via Halifax, Trepassey Bay, and the Azores to Lisbon and Plymouth, England, from whence *Mayflower* had sailed three centuries before. When the flying boats were at last ready to proceed north, Towers invited Byrd to navigate NC-3 as far as Newfoundland. Richard detected a hint that he might be kept on at least for the Azores leg of the journey. The delighted young navigator spent the flight north, in Towers's words, "vibrating" between the forward and after cockpits, trying out instruments, dropping smoke bombs, and tying himself up in communication wires. Between Cape Cod and Halifax and again between Halifax and Trepassey Bay, the flying boats navigated out of sight of land for the first time. At one point, vicious side winds forced Towers and Byrd to rely on the drift indicator, which worked perfectly. Bouncing and bumping through the extremely rough weather common to the area, NC-3 made precise landfall on the tip of Newfoundland. But whatever satisfaction Byrd got from navigating safely through heavy weather quickly evaporated upon landing when he learned that his hope of flying on to the Azores had been dashed. A cable awaited from his "nemesis," Irwin, expressly forbidding him from accompanying the seaplane contingent on its over-ocean flight.[28]

But the dirigible C-5 remained a possibility if all four seaplanes failed to make it from New York to Plymouth. So Towers and Irwin sent the "fragile non-rigid gas bag of only about 200,000 cubic feet of capacity" north in the wake of the seaplanes. The airship, under the command of Lieutenant Commander Emory Coil, flew nonstop the 1,050 nautical miles from Montauk Point, Long Island, to Newfoundland in just under twenty-six hours on May 14–15, 1919, setting a record for the time. Suspended beneath the gasbag of the ship was a bullet-shaped gondola perhaps 50 feet in length that carried three or four men in two cockpits. Two tiny motors were mounted on either side of the gondola. Some speculated that even if the dirigible lost all power, it might be possible to just drift across the Atlantic. Good navigators like Dick Byrd knew such thinking was fallacious, but when he was offered a chance to join C-5's crew at Trepassey, he jumped at it. For its time the "C"-class dirigible was reasonably advanced technology, and within a few years, the navy would equip the C's for bombing, mounting several missiles on the gondola's hull. However, almost immediately upon reaching the windy coast of Newfoundland, C-5 blew away from its moorings and perished in a storm. With it went Byrd's last chance to be among the very first to cross the Atlantic. It was a disheartened, grounded aviator who climbed the hill behind Trepassey Bay shortly before dinnertime on May 16, 1919, and watched American seaplanes take off, bound for glory and history. A sharp wind cut down from the Arctic, and out on the blue sea, huge white icebergs dotted the dark waters. "To be here on the spot and see three planes hop off for Europe for the first time in history and, after all my hopes and work, not be in one of them, was a cataclysmic actuality that no amount of philosophy could efface."[29]

Only seaplane NC-4 would make it all the way to Plymouth, England, eventually splashing down on May 27 after a total elapsed flight time of twenty-seven hours. One of its four crewmen was Lieutenant Walter Hinton. Despite his own adversity, Dick Byrd had obviously kept the pledge he had made to his mate. Nineteen days later, on June 15, John Alcock and Arthur Whitten Brown officially "won" the Newfoundland-to-Ireland leg of the great Atlantic air race. Sixteen and a half thrilling and exhausting hours after leaving the cliffs of the New World, the two men semicrashed into an Irish peat bog after flying through almost perpetually stormy night and daytime skies.[30]

Dick Byrd had done well and received numerous letters of commendation, including one from his good friend and acting navy secretary, Franklin Roosevelt, who praised the flier-navigator for "the energy, efficiency, and courage" he had demonstrated in contributing to the success of the transatlantic flight.[31] But Dick was discouraged. He had just suffered what he considered a devastating personal and professional setback; he was permanently on the retired list and could expect no further promotion. The country and the world were entering a period of general peace, and there were widespread cries to reduce military budgets and vast fleets. A prudent man about to start a family should contemplate life outside military and naval circles.

Within days of the flight, Dick began to look for opportunities. He contacted W. B. Miller, president of the Norwalk Tire Company and, though remaining on active duty, assumed the presidency of the Tire Store at New York Avenue and Twelfth Street Northeast in Washington. Byrd and his partner, J. W. Hefton, hoped to obtain a marketing franchise from Norwalk, and they compiled impressive endorsements from U.S. Senators Thomas Martin and Claude Swanson, several prominent Washington, D.C., bankers, and the assistant cashier of the largest bank in Winchester.[32] But the business soon ran into trouble. Richard assumed that as new franchise owners in town, he and Hefton would be given the same sales advantages, including distributing discounts, as the already established franchise. Norwalk expected spirited competition to boost sales. Richard apparently bailed out of the business quickly to concentrate exclusively on his naval work and career.

However much it may have galled or frustrated him, Dick Byrd quickly became the quintessential staff man for naval aviation. He possessed the ability to please and to accomplish, to get his work done in an atmosphere of pleasantness that made others like him and want to do his bidding if at all possible. He was aided immeasurably by the atmosphere in which he worked. Despite the recent war, Washington, D.C., in the early twenties remained in many ways a small and folksy town. The volume and range of public business was comparatively small and political life leisurely. Power resided, as it had in all but times of extreme national emergency, in the urban canyons and offices of central and lower Manhattan, 240 miles to the north. The federal bureaucracy was minute; representatives and senators were not yet buffered by layers of legislative and administrative assistants. Most got by with a secretary and a clerk. Determined lobbyists like Richard Byrd thus enjoyed easy access. Even this early he possessed sufficient dash, credentials, and, thanks to brother Harry and his own skills, the growing family name and political clout to champion naval aviation in public circles. In the six years between his return from Newfoundland in the early summer of 1919 and his departure for Greenland with the MacMillan expedition in June 1925, Richard became a savvy Washington insider with a thick file on all the right people to know and to cultivate. There may never have been a lieutenant commander in the history of the United States Navy who became as well connected as he.

Richard joined John Rodgers, Henry C. Mustin, John Towers, Bruce Leighton, and Kenneth Whiting in a coalition of ardent young fliers "who had become true believers . . . unswerving in their certainty that the airplane would revolutionize naval warfare." It is unclear whether Byrd went all the way as some of his colleagues did in proposing a naval air force completely separate from the surface fleet and submarine service, but he and they had plenty of work to do simply obtaining a safe administrative niche for aviation within the Navy Department. Their chief opponent was General Billy Mitchell of the Army Air Service, the American apostle of strategic bombing. Mitchell, Hugh Trenchard in Britain, and Giulio Douhet in Italy preached to ever wider and more appreciative audiences that all future warfare could, indeed would, be decided by fleets of bombers smashing cities, battle fleets, and entire nations to pieces from the air. Modern aircraft had rendered armies and navies obsolete, and a nation's national defense should be organized around an independent air force that included all elements of airpower, land and sea based. Mitchell's attacks on the concept of sea power were unending and caustic. They proved to be a godsend to Byrd and his fellow naval aviators. Besieged battleship admirals grudgingly conceded the need for sea-based aviation. But it was up to the fliers to solve the organizational problems or risk being absorbed into a united air service.[33]

As soon as he returned to Washington to work on the transatlantic flight, Richard was asked by his colleagues to help prepare legislation proposing a bureau of aeronautics within the Navy Department. He would later write that he was asked to draft the legislation alone and then was joined by three others in presenting it to his superiors. But Richard took the leading role, which for some reason he did not wish to acknowledge. The despised Noble Irwin suppressed the initial legislation. But Irwin departed as director of naval aviation in July 1919, to be replaced by Captain Thomas P. Craven, who worked tirelessly to promote aviation despite chafing under the direct administrative control of the unsympathetic chief of naval operations, William Benson. When Benson retired, Craven emerged as a doughty champion of naval air. Byrd and his friends found another champion on the Hill in Congressman Frederick C. Hicks from Long Island, who prepared legislation of his own, grounded firmly in the ideas circulating within the naval aviation community. Hicks found strong support among fellow lawmakers for the notion that the flying sailors must enjoy a substantial degree of administrative and operational independence.

But Billy Mitchell held Congress and the country in thrall throughout 1919 and 1920 as he continued his demands in the media and on the Hill for an independent air force and a department of national defense. When Captain William Moffett reported as director of naval aviation in March 1921, Byrd and his in-

creasingly impatient colleagues quickly collared him. Five days after Moffett assumed his duties, Byrd presented him with a memorandum containing a "point-
by-point case" for a bureau of aviation. The current Planning Division of Naval
Operations was no place for the director's office because neither the chief of naval
operations nor anyone else there had time to understand or pay attention to the
incredible number of details involving this new and revolutionary branch of the
service. Moreover, aviation suboffices and branches were scattered across ten Navy
Department bureaus, "each of which is a law unto itself." The new chief of naval
operations wanted a separate bureau for the navy's fliers, as did several members
of the House and Senate Foreign Affairs Committees.[34]

Moffett was readily convinced, as were Secretary Josephus Daniels and Franklin
Roosevelt, then in his last months as assistant secretary. Moffett's careful, low-key
testimony before Congress when combined with Mitchell's growing intemperance
carried the day, and on July 12, 1921, President Harding signed into law legislation creating the Bureau of Aeronautics within the Navy Department. Moffett was
generous in his praise of Byrd's work. In early 1922 he assured a correspondent
that "in 1919 [Byrd] wrote a bill creating a Bureau of Aeronautics in the Navy Department. Though at first violently opposed by both the Navy and Congress he
stuck to his guns and finally won over the Navy and then, almost single-handed
passed the bill through Congress, though opposed by the Republican leader who
was then in power."[35]

Many years later Byrd claimed that he had become Moffett's right-hand man,
acting "as a sort of a confidential assistant to the Captain, and thus worked very
closely with him and had an intimate knowledge of most of his problems." His fit-
ness reports from those years glow with approval, filled with such hallowed words
as "cooperative," "devotion to duty," "industry," "initiative," "judgment," "justice," "leadership," "reliability," "self-control," "discipline," and "loyalty" from and
to subordinates. In the fall of 1921, Moffett wrote that the young man exhibited
"remarkable good judgment" and "tact" in dealing with others.[36] Richard por-
trayed himself as Johnny-on-the-spot, intuitively perceiving when a crisis was
brewing and throwing himself into the breach, once rising from a sickbed to do
so. He raced up to and around Capitol Hill on many occasions, soothing feelings,
easing communications between rival camps, dramatically cornering key legislators at critical moments and persuading them to speak up for naval air and a separate aeronautics bureau at just the right time. Moffett's most scholarly biographer
grants Byrd credit for one major innovation. Billy Mitchell got to Senator Robert
La Follette with the proposal that, of course, any chief of the proposed navy aeronautics bureau should himself be a naval aviator; that was only common sense.
Mitchell well knew that naval aviation was so young that there were no senior officers available; the proposed bureau could be rendered stillborn by lack of suit-

able leadership. Hearing of Mitchell's impending coup, Byrd rushed to La Follette's office, found the senator, and offered an ingenious solution. Chiefs of the Bureau of Aeronautics need not be qualified aviators per se but must qualify as aviation observers. La Follette bought the proposal, the bureau was born, and Moffett duly went off to Pensacola for a brief five-week course of general aviation study. Moffett subsequently employed the aviation-observer billet to temporarily fill senior positions in the new bureau until a sufficient number of fliers obtained promotions to ease the problem.[37]

With the bureau at last a reality, Richard hastened to mend fences with its opponents. He wrote Representative Frank W. Mondell of Wyoming, thanking him for taking the time to listen to the bill's sponsors. "I have understood your position in the matter all along," Byrd added, "and I realize it was an unpleasant duty for you to oppose" the measure. Richard applauded the congressman for not carrying his opposition to the point of killing the legislation, which he could well have done. "You played the game squarely," Richard concluded with more than a trace of youthful pomposity. Mondell quickly dispatched a gracious reply: he hoped the bureau would efficiently and economically promote the aviation interest within the navy. "I congratulate you on the outcome. I feel that your earnest efforts had much to do with it." Others echoed Mondell's assessment. "I don't know what we would have done in aeronautics except for you," one rear admiral wrote the still-junior officer in 1924. "We certainly would have made little advancement. I wish we had someone like you to look out for us in other affairs."[38]

But when Moffett began staffing the senior levels of his new bureau, Richard's name was nowhere to be found. The "confidential assistant" with the glowing efficiency reports and wide contacts was not offered a position of power or influence. There are a number of possible explanations. First, Lieutenant Commander Byrd was still too junior to be offered a substantial job. But he could well have remained in some capacity as Moffett's official or unofficial adviser. Second, the fact that he was a retired officer recalled to the active list could well have told against him. But once again, bold and imaginative leaders like William Moffett always managed to skirt red tape and find places for valued subordinates. A third explanation is that Richard Byrd simply did not want to "fly a desk" in Washington, that he never surrendered his dream of crossing the Atlantic by air. Despite the triumph of Alcock and Brown, the two Britons "still left us the problem of a direct flight from America to Europe"—from New York to Paris or beyond.[39] NC-4 had not even overflown the entire Atlantic without pause. Thus, shortly after the epoch-making flights of 1919, New York hotel magnate Raymond Orteig offered twenty-five thousand dollars for the first nonstop flight between New York and Paris, touching off a frenzy of interest.

As the fight to create the Bureau of Aeronautics reached its climax late in 1921,

Richard determined to have a go at Orteig's prize in a single-engine aircraft. The new secretary of the navy, Edwin Denby, wisely vetoed his request; single-engine planes of the early twenties were simply too fragile and limited to make the attempt worthwhile. So the determined aviator turned his mind to doing the job with a larger multiengine plane. Unfortunately, that technology also remained too crude and uncertain. The frustrated young officer was once more left in limbo. His dreams always seemed to outpace reality.

Richard returned to the routine work of answering correspondence and responding to or deflecting the efforts of lobbyists trying to get the new aviation bureau's attention. Amid the summer heat and administrative doldrums, the British suddenly offered a glimmer of hope that Richard might yet realize at least one of his aviation dreams. Despite the amazing advances in propeller driven heavier-than-air-craft technology, interest in dirigibles remained high throughout the world. No one had a stronger belief in the future of "airships" than Moffett, who would perish in 1933 aboard the navy's ill-fated *Akron*. British and German technology was far ahead of that in North America. Just a month after Alcock and Brown had fought their way across the Atlantic, Britain's R-34 airship made a smooth and uneventful crossing from Scotland to New York City. The future of dirigibles seemed ensured, so in 1921 Moffett convinced the Navy Department to buy the newly constructed British airship ZR-2—subsequently designated R-38—and fly it across the Atlantic. R-38 was no gasbag like C-5 but, like sister R-34, a large, rigid craft with enormous lifting power, strong engines, and a sophisticated control car. It was, in sum, the type of dirigible that would culminate in the magnificent *Hindenburg* a decade and a half hence. Competition to crew the vessel across from Europe was intense, and Byrd had no reason to think that his application of August 4 would be favorably considered. Two days later, however, Moffett ordered his assistant to England for duty in connection with preparing R-38 for its flight and navigating it across the Atlantic. The appointment was undoubtedly a reward of sorts for the frustrated young pilot and also an acknowledgment of his formidable skills.[40]

But did Moffett also want to get his vigorous young colleague out of town? Byrd had exhibited a flair for self-promotion as well as hustle, even a tendency to amplify his importance and role a bit more than necessary. These traits would make him a superb fund-raiser in just a few short years. But they could also be off-putting, and they would make him a controversial figure later on. Byrd himself hinted that Moffett might have wanted him removed for a time. After spending ten pages in his first memoir, *Skyward* (1928), talking about his numerous and always successful activities in helping get the bureau legislation passed, Byrd wrote with questionable modesty that although "all this sounds very simple and easy; just a lot of running around and talking to people," he was nonetheless often "misunderstood." Some of his "shipmates" looked upon him as little more than "a 'politician,' a term of more than mild contempt in the Navy. Many thought I was grinding my own axe."[41] If Moffett felt this way, or was influenced by many of his new staff in this direction, then Byrd's assignment to R-38 was less a promotion than a banishment, however temporary, while the new bureau was being organized and put on its feet.

The rest of R-38's flight crew under Commander Louis H. Maxfield had been in Britain for some time working with the Royal Air Force (RAF) to test the new airship near Howden, a small town some twenty miles south and slightly east of York in northeastern England, not far from the city of Hull. A number of wives and family members accompanied their men abroad, and at least one mechanic met and married an English girl.

Sailing by steamship across the Atlantic, Richard reached Howden on the evening of August 22 but for some reason was immediately ordered to report to the naval attaché's office at the American Embassy in London. He arrived in the capital that night. The following afternoon tragedy struck R-38. Soaring aloft from Howden the airship headed eastward on a routine test flight. Passing over Hull at about four o'clock, the craft began to break apart and came down in two pieces over the Humber River. Only fourteen men out of a crew of forty-nine survived. Word was flashed to London, and three hours later the naval attaché convened a hasty meeting, sending Byrd and another lieutenant commander, Newton White, rushing back north to take charge of salvage operations. Upon reaching Hull, Byrd went immediately to the riverside and joined British authorities on a wrecking barge that set out to search for survivors. For the next eight days Richard worked around the clock with his British colleagues to salvage whatever could be retrieved from the disaster. His two reports to Moffett and an informal message to Commander Pence, the naval attaché in London, are models of brevity and clarity.[42]

According to Byrd, the commanding officer of the airship, Lieutenant Wann, Royal Air Force, having just completed satisfactory speed trials, began a fresh set of speed and rudder tests. Apparently, some very sharp turns made at about fifteen hundred feet above Hull overstressed the airship's frame. Suddenly, a large dent about sixty feet wide was seen to appear on the right side of the giant craft about three-quarters of the way to its stern. Obviously, one or more girders within the mainframe had collapsed catastrophically. For a long moment, Wann maintained a turn that took the airship over the river, away from the populated area. Suddenly, the fabric on and around the dent began to rip and tear. The ship's nose and tail both went up as its internal girders collapsed in a scream of metal. Then the nose went down and the ship tore apart, the after section drifting into the water while the forward three-quarters caught fire from ruptured fuel tanks feeding the motors. Falling rapidly, the huge nose section blew up several hundred feet above the river. The rest of the forward section exploded again just over the water. Wann, the only survivor in the forward section, later told one of Byrd's colleagues that everything happened so quickly that he could not react—a terrific crash, the nose suddenly up, an enormous explosion, incredible heat, a rush to the door, another explosion, and he lost consciousness. Byrd wrote Moffett that he, the American sailors not aboard the dirigible, and the British worked deep into the first night searching for survivors and wreckage and "began salvaging again early today." Operations were hampered by a paucity of men to work the cranes, barges, and tugs and by the vicious tides in the Humber that ran as fast as five knots and rose and fell about twenty feet, discouraging divers from going down.

As the days passed, the grimness of the work tested everyone's endurance. Nearly all the bodies were recovered, some from the river, a few blown as far as a mile away by the explosions. Several crewmen apparently donned parachutes, and eyewitnesses claimed to have seen at least two deploy from the stern of the rapidly falling ship. One, however, became trapped beneath the falling stern section. Byrd subsequently determined that some crew members died of drowning, burns, and shock. Most bodies were "terribly swollen"; many were mutilated. Commander Maxfield's body was found in a nearby village; Lieutenant Bieg's corpse was discovered "abaft the control car amongst entangled wires and girders." So important had dirigibles become to the Royal Air Force at the time that Air Commodore Maitland had come aboard R-38 for this particular test flight. His remains "were found in what was left of the control car; he went down with his hands grasping the water ballast lever" in a pathetic attempt to arrest the crash by releasing weight.

Richard had to deal with wives and families as well, most of whom "held up wonderfully well" until the bodies of their loved ones had been recovered. Richard's burden was further weighted by the fact that his old friend Emory Coil, who had commanded the dirigible C-5 back in 1919 before it was destroyed in the Newfoundland storm, was aboard R-38 that fatal day. Coil's new wife—an Englishwoman—was below in the city. A survivor stated that the unfortunate officer was at girder 100, precisely where the airship broke apart. He fell out and down a thousand feet or more into the water, where his broken body was later recovered. The British widow of an American enlisted man named Julius was not so fortunate. He had apparently remarried before his American divorce was final. Mrs. Julius thus faced penury because she could not claim any accident insurance. Byrd went around to the American and British salvage workers and raised sixty pounds for her; he also arranged for the YMCA in London to look after her. The other American widows were in somewhat better shape, but Byrd warned Moffett that they, too, would require support beyond their death benefits.

Between looking out for the wives, attending services, liaising with his British counterparts, and working hour after hour with the salvage crews, Byrd got very little sleep. "Today is Friday," he wrote Moffett on September 2, "and we will continue Salvage Operations at least until Monday night." Several of the wives would soon be returning home along with the bodies of fifteen crash victims. "I am arranging for Flowers and the proper escort. One of our officers will go with them to Plymouth, but the R.A.F. will provide the train escort." Byrd's only problem was with the American press, and in particular the Hearst correspondent who, Byrd claimed, would rather muckrake than report. At first he decided that the best course was to "beat" up the Hearst reporter verbally; then he chose the softer role of seduction, and that seemed to work. After it was all over, Richard returned to London where, as senior officer present, he drafted a form letter of thanks to various RAF and civilian officials and authorities. He mailed no fewer than a score.

Cooperation between the United States Navy and the Royal Air Force in salvaging the wreck and making preliminary investigations of the crash had been exemplary, and it was due in large measure to the words and actions of a thirty-two-year-old junior American naval officer. Air Vice Marshall A. V. Vyvyan wrote a graceful note to "My dear Byrd." Awful as the tragedy had been, it had been "made easier by the splendid way the aftermath has been shouldered together." Vyvyan promised to send a copy of his letter to Washington for inclusion in Byrd's official file. Anglo-American relations at the time were not the easiest. Washington was pressing London unmercifully to agree to naval parity and thus to a practical limit on British imperial power. Reaction at the Admiralty and on Fleet Street in London had been sharp. The prompt, efficient, and compassionate common response to the R-38 tragedy served to remind officials on both sides of the Atlantic how basic the ties between the nations had become in recent years of deadly war and uneasy peace. Richard's conduct materially advanced his nation's interests.[43]

He returned to the States aboard the cruiser *Olympia* in early November and resumed his tedious duties in the bureau only to find that Congress, in one of its many economy moves, was about to revoke the temporary appointments it had granted in wartime. Still on active duty, Richard was abruptly reduced to the rank of lieutenant. Once again, his eye wandered toward the attractions of civilian life.

Work brought him in contact with the Auto-Ordnance Company owned by New York industrialist and financier Thomas Fortune Ryan, and for some time in the early twenties Richard entertained hopes that Ryan might provide him a financial stake to enter the business world. He assiduously wooed Auto-Ordnance officials and lobbyists and had one apparently encouraging "long talk" with Ryan himself. Early in 1924, Richard wrote the industrialist that "I was ready to tell him what business I was going into." Ryan never replied, so Richard wrote another letter. Nothing came back from New York. Richard was humiliated and outraged.

"There is no man living who can treat me like that, and I resent it, and I hope you will," he wrote brother Harry. Ryan was the last person, Richard added, whose support he would ever request.[44]

Shortly before nine o'clock on Saturday evening January 28, 1922, in the midst of the biggest and hardest blizzard Washington, D.C., has ever experienced, the "massive" roof of Crandall's Knickerbocker Theater on Columbia Road collapsed with a roar "mighty as the crack of doom." A heavy accumulation of snow was the cause. The final death count was ninety-seven; nearly everyone else in the building was injured. Richard was either passing by or nearby and immediately joined those racing to the scene as doctors quickly installed a makeshift hospital in a nearby candy store. The falling roof brought down the theater's balcony onto the main floor, trapping several score people. As the injured and dying lay screaming and crying in the frigid, snowy cold, Richard and a navy doctor, Lieutenant Commander R. A. Warner, worked heroically to free those trapped. For "three or four hours" Richard concentrated on army captain Mills and his wife. Crawling on his hands and knees under the suspended portion of the balcony, he worked on both his back and his stomach with plaster falling on and all around him in an unsuccessful attempt to raise "tons of steel, concrete, and plaster" sufficiently to free the couple. All the while, he cheerfully assured them that rescue was on the way and that he would not leave them. Once they were freed, he moved on to help others. These acts received wide attention in town, among the military, and around the country. Once more, Richard had proved himself a fearless hero.[45]

His relations with Moffett, however, remained prickly, and when he rashly proposed establishing a naval aviation reserve unit at Squantum on South Boston Bay, the admiral rushed him out of town with orders to do it.[46] There could be no finer duty from a family standpoint, as Marie's parents had long made their home on fashionable Brimmer Street, "the water side of Beacon Hill," not far from the Boston Navy Yard. Dick and Marie had lived for a time in several temporary homes in and around Boston whenever they were in the city, but by the end of 1924 they were firmly ensconced at 7–9 Brimmer, a spacious, "old fashioned five story brick house" that they would make their home for the rest of their lives.[47]

Son Richard Jr. ("Dickie") had been born in February 1920, as his father settled firmly if not comfortably into duty at Washington. Three girls would follow in the next six years. Evelyn Bolling, always known by her middle name and whom her father often called "Bommie," was born in September 1922; Katherine Ames came in March 1924, and Helen Ames was born in October 1926. Marie's money and the security of Brimmer Street ensured a comfortable life for the children, though one disrupted by their father's frequent absences—and their mother's as well in the early years. Despite Byrd's modest rank, the Ames family fortune allowed Richard to play the 1920s version of the Washington power game, and in many ways he relished it. He was what contemporaries approvingly called a "club-bable man," and during his tours of duty in the capital he gained membership not only in expected organizations such as the Army and Navy Club but also in more exclusive circles, including the Chevy Chase Club, where, in early 1925, he hosted a lavish dinner dance. Soon he was writing a friend that he had resigned from the Army and Navy Club "because I am a member of so many other clubs." At the same time, he and Marie routinely invited "thirty or forty people to dinner" at their apartment on P Street Northwest and frequently attended Washington theaters. Richard also began investing in the stock market that had begun its fabled midtwenties boom. Eddie McDonnell of Smith and McDonnell brokerage house handled his affairs. A retired lieutenant commander who, unlike his client, had truly retired, McDonnell found Richard to be a cautious player, at least in the early years. At one point Byrd told McDonnell that he had "several hundred dollars to invest. What would you recommend that pays a good interest? . . . I don't want to have anything of a speculative nature." He wondered about Philips Petroleum.[48] How much money Byrd made or lost in the market is not clear.

Such a busy life, day and night, left little time for devotion to the children. Just before his son's fifth birthday, Byrd wrote brother Tom that "Marie has to go back [to Boston] temporarily, as Dickie has been sick, but he is O.K. now, I'm glad to say." Marie rushed back to Washington so quickly that she and Richard missed the boy's party. With the transparent awkwardness of the neglectful parent, Dick tried to make amends in a letter. Daddy and Mommy were sorry they could not be there. "We have sent you some birthday toys, and as soon as Daddie makes some money, Mommie and Daddie will come back to little Dickie, and we will take a ride in Daddie's car and choochy boat and a canoe boat, too. Where would Dickie like to go next summer?"[49]

In November 1923 Roald Amundsen, the famed polar explorer who with a handful of compatriots had reached the South Pole and lived to tell about it, announced that he was organizing an aviation expedition to the Arctic. Richard, who was still in Massachusetts, promptly filed a request to volunteer. Not only had he been connected with every transatlantic flight the navy had attempted, he reminded his superiors, but he also claimed that "for eight months I have studied the problem of flying in the polar regions." The navy ignored him. Instead, he was ordered on a series of trips to organize naval reserve aviation units on the East Coast and in the Midwest. At one point he returned to Washington to lobby Congress personally and successfully for sufficient funds to operate the aviation reserve stations. It was little wonder that his superiors continually frustrated his attempts both to leave the service and to pursue his own projects.[50]

The only way Richard saw to get ahead at this point lay in fighting to regain

the temporary rank of lieutenant commander that he and a number of colleagues
had lost due to congressional action two years before. Richard believed, or was advised, that his best opportunity was through private legislation that would allow
Congress to direct the navy to restore his rank. In late May 1924, he or a colleague
with legal experience drafted a short bill, House Resolution 9461, to this effect.
Old family friend Claude Swanson was easily persuaded to sponsor the legislation
in the Senate. Byrd's own Bureau of Aeronautics, however, resorted to legal nit-
picking, informing the judge advocate general that although Byrd's service had
been unquestionably "exceptional," the bill as drafted was "for the benefit of an
individual and not for the general service," thus falling afoul of the department's
general policy against permitting personal legislation. Theodore Roosevelt Jr., now
acting secretary, swiftly concurred. Richard nonetheless appeared before the House
Naval Affairs Committee the following day to plead his case. He had requested
separation from the service on several occasions, most recently two years before for
pressing family reasons. Each time he had been pressured to stay on. Since his value to the navy seemed unquestionable, simple justice dictated that he regain his
lost rank, as so many others had done through the general action of both the army
and the navy. The representatives, and soon thereafter the senators as well, were
convinced, and the bill passed both committees unanimously. But as Richard told
Franklin Roosevelt six months later, the legislation languished on the private calendar, "so far down that due to the press of business it will not be reached this
year."51

Richard's latest frustration led him to play partisan national politics as never before and, in the process, to intervene in the quarrel that was tearing apart America's most famous political family. By the midtwenties, the Roosevelts had fractured
badly, as ambition, competition, and personality drove Teddy Roosevelt's son and
daughter away from their cousin Franklin. The Oyster Bay Roosevelts out on Long
Island, led by Colonel Theodore Roosevelt Jr. and his sister, Alice Roosevelt Longworth, wife of an influential congressman, remained staunch Republicans and
scarcely if ever spoke to their Democratic Hyde Park cousins along the Hudson,
ably represented by Franklin and Eleanor. Franklin's appearance in 1920 on the
Democratic ticket had completed a rupture begun years before.

Four years later, FDR stumped rather frantically for John W. Davis, who was
widely and rightly considered to have no chance of victory over Calvin Coolidge.
In the last days of the campaign, FDR charged cousin Theodore with "gross inefficiency" in administering his naval office. By this time Richard had ingratiated
himself as thoroughly with new assistant secretary Roosevelt as he had with the
old, and he promptly bestirred himself on his new chief's behalf. The day after
FDR's speech, Byrd cabled Rear Admiral de Steiguer at the First Naval District in

Boston, stating that he had "advice from Colonel's managers speech hurting him greatly and must be refuted emphatically." It was "most urgent," Byrd continued, that de Steiguer "lay [the] matter" before Navy Secretary Curtis Wilbur "in strong terms and ask him to refute Franklin Roosevelt's statements in aggressive language." Perhaps the excitable Virginian could have been forgiven for zealously defending his service, for by attacking his cousin Theodore, Byrd added, FDR had attacked the "whole Navy." But Richard went one step further, stating that FDR's statement "may affect national situation in New York" and that Wilbur should take up this "matter" in his speech as well. By seeking, however indirectly, to influence the outcome of a national election, Byrd went well beyond the bounds of restrained and responsible conduct demanded of military officers in their dealings with the civilian world. Indeed, in a cryptic message from Oyster Bay the month before, Colonel Roosevelt had thanked "Dear Dicky Byrd" for a telegram of support, adding, "I wish you were in New York now and not in Boston to switch these southern democratic votes for me!"[52]

For the remainder of the year, Richard bounced back and forth between Washington, New York, and Boston as he continued his temporary duties in connection with the naval aviation reserve. But he and the department were always aware of his political abilities and connections. On December 1, the navy wired him at home on Brimmer Street: "Congress meets today. Reserve and Omnibus bills up Wednesday. Need your services soon as possible."[53]

As he rushed back to Washington, Richard determined to employ his power and influence once more to regain the rank that had been taken from him. He again enlisted Swanson in his crusade, and the Virginia senator wrote the navy judge advocate general in mid-December, arguing that the only way to ensure passage of his client's personal legislation was to redraft it in such a way that it did not mention him by name, then attach it to the pending naval reserve bill as an amendment, as "has been done a number of times." Richard also mobilized brother Harry, who was about to win the Democratic nomination for the Virginia governorship, and also, without a moment's hesitation or embarrassment, enlisted all three of the feuding Roosevelts on his behalf. Whether or not Franklin knew of his old friend's recent activities against him, he responded handsomely: "Of course, I will do everything possible in regard to the Naval Committee. I am writing today to Senator Copeland and I am also dropping a line to Gerry and Broussard. I do hope the amendment will go through. You certainly deserve it." Richard was effusive in his thanks, telling FDR how "uncommonly nice" he had been not only in sending the letters but in going to some unspecified "further trouble" on his behalf as well. "If you hear from any of the Senators," Richard added, "will you please pass their answers to me?" The Oyster Bay colonel who had become assistant secretary of the navy was equally helpful, especially in obtaining the support of his brother-in-law, Congressman Nicholas Longworth.

But Richard took no chances. He drafted letters for Harry to sign praising his achievements, and he added a new weapon to his political arsenal—apples. Shortly before Christmas he wrote brother Tom in Winchester, asking him to send a box of apples from the family orchards "to the following people," including two rear admirals and one congressman. This could be considered cheeky enough on the part of a junior naval officer, but Byrd went further. Franklin Roosevelt was also on the dozen-person list, as were Alice Roosevelt Longworth and her brother the colonel. Taking no chances, Byrd also sent his assistant secretary a ham. The fruit of the Byrd orchards was always of the highest quality, and the recipients expressed delight in receiving it. Shortly after the New Year, Richard wrote Tom gleefully that the apples were making him very popular. "I believe I could be elected President if I had enough of your apples to send around," and he bought "thirteen or fourteen" additional boxes to send to personal and political friends. Thereafter, Richard sent boxes of Byrd apples yearly at Christmastime. By 1937, the holiday "Apples List" had grown to more than eighty people, and a decade later he reminded Harry what "a tremendous thing to me" the Yuletide apple giving had become. "It has actually allowed me to keep my friendship with people that I am very fond of but whom I am not able to see because of my very busy life. And further," he added, without a trace of self-consciousness, "it actually helps me with my business associates."[54]

The ambitious young officer was clearly interested not only in regaining his former rank but also in becoming a power behind the scenes within the Democratic Party. Some sort of North-South alliance based on the antebellum Virginia–New York axis was logical if not essential in the wake of John Davis's woeful showing in the 1924 presidential election. Richard seemed eager to forge it. "Harry will certainly look you up if he comes up in January," Byrd told FDR at the end of the year, "and I will try to come with him. You don't know how very much pleased I am that you and he have become friends." Demonstrating that he knew how to polish apples as well as send them, Richard added, "Harry says that you have the most pleasing personality he has ever come in contact with. Be sure and give my best love to the family."[55]

The private calendar with Richard's legislation on it came before the House of Representatives on January 22, 1925, and after some perfunctory questioning, which young Carl Vinson of Georgia quickly beat down, the measure passed. Nine days later the Senate acted with equal dispatch, and Richard E. Byrd was once again a lieutenant commander, though with the provision that he would receive no back pay for the months and years of his lost rank. Richard promptly wrote

Vinson the kind of fulsome letter of thanks that would become almost a boiler-plate in later years. Vinson had fought the good fight on Dick Byrd's behalf and had won. "I honestly don't believe that any other man in the House could have done it." Vinson had done "a big favor for me, and as long as I live I will never forget it, nor will any member of the Byrd clan." Richard was deeply grateful, and Vinson would "always be one of the ranking members on my list."[56]

The frustrating years were coming to an end for Richard Byrd, though he could not know it. He had gotten back his rank, but the navy continued to block his every proposal to fly—solo over the Atlantic, around the Arctic, wherever. As Raimond Goerler has observed, Byrd at age thirty-six had achieved much, but not fame. He had demonstrated courage at sea, innovation in the air, and striking leadership and competence in every bureaucratic post he had held. In the halls of Congress he had "attracted the favorable attention of powerful and influential men."[57] But for all his effort, he had not passed much beyond the status of a junior military bureaucrat. And then suddenly in the winter of 1925, fortune began to smile. His golden years were about to begin, yielding fame and fortune that not even he could have imagined. The portal to glory lay in Greenland, the world's biggest and most frigid island.

Chapter 3

Breakthrough

ate in 1923, rumors began to circulate in Washington that Billy Mitchell and the Army Air Service were planning a dramatic new initiative for the following year: a round-the-world flight that would consume many weeks and fix the world's attention on long-range airpower. The navy needed a counter. According to one knowledgeable contemporary, Bob Bartlett, who had played a major role in breaking the trail for Robert Peary's final, and ostensibly successful, rush to the North Pole back in 1909, saw a chance "to sell the Navy a bit of Polar exploring enthusiasm. He quickly teamed with Dick Byrd and other Navy dirigible balloon enthusiasts to plan a Polar exploration" using the navy's huge new dirigible, *Shenandoah*. Moffett proved receptive, and Navy Secretary Edwin Denby, with President Coolidge's approval, directed his chief aviator to chair a seven-man commission to study the feasibility of reaching the North Pole by air.

Byrd was named to the commission along with Bartlett and Fitzhugh Green, a navy lieutenant commander who had been out on the polar sea and was considered a great Arctic expert. Moffett ordered Byrd to take the lead in coordinating plans for *Shenandoah*'s Arctic trip on which he would be chief navigator.[1] The Moffett committee reported to Denby in mid-December with a proposal to send the airship out to San Diego and up the coast to Alaska. From Nome, *Shenandoah* would fly to the pole and either return to Alaska or pass on to the island of Spitsbergen, in the Svalbard archipelago north of Iceland. From there *Shenandoah* would fly home to Lakehurst, New Jersey. However, early the following month a seventy-mile-an-hour gust tore the dirigible from its mooring mast at Lakehurst, and Congress began to voice concern over an Arctic flight: the project would be costly, the weather questionable, basing arrangements difficult, and hazard to the

crew high. In mid-February 1924, President Coolidge himself killed the operation. Moffett, Byrd, and their fellow crusaders were crushed as they watched
Mitchell and the Army Air Service take control of public relations. Seven months
later army pilots successfully completed their global mission. Naval aviators would
have to accomplish something equally spectacular if their service wasn't to fall into
permanent eclipse.

Donald MacMillan thought he had the answer. Like Bartlett, MacMillan had
been one of Peary's men on the admiral's controversial 1909 Arctic expedition,
turning back above 84 degrees north with frozen heels. With his Arctic credentials
firmly established, MacMillan became one of the great, if unsung, polar explorers,
returning to the Far North as either leader or participant in thirty-one expeditions
over the next forty-five years, concluding his last adventure when he was eighty.
Widely perceived as a weighty, quiet man of great force yet calm temperament,
MacMillan specialized in biology and the linguistics of Arctic native peoples. A
lieutenant commander in the U.S. Naval Reserve, MacMillan had developed a
long-standing connection with the National Geographic Society, and had just bur-
nished his growing reputation with a two-year expedition to northwest Greenland
and adjacent Smith Sound and Ellesmere Island.[2]

Early in December 1924, while Mitchell's fliers were rightly being treated as
public heroes, MacMillan wrote Moffett, expressing disappointment over the
scrubbing of the *Shenandoah* mission and offering the navy any help it needed in
furthering its aviation objectives in the North Polar region. In response, Moffett
urged MacMillan to continue to speak out on behalf of naval aviation's role in the
Arctic. Moffett's letter galvanized MacMillan. Following a radio address about his
North Polar adventures on a Chicago radio station, MacMillan sat down with Eugene F. McDonald, head of the fledgling Zenith Radio Corporation, to plan another Arctic journey. Like MacMillan, McDonald was a lieutenant commander in
the U.S. Naval Reserve and an intelligence specialist as keenly interested in expanding the uses and applications of radio as Richard Byrd was in expanding the
role of aviation. Following his consultations with McDonald, MacMillan in February 1925 dispatched a three-page proposal to Moffett. The navy should spend
the coming summer exploring the Arctic by airship—certainly *Shenandoah* and
perhaps another craft, if available. Based on tenders riding at anchor off the west-
central Greenland village of Godhavn, the great dirigibles would explore the two
million square miles of North Polar wastes not yet seen by man. If weather and ice
conditions permitted, the dirigibles and their mother ships might even move as far
north as the Inupiat village of Etah in far northwestern Greenland on Smith
Sound, some sixty miles above the later cold war American strategic air base at
Thule.[3] MacMillan was a marvelous ally for the navy to have. But in the early win-

ter of 1925, his plans collided with ambitions expressed by Dick Byrd as well as by MacMillan's old Arctic colleague Bob Bartlett.

On the first day of 1925, Byrd wrote in his diary that he had been "dreaming all winter of a trans-polar flight. I wonder if it will materialize? . . . When Congress adjourns, I shall wire Bob Bartlett and try to work out some scheme with him." Richard waited seven weeks, then at the end of February wrote Bartlett that he had "never given up the idea of flying across the Pole. I think it would be dangerous in an airplane, but not so in a dirigible." Byrd added in confidence his opinion that the navy would not send the brand-new airship *Los Angeles* to the Arctic during the coming summer. If that were the case, he would try to get a smaller TC type of dirigible to Spitsbergen "and shove off from there for the Pole and back." The same day Byrd wrote to the commanding officer of *Shenandoah,* stating that he was considering "making an interesting flight in a dirigible" and wanted to know if Lieutenant C. E. Bauch could offer him advice and wished to join the expedition.[4]

Moffett, now a rear admiral and recently reappointed head of naval aviation, owed much of his good fortune to Dick Byrd. A consummate political fixer by this time, Richard had arranged through one of his reserve fliers with superb Washington connections to have a close friend of Coolidge suggest to the president that he tell Secretary Denby of his personal interest in having Moffett remain in his post. Everything fell smoothly into place, and in evident appreciation Moffett in early March wrote to Philip K. Wrigley, the chewing gum king of Chicago; P. W. Litchfield, vice president of Goodyear Tire and Rubber in Akron; and Henry Ford in Detroit. Would they see his young protégé, Dick Byrd, within the week about a "proposed airship flight to [the] Arctic regions?" In his letter to Ford, Moffett added that "the National Geographic Society thinks that the trip will be of great scientific value. I think that Byrd has the ability and determination to succeed in this undertaking," Moffett continued, "and I want to assure you that you could make no mistake in putting the utmost confidence in him. He is the kind who enjoys life most when there are difficulties to overcome." Moffett told Litchfield substantially the same thing.[5]

The admiral was fully aware that in backing Byrd, he was for all practical purposes compromising if not rejecting the steadily advancing plans of MacMillan and McDonald, who had suddenly appeared in Moffett's office on February 28 with a wholly new proposal. Obviously impressed by *Shenandoah's* fragility and undependability in heavy weather, MacMillan now proposed that aerial exploration of the Arctic be accomplished with heavier—rather than lighter—than air craft. He and McDonald were in contact with Grover Loening, an innovative manufacturer of amphibious aircraft. Moffett took the two men in to see Navy

Secretary Curtis D. Wilbur, where they baited their proposal with specifics. The proposed four-month expedition would explore the interiors of Baffin Land, Axel Heiberg Island, and Ellesmere Island as well as North Greenland and much of the Greenland ice cap. Men would see in minutes from an airplane what those on the ground would take months and even years to experience. Moreover, MacMillan put forth the alluring prospect of a possible continent lying between Point Barrow and the pole that might also be the subject of search and identification. "Here at least twice," MacMillan later wrote, "land has been reported and here tidal experts have predicted that it would be found." The existence of "Crocker Land" had been the subject of a prolonged but inconclusive expedition between 1913 and 1917. "Inaccessible by ship and extremely difficult to reach with dogs," the mysterious island or minicontinent "awaits exploration by air." Wilbur was noncommittal; he feared for the lives of any fliers trying to penetrate the upper Arctic, and he knew the navy had no amphibious aircraft of the type that his visitors wanted to employ. Undaunted, MacMillan and McDonald went to the Hill, lobbied several key congressmen, and got one of them to wangle an appointment with President Coolidge himself three weeks hence.[6]

The navy's coolness to MacMillan's insistent proposals for a polar aviation expedition is striking. Both Moffett and Wilbur kept the explorer and his colleague at arm's length. There were a number of compelling reasons for doing so. Pilot safety was an obvious consideration with respect to the fragile heavier-than-air craft of the time. Moreover, Moffett was a devout champion of the airship; he believed in it, and he pushed for it. Finally, there was the matter of Richard Byrd, not only fanatically loyal and hardworking but also (as he had repeatedly reminded people in the department and in Congress) profoundly frustrated at being on the retired list yet not being permitted to retire. Moffett had already assigned him a very substantial planning role in employing naval aviation for Arctic exploration well before MacMillan submitted his proposal. If *Shenandoah* had been sent north in the summer of 1924, Byrd would have been aboard as navigator. Now Byrd—and Bartlett—was as keen as MacMillan to revive the airship's mission. No one could accuse Moffett's protégé of either thinking small or being averse to risky adventure.

Caught between MacMillan's genuine willingness to do good for the navy and his subordinate's bulldog loyalty, Moffett essentially gave in to both men. Perhaps he was cold enough and tough enough to play them off, to let them plan and propose and then pick out the best elements in both their thinking.

Throughout March, Byrd proceeded determinedly with his plans for a dirigible mission to the pole. He had obviously read widely in the comparatively thin literature of Arctic exploration and was especially conversant with Peary's explorations, most of which had been staged out of the primitive settlement at Etah. On the seventh he wrote Bauch again that it appeared likely that a temporary wood and canvas hangar could be built on the beach there to house the TC dirigible and that a "cache" could somehow be placed 150 miles from the pole to ensure that the small airship could make it there and back to Greenland. Again, he urged Bauch to keep everything confidential. Bauch soon wrote back, questioning both Byrd's plan and his optimism. The budding polar explorer replied with a qualified dismissal of Bauch's concerns. "I like your conservatism," he said, but then largely discounted Bauch's reservations.[7]

Just hours after Moffett wrote to Litchfield and the others, Richard was on his way west to Akron. He returned to the capital four days later to join his chief in bombarding Goodyear officials with correspondence. Byrd had not only spoken at length with the Goodyear people in Ohio but also had a long talk with the company's president on the train from Akron back to Washington. Mr. Wilmer assured Dick that he would be "in hearty accord" with any decision that Litchfield reached in providing Byrd with a TC airship bag, the navy already having agreed to supply the control car. Byrd subsequently told Litchfield that he had assured the Goodyear president that publicity could be so arranged that the company would be protected in case of failure and praised unstintingly in case of success. "I would, of course, play the game straight with you in every way and consider it a matter of honor to do so," Dick concluded. Moffett both wrote and cabled Goodyear officials. He would "personally appreciate" anything the tire and rubber people could do for his protégé. "I have a high regard for him, and you can put every confidence in him."[8]

On the sixteenth, Byrd and Moffett met with Gilbert Grosvenor, president of the National Geographic Society. Richard formally submitted a two-and-a-half-page proposal that concluded with a request for forty thousand dollars from the society "to enable me to execute the project." The navy would provide important material support; the airship bag could be gotten from Goodyear for fifteen thousand dollars; a Newfoundland ice steamer could be procured for five thousand dollars a month. The vessel would take Byrd's party and a disassembled TC dirigible (air bag and control car) up to Etah, "713 miles from the Pole." There, Byrd's party would take about two weeks to erect a canvas hangar, "and several days later the airship would be inflated and ready for the trip." A cache of fuel and food would first be laid at Cape Columbia, which juts out into the frozen polar sea from the northernmost tip of Ellesmere Island. "We would then be only 400 or 500 miles from the center of the unexplored region" between Point Barrow, Alaska, and the pole, "with enough gasoline aboard to make 2,500 miles." Summertime visibility could be expected to be "remarkable," and Byrd and his companions would fly over the North Pole, then turn south toward Alaska to "solve once and for all that question which has been interesting the world for so long—whether or not there is land in that unexplored region. I am personally convinced that land is there." Summer breezes should be moderate; the fragile airship would neither be blown off course nor be brought to a virtual standstill by stiff headwinds. "I would play the game safe in every way," Richard emphasized.[9]

He apparently sensed or had been told of the MacMillan initiative, for he began hectoring his potential benefactors at Goodyear. The day after his meeting with Grosvenor, Dick wrote Litchfield that when he had left Akron, "Mr. Wilmer told me that I would get a decision from you last Saturday. I called Akron Monday, and was told that a wire would be immediately sent me. Wednesday has come, and still I have no word." He amplified his concerns to W. C. Young, another Goodyear contact. The company's silence "has been a serious handicap to me in my negotiations with the National Geographic Society. You think that I have hurried matters too much," he added, "but in order to embark on the steamer to Etaw [*sic*] by the 20th of May I will have to start preparations almost immediately." While Byrd stewed, Grosvenor called Moffett in for another conference. The society was obviously less than overwhelmed with the navy's proposal. On the nineteenth Grosvenor replied that although Byrd's project undoubtedly had great scientific merit, insufficient time remained to prepare carefully for the kind of expedition that would yield results. Moreover, the society's Research Committee had developed a fine program of its own for the coming year before its chairman had left for the West Coast. The society, Grosvenor concluded, could not approve any new projects without summoning the man back from California, which it was clearly unwilling to do.[10]

The moment Moffett received Grosvenor's letter, he contacted Henry Ford and got Byrd an interview with Henry's son, Edsel. Thereafter, events moved swiftly. Richard's interview with Edsel Ford obviously went very well, for on March 23 Edsel wired Moffett that he had cabled John D. Rockefeller Jr. on Byrd's behalf. Moffett, meanwhile, had written to Raymond Fosdick, now representing the Rockefeller family, just as soon as the navy received the National Geographic's letter of rejection. Moffett's letter formally "introduced" Byrd, who, of course, had known Fosdick for years, and Richard took the train directly from Detroit to New York to meet with his old colleague. Richard had also contacted Franklin Roosevelt aboard his Florida houseboat, and this time FDR responded promptly, directing his chief lieutenant, Louis McHenry Howe, to write Fosdick on Richard's behalf. Forty-eight hours after the National Geographic Society rejection, Byrd handed an almost identical proposal to Fosdick. He would use a TC-type dirigible, he told the Rockefeller family agent, to fly to the North Pole and from there fly south and west, exploring the million-square-mile unknown area toward Alaska. Richard informed Fosdick that Edsel Ford had pledged fifteen thousand dollars and that Marshall Crane had donated another five thousand, leaving forty thousand to raise. On March 24, Edsel Ford received a cable from young Rockefeller. He was sorry to have been out of town when "Commander Byrd" called. "I know but little about his project," the young millionaire told the other young millionaire, "but if you fully approve it and would like to have me do so I will be glad to join you in the enterprise and duplicate your contribution which I understand was in the amount of fifteen thousand dollars."[11]

Richard immediately cabled Litchfield out in Akron. He had the money to go ahead with his project if Goodyear would sell the bag for fifteen thousand dollars and "erect it at Akron for the trial trip." Then Byrd wrote William C. Young, the other Goodyear official involved with evaluating his project, informing him that sufficient funds were available, "provided you can let us have the bag for $15,000." He added, "I guess you thought that I was rushing you too much on your decision when I was in Akron, but I knew the situation with the National Geographic Society; as a matter of fact the delay in getting a decision from you people caused them to reverse their decision to give us $40,000." Not only was the charge untrue, but Byrd committed an act of incredible folly in making it. If he hoped to pressure Goodyear into giving him what he so desperately wanted, he went about it exactly the wrong way. It is probable that Young did not see the letter until after his colleague Litchfield informed Richard by return wire that Goodyear saw "no possibility of meeting the fifteen thousand dollar limitation." Litchfield promised to provide a firm cost figure for the bag within twenty-four hours.[12]

His hopes dashed yet again, Richard pressed on. Without mentioning the setback with Goodyear, he wrote Edsel Ford a note of deep appreciation for his contribution and for intervening with Rockefeller, adding, "I am now ready to go ahead with the expedition." On March 26, two days after Litchfield's discouraging cable, Richard wrote a "dear Fitz" note to Fitzhugh Green, his colleague on the Moffett commission, stating that he was "contemplating a trip to the Polar regions." For the first time he mentioned airplanes, and asked Green's advice on a number of matters: Could one land a seaplane safely in an open "lead" in the ice pack in case of engine trouble? Should a seaplane be equipped with skis? Would it be possible to establish by airplane a cache at Cape Columbia "or thereabouts"? Richard concluded by asking Green not to tell Bob Bartlett (whom Green saw frequently) "that I have asked you these questions, since I asked him when he was down here."[13]

Polar politics and personalities have always divided historians and distorted history, so perhaps it is not surprising that MacMillan partisans have emphasized

Byrd's "apparently conscious manipulations of the truth" in claiming "authorship of the plans for the 1925 MacMillan expedition." Several commentators have been quick to accept the authors' questioning of Byrd's "veracity." Certainly, what transpired in the week to ten days following Byrd's letter to Fitzhugh Green remains a matter of bitter controversy and "would contribute to a lifetime of enmity between Byrd on one side and MacMillan and McDonald on the other."[14]

On March 26, the same day Byrd wrote Green asking for information about aircraft flight in the Arctic, MacMillan and McDonald returned to Washington for their interview with President Coolidge. Two days later they came to Moffett's office to talk about their project. In the meantime, Byrd had further queried Green, and had informed both Fosdick and Theodore Roosevelt Jr. that Rockefeller had come through with handsome financial support and that his enterprise was "going through." Now in Moffett's office, Richard heard MacMillan out, then informed the meeting that he, too, had plans for an aviation expedition to the Arctic, but they were not yet formalized. What he meant by "formalized" is unclear. He had clearly abandoned the idea of employing a dirigible and had switched to heavier-than-air craft. But his objectives remained firm. The navy was behind him. The question was whether he could win essential presidential and congressional approval. In that sense, no one's plans were "formalized." Either just before or after the meeting (MacMillan partisans insist it was after), Byrd submitted two papers for an Arctic expedition employing aircraft in a manner suspiciously close to his rivals' project. A careful perusal of the documents suggests that the first, undated, memorandum was submitted to the chiefs of the Bureaus of Navigation and Aeronautics and probably received their quick approval. The second, handstamped March 28 and signed "Byrd," was from the Bureau of Aeronautics directly to the secretary of the navy. In these papers, Richard reiterated his now frequently stated objectives to explore the two million square miles of unexplored Arctic territory between Alaska and the pole to determine if land existed there. If it did, the United States should claim it.[15]

In another memorandum, presumably written just after the meeting in Moffett's office, Byrd begged his chief not to make a decision on giving MacMillan any "additional" planes until Moffett returned from an unspecified out-of-town trip. Two days later, on March 30, Byrd first made the charge that he would later repeat rather widely that MacMillan had come to Washington, "found what our plans were . . . immediately changed his plans and now has adopted ours." Richard's response was strange in more ways than one. He also told Bob Bartlett that although the chief of naval operations and the secretary of the navy had approved "our" plan, the latter insisted on taking it up in a cabinet meeting in a few days. "I regret extremely," Byrd added, that the secretary felt it necessary to "take such a small matter up with the President." Surely, the question of government support for a major polar expedition designed to determine if unknown land existed in the Arctic and to claim it if it was there was no small matter. But the major bone of contention lay elsewhere. Byrd was quite right to assert the impracticability of two expeditions attempting to accomplish the same thing in the same place. But what angered him was that MacMillan was not interested in the same objective. According to Byrd, who did hear MacMillan out at the March 28 meeting, the seasoned Arctic explorer "does not intend to try the pole," though he did intend to put down a cache somewhere north and west of Greenland to explore the unknown region. By winning out, MacMillan, in Dick Byrd's eyes, reduced the scope and the grandeur of the proposed expedition.[16]

MacMillan partisans, of course, tell a different story. Their man was completely unaware of Byrd's proposals submitted immediately following the March 28 meeting. On March 29 or 30, McDonald and Congressman Britten went to the White House to brief Coolidge on their plans. The president promised to take the matter up with the cabinet on April 2, which he did. The result, formally announced by the navy on April 6, was the "MacMillan Arctic Expedition under the auspices of the National Geographic Society." The historians of the expedition do not explain exactly how or why the society changed its mind and came to support a costly research project it had earlier rejected. Byrd's March 28 proposal to employ airplanes rather than an airship may in fact have been instrumental in stimulating further consideration. The society merely announced that it would provide partial support for exploration of one of the world's last great unknown areas that lay between Alaska and the North Pole as well as an aerial survey of the inner parts of Baffin Land and Ellesmere Island. McDonald was able to emphasize the importance of the radio experiments he wished to conduct, communicating with the "outside world not only in code but also by voice." The navy's Bureau of Aeronautics would provide the aviation component.[17]

Who would lead the fliers? Certainly, MacMillan and McDonald would have preferred anyone but their nemesis. But Byrd had been too long and too closely associated with naval aviation's plans for the Arctic to be ignored. There was no one else in the aeronautics bureau that had done so much. Richard himself later wrote that although he possessed absolutely no polar experience, he promptly applied to the secretary of the navy for the aviation command position. "I struggled through a maze of red tape" to get to Wilbur, but when he did Wilbur replied, "I will go to see the President." Convinced that "I had reached the last barrier," Byrd waited impatiently. "The critical moment had been reached, the moment I had been dreaming for years. If only I could go on this one expedition, I knew I might have a chance in the following year to realize my cherished hope of some day flying to the North Pole," thus entering the pantheon of great explorers. In the Oval Office, Wilbur went thoroughly into detail about Byrd's plans. "There is still a great deal of blank space on our polar map, Mr. President," he concluded. "Don't you think we ought to let Byrd go?" The impassive president sat for a moment. Then: "Why not?"

Byrd—and Wilbur—must have moved swiftly, for just two days after the navy's official announcement of support for the MacMillan expedition, the secretary called a meeting in his office attended by a representative of the National Geographic Society and "others concerned" with the forthcoming Arctic flight program. The *New York Times*, that authoritative record of American history, reported that "Lieutenant Commander Robert Y. Byrd" would not only head the air unit but "at all stages of the expedition" be "under the sole direction of the Secretary of the Navy." As Wilbur's on-site representative, Byrd had the power to "decide whether weather conditions are propitious for flights and when the hop-off should be made" once the expedition reached northwest Greenland.[18]

The navy's decision to give operational command to Byrd but under MacMillan's overall guidance was a recipe for disaster. Richard was bitter and frustrated; MacMillan and McDonald were understandably uneasy at best and alienated at worst. At the end of March, Richard poured out his heart to Judge A. C. Carson, his old patron from Philippine days who had become a firm older friend and mentor, with whom he was trying—and would fail—to develop a brick business in Manhattan. Rockefeller had come through "very nicely," but upon returning to Washington, Richard had researched the matter thoroughly and had concluded that dirigibles would not be feasible for Arctic research, so he had turned to heavier-than-air craft only to be blindsided by the usurpers, MacMillan and McDonald. MacMillan was jealous and small-minded; all he envisioned was "a very modest plan of exploring 500 miles south of Etah. . . . He even went so far last night as to give a lecture for Cabinet members and to have Congressman Britten make a speech for him." Richard told Carson he felt constrained by "ethics . . . not to use political influence, nor have I got three big bugs going around promoting for me." In his despair, he contemplated rejecting the MacMillan expedition, and he turned to Marie for advice and support. She had gone back to Boston, possibly to be with young Dickie, still recovering from his recent illness. "Come immediately," he wired 9 Brimmer Street two days before the formal navy announcement of the MacMillan expedition. "Undecided but want to be with you." On April 8, Carson weighed in with some badly needed fatherly advice that indicated how well he knew his young protégé. "If you have the backing of the Department and control of 'flight operations,' as it seems you have, you need not worry, and there will be plenty of glory in the doing of your job as it ought to be done and must be done."

Richard must make up his mind from the outset to "play the game" to the limit. Neither jealousy nor envy nor personal or professional ill will must be permitted to affect his judgment or reduce his effort on behalf of the cause. Soon a clearly abashed junior naval officer wrote back, thanking Carson for his good advice.[19]

But relations between Byrd and his new colleagues continued to deteriorate as Richard poured out his anger and frustration at the other men. He begged his correspondents to keep everything he said confidential, then let loose. He told Green that MacMillan had stolen not only his plans and planes but his ship as well. MacMillan had originally planned to use just his own little Arctic schooner *Bowdoin* (named for his alma mater). Though the vessel was propelled by a powerful engine in addition to the traditional rigging, it was much too small to carry even one disassembled aircraft and did not possess the ice-breaking capabilities to get into Etah Fjord. As soon as he got the go-ahead, however, MacMillan also grabbed the far more capable vessel that Byrd planned to use. *Peary,* a former French minesweeper, was a big steamer with substantial stowage space for aircraft and other supplies. Moreover, its strong steel hull might be capable of limited ice breaking. Worse, "When McDonald and I had a conference to combine he insisted on relegating me completely to the background and taking away all rights and not even agreeing to my being second in command. In order to make harmony," Richard continued, he had surrendered every point but one. McDonald had demanded that Byrd not engage in any public relations activities relating to the expedition after its conclusion. Richard shot back that he would have to take up this matter of "being entirely tied up as to the aftermath in the matter of writing, talking, etc., with the Secretary of the Navy." Wilbur supported him completely. "Now I have the impression quite strongly that I am up against an extremely selfish outfit that drives an extremely hard bargain." McDonald seemed unable to give an inch on any point, "and I rather imagine MacMillan is the same type."[20]

But Richard Byrd was resilient and buoyant beyond most men. He wrote Edsel Ford about the origins of the MacMillan expedition in surprisingly soft tones. It did not seem ethical to ask the industrialist for money now that he had "combined with" MacMillan, Richard said, and he had made suitable "arrangements" with the explorer in this regard. If Ford had any qualms about the matter, Richard begged to know of them immediately. "I will be able to gain on this trip considerable knowledge of flying over the Polar Sea and in the Arctic regions which will be of great value to me in the future, and in case there is still left next year much to do for science I trust you will still hold out to me the fine offer you made this year." He told Ford that Fosdick had assured him John Rockefeller would "be entirely guided by any decision you made or any thought of yours."[21]

Byrd now focused his attention and energies on the expedition. His first task was to find suitable aircraft. Not surprisingly, Grover Loening's amphibious planes had already been sucked into the ongoing maelstrom of army-navy aviation competition. Billy Mitchell had decided that the aircraft would be perfect for coast artillery spotting and search and rescue. Moving quickly, he had secured the first order of ten Loening aircraft for the Army Air Service before Moffett could act. As matters stood in April 1925, the navy would not receive its initial shipment of amphibians for nearly a year. MacMillan's partisans claim somewhat lamely that "available records do not explain exactly how the navy was able to persuade the army to loan the MacMillan expedition the precious Loenings."[22] Grover Loening himself, however, had no doubt how it was done. Moffett immediately called on Richard Byrd, who became the navy's "star performer" in convincing not only Coolidge but also the appropriate congressional committees of naval aviation's "urgent need" for three of these aircraft "so well suited for the Arctic." According to Loening, Byrd went further. A worldwide rivalry was developing in aviation, the naval officer told everyone, and American prestige was on the line. The army's global flight, spectacular as it had been, could not in and of itself sustain American stature and prestige. Ongoing aviation spectaculars were required. The United States would pioneer polar aviation through the MacMillan expedition. "That was Byrd's line of talk," Loening remembered years later, and "his exciting and grandiose plans" won the day. The army grudgingly surrendered two planes, then, at the last moment, a third.[23]

The decision-making process was doubtless hurried along by continuing news of Roald Amundsen's rapidly materializing expedition. The year before, the monarch of polar explorers joined forces with a wealthy young American sportsman and flier named Lincoln Ellsworth to form an aviation expedition to the Arctic. This was the project that Byrd had volunteered for, only to be stifled by Moffett, who brought him back to Washington to work on a possible airship mission to the Far North. Amundsen and Ellsworth planned to fly two German Dornier Wal flying boats from Spitsbergen to the North Pole in a matter of days. Amundsen's idea was superficially plausible. Flying boats capable of landing in open water could reach the pole by incremental flight, as Byrd himself had suspected when querying Fitzhugh Green on the matter. Engine problems and failures could be addressed and repaired by landing in the open water "leads" and pools ("polynyas") that were always found in an Arctic ice pack softened by spring and summer sun and constantly shifted and moved by wind and tide. But Amundsen proved too clever by half, his knowledge of aviation always too sketchy to match his dreams. The Dorniers were big craft, much larger than Grover Loening's small, efficient planes, and like many aircraft of the time they were underpowered. Lifting off from Spitsbergen on May 21, 1925, Amundsen and Ellsworth soon ran into fog and storms. The expected leads in the ice along the route never materialized, and although they flew as close as perhaps 120 miles from the pole, they encoutered disaster in attempting to land in an open lead. "Amundsen's plane lost its rear engine into an ice pack," while Ellsworth's aircraft landed three miles away and promptly began to fill with water. Within forty-eight hours the world feared that tragedy had befallen the world's greatest polar explorer.[24]

The Amundsen-Ellsworth expedition was still a bright promise when Richard Byrd and the rest of his Naval Air Unit gathered in early May at Grover Loening's New York City factory at the foot of Thirty-first Street, fronting the East River, to spend "many days in training and preparation." Byrd himself was in and out, spending much of the month traveling up and down the East Coast on various bits of business, all at his own expense. Much of the time he was at the Navy Department, working up the navigational part of the mission. He told an old friend and aviation pioneer, Pat Bellinger, that whereas there had been about ten or twelve officers working on the transatlantic flight back in 1919, "I have only one assistant, so you know what I am up against." He was shocked to find that no progress had been made in developing advanced instrumentation. "As a matter of fact the best instruments I can find are the ones used on that flight." The problem was to come up with specific methods to navigate in the polar regions.

Up in New York, Byrd's repeated absences left much of the work in the hands of his junior officers and enlisted people. Loening was impressed by all of the flier-mechanics, but two stood out. Chief Aviation Boatswain E. E. Reber was a beefy-faced, stocky man in his thirties, a "forceful, and highly competent all-around pilot, mechanic and navigator" who "would stand for no nonsense." Reber nonetheless possessed the kind of rough humor often displayed by career sailors, and he got away with kidding Byrd "unmercifully to his face." The other was Floyd Bennett, another enlisted man who had learned to fly. Loening found Bennett, a slender, good-looking chap in his twenties, to be a "keen, able, sensitive technician." So did others. In early June, the navy took command of the three planes and flew them to its aircraft factory at the navy yard in Philadelphia for final preparations. Mechanics discovered each one required new feeder lines in the reserve oil tank. "I think Bennett understands the method of installing the new oil line," a yard official assured Byrd. Loening saw that Bennett obviously harbored "great respect for Byrd." So did Loening, who concluded that the head of the Naval Air Unit possessed "that indispensable attribute of great leadership—the ability to pick excellent men."[25]

Reber, Bennett, Lieutenant (jg) Meinhard "Billy" Schur, and the other men under Byrd's command performed prodigiously in preparing their brand-new aircraft for the expedition. In little more than six weeks, first in New York and then in

Philadelphia, the planes were examined, preflighted, and flown several hundred miles to the factory, where they were modified for Arctic service, airframe and engine spares were collected, lightweight camping and survival gear was purchased, and food, clothing, and medical supplies were obtained before the aircraft were flown another 400 miles through heavy fog to Boston, where they were again tested intensively, barged to their mother ship, *Peary,* disassembled, loaded aboard, and safely cradled. The whole exercise was vintage Byrd. He worked his men hard, sometimes ruthlessly. At one point he brought in a naval photographer and a movie cameraman from Pathé News to take publicity shots of himself with the planes, which did not amuse at least some of the frantically busy naval airmen.

During the last hectic weeks, Byrd took time out to secure permission from both the National Geographic Society and MacMillan to write several articles about the expedition. He would make his mark with the public, come what may. He also kept a close eye on his financial portfolio, instructing his broker, Edwin McDonnell, to buy and sell several stocks.[26] But amid these distractions he got the job done, demonstrating once more his remarkable skills as an organizer, administrator, and leader. When MacMillan and McDonald were ready to leave Boston in mid-June for the final port of departure, the charming fishing village of Wiscasset, Maine, the Naval Air Unit was on board and geared up.

By then the fate of the Amundsen-Ellsworth expedition had become a massive distraction. Were some or all of the men alive? Where, in all the immensity of the frozen North, were they? Could they be rescued? Amundsen had chosen to dispense with radios to save weight, and in any case the primitive state of the technology in those days was such that no signal could be guaranteed to travel far. On May 28, in the middle of frantic preparations to get their expedition under way, MacMillan and Byrd were summoned to Washington by Secretary Wilbur.[27] Even this early the antipathy between Byrd and MacMillan was so great that Wilbur had to hold separate meetings with the two men. The secretary apparently first met with MacMillan; Byrd and Moffett were present but said little or nothing. Later, Wilbur met alone with Byrd. MacMillan told Wilbur and later members of the National Geographic Society that if Amundsen had gotten close to the pole before his aircraft gave out, "he will never come back." Summer was approaching; the Arctic pack ice was beginning to soften, thin, and disperse; and there was no way to walk out. However, MacMillan held out the hope that the Amundsen party might have flown to within 50 miles or so of the pole, then decided to walk the rest of the way north before returning to their planes and flying home. If so, "all may be well with these brave men."

In his own meeting with Wilbur, Byrd was skeptical about using the MacMillan expedition to find the lost explorer. Amundsen had disappeared almost a week before. He was undoubtedly near the North Magnetic Pole, where the possibilities of losing one's way were "vastly increased." The secretary subsequently told the press that Byrd had shown him a map of Amundsen's proposed operating area prepared by the navy's Hydrographic Office. After hearing Byrd out, Wilbur had concluded that "a search for Amundsen would be long and hazardous"; it would be undertaken only after "the most careful consideration." Nonetheless, he conceded that public pressure on both sides of the Atlantic to rescue the world's most redoubtable polar explorer might prove irresistible. Amundsen's fate was still unknown at the moment the MacMillan expedition sailed north, and authoritative press reports stated that the commanding officer was prepared for a "double quest" to find Amundsen "with airplanes" and then explore the "blind spot of the Arctic . . . north of Canada and Alaska."[28]

On the eve of MacMillan's departure, the New York Times devoted a major headline and story to the project. Reporter Howard Mingos described the expedition and its objectives in military terms. MacMillan and his men were mounting "the most completely organized and the most comprehensive attack on the polar regions since the first explorer dared the terrors of the Far North in a search for the Pole." Mingos mentioned Byrd just once in the course of his lengthy article; his focus was on MacMillan. It was MacMillan's expedition, MacMillan's planes, and MacMillan's plans. What MacMillan hoped to do was to reach Etah with his two vessels, off-load and reassemble the aircraft, and fly them to a sandy, usually snow-free beach at Cape Columbia at the northern edge of Ellesmere Island. It was from this spot that Peary had raced toward the pole in 1909. Should weather and ice conditions permit, MacMillan would then order the three aircraft to shuttle back and forth to the ships at Etah, bringing back men and supplies for the establishment of a weather station and reconnaissance base for the brief three months of summer. From that base, the planes would fly deep into the Arctic pack ice, exploring the area between Alaska and the pole. MacMillan never emphasized the pole itself as an objective—indeed, he and Byrd had been increasingly preoccupied with the probability that they would first have to rescue the Amundsen party. MacMillan told Mingos he hoped that if Amundsen's planes had come to grief, the Norwegian would be able to lead his men the 420 miles from the pole down to Cape Columbia and would be waiting for the MacMillan party there when it arrived. He reiterated that the loosening of the summer ice pack made such a prospect doubtful.[29]

Then word came from Oslo that Amundsen and his entire party had managed their own rescue. When the big Dornier Wals had been forced down on the pack ice within three miles of one another, one of the big planes was still capable of flight. The men waited patiently on the ever shifting floes for conditions to work in their favor. At last the ever shifting winds opened a 500-meter-long stretch of ice-free water. Everyone crowded into the single operational Dornier and took off for Spitsbergen, where they were forced down just off Brandy Bay. Fortunately, the plane taxied toward a sealing ship that rescued the party, all of whom were somewhat crestfallen at the failure of their mission.[30]

The dramatic news from Norway did not lessen popular enthusiasm for MacMillan's expedition. As his two ships sailed down Maine's Sheepscot River on June 20 and set course northeastward toward Greenland, they were sent on their way by a delirious public. An assistant secretary of the navy had come up from Washington to Wiscasset to bid Godspeed; the governor had traveled down from Bangor for the same purpose. As *Bowdoin* and *Peary* prepared to cast off, army troops had to rope off an area of the dock so that friends, well-wishers, and officials could get aboard for hasty final farewells. The entire state seemed to be at dockside, including the faculty and student body of nearby Bowdoin College, where MacMillan had matriculated. Hawkers pushed through the festive crowd, selling ice cream, popcorn, and candy. There was cheering and songs, and then, shortly before three o'clock, the ships steamed away and the crowds left. Dick Byrd was starting on his lifework at last.

He was not a happy man. Departing Boston for Maine he had wired Secretary Wilbur that the "Naval Aviation Arctic Unit" was ready in all respects for duty, then added the sly and undoubtedly sad acknowledgment that "E. F. McDonald, President Zenith Radio Corporation appointed second in command will be assigned to *Peary*." Not only was Richard out of the command loop, but he was also aware that his driving ambition had divided the navy hierarchy as well as the middle levels in the department. Moffett wired best wishes, "knowing that you will do everything in your power for the glory and honor of the Navy and our country." But another superior in the aeronautics bureau ominously reminded Byrd of the fragility of his reputation among his colleagues. "You know exactly how I feel about the whole expedition," A. W. Johnson wrote. Byrd's success would be judged by his "actual accomplishments rather than upon any spectacular features. I believe that your success depends absolutely upon your good head work rather than upon any desire for notoriety."

Leaving Marie and the children behind was another burden for the fledgling explorer. Marie and Dickie had come up to Maine to see him off, filling him with "this terrible ache I have tried so far to hide." He was doing his wife "a dirty trick," he confided to his diary. She had worried for weeks about the expedition; now she would be left to worry for untold weeks more while he was away. "I feel mightily low and wicked today on account of it and the wonderful send off we got from thousands of people has meant absolutely nothing to me. . . . Dear little Dickie

didn't realize what it was all about and that made me feel still more useless." Byrd
flagellated himself unmercifully. The "poor little fellow" was too young to realize
what an irresponsible father he had. "Marie as always was a wonderful sport." Just
before sailing Byrd made a speech on the Wiscasset City Common to "hundreds
of people" and accepted "wonderful hunting knives" for the entire unit presented
by the National Aeronautical Association of Maine.[31]

Once at sea, Byrd chafed at MacMillan's caution. Concerned about the looming polar ice pack, MacMillan ordered *Peary* into Sydney, Nova Scotia, to have its
portholes sealed and to top off its fuel bunkers, while he proceeded up the Newfoundland coast with *Bowdoin.* The two ships joined up at Battle Harbour on July
2, but did not proceed northward for another seventy-two hours, leaving the crews
free to roam the crude little fishing and commercial port with its substantial white-
frame dwellings perched on a rocky promontory. The town boasted the northernmost year-round radio station on the east coast of North America. When the two
vessels reached the settlement at Domino Run on the fifth, more time was consumed purchasing native sealskin boots, "much lighter and warmer for northern
work," MacMillan later wrote, "than our homemade product."[32]

Byrd spent much of this time drafting a lengthy "tentative plan of operations"
for his Naval Air Unit, which he completed on June 29 and wired to the chief of
naval operations soon thereafter. He emphasized that since the difficulties of polar flight were largely unknown, it was necessary to avoid "spectacular dashes" out
into the polar sea. Byrd assured his superiors that all three aircraft would be
equipped with radios; that most if not all missions would be flown by two aircraft,
one of which would have a mechanic aboard "to repair the engine if possible in
case of a forced landing"; and that "all members of the Naval Unit are being required to learn to send and receive radio." The navy and the National Geographic Society were so relieved by these assurances that they each issued lengthy press
releases that practically quoted Byrd's draft plan verbatim. The navy release also
stated that "one of the most interesting tasks before the Naval air unit" would be
to decide whether Peary had in fact seen a body of land "never reached by man."[33]

Moving up the Labrador coast, the two vessels met the ice pack for the first time
near Cape Harrison, "lying close against the land and extending north in an almost unbroken sheet."[34] The previous winter had been unusually cold, and the
expedition would periodically encounter heavy pack ice on both sides of Davis
Strait and up Baffin and Melville Bays most of the way to Etah. Open water leads
were hard to find and even harder to spot, despite *Peary's* high crow's nest. MacMillan continued to fret about *Peary.* Only a decade had passed since *Titanic* had gone
down, and sailors now knew that contact of steel hulls with ice resulted in popped

rivets. Moreover, the central Newfoundland coast was filled with rocks and shoals that could rip out the bottom of either a steel- or a wooden-hulled vessel.

MacMillan took the lead in *Bowdoin,* determined, as he wrote, to move the little schooner carefully. *Peary,* with its 600-horsepower (HP) triple-expansion engines, nine-foot propeller, and triple-plated bow, stood up well in the pack, and MacMillan and McDonald were soon satisfied that it was a good ice ship. But "the most difficult bit of navigation of the whole trip," the inside run from Cape Mokkovik up the Labrador coast to the Moravian settlement of Hopedale, now loomed. MacMillan had been here before with *Bowdoin* but not *Peary,* and Captain Steele proved "a bit overcautious" and promptly ran his ship aground near Flagstaff Tickle.[35] Pulling it off the rocks by kedging proved a formidable and lengthy task. At one point, according to MacMillan, some of *Peary*'s crew prepared to abandon ship; MacMillan professed amusement. The little convoy at last reached Hopedale on July 7.

There Byrd was almost electrocuted. Two of his sailors had run a heavy copper uninsulated wire cable from *Peary*'s radio room across the ship's gangway at head height. The radiomen were testing the cable by shooting 100,000 volts, while watching and listening for anyone passing by. Byrd came up behind them wearing rubber-soled shoes. At the last moment, his men spotted him and yelled at him to stop. "My head got six inches from that wire," the shaken aviator wrote soon thereafter in his diary, "and the 100,000 volts would have jumped to my head if I had gotten one inch nearer!" His sailors were white as a sheet. "There's another narrow squeak," Byrd added. "The gods of chance have been good to me. That wire will have to be well insulated."[36]

Four days later the expedition avoided another potential tragedy. While *Bowdoin* remained at Hopedale, *Peary* set out across Davis Strait toward Greenland. As the steamer sailed through calm, ice-free seas, a pile of life preservers caught fire near one of the wooden wing crates for the planes. The nearby fuselages were soaked in oil and kerosene, and the entire aviation unit could have been wiped out. Indeed, the entire ship, loaded with 7,600 gallons of gasoline about its decks, could have gone up like a torch. Byrd was standing on the bridge when he saw smoke and raced aft "in a jiffy" to put out the flames by throwing some preservers overboard and putting a fire extinguisher on the rest. Byrd intimated that he had already raised the fire issue with McDonald, who had been rather casual about the whole thing. As a result of the fire, McDonald agreed to station a permanent watch about the decks, "including the naval personnel and the doctor."[37]

By now Byrd and McDonald were at loggerheads. Shortly after leaving Hopedale, Byrd sent a memorandum to MacMillan aboard *Bowdoin,* admitting that when he ordered gasoline for the expedition he did not take into account the fact that it would be used to run motorboats and the motors aboard *Peary.* Although there would "probably" be plenty of fuel, Byrd asked that the frequent motorboat trips ashore be somewhat curtailed in the future. The following day he dispatched a stiff memo to McDonald requesting that any and all radio communications from the Navy Department be passed to him. McDonald may have been miffed by this time over the fact that Byrd's messages back to Washington on the expedition's progress were quickly finding their way into print. He was becoming identified as a major player. Obviously, McDonald said something to Richard about reciprocity, for the aviator promptly forwarded to his immediate superior a copy of the memorandum he had written to MacMillan in regard to gasoline conservation.

But McDonald could not let matters rest. On the eleventh he sent his nominal subordinate a lengthy, nasty letter in which he "compliment[ed]" Byrd for his "apparent decision to reduce to writing all material communications, and I shall also in the future reduce all my material communications to writing." McDonald then proceeded to take up each of the points Richard had raised regarding fuel conservation and radio communications. He also took a brief paragraph to acknowledge Byrd's internal communications to his men regarding the necessity for them to master both Arctic navigation (insofar as possible) and radio communications. "You will recall," McDonald added smugly, "that I told you that during your absence in Washington I directed a letter to Admiral Moffett requesting that you be requested to issue instructions to each of the Navy personnel to spend at least one half hour each day in intensive work brushing up on the [radio] code." Byrd's dutiful issuance of such orders, McDonald concluded, would ensure not only that the navy men understood radio and radio code but also that they would have "a means of diversion and occupation which is best if we are to keep our personnel happy."[38]

On the eve of the ships' departure for Greenland, *Bowdoin* suddenly came to a stop and refused to budge. Since there was no decent place along the rocky coast to beach the vessel in order to check its propeller shaft, MacMillan decided to tow it back to Hopedale by means of its own small boats while McDonald and Captain Steele took *Peary* on to Disko Island, just off the central Greenland coast. The day before *Peary* reached Disko, McDonald informed Byrd that MacMillan had ordered the bigger ship to wait for *Bowdoin.* "I am so anxious to get to Etah" and start flight operations, Byrd recorded, "that every day's delay seems like a week." Now with the prospect of further delay, he became incensed. "I had told McDonald that the project might be a failure if we had to" wait for the other vessel, "for it would probably be another two days before the *Bowdoin* would leave Hopedale and probably five or six days more getting here." A further day or two wait at

Disko, "and we would get up at Etah too late to accomplish our mission." Byrd "urged McDonald in the strongest terms" to call MacMillan's "attention to the urgency of the matter." MacMillan should allow *Peary* to push on ahead, leaving Disko as soon at the ship could be coaled and watered. McDonald promised to cable MacMillan, but his impatient subordinate refused to wait. On July 22, Byrd dispatched a long message to the expedition commander aboard *Bowdoin*. "Feel it is my duty to call your attention to extreme seriousness of situation from an aviation standpoint that has arisen from the valuable time now being lost. I tell you most solemnly that unless we leave immediately for Etah all the aviation personnel consider that the superhuman effort they are ready to put into their jobs will probably avail nothing." The most "heroic efforts" must be made to get *Peary* to Etah posthaste. MacMillan took a more responsible view. *Bowdoin* carried all the aviation spare parts, three Liberty engines, and 1,500 gallons of gas. Byrd and his pilots could come to grief by rashly flying in a wholly new, harsh, and unfamiliar environment without sufficient spares and fuel. The commander refused to rescind his orders.[39]

Peary lay off Disko Island and Godhavn village until the end of July while *Bowdoin* was repaired at Hopedale, then clunked its way across the Davis Strait. The entire north-south sweep of coast up to Etah offered a stark and forbidding scene. The vast dome of the Greenland ice sheet, hundreds of miles across and thousands of feet deep, with its frigid winds and storms, began just beyond the narrow strip of low coastal hills and mountains that swept down to the sea. Great glaciers cut through the monochromatic brown-black rock, dumping millions of tons of bright white ice in the form of great bergs into Davis Strait and Baffin Bay, from whence they drifted southward into the North Atlantic shipping lanes. One such berg on a cold and lonely night thirteen years before had ambushed and killed *Titanic*. Only a few harbors, sounds, bays, islands, and rocky beaches, most of them tiny and cramped, afforded a bit of shelter for the handful of widely scattered native settlements and villages that dotted the landscape as far north as Etah.

As the men of *Peary* impatiently awaited *Bowdoin*'s arrival, a new crisis arose. The Danish district governor at Godhavn insisted that although coal mining was going on nearby, he could spare none for the two ships because of looming winter needs. Byrd vowed that the expedition would not founder at this advanced stage: "we'll get that coal somehow." He bombarded the Navy Department with brief but pungent messages requesting that the Danish government be asked to order its governor to provide the precious fuel. Byrd got MacMillan to enlist the National Geographic Society in the same effort. For a week Governor Rosendahl refused to budge, even though Byrd at one point showed him a message transmitted through an amateur radio operator indicating that Copenhagen had indeed instructed him to release sufficient coal supplies to fill *Peary's* bunkers. Not until the evening of July 24 could Byrd send a message ashore to Rosendahl from the department, passing an order from Copenhagen to "deliver necessary coal to Peary at once." Orders in hand, Rosendahl proved most accommodating. According to Byrd, he spent the entire night "negotiating" with his Inuit workers, and at last got them to agree to take an entire day to mine coal exclusively for the American vessel and then fill its bunkers. In his message to the navy secretary, Richard emphasized that the "inconvenience" that Rosendahl "put himself to was out of consideration for a statement from the Commanding Officer of the Polar Unit that much further delay would very seriously jeopardize the chances of success of the Navy's effort." In other words, Richard Byrd, not McDonald or the still-absent MacMillan, had saved the expedition.

The ever fastidious Virginian was also bedeviled during these unhappy days by an inability to get his laundry done. The native inhabitants of Godhavn had come down with a ferocious case of whooping cough, and no one wanted the disease carried north with the expedition. At last, shortly after four o'clock on the morning of July 27, its bunkers full of coal, *Peary* followed the recently arrived *Bowdoin* out of the bay and headed north. "Seven more precious hours lost," Byrd recorded in despair. "I wish I could see this thing as MacMillan sees it."[40]

The two ships soon encountered more pack ice. It began as flat cakes, but within several hours became an "apparently unbroken field." As the wind shifted and leads opened up, the vessels bulled ahead. But after twenty-four hours they hit a new field, surrounded with fog. Byrd and several others got off their beset ship and walked out onto the tightly packed floes for nearly a mile. One had to be careful, for the "snow," as Byrd described it, was slushy in spots, and one of his colleagues sank to his knees. Richard was pleased to have his new waterproof boots. Still, he fretted even when the pack loosened and the ships were able to get under way. "The trouble is that we are heading for land too far to the eastward. We are bound to get into [more] ice." Byrd did not keep such second-guessing to himself.

Soon after entering the pack, he cabled MacMillan on the nearby *Bowdoin:* "I have been talking to the boys and we all want to ask you if you will please try to have the *Peary* anchored in Etah harbor by seven o clock day after tomorrow morning the thirtieth." If possible, "that would give us two full days this month." Should *Bowdoin* not make it, would MacMillan release *Peary* to go ahead? "Every minute seems very precious to us now." Congratulating MacMillan for his fine ice seamanship to date, Byrd closed with the admission that "am sending this without McDonald's knowledge as he is taking a much needed sleep and I don't want to awaken him." MacMillan ignored the request, but Richard thought he had scored with his equally impatient fliers and mechanics. "I am the little ray of sunshine on this ship," he wrote that evening, "for I am continually after McDonald and MacMillan not to lose time. Of course we have been in ice. Should not have played the game so damn safe." MacMillan was undoubtedly enraged by Byrd's cheekiness and rightly so; he was the experienced Arctic hand, Byrd the novice. If Byrd was wrong, it would go hard for him; if he was right, he had made matters even worse.[41]

For four days, the vessels struggled to escape the tight pack that also imprisoned several large icebergs. Wet snow, fog, and mist lent a further depressing cast to the gray and white environment. Then the wind shifted, the sun came in and out, and the ships fought through to broad leads, at last crunching into Etah on August 1 in the midst of a snowstorm. Byrd cabled Washington that *Bowdoin* and *Peary* "followed close to the coastline and had good view of many gigantic glaciers" through the gloom. The expedition had arrived "three hours ahead of schedule," MacMillan later proudly claimed. Byrd, sending daily and sometimes twice-daily reports to the department on the expedition's progress, believed the ships could have arrived a week earlier or more. Still, as the high brown-black hills of Etah came over the horizon, lightened by bright-orange lichens and dappled with gray patches formed by the droppings of millions of little auks who summered there, his unquenchable optimism quickly returned. "Flight operations will begin soon," he said in one of his reports, "and I am extremely desirous of maintaining quick communications with the Department. Have sent lengthy messages last few nights giving some interesting facts. Have they been received?"[42]

Byrd's ongoing concern over communications was understandable. McDonald (and his later defenders) laid great emphasis on radio's invaluable contribution to the safety and success of the expedition; he had chided Richard directly on the matter. Yet radio was, on a personal level, letting the commander of the polar air unit down. "Have not heard directly from my family by radio since I left the States," Byrd cabled acting navy secretary Theodore Robinson on July 29. "All other personnel on Peary have received radio from home." This was not quite true. Richard cabled Marie from Nova Scotia on June 27 that he had received "all your telegrams and letters," which would have included news that she and the children had reached their temporary home in Atlantic City safely and that young Dickie had had his tonsils removed (not always a routine operation in 1925) without incident.

Thereafter, however, communication between husband and wife broke down, despite the best efforts of both to stay in touch. McDonald had asked Zenith to provide Marie with a new shortwave radio, and at one point the company had written her that she could send messages of any length to Zenith's headquarters in Chicago for weekly transmission to the Arctic on the radio program that Mc-

Donald had established to keep the public informed and excited about the expedition. But on July 19 and again two days later, Dick sent out a birthday message to his wife in which he complained that he had received "no radio from you. All is well here," he cabled in obvious concern. "How are you and the children?" A week later, Richard wired Marie that he had cabled the acting secretary, "asking him to help you get a radio message through to me." Had she tried to reach him? Byrd queried anxiously.

Marie was as frustrated as her husband. She had written him several long, deeply affectionate letters and had been in contact with both the Navy Department and Zenith about the lack of radio communication with him. McDonald's heralded communication system had broken down. Not until August 6 did Byrd learn from his wife that she had at last received his cable of July 29 "forwarded from Seattle." Had he received any of her messages? "Do you listen to Zenith program Wednesday night when they read my weekly letter to you?" The Byrds never did establish the satisfactory communication links enjoyed by everyone else aboard the two ships. Marie got a few messages from Etah via "ham" radio operators, but that was all. The communication failure was undoubtedly another source of tension between McDonald and his chief subordinate that continued to grow worse as the expedition at last prepared for polar operations.[43]

Time was of the essence. MacMillan wanted to be on his way home by August 25, September 1 at the latest. The expedition had made no provision for wintering over, and ice conditions would worsen rapidly after the middle of the month. The sailors got to work. The aircraft were quickly uncrated and assembled one by one aboard *Peary,* then lowered over the side and run onto the rocky little beach that fronted the wide bay. There an attempt was made to fashion an acceptable runway out of wooden materials from the crates. Byrd was able to enlist the help of not only the civilian crews from the two ships, plus MacMillan and McDonald, but also several "eskimos" from the nearby village. The natives fascinated Byrd. The few families in Etah lived "in most primitive possible way," he cabled Washington. "They are the northernmost living people and their struggle for existence is so intense that it takes considerable intelligence to survive."

After a few hours of planning and work, it became apparent that the small, rocky beach could not support an adequate wooden runway. Byrd ordered the three aircraft pushed back into the water, where they would be employed exclusively as seaplanes. This decision created other hazards. Each plane was initially secured to an anchor. But wind and tide soon caused the anchors to drag, threatening either to beach the planes or to bang their fragile wings against the hulls of the two ships. Byrd then ordered the aircraft snubbed closely to mooring buoys and later to the sterns of the vessels themselves. But this solution increased the chances of structural damage, as the aircraft continually butted against the ship's hulls. The harried air unit commander had no choice but to order a continual watch over the planes whenever they were secured alongside. Despite these problems, Richard found time to visit *Peary*'s radio room and send brief messages to his allies in Congress, including Carl Vinson ("Only seven hundred miles from pole. It is a bit colder than Georgia. We will begin flying soon"), Senator Hale of Maine, and brother Harry.[44]

On August 3, "with the first sunlight since arriving here," the planes were revved up. The frigid waters of Etah Fjord and the surrounding hills echoed to the roar of aircraft engines. Soon Billy Schur took off on the first test hop. With him went MacMillan and mechanic Charles Rochefort. In reasonably clear weather Schur took NA-2 up over Smith Sound, the snowcapped, partially obscured mountains of Ellesmere Island looming before the three men in the open cockpits of the Loening Amphibian. Then Schur looped back to become the first man to pilot a plane over the Greenland ice cap before touching down on Etah Fjord. The following day Byrd and Bennett roared aloft in a spume of spray in NA-1, followed by Reber and two mechanics in NA-3 for a slightly longer ride. The air unit next concentrated on testing the aircraft radios (including long-wave transmissions from the battleship *Florida* lying in the North Atlantic) and loading the aircraft.

While awaiting MacMillan and *Bowdoin* down at Disko Island, Byrd had whiled away some of his enforced leisure drafting "General Order Number One," an elaborate, detailed eight-page list of materials to be carried on polar flights. It covered everything from emergency supplies (salt, cod liver oil, bread, and bacon) to tools (wrenches, pliers, chisels, and cotter pins), sleeping bags, rafts with paddles, sextants, rifles and knives, primus stoves and fuel, and a radio. Now that list would have to be tested and revised on the basis of what the planes could actually carry. What was the maximum feasible load, and how should it be distributed when one was taking off from frigid waters and might be landing on the ice? On the sixth they began to find out, as the planes failed to lift off with materials placed in the stern. That night as the aircraft were restowed, Byrd wired the Navy Department that he hoped to send a flight over Ellesmere Island the following day to investigate landing conditions. He hoped an advance base for aerial reconnaissance of the unknown portions of the polar sea could be established within two or three days.[45] But the weather suddenly turned vile. Heavy snowstorms were followed by fog and pouring rain, then by a full-blown gale. Byrd and his men rightly concluded that this Greenland year would scarcely see summer at all. Not until the eighth did the skies clear sufficiently for a short flight.

In the following two and a half weeks until the expedition left Etah, Byrd was filled with despair. Flying conditions were too often minimal, but MacMillan consistently failed to exploit what fleeting opportunities appeared. He refused to heed the advice of his flight commander, who may not have known much about the Arctic but knew a great deal about aircraft. In fact, MacMillan was in a hurry to bail out and go home because of a persistent coal shortage.

But Byrd remained most frustrated by his relations—or lack thereof—with McDonald. "I do not invite any confidence as long as McDonald is in power." The second in command "seems to be suspicious of everything and every one." This may have been due, in part, to Byrd's own success with shortwave radio. Peter Freuchen, a longtime Danish resident of the West Greenland coast, recalled that while members of the 1913–1914 MacMillan party tried to make radio contact with New York from Saunders Island, "more than ten years later Admiral [sic] Byrd tried the same thing at the same place and succeeded in getting in radio contact with Australia."[46]

Despite tensions and frustrations, the aviation unit accomplished some remarkable flying. Byrd proudly recorded that his three aircraft flew more than 6,000 miles, 5,000 of which were out of Etah Fjord over Smith Sound and the interior parts of Ellesmere Island. He and Bennett bore the brunt of flight operations because of severe damage to the other two aircraft that fortunately occurred on the ground rather than in flight. Byrd admitted that although he was a qualified pilot, Bennett, "being the better" airman, "did most of the flying while I navigated and flew from time to time when I was sure of our location and could let the navigating go for awhile."[47] The two men's confidence in each other's abilities became complete; Byrd would never find another aviator in whom he could repose such total trust.

Once the gale subsided on the evening of August 8, Byrd ordered his men aloft. Schur piloted NA-2, while Reber flew NA-3 with Byrd as navigator. Shortly after nine o'clock as the aircraft began to maneuver for takeoff, a herd of a dozen walrus surfaced a few feet from NA-3. "They apparently became enraged at" the plane, Dick wrote in a private memo, "and dived toward us." Reber promptly gunned the engine. The aircraft bucking and bouncing through the waters of the fjord scattered the animals, for Byrd "could not see them when they arose to the surface again because of the spray kicked up by the propeller."[48]

Clawing upward, the two aircraft passed over Cape Sabine, 30 miles northwest of Etah. Byrd immediately found himself struggling with navigation. The North Magnetic Pole lay off to the south of the aircraft, while the North Pole was on the other side. The force of the earth's magnetism operating on the standard compass needle was very weak. The steering compass was stuck on due east, and bearings taken at the cape indicated a 103-degree error and an additional 30-degree error of deviation. Fortunately, officials at the National Geographic and the Navy Department already understood the devastating effects of the magnetic pole, and Albert Bumstead, the society's chief navigation specialist, had developed a very effective sun compass that in clear weather provided precise navigation. With the sun obscured, as it was during much of this flight, Byrd simply flew "east" in order to fly northwest, and "west" in order to return to Etah.

As he finished his calculations, Byrd gazed over ice-choked Smith Sound from the open cockpit and could see at a glance the area in which Peary and Bob Bartlett had experienced such a difficult time back in 1908 getting their ship *Roosevelt* through the pack. Looking down and around at perhaps 100 square miles of Arctic wasteland, Byrd realized how immeasurably helpful an aircraft would have been then in searching out leads "so easily visible to us, but so difficult to locate even from the crow's nest of a ship." He was impressed, too, with the fact that he and Reber were traversing in a few moments areas it had taken Peary and his men days to cross.

Soon Reber, Byrd, and the others saw a magnificent vista open up before them as the glacier-clad mountain ranges, fjords, coastline, and inner lakes of snow-covered Ellesmere Island loomed through the whirling propeller blades. The day was generally gray, with intermittent low clouds, but "we were stirred with the spirit of great adventure—with the feeling that we were getting a comprehensive idea, never before possible, of the Arctic's ruggedness and ruthlessness." (Fifty-five years later, the author flew over the same general area with the U.S. Navy in a large, warm, enclosed prop-jet on a ten-hour journey from Thule to Eielson Air Force Base outside Fairbanks, Alaska, stunned by the same vista and stirred by a vague fear that the four engines might quit altogether and pitch everyone aboard into a frightful situation.) Flying over the coastline and into the interior of Ellesmere Island, Byrd did not see "a single place" where it would be possible to put an aircraft safely down in case of emergency. The "irregular" topography and ice-choked waters of sound, fjord, and lake precluded landing. Soon the weather closed in both ahead and astern, and Byrd ordered the two planes to turn and race for Etah. Fortunately, they spotted a hole in the clouds over Smith Sound and were able to return to the fjord, dodging fog banks most of the way.[49] The airmen returned exhausted and shaken by cold. At 4,000- and 5,000-foot flight altitudes, the temperatures around their open cockpits reached below zero Fahrenheit, and icy slipstreams compounded the discomfort manyfold.

Impressed with the rigor and rapid variability of the weather, Byrd called his men together "and told them that I would never order any of them to fly over that land again."[50] Secretary Wilbur, it is true, had urged Byrd not to take foolish risks, but the commander himself was demonstrating a sincere concern for his men and their safety that he would exhibit throughout his polar career. He took prudent risks, but he did not want blood on his hands. Of course, he would never prevent men from volunteering, and so they did that day in Greenland, and later in the Antarctic, as he knew they would.

MacMillan was more eager than Byrd would admit to at least get a glimpse of the unknown area to the north and west of Ellesmere and its immediately adjacent island, Axel Heiberg. But the planes became aerodynamically unstable above certain loads. Moreover, the cruising radius of the Loening Amphibians was markedly reduced whenever they were forced to take off from water. The drag associated with getting aloft greatly increased fuel consumption so that the aircraft's range was closer to 1,000 miles rather than the 1,400 miles that Grover Loening and the navy had promised. On August 10 MacMillan sent a memo to Byrd reiterating that the expedition must depart for home no later than September 1. That being the case, would it be possible to establish "an intermediate base" on the south side of Bay Fjord on Ellesmere Island about 150 miles away? From there the expedition could make an advance base at Cape Thomas Hubbard, 320 miles from Etah, "and hence one flight out over the Polar Sea to at least a point 200 miles from land."

MacMillan summoned Byrd and McDonald for a conference to discuss the proposal. In his public report of the expedition, Byrd noted that "Commander MacMillan had confidently believed that the fjords would be free of ice. That they were not was due probably to the fact that we were having scarcely any summer." These careful words hid a deep division within the expedition that led to a flaming row between Byrd and the other two commanders, for the airman did not want to risk creating a base in ice-choked fjords that could damage or destroy his planes. Already his mechanics and pilots had had to leap onto the tethered aircraft and maneuver them out of the way of errant bergs that had drifted into Etah Fjord with the recurrent gales. A calamitous collision with a berg in one of Ellesmere's ice-choked fjords 100 and more miles away would doubtless be disastrous. As Byrd recorded in his diary on the evening of August 10, "I pleaded today with MacMillan to go [that is, fly] north along the coast [of Ellesmere Island] instead of over land. I believe there will be landing places here and there along the coast. McDonald knew of my desire to stick to water and so he preceded me to the *Bowdoin* and had everything cut and dried before my arrival. He always does this. I was most vigorously turned down. This will probably mean the failure of the whole plan."[51]

Nonetheless, Byrd and his men dutifully carried out their orders. That afternoon, as the gale subsided, the airmen took off again.[52] But they ran into a snowstorm over Cape Sabine and found Ellesmere Island completely covered with fog and snow. That evening they tried again in clearer weather. Climbing over Cape Sabine, the three aircraft flew across Smith Sound to the island. Byrd and Bennett were at 7,000 feet in NA-1, and the other two aircraft, with MacMillan aboard NA-2, were 3,000 feet below. The fliers, already suffering in their open cockpits from "bitter cold," reached the western end of Flagler Fjord twenty-two minutes later. The day was incredible, bright and clear. Byrd saw "hundreds" of mountain peaks to the left gleaming with snow, while clouds covered everything to the right. The mountains were obviously much higher than the 7,300 feet shown on existing maps. "Much land probably never seen before," he would later wire the Navy Department. Soon MacMillan's NA-2 disappeared in the clouds, and NA-3 reported it could not gain altitude and was heading back to Etah. Byrd and Bennett pressed on across Ellesmere Island to find a marginally acceptable landing spot at Eureka Sound, 200 miles from Etah, before being forced back by bad weather.

Flying home, worried about the other two aircraft that had been forced back, Byrd and Bennett saw Beitstad Fjord, just 100 miles from Etah, clear of both weather and bergs. Beitstad cut deep into the interior of the island, and that may have accounted for its lack of ice. If so, MacMillan had been right and Byrd wrong. Byrd was decent enough to send a wire to Secretary Wilbur praising Beitstad as a "magnificent" location, with cliffs rising 2,000 feet straight out of the water. But the two fliers were not through. They flew on to Hayes Fjord and actually landed on the western end, but strong winds rushing down from the adjacent glacier made anchoring or maneuvering the plane up the rocky coastline impossible. The two men took off through heaving waters. Still doggedly looking for the perfect site, Byrd and Bennett glanced down at Flagler Fjord once more as they prepared to leave Ellesmere and found its mouth ice free. So MacMillan would have two alternative base sites to choose from. The other two planes had already returned to Etah by the time Byrd arrived.

The men were beginning to wear down. Reber reported not only extreme cold but some snow blindness as well. Reviewing this first substantial flight in the high Arctic, Byrd was struck by the fact that although "at last we had been able to land in the interior of Ellesmere Island . . . the water had been dangerously rough." He was also impressed by the behavior of the catabatic winds that flowed off the glaciers. "We . . . found that no matter what the direction of the wind elsewhere it generally flowed down the glacier and then subsided or changed its direction some miles beyond the foot." Byrd also discovered that distances in the "Far North" were consistently deceiving. Landing in Hayes Fjord, he and Bennett thought they were but a few hundred feet from the shoreline at the foot of the 2,000-foot cliffs, "whereas to our great surprise we found ourselves more than half a mile away."[53]

MacMillan promptly chose Flagler Fjord for the advance base, and the fliers were eager to press any advantage they had won against the Arctic as long as they could. But on the thirteenth, "everything seemed to go wrong." A gale suddenly blew in, causing heavy seas that opened up a seam on NA-2, moored astern of *Bowdoin*. The plane began to sink until the motor was three-quarters submerged. Byrd later wrote that "MacMillan and his crew, by prompt and heroic effort, saved the plane." But when the plane was hoisted aboard *Bowdoin* for safety and repair, the boatswain mate accidentally let the aircraft fall heavily to the deck, breaking its keel. NA-2 never flew again. As NA-2 was slowly sinking in the swelling seas and high winds, an errant gust tore an engine cowling out of the hands of Floyd Bennett and another mechanic, Peter Sorenson, who were working on repairs aboard the nearby NA-1. Before the men could save the heavy piece of duralumin, it flipped overboard and sank. The two sailors worked all night on the deck in the cold making a new cowling out of scrap duralumin. Byrd later reported proudly that they did not finish their work until nearly six the next morning, then insisted on reporting for the next flight.

MacMillan, however, was losing faith in the potential of polar aviation. He told his patrons at the National Geographic Society that "science has not solved for Arctic explorers all the difficulties of the past. While airplanes annihilate time and distance, aviators experience other handicaps which never thwarted explorers who relied solely upon the sledge and the Eskimo dog team." Fog and low-hanging clouds, he continued, had consistently frustrated the aviators' attempts to establish advance bases in the interior or on the coast of Ellesmere Island, to say nothing of adjacent Axel Heiberg Island. Thus, prospects were rapidly diminishing for even a single "dash" out over the polar sea to "the great blind spot of the Arctic to ascertain whether or not there is land in the unexplored area."[54]

On the morning of August 14, Byrd and Bennett in NA-1, with Schur piloting NA-3, shot aloft again in a spume of spray and headed back to Flagler Fjord, 107 miles away. Setting down, the pilots were able to maneuver their aircraft to within 50 feet of an ice-free beach, and the four men waded ashore through the frigid waters with 200 pounds of food, 100 gallons of aviation fuel, 5 gallons of oil, a primus stove, a camping outfit, smoke bombs, a rifle, and ammunition. A large block of ice drifted into NA-1, but after a half hour the crewmen of the two aircraft were able to push it off and get back in the air. They raced back to Etah for more supplies. It was too late. Reaching Flagler again in the deepening twilight of an Arctic midnight, Byrd and Bennett in NA-1 and enlisted pilot A. C. Nold flying NA-3 found that in just a few hours, "the ice had closed in and completely covered our landing place." The two planes cruised fruitlessly about for some 60 miles, hoping to find an alternative base site, but could not. In the gloom of the fjords, Byrd and Bennett lost sight of Nold. Frantically, they cast about until at last they saw him far off, "just a speck in the distance," completely disoriented and fly-ing straight north toward the pole. Bennett crammed on speed and took off after the errant flier. Slowly, slowly, as they raced above Ellesmere's dark terrain, they gained on their colleague and overhauled him. "What Nold's compass was doing or what he was about, I have never found out," Byrd later wrote. But the two planes got back safely to Etah.

Determined to find a new site, Byrd and Bennett in the faithful NA-1 set out once more at midnight, with Schur piloting NA-3. The two aircraft scouted the eastern portions of Ellesmere once more. Flagler Fjord was still blocked, and the fliers soon "ran into fog and low clouds. . . . Mountains completely covered with fog and so impossible to get over them." Sawyer Bay had "some open water," and Bennett and Schur put down. But the weather closed in, so Byrd ordered the planes beached, and the fliers had a picnic lunch while waiting for the clouds and fog to lift. "The appearance of Cannon Fjord near us was water dropping a thousand feet into a bowl." Finishing their lunch, the men cleared out some scum ice that had formed around the aircraft, then took off to climb over the low mountains near-by. But Schur reported that NA-3 had a developed an engine knock, and he re-mained behind while Byrd and Bennett, the latter nearly exhausted by nonstop flying, pressed on. The two aviators first investigated Cannon Fjord at an altitude of 5,000 feet, but for some unexplained reason they found it unacceptable. They cleared the nearby mountains "and got over unexplored regions of Grinnell Land. Found high uncharted mountains. Saw many square miles never seen before by man, covered with snow. There was an uncharted lake frozen over." The men were both moved and frightened by the scene before and around them as their tiny open-cockpit aircraft bucked and wobbled and bounced through "the roughest" air "ever experienced by us." The "jaggedness, irregularity, and many deep valleys presented a magnificent but awful spectacle." Suddenly, high peaks "completely covered by clouds" rose before them. "Made effort to get through but it was im-possible," Byrd reported. Bennett turned NA-1 back to Sawyer Bay and deposit-ed 100 gallons of aviation fuel, 5 gallons of oil, and some pemmican. Then the shaken fliers lifted off with NA-3 for the trip to Etah.[55]

And that was all. A gale blew up soon after the aircraft returned and kept them grounded. On the seventeenth, gasoline on the water around *Peary* ignited, threat-ening to blow up the ship and destroy NA-3, which was tied up astern. Sorenson and another mechanic, A. C. Rocheville, immediately cast the burning plane adrift with Nold aboard. Schur promptly threw Nold a rescue harness, calming and en-couraging the sailor until he could escape the licking flames. That evening, Byrd wrote of his enormous respect and admiration for the men. "They have been in-

defatigable and courageous and whenever there has been a job to do they have
needed no commanding officer to tell them to do it [or] to spur them to greater
effort."

It would take three days to repair the aircraft, but MacMillan had already had
enough. Earlier that day he and his aviation commander had engaged in a furious
exchange of formal memos. Writing two notes, one to "My dear Commander
Byrd," the other to "My dear Byrd," MacMillan laid down the law. Two of the
three planes were now out of commission. "Considering that I am to be held responsible for the success or failure of our plans and that if any plane fails to return
one of my two ships must remain in the north for fifteen months it is against my
orders for any plane to cross Smith Sound alone." He instructed Byrd to let him
know whenever NA-1 or -3 was leaving Etah Fjord "and the object of the flight."
In his second note, MacMillan told Byrd he was giving "you and your men" one
more week to put down a cache of provisions on Ellesmere Island, either at Bay
Fjord or Eureka Sound. If after that week Byrd believed that within another three
days they could reach a point "on the Polar Sea" at least 200 miles west of any part
of Axel Heiberg Island, "I will gladly remain." Otherwise, the expedition's flight
plan was over. MacMillan asked Byrd for a reply, including a report of depots already established on Ellesmere Island. Since no real "depots" had been established,
Byrd was in a bind, but in a lengthy response later in the day he insisted that "if
we have fair weather and can find two bases that stay clear of ice," then a one-shot
trip out across the polar sea was still imaginable. "We cannot, of course, get over
the mountains if they are covered with cloud." Both Byrd and his commander were
aware that "fair weather" had never consistently blessed the expedition, that no
base or depot had been found clear of ice for long, and that Ellesmere's mountains
had been continually blanketed by cloud and fog.

The following day MacMillan radioed the National Geographic Society that
despite laying caches at Flagler Fjord and Sawyer Bay, the 7,000-plus-foot mountain peaks on Ellesmere Island blocked all attempts to get to Cape Thomas Hubbard on adjacent Axel Heiberg Island from which flights over the polar sea were
to have been staged. The society immediately released the messages to the press,
which put enormous pressure on the navy to support MacMillan. Secretary Wilbur
radioed Byrd, asking whether the expedition should abandon its major purpose
"of flying this year over the frozen Polar Sea in search of an unknown continent."
Should MacMillan agree to end operations at Etah, the expedition would use its
two remaining aircraft to "explore regions further south where the naval aviators
will not be balked by weather and ice conditions." The Norse ruins in southern
Greenland and the interior of Baffin Island, which no "white man" had ever seen,
seemed suitable candidates.

Wilbur's message decided the matter for MacMillan. On August 19 he recommended "withdrawal from Etah because unexpected Summer snowstorms, continuous fogs and unprecedented weather conditions have rendered it impossible to establish an advance base at Cape Thomas Hubbard this season and explore the polar region." The Navy Department concurred, and the explorer was directed to pack up as quickly as possible and head back down the Greenland coast. The National Geographic issued a formal press release fully supporting MacMillan's decision. Persistently foul weather justified releasing the Arctic expedition from its duties around Smith Sound. MacMillan and his men "would proceed immediately from Etah to accomplish other objectives of the mission." MacMillan quickly passed the order to Byrd via the usual formal memo. The commanding officer took the opportunity to get in a dig at his subordinate: "All other work as planned by the National Geographic" was "being prevented" by the air missions, and so it was time "to prepare for home at once."[56]

At least publicly, Byrd took it all with good grace. With the perfect correctness of the good subordinate he informed the navy that he would "withdraw and cease attempts to fly over Polar Sea as directed." He would make "such flights in secondary explorations as may be requested by MacMillan and that are practicable." Byrd told Wilbur that he had communicated his great disappointment to MacMillan. "But do not presume that I question Commander MacMillan's good judgment nor do I fail to sympathize with him in his position and I know that it is with great reluctance that he gives the orders to abandon our flight. He has never failed to put the greatest effort into making the aviation program a success." In a brief article appended to MacMillan's longer report on the expedition published later in the year in *National Geographic Magazine,* Richard wrote that his commander had emphasized concern that the mouth of Etah Fjord had frozen over; should the planes or a plane have to make a forced landing on a fjord somewhere on Ellesmere Island, it would probably be frozen in permanently. MacMillan "was right. He knows the Arctic, and it is due to his good judgment that the personnel and the planes got back to this country safely."[57]

Privately, however, Richard's thoughts darkened again. MacMillan had, after all, promised the fliers a week, perhaps ten days, to accomplish their mission. In the midst of their exchange of notes on the seventeenth Byrd had "begged" his commander "to let Bennett and me go today to Cannon Fjord but he would not agree. Wonderful day. Probably last chance." Two days later Byrd was led to believe, rightly or wrongly, that MacMillan had reconfirmed the commitment to remain at Etah when in fact the commander was preparing to pull out. "I have just received your letter stating that we must prepare to go home at once," Byrd wrote MacMillan the next day. "I am distressed beyond measure that we won't try again for the polar sea and I beg of you to reconsider your decision." Yes, Byrd readily admitted, his commander was far more conversant with Arctic conditions than he. Nonetheless, "I do feel that we still have a chance to succeed." But the flight commander was now isolated, and MacMillan knew it. His order stood, and within hours after Byrd submitted his despairing note the navy released a statement that "the Department considers further attempts to fly over the Polar Sea are not advisable this season."

MacMillan then weighed in with a last devastating message to the National Geographic Society. Reiterating his decision to end flight operations because of foul weather, MacMillan told his patrons that Byrd was begging for a last chance. "I admire his courage as I do that of every man under his command who has been flying over ice-strewn waters and ice-capped hills [!] where safe landings are utterly impossible." Someone, either in Greenland or Washington, deleted the sentence. Having set up Byrd and his boys, MacMillan delivered the kill. If navy officials could see Arctic conditions from the air, "I am confident that orders would be issued to stop all work at once." MacMillan was "more convinced than ever that far northern Arctic work will never be done by heavier than air machines simply because landing places are uncertain and caches of food and gas cannot be depended upon. . . . A lighter than air machine [that is, a dirigible] can do the work and should do it at the earliest opportunity." Two days later, with departure imminent, the despairing Byrd thought of "a remorseless cruel universe grinding out its destiny." The following day he brightened a bit: "To have Marie in the midst of chaos, that is enough."[58]

One thrilling flight remained for Bennett and Byrd. While the expedition was packing up at Etah, MacMillan ordered the fliers to make several photographic surveys over the adjacent ice sheet. On the twenty-second, NA-1, with Bennett, Byrd, and an enlisted mechanic aboard, started out for Igloodahouny beach, fifty miles to the south, along with NA-3, piloted by Reber and carrying Nold and a National Geographic photographer. A half mile out of Etah, Reber's plane threw its connecting rod, doubtless the source of the earlier "knock" that had forced Schur to return prematurely from Ellesmere Island. Reber managed to get NA-3 down in the water, and it was towed ignominiously back to base by ship's boat. Byrd and Bennett landed to make certain that the NA-3 crew was all right, then rose again to head toward Igloodahouny, "where we found a fine beach. We landed and made camp."

Several hours later, Bennett and Byrd left their mechanic behind and in cloudless weather headed toward the vast ice sheet that covers all but the narrow coastal strips of Greenland. The glaciers near the foot of the low coastal mountains were deeply crevassed, but they became smooth and firm farther up as they blended into the ice cap. Bennett climbed to eleven thousand feet, passing into and through a warm-air stratum. Reaching the frigid air above was a shock to both men. Freezing and somewhat oxygen deprived in their open cockpits in the thin, cold air, Byrd and Bennett could see a hundred miles in every direction. "As we got further in over the ice-cap it grew bitterly cold." Flying south and east over another Arctic area never before explored, the men gazed down from their moving perch in the high, clear northern sky at an ice sheet that had become as smooth as the crystal on a watch. Looking eastward they saw the Greenland ice cap gradually rising until it reached their eleven thousand–foot height, "higher than any altitude heretofore reported." The airmen returned to the beach at Igloodahouny "frozen stiff" but exultant at what they had seen and grateful to a remarkable aircraft, NA-1, that in more than twenty-five hundred miles of rugged polar flying had never failed them. Their mission was finally over.[59]

But the expedition was not, nor were Byrd's troubles with MacMillan and McDonald. *Peary* and *Bowdoin* moved slowly down the Greenland coast for several weeks through often heavy pack ice while the National Geographic photographers and scientists did their work. Byrd was impatient. He had hoped to be home soon with his wife and children, who continued to wait in Atlantic City. But the National Geographic people were in no hurry, and MacMillan was apparently in no mood to hurry them. Bursts of bad weather also set the schedule back. The long voyage home soon began to wear on everyone, and at one point Richard had to remind his men "that the prohibition laws of our country apply to this vessel and the personnel of the Naval Unit will be careful to observe them to the letter."[60]

At last the two vessels made their way against heavy gales across Davis Strait to the Newfoundland coast and the small port of Battle Harbour, where Dick found a "long" telegram from Grover Loening. The word in Washington and elsewhere was that Loening's amphibious aircraft had failed. The National Geographic seemed to think so, MacMillan surely did, and now Billy Mitchell had taken up the allegation in his usual flamboyant fashion, charging naval aviation in particular and the U.S. military establishment in general with treason.

Mitchell was provoked into making the charges that would lead to his court-martial by the spectacular breakup of *Shenandoah* over Ohio on September 3 in the midst of a goodwill tour. Fourteen crewmen were killed. From his post in Texas the maverick airman issued a six thousand–word statement in which he sputtered that the loss of the great airship was the result of "incompetence, criminal negligence, and the almost treasonable negligence of our national defense" on the part of the War and Navy Departments. Turning to the Greenland expedition, Mitchell stated that the navy had sent MacMillan and Byrd into the Arctic with underpowered "jitneys" to attempt a flight to the North Pole. Moffett had "borrowed" the planes from the army, knowing they were "inadequate to the work." As a consequence, the planes "got nowhere, did nothing. Another example, says the Navy Department, of the incapacity of aircraft." Unfortunately for Mitchell, it was widely known in Washington circles that he had tried to corral for the army all of the planes he now so contemptuously dismissed. Nonetheless, Byrd was outraged at Mitchell's charges. "Can't you stop [him] in his misstatements of facts?" he asked Loening. "Men with me did superhuman things and Mitchell is unjust and hurting his own game, because really planes showed what can be done by aviation under very adverse operating conditions."

Despite his anger and concern, Dick sought to reassure the aircraft manufacturer. The National Geographic was in "entire accord" with Loening's insistence that the planes had worked well. MacMillan had sailed on to Nova Scotia and could not be reached for comment, but "your planes did not fail and MacMillan has not said so." The commander had complained about the engines and the lack of decent cruising range, but "I don't agree . . . that that had anything to do with the outcome." Emotions and feelings within the expedition were "delicate," Byrd continued, so Loening should not reply to his critics "until I see you." Richard promised that he would ride the train from Wiscasset to Boston with Loening, and the two men could resolve whatever questions and problems remained. The navy's agreement with the National Geographic Society precluded giving out any stories about the expedition at the moment. Byrd closed on an encouraging note: "Don't worry everything will come out okay. Be sure that you don't quote me to newspapers." Despite his brave front, Byrd was clearly a worried and angry man. Somehow, Mitchell had gotten hold of MacMillan's critical comments about the aviation unit. One more breach had been opened between Byrd and his commander.[61]

Relations deteriorated the longer the expedition took getting home. While the two vessels loafed in Battle Harbour, Newfoundland officials approached MacMillan with a request. The steamship *Home* was missing offshore. Would the commander use his last remaining operational aircraft to search for it? MacMillan agreed and cabled the National Geographic regarding his intentions without consulting Byrd. When he summoned his chief flier from ashore to tell him of the commitment, Byrd demurred. NA-1 had been run hard, and he no longer trusted it. He cabled Marie the following day that he had "no flying plans. Will not fly planes if they are unsafe." MacMillan huffily deferred to his airman and told the Canadians that *Peary* itself would search for the missing ship. The public was now aware of the situation, and Richard was forced to cable the Navy Department that if *Peary* was unsuccessful, NA-1 would be used to widen the search. *Home* was soon discovered, "windbound" in an adjacent coastal harbor, and the incident passed, but tensions within the expedition command structure continued to build.[62]

They boiled over several days later. Late in the evening of September 26, while *Peary* was docked at Bonne Bay, Newfoundland, Byrd received a letter from McDonald replying to the airman's earlier verbal query as to future plans. The waters within the harbor had been "very rough" that afternoon, and at one point the ship's gunwales dipped under the water, injuring the wings of the already damaged NA-2. After stating that the ship would leave the following morning, weather permitting, McDonald criticized Byrd for not properly securing the navy material aboard, "this being a reiteration of my request of five p.m." Richard hastened to McDonald's cabin to explain "that he was mistaken—that Rocheville, Bennett, Nold and Francis had in accordance with my instructions put extra lashings on the wings—the Navy gear in question." McDonald would have none of it, and shortly thereafter he appeared outside Byrd's stateroom "apparently in an excited state of mind." He summoned his subordinate to look at some other allegedly loose bindings that when examined seemed firm to Byrd. After further "unintelligible remarks" McDonald led Byrd back to the lashed-down wings of NA-1 and by word and manner indicated that the air-unit commander had been consistently lying to him. McDonald then "requested" that the officers and men of the air detachment be brought on deck to see the lashings for themselves. Byrd rousted them out, and while they were dressing McDonald "threatened . . . a court of inquiry using profane and uncontrolled language." The airman noticed that some of the lines around the wings did show a slight slack due to continual and heavy wetting in the heavy seas coming down the coast from Battle Harbour, but the slack was not sufficient to cause movement of the equipment. McDonald, however, claimed "criminal negligence." As soon as the officers and men appeared, McDonald called for a stenographer and began asking questions. The sailors' testimony fully vindicated Byrd, but McDonald was determined to press on. He reconvened his court of inquiry in the ship's dining cabin, where, in Richard's words, "the heat of the room soon disclosed the fact that McDonald appeared intoxicated. The fact became evident to everyone." Schur suggested the ship's doctor be called to ascertain everyone's "general health," and McDonald abruptly closed the meeting. He refused to continue the questioning or to give Byrd a copy of what the stenographer had taken down. "In a few minutes," Byrd concluded, "McDonald returned to the mess room and in the presence of the Naval Unit said that he did not like us."

Byrd immediately wrote a report of the incident, claiming that "McDonald is after me and I believe that he would not hesitate to do the whole Navy injury to gain his ends. He is vindictive towards me because I have not made myself a pawn in his hands." The previous week McDonald had threatened "dire punishment if I tried to bring anything out against him," stating that he had "gradually built up a case" against Byrd "and would get me if it should ever be necessary." McDonald had no character or ethics, Byrd continued, and at one point had criticized his air commander "for not throwing several cans of food ashore at Hayes Fjord and stating that we had formed a base." Richard then circulated his draft report around the aviation unit and had all the officers and senior petty officers sign an affidavit as to its truthfulness. The next morning McDonald wrote Byrd a brief note, congratulating his subordinate for ordering three of his men to make fast the lashing on all navy equipment.[63]

Peary reached Curling, Newfoundland, on the last day of September, and all hands went ashore to register for a meal at the Glynn Mill Inn in nearby Corner Brook. Byrd later claimed that when he returned to the front desk he noticed that someone had written "Vice Admiral" before his name. Bennett and Sorenson were nearby, and Byrd called them over. The writing was evidently not his, and he scratched out the rank before his name. But others had seen it, and McDonald was incensed. There was a big dance in the building that evening, and McDonald wrote Byrd of his mortification "when even Americans asked to be introduced to the Admiral," and he was "forced to tell them there was no Admiral on board the *Peary*." Because the two men had obviously not been speaking to each other for some time, Richard sent back an immediate note in which he claimed he had been the victim of a joke and that he had obliterated the offending title. He also got Bennett and Sorenson to back him. After insisting that the two words were written in a hand other than that of their commanding officer, the two added that the whole matter was "just another indecent move on McDonald's part to get some technicality on Commander Byrd." Two days later, McDonald replied with a stiff little note that mingled acknowledgment that he could have been mistaken with the reminder that the acting hotel manager had made a statement to the effect that Byrd had written his rank when registering.[64]

Riven with ill-concealed dissension, the MacMillan expedition at last came home on October 12, 1925, to an enthusiastic welcome at Wiscasset that matched the departure ceremonies four months before. A brief flurry of news followed, but thereafter the expedition quickly faded from sight. There were no ticker-tape parades down Broadway, no lavish White House receptions, no extended lecture tours by the principals. Byrd angered McDonald by including in his draft report an account of *Peary*'s grounding off the Labrador coast on the way north. McDonald argued that Byrd had blown the incident far out of proportion and insisted that the flier delete the offending passage. Word leaked to the press that McDonald had "suppressed" his subordinate's account. Byrd talked out of both sides of his mouth when the press got to him, first saying that "Mr. McDonald's statement is correct," with respect to causing needless alarm, then adding that *Peary* had listed "to a dangerous angle, but righted itself on the rising of the tide," and that "had she struck the reef at high tide she undoubtedly would have plunged to the bottom." Later, Byrd and MacMillan clashed when the latter picked up McDonald's story of Byrd's naming himself a vice admiral in the Corner Brook hotel registry. Byrd once again dismissed the entire incident as a joke. Less amusing or juvenile was the charge leveled by rival Canadian explorer G. P. MacKenzie that MacMillan's pilots had flown over Ellesmere, a Canadian possession, without permission. Both Byrd and MacMillan denied the allegation, and press investigations suggested that the State Department had "pigeon-holed" MacMillan's formal request to Ottawa for overflight privileges.[65]

If the expedition faded quickly from the public mind, Richard Byrd did not. Billy Mitchell saw to that. Even before reaching Maine, Richard was detached from the Naval Air Unit (which he turned over to Schur) and ordered to Washington to prepare a rebuttal to Mitchell. The toughest critics could not deny the polar airman his achievements. Byrd and his Naval Air Unit had attempted the most difficult noncombat flying up to that time; everyone had worked and flown tirelessly. The expedition historians, no friends of Dick Byrd, nonetheless concede that his "unquestionable personal bravery and determination to complete the mission . . . virtually leap from the pages of the record."[66] Men had been flying seriously for only a decade; the vast, turbulent atmosphere above the earth remained a great mystery. Venturing above ten thousand feet was still a daunting prospect. Byrd and his pilots and mechanics, operating in the wholly new polar environment, experienced the rigors and treacheries of its weather while tracing thirty thousand miles of Arctic terrain. They had been true discoverers, and Byrd returned home, if not a hero, at least an apprentice explorer. He would never again be misidentified as "Robert Y. Byrd." He had broken the shackles of a frustrating naval career.

Three days after *Peary* docked at Wiscasset, Richard was in Washington, where he appeared before the special board convened by President Coolidge to investigate military aviation. So effective was he that the navy quickly tapped him as chief spokesman at Mitchell's court-martial. No one wanted MacMillan, who might scuttle naval aviation with one ill-timed comment. The young flier performed brilliantly, ably assisted at crucial moments by Mitchell's blundering defense counsel, Senator Reid ("I went up to the Mitchell Court the other day and gave that scoundrel Reid one in the eye," Dick wrote a cousin exultantly). Under close questioning by the trial judge advocate, Major Gullion, Richard outlined the careful planning and preparation of the expedition and, with the able assistance of aeronautical engineers from the Naval Aircraft Factory in Philadelphia, effectively defended the Loening Amphibian as the best plane for a job well done.

In other areas he was not so effective. His part in originating the aviation component of the Greenland expedition left everyone confused: had he contemplated the use of heavier-than-air craft before MacMillan came forward or not? Nor was he especially persuasive in his philosophical defense of naval aviation. Byrd later quoted a part of his testimony in his first autobiography, *Skyward.* The effort was labored, rambling, diffuse. Only towns and ships were suitable military targets, Richard had testified, and though both could be bombed from the air, armies had to seize cities and navies had to capture ships. Richard even brought in submarines to argue that their only true targets were other submarines. This was the rankest sophistry, and Byrd doubtless knew it. In theory, bombers could obliterate both cities and ships, thus canceling the need for armies and navies. The problem, of course, was that in 1925 and for much the greater part of the twentieth century, bomber formations could not do what Mitchell, Trenchard, Douhet, and others insisted that they could do. But Richard Byrd, himself a product of the earliest air age, was not sophisticated enough—nor was anyone else—to grasp the argument.[67]

Nonetheless, Byrd's testimony helped convict Mitchell and drive him finally from military life and politics. As always, Richard was careful to mend fences, promptly writing to General Mason Patrick of the army to thank him again for helping secure the Loening aircraft for the navy in the first instance. "I attempted to introduce into the evidence before the Mitchell Court the other day the statement that I consider your giving us priority on these planes an extremely generous and cooperative thing to do," he wrote. Unfortunately, though Major Gullion asked the question that would have brought that answer, the court determined that Byrd could not reply. "I am very sorry indeed for that," he told General Patrick.

Richard's article in the *National Geographic Magazine* that November kept him in the public eye. He began to be offered the first of many rewards and perks that would accrue naturally to celebrity in coming years: complimentary tickets to the Washington concert season and an invitation from Detroit's University of Michigan Club to watch the Navy-Michigan game at Ann Arbor, all expenses paid. Signing the letter of invitation on behalf of the club were the mayor of Detroit and a U.S. congressman.[68]

But Richard's appetite for achievement and glory was unslaked by such modest rewards. He had, after all, not even gotten to the polar sea much less to the pole itself. The tantalizing prospect of discovering a great landmass between Alaska and the top of the world remained unrealized. MacMillan's dismissal of the effectiveness and usefulness of airplanes in polar regions represented a multifaceted challenge and one last personal insult that Richard Byrd simply could not ignore. He had cut his aviation teeth in airplanes; his brief dalliance with dirigibles and airships had been for convenience' sake. They were for a time the most readily available craft to explore the Arctic, and Moffett loved them. But if heavier-than-air craft could function effectively in the harsh environments at the top and bottom of the world, then they could function everywhere—they would remain the cutting edge of what everyone agreed was aviation's unlimited future. Richard was eager to prove the point.

Moreover, he had demonstrated once again to himself and to others that he could lead men effectively under rigorous circumstances and conditions, that he could organize at least a substantial portion of a complex expedition at short notice, and that he could pick the right people upon whom he could rely to help him get the job done in the planning, preparation, and operational stages. He had established an impressive network of invaluable contacts among the men of politics and business at the apex of American society and had shown that he could tap them for money and support. And after his help in disposing of Mitchell, the navy's debt to its young officer was greater than ever. Byrd observed MacMillan carefully, noting how well the seasoned explorer appealed to American business for essential goods provided either gratis or well below cost: Johnson and Johnson for medical supplies, the Campbell Company for soups and other foods, Bell and Howell for movie cameras and film, the Jensen Company for outboard motors for small boats and skiffs. He observed MacMillan and his patrons at the National Geographic Society, employing the most advanced tools of technology and communication—the radio and still and motion picture photography—to attract, entrance, and entertain the general public. He brought in newsreel cameras to dramatize his own work in preparing the Loening Amphibians for their arduous Arctic duty.

At the same time, the Greenland expedition put the last pieces of iron into Dick Byrd's soul. For years he had labored mightily for Moffett and the navy with little real reward. His chief and the service he truly loved might have owed him, but there was no indication when, if ever, he would be satisfactorily paid. When at last Byrd had had the opportunity to make an independent reputation, Moffett had allowed him to be abruptly shouldered aside at the last moment by two men of perhaps lesser ability, who subsequently frustrated his dreams, systematically condescended to him, then demeaned his not inconsiderable achievements and those of his men.

To the restless, ambitious adventurer who grew up climbing trees, crossing roofs, and swaggering down the streets of Winchester with his brothers looking for a fight or a frolic, it was time to seize the moment that the Greenland experience had provided. "Aviation will conquer the Arctic—and the Antarctic, too," he confidently informed the readers of the *National Geographic Magazine* shortly af-

ter his return. The task would be difficult, but such a challenge could "only increase the lure of the Polar regions."[69]

Richard Byrd was plainly eager to get started. Never again would he be someone else's lackey. Never again would he allow someone to take the prizes that
should have been his to win. Never again would he allow someone else to determine his place or his reputation. From now on Richard Byrd would break his own
trails across the world; he would make his own reputation, and determine how it
would be presented to a public seemingly insatiable for heroes.

Chapter 4

Triumph

On the last day of January 1926, Richard Byrd announced he was returning to the Arctic as soon as spring arrived in an "independent attempt to
explore the North Polar regions from the air."[1] In his statement, Byrd said that his
experience in the Arctic the previous summer had "convinced me of the entire
practicability of exploration by aircraft in this section of the world which has hitherto been inaccessible." He added that "we are now trying to reach a decision as
to whether an airship or a specially designed plane gives the best assurance of a successful outcome of the venture."

He had spent most of his time since the close of the Mitchell hearings on the
lecture circuit, inaugurating what would be a lifetime of speaking tours. "It is astonishing," he wrote to a sponsor, "the interest people take in Polar things."[2] At
the beginning he stumbled badly over the very technologies he relied on to connect with the public. His chief aerographer, who had been responsible for the photographic activities of the aviation unit, warned that both the still and the motion
pictures from Greenland were not much good. The strength of the light north of
the Arctic Circle was greatly affected by filtering through high clouds, even though
the actual light remained strong enough to cast shadows on the ground. Since
MacMillan had deemed it "imperative" to capture operations as they occurred, often at midnight or in the midst of sudden snow squalls, "a great many" exposures
of both still and movie film were not of the highest quality. Richard also proved
to be a less than dynamic speaker; his chief failing was an inability to synchronize
his talk with the motion picture images that were quietly flickering and spooling
at his side. After his first set of lectures, he wrote one sponsor, "I am, as you know,

not used to talking to movies." He promised to improve "100%." Shortly there-after, he told Gilbert Grosvenor that in future lectures he would provide more nar-rative, synchronize his talk more precisely with the movies he was showing, cut out a bit of the ice scenes, and "tell briefly of the scientific work accomplished by the National Geographic."

He used these early contacts with the public to determine not only his persona but also what people wanted to know and to see—and what they wanted to see and know was not only the drama of exploration but the value of science as well. Always the apple polisher, he also informed Grosvenor that part of the improve-ment would be to "include you in the movies." Nonetheless, the public was clear-ly enthralled with Richard Byrd and his dim, flickering films of the Far North. When he showed his movies in Winchester for the first time, "a quarter of the city turned out." By the end of November, invitations to lecture and to dinners in his honor began to roll into his office at the Navy Department, and in late January 1926 he told a correspondent that "I have been traveling all over the country."[3] He rented a house in Washington for the winter, but clearly Marie and the chil-dren did not see him much.

In February the *New York Times* formally anointed both him and brother Har-ry as public figures with a short article in its prestigious Sunday feature section. Both men could only have been pleased with the title: "Virginia Byrds Again to Fore." Although the bulk of the article was given over to a history of the family, with heavy accent on its colonial origins, the unknown writer began by remind-ing his readers that just two weeks previously, Richard had announced plans "to lead an aircraft expedition to the Arctic regions," while Harry had been inaugu-rated as governor of Virginia the previous day.[4]

If Arctic flight remained Richard's obsession, it was for others as well. Follow-ing the Amundsen and MacMillan expeditions, the idea fired the imaginations of explorers and scientists everywhere. Roald Amundsen and Lincoln Ellsworth an-nounced their intention to make another attempt to reach the pole, using the new-ly designed Italian airship *Norge*, sold to them by Mussolini. The two obtained fi-nancial backing from the Aero Club of Norway and also through an exclusive contract with the *New York Times*. (The *Times* would later back one of Ellsworth's expeditions to Antarctica, prompting Byrd to label the journal as "my enemy pa-per in New York.") The French were also thought to be mounting a "polar flight," as was George Hubert Wilkins, a well-known Australian naturalist and pilot who was determined to employ motion pictures as the medium of record in polar ex-ploration and had obtained lucrative contracts from the Detroit Aviation Society and the North American Newspaper Alliance. Wilkins and a Frenchman named Guy de Bayser wanted to fly between Alaska and Spitsbergen; de Bayser planned to go east to west, Wilkins west to east. Both seemed more interested in finding Crocker Land, or any undiscovered Arctic landmasses, than in reaching the pole itself.

Late the previous year, W. H. Hobbs, chairman of the Department of Geology at the University of Michigan, had invited Byrd to help mount an expedition using aircraft to expand physical knowledge of the Arctic. Hobbs particularly desired Byrd's assistance in obtaining a vessel large enough to transport one or more planes to northern Greenland. Byrd got Hobbs the ship, but refused his invitation to go north. Several weeks later Richard informed journalist David Lawrence in confidence that he had received an invitation "to go as second in command of the Wilkins Expedition." Richard added, "It is not yet decided whether or not I will go," which suggests that he still felt himself bound in some manner to the navy. Two days later, however, he wrote Wilkins, declining the offer as gracefully as he could. "I have enjoyed knowing you, and I hope that we may see more of each other in the future. I am extremely anxious to do anything that I can for your expedition and therefore I beg of you to call on me if there is anything I can do." Once Wilkins reached the North, Richard added, if there was "anything you would like to have sent up there from this country, send me a wire." Byrd was being somewhat disingenuous, for he had already indicated to Lawrence that "I have raised some money but what I can do with that will depend upon what is decided with regard to the Wilkins crowd."[5]

His nascent celebrity status enabled him to approach both his service chiefs and his contacts in American business and industry for support. He required from the navy only a prolonged leave of absence for himself and as many fellow servicemen as he could recruit. Material assistance would be welcome but not essential. The department gave Byrd the furlough, but, as Billy Mitchell acidly noted, it had no aircraft capable of flying to or near the pole. As for dirigibles, even before the *Shenandoah* disaster Secretary Wilbur had turned aside a request from Dr. Hugo Eckner, Germany's foremost lighter-than-air expert, to mount a joint airship assault on the Arctic from Point Barrow, Alaska.[6] So Richard would have to look elsewhere for financial and material assistance. "The first man I tackled was Edsel Ford. He was near my own age, a big man with ideals, and son of a father who thought in terms of America's tomorrow." Precisely Dick Byrd's kind of chap. In November 1925 the apprentice explorer began knocking on the automaker's door. He found young Ford to be a dreamer, too, one who had quickly grasped the possibilities of both commercial and private aviation.

Critics of both Byrd's North Polar flight and his transatlantic jump the following year often missed or ignored what the man was trying to accomplish. He viewed both efforts as "clean sport" and good adventure. But his far more important "practical objective," he told the American press, was "conquering the Arctic [and later the Atlantic] with multi-motored planes" that would "give an impetus to commercial aviation. . . . [T]he multi-motored plane is the answer. Science has made aircraft safe enough for commercial use. The stage is set. Confidence is all that is needed to lift the curtain on an era of rapid development in air commerce."[7]

Edsel Ford was in perfect agreement with Byrd's dream. He had already set his designers to work not only on big three-engine ("trimotor") passenger planes but also on development of a mass-produced, standard-parts "flivver" aircraft that could eventually put every American adult behind the throttle of his or her own plane. Early in 1926, Byrd approached his young benefactor for "your approval" in mounting an aerial expedition to the high Arctic using a "multi-motored plane." The objective was not the pole, but Cape Morris Jesup, 375 nautical miles to the southeast and the northernmost point of land in the world. No one had traveled from Spitsbergen to Morris Jesup and back, and "by following this route," Byrd emphasized, "I would be taking 60,000 square miles of unexplored region off the map." A week later, Byrd cabled Ford that he "would much prefer to use your three motored plane than any other." Within hours the discouraging news came back from Michigan. The company's "experimental three motored plane" had been destroyed in a recent factory fire. Richard had no choice but to turn to Tony Fokker, the only other trimotor airplane builder in the world. One of the thirty-five-year-old Dutch aeronautical engineer's big planes had recently flown 15,000 miles, "long enough to get the usual kinks out of it."

Fokker's 1925 trimotor was a huge craft for the time, powered by three Wright 220-horsepower air-cooled engines and with room for two pilots and ten passengers. Manufactured in Holland, the aircraft had won Edsel Ford's own Reliability Trophy for 1925. Nonetheless, Byrd found it a "ticklish moment" asking his new young friend to finance a scheme that could not help but be an advertisement for Ford's chief competitor. But Edsel was shrewd. At this early moment in aviation, the industry itself had to be promoted. So he told Byrd that he certainly would help. "I believe your expedition will do a lot to increase popular interest in aviation in America," he reportedly told Byrd, who responded to this calculated generosity in kind. The Fokker aircraft he flew north from Spitsbergen toward the pole carried not only the manufacturer's name in bold letters but also, in equally boldface, the words JOSEPHINE FORD: BYRD ARCTIC EXPEDITION. Josephine was Edsel Ford's young daughter.[8]

Ford's help proved essential, especially when he pulled John D. Rockefeller Jr. into the enterprise. But even the support of two of the nation's biggest businessmen and philanthropists proved insufficient. Richard had to go begging elsewhere.

At one point, his credit "strained to its breaking point," the fledgling explorer "put . . . my pride in my pocket [and] called on the president of one of our great corporations, a Crossian cliff dweller on Broadway. In my pocket I fondled a warm letter of introduction from an old friend of the great man." It did no good. Byrd appeared at nine. At noon, the "great man" slipped out a side door for lunch, promising to see his supplicant in the afternoon. "I waited. As the sun was sinking over the Hudson I got my final word—of dismissal. A colored messenger came out and told me that Mr. Blank had decided he couldn't see me at all." But Rockefeller, Vincent Astor, banker Dwight Morrow, department store magnate Rodman Wanamaker, and, perhaps of greatest importance, *National Geographic Magazine* joined Ford in underwriting Byrd's project. Gilbert Grosvenor had become quite taken with the younger man as a consequence of the MacMillan expedition, and he had developed a special fondness for the ever loyal Marie. The previous summer, Grosvenor had gone as far as Labrador to see MacMillan and his people on their way and upon his return to Washington had written Byrd's wife, assuring her of her husband's continued good health and of his own esteem for the young aviator-explorer.[9]

Richard sought to portray the developing race for the North Pole in the most benign terms possible. He told the press that his expedition "has no connection with any others that are in competition and has no 'commercial backing' in the strict sense of the word, being an undertaking that will be financed and managed by private individuals. My plans do not put me in competition with the Detroit expedition," which "has a splendid leader in Captain Wilkins and should give a good account of itself." Byrd was obviously more interested in maintaining good relations with Wilkins than in forging them with Amundsen. The Norwegian was getting old; Wilkins was still young. He and Byrd might contend for years to come on the global stage. Wilkins's friendship seemed much more valuable than Amundsen's. Byrd was, in fact, shortsighted. If the North Pole venture was to succeed, it was far more important to secure Amundsen's friendship, or at least neutrality, than that of Wilkins. In warmly endorsing Wilkins's expedition, Byrd might well have sown the seeds of the enmity that would nearly wreck his mission once it reached Spitsbergen.

Press reports indicated that the navy was not particularly happy with its maverick aviator. Secretary Wilbur, by now thoroughly skittish about aviation, had "advised" Byrd on the difficulty of his mission and urged the nascent explorer "not to hasten too much in the necessary preparation of his flight but to take sufficient time to insure a successful outcome of the expedition." Speculation was that "the expedition could not be ready to leave before August."

Byrd had no intention of waiting, and he must have been heartened and spurred by the generosity of his private backers. One of Rockefeller's "associates" confirmed to the *New York Times* that the philanthropist had donated lavishly to the expedition and that "three others also took a similar share in financing . . . so that the financial backing thus far totals $100,000." The *Times* emphasized that this was the first gift of its kind that Rockefeller had made and noted his interest in expanding the limits of human knowledge by determining once and for all what existed in the broad Arctic area so far unseen. Backers of the enterprise were reportedly "not very hopeful that a body of land, or even small islands, will be found in the polar area, but they want the facts about the region to be definitely determined."[10]

Exploiting the knowledge and experience he had gained through his affiliation with MacMillan, Richard pressed on to complete arrangements not only to finance the expedition but to publicize it as well. Publisher George Palmer Putnam readily agreed to handle contract negotiations concerning film rights and soon closed a deal with Pathé News in which Byrd gave the company an "exclusive right to take motion pictures" of the forthcoming expedition, and pledged to prevent "by every means possible" other companies or cameramen from filming "any of its operations." In return, he received a cash advance of twenty-five hundred dollars to defray immediate expenses. (Putnam briefly toyed with "devil[ing]" Pathe News "up" to five thousand dollars but concluded it would be too difficult.) Byrd was also guaranteed a percentage of the earnings from Pathé's newsreels about the expedition, and two prints of the film to use on the lecture circuit. Richard was delighted. Pathé had given the same terms to Amundsen, but not the twenty-five-hundred-dollar cash advance. The nascent explorer quickly pronounced his agent a "genius."[11]

In arranging press coverage, Byrd worked through David Lawrence of Current News Features, signing a contract on February 13, 1926, that Lawrence then used to license the *New York Times* and *St. Louis Post-Dispatch* as exclusive news distributors. Subsequently, the *Times* and Pathé also put up a "substantial" share of the funds Byrd required for purchase of the Fokker aircraft that he hoped to fly to the pole. Under the original arrangements with Lawrence, Richard would make two Arctic flights, one a round-trip between Spitsbergen and Cape Morris Jesup, the other between Spitsbergen and Alaska via the pole. In the event, Amundsen's pressing competition for the polar flight induced the apprehensive American to make a straight shot from Spitsbergen to the pole and back. Finally, Byrd signed a contract with the Pond agency for a postexpedition lecture tour that would, he hoped, clean up any and all remaining expedition debts.[12]

A week before Byrd's departure, the *New York Times* gave Richard the entire front page of its feature section to explain his forthcoming venture. Six columns were broken only by several flattering photos of the Virginian and the Arctic landscape. The paper assured readers that "all news and scientific articles from the expedition" would appear in the *Times.*

Richard reviewed the detailed and meticulous plans he had developed for a successful aerial assault on the pole.[13] Spring was the best time to fly in the Arctic because the comparative lack of fog and the hardness of the ice permitted a heavy, ski-equipped Fokker to easily find and safely land on the few smooth spots that Peary had found in widely scattered pockets throughout the pack ice. Richard would fly the plane roughly four hundred miles toward the pole from Spitsbergen to an interim spot on the ice at Cape Morris Jesup at the extreme tip of Greenland. Landing by skis on the first patch of smooth ice to be found at or near the cape, he planned to deposit a cache of food, gasoline, and other supplies before flying back to Spitsbergen. A second flight would bring more supplies to the cache, and Richard would then hop off from there to fly the last four hundred miles up to and around the pole.

The expedition required a knowledgeable fuel specialist, because oil and lubricants would break down easily in the springtime Arctic cold. Byrd recruited the best man in the business. George Noville of the Vacuum Oil Company would fashion a correct mix of fluids, thin enough to work efficiently at high altitude yet thick enough to remain effective closer to sea level.

Loyal and competent subordinates were essential to the mission's success at all levels. Floyd Bennett would go along, of course. "He is a man of the greatest energy, endurance and skill both as a navigator and as a mechanic. I would not like to be in the Arctic without him and I would take him before any other man in the world."

As for the aircraft, the Fokker was no "jitney" (an obvious swipe at the disgraced Mitchell) but a huge aircraft by the standards not only of its time but of several decades to come. Its three big Wright engines should ensure a successful flight. If one failed, the plane could fly on with the other two. If two engines failed, the aircraft could still stay aloft if lightly loaded.

But how would Byrd *know* when he had reached the pole? The ever shifting magnetism that pervaded the region required the most delicate and precise instruments. Byrd assured the public that he possessed them. Albert H. Bumstead's sun compass had worked flawlessly in Greenland during clear weather the previous summer. The chief cartographer of the National Geographic Society had constructed what was essentially a sundial combined with a clockwork mechanism that caused a hand to move around the dial once in twenty-four hours. The sun itself causes a shadow to travel in a circle each day. Setting a course by the sundial caused the sun's moving shadow to fall on the moving hand, and as long as the shadow continued to fall on the hand, the navigator knew he was on course.

Navigating accurately through murk required another new device, the earth induction compass developed by Pioneer Instrument Company of New York. The compass consisted of a coil driven by a small motor. Revolving at right angles to the earth's magnetic field, the coil would produce an electric current. The trick was to set a course, then adjust the compass so that no current was produced; so long as no current was produced, the navigator knew he was still on course. As soon as a current materialized, the navigator knew he was off course, and the strength of the current would indicate how far. Byrd planned to use both the sun and the earth induction compasses in clear weather as mutual checks.

Finally, Byrd would employ the tried-and-true bubble sextant that would enable him to obtain an artificial horizon if foul weather obscured the real one. "From the sun's position with reference to this artificial horizon, we can calculate our own position."

With these instruments, Richard was confident that he could stay on course to the pole "under all conditions" but one. Strong winds aloft could push any plane astray. Unless the drift caused by these winds on the aircraft was accurately understood, "it is no simple matter to determine our position." Thus, the pilot or his navigator must constantly measure and allow for drift by employing a wind indicator now as dependable and routine as the bubble sextant. "If we reach the vicinity of the Pole," Byrd wrote confidently, "our instruments will enable us to determine while in flight our location within a margin of twenty miles. To make sure that we have reached and passed the Pole we will make a wide circle around it. This circle would be less than a hundred miles in distance, but it would be a complete circumnavigation of the globe." Byrd went even further in his commitment to accuracy. If he and his companion(s) should sight a suitable landing spot beneath them once they reached the pole, "we would come down. Once safely on the snow we could take careful observations and locate the Pole exactly. If it were within twenty miles we would travel to the Pole and back on foot, weather conditions permitting."

What if the plane crashed, or became disabled in some way, as had Amundsen's and Ellsworth's aircraft the previous summer? Byrd prepared for this contingency as well. "If we should wreck our plane at the North Pole and be forced to march back over the ice, I believe that we would be able to see it through." The Fokker would carry both "sleds that carry boats and boats that carry sleds." The collapsible boats were made of balloon cloth and weighed but twelve pounds. Tests the previous summer indicated they could be inflated in three minutes. "We will carry rations for sixty days—two pounds a day for each man, more than sufficient." The food was light and high-energy—chocolate, pemmican, erbswurst, "which is a kind of pea soup," powdered milk, and bacon, the latter "an innovation and some explorers would object to it as a luxury, but I believe in it." Sleeping bags and a tent were, of course, essential, as was a primus stove that could be fueled by gasoline from the downed aircraft. Byrd also planned to take along a shotgun and pistol with one hundred rounds of ammunition apiece and a high-powered rifle with two hundred rounds together with binoculars, a sextant and a pocket compass, ice axes, a camera, maps, and waterproof matchboxes. Warm foul-weather clothing was provided from Alaskan sources by Lomen Brothers clothiers.

Why the flight? "The sporting element" involved in being first over the pole "appeals strongly to me, but I am also deeply interested in proving that the airplane can do the job." Even successful flights from Spitsbergen to the Cape Morris Jesup jump-off point without a subsequent flight to or toward the pole would be sufficient to demonstrate beyond question that airplanes could operate successfully in the harsh Arctic environment. The public would "awaken" to aviation's "vast possibilities." Byrd had approached Ford, Rockefeller, and the other big philanthropists in this spirit and had been warmed by their response.

Byrd's earlier *National Geographic Magazine* article on the MacMillan expedition had given the appearance of an add-on, an addendum to a greater man's story. With the *New York Times* piece, he inaugurated what would become an ongoing dialogue with the public about his own life and aims. He would be no lone eagle, no remote figure on a distant hilltop, but a public creature of his own making, inviting the people to share his adventures, however vicariously, through print, radio, and film. One can see in these months and years of the midtwenties a man learning how to be a public figure, how to both exploit and enjoy what he would soon label "this hero business."

On the eve of his departure for Spitsbergen, Richard hosted a luncheon on board Vincent Astor's yacht. Astor was detained by a family funeral; business prevented Edsel Ford's attendance. Unfazed, Byrd put young Rockefeller at the head of the table. The flinty, old oil magnate's son had developed a strong spiritual impulse and at one point begged leave to make some remarks. It was "a wonderful talk," Byrd recorded that night in his diary. "He referred to my great interest in the Pole. I know no man who is more interested in the progress of mankind than Mr. Rockefeller." In a letter several years later, Byrd told Rockefeller that the speech "convinced me" that the youthful philanthropist "understood to a degree what I was aiming at." Byrd reminded Rockefeller that after the luncheon the two men stood aside and Byrd said "something about what I was driving at, that is, my desire to devote myself ultimately to international amity and coordination."

Richard's interest in becoming an apostle of world peace had apparently been gestating for years, stimulated perhaps by the interest in philosophy that he had developed as a teenager rummaging through his father's library and later by some

classes he had taken at Harvard during his days as commander of the naval aviation reserve unit at Squantum in South Boston Bay. At Cambridge he struck up a
friendship with W. E. Hocking of the Harvard Philosophy Department, writing
the professor shortly after his return from Greenland that while away in the Arctic, "I read only your book on the 'Remaking of Human Nature.'" Richard had
also given at least one speech on war, and he lent the manuscript to an acquaintance in Newfoundland on his way north. Howard Cox professed amazement at
the breadth and incisiveness of Richard's learning and begged him to publish the
speech as an article or series of articles. Still later, in the midst of his lecture tour,
Byrd found himself seated one night next to Gertrude Lane, then editor of the
Women's Home Companion. The two discussed the notion and concept of war,
which Richard said "interested me very much." Miss Lane, too, received a copy of
Richard's speech. He was thus beginning to articulate a dream that would eventually become an obsession for him: to serve humanity through his expeditions
and otherwise as an apostle and icon of peace. In his 1933 letter to Rockefeller recalling the luncheon aboard Astor's yacht, he confessed that "my method has been
apparently a very indirect one. That is, I have been working away from the center
in order to make my work in the center more productive when I finally reached
that stage of my plans."[14]

On Monday, April 5, 1926, shortly after three in the afternoon, USS *Chantier,*
a three thousand–ton war-surplus steamer leased from the United States Shipping
Board, cast off its lines at the Brooklyn Navy Yard, headed for the entrance of New
York Harbor, then turned north and east toward Norway and the Arctic. Some
fifty volunteers were on board, the vast majority of whom were U.S. Navy and Marine Corps men on extended leave, the rest civilians who were going "for the sport
and adventure." Byrd was as giddy as he ever allowed himself to be at "one of the
most remarkable send-offs I have ever seen." He professed astonishment "that
there is so much public interest in our expedition." He knew better. He had anticipated having to work hard to obtain the necessary volunteers, but literally hundreds of men—and not a few women—stepped forward. A letter from "a lady—
young or old I do not know," was typical, and Byrd shrewdly quoted from it in his
official article on the expedition, for it encapsulated the enduring attractiveness of
himself and his work. "'Little do you realize that thousands of people who have
no chance of adventure live your adventure with you. Probably you have no idea
what pleasure you give us.'"[15]

Among the volunteer crew were several men who would form the nucleus of
"Byrd's boys" in the following years. There was Floyd Bennett, of course, who
would do the bulk of the flying to and from the pole; Byrd had pulled every wire
he could within the navy to ensure that this most gifted of enlisted aviators was

also furloughed long enough to join the expedition. Also on hand were George Noville; Marine Corps pilot Alton Parker; Malcolm Hanson, a civilian shortwave radio expert from the Naval War Research Laboratory, who, according to Byrd, came along as a stowaway; meteorologist William C. Haines of the U.S. Weather Bureau; and an obscure young mechanic named Pete Demas, who would steadily rise to positions of responsibility in Byrd's later expeditions to Antarctica.

Several days out, the ship began rolling steeply, and Captain Mike Brennan ordered all hands on deck when he heard something break loose in the fore hold. Struggling to retain the commanding officer's sangfroid, Byrd later wrote, "This was an interesting moment for me." If the pitching deck had torn some barrels or other cargo from their restraints, the plane's huge wing would have surely been smashed, ending the expedition in "failure—with a capital 'F.'" Fortunately, a wooden bracing beam was all that had come loose, ripping an easily repairable hole in the wing. Byrd ordered double lashings on the barrels as a precaution, and the seas soon calmed, leaving tired, seasick men after the stress and strain of making the quickly loaded *Chantier* shipshape.

While *Chantier* worked its way slowly north, Richard spent most of his time "pondering the problems ahead, laying down my courses, etc." The aircraft's weight "has to be kept down to a minimum and yet there are so many things we should have to add to our safety." If the manifest could be kept to fourteen hundred pounds, including pilot and navigator, "we think this may leave us with 1800 miles cruising radius but . . . we can't tell until we reach Spitzbergen and actually try out the plane."

As the days wore on, Byrd's frustration grew. *Chantier* had been laid up for years, and it showed. The vessel could scarcely make eight knots in the heavy seas that often prevailed in the springtime North Atlantic. "I shoveled coal in the morning and spent the afternoon working out instructions for the main base to observe after we leave on our flight," Byrd wrote on the seventeenth. He knew that Amundsen and Ellsworth were undoubtedly already on the island, preparing their airship for the trip to the pole and beyond. "We are flying in dangerous country," Byrd fretted. He still anticipated establishing an advance base, and "the 300 miles [from Spitsbergen] to Greenland is the most hazardous region in the world to fly over. If we should have a forced landing there [that is, on the polar ice pack] we should be swept in to the Atlantic before we could cover 50 miles and the ice would melt under us."

At last, on April 24, the expedition reached Saetimo Light, some eighty miles down the Norwegian coast from Trondheim, to be met by an ice pilot, a *New York Times* representative bringing "about $1,000 worth of supplies we had radioed ahead for," and the London representative of Pathé News. "Flares were lighted and moving pictures were taken" of the three of them coming aboard. Then it was off, at last, to Kings Bay, Spitsbergen.[16]

Richard was now consumed with flight preparations in all their contingencies. "Noville has been a trump. He has relieved me almost entirely of the details of administering the ship." But it was Amundsen who obsessed Byrd's waking moments, and perhaps his dreams as well. The great Norwegian was "hurrying as much as possible. I am afraid Wilkins and I have hurried him unduly." Wilkins's threat seemed to dissipate as Spitsbergen came up over the frigid Arctic horizon. A radio message to *Chantier* reported the Australian thirteen days overdue. "Hope he is o.k.," Richard noted. Wilkins appeared in Alaska soon thereafter, delayed by bad weather but in good shape and fine spirit. Amundsen, however, was the immediate competitor. On the twenty-eighth, in anticipation of an arrival on the morrow, Richard extended an olive branch to the Norwegian, cabling an offer of "help of our crew if he should need it." Byrd coupled the offer with a request "to arrange for us to go alongside dock" so that *Chantier*'s crew could unload the *Josephine Ford* and a smaller aircraft brought along for reconnaissance and photographic work. On the twenty-ninth, some hours in advance of schedule, *Chantier* sailed into Kings Bay to find sullen, if not hostile, hosts.[17]

More than eighty years later, Spitsbergen and the Svalbard archipelago, of which it is much the greater part, enjoy a modest summer tourist boom. The mountainous, heavily glaciated island, snowy and cold in the winter despite the presence of the uppermost sweep of the Gulf Stream, warms considerably under the weak summer sun, offering tourists stunning vistas of ice and rock under usually clear skies. The towns of Longyearbyen and Ny Aslund contain several modern hotels, and a regular ferry service connects the settlements with the northernmost villages of Norway, some four hundred miles to the east-southeast.[18] But in 1926, Spitsbergen remained a remote, little-known place where crude human settlement was only twenty years old, as a handful of Norwegian miners and their families worked the island's rich coal deposits.

Byrd would always insist publicly that relations with the Amundsen party were cordial, but he provided incontrovertible proof in private notations that they were anything but. For much of the time, contact between the Norwegians and Americans was barely civil, as Amundsen's men placed every possible obstacle in the Americans' way.

Chantier's appearance with the fuselage of an aircraft on its deck sobered and even depressed everyone in the Norwegian camp; any long-range airplane was at least twice as fast as *Norge*. All work halted as the men stood in silent groups along the snowy bluff above Kings Bay, watching as the black-hulled American ship rounded the point, moved into the mouth of the fjord, and sailed carefully up ice-choked waters.

One of those brooding Norwegians was a handsome, stocky, reddish-blond young man nearing his twenty-seventh birthday, Bernt Balchen. A 1919 graduate of the Norwegian Military Academy, Balchen had won his wings two years later at his nation's Military Flying School. An avid boxer, skier, and rifleman, the young flight lieutenant was assigned by the Royal Norwegian Air Force in 1925 to help in the desperate search for Amundsen and Ellsworth. Balchen flew for many hours over the North Polar ice scape, hundreds of miles from help should he himself go down. Thereafter, the young flier considered himself an expert on polar aviation and a top-notch pilot: he would prove the accuracy of these assumptions over and over again during the course of a long career of remarkable and varied achievement. Once Amundsen and Ellsworth emerged from their ordeal, Balchen went to work with them preparing to take *Norge* to the pole. Amundsen now placed his formidable prestige and resources behind dirigibles. Balchen was assigned as a reserve crewman and also to oversee construction of *Norge*'s mooring mast and hangar. In the midst of preparations, the Americans suddenly appeared. "We resent this foreign ship coming here to our country," Balchen would later remember. "Now we know it is a race, and the odds are against us." As the group watched *Chantier* slowly make its way up the harbor through the ice floes, one of the Norwegians nudged his mate, and all eyes turned to the hill behind them, where Amundsen himself had suddenly appeared, standing at rest on his ski poles, a tough, weathered, gnarled Viking in his midfifties still "vigorous as a young athlete." Slowly, Amundsen pushed back the visor of his ski cap, watching the rivals approach. He kept his face and eyes expressionless, said nothing, then pivoted on his skis without a word and went back to the headquarters building.[19]

Even before the Americans arrived, Amundsen had warned Byrd by radio that *Chantier* would be unable to use the single dock of the bay because two Norwegian ships were moored there. One of those vessels was a gunboat, and as *Chantier* sailed in, the small warship sent out a lieutenant to inform the Americans that it would be impossible to know when a docking area might be free. Accounts differ sharply over what happened next. Byrd wrote in his diary that night that he asked the gunboat's captain if *Chantier* could moor alongside the warship. "He reluctantly consented." Balchen had no such recollection: *Chantier* anchored about three hundred yards out. Wherever the American vessel found berthing—and it was probably next to the gunboat near the dock—Byrd immediately went ashore to meet his rival, "but he was [away]," so the men returned to the ship for a time, then came ashore again. Balchen saw a few curious families from the Ny Aslund mines walk down to the water's edge to see the foreigners. They stepped back quickly as Byrd and his party passed by. The barking of sledge dogs quartered behind the few houses that composed the settlement was the only sound of greeting the Americans got as they trudged along the long, flat ground toward Amundsen's camp. "Hostile" workers watched them "in sullen silence."

Balchen was standing by the machine shop as Byrd came up to him, introduced himself, and asked after Amundsen. Without a word, Balchen wiped his greasy hands on a ball of waste and led the way up the hill toward the headquarters building. Byrd, he decided, looked like a slight, youthful, clean-shaven high school principal with his small, rather prim mouth and natty outfit. Balchen saw Amundsen rise up ponderously from behind a desk as the younger, smaller American entered. "Glad you're here safe, Commander. Welcome to Spitzbergen." Byrd was at first reserved as he introduced his men: Noville, his executive officer; Robb Oertell, who handled supplies; and Floyd Bennett. Lincoln Ellsworth stood shyly in the shadows, saying nothing as Byrd and Amundsen set to work unrolling maps and exploring mutual problems. Bennett, a plain-faced, "gawky country boy," lounged against the doorjamb, hands in pockets.

According to Balchen, Byrd was clear about his route, but wondered where he could find a sufficiently level spot to get the heavily loaded *Josephine Ford* aloft. Use the flat area in front of the Norwegian camp, Amundsen replied, and when Byrd cautiously ventured that his Norwegian competitor was being very kind, Amundsen corrected him. The two men were not rivals, he insisted, but compatriots, "collaborators in a joint assault on the polar regions, an attack by two vehicles, one lighter and one heavier than air." The giant Viking stood up, towering over the American. "We are partners in this venture together." Dick Byrd was, at last, anointed as a full-fledged polar explorer. That night he merely recorded in his diary that he met Amundsen "later and went to his quarters with him."[20]

If Byrd was taken in by Amundsen's rhetoric, he was soon reminded of the reality of life on Spitsbergen. A 1920 treaty had largely internationalized the Svalbard archipelago but left local jurisdiction in Norwegian hands.[21] Returning from his visit with Amundsen, Byrd called on the captain of the gunboat alongside which *Chantier* was moored. When would the gunboat be able to move so that the American ship could get along dockside and get its aircraft ashore? Monday, the captain replied. Well, Byrd responded, he had been told that the gunboat was going to leave the dock that "night" (there were nearly twenty-four hours of often gloomy light at the time) to provide coal to another vessel. Could *Chantier* use the dock then? No, the Norwegian captain said, "he would not do that." Then Byrd called on Smithmeyer, the director of the coal mine, who told him that the gunboat would be coaling a Norwegian whaler alongside the dock, not out in the bay.

Chantier would have to move from alongside the gunboat immediately. Richard finally lost his patience. The four days until Monday were simply too long to wait to unship the *Josephine Ford* and the smaller aircraft. He ordered *Chantier* three hundred yards out into the bay and, as the Norwegians watched impassively, set his men to rigging a pontoon raft from planking and four of the ship's boats. He also had his sailors cut a lane through the heavy ice floes that extended from the ship to the beach.

It began to snow; the air was raw and cold as the men worked all through the night of April 30–May 1 "at top speed to meet the emergency of a landing that was far from safe." The movie cameramen that Byrd brought with him ground away on their instruments, recording the operation. Amundsen and Balchen came aboard at one point to watch. Balchen was impressed with the boisterous efficiency of the Americans, who wore all sorts of makeshift cold-weather apparel and came from every walk of life: doctors, lawyers, merchants, college boys, naval officers, and enlisted men. "These Americans are not to be discouraged by any new difficulty, I think; they never worry about a problem beforehand, but when it develops, that is the time to take care of it." This pioneering spirit, which he had heard so much about, Balchen added, would open the entire Arctic to commercial air travel one day.[22]

With the pontoon raft completed, Chief Engineer Tom Mulroy, Alton Parker, and several others got the small plane ashore first. Byrd ordered a stand-down at breakfast time, and everyone slept. He ordered all hands to turn to again after lunch. "We seem to have either no ice and wind or no wind and ice or both," Richard recorded that night. The first task was to carefully raise the *Josephine Ford*'s big wing out of the hold and place it on deck. Next the first mate, with infinite care, raised the body of the aircraft from the ship's deck in a swirl of snowflakes and delicately brought it to rest on the pontoon structure. As Byrd's movie cameras continued to record the scene, sailors aboard the raft managed to prop the awkward body of the plane on frail wooden supports, then waited for the big wing to be lowered so they could bolt it to the top of the *Ford*'s fuselage. A heavy gust of wind suddenly sprang up, and sailors raced to hold the wing down until the wind subsided. Byrd and Bennett undoubtedly remembered the cowling that blew out of the latter's hand at Etah the summer before. But whereas it was comparatively easy to fashion a spare cowling for a small aircraft such as the Loening Amphibian, a big, heavy wing like that of the Fokker was irreplaceable. "As we had only one plane for our polar flight," Byrd later wrote, "a serious accident at this juncture would have been fatal to the whole project." Noville, Bennett, and others urged their commander to wait out the capricious winds and moving ice, but Byrd would have none of it. *Norge* might appear through the windy gloom at any time. With some fanfare, the Norwegians had just raised the massive mooring mast for the dirigible. "We may be licked," he confided in his daily diary, "but don't want to be licked waiting around and doing nothing."

As the wind abated briefly, sailors hastily bolted the Fokker's wing to its fuselage and set out to the beach in the wobbly pontoon raft. Byrd sent another of *Chantier*'s small boats ahead to clear as much of a path through the ice as possible. With "a dozen men shoving off ice cakes as we went along," the Americans managed to ferry the now largely reassembled *Josephine Ford* to the beach before the wind returned, either to crush the awkward raft against the heavy ice floes or to blow it helplessly out to sea. "Finally got ashore and had a lot of fun doing it," the irrepressible commander wrote. "Got a cheer from the Norwegians, which we returned. Norwegians didn't think we'd make it." Once ashore, Byrd had his men cut a slope in the ice face up from the beach, and the plane was hauled up on its skis to a hastily assembled shelter adjacent to the snowy plain with a "very gentle slope" that Amundsen had recommended as a perfect runway.

The "nerve wracking" days at the end of April and early May tested everyone's mettle and endurance, Richard later wrote. "No wage or ordinary urge could have evoked such enthusiastic industry and courage" as that displayed by his young American colleagues.[23] With the fuel drums, heavy parts, equipment, and instruments for the polar flight now ashore along with the smaller aircraft for taking aerial motion pictures and rescuing the polar party should it come to grief, Byrd was ready for the North Pole.

But he was fuming. The Norwegians had behaved abominably. Byrd's determined good humor and patience at last broke when the Pathé cameraman who had gone to the beach to film the final dramatic moments of the reassembly and transfer of the two aircraft from ship to shore was approached by Amundsen's "representative" and told "that we could not take movies of our own operation." "Great sportsmanship," Byrd wrote that night. "They deny us dock. Make us move out in the stream."[24] Fortunately, the cameraman had recorded most of the operation from a boat in the water. But Byrd was still angry the next day. "In spite of everything the Norwegians do I intend to be a sport and be dignified and calm," he wrote. "They have made it very difficult for us."

The Norwegians had grievances of their own. "Problems with photographers," Balchen recorded in his diary that night. "We have a clause in our agreement with the syndicate which had brought the news rights against any pictures being taken by outsiders." Unfortunately, Byrd's "projected runway was right in the middle of our camp." Under the circumstances, fulfilling the syndicate agreement "was a rather unpleasant thing to live up to" in light of Amundsen's earlier suggestion that

Byrd place his runway where he did. "We did not adhere to" the agreement "very strictly in any way," Balchen wrote.

Amundsen apparently concluded that he—or his overly loyal men—had gone too far in obstructing the Byrd party. Certainly, denying the Americans the right to take movies of their own operation flagrantly violated the recently concluded Svalbard treaty and might well have provoked a stiff diplomatic note from Washington to Oslo had Byrd, or the State or Navy Department, cared to create an issue. Amundsen changed policy, and when the "foreigners" got into trouble he quietly instructed his men to help them. An embittered Richard Byrd blinded himself to the new reality. The day after the Americans got themselves ashore, Byrd had lunch with Amundsen, "who professes great friendship but gave Lt Balchen (who is a peach and wanted to help us and has helped us) orders not to come near us again." Balchen would provide essential assistance, but in his formal article about the polar flight Byrd never mentioned it.

While the rival communities maintained a stiff and correct civility, a miniwar broke out among the reporters and cameramen from the two sides. Each expedition had sold the exclusive rights to its story to different newspaper syndicates in the States, and the syndicates had agreed not to try to scoop one another. But journalists and photojournalists have always been a notoriously competitive, often unscrupulous, crew, and now they began to clandestinely creep around the rival camps. It was a kind of guerrilla war "with undercover operations and secret infiltrations," Balchen recalled. "Scouts from the rival syndicates creep past each other, the Amundsen raiders disguised in American sailor hats, and the Byrd snipers wearing Norwegian ski caps." Each side sought a superior vantage point, and when it thought it had achieved one, movie cameras whirred and flashbulbs popped. "A skulking still photographer pops out of an empty crate to click a close-up of the *Josephine Ford* or as we enter the dirigible hangar we see a pair of heels disappearing out the other end, the scurrying figure staggering bowlegged under a heavy camera and tripod."

The press and publicity war placed further enormous pressures on both camps. Follies and accidents might well be recorded that could forever ruin the hopes and reputations of explorers whose rivalry had now reached a fever pitch. On May 4 Bennett, Noville, and two others climbed aboard the Fokker for the plane's engine test. The aircraft failed to budge even under full power from all three engines. The front set of skis broke. Fifteen hours later, the big trimotor lurched its way down the runway the Americans had tramped out of the snow, and one of the second set of skis broke, bending the adjacent landing-gear strut.

At this moment Balchen began to endear himself to the Americans. He and a few of his colleagues worked through the night in the coal company's machine shop "to put things right" while the anxious Americans critiqued the takeoff and concluded that the plane had been grossly overloaded. Pound after pound of equipment, a good bit of reserve fuel, and even the light commemorative flags Richard planned to drop over the pole were removed from the aircraft, drastically reducing its takeoff weight. Balchen also claimed that Byrd's survival gear was inadequate, and loaned him some more. As the Americans prepared their plane for another test flight, Balchen wandered by and noticed Oertell smearing a standard wax polish on the plane's skis. Balchen warned him that the substance would fail in the hard, crystalline snow and urged him to use another preparation that should be applied with a blowtorch. Oertell ignored the advice, and as a result the *Ford* once again came to grief. Bennett, Byrd, and one or two others climbed aboard, and Bennett gunned the engines. The plane began to move ponderously down the runway when one of the skis stuck in the snow. The *Josephine Ford* spun on its axis, lurched to the side, and wound up in a snowbank, the stuck ski a shattered wreck. Byrd and his men were stunned. Where could they obtain new skis? Was the expedition doomed? Balchen "went to help" and found the American commander in the "wreckage," making repairs. Balchen suggested using oars from *Chantier*'s lifeboats. Captain Brennan immediately protested, but Byrd and Bennett overruled him. Soon the *Josephine Ford* was aloft on its test flight, with Bennett at the controls and Byrd watching anxiously below. The aircraft was fitted with new and better skis shaped with the advice of Bernt Balchen and also freshly waxed with the compound that Balchen had suggested to Oertell.

As the Americans prepared a new series of tests, the weather cleared. The contest for the pole abruptly intensified. Amundsen ordered *Norge* to come on into Spitsbergen from Leningrad. Wilkins, over in Point Barrow, radioed that after days of fog and storm he and copilot Ben Eilsen were prepared to fly to Spitsbergen via the top of the world. Early on the morning of May 7, a speck materialized on Spitsbergen's southern horizon. Soon *Norge* hovered over its mooring mast. Colonel Umberto Nobile descended to embrace Amundsen.[25]

These developments caused Byrd to make "a complete and sudden reversal of our plans."[26] The *Josephine Ford*'s initial trial flight—a smashing success—had demonstrated "that we could probably take off the snow with sufficient fuel to visit Cape Morris Jessup [sic] and the Pole in one non-stop flight." But with the Norwegians and Wilkins breathing down his neck, Byrd decided to reverse the flight schedule he had earlier announced in his *New York Times* article. The Fokker aircraft would make directly for the pole, then visit Cape Morris Jesup on the way back to Spitsbergen.

The following day, meteorologist Bill Haines gave Byrd the word he had been waiting for, stating that a high-pressure area had developed over the entire polar basin. It was time to head north. "No announcement is made, but everyone senses the moment is at hand," Balchen recalled. Minutes later Bennett, red-faced and perspiring in his heavy flight suit, and Dick Byrd, slim and immaculate in his, walked through the crowd gathering around the Fokker. The two climbed up the ladder and got ready to go. Bennett gunned the engine, but the plane moved only slowly, balking at leaving the ground. Bennett turned the craft around and tried again. No luck. Was the craft still fatally overloaded? Was it underpowered? Byrd, grim-faced, descended the ladder and sought out Balchen. What was wrong? Balchen thought he knew. The sun was too high, the day too warm, the snow too sticky. Wait till midnight, he advised Byrd, when the sun is lower and the snow freezes hard again. Byrd and Bennett returned to their quarters.

Toward midnight, a restless Balchen pulled on his boots and parka and went out into a molten-gold evening created by the ball of the midnight sun. "The *Josephine Ford* throws a long black shadow at the far end of the landing strip and the padded figures of the ground crew look like creatures from another planet as they swarm over the plane." Suddenly, Byrd and Bennett appeared once more, their boots crunching on newly hardened snow. They exchanged a brief sentence with the crew chief, climbed aboard, and started the engines once more. A few sleepy and surprised faces appeared at the windows of the Norwegian camp as Bennett maneuvered the Fokker for takeoff, then once again gunned the engines. The journalists were completely surprised; perhaps that was Byrd's intention in order to defeat any attempts by the European reporters for a scoop. One Norwegian cameraman, however, managed to stumble out into the frigid evening with his bulky gear. As the big, heavy Fokker moved smoothly down the snowy runway, he was the only one to record the event. (Byrd's cameramen would later restage it.) The trimotor leaped into the air at thirty-seven minutes past midnight, Greenwich time, May 9, 1926. The ground temperature at takeoff was 14 degrees Fahrenheit. Richard Byrd and Floyd Bennett had begun perhaps the most controversial flight in aviation history.[27]

The night was crystal clear, and the coming day would remain so, allowing Byrd to employ the sun compass to maximum advantage.[28] The aircraft was superbly equipped. An enclosed cockpit—after their experiences in Greenland the summer before, Byrd and Bennett would wisely never fly open-cockpit aircraft again—included a double set of controls, ensuring that pilot relief could be accomplished without inconvenience. The Pioneer earth induction compass sat above and a little in front of the pilot's head, so that at all times he could see the exact course he was flying. Underneath the seats for pilot and copilot were racks for provisions and spare parts. Radio equipment had been installed back of the cockpit, in the forward section of the aircraft, with a trailing antenna extending from beneath the fuselage. Byrd's chart table sat nearby. Behind the radio compartment stretched a narrow companionway with big extra gasoline tanks bolted on either side. The tanks connected with two pumps, one automatic and one cranked by hand power, to force gasoline to the working tank in the center of the wing. The working tank was in two sections, each holding one hundred gallons. Back in the fuselage, behind the extra gasoline tanks, were the emergency rations—pemmican, chocolate, tea, and canned food. The walls of the fuselage behind the gas tanks were lined with light metal racks containing rifles for hunting game should the plane be forced down, as well as cameras, plates, reels of film, and Byrd's navigational instruments. Fokker's people had installed a raised observation platform just behind the middle of the aircraft, with a manhole cut through the top of the airframe from which Byrd could raise his head and shoulders out into the freezing slipstream and take his sights and observations as well as film whatever he thought important. Additional materials were stowed in the back of the plane, though Byrd and Bennett were careful after their Greenland experience not to weigh down excessively the rear of any aircraft taking off from water, ice, or snow.

As Bennett swung the plane on course for due north, Byrd busied himself at the chart table or the observation platform, making preliminary sightings and calculations. Often he gazed downward through an open trapdoor on the floor of the aircraft to check the drift indicator slung there. Quickly, the *Josephine Ford* raced past Amsterdam Island, a bit of bare rock at the very tip of Spitsbergen. The plane made excellent speed, skimming over cold and blue open water. Then the ice pack appeared. Byrd was surprised at how close it lay to the Svalbard archipelago, and looking eastward he saw that some of the pack had actually attached itself to a portion of Spitsbergen Island itself.

Bennett maintained a fairly steady altitude of 2,000 feet as the big Fokker pushed north, a vibrating box filled with deafening noise, suspended in space above a frigid, inhuman, empty ice scape by one broad wing, a tail assembly, and three steadily pounding engines. The featureless pack stretching to the horizon in every direction impressed the two fliers. Gleaming in the bright polar sunlight, the ice and snow provided no landmarks, neither roads nor villages, nor even icebergs, for if Antarctica is a continent of ice surrounded by an ocean, the Arctic in 1926 was an ocean of ice surrounded by continental landmasses. All the glaciers and ice shelves that give birth to bergs of various sizes and shapes through the "calving off" process were in Greenland, far south of the route Bennett and Byrd were taking to the pole. Only the steadily receding mountains of Spitsbergen provided a north-south bearing as long as they remained in view. A bit of wind struck the aircraft from the east but had no decisive effect on speed, which Bennett maintained at between 74 and 77 *nautical* miles per hour, or roughly 83 to 88.5 statute miles per hour. The Far Northern air was as smooth as Byrd had anticipated. Still, the aircraft exhibited a tendency to drift to the right; Bennett at first paid no attention. Byrd, constantly monitoring the drift indicator, moved often to the cockpit door, reaching up and tapping the pilot on the shoulder, motioning him with a wave of the hand to steer slightly left. When hand communication failed, Byrd used another method. The roaring engines and lack of insulation made voice communication impossible, so he passed up hastily written notes torn from a calendar pad: "You are keeping to the right 5° too much," and, later, "You MUST not persist in keeping too far to right." After a time, Bennett mastered the plane's idiosyncrasy, settling down and steering "with astonishing accuracy." Byrd returned to his chart table and observation platform. Every few moments for the first three hours, he thrust his upper body out into the slipstream to make sun readings, freezing his hands and face in the process. He alternated three pairs of gloves but had to remove them whenever he wrote on the chart. At last satisfied that all his calculations placed the aircraft on a direct route to the pole, Byrd returned his gaze to the great ice pack moving beneath the plane. Pressure ridges crisscrossed the surface, interrupted here and there by open leads of water and smooth stretches that beckoned the unwary aviator to land. Byrd searched for any sign of life; a polar bear, a seal, birds flying. Nothing moved on this bright, icy day as the temperature steadily dipped to 8 degrees Fahrenheit and then colder as they headed north.

Now it was time to relieve Bennett at the controls so that the younger man could stretch his legs and also begin pouring the gasoline reserve from five-gallon tin cans scattered all over the plane's interior into the tanks. It was a hard, physically demanding task in the cold and vibrating cabin. With Bennett back in the pilot's seat, Byrd returned to his chart table and continued his various sightings and calculations. He scribbled on his pad: "Radio that we are 230 miles from the Pole. Radio nothing but ice everywhere—no sign of life, motors going fine." At one point Byrd felt snow blindness coming on and donned his goggles.

Seven and one-half hours into the flight, as the Fokker trimotor passed beyond the point at which the Amundsen-Ellsworth aerial party reached farthest north before being forced down on the ice, Byrd noticed an oil leak in one of the engines. He pointed it out to Bennett, who, after checking it himself, said that the engine would soon go out and suggested landing for repairs. Byrd objected. The aircraft could fly on two engines, and Amundsen's experience the year before was a cautionary tale. Landing on the North Polar ice pack was far worse than a water landing. It was a dangerous enterprise that should be undertaken only in an extreme emergency. Byrd proved to be not only right but lucky too. The oil leak was caused by a rivet popping in the bitter cold. Once the oil level fell below that of the rivet hole, the leak stopped. The *Josephine Ford* soared on above the empty Arctic pack ice, all three engines roaring steadily.

The pole was within reach. In the bright sunlight at roughly 3,000 feet, visibility was roughly 100 miles in any direction. There was no land. If any existed in the barren ice scape of the high Arctic it was not visible to these men, and the two fliers were looking down at terrain never before viewed on such a scale. Byrd's appetite for viewing the unknown had become voracious; only the airplane could satisfy it.

Eight and one-half hours from Kings Bay, Byrd scribbled another note on his calendar pad. By his calculations, the plane had averaged 85 *statute* miles per hour, thus having traveled 722 miles. His sightings suggested that a very mild tailwind must have pushed it along slightly above recorded speed. He wrote, "20 miles to go to Pole." Shortly after nine in the morning, Greenwich time, Byrd announced to Bennett that they were at 90 degrees north. They had reached the very top of the earth. Below them the pack was tightly if smoothly compressed except for one long open-water lead lightly frozen over. Whatever thoughts Byrd may have had of landing at the pole were banished by the forbidding ice scape below and memories of the recent Amundsen-Ellsworth debacle. The thickness of the ice pack and, indeed, its actual smoothness could not be determined. To attempt to land would be foolhardy. Instead, Byrd later reported that he and Bennett flew in a broad circle for roughly thirteen minutes before heading directly back to Spitsbergen. The oil leak had not yet stopped; it was still possible that they would have to shut down the third engine. Under the circumstances, a dogleg flight to Cape Morris Jesup was unthinkable.

Byrd would also report that on the way home the easterly breeze that had picked up somewhat in the past hour or so before the pole provided a tailwind for the flight back. Also, the plane itself became progressively lighter—and thus faster—as more and more fuel was consumed and the empty tins were thrown out the trapdoor into the slipstream and down onto the ice. Racing back to Spitsbergen with the aid of the sun compass (the sextant fell off the table and broke shortly after the return flight began), Byrd remained confident of his navigation, and was rewarded shortly after half past two, Greenwich time, when the mountainous island loomed far in the distance roughly five and a quarter hours after he and Bennett had left the pole. The *Josephine Ford* swept over Grey Point, doglegged south and east to Amsterdam Island, and landed at Kings Bay to a rapturous welcome at 4:34 P.M. Amundsen was the first to greet Byrd as he stepped from the *Josephine Ford*. "I have never seen him display so much emotion," Balchen reported. "He cannot speak. His stern Viking face has broken into a rare and wonderful smile, and the tears run from his eyes as he puts his arms around Byrd and Bennett, drawing them both to him in a giant embrace, and kisses them on each cheek." What next? the giant Viking supposedly asks his slender rival and colleague, who replies, The South Pole.[29]

Amundsen left Kings Bay aboard *Norge* within hours after Byrd and Bennett returned from their flight. As the great airship took off north, Bernt Balchen was left behind, gloomy and depressed. Hanging around Spitsbergen, he talked Bennett into making two flights in the *Josephine Ford*. After the latter flight Byrd brought Balchen aboard *Chantier* and told the Norwegian he planned another Arctic flight and needed someone with cold-weather experience. Would Balchen be interested in a job? Balchen would need a year's leave of absence from the Norwegian Navy and would be spending most of that time in the States. The Norwegian was sorely tempted; he badly wanted to see America, but felt a residual responsibility to Amundsen. He would like to wait, he told Byrd, until he knew *Norge* had reached Alaska. Three days later, with the Amundsen mission a success, Balchen was on his way with the triumphant Byrd party to the New World.[30]

Like the tale of his action-filled trip around the world alone at age twelve, Byrd's North Polar flight is a wonderful story. But is it true? Many at the time thought not. Balchen himself claimed to harbor doubts that matured into conviction once he reached the United States. Others at the time recalled that the Amundsen-Ellsworth attempt to reach the pole the year before had come to grief because after eight hours of flight, the two aircraft were still 120 nautical miles from the top of the earth, having drifted badly off course. Could not the same thing have easily happened to Byrd and Bennett? Skepticism and outright disbelief echoed down the years. To understand what the two Americans may or may not have accomplished, it is necessary to peel off layer after layer of fact, conjecture, prejudice, and, at bottom, outright malice.

European critics led by the Italian and Norwegian press went after Byrd even as he and his men wended their way triumphantly homeward. Their pique was understandable. Polar exploration had traditionally been a European endeavor. Amundsen was widely recognized in 1926 as the king of his trade. Mussolini, Nobile, and the Italian nation were anticipating a great deal of reflected glory from *Norge*'s expected voyage to the top of the world. Then a young upstart American suddenly appeared out of far North Atlantic mists in his black-hulled ship to land on Spitsbergen and steal all the glory. Balchen remembered how down everyone was in the wake of the American triumph. Dismay was compounded by the blatant rivalry not only between the two camps but also between the two press corps.

Byrd and Bennett exacerbated the misery in their articles for the *National Geographic Magazine* and *Aero Digest,* mentioning neither Balchen's critical contribution of an effective wax to grease the skis for the *Josephine Ford*'s takeoff nor the

Norwegian's suggestion to wait until the snow froze hard again at midnight before setting off for the pole. Nor did Byrd describe Amundsen's graceful, indeed emotional, acknowledgment of his achievement. Instead, Richard gushed about the joy of being the first to view thousands of square miles of polar ice scape, conveniently forgetting that Amundsen, Ellsworth, Riiser-Larsen, and other members of the Norwegian-American 1925 polar aviation expedition had seen much of the same territory before being forced to land less than 2.5 degrees from the pole. Whether Byrd and Bennett wrote as they did out of careless enthusiasm or to ensure their place in the pantheon of polar heroes, the two men did nothing to endear themselves to the skeptics across the Atlantic.

Early critics focused on one point that would be embellished by later debunkers and scoffers: the *Josephine Ford* had simply not been aloft long enough to reach the pole and return. Balchen first publicly raised his own doubts in 1958, thirty years after Bennett's death and a year after Byrd died. Balchen's memoir, *Come North with Me,* set forth his charges, which were questioned by Byrd's family and friends. Publisher E. P. Dutton forced the Norwegian to excise the most controversial passages, but Balchen kept the issue alive by recruiting friends and sympathizers in Scandinavia and the United States to spread and justify the story.[31]

A decade later, journalist Richard Montague picked up Balchen's tale. Relying almost exclusively on Balchen's assertions, Montague argued in *Oceans, Poles, and Airmen,* published in April 1971, that a flight that should have lasted twenty hours was completed in fifteen and a half. Byrd and Bennett never even tried for the pole. Spotting an oil leak in one engine shortly after takeoff, Byrd had panicked and cravenly ordered Bennett to circle around the north Spitsbergen coast for hours before flying the 40-odd miles or so back to Kings Bay.[32]

Montague encouraged and goaded Balchen into making the kind of charges that would result in a sensational book. After closely reading Byrd's formal flight report to the navy, subsequently passed on to and published by the National Geographic Society, Montague wrote Balchen that he had

> no way of judging whether the data described in the report is adequate or whether the men who studied it were really able to substantiate Byrd's claim that he reached the Pole. Certainly the statement by the National Geographic's three-person Board of Reviewers that "the successful landfall at Grey Hook demonstrates Commander Byrd's skill in navigating along a predetermined course in our opinion is one of the strongest evidences that he was equally successful in his flight northward" means nothing if he was just flying back and forth across the [Spitsbergen] coast. . . . Now here are the things I need to know more about: Exactly what Bennett said, as far as you remember, about the phony flight. . . . Well, thar she is. It sounds sketchy to me but

it has scared me some all the same. I'm counting on you to shoot it [the report] full of holes.[33]

Montague harbored his own long-standing animus against Byrd, telling fellow journalist Budd Boyer in 1972 that as "a young reporter for the New York Evening Post" back in 1927, he had met "the man . . . numerous times . . . during the weeks I was waiting for him to take off from Roosevelt Field, Long Island, on an attempt to fly the Atlantic." Montague had concluded "that Byrd (1) was handing out hokum by the barrelful about the great things he was doing for aeronautical science, (2) that he was making test after unnecessary test, probably as a stall to get more publicity for his sponsor, Rodman Wanamaker, and (3) that he was far too considerate of, not to say deferential to, reporters." Montague subsequently told Balchen what he had written to Boyer, adding, "Maybe I'm somewhat unreasonable but I've been so mad about the whole Byrd thing that I tend to strike out hard when somebody takes Byrd's side." Montague published a virulent letter against the Byrd family in the *Washington Post* just before his death in early 1972, then wrote Balchen triumphantly that "it should do us some good. Certainly it will show that you are not alone in charging that Byrd was a fraudulent liar."[34]

According to his widow, "Bernt was in great and horrible pain much of his last years, and terribly weakened by severe anemia." Exhausted from major surgery, yet determined that Montague's sensational charges should stick, Balchen told Associated Press (AP) writer Vern Haugland late in 1971 that Byrd's claim of having reached the North Pole "was an out-and-out lie. Byrd's whole fame was based on that story—based on a fraud." Balchen charged that Bennett himself had confided privately that the claim of crossing the North Pole was false. "Floyd told me the whole story," Balchen confided to Haugland. "They never got that far away from their base at Spitsbergen, and if Byrd flew toward the Pole he didn't get as close to it as Roald Amundsen did a year earlier—130 miles from the Pole." Begging the obvious question as to whether Balchen was admitting Byrd made a good-faith effort to reach the pole or condemning him for making no effort, Haugland's sensational AP story was immediately picked up without comment by both the national and the international press. When Haugland's story appeared in the *New York Times,* Balchen released a statement confirming and amplifying his charges. Everything that Montague had written about Richard Byrd in *Oceans, Poles, and Airmen* was true, he declared. Flying the *Josephine Ford* 8,000 miles around the country with Bennett after the North Polar flight had convinced Balchen "that the plane could not average more than 67 miles an hour." Moreover, there had been "Floyd's admission to me that they never got further north than about 20 miles above the north coast of Spitzbergen." Balchen challenged Harry Byrd to read

Montague's book before seeking to refute the claim that his brother Richard "was a fraud." He closed by reminding readers that the *Boston Globe* and the *Sunday Times* of London had reviewed Montague's book and had asked the National Geographic Society "to comment on the charges of fraud," but the magazine had remained silent.[35]

Balchen got what he wanted, but it left him more remorseful than vindicated. Just before he died the old airman confided to an upstate New York reporter that although he stood by his charges, he wished the issue had never been revived. "After all Bennett is dead. Byrd is dead and cannot defend himself. This will hurt his widow, a fine woman, and others. And what good can it do?" Years later, one of Balchen's ex-wives would deny he ever said what he clearly did say to Haugland and subsequently to the *New York Times*.[36]

Balchen's charges, swiftly amplified by Montague and later repeated by freelance Baltimore astronomer Dennis Rawlins, created a cottage industry of scoffers that has flourished for many years, staining and obscuring Byrd's undeniable contributions to polar and aviation history and making of him something of a public fool. Rawlins has been particularly insistent, changing assumptions and shifting charges as necessary to keep the notion of Byrd's fraud firmly fixed in the public sight.

In 1979, one of Byrd's former colleagues, Finn Ronne, wrote that Byrd had admitted to Isaiah Bowman, president of the American Geographical Society (a natural though usually friendly rival of Gilbert Grosvenor's organization), that the *Josephine Ford* had gotten no closer than 150 miles to the pole. If Byrd and Bennett in fact got no closer to the pole than the Amundsen party, they saw *nothing* new in their flight, thus adding to the duplicity. In a 1998 television interview, Bess Balchen Urbahn reiterated her late husband's insistence that barnstorming around the country with Bennett in the *Josephine Ford* shortly after returning from Spitsbergen convinced him that the plane was simply too slow to have made the flight to and from the pole in fifteen and a half or even sixteen hours. According to Mrs. Urbahn, her late husband boldly raised the matter with Bennett, who *then and there* stated that he and Byrd had not reached the top of the world.

Montague and Rawlins ascribed an overriding commercial motive to Byrd's deceit and that of the National Geographic Society. (They, Balchen, Ronne, and others never discussed Floyd Bennett's account of the North Polar flight in the September 1926 edition of *Aero Digest* that supported Byrd in every particular. Perhaps all were unaware of it.) Byrd *had* to make good his polar dash in order to fully realize media commitments and pay off debts. Moreover, in the increasingly intense battle between proponents of the airplane and the airship, Byrd had become the unequivocal champion of airplanes. Through his connection with Edsel

Ford, Dick Byrd had staked his reputation on the airplane not only as a major tool of polar research but also as the future of commercial aviation. Donald MacMillan had openly challenged Byrd, and Amundsen and Ellsworth had abandoned the airplane in favor of a return to the airship in their own quest to be the first to reach the top of the world. Should Byrd admit that his own effort had failed, his critics' claims would be validated and he and his powerful supporters would be discredited. As for the National Geographic Society, it was in that organization's interest to deceive foreign critics in order to promote American pretensions in an area of human endeavor—polar exploration—traditionally dominated by Scandinavians and Englishmen.

According to Rawlins, Grosvenor and his staff *"deliberately doctored"* Byrd's navigation report, just as they had earlier assisted Peary in his equally bogus claim to have reached 90 degrees north. The society was willingly aided and abetted by the navy, the Byrd family, and the society's powerful allies in Congress. Rawlins went so far as to claim that he had "obtained elsewhere" (presumably from Balchen) a copy of Byrd's original report proving that he and Bennett had not reached the pole. In 1996 Ohio State University archivist Raimond Goerler discovered what soon came to be called Byrd's flight "diary" buried deeply within the explorer's papers at Columbus. Upon examining the document, Rawlins found what he thought was *the* smoking gun that vindicated his attack against Byrd. At 7:07 A.M. on May 9, 1926, nearly seven hours into the flight, Byrd had imperfectly erased a sextant reading indicating the aircraft was only "377m into the flight," or about 165 miles south of where Byrd would later claim the plane had to be to reach the pole and return. "Squinting to read the nearly-erased solar altitude, 19°25′300″ . . . I leapt upon a copy of Byrd's typed report to NGS [National Geographic Society] that was sitting just to the left of the diary and feverishly fingered through the pages until finding the 7:07:10 GCT [Greenwich Civil Time] solar altitude in the official report. There it was: 18°18′180″—*a completely different figure.* I instantly learned how the expression my-skin-froze came to be. From this time on, the Byrd claim was irreversibly doomed."

Rawlins concluded on the basis of this one partially erased observation that a "shocked" Byrd quickly realized that instead of being pushed off consistently to the right (for which he continually prodded Bennett to return to base course), "the plane's progress toward the Pole was being seriously slowed (down to merely 70 mph) by a wind with a strong north component. This 7:07 [sextant] shot is the key one that Byrd kept secretly sculpting" while "preparing to hand in his 'data' to the NGS judges. . . . Byrd was fine-sculpting his ultra-smooth story" from the instant he discovered his error at 7:07 A.M. local time on May 9, 1926, to the end of his life. Rawlins concluded that his earlier assertion that Byrd and Bennett "turned back" some 150 miles short of the pole was wholly vindicated. "I wished that the incomparable Roald Amundsen and the great flier-navigator Bernt Balchen had been still alive to be here with us, at this archivally precious moment-of-truth." Rawlins's ostensible triumph was picked up by the national press soon thereafter on the seventieth anniversary of the flight, and he elaborated his argument and condemned any and all defenders of Byrd and Bennett in a lengthy, rambling article in his personally published and distributed pamphlet, modestly titled *DIO: The International Journal of Scientific History*.[37]

What are we to make of such claims? The first task is to look at the claimants. During the course of his long and active life, Richard Byrd made a number of powerful enemies, Balchen, Ronne, and Montague obviously chief among them. Emboldened by his death—but not before—they proceeded to blacken Byrd's reputation with relish—and by implication the reputation of Floyd Bennett as well. Balchen and Ronne not only chafed under Byrd's leadership but also became convinced that he was out to thwart their careers, blight their reputations, and trivialize what they believed to be their own not inconsiderable contributions to polar exploration and science. Balchen was particularly insistent that after World War II, Byrd, working through brother Harry, blocked Balchen's promotion to air force general no fewer than seven times. Montague repeated this charge in his book and at least once to the press, which invoked Haugland's sympathy and that of many others.

In fact, the charge appears baseless. In the spring of 1973, Senator Barry Goldwater, U.S. Air Force Reserve, whose understanding of the institution's history and inner workings was unmatched, wrote one particularly virulent Balchen partisan as follows:

> I have made vigorous efforts to have him receive the rank I think he was entitled to, but many complications crop up, none of them related to any animosity from the Byrds or anyone else. Somewhere along the line in World War II as a Colonel, [Balchen] stepped on the wrong toes and I have been unable to find out who they belong to, and I have been up as far as General Spaatz, who would like to see him promoted also, but once a man has retired from the service, receiving those promotions is not easy.

Goldwater promised, however, "to keep after it."[38]

Nine years later, Byrd's longtime associate and sometime critic Charles J. V. Murphy, amplifying an earlier claim, wrote that "when I was Special Assistant simultaneously to both [U.S. Air Force] Secretary Finletter & the Air Chief of Staff, Vandenberg, friends of mine as well, I discovered that the high command of the Air Force was fed up with Balchen. The CIA had complained of his indiscretions and the Assistant Vice-Chief for Operations to whom Balchen reported, wanted to be shed of him."[39]

Balchen's initial charge against Byrd hinged on an alleged exchange between himself and Floyd Bennett while the two were flying the *Josephine Ford* on a rescue mission to Labrador following the North Polar flight. According to Balchen, he flew the aircraft while a deathly ill Bennett sat "slumped" in the copilot's seat. Suddenly, Bennett burst out, "It makes me sick to think about it!" "Think of what?" Balchen allegedly replied. "That North Pole flight," Bennett responded. "If you knew the truth, it would shake you to your heels." According to Balchen, "Floyd's eyes were hollow and his cheeks were blazing hot. I could see that he was a very sick man. . . . At Murray Bay he was taken off the plane in an advanced stage of pneumonia and I continued the flight to Labrador alone. . . . I was on my way back with the *Bremen* fliers when I heard the news of Floyd's death. I never mentioned Floyd's remark as long as Admiral Byrd was alive," Balchen added; he waited years for Byrd himself to make the admission of fraud. Setting aside the question as to whether a pilot and copilot could conduct a normal conversation in the roaring, uninsulated cockpit of a 1925 Fokker trimotor, surely any reasonable man would not take Bennett's vague ravings as a confession of guilt, of not having reached the pole. Who knew what was in the dying man's feverish mind? Yet from that alleged incident, Balchen—and others—concocted varying tales of failure and fraud.[40]

Ronne over the years proved to be a turbulent, imperious, chronically suspicious man who some came to believe was at best marginally competent in the polar setting. Among a number who felt that way was Stuart Paine, who worked closely with Ronne on the second Byrd Antarctic expedition. Ronne was a "goddam shiftless slacker," Paine wrote during the midst of that strife-torn expedition. "A person I cannot tolerate is one who deliberately permits his mate to do his work for him. Such is Finn Ronne." Charles Passel, who encountered Ronne on the United States Antarctic Service (USAS) expedition of 1939–1941, became as apoplectic as Paine, railing against "that @#%$ Ronne" who "screwed up" the supply situation on the several occasions when he did work and otherwise "skis around during our watch hour like he is an over-seer when he ought to be working like the rest of us. . . . [J]ust a stubborn Norwegian, he can't be told." Ronne himself admitted that his behavior as commander of the U.S. Ellsworth Scientific Station during the austral winter of 1957–1958 was such as to generate a near mutiny among the scientific staff. Subsequent memoirs and histories of the first year at Ellsworth not only substantiate but greatly amplify Ronne's character and leadership flaws.[41] As their bitterness grew and deepened over the years, Balchen and Ronne naturally became susceptible to all the skepticism and criticism leveled by contemporary critics of the 1926 polar flight.

The second task is to look at the evidence, and, indeed, there is something to tantalize and titillate credulous skeptics and conspiracy theorists. The *precise* duration of the Byrd-Bennett flight is difficult to pin down. In his formal report to the navy, Byrd claimed that the *Josephine Ford* departed Spitsbergen at 12:37 A.M., Greenwich time, on the morning of May 9, 1926, and returned at 4:34 P.M., fifteen hours and fifty-seven minutes later. In the brochure accompanying the exhibition of the *Josephine Ford* in the great court of his Philadelphia department store some months after the return of the Byrd party from the Arctic, Rodman Wanamaker claimed that Byrd and Bennett had departed Spitsbergen at 12:50 A.M. and were *sighted* returning at 4:20 P.M.—apparently a fifteen-and-a-half-hour flight, which Wanamaker's writers then claimed was actually fifteen hours and fifty-one minutes from takeoff to landing. Balchen agreed that Byrd and Bennett departed Kings Bay at 12:37, but stated that the two fliers touched down at 4:07 P.M., their flight thus lasting twenty-seven minutes less than Byrd said. Rawlins agrees with Balchen. Finally, Pete Demas told a California paper in 1971 that *everyone* else was wrong and that Byrd and Bennett were actually gone sixteen hours and fifty-five minutes. Rawlins readily brushed this aside, writing Demas that he had incorrectly relied on mid-European time, one hour east of the Greenwich time used by everyone—Byrd included—in chronicling the North Polar flight.

But Balchen knew of and should have acknowledged Byrd's insistence that he and Bennett had been airborne nearly sixteen hours, because the Norwegian at some point obtained and kept a copy of a document titled "Navigation Report of Flight to Pole" signed by Byrd, which was the formal report submitted to the National Geographic Society. In it, Byrd states, "Left King's Bay, Spitzbergen for North Pole at 00.37 Greenwich Civil Time, May 9 in the Josephine Ford with about twenty one hours gasoline aboard. . . . We reached King's Bay at 16 hours and 34 minutes Greenwich Civil Time."[42] Balchen may have based his initial skepticism of Byrd's achievement on the assumption that the navigator and his pilot flew from the pole to Cape Morris Jesup, as they earlier said they would, before returning to Kings Bay. Balchen, Rawlins, and Montague were obsessed with the notion that the Byrd-Bennett mission could not be completed in less than seventeen hours. A dogleg on the home flight to at least overfly Cape Morris Jesup would yield a seventeen-hour-plus flight. But Byrd and Bennett did not fly the dogleg.

Critics were greatly aided by Byrd's unwillingness to share his data with any but the National Geographic Society, which formally published his navigation report only after its own board of experts had examined and blessed it. Raimond Goerler's 1998 publication of what quickly came to be known as Byrd's diary and flight notations fails to resolve the central question of the flight's duration. According to Byrd's flight notes, which correspond with the report published by the National Geographic Society, the *Josephine Ford* reached the pole at two or three minutes past 9:00 A.M., Greenwich time, on May 9, or eight hours and thirty-four or thirty-five minutes after leaving Spitsbergen. Byrd claimed that their average speed up from Kings Bay was 85 statute miles per hour, which would have left the *Ford* roughly 40 miles short of the pole, unless, of course, it was aided by a mild tailwind that Byrd failed to record. At least some Byrd critics and partisans agree that weather conditions that day were such that at least a 5.5-knot tailwind would probably have been present, thus pushing the *Josephine Ford* to the pole in the time Byrd claimed, though he did not carefully relate speed to distance.[43] Byrd wrote that Bennett then made one or several circles around the pole so that Byrd could confirm his sightings. The total elapsed time for this maneuver was about thirteen minutes. This meant the aircraft left the pole, or at most 20 miles south of the pole, around 9:15 A.M. Byrd then claimed that he first sighted Spitsbergen five and a quarter hours later, at 2:30 P.M., Greenwich time, and landed at 4:34 P.M.—a total elapsed time of fifteen hours and fifty-seven minutes.

If we assume that Bennett and Byrd were gone three minutes shy of sixteen hours, how fast did they fly? The distance from Kings Bay to the North Pole on the 11.04 East Meridian route that Byrd employed is 662 nautical, or 762.36 statute, miles. His return distance, after circling the pole for some thirteen minutes, then returning along 15 East Meridian, is about 670 nautical miles, or 768 statute miles, for a total of 1,332 nautical (1,530 statute) miles. This meant the Fokker *averaged* 95.6 statute miles, or 83.3 nautical miles, per hour. If Byrd's calculations are correct, then he and Bennett flew the 670 nautical miles back from the pole to Kings Bay in seven hours and nineteen or twenty minutes, at an average speed of 104.33 statue miles per hour, or roughly 90 nautical miles per hour.

Whether Byrd and Bennett reached the pole thus revolves around two questions. Were *Byrd's* calculations of the distance from Kings Bay to the pole correct, and could the Fokker trimotor have flown as fast *back* from the pole as he claimed? This latter question came to form the heart of Balchen's slowly evolving criticism of his former colleague and became the basis of Rawlins's initial argument as well.

Any analysis must give the critics their due. Richard Byrd was not always the near-flawless navigator that he claimed. Wendell Summers, who flew with the admiral on Operation Highjump in 1947, recalled years later a disturbing incident from one of his missions.

Admiral Byrd liked to do his own navigating, so we navigated side by side— he using his hand-held sun compass and I using a modern, Navy astro-compass. We had flown about 3 hours when we came to the mouth of a glacier. The Admiral exclaimed, "There's Scott Glacier! It will lead us right up to the polar plateau." My plotted flight line from Little America to this point indicated we were far from that glacier, maybe as much as 75 miles. The Ad-

miral insisted we were at that point, saying he had seen that glacier on a previous expedition and remembered it well. Major Weir, who was the pilot, and
I spent the next few minutes deciding how we would handle the ticklish situation. We decided I should recreate a new navigation chart and start a new
flight line, assuming our correct position was over Scott Glacier and our original navigation up to this point was in error. We would then track the remainder of the flight from where Scott Glacier was pinpointed on the map.
HOWEVER, we also decided to secretly retain the original plot and track the
flight on it as well. Thus, we were using two navigation charts. We hid my
original chart under the new chart. I would update it when the Admiral
wasn't looking. As we approached Little America on our return, we steered
well to the left of it, almost toward Discovery Inlet. Regardless of which plot
was correct, when we reached the shoreline, we knew LA [Little America]
would be on our right. When we arrived back at Little America, we had a
dilemma. Should we use the "Admiral's plot" as the one to turn in with the
photos or mine? You can guess which one we turned in. A junior officer does
not embarrass an Admiral.[44]

Moreover, flying in the Arctic, at least through 1950, was a very uncertain business. Much of the area had never been seen. There were literally no maps. In February 1947, a B-29 bomber belonging to the Forty-sixth (Very Long Range)
Squadron of America's fledgling Strategic Air Command that pioneered North Polar routes and navigation became lost and strayed 1,500 miles off course to land
in a remote part of Greenland, necessitating a dramatic rescue mission.[45]

Finally, there is the damning conclusion reached by Rawlins regarding Byrd's
erasures in the flight "diary" discovered by Raimond Goerler in 1996. Are the concerns and reservations over Byrd's competence and honesty valid and of overriding importance?

The Admiral Richard E. Byrd of 1947 was not the anxious, even desperate,
Lieutenant Commander Dick Byrd of 1926. Admiral Byrd, his reputation secure
(at least for the moment), could afford to be carelessly imperious during Operation Highjump, and on Major Robert R. Weir's flight he was not aiming for the
South Pole. Moreover, he had not navigated for years, and detailed, accurate navigation, on the surface and in the air, is one of the first skills to atrophy with dis-
use. Flying with Bennett twenty-one years earlier, Dick Byrd was an authentic, acknowledged aviation pioneer, an experienced Arctic navigator and young explorer
out to make a legitimate reputation and thus could take no chances. Nonetheless,
in his frigid, vibrating iron box he made some mistakes over the course of nearly
sixteen hours.

His chief error was in not heeding the pitfalls and perils inherent in his accomplishment. His reputation—already shaky by the last decade of the twentieth century—would be further tarnished by erasures in the flight "diary" unearthed by Goerler of what appears from all the evidence to be hasty computations and what Byrd clearly thought were questions of only momentary value. Navigational errors are common among mariners and airmen alike, but in maritime and scientific circles, erasing them is considered to be very bad form. Young navigators at Annapolis and elsewhere have been taught for generations that one crosses out invalid computations; one does not erase them. But this holds firm only for surface navigation; aerial navigation at speeds up to 1.5 miles per minute (90 miles per hour) causes many a navigational error, which is why aviators in the 1940s welcomed radio direction finders and those in the eighties and nineties embraced inertial navigation systems and satellite-based global positioning with fervor. Richard Byrd in the cold, pressure, and fatigue of his flight, totally bereft of advanced aids, made errors, questioned, and erased them. Yet the erasures and questions were never completely effaced. They are rather easily read. Surely, a young man undoubtedly on the make who wished to fudge the data on which his entire reputation would rest would never have kept such incriminating evidence. He would have either destroyed it or sought to make the erasures complete. Why did he not do so if the diary *was* incriminating?

Because the "diary" was *not* the flight log—a fact that at least one recent critic reviewing Goerler's book has completely failed to realize.[46] The diary is episodic at best; in no way does it represent the carefully structured creation of a mission that the most novice navigator is required to write and turn in to proper authority for review. What Dr. Goerler discovered in the Byrd Papers in 1996, however fascinating, is a series of notes, queries, and questions jotted on a calendar pad that Byrd occasionally employed throughout the long flight to record some but not all computations and ask questions of himself and Bennett.

The diary, in fact, strongly resembles—indeed, appears definitely to be—what mariners for centuries have called a "scrap log," "intended to be kept at the time . . . as things happen." Scrap logs then form a part, but only a part, of the formal written log prepared by each watch at the end of its responsibility. To take but one example among thousands, in 1986 the bridge watch aboard the U.S. Navy helicopter assault ship USS *Tarawa,* cruising western Pacific waters, wrote a hasty scrap log covering perhaps thirty minutes when a helicopter making a nighttime on-board approach missed the flight deck and crashed close aboard. Fast-moving events had to be recorded as quickly and fully as possible and only later checked and refined as to time, accuracy, and detail before the final, definitive, log was written up.[47]

It is clear from his navigation report to the navy, subsequently reviewed by the

National Geographic Society, that Byrd did keep a more detailed and accurate formal flight log as he went along, updating and revising periodic calculations from
the scrap log. Certainly, he was not required to make, nor, indeed, should he have
made, the flight log available to clearly hostile critics in Norway and Italy on his
way home. It is in the official report to the navy, included in Goerler's useful book
about Byrd's flights around Greenland, to the pole, and across the North Atlantic,
that we may find an accurate account of Dick Byrd's effort to reach the North Pole.

A reading of Byrd's official report supports a contention that he made errors
even in his careful computations. Eight and one-half hours into the flight, he calculated that the Fokker had gone 722 statute miles with 20 miles more to go to
the pole, for a total distance of 744 statute miles. But the actual distance to the
pole was 762.36 statute miles. Presumably, the *Josephine Ford* thus missed the Pole
by slightly more than 18 miles. In fact, if his calculations had been correct and the
Fokker had flown an average of 85 statute miles an hour for eight hours and thirty-four or -five minutes, Byrd and Bennett would have still been 40 miles short of
their destination unless, of course, Byrd was aware of a slight tailwind pushing him
to the exact top of the earth, which, in fact, he was. "Traveling north he reported
a light tailwind component of about 4 knots." Shortly before reaching the pole,
however, he reported that the wind was "'freshening from the north,'" thus becoming a headwind that slowed the Fokker down. Byrd confirmed the change in
speed by a sun-line reading that he took with his sun compass at eight hours, thirty-five minutes, and twenty-five seconds. This "showed him to be 31½ nm [nau-
tical miles] from the Pole. He claimed to have reached the Pole at 9:03. His ground
speed for this last 3188½ miles was 67K [knots]," down from the 80-knot average
that he had reported earlier.[48]

Byrd apparently determined to take no chances with his navigation; he insisted in his report that having reached the pole he directed Bennett to bring the
Josephine Ford around in a wide thirteen-minute-long circle as he took more position sights. If he had not yet reached the pole, somewhere along the farthest point
of the circle the aircraft almost certainly did so. As for the flight back to Spitsbergen, Byrd wrote that "the average speeds for the first six hours of our return were
91, 89, 93.5, 92.5, 92, and 94.5 m.p.h." Byrd had carefully noted earlier that all
his recorded speeds on the return flight were in *nautical* miles per hour.[49] The
Fokker was thus making speeds of up to 107 statute miles per hour. Was this possible? Critics from 1926 on have laid their claims squarely on the assumption that
it was not.

Much of Byrd's claim of a quick return from the pole rests on a point of navigation to which Balchen and Rawlins gave short shrift. In his official report of the

flight—a copy of which eventually wound up in Balchen's files—Byrd wrote the following:

> There was another splendid check of our position. Soon after leaving the pole when I took the wheel to relieve Bennett my sextant which I had inadvertently left on the chart board slid off to the floor breaking the horizon glass. So it became essential to get back to Spitzbergen without a sextant and by dead reckoning alone. At eleven hours Greenwich Apparent Civil Time (one and three quarters hours after leaving the pole) when the sun would be crossing the meridian we were flying along 15 East. I got Bennett to head the plane as accurately as possible towards the sun. At the same time I checked the sun compass and found the shadow exactly bisected by the line on the hand of the clock. That proved we were exactly on our course—that we had steered a straight course from a known position.[50]

In other words, Byrd and Bennett were flying with the sun and not relying on any ground features to guide their flight. Bumstead's sun compass had already proved invaluable for accurate aerial navigation; it would continue to be an invaluable tool throughout the age of pioneer flight.

Bennett and Byrd were flying Anthony Fokker's hottest aircraft, the FVIIa-3m that had so impressed Edsel Ford (and Dick Byrd) when it handily won the Ford Reliability Trophy around the central United States in the summer of 1925. According to the authoritative *Jane's All the World's Aircraft, 1927,* the *standard* FVIIa-3m's *cruising* speed was 102.5 statute miles per hour, and the maximum speed at sea level was 118 statute miles per hour. Rodman Wanamaker, who exhibited the *Josephine Ford* for a time on the grand concourse of his vast department store in Philadelphia, claimed in a two-page brochure accompanying the exhibit that the aircraft's speed was 100 statute miles per hour—surely not an excessive boast. However, Balchen maintained that whereas the standard FVIIa-3m carried three engines of 250 horsepower apiece— a total of 750 HP—the *Josephine Ford* carried three Wright Whirlwind J4-B engines rated at only 210 horsepower each, for a total of 630 HP. Clearly hoping that this would be a decisive element in his charges against Byrd, Balchen invited Charles Froesch, Eastern Airlines' vice president in charge of engineering, to lunch in the spring of 1958 and gave him the navigation and performance records he had been able to garner about the North Polar flight. Froesch got back to Balchen some days later with conclusions that could only have been discouraging to Balchen. "I have looked over the North Pole flight data of the 'Josephine Ford' which you left with me and find nothing wrong with it." Froesch added, "I have also checked" the *Josephine Ford*'s performance "against the performance of [famed 1920s airman Charles] Kingsford Smith's Southern Cross which was equipped with three [Wright Whirlwind] J5C's of 220 HP each. That aircraft had a top speed of 104+ knots (120 mph), and a cruising speed of 81.5 knots (94 mph), 1650 RPM [revolutions per minute], which checks pretty well with the performance of the Josephine Ford." In other words, Byrd's plane could have readily reached the North Pole and back in the time and under the flight conditions that Byrd had stated.

Despite Froesch's conclusions, one of Balchen's earliest Scandinavian champions, Gösta H. Liljequist, insisted in an article two years later in a prestigious international aviation journal that the *Josephine Ford must* have been as underpowered as Balchen claimed. A meteorologist (at the University of Uppsala), not an engineer, Liljequist dismissed as business propaganda designed for "sales value" authoritative published accounts of the aircraft capabilities. "It is doubtful whether [the Fokker's speed] could have been maintained throughout a long flight."[51] To which a skeptic is entitled to reply, "Why not?"

Moreover, on the polar flight the *Ford* was far from a fully loaded commercial aircraft. It could never have gotten off the snow and ice of Spitsbergen if it had been. As earlier noted, the breaking of the plane's strut on the first takeoff attempt from Spitsbergen prompted the Byrd team to remove all but the most essential gear, and that which remained aboard was for survival, and thus necessarily lightweight. Because it was much lighter from the start than the standard model in commercial service, the *Ford* may well have been capable of speeds as much as 5 to 7 miles per hour faster than the officially rated cruising speeds attained by its standard FVIIa-3m sisters when fully loaded. Additionally, of course, the plane would have gotten progressively faster as it lightened still further due to fuel consumption. "The plane was much lighter than when we started," Byrd wrote in his report regarding the return flight, "and was getting lighter all the time" as it winged its way back toward Spitsbergen. Thus, only the slightest tailwind would have been sufficient to push the aircraft to the speeds that Byrd recorded were such to get back to Spitsbergen in seven and one-third hours. In fact, Byrd may have been too conservative in his estimation of the airplane's speed on the way up to the pole. If Byrd's navigation was correct—atmospheric conditions were optimal throughout the flight—and the *Ford* did reach the pole in eight hours and thirty-four minutes, then the average flying speed would have been 89 statute miles per hour, still certainly well within the aircraft's design capabilities.

In 1979, Finn Ronne raised another factor, arguing that the *Josephine Ford's* performance was affected by the drag exerted by its ski landing gear. How critical an element were the skis in reducing the plane's airspeed? Ronne accepted the fact that the trimotor was capable of flying 100 statute miles an hour. But with skis, he argued, without adducing any evidence, the plane's "average speed during the flight was probably no more than 70 knots (78 miles) per hour." Thus, according to Ronne, the skis exerted a drag of slightly more than 21 percent on the *Ford*'s top speed. Ronne's assumption was excessive. In March 2002, Wendell Summers told me that on his 1947 flights in the other polar region—Antarctica—his R4D two-engine transport plane (the military equivalent of a Douglas DC-3/4) flew at an average speed of 145 statute miles per hour with skis, while its top-rated speed without skis was 160 statute miles per hour. The skis thus produced a drag rate of around 10 percent.[52] Most important, however, the ski configuration on the *Josephine Ford* in 1926 was slightly "up," thus providing added lift to the aircraft by facilitating airflow over the plane's big fixed-wheel undercarriage. The skis that Balchen had recommended fashioning from oars aboard *Chantier* enhanced rather than detracted from the plane's speed.

The major element that remains to be considered is wind. Ronne's contention (and that of others) that "winds were not a factor, for meteorological records prove there were almost none in the entire polar basin the day of the flight" is highly questionable on several grounds. First, there were absolutely no weather-reporting stations on the line of flight between Spitsbergen and the pole, and we now know (as Ronne perhaps did not grasp back in 1979) that world, regional, and even local weather patterns are highly unstable, with each region and locale possessing often a multitude of microclimates and microweather patterns. Byrd carefully assessed changing wind patterns around the pole, and the "freshening" breeze "from the north" that slowed the plane down near the pole would have become a tailwind as Byrd and Bennett headed homeward. Since the plane was slowed near the pole from 80 to 67 knots, or about 17 statute miles an hour, it is fair to assume that such a wind, along with a steadily lightened fuel load, pushed the Fokker briskly homeward.

But what of Rawlins's conclusion that Byrd and Bennett never reached the pole, never even came close, because of brisk headwinds? Like all of Byrd's critics, indeed, like conspiracy theorists everywhere in every age, Rawlins seeks to divert attention from *his* untenable thesis by debunking, dismissing, and otherwise denigrating the efforts and conclusions of others. For all his windy rhetoric and elaborate theorizing regarding this element of the flight or that, Rawlins asks us to accept a truly incredible conclusion: that for the first six hours and forty minutes of steady flight, two aviation pioneers (one of whom had also been a prime innovator of aerial navigation) who had successfully flown many hours through wind, fog, rain, and snow in the high Arctic just scant months before did not recognize or even sense that "a wind with a strong north component" was fatally compromising their mission. We are asked to accept that not until 7:07 A.M. did Byrd to his "shock" realize that his aircraft was flying at roughly one-third less than its designed speed and only 15 statute miles an hour above stall speed (the landing speed for the Fokker VII3a was 55 miles per hour). Moreover, Bennett at the controls with his own instruments before him supposedly never did realize what was happening until Byrd apprised him.[53] Such a conclusion simply beggars belief, for it must also be borne in mind that although there were no *geographic* features (mountain peaks, rivers, glaciers, and so on) to help assess speed, the open leads and frequent pressure ridges of the polar pack passing below the aircraft on this crystal-clear day would have given both Bennett and Byrd a clear sight indication as to whether the *Josephine Ford* was maintaining satisfactory speed over ground.

Upon reading the "diary," Rawlins abruptly abandoned his insistence that Byrd was a charlatan. He fawned over an explorer who made an "amazingly dangerous real-life flight into the unknown (*far* into the unknown)." In fact, of course, had Byrd and Bennett gotten no farther north than Rawlins maintained, their flight was not far into the unknown at all, since Amundsen, Ellsworth, and their aerial party had gone just as far before going down on the ice the year before. In a typically convoluted single-spaced, fifteen-page letter deposited in the Byrd Papers at Ohio State University shortly after reviewing the diary, Rawlins anticipated his headwind claim by first questioning the performance capabilities of the *Josephine Ford*. "Pilots Bennett and Alton Parker had privately tested *Jo Ford* on 1926/3/29 [at Mineola, Long Island; a carbon copy of the test results is now in the U.S. National Archives]—speed 87 mph or 76 knots. This verifies Balchen's assertion that the skis (which he personally helped get onto the *Jo Ford* in 1926 at Kingsbay) slowed the airplane a few knots" to the speed that Rawlins calculated had to fit in with his own stubborn insistence that Byrd and Bennett actually got no closer to the pole than 150 miles (135 nautical miles) before turning back.[54]

No one has ever denied that Richard Byrd was a prudent and careful aviator—indeed, he has been labeled by some a coward in the air. It is quite proper, then, to ask if he would have accepted, flown aboard, and navigated an aircraft whose performance was so shoddy, so far below design specifications for its type—at least 15 to 20 miles per hour slower—as to raise questions about its overall airworthiness in any kind of flight. Doubtless, Bennett and Parker did fly the *Josephine Ford* on March 29, 1926, and, doubtless, they recorded its performance accurately—no one has ever asserted that either pilot was ever dishonest. But "test" flights are undertaken for a variety of reasons, not all of them having to do with speed. Did Bennett and Parker fly the plane to its limits? Or even to its cruising speed?[55] In all probability, they were merely giving it a routine systems check, in which case flying to even cruising speed was unnecessary. Moreover, would manufacturer Tony Fokker have allowed Byrd to fly such a questionable aircraft on the most important flight made to date by an airplane? It is highly doubtful. In the end, despite some gracious admissions that he had been frequently misled by Balchen's bitterness, Rawlins continued to desperately clutch at any explanation that might support the shopworn but always attractive charge of fraud.

According to retired air force navigator William Molett, who has flown "to or near the vicinity of the North Pole" on "91 flights," Byrd's official report of his flight contains no fewer than "3 evidences of authenticity."

> The first is triangulation on the Spitzbergen mountains which [Byrd] did on the first hour north of Amsterdam Island. This triangulation fixed his position accurately and enabled him to check his drift meter speeds for accuracy. The second is heading directly at the sun when it crossed the 15 E Meridian which confirmed his position by the shadow on his sun compass. The third is his reporting of a strong north wind making white caps in the bay when he returned to Amsterdam Island. White caps begin at about 15 *nautical* miles of wind and their presence confirms that the high pressure sitting north of Spitzbergen (as reported by expedition meteorologist William Haines) had moved to the west while Byrd was traveling north and gave him a very favorable tail wind for his return and accounts for the fact that he returned about one hour shorter than he had predicted.

Colonel Molett dismisses speculation that to have even reached the pole Byrd and Bennett required a 15-knot tailwind, increasing to 40 to 50 knots on the return trip, because "fresh winds could have occurred only during the first half of the homeward flight." Why, Molett asks, would not a tailwind of 15 nautical miles per hour getting Byrd and Bennett *to* the pole not have been sufficient to get them back as well? And even if higher winds had been required to get back earlier, why would they have occurred only during the first half of the return flight? A moderate 22-knot tailwind throughout the return flight would have been sufficient to get Byrd and Bennett back to Amsterdam Island at the time they did, particularly since the plane became progressively lighter, and thus faster, as it burned off ever more of its fuel. Since Colonel Molett is an experienced high Arctic flight navigator, whereas Byrd's critics (Balchen excepted) most emphatically are not, his argument commands attention.[56]

Simple justice demands that skepticism be extended not only to the subject but also to the author of any charge dealing with a man's alleged dishonesty. Balchen had more than one ax to grind. Not only did he come to dislike Byrd, but joining Byrd so quickly after Amundsen's departure for the pole also identified him with an American triumph over his home country of Norway. One way to remain on good terms with his fellow Norwegians—who immediately expressed skepticism over the Americans' claim—was to agree that Byrd, in fact, had not reached the pole first by air, therefore giving the triumph over to Amundsen.

Bennett never indicated to anyone else that he and Byrd had not reached the pole. Indeed, he wrote his own account of the flight that corroborated Byrd's report, publishing it just shortly before his alleged confession to Balchen. Nor, given Balchen's bitter bias, can we automatically take his word that the *Josephine Ford* could fly no faster than 63 to 67 knots on its return to this country. The only man who could corroborate or refute Balchen's claims, first made public in the late 1950s, was Floyd Bennett, who had been dead for thirty years.

Beyond his formal report, Dick Byrd left behind his own accounts of that memorable day and of his general impressions of Arctic flight and its challenges. Unfortunately, the account he chose to publish in *Skyward* is sketchy, probably due to publication cost considerations, and thus opens the door to critics, scoffers, and conspiracy theorists. But two apparently unpublished manuscripts, one of twenty pages, the other thirty-five, both clearly written soon after the North Polar flight, demonstrate Byrd's impressive grasp of the dimensions, dangers, and pitfalls of high Arctic aviation. Among many topics and considerations, he wrote of using graphite rather than grease to keep the dashboard instruments from becoming "sluggish," the dangers of fog in obscuring sun and ground, its absence at both Etah and Spitsbergen in early May, and its "peculiarities" that allow airmen to fly around it. He dilated at length on the difficulties of high Arctic navigation—of sluggish compass needles, faulty readings close to the North Magnetic Pole or due to the metal surface of the aircraft, and the absolute need to know the compass variation at every point of the flight. Most if not all difficulties could be resolved, Byrd wrote, by employing the advanced instruments of *his* time, the drift indicator and especially a sun compass, which, of course, required the kind of consistently clear day that he and Bennett encountered on the polar flight. The manuscripts reflect Byrd's truly scholarly interest in flight and of the intellectual challenges it posed during the pioneering era. When he chose he could be a teacher, and a good one.[57]

No one in the days before sophisticated positioning equipment could ever be *precisely* certain that he or she had reached an exact geographical point or spot on the face of the earth. The map of Antarctica would be redrawn many times in the thirty to forty years after Byrd's first expedition in 1928–1930 as photographed features were plotted with ever greater precision, thereby supplying cartographers the ground truth necessary to create increasingly accurate depictions of the continent. Antarctica was much easier to plot than its polar opposite, of course, because there *were* continental features that could be used as reference points, unlike the North Polar region, a frozen sea in which no ships ply to provide precise plotting through radio direction finding. The South Polar plateau is much like the Arctic in its lack of feature. When Amundsen reached what he thought was the South Pole in 1912, he split his group and had men walk an additional 5 miles in each direction, a 10-mile circumference in all, just to make sure that *somewhere* in that flat snowy plain, one of them had "reached" the pole. Byrd did the same thing on his North Polar flight. The man did as well as he possibly could with the still-crude instruments at his disposal; he honestly believed in 1926 that he had reached the North Pole. There is no reason to think that he, or his pilot, committed fraud. Although the possibility that Byrd somehow went inadvertently astray like the Strategic Air Command B-29 bomber and flew off in another direction altogether from the pole cannot be wholly discounted, it must be emphasized that he made landfall back at Spitsbergen just about where he calculated, which would indicate that he aimed for a straight-line shot to and from the pole and achieved it.

This leaves only the charge that he never even attempted the pole, that he panicked (or coldly calculated) when the oil leak was spotted early on and directed Bennett to fly just over the horizon from Spitsbergen, returning to Kings Bay as soon as he decently could to claim a bogus triumph. Such fraud is not unknown in the annals of air or sea. At least one sailor in a recent round-the-world competition apparently sat alone in the South Atlantic for some weeks fabricating data indicating he was continuing on, when in fact he planned to return to England as soon as possible to claim victory. Apparently, the poor devil was eventually overwhelmed by both his isolation and his deception and threw himself overboard, leaving the incriminating evidence behind.

But this charge is the easiest to rebut. Byrd had chosen a trimotor precisely because it could continue to function on two engines, and in an all-out emergency even on one. And, of course, all evidence points to the fact that the oil leak began—or was discovered—only an hour from the pole.

Finally, and most important, Richard Byrd had one compelling motive to play the polar flight absolutely straight, a motive that neither his critics nor his defenders have ever emphasized but one that was, in fact, overriding. It was the possibility of land somewhere between the northernmost point the Amundsen-Ellsworth party had reached the year before and the pole. Peary had supposedly marched to the top of the world; Frederick Cook claimed to also. But neither man had taken the route that Byrd, Bennett, Amundsen, and Ellsworth had chosen. The notion that there might be some sort of landmass, however small, in the high Arctic near the North Pole had bewitched the polar community and the general public for years before the Byrd-Bennett flight to the top of the world and, indeed, for some years thereafter. In fact, one of Byrd's major stated objectives was to determine if any land existed in the high Arctic region, and it is clear from his unpublished account that he and Bennett constantly searched for signs. The general assumption was that if such a landmass did exist, it lay in the vast unexplored quadrant between Alaska and the pole.[58] But no one could be sure there might not be some sort of small land features elsewhere near the pole.

Amundsen was coming right behind Byrd in *Norge.* The world's leading polar explorer left Spitsbergen aboard the huge Italian airship shortly before nine in the morning on May 11 and reached Teller, Alaska, via the polar route seventy-one hours later.[59] (No one, incidentally, ever subjected Amundsen's flight to the brutal skepticism accorded Byrd; perhaps simple fairness dictates that they should.) The Norwegian and his flight crew aboard the big dirigible would surely check every mile, indeed every inch, of his competitor's claimed route. If there had been any unusual feature to be found in the polar sea ice field between Amundsen's farthest north penetration the summer before and the pole itself—a small, ice-encrusted island or two, perhaps, or even a point of rock in an open area of water—and Byrd had not reported it because in fact he had not been there, Amundsen would have revealed it in a heartbeat, and the American's reputation would have been irretrievably ruined. Richard Byrd would have gone down in history as the all-time fraud, *the* charlatan, of polar exploration. He thus had to try for the pole—to go all the way—or risk utter disaster in claiming a feat he had not, in fact, accomplished.[60]

Taken measure for measure, fact for fact, inference for inference, all evidence indicates that on May 9, 1926, Richard Byrd and Floyd Bennett flew to the North Pole—or close enough to it, say within three to five miles—so as to render any and all doubt churlish in the extreme. Byrd could satisfy himself that he and Bennett had passed well beyond the point reached by Amundsen and Ellsworth the year before and that Amundsen, coming along behind in *Norge,* would see nothing that Dick Byrd and Floyd Bennett had not seen. To claim that the two Americans failed to reach the top of the world is simply wrong. Doubtless, controversy will continue to rage within the steadily diminishing portion of the polar research and scientific community that cares about the matter. Conspiracy theorists such as Balchen, his wives, Rawlins, and others are adept at creating and rigidly maintaining alternative realities based on a single highly questionable assumption, be it that Byrd and Bennett could never have reached the North Pole, Harry Truman dropped the atomic bombs as a military demonstration against Stalin, or John F. Kennedy was the victim of a plot by the CIA and Soviets or perhaps FBI director J. Edgar Hoover. Such people will raise new perspectives and propose fresh arguments. Theories and theorists are seldom if ever amenable to reason or common sense.

The fact remains that two intrepid airman in the pioneer days of manned flight steered a powerful but crude experimental aircraft more than 700 miles across the sun-drenched, empty, and treacherous North Polar wastes to the top of the world and back. Their single fragile aircraft could have come down at any point far from civilization; rescue, had the fliers survived, would have been at best hazardous in the extreme. Despite elaborate survival gear, their chances of walking and paddling to safety across hundreds of miles of ever softening, ever shifting pack ice that characterizes the springtime Arctic were almost nonexistent. Within two years Amundsen would perish trying to find and rescue his fellow downed airman, Umberto Nobile. Who is to say he might not have died earlier trying to find a downed Richard Byrd and Floyd Bennett?

With his North Polar flight, Richard Byrd put to rest once and for all the canard that heavier-than-air craft—airplanes—were not suitable for polar conditions. Eighty years and more after the event, as we wing our way comfortably through the skies above upper earth in huge, fast-moving jet aircraft across the polar route from Asia to Europe, we might chance a glance downward on the same ungodly ice scape that Byrd and Bennett braved. If we are lucky we can glimpse the fleeting shadow of a noisy, roaring trimotor aircraft, impossibly small and fragile against the white polar sea, struggling northward toward a mathematical abstraction humanity calls the North Pole. Floyd Bennett and Richard Byrd deserve a lift of the plastic cocktail glass or Styrofoam coffee cup in salute to a harrowing venture accomplished, to a job well done, that for good and ill brought our impossibly complex world one step closer to realization.

Chapter 5

Hero

The Byrd party entered New York Harbor on the morning of June 22, 1926, to a tumultuous welcome that would become routine for returning heroes within the next few years. Yachts, sailboats, and steamers filled the huge anchorage, proudly bedecked in national bunting, pennants, and signal flags. *Chantier* steamed slowly toward the dock next to Battery Park through a din of cheers and sirens, the waters rocking and heaving as fireboats spouted great jets into the clear blue sky. The little steamer was accompanied by Mayor Jimmy Walker's official tug, *Macon,* filled with state, national, and local officials, including several U.S. senators and representatives. Press boats raced out from the Manhattan and Brooklyn shores, those on board determined to get the first direct story of the polar flight from the gallant aviators. Battery Park was black with people as *Chantier* arrived. Immediately, New York police commissioner Grover Whalen, Walker's chief greeter and himself well connected to the powerful Manhattan merchant princes, strode aboard, his signature white carnation neatly placed in its usual buttonhole.

Whalen swept Byrd and his men ashore into mass confusion. The explorer felt himself "tossed about like a leaf in a storm." The scene "resembles a riot." Perhaps he had a moment with Marie, perhaps not, before Harry Bruno, who handled all Byrd's arrangements, raced to him through the crowd and began chattering in his ear an impossibly busy schedule that included a parade, a civic honor at city hall, a luncheon banquet (where Richard would speak), a brief rest at the Hotel McAlpin, a rush to the train station, and a hasty trip down to Washington, where that evening President Coolidge would greet him with a gold medal. Suddenly, Byrd was whirled about to look at an airplane in the sky pulling a message, someone else yelled in his ear that he must meet Mr. So-and-so, a very prominent . . .

and he was whirled about again to be told that the press wanted pictures of him and his mother. Amid the din and crash of voices the parade formed, ready to march uptown through the canyons of Manhattan, where several million lined the sidewalks or waited in windows to throw tons of confetti down on the new hero. Bennett came in close behind, followed by the rest of the expedition, including the ship's crew.

Aboard *Chantier* Captain Mike Brennan was the last off but one. Striding down the gangplank he glanced up at the lone figure on board. "Balchen, you've got the watch," he called over his shoulder as he gave a final hitch to his pants and hurried to catch up to the parade. Balchen, after all, was not part of the expedition that got Byrd and Bennett to the pole. The bands began to blare, and the parade started off across the park. Long years later Balchen remembered it all and how "the roar of the crowd tracks into the echoing canyon of Broadway," the drums and trumpets suddenly muffled by the high buildings.

Striding along in a blizzard of torn newspapers and telephone books behind the blaring bands with Bennett nearby, Dick Byrd experienced his first ticker-tape parade as a surreal wall of noise and people and stopped traffic. It is not a triumph so much as a bewilderment that he will get used to. This is the first of three such events. No one before or since has had three ticker-tape parades down America's most famous street. Back at the battery, Balchen found himself alone, "the only sound . . . the mewing of sea gulls and the monotonous creak of the *Chantier*'s hull against the pilings."[1]

Reaching the capital that evening, Byrd and his men were promptly hustled over to the Washington Auditorium, where before a glittering crowd of six thousand, including President Coolidge, the leadership of the army and navy, members of Congress, and members of the foreign diplomatic corps, Byrd and Bennett received from Coolidge's hand the National Geographic Society's Hubbard Gold Medal. In his remarks Gilbert Grosvenor stated that a committee of the society had already examined Byrd's flight records and found them to be "carefully and accurately kept." Many critics and skeptics raised eyebrows at how suspiciously soon after the event the review and conclusion followed. In rather rambling remarks, Coolidge tried to define Byrd's feat. The naval officer had added undoubted luster to his service and to the country that had invented the heavier-than-air craft. He had demonstrated "superb courage" in setting out "on such a great adventure in the unexplored realms of the air." But most striking was his persistence in following and fulfilling a dream from "his Naval Academy days." In good old American fashion, Richard Byrd had "brought things to pass." In his own remarks, Byrd took care to define his achievement in a broader context of developing competence. The polar flight had been a natural outgrowth of the success that he, Bennett, Schur, and others achieved during the 1925 Greenland expedition. As he would always do, Byrd praised his men—especially "my flying mate," Floyd Bennett—and those captains of industry who had bankrolled the enterprise, Ford, Rockefeller Jr., Astor, Wanamaker, "and others."

It was left to Secretary Wilbur to at last bring Marie into the picture with the kind of salute that would leave later generations of feminists grinding their teeth. Earlier Wilbur spoke of the guest of honor in terms one would address an errant schoolboy. When Byrd came for permission to "undertake the flight" (Richard had asked for leave, not permission to fly), the secretary had asked about his family. Was he married? Yes. Did he have children? Yes, three. Did his wife "consent to your expedition?" "Yes, she said that she was willing that I should do whatever I considered my duty." Well, then, Wilbur, replied, he had permission to go. Now the bumbling secretary laid one more humiliation on the Byrds, intoning, "I am sure we will not do justice to ourselves or to our inmost convictions if we fail to do honor on this occasion to the heroic little woman who had so little to gain and so much to lose in this undertaking." He asked Marie to stand up and be recognized. Marie apparently remained determinedly in her seat, for after a moment Wilbur stammered amid some embarrassed laughter that "so many women are standing that I fear we will have to postpone our effort to identify Mrs. Byrd." Little wonder that Marie wished to avoid the limelight when she was treated in such a manner.[2]

At some point, either in New York, on the train, or in Washington, Richard must have realized that Bernt Balchen had been callously ignored, for he promptly made an effort to amend. The next morning Grover Whalen appeared at the Battery Park dock in his limousine and gave the Norwegian a personal guided tour of the city on a quiet Sunday. Balchen noted the tons of confetti piled up on the curbs. Despite the belated gesture, he felt belittled.

Byrd soon claimed that the North Pole flight represented a kind of epiphany. Everything he had done before was for the navy, or science, or the national good. His first experience of a ticker-tape parade down Broadway surrounded by madly cheering throngs, he said, changed him forever. He decided that as a national hero he was more than just "someone who's worth two columns and a front-page streamer, fireboats, and a basket of medals." He had become (for as long as he could sustain it) larger than life, a transcendent figure who for good or ill embodied for hundreds of "sad little mothers" and millions of other little people not just "the success that might have been their own" but also "the living memory" of good and productive relatives gone to often premature graves. "In us," he added, speaking for himself, Bennett, and the entire support staff of the North Polar flight, "America for the moment dramatized that super, world-conquering fire which is American spirit. For the moment we seemed to have caught up the banner of American progress." Byrd and his mates "typified" America for the Americans. He was, he readily acknowledged, now in "the hero business."[3]

There never had been a better time to ply the trade. The United States in 1926 was in the midst of what social observer Frederick Lewis Allen called the "Bally-hoo years." The nation had finally moved symbolically from the country to the city, where entertainment and information distributed by national newspaper chains, Hollywood, and the new medium of radio could be readily produced, standardized, and debased to meet the lowest possible standards of taste. These new forces created the rough outlines of a national mind at once hungry for information and avid for sensation, scandal, and trivia. The successful tabloids quickly discovered that the public tended to become excited about one thing at a time, whether it was the Scopes "monkey trial" in Tennessee, the crash of an airship, or Babe Ruth's annual attempt to remake the baseball record book. But the attention span was short. The national sleeve needed constant plucking; hucksters had to remain in the public's face, shouting the latest scandal or achievement. In the absence of jarring international crises or domestic tensions, a sporting event, a murder trial, or a long-distance flight became the equivalent of Armageddon. "Outlined against a blue-gray October sky, the four horsemen rode again," Grantland Rice wrote about an ordinary football game between Notre Dame and Army in 1924. "In dramatic lore they were known as Famine, Pestilence, Destruction, and Death. These are only aliases. Their real names are Stuldreher, Miller, Crowley, and Layden."[4]

Prohibition had unleashed a nationwide crime wave, and in reaction the public yearned for genuine heroes, modest men and women of real accomplishment. The gridiron, diamond, ring, and links were natural habitats for those seeking achievement and glory. Aviation was even better. Reaching the top of the world by airplane was a stunning achievement, and in the pre-Lindbergh era Byrd and Bennett, along with Peary, were the only Americans to challenge successfully European supremacy in exploration. Perhaps the Peary-Byrd North Polar claims seemed brighter, stronger, surer in American eyes precisely because chronically condescending Europe immediately dismissed or questioned them.

Just how Richard Byrd defined the "hero business" became clear in an interview he granted to Robert H. Davis of the *New York Sun*. With transparently calculated modesty, he told the fawning reporter for public consumption what he had haltingly confided to Rockefeller in privacy on Astor's yacht.[5] Davis asked him what he had been thinking as he and Bennett had "crossed the pole in the air." "For one transitory second," Davis wrote, "the eagle folded up his wings and dropt [*sic*] his fine dark eyes in humility. 'Do you really want to know?' he asked." When Davis gamely replied that he did, Byrd let loose with a prolonged monologue. He had thought, he said, of "the infinitesimal proportions of mortal man, of the frailty of the atoms that occupy the spaces, of the limitations of those who have taken over the conduct of civilization. I caught for the first time as in a flash of understanding, the inadequate results of the effort to solve not the enigmas of space and duration but the problems of mankind." At any point on the earth's circumference, Byrd continued, at any given elevation, human vision encountered its limitations, but one could and must cast one's mind back to the beginnings of both man and nature. Slowly, out of the chaotic beginnings of both, "the units became interdependent, the races began to unite, the responsibilities of each increasing as the mutual interests expanded. Figuratively the world became smaller," but the "swords" also became longer. Each human unit, each race, each community "began to feel the effect of conflict." The healthy gaps between countries that kept them in isolation and out of conflict disappeared. "The strong came to the weak and possess [sic] them. Foreign armies conquered other lands. Flames were visible across the seas. War, destruction, hatred took the saddle at the peak of civilization. To-day, a shot fired in any country is not only heard but felt around the world." Humanity had improved, progressed, and developed, but still fell far short of what it could be. "The sum total of our occupation of this shrinking planet is a pitiful demonstration of weakness. . . . We are still a horde of pigmies, selfish, and envious, each striving for individual supremacy." The international explorer had a decisive role to play in trying to resolve this dreadful state of strife. "It is not the geographic but the moral limitations of the world that must be charted, and the really great explorers will be those who find the way to universal reconstruction, the first step in which is the abolition of war and the needless destruction of human life."

If these thoughts flashed across Byrd's mind as the *Josephine Ford* shot across the top of the world, he must have been a busy man indeed. They were the sentiments that made him so attractive to the Rockefellers and Wanamakers, men in whose lives wealth, power, and business mixed inextricably with religion, idealism, and good deeds. Rodman Wanamaker's father, John, was the first full-time paid secretary of Philadelphia's Young Men's Christian Association just before the Civil War, even as he began his ascension in the ranks of the city's—and nation's—merchant princes. Rodman expanded his father's department store empire while dabbling heavily in philanthropy, his most serious and prolonged venture being an ultimately futile effort to reform national policy toward Native Americans. Young Rockefeller became deeply involved in his Men's Bible Class in New York City, and shortly after Byrd returned from his first journey to Antarctica, Rockefeller asked him to address the group. When Rockefeller tried to press an honorarium on the explorer, Byrd hastened to assure his patron "that this occasion was a delight to me." Byrd's sense of the sacred was genuine. Although he seldom if ever attended church or discussed religion "in a credal sense," he was nonetheless, according to daughter Bolling, "a deeply spiritual man."[6] But like the wealthy friends and supporters with whom he was becoming increasingly comfortable, Richard seamlessly blended secular piety and spiritualism with the main chance.

As Richard's ship steamed slowly homeward from the Arctic, brother Harry, now governor of Virginia, pressed the state's national delegation to have Congress vote the country's newest heroes a Medal of Honor (normally reserved exclusively for battlefield heroics) and, for Richard, a handsome promotion. Congress quickly responded with both the medals and Byrd's promotion to full commander on the retired list. As soon as he reached New York, Richard dashed off a hasty note of appreciation to his brother. "It is mighty good of you to take so much interest in my promotion. I still feel that I prefer 'Commander' with the highest pay of the grade to a 'Captain.'" Asking friends in both houses to press for a promotion beyond captain to commodore would, Richard added, "cause a fight on the [Senate] floor or in Committee and I believe that would not be wise." Richard urged Harry to meet him in Washington as soon as possible to share in the glory and make valuable political contacts on the Hill. "I have a great many friends up there, Senators Oddie, Keyes, Wadsworth, Hale, Walsh, Pitman and so forth. In the House nearly the whole Naval Affairs Committee from Butler, McGee, Britton [*sic*], all the way down. Nick Longworth is a good friend of mine." The hard years of bureaucratic scrabble and scramble on behalf of a navy indifferent to his own interests and career development had at last paid off. But in seeking the medal and the promotion, "I must evade the appearance of seeking action."[7]

From this moment on the brothers forged an inseparable bond that lasted until Richard's death thirty-one years later. They praised each other's accomplishments, worked to advance each other's careers, and consoled each other over every setback and adversity that the other suffered. Even before he set off for Spitsbergen, Richard had taken time from a busy schedule to write his older brother, praising Harry's inaugural speech as governor. "If you keep up the standard you have set," Richard continued, "you will emerge head and shoulders above the half hundred most prominent Democrats you are now classed with, and will be in a position to secure the Democratic nomination for President. That mark is worth shooting for, and if I were in your place, I would do so." Now, in the days and weeks following his brother's triumphal return from the North, Harry carefully protected and promoted Richard's career. The hasty note of appreciation that Richard had penned on the day of his return crossed a telegram that Harry dispatched northward from Winchester: "Tom and I think it very important you meet us [in] Washington this week." Whatever the three brothers concocted,

Richard gave his first public talk at Richmond several days later under the aegis of lecture impresario James Pond. Harry wrote Richard the next day, urging him to write letters of thanks to the editors of Richmond's two leading newspapers, the *Times-Dispatch* and the *News-Leader*, for their laudatory articles about the speech and Richard's achievements. Harry had already gotten authorization from the legislature for a statue of his dashing brother, and both Richard and Pond donated their shares of the honorarium to the project.

Several days later, Richard sent Harry a copy of the long-term contract that Pond was offering. Richard thought it was fine, though he was disappointed that Pond had not tried to set up a fuller schedule. Nonetheless, "I am going to be guided by your judgment in this matter." Harry replied several days later. He did not like Pond and thought the man had a poor reputation. The governor wanted to meet the impresario and size him up. Harry also approvingly quoted a friend experienced in public relations who warned that Richard was "making a great mistake in delaying your lecture tour, as three or four months from now people would lose interest." In the event, Richard fended off any confrontation between his brother and Pond by pleading a trip to Detroit to see Edsel Ford, and soon signed with the Pond Bureau.[8]

Richard reciprocated his brother's solicitude. Deciding to rest and relax throughout the remainder of the summer of 1926, he rented "the home of a millionaire" in Waltham, a wealthy Boston suburb, and invited Harry up for a stay. Richard had made the acquaintance of Van Lear Black, who was "the salt of the earth" and whom Richard was anxious for Harry to meet. "He is worth only about sixty or seventy millions." Richard promised Harry that the Byrds and Black would sail down to nearby Marion on Black's yacht to spend the day with Franklin Roosevelt, who was vacationing there. In October, Richard wrote Harry again, complaining that his older brother was reneging on attending a banquet given by the Southern Society and the Virginians. "I cannot face all those people alone," and it was most important that Harry meet "all the distinguished people who will be present. Those fellows wield a big influence politically."[9]

By mid-November 1926, Richard was out on the national lecture circuit, where he remained until the end of February. But he had already laid the foundation for his next big adventure. In fact, it had been handed to him. Rodman Wanamaker had tendered the Byrd expedition members a special luncheon during which he stood up and all but challenged Richard to have a go at crossing the Atlantic in a single bound. Wanamaker read the letter he had first sent to the Aero Club of America back in 1914 proposing such a venture and stated that he was as eager as ever to see it through to fruition. Wanamaker's interests extended beyond business and philanthropy to sports. He was not only a charter member of the Professional Golfers Association but also one of the founders of the Millrose Games, the country's premier indoor track and field event held each year in New York's Madison Square Garden, in which the Wanamaker Mile Run was a prominent feature. Flying the Atlantic was as much a sporting adventure as a serious technical feat, and it held endless commercial possibilities.

Now in the vanguard of man's growing mastery of the air, Byrd had little choice but to accept Wanamaker's challenge. Indeed, the entire incident may have been set up to release Richard from his ostensible promise to Amundsen to fly to the South Pole next. Revising reality, Byrd soon claimed to have told Bennett as they left Spitsbergen, "Now we can fly the Atlantic." According to Byrd, he and Bennett huddled for hours over a planning table aboard *Chantier* as the vessel wended its way slowly homeward from the Arctic, elaborating the details of the ocean crossing. Whatever the source, his ancient dream, frustrated in 1919 by the navy and frustrated again two years later when FDR, as acting navy secretary, would not permit a solo flight in a single-engine aircraft, was again within reach.[10]

Meanwhile, someone from the expedition had to stand by the *Josephine Ford* and answer questions while Wanamaker displayed the plane. Byrd settled on Balchen. "Of all the things I wanted least in the world," the Norwegian later wrote, "this is it." Day after day he stood beside the aircraft, "caged inside a red velvet rope, on a flag draped platform, in the middle of Wanamaker's store," while crowds gaped and gawked. Teenage girls with "horrible" New York accents giggled at the handsome young Viking, regarding him "like a prize bull at a country fair." Byrd's chief publicist, Harry Bruno, finally saved Balchen, introducing the Norwegian to members of the American flying community, including such future military leaders as Carl Spaatz, Jimmy Doolittle, and Ira Eaker. Balchen was most impressed with the disgraced but stubborn Billy Mitchell. The Norwegian also met a short, surprisingly young, "peppery Hollander," who turned out to be Tony Fokker. The airplane manufacturer immediately offered Balchen a job anytime he wished at the new Fokker factory in New Jersey.[11]

Shortly thereafter, Bruno told Balchen that the Guggenheim Foundation had agreed to finance a national tour by the *Josephine Ford* to make America more airminded. Balchen attributed the blessed intervention to Bruno. But the publicist worked for Byrd, not the Guggenheim people. Byrd owned the plane, which he lent to the Guggenheim Aviation Fund before later donating it to the Ford Museum in Michigan. It may well have been Byrd who saw to it that Balchen went on the tour with Floyd Bennett, another handsome if never acknowledged apology by the Virginian for his neglect and humiliation of a young man he had lured across the Atlantic with the promise of future polar flying.

Shortly before Byrd left on his lecture tour late in 1926, he secured Wanamaker's agreement to build an entirely new plane to cross the Atlantic nonstop some-time the following spring or summer. It would have a larger wingspan than the *Josephine Ford*. Byrd insisted from the outset that his only wish was to advance the science of aviation, not to engage in some air race to the Old World.[12] If this was true, he stood alone as the "wild and incredible summer of 1927" approached.

Suddenly, everyone wanted to fly the oceans—across the Pacific from San Francisco to Honolulu or across the Atlantic from New York to Paris. In a *Saturday Evening Post* article appearing at the end of May 1928, Byrd estimated that in the previous year and a half, "about thirty-five fine young pilots, mechanics and passengers have lost their lives in connection with ocean flying," a mortality rate "far higher than that in the trenches in the Western Front in 1918."[13] The Atlantic "hop" proved most enticing. No matter that Alcock and Brown had first accomplished the feat eight years before, followed in short order by the U.S. Navy. It was one thing to fly from the remote cliffs of Newfoundland to crash in an Irish peat bog, or to cross the water in comparatively short hops from the States to Newfoundland to the Azores to England. Now another far more glittery prize—Paris—beckoned aviators who had steadily developed the art of flying since the raw, crude days of 1919.

Paris in the twenties was an icon of joyous freedom. So was flying. The long-unclaimed Orteig Prize blended the two images into a single romantic dream, and as springtime came to America's eastern seaboard in 1927, the few muddy airfields dotting Long Island became magnets for fliers eager to cross the Atlantic. At the end of February the National Aeronautical Association in Washington, D.C., announced two formal entries for the Orteig Prize. Lieutenant Commander Noel Davis, United States Navy, planned a June crossing in his powerful single-engine *American Legion*. "C. A. Lindbergh," an obscure "St. Louis mail pilot," would fly a Ryan single-engine monoplane. Two days later, front-page stories in the nation's press confirmed that Wanamaker had written Richard Byrd a check for one hundred thousand dollars, most of which would be devoted to building a new Fokker trimotor that the ever patriotic Wanamaker wished to be called *America*. The department store king added another resource to the Byrd camp—Grover Whalen. New York City's police commissioner and chief greeter was also on the Wanamaker payroll, and his boss designated him chief publicist for the Byrd flight. Byrd promptly leased Roosevelt Field out on Long Island, where he and his men spent hours filling in and tamping down the pockmarked dirt runway until it was as smooth as a golf course and as even as a billiard table. They also graded the runway to provide a slight inclined hill at the beginning to aid in airplane speed at takeoff, as had earlier been done in Spitsbergen. Within a week of Wanamaker's announcement, businessman Charles Levine, owner of Luigi Bellanca's splendid single-engine aircraft *Columbia,* announced that renowned fliers Clarence Chamberlain and Bert Acosta would fly his plane to Europe sometime in the early summer. Two French war heroes, Charles Nungesser and one-eyed François Coli, added piquancy to the competitive juices rising on the western side of the Atlantic by announcing that they would have a plane filled with eight hundred gallons of fuel ready by early summer to fly the broad, stormy ocean east to west, from Paris to New York. By the end of March, the American media were caught up in "Atlantic fever," which it ballyhooed to every corner of an increasingly mesmerized country.[14]

Then the aircraft began to crash. "Every plane that attempted a trans-atlantic flight from the States last summer," Byrd recalled, "was loaded to the danger point. Lindbergh's was. Chamberlain's was. Ours was. And so on."[15] One aviator, Paul-René Fonck, had tried the Atlantic crossing in the summer of 1926, but crashed his trimotor in flames taking off from Roosevelt Field; fire had consumed two of his mates. He never thought of flying the Atlantic again, but remained a kind of morbid presence on the fringes of the Long Island and New Jersey airfields where the transatlantic planes were being tested.

Byrd prepared for the Atlantic journey with his usual thoroughness. The *America's* larger wing permitted greater fuel capacity and thus a larger cargo, which Byrd wanted to carry to prove that contemporary trimotor aircraft were capable of establishing routine transatlantic passenger service. The big wing also permitted the stowage of mail, and Byrd was sworn into the U.S. Post Office Department as a transatlantic mail carrier. Should the plane be forced down despite its advanced design, Byrd placed a powerful radio set aboard designed by two specialists from the Naval Research Laboratory in Washington, D.C. He also saw to it that special insulation and rubber rafts were placed aboard, together with emergency rations, an extra sextant, and hand compasses for navigation. "We even went in for a kite with which our wireless antennae would be kept in the air if we settled on the ocean." The huge twelve hundred–gallon gasoline tank was rigged with a dump valve so that it could be emptied almost instantly in case of an anticipated crash, thus forestalling a fire-induced explosion. Bennett designed a switch to cut out all three engines at once to further forestall the prospect of fire in case of a crash. Finally, the plane was so big that an internal catwalk could be built into each wing leading to the outboard engines so that if one or two failed in flight they could be repaired while the aircraft labored on.

Byrd's most brilliant stroke, however, was the creation of a transatlantic weather-reporting service. He and Noel Davis had previously approached the secretary of agriculture (whose department then housed the U.S. Weather Bureau) and gained the cooperation of the federal meteorological corps. Early in 1927, James Kimball, head of the Weather Bureau's New York office, began making transatlantic weather predictions based on a new system of reporting from ships at sea through RCA, the Radio Corporation of America.[16]

But all the preparations would be for naught if the *America* could not fly, and in late April Tony Fokker took his plane up for the first time in a "factory test" with Byrd, Bennett, and George Noville aboard.[17] The aircraft took off beautifully and at level flight performed superbly. As Fokker made his landing approach, however, a fatal flaw suddenly appeared. The plane was inherently nose-heavy, and the huge gasoline tank that took up the entire center of the aircraft prevented crewmen from moving aft to provide sufficient balance. Fokker managed to abort the first landing attempt, but he and his passengers had little time for troubleshooting, as there was not much fuel aboard. Fokker had to get the plane down. As he brought the *America* in again at sixty miles an hour, Byrd along with Noville clung to a stanchion just behind the pilot's seat. Bennett was sitting next to Fokker, whose body blocked the single exit. Byrd watched as the plane struck the ground. Fokker instantly leaped for the single exit. The plane pancaked down, then flipped over. There was a terrific booming crash, and Byrd felt the entire plane coming apart around him. Then he was struck a heavy blow as Noville, standing just behind, was thrown violently into his back. Byrd claimed that Noville's body snapped his arm; others claim it was his wrist. Noville did strike Byrd's head hard enough to send the Virginian into temporary unconsciousness. Byrd awoke moments later to hear Bennett cry out feebly, "Look out for fire." The three men found themselves in a tangle of wires, broken rods, frames, and seats, reminiscent of the wreckage surrounding poor, dead Air Commodore Maitland after the crash of the R-38 airship at Hull less than six years before. Helpless, Byrd thought of Fonck's men the year before, trapped like this and burned to death when their plane burst into flames. But as Noville frantically smashed a hole through the fuselage and dove out, writhing on the ground in agony from internal injuries, no fire appeared. Bennett had managed to toggle the engine cutoff switches. Byrd also burst out of the wreckage and struggled forward to where Bennett hung upside down. He waited with the badly injured man until help arrived, then claimed that he set his broken arm on the way to the hospital. Byrd never mentioned Fokker's behavior in his own account of the crash, but rescuers later said they came upon the two men not surprisingly screaming at each other.[18]

Although Bennett never fully recovered and died of pneumonia a year later, the *America* was not totally destroyed, as Byrd initially thought. Wanamaker remained a source of sturdy support, and Byrd and Whalen minimized the accident to the press and public. Still, Richard and his men and backers could not help but be sobered by the fact that the first two North Atlantic aircraft to crash—Fonck's and their own—were both trimotors. Levine's Bellanca, Lindbergh's Ryan aircraft, and Noel Davis's *American Legion* were all single-engine planes. Was a multiengine aircraft inherently unsafe?

Rebuilding the plane was Tony Fokker's responsibility, but Richard had to find a new pilot. He had tentatively planned a transatlantic flight in early May when the moon was full. With the *America* "scattered all over the factory floor, to be redesigned and completely rebuilt," Richard had only a few weeks to find a replacement for Bennett. Other eager fliers were now crowding into Long Island, straining at the leash like nervous thoroughbreds while they made successful test flights. Even before the Fokker's disaster, Clarence Chamberlain and Bert Acosta had taken Charles Levine's Bellanca aloft and set the world's endurance record. The plane was clearly capable of flying to Paris and well beyond.[19]

But tragedy continued to dog what an increasingly excitable press called "the Great Atlantic Derby." With Byrd's crash, Noel Davis and copilot Stanton Wooster seemed to have the inside track. On April 26, however, the two "splendid flyers and gallant officers" died when their plane, carrying two thousand pounds more than the engine had ever before lifted, went out of control on takeoff from Langley, Virginia, and crashed into a salt marsh, ramming the bank of a saltwater pool. Twelve days later, in the pearl-gray and rose dawn of a Paris morning, Nungesser and Coli climbed aboard their plane, *White Bird,* and started the engines. Everyone knew that an east-west flight over the Atlantic was much more risky, indeed foolhardy, given the prevailing west-to-east winds over the ocean and the weak engine power and fragile airframes of the aircraft of the day. But the two fliers were determined to make the effort. They announced that to save weight they would jettison their landing gear as soon as they reached the ocean, bringing their bird down in New York Harbor like a seaplane. Young Mrs. Coli kissed her husband with a smile, then burst into tears as he walked toward the aircraft. The *White Bird* trundled down the runway slowly, too slowly, it seemed to many, rose briefly, fell back to the ground, increased speed, and at the last possible moment struggled aloft and quickly disappeared. Some later claimed to have seen the aircraft pass over the Atlantic coast of Ireland some five hours later and head out to sea battling stiff headwinds. It was never seen again. Lloyds of London had already quoted odds of ten-to-one against any successful transatlantic flight that year.[20]

While the press speculated, Lindbergh arrived at last on Long Island with his single-engine monoplane, the *Spirit of St. Louis.* Nonetheless, Chamberlain and Acosta now held the inside track; they could, it was clear, take off at any time. But the two quickly fell out with the Bellanca's owner, Charles Levine, who wanted not only to be part of the crew but to pick it as well. The quarrel grew into a court injunction denying *Columbia* the right to take off. In the midst of this excitement,

Byrd's *America* emerged from the factory rebuilt, and Acosta, in a huff, accepted Byrd's invitation to fly the *America* to France. Wanamaker, however, insisted on more test flights.

Fokker soon lost patience. The *America* was ready to go; the flaws had been corrected. Why did not Byrd take off? Had he become afraid? The press began to wonder also. The following year, Byrd would write in justification that he was planning a scientific experiment in flight, not competing for the Orteig Prize by rushing pell-mell across the ocean. His and Fonck's trimotors had performed badly so far. A full testing of plane, equipment, fuel, and engine was the only way to determine "what our machine could do." To hasten this laboratory work for the sake of notoriety was to undermine the scientific character of his expedition. Lindbergh, Chamberlain, and the others were all using single-engine aircraft for which there were "ample data available." But no one knew the exact performance characteristics of a multiengine aircraft, how much it could lift, or its radius. "We had to find out."[21]

One person who did become openly fearful of the forthcoming flight was Acosta, who Balchen thought was "one of the top pilots in America if not in the whole world." On one of the Fokker's test flights over Long Island, Acosta froze and nearly crashed the aircraft because of disorientation when the plane entered bad weather. Balchen was aboard and grabbed the controls. As he did so Acosta readily admitted that although he might be a great stunt pilot, he was strictly a clear-weather aviator, incapable of flying comfortably or ably on instruments. According to Balchen, Bennett and Fokker became increasingly concerned about a three-man crew flying to Paris, and it was Fokker, not Byrd, who immediately after the Acosta incident invited Balchen to join the *America*'s flight crew as pilot. Four men would fly to Paris: Byrd, Balchen, Acosta, and Noville as radio operator.[22]

By mid-May, the New York to Paris derby had developed into the story of the year. Daily, thrill seekers in their roadsters, jalopies, and flivvers jammed the dirt roads of Long Island out to Roosevelt and nearby Curtis Fields. Either Byrd or Wanamaker or both offered Roosevelt Field to Lindbergh and Levine. Lindbergh, clearly on the verge of leaving, gratefully accepted.

At last, Byrd, Fokker, and Wanamaker agreed that the *America* was airworthy and planned a public rechristening party for Saturday afternoon, May 21. "Two thousand guests including the French Ambassador and his staff" were invited. A speakers' platform prominently crisscrossed with French and American flags was erected at one end of Roosevelt Field's big wooden hangar. On the evening of the nineteenth Balchen learned that although it continued to drizzle heavily along the East Coast, "Doc Kimball," the U.S. weatherman in New York, was predicting clearing over the Atlantic extending all the way to Paris. Was it not time to go? But at the *America*'s hangar all was quiet. Instead, Lindbergh suddenly appeared in the middle of the night, obviously eager to get aloft. Byrd came soon after, as did Chamberlain, Fonck, and Acosta. The crowd of thrill seekers, reduced by the rains, began to grow again as word got out that "the flying fool" might indeed be ready to make the great leap to Paris. Men and women going to work in the city stopped by the field, joined by revelers on their way home. Balchen strolled over to the growing crowd. "As if to prove that he could have made the journey that day," Balchen sarcastically remembered, "Byrd asked Lindbergh if he might borrow his own runway to make a trial flight in the *America*." For nearly two hours, in the predawn gloom from 5:30 to nearly 7:30 A.M., Byrd himself put the Fokker through its paces, flying in and out of fog and landing just as Lindbergh was about to embark. Ten minutes later Byrd was at the tiny door of the *Spirit of St. Louis* to be the last to shake Lindbergh's hand as "Lucky Lindy" got aboard. Bouncing down the runway, barely clearing the trees at the end, Lindbergh was off on his lone quest. Moments later, standing by the *America,* Byrd intoned, "God be with him" for the press pool. Chamberlain, standing nearby, gave Lindbergh a three-to-one chance of success.[23]

Thirty-six hours later, as the festivities at the Byrd hangar neared a close, the commander mounted the rostrum to give the final speech. Balchen watched Harry Bruno rush up and hand Byrd a message. The commander read it, stuffed his prepared remarks in a pocket, raised his hands for silence, and announced that Lindbergh had reached Paris. Soon after, Chamberlain and Levine resolved their feud and flew off over the ocean together. Levine announced the long-range Bellanca would fly as far as fuel held out. Forty-two hours later, the two landed southeast of Berlin, their flight made entirely by dead reckoning.

Now only the *America* remained of the original North Atlantic entrants, but Lindbergh's triumph gave Byrd pause. Telling the press that it would be unseemly to try his own Atlantic hop while Lindbergh was still garnering his laurels, Byrd privately wrote the same thing to Wanamaker and proposed a wholly new objective: "The flights of Lindbergh and Chamberlain-Levine will undoubtedly be made again and again until the day will perhaps come when this will be a regular commercial undertaking. . . . [T]he pioneer job in this particular line has been done. . . . [N]ew pioneering lies ahead." The Pacific Ocean was obviously the next arena for the further advancement "of the science of aviation," and Byrd proposed flying the *America* west for a California-to-Hawaii flight.[24]

Wanamaker would have none of it; Byrd must fly to Paris, so the polar hero kept testing and waiting until Balchen was ready to scream in frustration. At last, late on the night of June 28, Doc Kimball awoke Byrd in his New York hotel room to say that weather conditions along the planned route to Paris were about as good as they would be for the rest of the summer. Byrd promptly headed for Roosevelt Field, collected his men, received a quick weather briefing, saw that the U.S. mailbags were properly stowed in the wing compartment above the fuselage, and shepherded Balchen, Acosta, and Noville into the airplane. A crowd gathered, growing in size. While the sky steadily brightened under a rainy fifteen hundred–foot ceiling of clouds, Acosta ignited all three engines. Sitting at the top of its low rise, the plane was tethered by a rope, the intention being to hold it in place while Acosta got the engines to full power, then cut the line, sending the plane down along the runway at full power. But as the engines rose, the weight of the straining aircraft broke the rope, and the *America* started on its way sluggishly. With cool, perhaps desperate, courage, Acosta slammed the throttles wide open rather than abort the takeoff. Slowly, the Fokker accelerated as it gobbled up the rain-slick, muddy runway. Like Lindbergh, it appeared for a moment that Acosta would not make it. At one point he raised an arm to warn Balchen sitting next to him to hit the gasoline dump valve. But he never gave the command; committed to takeoff, Acosta kept the engines roaring, and at the last moment the *America* lunged skyward, barely cleared the trees, and was off.[25]

What happened on that wild forty-two-hour ride to Paris and back to the Normandy coast will never be precisely known. All that the participants could agree on was that Doc Kimball's weather forecast proved disastrously wrong. Flying up to Newfoundland through alternate murk and clear weather, the *America* turned eastward, soared out over the Atlantic, and into skies filled with fields of high storm clouds that the heavily overloaded Fokker simply could not climb or stay above with any regularity. Rain, darkness, and turbulence were the airmen's constant companions. An irresistible sense of unreality gripped the fliers. "It was utterly impossible to navigate," Byrd wrote several months later. "We could not tell which way the winds were blowing, which way we were drifting, or what sort of land or water was below us." For all they knew from vision and sense, they could have been flying in circles—or due west, or south. "Our chief safety lay in watching our instruments closely so that we should not be carried too closely to the land or sea that we might crash without warning," as several of the inexperienced transoceanic fliers were to do later that hectic summer. "Our lives hung on our altimeter."[26]

For hours after departing the Newfoundland coast Byrd and his pilots were unable to see anything as the Fokker plunged along. "5:30. Thick fog for nearly hour. Can hardly see wing tips. Can't navigate. 6:30 impossible to navigate. Wonder how long this will last. 7:30 Impossible to navigate. Situation terrific. 8:30 Impossible to navigate." Four hours later a beautiful dawn shone through the clouds, but then, an hour and a half later, "2:00 Clouds are right up to us. Nothing seen below for 10 hours. 3:30 Ice began to form. 5:00 Dense fog that can't climb out of. Terribly dangerous. No water yet." And a bit later, "Haven't seen water or land for 13 hours."27

Because they used their radio and compass accurately, the four reached the French coast more or less on schedule in rapidly improving weather. Balchen took the controls, and soon they spotted Brest. In his 1958 autobiography, the Norwegian asserted not only that had he done most of the transoceanic flying but also that Byrd had compromised the mission once they reached Normandy by insisting on heading north from the landfall at Brest to find the mouth of the Seine and follow it to Paris rather than simply using the railroad line from Brest as a direct marker to Le Bourget. Had his advice been taken, Balchen added, and the latter course pursued, the *America* could have slipped safely into Le Bourget. As it was, the fliers remained in the sky many minutes longer, striking more fog and heavy rains over western France that followed them down the Seine Valley to Paris. The compass apparently gave out about this time, and Balchen flew over the socked-in city before anyone realized it. "Blind men in the air."28 Byrd ordered Noville to send out an SOS, probably the first ever sent from an airplane. Having at last found—and lost—their destination (French aviators and officials later claimed that had the Americans tried to land at Le Bourget, they probably would have killed a large number of spectators), Byrd, Balchen, Acosta, and Noville headed back westward to Normandy, hoping to find clearer weather and a decent beach to land on. Balchen states that as pilot he unilaterally made this decision, but other accounts suggest it was by consent. Luck proved as elusive over Normandy as over Paris. Balchen saw that every bit of sand on the coast was adjacent to a fishing village and was thus a natural storage place for fishing boats. At last, with fuel finally running out, rain pelting down, and the pitch blackness of a late European night hemming them in, Balchen, with the sure hands of a born flier, settled the *America* into surf lit by flares dropped by Byrd. Within months, Byrd saluted Balchen in print for his "kind of soul, cool and courageous in emergency."29 In a fortunately receding tide, the men struggled ashore with the mailbags and a flag that Byrd wanted to give to French officials. Crossing a bit of sand that almost exactly seventeen years later would become one of the British D-day invasion beaches, they headed toward the small settlement of Ver-sur-Mer, a mile away to the south.

Byrd was at first bitterly disappointed in the mission, saying that he felt as if he ought to be kicked for not reaching Le Bourget Field, as Lindbergh had done. But the *America*'s engines had functioned perfectly. Indeed, every piece of equipment functioned perfectly until the compass gave out over France. The self-discipline required to maintain one's orientation, sanity, and efficiency hour after hour, tossed about in a cramped, often bouncing iron box wrapped in a world of constant wet, gray gauze, was stunning. Nonetheless, controversy rather than self-congratulation defined the mission.

No fewer than seven accounts of the flight exist. Four are by Byrd (*Skyward* [1928], a brief *National Geographic Magazine* article published three months after the flight, an even shorter recapitulation in a *Colliers* article appearing at the same time, and his "diary" notes found and published by Raimond Goerler in 1996—the only immediate account). Balchen wrote one (his autobiography, published thirty years after the event). Charles J. V. Murphy wrote another in the course of his brief but highly informative 1939 sketch of Byrd for *Life* magazine. Finally, Norman Vaughan, who accompanied Byrd and Balchen to Antarctica in 1928 and came to know both men well, provided yet another story line in 1990, based on what Balchen allegedly told him years before.[30]

In his fullest account, *Skyward,* Byrd concentrated on his own navigational problems and errors, due, he claimed, to strong winds that pushed the aircraft from an expected landfall on the Irish coast all the way south to Cape Finisterre, together with a compass malfunction that sent the aircraft in a wide circle around the French coast when Byrd thought the plane was over Paris. He emphasized that both Balchen and Acosta deserved enormous credit for superb flying under impossible conditions.

In his own lengthy account thirty years later, Balchen scarcely mentioned Byrd, except to note that when Noville's erroneous calculations indicated an excessive consumption of gasoline early in the mission, Byrd asked everyone if they should turn back. All agreed to press forward. Byrd's states that he and Acosta relieved Balchen of flying duties periodically, but Balchen argues that he did the bulk of the piloting over forty-two hours because Acosta was simply incapable of instrument flying. Balchen does not mention that Byrd took the controls for a time, though Byrd asserts that he did.

Murphy further complicates matters. Twelve years after the event, the journalist—who wrote about Byrd with remarkable balance—contended that Acosta did all of the flying for the first thirty-eight hours, then went to pieces from the strain, sending the aircraft in a circle back out to sea just as it reached the European coast.

> Whether it was Byrd himself or Bernt Balchen who knocked Acosta from the controls, and whether the weapon used was a flashlight or a wrench, no one but the four men in the *America* can say; and they have seldom discussed the episode. In his official log of the flight, Byrd, who has a deep respect and liking for Acosta, never mentioned it. As a Virginian, Byrd esteems loyalty above all other qualities and many of the men who have served him know that they can count on his help in any emergency "on the beach."

Vaughan's account is the most bizarre of all. He claims that "one day," Balchen told him what really happened on the flight. Acosta flew the first several hours over the ocean, then Noville relieved him and was forced to fly low, nearly clipping the waves because of poor visibility. "'We can't see anything but ocean,' one of them groaned, 'We need to turn back.' 'Let's have a drink,' the other said, 'I think it will steady our nerves.' 'Good idea,' the first one agreed." Byrd and Balchen were offered a drink. Neither accepted, so Noville and Acosta had one, and another, and another, continuing until both got drunk. Then the two begged Balchen and Byrd to turn back to escape the hellish prison of ocean and sky that offered no respite. But the commander and the chief pilot refused. They got the two drunks out of the cockpit and back into the fuselage while Balchen took the controls. Noville and Acosta kept drinking and getting more and more obstreperous until Byrd at last picked up a wrench and knocked both men out. "They lay on the floor of that plane for the rest of the trip."

The confusion and condemnatory contradictions found in accounts of the flight are unfortunate, for it was a magnificent feat. Balchen's self-serving recollections are particularly suspect. Thirty years later he remembered many exact moments of the flight—striking land features over North America, gazing up at dark and towering clouds over the Atlantic fitfully lit by rays and shafts of sunlight, brief glimpses of windswept water—not only in such detail but also in such a precise time frame as to provoke skepticism. Can anyone remember that much that exactly so long after the event? Had Balchen himself written an informal log from which he could later refresh his memory, his account might be more persuasive. But if the man flew as much and as intensely as he claimed, he would have had neither the time nor the energy to record in such detail. The times he cites as headings to various passages do not jibe with Byrd's own rough notes.

In 1928 Byrd called the flight to Paris and the French coast "the toughest air battle, I believe, that has ever taken place." Nine years later Murphy concurred: "The transatlantic flight makes even the Hollywood air epics seem pallid by contrast." Both were right. The battle up and down the Atlantic skies in a heavily overloaded aircraft from Newfoundland to the French coast through cloud and fog, persistent storms, and potentially fatal icing demanded the best from all four men. They gave it. No evidence supports Vaughan's story that Byrd knocked Acosta and Noville unconscious for the last critical hours of the flight and then told the European press that their injuries had been sustained in the crash. If Balchen indeed told such a tale as Vaughan insists, the Norwegian's reputation suffers further.

The public had followed the flight as avidly as it had Lindbergh's. Byrd shrewdly never surrendered Paris as his objective. Chamberlain and Levine might fly farther, but the small German village where they landed and even nearby Berlin were poor substitutes for the romantic boulevards and gay throngs of Paree. As the *America* swept up the North American coast toward Newfoundland and the Atlantic journey, the press handled the story as Byrd wished. According to a signed article by Noville released as the trimotor left the ground, the crew was "Gay over Order to Begin Cross-Sea Flight." Now the "Giant Plane" was "Winging over Sea on Scientific Hop: Radio Flashes Give Position." The Marconi wireless station in Lewiston, Maine, picked up Byrd's signal: "Dense fog covers all Newfoundland. Getting above it. Have had adverse winds. Impossible to navigate. Can hardly see wing tips. Running into another one now."

The following day in summertime Paris, which boasted several American overseas newspapers, the late-afternoon edition of the *New York Herald* (precursor of the current *International Herald Tribune*) announced worrisome news: "Byrd Plane Battles Fog for Twenty Hours." Aboard the storm-tossed aircraft, Noville assumed that Byrd's frequent messages were not being received anywhere, but they were. The *Herald* picked up a flash sent by Byrd during the middle hours of the flight; his colleagues were "doing [their] jobs like men." The *Herald* prepared a detailed flight log of the *America*'s progress based on Byrd's reports, which appeared in the following day's editions as the weather began to deteriorate over the French capital. For the moment, the *Paris Times* said, the "Fokker monoplane" was 250 miles from Ireland, and authorities at Le Bourget had been "informed." Readers were assured that although adverse winds had lowered the plane's speed, "Motors Work Perfectly as Record Weight Is Carried across Ocean." Byrd had persuaded the international press that his "Attempt Not Just 'Stunt' but for Science." He had permitted neither weather nor men to hurry preparations for the "Hop-off"; this was no "Sporting Chance"; the Virginian had never cared about the Orteig Prize. Rather, it was a serious endeavor that "Anticipate[d] Regular Air Crossings of Atlantic by Commercial Planes."[31]

Late on the evening of June 30 several hundred "anxious" Frenchmen gathered at Le Bourget, whiling away the time watching soldiers parade and listening to loudspeakers through the growing mist and dark. Then, as the storm appeared after midnight and the rain came down heavily over the city and airfield, news came in fast and grim and often wrong. "Byrd in Paris Region Vanishes in Rainstorm: Flashes Plane Is Lost and Compass Disabled after 40-Hour Air Battle; Report of Crash Nearby Proven False"; "Byrd Lost: Reports Are Vague after Fliers Reach French Coast; Miss America [*sic*] Loses Course in Passing over Channel; Heard above Brest, Rennes, Then South of Paris." Had Byrd and his three comrades "shared the fate of Nungesser and Coli? This was the question that thousands of late watchers in the United States and Europe were asking at 4 A.M. today when the steady reports from the Miss America had ended in silence and contradiction."[32]

At Ver-sur-Mer, the four men stumbled through the July 1 predawn murk into the sleeping village to find all the house gates locked. A boy on a bicycle came by, took one look at the rain-soaked and exhausted apparitions before him, and peddled frantically on. At last, the four found the lighthouse and, with Noville's execrable French, managed to convince the operator and his wife who they were. The floodgates of French hospitality opened wide, while back in New York the "aviation enthusiasts" at Roosevelt Field and "thousands" more in the city who had remained awake all night in front of bulletin boards went wild with "inexpressible joy." Like the waiting hundreds at Le Bourget, the New Yorkers had been on an emotional roller-coaster. Byrd had been lost, and then the late editions reported he had landed at Issy-les-Moulineaux. The report was false, and he was lost again. Finally came the news from the Normandy coast that the "haggard and weary" men had washed ashore from their crashed aircraft and were resting at Caen before proceeding on to Paris. On Saturday morning, July 2, the Parisian press headlined: "Byrd and Mates Coming Here Today . . . Trans-Atlantic Heroes Given Great Welcome in Normandy." An American reporter named Levit claimed that, rather than trudging the mile into town, Byrd had been found asleep on the beach by a fisherman. The story, if true, was soon buried under adulation.[33]

In Paris, the four men received almost as delirious an ovation as had Lindbergh scant weeks before. The French have always revered the gallant gesture, and Byrd and his men had certainly provided that. Wilbur Forrest, Paris correspondent of the *New York Herald Tribune,* gushed that whereas Lindbergh, "the unforgettable pioneer of all!" was taken straight into French hearts "because of his fresh, youthful modesty and above all because of his engaging smile," Byrd, "more mature, handsome, and the perfect type of officer and gentleman," had won France "as greatly as Lindbergh did." And there was his crew: "Rough-and-ready Noville, big, dashing Acosta, and that little hunk of Northern granite, Balchen" (who had been forced to quickly take out American citizenship in order to satisfy Wanamaker). All three subordinates

> have missed no occasion here to tell what a great fellow and valiant man their commander is. . . . Paris has embraced all four of them as the purest gold and has learned from them, as from Lindbergh, what America is. . . . Many believed that after Lindbergh left Paris there would never be another reception to an aviator here equaling his. But along came this erect figure in navy white with a charming personality seconded by the characters of his crew. . . . Frenchmen believe that they know America better than they have at any time in history.[34]

As the four fliers went from reception to luncheon to ceremony to banquet to train station, they were cheered on by throngs who rushed at the cars, denting fenders, breaking a windshield, and getting hurt in the process. They met France's greatest war hero, who later cabled Byrd that "Marshal Foch is by heart and spirit with the citizens of New York and their mayor in their welcome to you and your shipmates . . . for your wonderful flight between our two sister countries." Ferdinand Foch signed off with "affectionate regards." Byrd laid a wreath at the Tomb of the Unknown Soldier and along with his mates met Louis Blériot, the first man to cross the English Channel by air back in 1909. The four also paid the obligatory condolence call on Nungesser's widow. Perhaps the most piquant *salut* of all that Byrd received that unforgettable week was from "Boris, Parfumeur" and "Masseur Diplomé" who had been given the privilege of rubbing down the exhausted American hero on several occasions. Boris sent his distinguished customer home with four good-luck dog figurines for Byrd's children "as a token of deep gratitude." And Boris had a request. His other patrons were clamoring for the liniment that he had applied to the hero's skin. "I would be very proud to call my embrocation 'Com. Byrd' if you have no objection."[35]

While Byrd, Balchen, Noville, and Acosta basked in the adulation of the French, they received heartfelt cheers from their own people. Secretary of War Dwight F. Davis congratulated the commander for a flight that "again link[ed] Science and Aviation." Secretary of State Frank Kellogg echoed his colleague. "The accomplishment which you and your companions share marks another milestone in the progress of aviation science." Kellogg added a thought that would grow ever larger in the American public mind as Byrd's career continued to advance from success to success. The Virginian had made an "effective preparation" for the flight; for all his daring, he was a careful explorer, not a daredevil. The greatest compliment of all came out of the prairies of eastern South Dakota, where Calvin Coolidge was vacationing. "I have followed your distinguished and courageous career in aerial navigation with interest and admiration," the president informed the hero. The North Polar flight proved the effectiveness of the airplane in advancing human exploration, the president wrote, and the transatlantic hop had illuminated and dramatized the formidable conditions that had to be overcome before transoceanic travel could become "commercially practicable and safe." Responding on behalf of his "shipmates," Byrd thanked American officialdom and emphasized at every opportunity "the great work" that Balchen, Noville, and Acosta had accomplished "throughout the flight."[36]

Everything worked out perfectly for Richard Byrd. His transatlantic flight set in concrete a style of leadership, behavior, and response that he would display for the rest of his life. Balchen, Acosta, and Noville suppressed whatever unhappy impressions they may have had about the journey and about their commander, providing a backdrop of esteem that further enhanced his towering reputation.

Having won the hearts of all France and his own countrymen, Byrd kept the sensation mill grinding. "Next—the South Pole!" America's influential intellectual journal raved. "And after that," asked the *Literary Digest* rhetorically, "what new and perilous enterprise to tempt the vaulting spirit of our tireless Byrd of passage?" Byrd told eager listeners in and beyond the international press corps that he had "mapped out a rough program" of aviation exploration after Antarctica: "to soar across the Arabian Desert, the Brazilian jungle—in fact, wherever danger, mystery and virgin remoteness baffle the ken of civilization this Byrd aspires to fly." There were two Richard Byrds, the *Literary Digest* said, the adventurer and the scientist: the boy who at "twelve" "set out from Virginia by himself" to journey around the world and the man who had devised the bubble sextant, drift indicator, and other essential instruments that had "revolutionized aviation." In a long article for the *New York Times* just after his transatlantic hop Byrd promised to explore Antarctica far more thoroughly than he had the Arctic. He would not "merely" fly to the South Pole, "far from it. We shall stay there for months, perhaps for more than a year in an effort to procure more scientific information than now exists about that unknown continent." He would take at least ten or a dozen "'ologists—biologists, zoologists, ornithologists, meteorologists and so on," as well as experts to study the magnetic force fields around the South Pole.[37]

Byrd's heroics lent credence to his audacity, for the world in general interpreted the Atlantic flight as "a successful failure"—and more. To the *New York Times* the story was "the most stirring record of adventure in the air ever told." Thousands throughout the eastern United States had remained awake all night, straining through the static of their primitive radios to hear the latest bulletin, and the news from France "gave all a new thrill." The *New York Evening Post* reminded its readers that there had been, after all, "something of luck in Lindbergh's great flight." The *South Bend Tribune* concurred. The ordeal of man and machine under Byrd's leadership proved valuable "in dispelling the cocksureness stirred in some by the Lindbergh flight." The *San Francisco Chronicle* finished the thought: it is "upon such work as Byrd has done that the development of aviation depends." If routine transatlantic air travel was ever to become a reality, the *Springfield (Ill.) Republican* added, "it must be made possible to cross under just such conditions as the crew of the *America* experienced." The *Newark News* agreed: progress and wisdom in the air as elsewhere came as much by winning through against mistake and miscalculation. Yes, the *Cincinnati Post* added, Byrd had proved again in Lindbergh's wake that transatlantic flying was possible, but the Virginian and his men had "proved even more decisively how much more there is to be done in the field of aviation before ocean voyages by air become a part of everyday life."[38]

Regrettably, several score pilots chose to dwell on the glory rather than heed the lessons of the Byrd and Lindbergh achievements. Six weeks after the *America* crashed off the French coast, the first of seventeen more "Atlantic bids" got under way. The vast majority failed miserably. Four years later, Frederick Lewis Allen waxed caustic about the profits of aviation heroism:

> The formula was simple. You got an airplane, some financial backing, and a press agent, and made the first non-stop flight from one place to another place (there were still plenty of places that nobody had flown between). You arranged in advance to sell your personal story to a syndicate if you were successful. If necessary you could get a good deal of your equipment without paying for it, on condition that the purveyors of your oil or your flying suit . . . might say how useful you had found it. Having landed at your destination—and on the front pages—you promptly sold your book, your testimonials, your appearance in vaudeville, your appearance in the movies, or whatever else there was demand for.

Allen did not ignore the usefulness of a New York ticker-tape parade. The ultimate expression of ballyhoo, Grover Whalen's creation rested on "the great discovery that anybody riding up Broadway at noon with a motorcycle escort would find thousands of people gathered there in honor of luncheon."[39]

No one lamented the folly more than Richard Byrd. The following spring he wrote an article for the *Saturday Evening Post,* titled "Don't Let Them Die," which was an impassioned plea to save aviation and its limitless commercial promise from the fools who through their deadly rashness might strangle the profession in its infancy. Byrd remembered his heart sinking as he saw "plane after plane get ready and go" on a feckless attempt to fly the Atlantic "when we felt their chances of success were so pitiably slight. Yet whenever I undertook to point out the lack of planning and equipment in some of the other flyers I was met with: 'Well, you took big chances didn't you?'" When Byrd tried to warn one pilot about ice, the man replied innocently, "It isn't winter, is it?" The trouble that year was that "we were all lumped together as a sort of fraternity, of which the members were heroes in public and clowns in private; idols if they lived and quickly forgotten if they died." Confronted with that kind of wild-blue-yonder lunacy, Byrd's essential care and maturity shone through. There were decided limits to this hero business, and they were quickly reached when caution and prudence were cavalierly thrown to the winds.[40]

Ten days after their arrival in Paris, Byrd and his compatriots boarded the liner *Leviathan* for home. Perhaps in all the excitement and stress surrounding his flight and the whirlwind tour of northern France it was inevitable that Richard would wound some sensibilities through simple carelessness or neglect. Herbert

Adams Gibbons felt himself such a victim. Wanamaker's agent in France, Gibbons had knocked himself out to see that Byrd's hectic schedule had been completed and his every need catered to. Shortly after the two men returned to the States, Gibbons sat down in his New York hotel room and poured his heart out to Byrd in a self-described farewell letter. "Your speech last night at the big banquet, in which you mentioned everyone who had any connection with the America and the voyage except those who prepared the way and welcomed you to France, made things rather hard for me," Gibbons began. Friends and reporters instantly noticed the omission, as did many in Byrd's radio audience, "to judge from the calls that kept coming in here long after you left my room." A reporter had followed everything that Byrd and his mates had said in interviews and in signed written articles from their arrival in France to their return to New York. "Never once" did Byrd or his men mention the many services and kindnesses that Gibbons and his wife had provided. Gibbons was deeply wounded, but he and Wanamaker had decided the best thing to do was simply drop the entire matter. However, Gibbons wanted the ungrateful commander and his boys to know all that Gibbons and his wife had done for them. Wanamaker had sent Gibbons to France to provide emergency assistance and then to act as "host" and "professional publicity man or courier . . . solely . . . to give you the best break possible." Mr. and Mrs. Gibbons "had no thought other than your safety first, and when that strain was over, your comfort and your making everything possible for yourselves out of your glorious feat." Gibbons had advanced money to the four men and had paid the bill "for an expensive valise" for one of Byrd's crewmen. The cost of Byrd's radio broadcasts back to the States, amounting to nearly three hundred dollars, was "paid out of my personal checkbook because I had the impression when I was talking with you that you were rather hard up." As "her little personal farewell to the other three of your crew," Mrs. Gibbons had arranged for the dinner at Rouen en route to Cherbourg and the passage home, including an expensive wine list. Gibbons closed by reiterating his hurt and bewilderment at the cold treatment he and his wife had received from men for whom "I have a real affection. . . . [T]he slight last night struck pretty deep after you had been lauding Grover Whalen and many others."[41]

There is no indication that Byrd ever replied to Gibbons. But in *Skyward,* which appeared the following year, he mentioned that it had been his "good friend Herbert Adams Gibbons" who had rescued him and his mates from the Paris mob that had attacked his auto with such exuberance and thereafter "helped us through the balance of our exciting stay in France."[42]

Byrd seldom if ever again made the mistake of failing to acknowledge those who helped him. He could not afford to, for he was beginning to realize that his latest achievement had elevated him even beyond hero status. The obscure lieutenant

commander who a few short months before struggled to keep his rank now abruptly metamorphosed into a new kind of public figure—the celebrity—created by
the ballyhooers and the new mass-market radio technology of the twenties. He was
in the process of surrendering the freedom and frustrations of obscurity for the in-
toxication and bondage of fame.

Chapter 6

Celebrity

The publicity mills began grinding even before Byrd left Europe. "Congratulations to you and your crew on your splendid achievement," O. K. Bovard cabled. "If agreeable please reserve St. Louis newspaper rights to your South Pole expedition for Post Dispatch." "Triumph here outshines everything," one of Wanamaker's flacks telegraphed to Paris exuberantly. Aboard ship the cable office kept busy receiving a flood of messages from New York and all around the United States asking Byrd for articles about the flight, begging him to address this club or that organization, and informing him where and when he would speak. Everything was being orchestrated by Grover Whalen, acting on Wanamaker's orders. Finally, a weary Byrd cabled Whalen care of Wanamaker's Department Store in New York City: "Am referring all invitations to you. We don't want to do unnecessary things. Can you send us schedule of receptions." Fitzhugh Green, who had joined Putnam's publishing house, became his contact in the literary world. Byrd telegraphed his old navy comrade that he would try to write a story for *National Geographic Magazine* on the flight and asked Green to contact editor John LaGorce to "start collecting photos from newspapers. Lost ours in water." Byrd added that he would also write an article for *Colliers* but stated, "Don't wish to write about emotions. . . . Sorry."[1]

He returned in the late July heat to another tumultuous New York welcome. Once more he went up Broadway under a blizzard of paper amid a steady roar of cheers from thousands of throats. Then it was down to Washington for the whole crew and lunch at the White House and back to New York for a banquet at the Astor Hotel hosted by navy secretary Curtis Wilbur. The weeks of sustained adulation on both sides of the Atlantic had an impact on Byrd's self-esteem and ego that can only be imagined.

At the Astor dinner Wilbur awarded Distinguished Flying Crosses to Byrd and Noville, but not to Balchen or Acosta. This caused consternation in the audience, which erupted with several loud comments and even a few boos. Under prodding from Mayor Jimmy Walker, Wilbur explained that such decorations could be awarded only to members of the U.S. armed forces. Since Balchen was still a Norwegian naval officer (despite having taken out American citizenship) and Acosta had not flown for the military since the Great War, they were not eligible. Walker pursued the matter for several weeks, but Wilbur would not budge. It was an upsetting end to a controversial enterprise.

Returning to his hotel room, Bernt Balchen found Tony Fokker waiting. The manufacturer wanted to know how the flight had really gone. He was pleased to hear from Balchen that the plane performed brilliantly. According to Balchen's biographer, Fokker also confided that he was fed up with Byrd for having waited so long to cross and urged Balchen to come back to work for him if it did not conflict with firm commitments Balchen had made to Byrd. The Norwegian assured him there were none pressing. Balchen was beginning to move out of Byrd's orbit, the first of the explorer's "boys" to do so.[2]

Richard played on the interests of the press and public brilliantly. He understood, as Lindbergh never wanted to, that people were avid to see and touch and hear from their celebrities. He intuitively plugged into the ethos of the 1920s: its showmanship, its love of heroes, its veneration of the businessman and of boosterism. In a time and place when public life was defined by a fix that seemed eternally on and honor and fair dealing were always in question, plausible heroism demanded unblemished conduct.[3] Byrd's prickly lifelong obsession with the honesty and integrity of his endeavors—his outrage whenever his achievements were questioned—was grounded in a realization of the corrupt world in which he operated as essentially a public entertainer. The role of public hero fitted neatly with his own self-conception as a traditional southern gentleman of ironclad gallantry, integrity, and fidelity.

In his early forties now, he remained a handsome man, slim and trimmed down through daily exercise. To Merle McBain, a professional publicist who knew all three, Byrd was better looking than either Rudolph Valentino or John Barrymore: his features were "perfectly medallion, like those on a Roman coin," his hair "crisp and blond." His tenor voice was a bit high-pitched, yet not unpleasant. Above all, he had a contemporary air about him that F. Scott Fitzgerald, in another connection, captured perfectly. "If personality is an unbroken series of successful gestures, then there was something gorgeous about him, some heightened sensitivity to the

promises of life, as if he were related to one of those intricate machines that register earthquakes ten thousand miles away." Like Jay Gatsby, Richard Byrd projected "an extraordinary gift for hope, a romantic readiness such as I have never found
in any other person and which is not likely I shall ever find again."[4]

In the year and a half between his return from Paris and his departure for
Antarctica, four articles appeared over Byrd's signature in the *Saturday Evening
Post,* which in the pretelevision age was the country's premier medium of public
thought and communication, and one for *Colliers,* which was not far behind. He
also published the first of his four best-selling books, *Skyward,* which he and his
publisher characterized as partly a history of the conquest of the air and partly an
autobiography by Richard Byrd. It was often difficult to determine where the one
ended and the other began. The book was probably ghostwritten by Fitzhugh
Green, perhaps by Charles J. V. Murphy, an up-and-coming journalist. It contained some verbatim passages from his magazine articles, together with a thinly
veiled rationalization for busy men engaging ghostwriters to help them. Finally,
Byrd allowed Murphy to write a somewhat fuller biography, titled *Struggle,* with a
fulsome introduction by Edsel Ford.

A central theme throughout his writings was encapsulated in the title of his *Colliers* article—"It's Safe to Fly." He believed himself to be, and in many ways he
was, an aeronautical scientist. He and Edsel Ford shared the dream of mass travel
in the skies, although Ford's notion of a nation graduating from the automobile
to the small aircraft as a means of daily transportation was beyond realization for
many reasons. Murphy was not altogether wrong in defining Byrd—or in accepting Byrd's definition of himself—as a blend of mystic and scholar, "deeply concerned with the meanings of life" but in a scientific rather than poetic sense.[5]

If his early letters and memoranda are any indication, Byrd could write well on
his own. But a good ghostwriter could save him an enormous amount of time, and
time was something that Richard Byrd never had enough of in the course of an extraordinarily busy and eventful life. In between his Arctic expeditions, Richard got
good advice on how to employ ghostwriters most effectively from *New York Times*
journalist Howard Mingos, who was helping him with an article on his Greenland
adventures: "It has been my experience that you men of action often find it ex-
ceedingly difficult to write several thousand words quickly." Part of the problem
lay in the innate modesty and self-consciousness of the explorer, and some of it "is
that haunting fear that the reader is not going to be interested in what you have
to say. Please," Mingos begged, "forget all that." Byrd should learn to "write at
length, quickly and speedily, setting down without regard to grammatical construction, spelling, form and sequence everything you have to say or can think of."
He was then to send the material on to Mingos, who would polish and burnish it

for publication. "After two or three days I will have it ready for you to scan again, and all corrections can be made by you at that time."[6] Byrd opted to write in a personal vein about personal matters—the constant need and difficulty of raising money, life on the lecture circuit, how he picked his men for hazardous expeditions, and, as we have seen, the folly of dashing, thoughtless flight. Yet the personal was not the intimate; he kept his readers and listeners at arm's length.

The lecture tour was where Byrd chiefly made money and interacted with the public. He was wildly popular throughout the late twenties, as indicated by the three-page list drawn up by the Pond Lecture Bureau in August 1926, detailing all of the invitations he had been forced to turn down between June 12 and the end of the year. They totaled fifty-five in all. He allowed—indeed, encouraged—James Pond to book long tours, and he stuck with them. Writing from Kansas City in mid-February 1927, Byrd informed an Ohio editor that "I contracted to lecture because of a deficit in the [North Pole] expedition of about $32,000.00 and though that deficit is made up now, I must live up to my contract." Byrd seems not to have enjoyed lecturing particularly, but it was the basis of a steadily escalating level of comfort and security for himself and his family. At some point early in his stage career, Byrd drafted a "Memorandum of Instructions for Preparing for a Lecture by Admiral Byrd." It was "absolutely imperative" that his hosts provide him with "a good loud speaker [presumably he meant a microphone and speakers] and two good 35mm. moving picture machines that are not the so-called small portable ones." He felt so strongly about these props that, with suitable apologies, he mailed a copy of his memorandum to hosts at each stop on his forthcoming tour. "Please do not think I am being too aggressive. It is futile for me to lecture for you unless I do my best." Byrd added that he had had "some very disastrous times" as a result of bad film projectors, and he reminded hosts that his films of Greenland, Spitsbergen, and, later, Antarctica were extremely valuable, especially as he had no copies made.

He was also very shrewd about money. From the beginning, he warned hosts that he would make no public appearances prior to his lectures because, as he informed the Ohio editor, it had been the universal experience of both lecturers and lecture managers that whenever a celebrity did so, few if anyone attended the lecture. Byrd and Pond began by charging five hundred dollars a lecture, a princely sum in the twenties, and a rate that would constantly increase as the years passed, no matter the state of the economy. They usually demanded "large auditoriums," which were often full. "The lecture," a Pond representative informed an inquirer from the British Empire Club, "is illustrated with lantern photographs and motion pictures and it is necessary for the local organization to provide lantern and operator."[7]

Things did not always go well. "Don't worry about Minneapolis being a loss," Pond wrote his client, then in Chicago, in the middle of November 1926. Both men would have to take the bad with the good. Business was a bit slower than either would like, but they were making enough money to show a profit. However, Pond did ask Byrd to waive the minimum guarantee of five hundred dollars on his forthcoming swing through the western and Pacific Coast states because most towns and cities there did not have a sufficient financial base. "In order to make such a trip profitable, I ought to include every city that can pay a reasonable amount of money. For instance, we ought not to pass up towns like Grand Junction and Boulder, Colo. if they can pay $350 or $400 or thereabouts." Pond reminded his client that "I have to play quite a number of dates on a percentage, so if I am giving you the high guarantee on the small business which I must accept" in the western towns, "it will wipe out the big dates" in San Francisco and Los Angeles.[8]

Big dates and small, bad days and good, Byrd stuck it out. He wrote one correspondent that "for some weeks past I have been travelling all over the country and have scarcely had one single minute to myself. Practically every night has been spent on the train." Occasionally, he tired of the brutal schedule, but Pond kept him at it. Byrd was a moneymaker, and Pond had signed him to a tightly controlled contract. "I will be able to talk there only by permission of my lecture manager, Mr. James B. Pond of 25 West 43 Street, New York City, and the National Aeronautic Association, under whose auspices I am appearing in Akron," he somewhat primly informed the Ohio editor. "You say you would like to have some days around March 13th clear," Pond wrote at the end of November 1926. "I think you ought to know that I am planning to take you into the near south at that time. . . . In the latter part of the month I am taking you out to Ohio and that part of the country again." This was at a time when Byrd was negotiating intensively with Wanamaker and Fokker to get his transatlantic flight under way and also laying advance preparations for Antarctica, but Pond was remorseless.[9]

On January 3, 1927, Richard left New York on a 6:40 evening train, the Crescent Limited, bound for Charlotte, North Carolina. From then until February 5, his schedule was daunting: Charlotte to New Orleans to San Antonio to Austin, back to San Antonio, to El Paso, to Maricopa (Arizona), to Phoenix, to San Diego, to Los Angeles, Glendale, Long Beach, Pasadena, Santa Barbara, Bakersfield, San Francisco, Eugene (Oregon), Portland, and Tacoma (Washington). He lectured every night except January 29–30 and February 1; his world was essentially confined to trains, auditoriums, and hotel rooms. What little spare time he had was largely consumed in drafting articles, keeping in touch with his powerful friends in the business world, and answering the many queries Pond sent on to him about further lecture engagements. He told one correspondent in mid-January that "I do travel fast and far . . . and will not return to Boston until sometime in March." He returned east through Chicago and Ohio. The first day of March found him back in Virginia, where he thanked Lincoln Ellsworth for a recent telegram informing him that he had been given yet another award—the Polar Legion Insignia. "I am still on the wing making one night stands and still don't know whether I am coming or going. . . . I am so sorry that I have not been able to see more of you in the last several months, but believe me I have been on a terrible rush." Lecture schedules in the Byrd Papers for 1930 (immediately following his return from Antarctica) and later indicate that he followed equally hectic tour schedules down to the eve of World War II.[10]

Byrd's only trace of rebellion in his ironclad relationship with Pond involved his willingness to occasionally lecture outside the boundaries of the contract. David Lawrence, his contact with the press, had the same problem. The two had signed a tentative contract regarding exclusive news rights to the forthcoming Antarctic expedition as early as February 1926, though final agreement was not reached for another twenty-two months. During that time, Richard not only wrote magazine articles but also gave numerous "spot" interviews to what Lawrence interpreted as "unauthorized media outlets." Such interviews provided a little ready cash for the chronically strapped explorer, but Lawrence believed his client was cultivating the trees and not the forest. The media man had become an expert in crafting news stories that might extend for months or even several years. With his long planning and promotional campaigns and equally long sojourns on the ice, Byrd was a godsend. Lawrence was not pleased when his client kicked over the traces. By the spring of 1928, with the first Byrd Antarctic expedition only months from sailing, Lawrence cabled his client that "the small amount you are getting from syndicating articles does not compare with what we will get." Articles and stories released through Current News Features had yielded a hundred thousand dollars, and Lawrence "fully expect[ed] this to go up at least fifty thousand dollars more." But Richard would not be contained; he and Lawrence entered into a period of prolonged stress.[11]

Pond reacted similarly every time Byrd gave in to the requests of old friends to talk free of charge. More often, the explorer offered to lecture gratis when business or media giants who could help him along in his career came calling. Joseph Pulitzer wrote to congratulate Byrd on his recent Congressional Medal of Honor for flying to the North Pole and asked if the explorer could give a talk at Pulitzer's old school, St. Mark's, outside Boston. Richard replied that he was "pretty busy now getting ready for another expedition" (that is, the transatlantic flight), "but I still have some open dates and to show you my appreciation for the big things you have done for the progress of our country, I not only will not want to charge you for the lecture at St. Marks but will consider it a pleasure to do it for you and the boys there." Byrd evidently made this decision known to Fitzhugh Green, who passed the word on to Pond. The impresario immediately wrote Green a "dear Fitz" letter in which he let his unhappiness be known. Byrd should not be given "carte blanche" to make separate lecture arrangements "for many reasons." Pond had ceased booking his famous client because Richard wanted the time to prepare for his transatlantic flight. "If he has the time to do free lecturing, there is no reason why he can't do it for me professionally." And if Richard "goes around for himself without any reference to what I have been doing, we are going to get into some nasty complications." One had already arisen in connection with the explorer's recent lecture at Newburgh, New York, when he had let slip that he would be giving a free talk at the military academy in nearby West Point. "I have tried to be fair with Dick in all things," Pond concluded, "and if there are special places he wants to go, have him get in touch with me, and if it can be arranged, I will not object. There must be control, however."[12]

Out on the circuit once again, Richard wrote Pond a flattering letter ten days later. He thanked "your good self" for agreeing to suspend booking while he took time out to begin preparations for the Atlantic hop. The last dozen or so lectures had "all been bulls eyes, and enthusiasm on our trip seems to be just as keen" as ever. Three thousand people had greeted him on his arrival at Grand Rapids, Michigan, "and we had a large house." But Byrd also reminded his manager just how difficult life on the road could be. There was no movie machine or operator at the Union Club lecture in New York, and at Grand Rapids no movie machine had been installed when he arrived at the theater. When it was finally up and running, it broke down several times and "threw a very poor picture on the screen." He was not complaining, Byrd hastened to assure Pond. "I know you cannot help it. I am only giving it to you for your information."[13]

Despite the tensions, Richard stayed with Pond, who reengaged him following the transatlantic flight and sent him on at least one lengthy tour before preparations for the Antarctic expedition accelerated. But Byrd may well have indicated to friends and acquaintances his impatience with Pond, for at the end of February 1928, Louis Alber and Elbert Wickes, who modestly billed themselves as "Manager[s] of World Celebrities," contacted the explorer, using Isaiah Bowman of the American Geographical Society as a point of introduction. Alber informed or reminded Richard that the firm had managed the recent lecture tours of renowned naturalist and explorer Roy Chapman Andrews, Arctic veteran Vilhjalmur Stefansson, globe-trotter and commentator Lowell Thomas, Prince William of Sweden, and chief justice and former president William Howard Taft.

Richard at first seemed interested, thanking the men and expressing appreciation for their "going into this so thoroughly." But either Pond stroked his skittish client sufficiently or Alber and Wickes became too ardent in their pursuit, for by the autumn of 1928 Byrd was fending them off politely. His expedition was now taking all his time; he could not consider further lecturing until he returned from "the South Pole." The more Richard evaded, the more pressing Alber and Wickes became, until at last his polite evasions wearied and convinced them that they could not land him. The chase ceased.[14]

"You know I don't like this lecture business," Byrd confided to one correspondent in the autumn of 1927, "but expenses of expeditions are enormous and it is one of the ways we have of making both ends meet." In one of his articles for the *Saturday Evening Post* that appeared several months later, Byrd contradicted himself, decrying "lecturing" as "a vastly overrated way of raising money for exploration." In a surprisingly unvarnished account he proclaimed what some would consider a rather romantically nomadic and carefree way of life "the most trying work I know. With its one-night stands, receptions, banquets, irregular hours, disorderly regime, long periods of standing and general nervous strain, it can well break the strongest man in a few months." This was particularly the case if "the active explorer" was carrying a heavy load of correspondence in relation to his next venture.

The "order of the lecturer's day" was monotonous in its predictability. He stepped down from his Pullman car sometime during the morning to be met by the usual delegation of friendly citizens. A luncheon that was really a daylight banquet was accompanied by speeches of welcome, culminating usually in an address by "the distinguished visitor" himself. A virtually obligatory tour of the town or city followed, "a vague method of pseudo entertainment that may mean anything from a series of cocktail parties"—never mind that Prohibition was still the law of the land—"to a hundred-mile motor trip over the local parkways." Often there was an afternoon reception "engineered by the ladies," then the big banquet and lecture in the evening. The explorer was lucky "if he gets back to his hotel by midnight and is free to plunge into the pile of telegrams, letters and long-distance telephone calls awaiting him." Of course, a hotel room was available only if he was to stay in a general area, like Los Angeles or New York, for more than one night. Otherwise, it was back aboard the Pullman for still another three hundred–mile trip to the next city, where he must once again alight in the gray or brightness of an early morning, friendly and alert, to greet a new set of strangers.[15]

The thousands of people whom Richard met or encountered through lectures, letters, and donations ensnared him "in an altogether new set of complications" that the average citizen never had to confront. Each audience had its own personality, which often defied expectation. He faced nothing but friendly faces one night in conservative Boston and an inexplicably cold reaction in New Orleans. "I am a Southerner, too," he complained lamely. "One audience will have a little sense of humor, another a lot. Some are serious and detached, others are gay and responsive."[16]

Schoolchildren were among the most "irresistibly enthusiastic" people that Byrd encountered either in person or through the mails. He quickly perceived them as a valuable source of public support and even funding, and encouraged them to mail in their pennies to help send him south in 1928. They "joyfully" complied. Byrd formed an alliance with the National Education Association (NEA) that devoted a substantial portion of one journal issue to publishing letters sent by the nation's students to the explorer down at Little America. Upon his return from the ice, the NEA at its annual convention in Detroit presented Richard with a tribute from the country's schoolchildren. He responded handsomely. Among other things, he told the NEA, the tribute "betokens your realization, as educators, of the high value of exploring and investigating scientifically the vast, mysterious wastes of the Antarctic Continent."

He dramatized his interest in youth soon after returning from his transatlantic flight by announcing that he would take a Boy Scout with him on his "expedition to the South Pole." Byrd, an honorary Scout, "thrilled . . . the whole world of Scouting . . . and the general public was stimulated to the greatest interest." Chief Scout executive James E. West immediately contacted the nation's 650 local Scouting councils and the 28,400 Scout troops and invited them to designate such Scouts "as they felt could meet the difficult requirements" through local courts of honor or special committees. Although "literally thousands of ambitious boys made application to the Local Scout Councils," Byrd had shrewdly stipulated that a candidate must be between the ages of seventeen and twenty—that is, in his very last years of Scouting. Byrd, or West, then laid down other requirements and restrictions that further reduced the recruiting pool to those boys who had merit badges in the widest possible array of activities, including astronomy, radio, photography, seamanship, carpentry, journalism, plumbing, surveying, and, interestingly enough, taxidermy. The winner was a brawny, ambitious, wildly overachieving college student named Paul Siple, whose days as an Eagle Scout were about to end along with his minority.[17] Siple would prove to be a jewel. No other colleague except the ailing, soon-to-be-deceased Floyd Bennett ever got so close to Byrd or served him so loyally, faithfully, and efficiently. To meet Paul Siple (as the author did on one memorable occasion) was to meet a born leader, a big bear of a man totally dedicated to the work of understanding Antarctica and convinced that any man who had been there was the better for it.

Richard used his trips to make invaluable lifelong contacts across the country. One of the chief benefits of his tour to the West Coast in early 1927 was his meeting with Robert S. Breyer, a Los Angeles businessman. Breyer and Byrd quickly became fast friends, and much more. By the early thirties Breyer was Richard's de facto West Coast agent, arranging transportation, talks, luncheons, meetings, and anything else Byrd wished or needed whenever he was in California. Breyer was smitten with Byrd's venturous spirit; Byrd thought Breyer the epitome of American enterprise. The two shared a common conservative political outlook and talked and wrote—often daily in later years—about what they believed to be the decline, if not fall, of American virtues and values. The Breyer children visited the Byrd summer home in Maine on several occasions just before and after World War II. In 1947 Robert Jr. married Byrd's second daughter, Katherine. Harold Byrd, a distant relative with whom Richard became acquainted during one of his early lecture swings through Texas, soon served the same functions in the Dallas area and southwestern region that Breyer did in California.

In all the rush and bustle Byrd kept in touch with his old friend Franklin Roosevelt. The two were close enough that Byrd did not feel embarrassed in asking FDR about his progress in fighting polio ("How high can you stand in the water now?"), and the explorer was eager to accept a speaking engagement in Poughkeepsie, close by Hyde Park, that Eleanor had arranged. Byrd's letters to Roosevelt were full of a warmth that could only be genuine. "I have been thinking of you a lot lately," he wrote in the autumn of 1927 when he and FDR were both in New York City, "but have not looked you up because I have been working day and night trying to write a book [Skyward]." Three days later he wrote again: "I got your letter this morning and it is extraordinary that just yesterday I wrote you trying to find out how you are getting along. You are dead right, old fellow. We must have a reunion soon." Byrd supplemented warm notes with the inevitable gifts and mementos: a flag that he had carried across the Atlantic and, at Christmas 1927, the now-expected box of Winesap apples from the Byrd orchards in Winchester. Along with sincere concern for the health of an old comrade, Richard harbored a not-so-subtle interest in Roosevelt's political future. FDR was struggling back toward a full life. His successful run for the governorship of New York was about to commence, and he was already working hard in Warm Springs, Georgia, to create a national organization to help fellow polio victims. "I have been following you in the newspapers," Richard wrote on one occasion, "and that is a great thing you are doing down there." FDR would obviously continue to be a very valuable ally for an explorer uneasily perched on the top rung of his career ladder and chronically in search of money and influence.[18]

The frenetic schedule of travel, writing, and correspondence placed considerable strains on Richard's family life and his own constitution. He almost certainly would have avoided or substantially reduced the strenuous, ongoing tour schedules if he could have done so. That he did not do so was due to conditions beyond his control and ambitions beyond aviation or the polar regions. "The professional explorer is an anachronistic fragment," Charles J. V. Murphy wrote with brutal candor in 1939, "caught, like the kangaroo, behind the evolutionary eight-ball. A romanticist, he is suspect in a materialistic world. Doomed by a shrinking geography to comb comparatively worthless vacancies, he may even be ashamed to justify exploring for exploring's sake."[19] Byrd had reached Murphy's conclusion a decade earlier, and felt no embarrassment in telling the public about the usually melancholy fate of explorers. Most "went on the rocks a bankrupt" and died poor or worse.

In the fickle world of ballyhoo the cheering could stop at any moment. Titus Oates, who perished with Robert Scott, had observed on the eve of their fatal trek that if Amundsen got to the South Pole first, "we shall come home with our tails between our legs and no mistake. I must say we made far too much noise about ourselves, all that photographing, cheering, steaming through the fleet, etc."[20] Not only did the public hero cum celebrity have to remain on display, but he or she (Amelia Earhart comes immediately to mind) had to constantly deliver. Moreover, *what* the hero-celebrity was supposed to deliver was always a slippery matter of great concern. Soon after Byrd received the first of his three Broadway ticker-tape parades, New York held another lavish spectacle for Gertrude Ederle, the swimmer who conquered the English Channel. Lindbergh's delirious coronation was just around the corner. Ederle soon faded from public consciousness, and Lindbergh might well have also had he not soon become the center of attention and a chief victim of the kidnapping and murder of his infant son in 1932, which ignited another, quite despicable, spasm of ballyhoo. If Richard Byrd's appeal resembled that of Jay Gatsby, his chosen profession rendered him something of a Willie Loman—Arthur Miller's eternal salesman out there in the blue, armed only with a smile and a shoe shine. If the public stopped smiling back, it was death.

Polar expeditions, particularly those to the Arctic in quest of the North Pole or a Northwest Passage, had failed spectacularly and disastrously, leaving behind ruinous financial debt and leaders who were either dead or disgraced.[21] The incessant need for money inevitably turned early-twentieth-century explorers into hucksters and showmen who had to be consistently successful to sustain their access to wealth and support. Luck and whim played decisive roles, and an explorer fallen from grace in any way faced a bitter epilogue.

Robert Peary scrimped and pinched for more than a decade to finance a rush to the North Pole that whispered rumor, even eighty years ago, insisted had been a failure. A heartbroken Roald Amundsen wrote soon before departure to his mysterious death in the Arctic of his suffering when a brother, who had been managing his affairs, threw him into bankruptcy over a personal loan of twenty-five thousand dollars. The suddenly destitute hero expected the people of "this little Norwegian nation, to which I had more than once brought a new fame by reason of my exploration," to help him out or at least understand his plight. Time and again in the past they had done him honor; surely, they would not shun him in his moment of need. They did. "Almost to a man," they turned on Amundsen "with such unbelievable ferocity" that he was lucky to maintain a roof over his head. "Men who had flattered me now stooped to circulating the basest scandal. The Norwegian press attacked me. They could not take from me the glory of the Northwest Passage, nor the discovery [*sic*] of the south pole, but the same lips that had described my career as a glory of the Nation did not scruple to repeat lies of the most transparent fabrication, in a cruel effort to besmirch my private character and tarnish my name." Stories were put about that Amundsen and his brother had actually concocted a conspiracy to defraud creditors and that the explorer had sired the two Inuit girls he had brought to Norway, "an invention so fantastic as to be merely amusing in the light of my known whereabouts in regions remote from their birthplace for years before and after the possible dates of their origin."[22]

Byrd knew these stories and their implications. One miscalculation, one mistake, and he was finished in a world that in the end understood and celebrated nothing but get and gain. "Columbus died penniless," Byrd reminded readers in 1927. "Scott, perishing on the Antarctic ice, penned a message to the English nation pleading that his family be cared for ["For God's sake look after our people."]. Shackleton, dying in harness [on his way to Antarctica in 1922] left an estate too slight to keep his wife and child. Amundsen, Rasmussen, Wilkins, Stefansson, Capt. Bob Bartlett and a dozen others who have devoted their lives to the spread of human knowledge through the medium of exploration are all poor men." Heartfelt as his complaint may have been, it contained a strong if implicit dose of criticism of his contemporaries in the exploration profession. Their desperate plight was due, he suggested, to their inability to "administer the business affairs of [their] expedition[s] economically."[23]

In the end, making noise, getting attention, and winning public support were what the great game of exploration had become in an age of fallen or declining monarchies and rising democratic capitalism. And explorers could not quit. In a personal message to Richard congratulating him on his 1929 South Polar flight, President Hoover wrote, "We are glad of proof that the spirit of great adventure still lives."[24] Even before he left for the ice, Richard knew that he would have to prove that it did, over and over again.

Chapter 7

The Secret Land

Antarctica was a dream long before it became a reality. The coldest, windiest, and one of the highest places on earth is a dome of ice (from the coast one travels "up" not "down" to the South Pole) millions of square miles in dimension, pierced by a high mountain range shaped roughly like a question mark and cut through with enormous glaciers. This empty theater of fog and storm, of shrieking wind and stunning silence, of tranquil beauty and raging tempest lay for eons undiscovered at the bottom of the world, wrapped in "billowy white robes of snow weirdly luminous with amethysts and emeralds of ice." Each year as the austral summer reluctantly gave way to polar night, "iridescent ice halos around the sun and moon" faded, and "horizons painted with pastel shades of pink, gold, green, and blue" turned deepest black. "The last greeting from the departing sun" was always spectacular. "The refraction of it appeared as a large red elliptical glowing body to the north-west, changing gradually into a cornered square, while the departing day seemed to revel in a triumph of colors, growing more in splendour as the sun sank, when the colors grew more dainty; and surpassed themselves in beauty." In the inky blackness temperatures dropped to inconceivable levels, and great blizzards lashed and scoured the dark, frozen terrain. All the while enormous sheets of frozen liquid imperceptibly flowed down the dome, forming the mountain glaciers and vast Ross and Ronne-Filchner ice shelves that at the coastal edges—or barriers—periodically calved off into the surrounding seas upon which they sat like great white cakes. The vast tabular bergs that resulted slowly drifted northward, grinding their way through the pack ice and out onto the world ocean where they became the steadily shrinking sentinels of an unearthly land.[1]

The ancients, with their passion for logic, had posited great landmasses on each side and at top and bottom of a flat earth. Their dream of an "antarctica" first took substance one clear, cool October day two thousand years later when a tiny Spanish sailing fleet commanded by Ferdinand Magellan prepared to enter the narrow straits that linked the Atlantic with the Pacific at the tip of South America. Glancing southward, the great navigator saw a "tierra del fuego," a land of fire, and assumed it to be the continent of classical Greek lore.[2] He was wrong. Tierra del Fuego is a large island separated from the South American continent by that narrow body of water through which Magellan sailed and which now bears his name. But subsequent discoveries of New Zealand and other southern lands fired adventurous Western minds to seek out the real Antarctica and learn its dimensions, its nature, and its secrets.

Between 1772 and 1775 the greatest seafarer of his age, Captain James Cook, circumnavigated the globe, spending much of his time sailing just below the Antarctic Circle. He endured stormy seas, fog, and pack ice before returning to England to report that any continent that might exist lay far below the ice belt and was of little worth to mankind. But his word was belied by the artist and naturalists who sailed with him and brought back tales of rich sea life. Whalers and sealers soon rushed southward in search of profit.

In the latter decades of the eighteenth century and the early decades of the nineteenth, Antarctica stole slowly into the human consciousness. The thin belt of islands that surrounded it was found, explored, and, where possible, lightly settled with whaling stations and processing plants. In 1820, Nathaniel Palmer, an American with the Stonington whaling fleet, and Russian admiral Thadeus Bellingshausen were the first to see the continent itself as they sighted the long peninsular arm that Antarctica flings out several hundred miles toward South America. Thereafter, the explorers rushed in, stimulated at midcentury by advances in electromagnetism that ignited a race to find the South Magnetic Pole. Great sailors, including Ross, Biscoe, Ballenz, Durville, and Wilkes, were followed after 1870 by steamship captains led by the Englishman George Nares in *Challenger*. These men and their successors began the arduous task of breaking through the formidable ice pack to map tiny portions of the Antarctic coastline. But viewing an icy coast from shipboard did not satisfy restless minds determined to unlock the world's final frontiers in the heart of Africa, the mountains of Asia, and the polar regions. With the South Magnetic Pole still undetermined, the Sixth International Geographical Congress meeting in London in 1895 declared that Antarctica remained "the greatest piece of geographical exploration still to be undertaken."[3] That statement would echo down the years and decades, shaping the course of international exploration deep into the twentieth century. The architects of the 1957–1958

International Geophysical Year reconfirmed it and set in place the infrastructure for ongoing South Polar research that continues to this day.

H. J. Bull of Norway was the first to set foot on Antarctica, coming ashore at Cape Adare hard by the Ross Sea just weeks before the 1895 Geographical Congress convened. Three years later, Adrien de Gerlache de Gomery of Belgium brought the exploration ship *Belgica* too far into the pack ice and was forced to "winter in." The vessel drifted for nearly a year off the coast of what is now Marie Byrd Land. Aboard were two young men, the American doctor Frederick Cook and a Norwegian named Roald Amundsen, who would make polar exploration their lifework. The British Antarctic Expedition of 1898–1900 was the first to deliberately occupy the white continent for a prolonged period, taking up residence at Cape Adare.

In 1902, Erich von Drygalski of Germany became the first to see the Antarctic from the air, ascending for an hour or so fifteen hundred feet in a balloon above Wilkes Land. Frenchman Jean Charcot explored the peninsula with sufficient thoroughness between 1903 and 1910 to be honored with a variety of place-names. But as late as 1912, little of the interior continent had been seen. A decade before, British naval officer Robert Falcon Scott, who had also viewed Antarctica from a balloon, took a small sledging party southeastward from his camp at Hut Point on McMurdo Sound at the western end of the Ross Ice Shelf. Relying on insufficient animal power to haul heavy sledges, Scott hoped to reach the bottom of the earth, though he had no idea of either route or journey. Once his handful of animals gave out (the comparatively heavy ponies quickly exhausted themselves sinking into the polar snows, and he had no idea either how to equip or train to harness the few dogs he had brought or how to educate men to run them), Scott was forced to rely on human power. Hauling the sledges with three companions, Scott trudged determinedly 400 miles down the Ross Ice Shelf to discover part of the trans-Antarctic mountain range in what became Victoria Land. One of his subordinates, Ernest Shackleton, climbed a "red mountain" in search of a highway leading south to the bottom of the earth and discovered iron in the rock. But Scott wisely had had enough. The great blocks of dark, forbidding stone stood as a barrier to any further advance, and man-hauling two hundred–pound sledges, no matter how "manly," was literally a killing job. Stumbling back to Hut Point in hunger, pain, and exhaustion, Scott's party nearly perished. Shackleton collapsed and had to be carried in a man-hauled sledge, further taxing the waning strength of overstrained colleagues. Though Scott was happy with his discoveries and the knowledge that he and his men had reached 250 miles farther south than anyone else, Shackleton seems never to have overcome his own humiliation and thereafter set himself to prodigious feats of polar exploration.

In 1909, deflecting the angry reaction of his former leader who wanted Antarctica for his own, Shackleton mounted an expedition to reach the pole. Ignoring the lessons of 1902, he also relied on ponies to reach his objective and soon rediscovered that in Antarctica their chief value was as food once they died in harness—as they did quickly. Nonetheless, Shackleton, in whom resolution replaced common sense, plodded grimly with his companions down the Ross Ice Shelf to the mountains, where they struggled up what would be named the Beardmore Glacier to the previously unknown polar plateau, hauling sledges all the way. With waning powers, the little party trudged to within 97 miles of its objective before turning back, utterly exhausted. In a rare burst of sagacity, Shackleton wrote his wife that he would rather be a live donkey than a dead lion. Not only did he penetrate hundreds of miles farther south than any other human, but his chief physicist and geologist, Douglas Mawson, reached the holy grail of international science, the South Magnetic Pole, which Professor T. Edgeworth David had earlier plotted from his own Antarctic researches at latitude 72°25′S and longitude 155°16′E. On his return, Mawson nearly perished, falling into a deep glacier.

The year 1912 proved the apex of South Polar disaster. Mawson, in charge of Australia's first Antarctic expedition, lost his two companions and all dogs and supplies to a crevasse and disease in a trek along the perpetually windy shores of Adélie Land. Starving and alone, the geologist walked the last 100 miles back to base across a polar waste ravaged by blizzards and strewn with crevasse fields. It was as epic a polar journey as any ever undertaken.[4] Nearly twenty years later Mawson returned to the Antarctic for another winter-over.

Meanwhile, plucky, foolish Scott again sought the pole, now in a desperate race with the phlegmatic Norwegian Roald Amundsen and his expert party of skiers and dog-team drivers. Disastrously victualed, and still relying on ponies and manpower rather than dogs, Scott and four companions at last reached their goal after weeks of freezing, backbreaking labor only to find Amundsen's cairn there to mock them. Heartbroken, the four Englishmen stumbled back toward home, once more manhandling heavy sledges across the polar plateau. Pausing at the top of the Beardmore Glacier, the men wasted precious time collecting rock samples, which they dutifully hauled down the great icefall and across the blizzard-lashed Ross Ice Shelf. Gasping, groaning with fatigue, their energies steadily drained and their pace slackened. At one point, Titus Oates, the weakest of them, roused himself from his sleeping bag and staggered out into the windy, snowy gloom. Scott, Bowers, and Wilson pushed blindly on for a few days, stolidly hauling their heavy sledges before being forced by an endless blizzard into the tent that would become their shroud.

Unlike Scott, Amundsen had trained as a polar explorer in the Far North. He believed in taking neither chances nor shortcuts. Nor was he much interested in scientific collection. The pole was his sole objective, and to attain it he would rely on tried-and-true methods of polar exploration, including the use—and if need be ruthless sacrifice—of dog power. As a consequence, the Norwegian and his men reached the pole a full month earlier than Scott and his party, consuming two weeks less in the journey than the Englishmen. Amundsen and his people tarried four days at the bottom of the earth, taking sun sights to confirm their location, walking a wide circuit around the pole to solidify their claims, and erecting the cairn whose distant appearance on the bleak polar ice scape so disheartened the approaching Britons weeks later. Amundsen and his companions then raced safely back the 800 miles to the Bay of Whales, collecting a few granite samples along the way. Reaching base, the Norwegians discovered that several of the eleven surviving dogs had actually gained weight.[5]

The last great expedition of the heroic age began in 1914 when Shackleton left England with nearly thirty men for the Weddell Sea. The Great War had just been declared, but all confidently believed it would be over by Christmas, so Shackleton and his party left Britain in good heart and with clear conscience. Their ship, the wooden-hulled *Endeavour,* would bring the expedition to the icy shore of the Weddell Sea. There Shackleton and five other fellows in six dog teams would leave the ship to trek up to the pole, then across the plateau to the top of the Beardmore Glacier, where a relief party coming up from the Ross Sea would have stashed the first of a series of food caches. These supplies would see Shackleton and his men down the glacier and across the Ross Ice Shelf to a base camp established by the relief party at McMurdo Sound, from which all would ship homeward. What in fact happened became legend. The vicious pack ice of the Weddell Sea gripped and crushed *Endeavour* before it ever reached the continent. After months adrift in the pack, the men set out in lifeboats for the nearest land, deserted Elephant Island. Arriving there with his exhausted and half-starving party, Shackleton and four others soon set out for the nearest inhabited island, South Georgia, 800 miles across the freezing, hurricane-lashed waters of the Antarctic Ocean. Forced by wind, current, and their own weariness to land on the empty side of the island, Shackleton and two others trekked across its mountainous spine in thirty-six hours to Stromness whaling station. After the briefest rest, they sailed around South Georgia to pick up their stranded companions, then after frustrating weeks got through to Elephant Island and rescued the main group. Shackleton had not lost a man (though two died in the Ross Sea relief expedition); it was a goal that all who came after him would strive to match.

From Bull and de Gerlache de Gomery's time onward, glory, science, exploration, and commerce coexisted in uneasy tandem. Every major venture after 1900 was mortgaged to the hilt, its leader begging wealthy benefactors for funds and goods, promising to write a postexpedition book or two and several articles, pre-selling any and all photographs and (after about 1905) motion pictures taken of the enterprise. Almost all expeditions, none larger than forty men, contained some mixture of geologists, glaciologists, oceanographers, meteorologists, and biologists who discovered that the white continent, far from being a geophysical anomaly, had surprising affinities with the rest of the earth. Scott's scientists were the first to suggest that the geology of the great trans-Antarctic mountain range harmo-nized with that of the present-day Southern Hemisphere, thus adding weight to the growing notion of a single ancient earthly continent (later called Gondwana-land) that had broken apart over eons due to continental drift. Sea life proved surprisingly rich and varied. Scientists began taking crude measurements of tem-perature, atmospheric pressure, and weather patterns. Through it all Antarctica displayed its splendors and its wrath indiscriminately.

On good days, beset in gray-white pack ice stretching from horizon to horizon under pearl skies, "there is the feeling of being alone in a vast, white sepulcher. . . . The only sounds are the winds whistling softly in the rigging" and "the lost voices of men beating against emptiness." The silence is "tremendous," Stuart Paine not-ed in 1933. "You can almost hear a person whisper back in the poop [deck]. Even the dogs seem to be silent tonight. It is as if all ye who enter here must keep silent." Then the winds shift, the mist lifts, and the clouds tear away, revealing a clear sky under a faintly glowing yellow sun. "Flashes of light come back from uplifted ice, bergs caught in the pack glow with color reflected from a sky that is like a mag-nificent batik of green and crimson and yellow and blue." "I have never seen such purity of color," Paine wrote. "It is the color virginity would have if it had a col-or." Beneath the spreading light and faint warmth the explorer "bask[s] . . . as when a boy you sat in the sun against the barn in the first warm days of spring." Ashore on such days, Antarctica was an "enchanted continent in the sky, like a pale sleeping princess." Out on the trail alone except for the dogs and a few compan-ions, one could hear a heart beat in the frigid stillness. The vast, clear, pure silence elevated those who experienced it far above the petty quarrels of nations and men.[6]

But the white continent also possessed a unique capacity for treachery. Even postmodern man with his fluorescent lights, instant international radio commu-nications, helicopters, multiengine airplanes, television, and video cassette record-ers often finds the place "a frightening, exhausting, often unreal utopia."[7] For those who first encountered its rigors a century and more ago, Antarctica was pure hell. "In all the world there is no desolation more complete than the polar night. It is a return to the Ice Age—no warmth, no life, no movement." The crew of de Ger-

lache de Gomery's *Belgica,* beset by ice in the Weddell Sea in 1898, fell into melancholy as the winter darkness descended on them. "Since entering the pack," Fred
Cook wrote, "our spirits have not improved." Appetites slowly diminished to the
point that "now we are tired of everything. We despise all articles which come out
of tin." A "monotonous discontent" soon arose that consumed and defined everyone. "This part of the life of polar explorers is usually suppressed in the narratives,"
but "it is natural that this should be so, for when men are compelled to see one
another's faces, encounter the few good and the many bad traits of character for
weeks, months, and years, without any outer influence to direct the mind, they are
apt to remember only the rough edges which rub up against their own bumps of
discontent. If we could only get away from each other for a few hours at a time,"
Cook moaned, "we might learn to see a new side and take a fresh interest in our
comrades, but this is not possible." Soon melancholy degenerated into depression,
which became despair, and finally madness. At the end of June, weeks into the polar night, with weeks left to go, Cook wrote that "there has been nothing to mark
time or disturb the gloom of the long black monotony." In time the men could
not concentrate and could barely eat. One perished of a heart attack brought on
by unreasoning terror; another became convinced that his mates were about to kill
him, and slept in a tight fetal position jammed in a far corner of the tiny vessel.
Still another succumbed to a hysteria so profound that he became temporarily deaf
and dumb. Shackleton, confronting the same conditions, pulled his men through
their inhuman ordeal by the sheer force of personality.[8]

Deliberate rather than accidental stranding in Antarctica in no way relieved the
dreadful stress on men's minds and emotions. C. E. Borchgrevink, a member of
the British Antarctic Expedition of 1898–1900, noted that even a few weeks into
the polar night, "we were getting sick of one another's company; we knew each
line in each other's faces. Each one knew what the other had to say." Realizing the
pressures they were under, each of the ten men deliberately "kept cheerful." But
as the weeks passed, "the darkness and the silence weighed heavily on one's mind.
The silence roared in our ears; it was centuries of heaped-up solitude." The "same-
ness" of each cold, dark night "attacks the minds of men like a sneaking evil spirit." Novelty became priceless but quickly palled. Reading helped, as did playing
chess and cards. Someone had brought a music box ashore from the long-departed
ship, "but we soon came to know the *repertoire* so well that we preferred for a time
to have it silent." (On the author's icebreaker, alternatively bashing through and
beset by the Weddell Sea ice pack early in 1957, the projectionist began running
the thirty-odd movies aboard backward as a novelty.) Perhaps most disturbing to
those who sought real knowledge of the Antarctic, "the monotony of the life

seemed to create amongst the members a most sensitive professional jealousy." Rather than sharing the hard-won fruits of their work on the cold, perpetually belligerent ice, individual scientists "guarded passionately against intrusion."9

With its whimsical tests and cruelties Antarctica seemed almost alive. Journalist Russell Owen remembered how out on the open sea, shrieking winds could blow so hard as to push a steamship under full power backward, its wake creaming past its bow, its hull coated with several hundred tons of ice. Ashore, blizzards blinded men listening desperately for the sounds of breakers on icy cliffs or looking frantically for shelter.10 One year the pack ice that girdles the continent even during the austral summer might prove benign, graciously loosening and scattering under the play of wind and water to open wide passageways to the usually clear austral summer seas that at once lap and flow under the edges of the great Ross and Ronne-Filchner ice shelves. The next year, or the next week, the same tides and breezes would jam the pack together in huge pressure ridges or tightly compacted and interlocking floes, blocking passage of or crushing to death even the stoutest ship. Then indeed might the religious recall the Book of Job:

> Out of whose womb came the ice?
> And the hoary frost of Heaven, who hath gendered it?
> The waters are hid as with a stone
> And the face of the deep is frozen.

As Shackleton's *Endeavour* lay in the Antarctic wastes nearly twenty years after the *Belgica,* one normally cheerful crew member wrote bitterly of the "delirium, induced by gazing too long at this damned infernal stationary pack that seems . . . doomed to drift to and fro till the Crack of Doom splits and shivers it N., S., E., & W. into a thousand million fragments—and the smaller the better. No animal life observed—no land—no nothing!!!" Several weeks later as the ship broke up around him, Shackleton wrote in his diary, "The attack of the ice reached its climax at 4 P.M. . . . At 5 P.M. I ordered all hands on the ice. The twisting, grinding floes were working their will at last on the ship. . . . I cannot describe the impression of ruthless destruction that was forced upon me. The floes with the force of millions of tons of moving ice behind them were simply annihilating the ship."11 Richard Byrd, looking back over nearly two decades of active South Polar exploration, saw Antarctica as an "ugly" place, "just as cruel and sinister as its beauty is harmonious."12

Explorers preached that only the fighters of this world could win glory there, and glory became for some a goal in itself. Britons condemned Amundsen for having no other object in 1911–1912 than a successful "dash for the pole" and quick return to civilization, whereas Scott "had a scientific mission in view, and his researches would naturally be carried out in a thorough and organized manner." But it was Amundsen who survived, whereas Scott so diversified his field operations in order to accommodate scientific inquiry that he and his men perished. The thirty-five pounds of rock samples from the Beardmore Glacier that they would not abandon fatally sapped their strength just eleven miles from One Ton Depot.[13]

Scott's stricken colleagues erected a nine-foot-high memorial cross. At its base they inscribed a line from Tennyson's *Ulysses:* "To Strive, To Seek, To Find And Not To Yield." In 1947 Byrd wrote that the men on his most recent expedition found a corked copper cylinder at Scott's wrecked hut at Cape Evans. It contained a single sheet of ruled school theme paper on which had been written a short, eloquent memorial to three other Englishmen who had perished in the brutal Antarctic environment and was followed by a few lines from Browning, a favorite of Scott, Shackleton, and, obviously, Byrd himself:

> I was ever a fighter so—one fight more,
> The best and the last.
> I would hate that death bandaged my eyes,
> and forebore,
> And bade me creep past

Of the great triumvirate of early Antarctic heroes, only Amundsen escaped its rigors. Scott died in harness, and Shackleton began his fourth expedition south in 1921 on the edge of death. He sensed that his terrible ordeal in the Weddell Sea seven years before had fatally stressed and drained his body and guessed that he was dying. Perhaps he would perish before ever reaching the Antarctic. Yet he was determined to press on. Shortly after noon on January 2, 1922, his ship, *Quest,* passed its first berg. "The old familiar sight" of blue caverns etched in the ice, shining with a "sky-glow snatched from heaven itself," together with green ice spurs showing beneath the water, moved him to tears. "Ah me!" he wrote. "The years that have gone since in the pride of young manhood I first went forth to fight! I grow old and tired but must always lead on!" Three days later, perhaps the fiercest polar fighter of all died peacefully in his bunk.[14]

Antarctica's brutal clime never ceased to govern human activity. The introduction of progressively advanced machinery modified but never altered this fact. The expense of getting and living there has always been prodigious. In the 1980s the National Science Foundation's U.S. Antarctic Research Program expended four of every five dollars spent on a research project just getting the scientists to and from their polar sites.[15] In the age before large, powerful aircraft permitted permanent occupation, the continent could be approached only during a short period of the year and had to be abandoned in an equally tight window of time lest an expedition be forced inadvertently to winter over again with dwindling, perhaps inadequate, supplies of food and fuel. The pack is impenetrable from mid-March to around the middle of November. Even the prime time of entry between Christmas and mid-February can, in bad years, pose great difficulty for ice-capable ships of either wooden or steel hulls. Once through the pack, expeditions are confronted by mighty ice barriers in both the Ross and the Weddell Seas that rise grandly out of the surrounding waters as much as one hundred feet. Breaching these barriers to attain the vast shelves of ice beyond is always difficult.

Since the pole is most readily accessible from the east side of the Ross Ice Shelf, Roald Amundsen and later Richard Byrd were attracted to the Bay of Whales, a narrow twenty-mile notch in the barrier that no longer exists. Many years, the bay remained choked with ice floes until late in the summer. Jammed against the great barrier ice cliff by the action of wind and water, the massive floes were compressed into great pressure ridges. Transporting thousands of tons of supplies across the floes and up the barrier ice cliff to a base site on the shelf by dog team and, later, gas-powered tractor invariably involved long days and weeks of backbreaking work. Sleds overturned in the uneven terrain; crevasses suddenly appeared or widened; carefully cut ice roads heaved and buckled as floes and pressure ridges rose and fell on the bay tide. Occasionally, a portion of the barrier ice cliff broke off under the strain of the heaving waters beneath, carrying a moored ship with it or flinging the vessel into a potentially fatal roll, spilling men and equipment into the frigid waters. The men were usually saved; the equipment was always lost. No one could ever be sure that a sizable portion of the shelf beyond the barrier might itself not "calve" (that is, break) off, to become an immense tabular berg, carrying with it a base or scientific station as it drifted out through the pack ice and into the clear waters beyond.

As base construction began, temperatures often varied dramatically, further straining men's bodies and leaving them gasping. Raging blizzards that stung the eye and froze the flesh suddenly leaped from nowhere and could last for days. Out beyond the encampments lay huge crevasse fields and pressure ridges created by the endlessly moving ice sheet. Several fields roughly fifty to seventy miles south and southeast of the Bay of Whales were an especially "frightful mess . . . a frozen whirlpool. Even under the softening influence of vertical vision and altitude," achieved through aviation, "the horrible nature of the surface was apparent. . . . [T]he shearing movement of the Barrier had wrought destruction of millions of tons of frozen ice and snow. Had the guns of half a dozen armies played upon the scene, they could not have worked as much destruction."[16] Trail parties that could not get around this dreadful terrain went through it slowly, roped together. Even open plains of ice and snow contained crevasses often cunningly hidden by snow bridges that might take the weight of one man or a single sledge team, only to collapse when the next unsuspecting animal or human tried to cross.

Blizzards and natural hazards completely foreign to newcomers in Antarctica did not exhaust the list of challenges that the white continent threw at careless or inexperienced explorers. Dramatic temperature variations turned slick snow to mush or to the consistency of soft sand, transforming sledging or man-hauling into killing ordeals. Mirages or the magnetic anomaly of the South Polar region readily lured men into blunder. Incessant, often inhuman, cold that could reach seventy or even eighty degrees below zero Fahrenheit, abetted by storms with winds sometimes reaching two hundred miles per hour, turned liquids into sludge. Kerosene poured like oil, and oil poured like molasses. Machines wore out quickly when lubricants congealed and engine metal became brittle; electrical systems failed as their rubber protection disintegrated. Antifreeze froze. When a man breathed the winter South Polar air his breath turned to ice before him, and as the frozen moisture drifted back across his face its crystals broke against his ears with the sound of hundreds of tiny tinkling bells. The uncertain light of the "white sepulcher" that so enchanted seamen caught in the pack ice often created a whiteout effect in which the horizon disappeared and the entire world turned into a cottony nothingness. Pilots frequently became nauseous and disoriented as they groped for a ground that had disappeared, while on the ground a man could not tell whether a dark spot ahead was a distant mountain or a matchbook cover on the snow fifty feet away. And the four months of total winter darkness when the only light was artificially generated by fire or weak currents of electricity continued to try the nerves and moral fiber of those already struggling to live harmoniously with one another in tight, freezing quarters.

Men could not help but be intimidated as well as enthralled by this vast, empty place in which screaming sound and the most silent stillness mixed capriciously. There were so many ways that Antarctica could kill you: stumbling about in a sudden blizzard, trying to rescue comrades or equipment or to find shelter and warmth; falling down a deep, icy crevasse; perishing of simple exhaustion or the wrong diet. A moment's carelessness in front of an airplane propeller or miscalculating a distance or a weight caused terrible injuries. And always there was the dreaded fear of fire that not only killed in its own right but was also capable of wiping out in mere moments every vestige of protection and support that an expedition needed to sustain itself.

If there was one man who came to know Antarctica as well as—perhaps even better than—Richard Byrd, it was his acolyte Paul Siple, whose pronouncements may be taken as a final, authoritative comment on the white continent. "Both a hateful and fascinating place," Antarctica "was cruel and heartless, yet its cold beauty, ominous silence, and weird phenomena" were haunting. "Once you've been here," he told a reporter in 1956, "there's something a little special about you—everyone feels it and so do you. I think this may be what draws people down here, and even though they hate it, they feel it's worth buying with a little time and a little discomfort. It will last them a lifetime."[17]

This was the land Richard Byrd sought to master by the advanced technologies of his time, aircraft and tracked vehicles. Existence was struggle. Life was not something you eased into and eased through. A man became his own hero through repeated searches for transcendent challenges, and in 1928 Antarctica was the greatest challenge of all.

Richard and his mother, Eleanor Bolling Byrd, at the U.S. Naval Academy, ca. 1911.
Courtesy Byrd Polar Research Center Archives, The Ohio State University, Columbus.

Young Marie Ames Byrd.
Courtesy Byrd Polar
Research Center Archives,
The Ohio State University,
Columbus.

Right to left: Tom, Dick, and Harry Byrd, ca. 1928. Courtesy Byrd Polar Research Center Archives, The Ohio State University, Columbus.

Bernt Balchen *(left)* and Floyd Bennett with the Ford trimotor, 1927. Courtesy Byrd Polar Research Center Archives, The Ohio State University, Columbus.

Lincoln Ellsworth. Courtesy Byrd Polar Research Center Archives, The Ohio State University, Columbus.

Etah Beach, Greenland, 1925. Courtesy Byrd Polar Research Center Archives, The Ohio State University, Columbus.

Byrd and his companions received by the city of Paris at the Hotel de Ville, 1927.
Courtesy Byrd Polar Research Center Archives, The Ohio State University, Columbus.

Commander Dick Byrd in Hollywood with Raymond Griffith (the "Silk Hat Comedian") and his leading lady, Ann Sheridan, at Paramount Studios, ca. 1928. Courtesy Byrd Polar Research Center Archives, The Ohio State University, Columbus.

198

First Byrd Antarctic Expedition. *City of New York* alongside the barrier near
Little America I. Courtesy Byrd Polar Research Center Archives, The Ohio State
University, Columbus.

Off-loading supplies onto the barrier for transport to Little America. Courtesy Byrd
Polar Research Center Archives, The Ohio State University, Columbus.

Radio tunnel at Little America I. Courtesy Byrd Polar Research Center Archives, The Ohio State University, Columbus.

Byrd poses with Gould's Geological Party after its return to Little America I. *Left to right:* Mike Thorne, Richard Byrd, Laurence Gould, Jack O'Brien, Norman Vaughan, and Eddie Goodale. Courtesy Byrd Polar Research Center Archives, The Ohio State University, Columbus.

A typical day during the early stages of the first and second Byrd Antarctic expeditions. Dog team and empty sled amid the pressure ridges on the trail from the barrier to the Little America I and II camps. Courtesy Byrd Polar Research Center Archives, The Ohio State University, Columbus.

Second Byrd Antarctic Expedition. Little America II looking southeast, January 1934. Courtesy Amory H. "Bud" Waite Papers, Byrd Polar Research Center Archives, The Ohio State University, Columbus.

Barquentine *Bear* departing the barrier during the second expedition. Courtesy Byrd
Polar Research Center Archives, The Ohio State University, Columbus.

Citroën tractors, Second Byrd Antarctic Expedition. Courtesy Byrd
Polar Research Center Archives, The Ohio State University, Columbus.

Members of the Second Byrd Antarctic Expedition gather in the mess hall at Little America II for their weekly movie at austral Mid-Winter Night, 1934. Courtesy Byrd Polar Research Center Archives, The Ohio State University, Columbus.

Alan Innes Taylor with husky pups. Courtesy Byrd Polar Research Center Archives, The Ohio State University, Columbus.

Charles J. V. Murphy in the broadcast room at Little America II. Courtesy Byrd Polar Research Center Archives, The Ohio State University, Columbus.

Ed Cox and Ivor Tingloff *(sitting)* taking their ease in the cramped carpenter shop at Little America II. Tingloff died suddenly in Australia soon after leaving the ice. Courtesy Byrd Polar Research Center Archives, The Ohio State University, Columbus.

The official caption from the expedition reads in part: "South of Little America. Rear Admiral Richard E. Byrd, the leader of the expedition, scans a book as he eats a meal he just finished cooking during his lonely four-and-a-half-months vigil 123 miles south of Little America." In fact, the picture may well have been posed during the final stages of Byrd's recovery at Advance Base just before returning to Little America. Courtesy Byrd Polar Research Center Archives, The Ohio State University, Columbus.

Tom Poulter and comrades depart on their first attempt to rescue Byrd. Courtesy Byrd Polar Research Center Archives, The Ohio State University, Columbus.

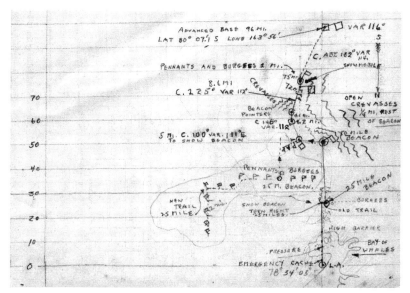

Amory "Bud" Waite's hand-drawn map of the rescue route to Advance Base.
Courtesy Amory H. "Bud" Waite Papers, Byrd Polar Research Center
Archives, The Ohio State University, Columbus.

Dick Byrd coming up the hatch of the hut at Advance Base. Courtesy Byrd
Polar Research Center Archives, The Ohio State University, Columbus.

Curtiss "Condor" over the Rockefeller Mountains. Courtesy Byrd Polar Research Center Archives, The Ohio State University, Columbus.

Byrd greets members of the second expedition's eastern party led by Paul Siple *(sunglasses and hands on hips)* upon their return from the field. Courtesy Byrd Polar Research Center Archives, The Ohio State University, Columbus.

Admiral Byrd coming down the gangplank from *Jacob Ruppert* at the Washington Navy Yard, 1935. Courtesy Byrd Polar Research Center Archives, The Ohio State University, Columbus.

At the 1939 World's Fair. Courtesy Byrd Polar Research Center Archives, The Ohio State University, Columbus.

Leaving the aircraft carrier *Philippine Sea* at Panama during Operation Highjump, 1947.
Courtesy Byrd Polar Research Center Archives, The Ohio State University, Columbus.

212

Admiral of the Antarctic, 1940s. Courtesy Byrd Polar Research Center Archives, The
Ohio State University, Columbus.

Working for the Reeves Brothers. Courtesy Byrd Polar Research Center Archives, The Ohio State University, Columbus.

Returning from the ice, 1956. Marie greets her husband. Courtesy Byrd Polar Research Center Archives, The Ohio State University, Columbus.

Chapter 8

Southward

In December 1927 Richard wrote an article for the journal *World's Work,* amplifying his earlier comments to the *New York Times* about the South Polar region. "Man cannot claim mastery of the globe until he conquers the Antarctic continent. It is the last great challenge. . . . [D]own there lies the greatest adventure left in exploring and aviation." He cast his eye on the future as well as the present, determined to remove from schoolchildren's maps for all time "that great white blank space at the bottom of the world." He reiterated that "the primary object of the expedition is scientific." With his first expedition, Richard established a pattern of exploration that he would continue for the next thirty years. Constructing the first of five "Little America" bases at the Bay of Whales, he explored the "Pacific Quadrant," the area stretching from the western edge of the Ross Ice Shelf up to the peninsula by ship, by plane, and on foot as vigorously as ice, sea, and atmospheric conditions permitted, while sending trekking parties more than four hundred miles down the broad shelf to the Queen Maud Mountains. He and his men eventually mapped vast swaths of territory from the air: glaciers, ice shelves, and mountains never before seen. At the same time they studied Antarctica's fauna, its natural resources, its weather, its geological structure. "My old and tried shipmate, Floyd Bennett, who flew with me over the North Pole will be second in command," Byrd wrote that December, but others, both American ("red blooded volunteers in whom the love of adventure and experience is strong") and Norwegian "Vikings" who "know and like the cold," would be going also. Many expedition members, such as George Noville, Pete Demas, Tom Mulroy (engineering officer aboard *Chantier*), and Bernt Balchen, were veterans of the MacMillan

Greenland expedition, the North Polar flight support group, or both. As always, safety was the prime consideration, and for that reason alone, "when we leave the States next summer it is our aim to have one of the most thoroughly planned expeditions that has ever gone into the Polar regions."[1]

Byrd's decision to form and lead such a large and chancy enterprise represented a major advance in his career. While he had briefly commanded a hundred or so men during the world war, he had been responsible for no more than a dozen as subordinates on the Greenland expedition and about fifty at Spitsbergen. Both Arctic ventures had been of short duration, and his wartime stint as head of an aviation unit had been within the context of a well-defined command structure. Now he was to lead two ships and some eighty men (forty-two of whom would winter over on the ice), together with the most advanced and elaborate machinery obtainable, for eighteen months in the most hostile and inaccessible region on earth through the grueling ordeal of a polar night, which he had never experienced. Despite industrial man's growing ability to create more or less secure secondary environments for himself in the world's harshest climes, Antarctica remained the supreme test of human character, of a man's moral code and fiber, of his conduct in society. Byrd would command alone, responsible or accountable to no one, but also bereft of support beyond that which he could immediately muster once on the ice through the force or persuasiveness of his own personality. Some thought the explorer was setting himself up for utter disaster. The *New York Times* wrote every man's obituary before the expedition left Norfolk.[2]

Byrd had obviously been reading everything he could about Antarctica, including the records of previous expeditions, and he rightly concluded that after 150 years of fitful human presence, "there has been little exploration down there." Half the coast at most had been very roughly mapped, whereas Scott, Shackleton, and Amundsen had developed two narrow lines of march to the pole from either end of the Ross Ice Shelf. Any real understanding of this vast expanse awaited an imaginative marriage of aviation and photography.

Antarctica's potential for generating and shaping the global weather system intrigued Byrd even as he pondered other pressing scientific questions. Were the Ross and Weddell Seas in fact connected under the massive ice sheet (which would suggest that Antarctica was in fact two or perhaps even more large islands)? Did the mountains at the foot of the Ross Ice Shelf directly connect in some way with the Andean range in adjacent South America? What more could be learned about magnetism near the geographic South Pole? How well and to what effect could man's advanced technologies operate in the Antarctic, not only aircraft and photography but also radio and gasoline-powered tracked vehicles? Scott and Shackleton had found coal and iron. Might Antarctica possess deposits of these and similar resources sufficient to fuel human material progress for centuries?[3]

There was so much to learn and to do in the twelve months between Byrd's announcement and his hoped-for departure in the summer of 1928. What kind of clothing would be needed, what kind of shelter? How much and what kind of food? What were the best ways of packing cargo to ensure that materials and supplies came off the ship when needed on the ice? What methods should be used to prevent or minimize devastating damage by fire? Where could dogs and dog-team drivers be obtained, and what about sleds? What kind of airplane or airplanes would best be suited for Antarctic exploration? What were the best kinds of petroleum, oil, and lubricants to use to maintain them at peak operating efficiency? How could the planes be safely stored so as to resist wintry blasts and be ready for a season of exploration? Where could one find the best equipment, the best maps, the best ships to take everyone and everything south? How many austral-summer round-trips between New Zealand and the ice were needed to establish and sustain the base camp, and how much fuel would be required in order to keep it sufficiently supplied? The answers required energy, diligence, and time while searching the world for suitable equipment.

Byrd mastered it all. In three short years the man had hit his stride. Preparing and carrying out dangerous Arctic and transatlantic flights plus two ticker-tape parades down Broadway in little more than twelve months will do that to a person. The frustrated but diffident subordinate who had suffered no little humiliation at the hands of MacMillan and McDonald just thirty months earlier now planned and operated his first Antarctic expedition like a supremely confident general of armies. He learned and applied the arts of administration, logistics, Antarctic geography, technology, and polar operations to the many problems at hand. Byrd knew that his Antarctic enterprise "will probably be seven times longer" than his North Pole venture "and will cost over three times as much." He was determined that the expedition be done right, that all advance elements of the industrial age be of top-notch quality and that the food, shelter, and other support materials be of similar value. In addition to the weeks and months spent raising money on the lecture circuit, he had to somehow find hours and days to pander to and plead with the nation's wealthy and self-absorbed business elite in ways that he himself admitted bordered on the very edge of shame. "The last dollar that I can beg is raised," he noted just days before his departure for the ice. "There is . . . an immense debt—I owe more money than I used to think existed."[4]

But Byrd exaggerated his plight, for the public was enthralled and came to him, often daily, with offers and proposals. The reason was not hard to discover.

Amundsen, Scott, and Shackleton had seemingly exhausted the dramatic appeal of the South Polar wastes. Another Antarctic expedition, no matter how large, varied, and dedicated to the advancement of knowledge, could not be expected to excite public interest unless it contained something more, something new, some compelling ingredient. A daring flight to the bottom of the earth by the same man who had just been the first to fly to the top was the answer. Byrd's media impresario, David Lawrence, first grasped the dramatic possibilities of a South Polar flight. According to Professor Robert N. Matouzzi, Lawrence first suggested it "off the record" sometime in late 1926 or early 1927. Indeed he might have. In opting for a single straight-shot North Polar flight back in 1926, the young commander had broken his contractual obligation to Lawrence to do two daring Arctic flights, one to the pole, the other a round-trip flight between Spitsbergen and the northwest tip of Greenland. Byrd was under a moral if not legal obligation to Lawrence to do more polar flying, and a trip to the bottom of the earth would fulfill that obligation admirably. "Though Byrd apparently felt pressured into performing what was essentially a media stunt" (as if the Lindbergh and North Polar flights were something else!), and at one point contemplated breaking his contract with Lawrence, he never stated his reservations publicly, and Lawrence's insistence paid off handsomely as soon as the Byrd Antarctic expedition was announced.[5]

Richard got cash and free equipment; he thanked the benefactors, unstintingly praising and hawking their products. Having named the plane that took him to—or within a few miles of—the North Pole after Edsel Ford's daughter, Josephine, Byrd "perceiv[ed] the human desire for even a small measure of immortality," and "tapped an entirely new stratum of polar patrons by offering to name ships, airplanes, and still-to-be discovered mountains and harbors after them." Rodman Wanamaker died a few months before the expedition's departure, but "Charles V. Bob, a mining impresario, gave $108,000. Rockefeller and Ford bestowed large amounts." The doggedly faithful Lawrence got the *New York Times* to pay $150,000 for news rights, including assignment of reporter Russell Owen to the expedition. A talented journalist jealous of the freedom of the press, Owen had covered Byrd's North Polar flight. The National Geographic Society once again bought exclusive magazine rights. Metro-Goldwyn-Mayer's newsreel division ("The World's Spotlight") waged a spirited battle with the opposition at Paramount studios for exclusive permission to film "a great dramatic picture" that would at once dramatize and advance the cause of commercial aviation in the United States. Paramount ultimately won out, and Byrd happily accommodated two of its most talented cameramen while pocketing a substantial check. He also signed a book contract with Putnam and a $50,000 minimum contract with Pond. Charles Evans Hughes, the Supreme Court justice, created a foundation through which further moneys could be channeled. Charles Murphy later estimated that total monetary contributions came to roughly $800,000 to $900,000, whereas the food, clothing, fuel, and other materials supplied gratis by an army of manufacturers could be valued at around $600,000. Moreover, "the Biltmore Hotel in New York was so delighted to have such a glamorous celebrity as guest of the house that it also put up his entire retinue free of charge" in a large suite.[6]

As a result of Byrd's first southern trip, the map of Antarctica would be graced by such names as the Edsel Ford Ranges and the Rockefeller Mountains (actually a set of low hills, few more than a thousand feet high). By the time he returned from his third trip to Antarctica in 1940, Byrd had bestowed the names of friends and benefactors across the width and breadth of the Pacific Quadrant: Sulzberger Bay (for the editor of the *New York Times*), the Horlick Mountains (for the malted-milk king), the Ruppert and Walgreen Coasts (for a beer baron and owner of the New York Yankees and the drugstore magnate), Roosevelt Island, and the Watson Escarpment (for Thomas Watson Sr., founder of International Business Machines). Mount Siple joined the Rockefeller Mountains and plateau and the Edsel Ford Ranges. Jacob Ruppert also gave Byrd $25,000 for his second expedition in exchange for having the lead ship given his name. Byrd painted *Blue Blades* on the side of his ancient Fokker to honor the Gillette Safety Razor Company's contribution. In his enthusiasm Byrd wanted to name Antarctic landmarks for everyone who had ever been nice to him. At one point he proposed naming a mountain after the manager of a Los Angeles hotel. His benefactors, of course, obtained significant economic benefits and enormous psychic fulfillment in associating themselves with this singular figure who either immortalized them in ice and rock or plastered their products' names on the nation's billboards and magazine pages.[7] Byrd kept meticulous records and refunded unspent funds. No backer ever accused him of cheating or profiteering.[8]

The Scott and Shackleton expeditions provided cautionary lessons to any polar explorer. Rashness and overreach had to be avoided—the human factor was supreme. The worth of subsequent expeditions would surely be calculated in large part on whether everyone survived. What kind of leader would Byrd be, and what kind of men would he choose to go with him on his great adventure? Characteristically, the explorer chose to mull the matter over in public. In the spring and autumn of 1928, he published several articles about manning his expedition. He clearly meant them as a kind of report to the public, which ranged from school-children to business executives who even then were pitching in, often at the last moment, to get him on his way. The articles were as notable for what they did not say as for what they did.[9] They also suggested the awful void that the Great War had left at the center of the Western soul.

An essential, blindly optimistic, element had gone out of Western life in the brief decade and a half since Scott and Amundsen had raced each other to the South Pole. The gentlemen who in two hundred years had built the European empires in India, Africa, and the Far East while exploring the last unknown spots in the Dark Continent and at the poles had been secure in their place. Good breeding and upbringing, they believed, created men of perseverance, fearlessness, honor, and patriotism. "Rome, in particular, was a shining example of a civilising empire whose achievements rested on the exploits of its natural leaders." Adherence to classic standards of virtue was leavened by profound religiosity. "Church memorials broadcast the virtues which distinguished a gentleman. In Bath abbey, the epitaph of Colonel Alexander Champion of the Bengal army announces that 'his Zeal, Courage, and Success were ever tempered by humanity' and that in his dealings with the world he was plain, open and unaffected.'" The gentleman of the Western world was expected to be "more than just a gallant dandy with an overdeveloped sense of his own superiority and personal honour. 'True courage blended with humanity' were the essence of the gentleman."[10]

Titus Oates went to his death in a stinging Antarctic blizzard in 1912 perfectly exemplifying these virtues. If he could sacrifice himself and the blizzard abated, his companions could share the remaining food and reach One Ton Depot without having to worry about him. "I am just going outside," he said quietly as he struggled out of his sleeping bag. "I might be some time." Out in the raging snow, the temperature was forty-three below as he trudged off into the polar void, never to be found. The next morning, with freezing figures, Scott painfully scrawled, "We have not seen him since . . . the act of a brave man and an English gentleman."[11]

Byrd quoted the incident approvingly. But the four-year slaughter on the western front that intervened between Oates's time and his had shot nineteenth-century idealism to pieces, as hundreds of thousands of gentlemen, steeped in true courage blended with humility, went over the top and marched to patriotic deaths for what their grieving survivors concluded was of little or no purpose. Byrd and the others who sought to pick up the fallen standard of the heroic life would have to develop new norms and values to carry on.

He claimed that nearly twenty thousand people volunteered for the 1928–1930 expedition (known in popular shorthand as BAE I). The pressures of inclusion or exclusion were intense. How would it be possible to determine in advance how an individual would function in an emergency? What traits should be looked for to mark the brave man? How old should he be? How big? How strong? Would he be *too* daring? When did courage shade imperceptibly into impetuous folly? "What about the married man? The smoker? The brilliant bookworm, gifted also with good muscles? The star athlete?" How far did family history count in medical and psychological terms? "And how do you get at it?" Byrd's article on picking his men was long on anecdote, short on assertion. But at last he began to zero in. Confronting danger was his first criterion. "I don't mean the sudden emotional situation men faced who went over the top in France. There the individual was sustained by a combination of mass emotion and excitement. What I have in mind is protracted peril, in which there is no stimulant of rapid and vital events." He was looking for men to whom "a peculiar indifference to continual danger" imparted an ongoing efficiency—men, in short, who would not crack under the tedious day-to-day strain of living in an Antarctic winter camp with several dozen others.[12]

Byrd also wanted men of imagination who possessed a "keen appreciation of what is going on." The phlegmatic individual might be temperamentally better in theory to face danger, but if he lacked imagination he was more likely to let things slide and to lack the initiative "of the more nervous yet imaginative man." He believed that youth was superior to age in providing not only unlimited strength but also, again, that precious element of ardor and commitment without which any polar expedition could fail. Finally, he had done his Antarctic homework well. The first man to perish on Scott's expedition had been Petty Officer Evans, who also happened to be the largest man. There was a reason for that. "The heavy man wears out footgear, chafes in heavy garments, and strains his heart if he must keep at a task for a long time." Lawrence of Arabia had been dismissed as "that runt" until "he showed he could outlast and outwork men twice his weight and stature" whose health records were equally good. All things being equal, Byrd concluded, "I incline to the slight, wiry man," like himself.[13]

Other critical traits were flexibility and the ability to learn. Byrd clearly harbored healthy apprehensions about flying across the remote, empty Antarctic. The plane might well be forced down hundreds of miles from base with men hurt and other men forced to take the controls and get the survivors out if at all possible. Byrd also worried about "hidden weaknesses." Drunkenness was reasonably easy to detect, but not so "those small but insidious foxes that tear at the vitals of a man without his being conscious of their presence: Overeating, under eating, too many stimulants, too much sugar, unbalanced diet, and so on." These vices might have been discarded months or even years before a man came up for expedition physical, but they might nonetheless have weakened him in ways that would not be apparent until he was exposed for prolonged periods to the rigors of the Antarctic ice.[14]

It was only when he at last came to describing the "antidotes" to human frailty and folly that Byrd touched on those elements of character and morality so central to the Victorian and Edwardian temperament. Even then, Byrd's essential lack of interest in formal religion inclined him to place it behind hobbies and just ahead of "habitual optimism and enthusiasm" in his list of private virtues. "I need not argue the value of religious faith as an asset," Byrd wrote with rather clinical dispassion. "The annals of exploration are full of heroism and sacrifice premised on a belief in God's will."[15]

Not until the eve of his departure, the expedition presumably filled with his kind of men, did Byrd at last settle on a common denominator that he insisted all effective polar explorers must share: a crusading spirit. The men who would sail on the expedition (about half as ship's crew only) were of various ages, sizes, weights, and shapes. They included blonds, brunettes, and four redheads, men who could play an instrument with skill and those who could not carry a tune, and did not care to. Byrd needed cooks, bakers, sailors, engineers, a doctor, dogsled drivers, pilots, mechanics, many "'ologists," and one Boy Scout. Forty-two in all would spend large parts of two austral summers and one long polar night on the ice. To a man, Byrd wrote with perhaps pardonable hyperbole, each of these "crusaders" "loves battle and is willing to drop everything and fight for the good of his kind, the rescue of the chalice of knowledge."

Antarctica constituted a battleground without destruction, where injury or death came as a consequence of mischance or miscalculation, and weapons included only peaceful machines such as airplanes and a crude motor tractor. But the warrior's temperament defined all. Tom McGuinness, first officer on the old wooden sailing vessel *City of New York* that would take Byrd and his men directly to the ice, summed up the crusader mentality perfectly. When Byrd asked him why he wanted to go to Antarctica, this veteran of the Great War in East Africa and the Royal Navy before that replied, "'If there'd 'a' been a dacent war goin' on, I wouldn't!" Byrd hired him on the spot.[16]

Yet Byrd was perhaps guilty of more than a bit of romantic self-deception. Pilot Dean Smith perceived his fellow crusaders somewhat differently. Once on the Antarctic ice sheet they proved to be "a heterogeneous group . . . each quite different from the other. If there was a single factor common to us all, one that might account for our being together on the expedition, it would be a desire for personal recognition and, whether we admitted it or not, a hunger for acclaim." Smith volunteered for another reason: money. When Byrd first interviewed him in New York City in the summer of 1928, Smith was "making about $1000 a month" flying professionally. Byrd, of course, was seeking unpaid volunteers, but that proved impossible where pilots were concerned. Smith was a man he wanted, so the two negotiated a $500-per-month arrangement. "My salary, accumulating in a New York bank with few withdrawals during my absence, would add up to a sizable sum by the end of the two year expedition." Smith proved a bit dense, since he failed to realize that his arrangement was about twice what Byrd had already agreed to pay the two other talented pilots, Bernt Balchen and Harold June. Smith found his flying companions rather testy companions until they, too, managed to get Byrd to raise their pay.[17]

One subject upon which the leader had little to say was leadership. "Few of us have not the germs of some weakness or other. . . . What the leader is after is the man whose potential defects are well buried in the first place and who is strong enough physically and nervously to remove the likelihood of those defects ever coming into view." Needless to say, the leader himself would have to possess such traits in abundance. "Probably the great leaders of modern exploration have, on the average, been the best examples of balanced temperament," Byrd continued. Amundsen, Peary, Scott, and Shackleton possessed rather laconic, even grim, personalities. "Yet their writings, their friends, their works, all testify to the heights of fancy their ardor could carry them to on occasion. It was this combination of dreamer and fighter that largely set each apart from his fellows."[18] Byrd, who had long viewed himself in the same light, was about to find out whether in the crucible of Antarctica he could measure up to these giants of yesterday.

Each expedition "nominee" signed a contract in which he pledged to "honestly and faithfully serve Commander Byrd" or his designated leader of the expedition "for the duration thereof." Byrd or the designated leader could terminate the agreement at any time, and it became null and void when the expedition broke up upon returning to the States. The expedition member agreed to assume all risks of damage to property or injury to person, "including loss of life of the member" from "all and every cause," and neither Byrd nor his designated leader assumed "any obligation to the member of the expedition or his estate for such damage or loss."

MacMillan and McDonald had taught Byrd well. "All pictures and photos taken by any member of the expedition shall be the property of Commander Byrd, subject to his editing and returning what he does not require." Moreover, no expedition member should give any interview or information to any corner of the media about the expedition for six weeks after returning to the States, and all members would have to wait two full years to "write or publish in any manner any story or book or deliver any lecture or address, relating in any way to the expedition."[19]

By the early spring of 1928 it became clear that a summer departure date was impossible. There was simply too much to do, including the raising of funds. Working out of his elegant Biltmore suite, Byrd and his business, shipping, and scientific consultants went all-out, nonstop, to complete the expedition while obtaining the cash to send it on its way. The hotel saved Byrd thousands of dollars, and Richard advertised himself and his enterprise shamelessly day and night. He became a frequent house guest of the wealthy and prominent as he cadged for money. There was even a popular dance that summer, the "Byrd Hop," designed to simulate the landing of an airplane, and no less an august institution than the *New York Times* publicly appealed for funds to support the expedition. The last weeks and days of preparation amid the deadening summer heat of New York City were hectic, as all last weeks and days before sailing would be on any Byrd expedition. Phones rang, typewriters clacked, and Boy Scout couriers raced in with news and out with orders as Byrd frantically sought to beg the last dollar and penny he could while seeking the last best men he could find.[20]

In the midst of chaos Byrd suffered two crushing setbacks. On April 26 Floyd Bennett died of pneumonia brought about by the injuries he had suffered in the crash of the *America* on its maiden flight the year before. Byrd was heartbroken. No man had been closer to him. For a brief time he was in seclusion, then emerged to announce that the big trimotor he was taking south would bear Bennett's name, as would some prominent Antarctic feature.

Five weeks later, George Hubert Wilkins suddenly announced that he, too, would be exploring Antarctica the coming austral summer with two aircraft. His goal: pure discovery unencumbered by scientific projects. Wilkins would presumably arrive at his proposed base site on the Antarctic Peninsula and begin overflights of the continental quadrant stretching westward to the Ross Shelf before Byrd even reached the ice. He probably did not possess aircraft that could reach the South Pole itself, but who knew for certain? Once again, a rival had appeared seemingly out of nowhere, threatening to steal Richard Byrd's glory. Richard had no choice but to welcome his fellow explorer. The two were, after all, members of an explorers' club even more exclusive than the New York organization that bore the name and to which each belonged. Whatever ache and misgivings may have raged in his heart, Byrd offered Wilkins the use of his own base facilities once they were up and running and even suggested that he could return Wilkins's small aircraft to New Zealand on one of his ships.[21]

Although Byrd proved that he could whip a large and sophisticated polar expedition together on reasonably short notice, he did it sloppily. In fact, his style was rather reminiscent of his nation's effort in times of modern war: get what you need, get it fast, and never mind the consequences. In the last weeks, the expedition took "everything that was offered, and in practically any quantity." Finally, the buildup of supplies got so bad that Balchen and June told their leader he had accepted nearly a thousand tons of cargo, all of which had to be loaded onto a single ship, the two hundred–ton barque *City of New York*. Moreover, there were three aircraft that also had to be shipped south, two big trimotors—a Fokker and a Ford—together with a smaller Fairchild to be used largely for short-range flights.

Byrd solved the problem in typical fashion: "he promptly wangled" another vessel, a steamer with a thin steel hull he renamed *Eleanor Bolling*. Finding even *Bolling* inadequate, he exploited Balchen's connections to charter two big Norwegian whale-factory ships, *Sir James Clark Ross* and *C. L. Larsen,* which stopped in the States en route to their annual Antarctic cruise. *Ross* and *Larsen* took the heaviest cargo, including the four planes and some of the dogs and sledges, as far as the jumping-off point for Antarctica, the New Zealand port of Dunedin.[22] Once *City of New York* and *Bolling* were reloaded with immediately needed machines, gear, and supplies at Dunedin, the two together with *Larsen* would sail to Antarctica, where it was planned that *Larsen* would begin whaling as soon as it reached the edge of the pack ice, standing by if necessary to tow Byrd's two ships through the pack ice to the Ross Sea and the Bay of Whales. *Bolling's* chief task thereafter would be to race back and forth the twenty-three hundred miles between the Bay of Whales and Dunedin, fetching auxiliary supplies as needed.

Eugene Rodgers, the distinguished historian of the expedition, observed that Byrd "seemed doomed never to have smooth going," a prophecy first uttered by a bearded old man clutching a Bible who stumbled aboard *Bolling* just before departure.[23] For a time the old man's prophecy seemed about to come true. Departing the United States with the advance elements of the expedition aboard, both *Bolling* and *City of New York* soon sailed into the jaws of one of the worst Atlantic hurricanes in memory, and Byrd spent long hours fretting that both might be lost. *Bolling* came through its ordeal in particularly bad shape, requiring hasty repairs at Hampton Roads. Two of its disgusted engine-room crew quit (before the engines were rebuilt, the ship was found to make five knots, not the posted fourteen), and several stowaways, including one attractive young lady, were discovered. They were put ashore promptly, to the dismay of the crew. There had also been some drinking among *Bolling's* largely inexperienced sailors, which did not improve their seamanship in the midst of the storm. At least initially, Byrd's crusaders failed to fulfill their commander's lofty ideals.

The cost of last-minute reconditioning of both *Bolling* and *City of New York* drove the expedition's debt back above $300,000. Rather than resting at home in Boston, Byrd spent his last days in New York on the telephone and telegraph, begging his backers for yet more money. Working day and night, he drove the debt down to $100,000 before he and Marie left on the Twentieth Century Limited and the Santa Fe Super Chief for California. As the trains sped westward, Byrd chastised himself in now familiar terms for once again leaving his young and needy family. "Home is back there now," he wrote in his diary, "but no, rather it is two years ahead of me." There were no good-byes, he added, only a casual "so long." A man who could confide his emotions to paper but not to people anguished. Young

Dickie, the usual "little soldier," solemnly handed his father $4.35 as his own contribution to the expedition. The "little rascal" had worked throughout the summer doing odd jobs and saving his money. Now the eight-year-old boy promised his father to make more money and send it down to Antarctica. Of the girls, only the eldest, Bolling, seemed to understand that her father was leaving for a long time, but a slight injury distracted her long enough for her father to beat his retreat.[24]

In California Byrd planned to board *Larsen* for a leisurely and comfortable voyage that would carry him in style from San Pedro to the expedition rendezvous in New Zealand. But the stress and tension of recent days and weeks finally caught up with him, and his wife had to nurse him carefully through a bad case of the flu in his Los Angeles hotel room. "Marie is the best of nurses," he later wrote. "We have seen more of each other during the past few days than in many many months. It has made me realize more fully how very busy I have been during the past ten years." When at last he boarded *Larsen* on October 13 he carried in his pocket a reassuring cable from Detroit industrialist L. P. Fisher that his request for $50,000 forwarded through Edsel Ford would be granted. Byrd could now only wonder how much additional expense the expedition might incur over the next twenty to twenty-four months.[25]

Managing that and other problems arising at home fell to his newly appointed business manager in New York. Hilton Howell Railey was a typical product of the ballyhoo business culture of the 1920s. The thirty-three-year-old New Orleans native and war veteran had come north some years earlier and settled in Boston, where he founded a promotion and fund-raising agency. He attracted Byrd's attention when the explorer decided to switch from a Fokker to a Ford trimotor for some of the Antarctic flights and sought a buyer for one of the two Fokkers he had in his inventory. Railey eventually sold the plane to young Amelia Earhart, who wanted a dramatic flight to ignite her career. Byrd then gave Earhart some lessons and information on transatlantic flying, and when the flight was a success Byrd was the first person Earhart called to thank. Railey, in the meantime, advised the explorer on the best means of raising needed cash from the public at large once the usual prominent butter-and-egg men had subscribed all they could or would. In the last hectic weeks before the advance elements of the expedition sailed, Byrd concluded that his second in command, Dick Brophy, was simply overwhelmed by the demanding pace, tasks, and schedules. Railey stepped in to help and became the obvious man to keep an eye on affairs at home while the expedition was isolated down on the ice. Byrd could not have picked a better man.[26]

Railey soon discovered that he had two Byrds to deal with, for Marie was as determined as he was to protect and, where possible, promote Richard Byrd's every interest. She traveled frequently from Brimmer Street to expedition headquarters at the Biltmore. "There has been a lot to attend to in New York," she wrote her husband in one typically undated letter. "Something coming up all the time." Railey was "very dedicated on the job," as was the Byrds' first personal secretary, Hazel McKercher. "She is very spunky and a regular treasure," Marie continued. "It was a splendid move putting her in with R, for they work together splendidly and are absolutely loyal and devoted to you."[27]

At sea, sullen men and a marginally competent captain kept the cramped and uncomfortable *City of New York* tense. It took thirty days and passage through one enormous storm for the ship just to reach Panama, then another forty days before a brief pause in Tahiti, and another month after that before reaching the jumping-off port of Dunedin. Perhaps because of the hurricane, much of the crew was drunk during several brief layovers in Panama (the ship had to return at one point because of engine trouble). Beyond Panama, preparations for the forthcoming months on the ice became necessarily intense. Readying and restowing hastily deposited cargo required heavy physical labor. Captain Frederick C. Melville was no help. Something of a martinet, he insisted that all hands stand one in four watches in addition to their other labors, which for many of the men resulted in steady eighteen-hour days. Water rations were short because the ship was overcrowded and its engines always suspect. Much of the meat quickly spoiled. One of the engine rooms flooded, presumably in the storm, and a fire broke out in the radio-battery storage room. Several would-be explorers threw in the towel, determined to leave the expedition at Dunedin and return home.[28]

As the expedition's ships approached New Zealand, a worried Brophy wired New York confidentially and without Byrd's knowledge that there would be a shortage of funds at Dunedin. "He did not say how great a shortage," a worried Railey wrote Marie in what would be the first of many such messages of alarm. "He merely warned me and said that he would rely upon me to make it up." Railey added that he radioed Brophy immediately to request specific information and to let the second in command know "clearly if delicately that the news is a shock." Brophy's cable came three days before Christmas, but an undaunted Railey immediately swung into action, and on December 26 he cabled Marie in a modest attempt at deception (doubtless to keep the press from learning of the crisis) that "aerogram returns show substantial profit on third day with promise of handsome margin." A "Christmas letter to subscribers has brought forth grateful and enthusiastic response. Plan has worked perfectly." Twenty-four hours later he added, "We are going to pass the thousand mark today, I think." On the thirty-first he told Marie that he might send out another telegraphic plea for funds.[29]

Chaos resulted when the expedition at last gathered in Dunedin. Food, clothing, shelter, communication equipment and towers, lights and flares, trail gear, instruments, dogs, sleds, a tractored vehicle, and one large (Ford trimotor) and one
small (Fairchild) aircraft were loaded apparently haphazardly on the decks of the
two ships, which seemed in imminent danger of capsizing even in port. What
would it be like when they reached the Roaring Forties, just south of New Zealand?
Like the old man with the Bible back in New York, many good folk in Dunedin
wondered if they would ever see Byrd and his men again. Some of Byrd's people
undoubtedly wondered the same thing.

Moreover, Brophy proved unable to fulfill the responsibilities of second in command. He lacked decisiveness, and with Richard Byrd decisiveness was everything.
Brophy was quietly sacked, taken off the ship's roster, and left behind in New
Zealand to oversee the minimal activities there while the expedition was on the
ice. Byrd assured him that his new position was essential, and, indeed, should the
expedition come to grief down on the ice, it would be.

Fortune at last began to smile on BAE I. After frantic day-and-night reloading,
the expedition at last got under way for the Ross Sea at dawn on December 2,
1928, before a small crowd on the dock that "gave us repeated lusty cheers." Byrd's
relief was palpable, but anticipation and apprehension battled for control of his
mind and emotions. On the way down from California, he and Captain Nilsen of
Larsen had reached "a most important decision." Rather than trying to ram both
Bolling and *City of New York* through the heavy pack ice to the Ross Barrier and
the Bay of Whales, *Larsen,* with its heavy steel hull and bow, would delay the start
of its own whaling activities to take the wooden-hulled, lightly powered sailing
vessel through. *Bolling,* after replenishing the schooner's coal bunkers at the edge
of the ice pack, would return to New Zealand to await better ice conditions later
in the season before trying to make the Ross Barrier on its own. But Byrd fretted
all the way down that Captain Nilsen would not wait long to penetrate the pack,
leaving the Americans to fight through on their own, which Byrd judged might
consume the better part of a month.[30]

Luckily, the passage from New Zealand south to the ice pack, which could be
a prolonged and brutal ordeal of raging seas and screaming skies, proved less than
that for the dreadfully overloaded vessels. *Bolling* towed *City of New York,* which
had its own small coal-fired power plant, through generally calm waters for the
first twenty-four hours, then cast loose to resume towing only intermittently. During the time it was on its own, the schooner made about seven knots under both
steam and sail.

Richard's spirits began to rise. How pleasing to leave civilization behind, with
its jarring telephones, "colossal mails, the financial difficulties, receptions, speech-

es, and autographs. No more of that now for at least a year and a half. It is a great feeling of relief." He and the men—"great fellows" all who suppressed their terrors and raced aloft into the rigging to break out the sails—would be twenty-three hundred miles from the nearest house, post office, "speed laws, prohibition, gasoline fumes, dust, city noises and dinner coats." Their only companions would be simplicity, hardship, and struggle as they bonded in a community of good fellowship.

As the days passed, oceanographer Ralph Shropshire began charting the seafloor south of New Zealand with a newly developed sonic depth finder, thereby inaugurating the important scientific program, which Byrd had insisted was the central feature of the expedition. Shropshire would continue his work all the way down to the Ross Sea and the Bay of Whales. "I have been observing the men closely at their arduous tasks," Byrd wrote soon after, "and everyone is happy and enthusiastic I am happy to say. I could not want a better crowd." The commander was particularly impressed with "how the land lubbers are being broken in as seamen. They are learning all of the intricacies of the lines and sails of a barque rig ship, which is no simple job."[31]

On its way to the pack, the two-ship convoy encountered only one major storm, but it was impressive. The seas swiftly swelled to "mountainous" proportions, whipped by a fifty-mile-per-hour gale. Few aboard either vessel got much if any sleep, and Byrd came on the barque's deck in the middle of the night to order double lashings on all deck gear and especially the dog kennels and supplies. Once again fortune smiled, for the gale blew along the ships' course, and so although the dangerously overloaded vessels pitched wildly, they did not roll excessively. Byrd endeared himself to his men when he joined them in the midst of the tempest to manhandle *Bolling*'s heavy towing cable that had snapped back onto *City of New York*. Everyone slaved uncomplainingly to save themselves, their ships, and the expedition. Despite Byrd's earlier assertions, the storm brought the first real sense of camaraderie if not brotherhood to a disparate group of men who, despite their commander's close observations, badly needed bonding. Pete Demas, who had been with his commander on Spitsbergen two years before, noted that "everyone is 100% Byrd."[32]

One week out of Dunedin the convoy encountered Antarctica. Because of magnetic declination, Byrd abandoned the compass to navigate solely by a wan sun that appeared only fitfully in skies that capriciously cleared, clouded, and wept snow and rain while the temperature began to drop. Pack ice was reported ahead, and Byrd scrambled up into the wet rigging but could see nothing in a steady murk as the first bergs began passing close by in the gloom. When the pack came into view, Byrd sent the ships into it, all the while ordering a keen lookout for *Larsen*.

For two days the little convoy prowled restlessly through a slushy pack under leaden skies before a greatly relieved commander heard the cry that the big whaler was sighted hull down on the horizon. Soon the three vessels were hove to while *Bolling* transferred coal to top off *City of New York*'s bunkers. Then *Bolling* set course back to Dunedin, while *Larsen* continued its initial whaling before pushing deeper into the thickening ice with *City of New York* in tow.

"Without a doubt this expedition is very trying on the composure of its leader," Richard wrote late in the evening of the twelfth. While *Larsen* spent the day absorbed with its catch, including a ninety-ton blue whale, *Bolling,* en route to New Zealand, did not respond to its hourly radio contact. Byrd had a fit. It had been hard enough on his nerves to split the expedition into four units on the way down from the States to New Zealand, he confided to his diary. Now the latest necessary division had caused more headaches. "This morning I guess I was the most disconcerted, and later the happiest man in the world." *Bolling* missed its regular 10:00 A.M. schedule, which was not too alarming at first because the operators had agreed to maintain contact every fifteen minutes by emergency radio. But when 10:15 brought nothing but silence on the airways, Malcolm Hanson, *City*'s radio operator, declared that *Bolling* had undoubtedly struck an iceberg in the prevailing gloom and gone down like a rock. In 1928 memories of *Titanic* were never far from seamen's minds. Byrd fretted and fumed for two hours until Hanson came running to his stateroom with word that *Bolling* was back on the air.[33]

Larsen at last completed its whaling on December 15 and set course through the pack, *City of New York* in tow. "That tow was something nobody who was aboard the *City* will ever forget," Russell Owen recalled a dozen years later. The next eight days were a nightmarish ordeal of constant noise and jarring, of backing, filling, and twisting amid crashing violence and the occasionally stunning beauty that is familiar to all who have gone through the Antarctic pack. The floes were heavy, tightly compacted, often "hummocky." Trying to bash, batter, and maneuver a big steel hull through them, while towing a small wooden vessel often navigating under its own power, posed a constant challenge for captains and helmsmen. Whenever *Larsen* stopped abruptly on a heavy floe, the barque threatened to ram into the bigger ship before engines in frantic reverse could take hold. As Byrd noted wryly, "something would have to give" in case of collision, "and I don't believe it would be the 'Larsen.'" If deck parties aboard *City* kept the towline tight, the risk of collision with the giant sister increased; if the towline were loosened to allow the smaller vessel greater maneuverability when the whaler suddenly stopped, the slack line might foul the bigger ship's rudder or screws. Richard tinged his unfeigned gratitude to Nilsen with apprehension. *Larsen*'s captain "is the prince of sports to do all this for us." The big whaler "unquestionably" made less speed towing the barque than sailing alone. It faced a "slight" risk of being struck severely by the smaller ship, and company owners would be far from pleased if they knew how their vessel was being used. "We therefore must not publish the fact that *[Larsen]* is towing us." Because he was risking his ship and his schedule, Nilsen might simply cut *City of New York* loose at any moment, a temptation that he expressed to Byrd on more than one occasion.

As the ships rammed and pushed and punched their way slowly southward, the pack thickened and tightened still more. *City of New York* was itself frequently buffeted and banged by thick floes that in Owen's words "made the ship groan in every timber." When the two vessels became totally beset, Byrd went over the side and onto the ice to inspect the barque's hull for possible damage. Fortunately, the wooden ship was stoutly built. The ice on this occasion did it no harm. One evening, however, as the little convoy moved ponderously through heavy, tightly impacted floes, *Larsen* lurched to a halt. Melville immediately backed the barque's engines to avoid collision and in doing so struck another floe with the stern of his own vessel, jamming *City's* rudder to one side, which spun the ship's helm wildly. A heavy wooden spoke caught Melville just below his left eye, causing a massive contusion and sending him tumbling to the deck. For several days the skipper was stiff and sore all over his body, and it took some weeks for the bruise to disappear. Richard, like his men, tempered his sympathy. Melville had proved to be the worst sort of captain. Working the men too hard on the voyage down through the tropics to New Zealand, he often did not appear on the bridge for hours, and earned Byrd's antipathy by not lashing down gear in heavy seas until almost too late. Perhaps Byrd remembered his own conduct being questioned in biting, unfair terms by McDonald three years before on the Greenland expedition. For whatever reason, Melville lost the trust of the entire expedition and its commander by the time *City of New York* reached Antarctic waters.[34]

Six days into the pack, Richard wrote despairingly, "Still in the ice, will we ever get out of it?" He was a novice. In later years he would learn a measure of patience, as the pack would often be far wider, stronger, and more tenacious than in 1928. Finally, on Sunday, December 23, after eight days, the pack ice gave the two vessels "some of the hardest bumps of the whole trip," then relented and released them into the open waters of the Ross Sea, some miles north of the barrier ice cliffs. *Larsen* promptly moved off to fresh whaling grounds, as *City of New York* alternately sailed and steamed eastward toward Amundsen's old base site at the Bay of Whales.

Because the barque crossed the international date line, Christmas came twice. During the first, the men arranged an elaborate midday dinner party, a midafternoon "jubilee," and a buffet dinner at six. Toasts, songs, skits, and shows accompanied the food, and Santa came down the stack; nearly everyone was teased. Master of ceremonies Charlie Lofgren, a seasoned navy veteran, sardonically saluted "Our Commander," who not only would soon be known for "having achieved the North Pole, flown the Atlantic, and delivered the South Pole on railroad schedule" but would also be "engaged in tunneling the earth from West to East in order to prove that the rotation of the earth is due to the instability of the Vernal Equinox." Larry Gould, a geologist from the University of Michigan, toasted the commander, which proved to have portentous consequences. With nominal number-two man Dick Brophy back in New Zealand, Byrd needed a second in command in the "field." He confided to his diary that evening that Gould, a man of steady temperament and usually unshakable common sense, would be that person.[35]

Beneath all the frivolity, however, tensions were beginning to rise. For whatever reason, Byrd chose Christmas to make several key field appointments that alienated as many men as they pleased. The commander was becoming dissatisfied with some of his mates, a dissatisfaction he could not always hide. Everyone had become rapidly stressed by shipboard life in the Antarctic. The perpetual daylight of the austral summer made sleep difficult. Barking and wailing dogs on deck together with a noisy radio room next to several cabins compounded the discomfort. Passage through the pack had been an exhausting ordeal of steady pounding and jarring. Nerves were taut. "The handling of personnel is certainly a vitally interesting thing," Byrd wrote to himself. "I am delighted that I enjoy this kind of work—otherwise things would not be very happy for me." One man particularly grated on the commander's nerves, though Byrd did "not like to even mention his name in these confidential pages, because I try to make it a rule not to criticize my shipmates." The commander believed this unidentified culprit, probably Russell Owen, possessed a surprisingly selfish attitude that made him inefficient. Byrd believed he had no choice but to "call attention to inefficiencies at times in vigorous terms."

But inefficiency was only one problem. Stupidity was the other. To his astonishment, Byrd concluded that several of the men who held important positions "I find extraordinarily dumb." They lacked foresight "because their minds do not allow them to visualize the situation." Byrd considered Captain Melville a prime example. When Richard ordered a fire drill, he found the equipment unacceptably shoddy. One main hose had a big hole in it. Richard first tried to call Melville's attention to this shocking deficiency quietly, but when that did not work the commander dressed the captain down. "It would have been better," Byrd admitted, "to have taken him aside afterwards and told him more quietly." And there was Brophy. Byrd did not mention him by name, either, but accused him of "utterly lacking in common sense." Brophy was "brilliant in books and mathematics," and

Byrd had trusted him "with a great deal to do in New York." But in New Zealand the man "failed on practically everything—only half doing the things." Now Gould looked all right, and Byrd made him second in command, entrusting to the geologist many details that the commander himself had been looking after.

Byrd announced other appointments. Balchen became senior flier, though "I myself will take active charge of the aviation unit." Balchen "beyond a doubt" deserved the "distinction" that Byrd bestowed. True, he had exhibited a tendency to allow "publicity" to go "to his head a bit, considerably" so "in New York." Fortunately, the Norwegian had "snapped out of it after several bawlings out, and I could not ask for a better attitude than his has been for weeks." Certainly, Balchen had been loyal ever since joining the Byrd retinue, and the man deserved his promotion for longevity of service if nothing else. Dean Smith, a superb airmail pilot and "a good fellow . . . felt a little hurt" by his exclusion, but "I have explained matters to him and now I believe he is O.K. in every way." Alton Parker became a test pilot. Byrd believed, not without reason, that his fliers were prima donnas, and on a Byrd expedition there could only be one prima donna. Parker remained "a splendid flier and the extraordinary good shipmate that I have found him in the past to be." Harold June, "an excellent mechanic" and a veteran of the North Pole support group in 1926, also hoped to be given charge of the aviation unit; instead, Byrd gave him responsibility for overseeing all unloading operations at the Bay of Whales and then for managing all aircraft maintenance. June's "spirit," however, was "disappointing. He seems to think mostly of himself." Certainly, the man had "given splendid service" and had displayed good form since leaving New Zealand, but "it was foolish of me ever to think that he could take Bennett's place." June had committed the unpardonable sins of "making some kind of contract in New York for a publicity manager" and then failing to tell his commander about it. He had been "a little premature on this," Byrd wrote. In fact, of course, the man had violated his contract. Everyone on the expedition should expect to better themselves out of the experience, Byrd added, and he stood ready to help them in every way—after the expedition left the ice.[36]

Whatever tensions Byrd saw or created were eased considerably by the prospect of getting ashore and getting to work. *City* reached the barrier on the second Christmas Day after passing the international date line. Byrd made for Discovery Inlet, a possible base site. There sailors made the barque fast to the ice, while Byrd, Balchen, and two others unshipped skis and traveled about twenty miles, scouting the area. At once Antarctica began to exert its lifelong hold over Richard Byrd. He became intrigued with the light, which shifted often and at one point "made it impossible to see the snow ahead of us." The men stumbled over small rises or little declines, not realizing that the terrain was shifting. Such perils might make aircraft landings dicey, but smoke bombs should take care of the problem. A day later, Byrd wrote of "learning something about the water clouds and the ice lights." The light streaks showing above the snow and dark clouds showing above water created an "extraordinary" effect far more pronounced in the South Polar region than up in the Arctic. Variables of light in the sky and off the clouds seemed "an almost infallible indication" of ice.

As the men returned to the barrier they discovered that a rising wind had created heavy swells that slammed the ship up against the ice. Byrd ordered an immediate departure, expressing remorse at leaving behind the bodies of about a dozen seals the men had killed. "I am against killing any living creatures unless it is for food." Once under way the commander ordered sails rigged "all the way down to the Bay of Whales in order to save coal. Coal is the valuable priceless thing with us now" because no one could estimate how much would be needed to crash out north through the pack ice at the end of the season if *Bolling* could not get down from New Zealand with replenishments.[37]

City of New York reached the Bay of Whales on December 28, arriving two weeks earlier in the austral summer than had Amundsen in 1911. It was a good omen. Not even word that Wilkins had managed the first flight in Antarctica (over the peninsula, hundreds of miles to the east and north) could darken the expedition's mood for long.

The first days and weeks were filled with wonder and work. Even at its best, the bay remained choked with pressured-ridged ice, at once thick and soft, frequently shifting, and filled with crevasses, which made getting to the barrier difficult. Nonetheless, a party, including among others Byrd, Balchen, and young Norman Vaughan, a recent Harvard student who had become an excellent and dedicated dog-team driver, managed to get up onto the barrier to scout out sites for the permanent encampment. They were entranced and awed by their new home, especially the "eerie lighting" that created flawed visions and illusions. Beyond the barrier the great ice shelf stretched endlessly south and west. Mountains were nowhere near. Yet "blurred shapes of icy hillocks, snowy peaks, vast, vague stretches of snow, the huge bulk of the barrier itself made up this deceiving world, in which nothing seemed quite so unreliable as the judgments of the eye." Men skiing blithely along suddenly found themselves plunging into a depression in the snow "when the surface seemed perfectly level. We would see a pressure ridge that appeared just ahead. It was, in fact, miles away." Wisely, Byrd insisted that since only a handful on the expedition had been to Antarctica before, those accompanying the dog teams on reconnaissance should be on skis rather than afoot.[38]

On January 1, 1929, Byrd selected a permanent site for "Little America," a name suggested by Brophy, who was concerned that the world press was referring to Byrd's proposed camp as "Framheim," Amundsen's base in 1911–1912 that lay abandoned nearby. Byrd unshipped a shovel from one of the sleds and had all four members of the party dig the first ceremonial hole.[39] He then placed Larry Gould in charge of construction. Byrd himself stayed aboard *City* in overall charge of the entire enterprise.

Soon the fifty-four men of the expedition and *City*'s crew began moving hundreds of tons of supplies from the ship's deck to the campsite. It was grueling, unending work, hauling supplies up the bay ice to the barrier and then fifteen miles across the shelf, digging big holes in the ground in which to place the huts and buildings, rigging the tall radio towers, and, later, constructing snow-block hangars for the planes once the initial flying season had ended. All hands worked twelve-hour shifts, but "since daylight was constant many men worked much longer, continuing until they almost dropped in their tracks."[40] One of the drivers, Jack Bursey, fell into a small crevasse and got wedged in, nearly dying of hypothermia before an alert lookout on *City* spotted him and raised the alarm. His teammate had driven on, thinking poor Bursey was yelling at his dogs, rather than for help. Though most of the men continued to live on ship, Vaughan and a few others roughed it in tents ashore.[41]

At one point in early January, winds brought heavy ice into the bay, and the barque had to get under way and maneuver to avoid it. The block of ice to which the vessel was moored broke away, and Byrd and Melville found another anchorage half a mile closer to Little America. A lead opened up in the bay ice several days later, necessitating yet another move, which placed the barque two miles closer to the emerging base.

Byrd kept a close eye on the dogs. He did not wish to kill them through exhaustion. Not only were they essential for the upcoming scientific fieldwork, but he admired them greatly for their willingness to pull until exhausted. He insisted that two teams make each run so as to keep an eye on each other, and he kept a lookout posted in *City*'s crow's nest with binoculars for added observation. As the days slipped by, however, and the temperature rose, the ice perceptibly softened, and the run from the ship to the camp became ever more treacherous. The dogs and their human drivers had to pull and haul big cargo sleds from the anchorage on the bay ice across treacherous floes separated by narrow gaps of water and up the barrier before heading out across the shelf toward Little America. Even the big, heavy fuselages and wings of the Fokker and Ford trimotor aircraft, together with the smaller Fairchild, had to be hauled to Little America by a combination of animal and human power. Base construction slowed, and Byrd wrote that he might have to freeze one of the ships in for the winter, employing it as the camp despite the risk of possible loss. He would send its crew back to the States on the other vessel. "I would rather do that than fail." The barque carried enough coal and food to maintain everyone on the ice for an entire year if *Bolling* could not break in or *City* break out.

In the meantime, Byrd ordered *Bolling* to bring down badly needed supplementary gear and equipment, including one or both of the big trimotor aircraft. On January 14 Captain Gustav Brown radioed that he had cleared Dunedin and was on his way. By this time Little America's light, strong, weather-tight, wind-resistant buildings—including a mess hall and an executive building complete with small laboratories and a library—had been put up along with several sleeping quarters. The more imaginative individuals built their own digs out of empty boxes and airplane crates. Machinist Czega constructed his shop in this manner, and several small sleeping quarters, an aviation workshop, and a radio storeroom materialized the same way. The doctor carved his storeroom out of the snow and roofed it over with a simple tarpaulin. Someone else used snow and tarpaulin to build a gym, though it was seldom used because of the cold. The men also dug snow tunnels and bridged them over to provide communication between the various rooms and buildings.[42]

During this hectic time, Byrd exhibited a trait that did not appeal to everyone. He supervised but would not labor.[43] Leaders were to be the brains of the outfit, not its brawn. Only in emergencies such as the night of wild seas on the way down should a commander lend a hand. Otherwise, he planned and directed the enterprise. Besides, he was anxious to complete the first season's planning and, above all, to get aloft. On January 14 he ordered that the one aircraft brought down on *City*, the high-wing Fairchild christened *Stars and Stripes,* be off-loaded and assembled. The men worked quickly and smoothly, and the next day the plane took off on its maiden flights, seven brief journeys in all to explore the shelf and barrier to the south and west of Little America.

In the first ten minutes aloft, Byrd viewed more of Antarctica than any footbound explorer could view in a month, including a "vast snow-covered ice field that the eye of man was scanning for the first time." It was a heady moment, one that gave Richard the first of his many "kicks" during the expedition. His usually sunny and optimistic nature was further buoyed by news that Wilkins had "given up his expedition" after only one significant flight. "It was futile for Hearst to offer him $100,000 to beat me to the Pole for he could not have made the distance." Moreover, the Australian had suffered "all sorts of difficulties." Byrd acknowledged that if his competitor had flown to Little America, "he certainly would have put some crimp in us," for "unless I miss my guess" the intervening fifteen hundred miles were probably full of "lots of good sized islands . . . and all sorts of interesting areas." Wilkins's failure was Byrd's prod. His next two expeditions (in 1933–

1935 and 1939–1940) would concentrate on exploring the region from Little America to the edge of the Eights Coast that he would name Marie Byrd Land.[44]

Thereafter, adventures in the air and on the ice came fast and furious: the first radio contact between New York and an airplane in Antarctic skies, the first lengthy flights north and east that uncovered a new set of mountain ranges (which Byrd named for Rockefeller), a frightening race by Byrd and several colleagues by motorboat to escape killer whales in the bay, and the arrival of *Bolling* at the end of January with one of the two big planes. *Bolling*'s arrival gave Byrd a particular sense of achievement since he had been bitterly criticized for allowing a steel-hulled vessel to penetrate the pack ice alone.

On the last day of January, the expedition almost came to an end when a small portion of the barrier to which *Bolling* was attached suddenly broke off with "a frightful crash." Richard, who had not yet moved to Little America, was in his cabin on *City* talking to *Bolling*'s first mate. He and the other man leaped up and raced on deck in time to see "the bottom of the reeling *Bolling*." The vessel should have capsized with the huge piece of ice on its deck but righted itself. Nonetheless, several crewmen had been pitched into the freezing water, and Byrd saw one of them, portly Benny Roth, an airplane mechanic, clinging precariously to a spinning ice cake and screaming that he could not swim. Richard promptly dove in after him while Melville ordered a boat lowered from *City of New York*'s deck. In their excitement, the barque's crewmen overloaded the boat, and to prevent it from foundering, radioman Hanson jumped into the water. Richard could not get to Roth because of intervening ice floes, but to his "indescribable relief" Roth and everyone were fished quickly out of the frigid water.

Richard later recorded these events for posterity.[45] Major personal crises remained confined to the pages of his diary and the minds of expedition members. The first involved Brophy. The man had been generally "calm and capable" in New York, "in short, a Rock of Gibraltar," until three days before departure, when the pressures got to him and he broke. "He barked at everybody, criticized them unjustly, tried to attend to every detail himself, and consequently got so balled up he hardly knew what he was doing. He antagonized every human being he ever came in contact with, and now, in spite of my efforts to make things right for him, he is thoroughly disliked." The man deserved "much better than that, but it is a curious thing about people, that no matter what one does one can undo it all by fussiness and the wrong kind of talk." A radio message from Dunedin early in the New Year indicated that "Brophy is still on a rampage." On January 9 Marie wrote from New York that she had "been going over everything with Railey and on my own responsibility, I have sent a message in code to you." Railey did not wish to worry Dick "with the way Brophy has been acting lately." However, Marie continued, "if B. is to be 2nd in command in n.z. at least you should know how he is now acting which you may not be aware of way down where you are." The man's messages had become so "unnatural that he must have been drinking or else absolutely lost his head."

Dick was gaining the same impression from Brophy's lengthy messages to the ice that suggested "an extreme nervous condition." A confidential cable from one of Brophy's subordinates suggested the same thing. Brophy had gone off to Wellington at just the moment the loading of critical supplies aboard *Bolling* had commenced. Should Brophy's authority be "overruled" in case problems arose? Byrd confided to his diary that night that he intended to "stick by" his second in command because of the excellent work he had done in New York up to the moment of his breakdown. "Otherwise I would wipe him off the slate in a moment."[46]

That sentiment was shared by Marie. Brophy had begun a letter-writing campaign of alarm to wives and sweethearts of some expedition members, who swiftly queried Railey in New York. Marie's ever alert antennae picked up the emerging crisis immediately. "It seems to me from what I saw in n.y. that things had quieted down a little in n.z. I do feel though there are very extraordinary ideas in a certain person's mind judging from the messages that keep coming in." But if Brophy was a problem, Marie quickly added, Railey was a treasure, "a very steady, dependable, utterly conscientious man. . . . The more I see him the better I like him—perhaps because we agree in most instances. He thinks the world of you and you can trust him." At the end of the month Railey wrote Marie how "weary" he had become "of the Brophy business," guessing that Brophy had become tired of working in New Zealand, had become disheartened that he could not join the expedition on the ice, and had concluded he wanted the next best thing—Railey's job. If this were indeed the case, Railey told Marie, it was "absurd" because his career as a promoter would go on long after the Byrd expedition had ended. "I am singly and primarily concerned with Dick's goodwill and public relations," Railey added. Marie replied the next day, urging Railey to calm down. Yes, Brophy's "unnatural messages" were disturbing, but "I am convinced B will be all right."[47] There the matter rested for the moment.

The second personal crisis involved *New York Times* reporter Russell Owen. In early January a viral-flu epidemic broke out aboard *City of New York,* striking down nearly half the crew. Dr. Dana Coman believed the dogs were the source. Owen, "short, slight, weak and bespectacled," was the sickest. Byrd gave the ill reporter his bunk aboard the barque, and the commander slept on the bathroom floor of the newly constructed command building at Little America. Pilot Dean Smith would later claim that Owen fell ill because from the start Byrd placed unendurable restrictions on Owen's reportage, censoring and rewriting the veteran reporter's dispatches to ensure that the commander received his proper due. In response, Owen started criticizing Byrd behind his back, which the commander found a totally unacceptable breach of the absolute loyalty that he expected from all who served with him. He had given up his bed to the stricken man, and this was how he was repaid.

Byrd promptly mounted a counterattack, claiming that Owen suffered from paranoia and would have to leave with the ships when they departed in early March. He got Dr. Coman to concur and to send the *Times*'s managing editor a telegram stating that Owen could not withstand the rigors of polar life. Byrd treated the matter circumspectly in his own "confidential" diary. On the last day of 1928, he recorded laconically that he had "got up a story for the New York Times,—Russell Owen being ill." Nine days later, as the incident reached its climax, Richard added, "It is extraordinary the changes that take place in some men when they go from civilization to the polar regions. One is frequently pleased at the change for the better and then one is some times shocked at the way men go to pieces."

After first stating that he did not have time or space to write about "the personnel" and then dilating at length about Brophy's shortcomings, Richard added that although "of course we have gone through some strains," they would be nothing compared to the coming polar winter night. He expressed pleasure when Owen came out on deck for a time. "I do not intend to squabble with him or to enter into any undignified discussion." Instead, he would simply uphold Coman's recommendation. "The doctor says Owen has a 'hatred complex.' I have noticed it before but never thought he would apply it to members of this expedition." For some reason, Owen also entertained an "implacable hatred" for Amundsen, "though Amundsen has just within the year sacrificed his life in trying to rescue one of his own enemies."

Owen quickly came around. According to Byrd, he said that his career would be ruined if he went back, that he had not completed an earlier Arctic assignment (due to Amundsen, perhaps?), and that this expedition was his one chance of atonement. Byrd relented and thereafter, according to Smith, had the reporter completely under his control. Byrd wrote Marie that "Brophy and Owen were the only ones who went haywire—but Owen has pulled out completely. . . . Now he thinks I have been very square to him and is, I think more loyal than ever."[48]

Byrd thus showed his hand early on as an iron-willed, even ruthless, commander. He has been criticized severely for it, especially when that ruthlessness was employed, as critics increasingly charged down the years, to press claims of personal achievement and glory that were not his to make. But Byrd had been schooled in the Old Navy tradition of command authority in which, to recall Lincoln's felicitous phrase in a similar connection, the captain held the power and bore the responsibility. There were for the men of BAE I months on end of unrelenting work, awful cold, dreadful isolation, the lack of any opportunity for the release of stress and tension through sexual activity, and a disturbing disorientation of light and dark, day and night. The four and a half months of total darkness were an obvious source of stress, as Byrd anticipated they would be.[49] Seasonal affective disorder due to lack of sufficient light is now well known. Less understood are the effects of total daylight. As this writer can attest from a later time, sleep can be very difficult in the Antarctic summer months. Even burrowed deep, one senses the sun and the light around one, which can cause an intense restlessness.

Byrd had no universally recognized law or legal system on which to rely. To this day the question of which, if any, laws apply across the Antarctic remains unresolved. Richard could rely only on the force and cunning of his own personality as expedition leader and the threat of handcuffs and straitjackets to dominate and discipline the group. "Losing control of his men was always one of his greatest fears" more than two thousand miles from the nearest civilization in the midst of a polar wilderness.[50] The fear was not unjustified. In general, he ignored contemptuous sniping so long as it did not escalate toward outright mutiny; he was, or seemed, comfortable if not serene in his decisions. When matters threatened to get out of hand, he suddenly appeared to drink with the boys, listen, and commiserate with them.

Charles Murphy, who played a key role in the second Byrd Antarctic expedition, subsequently wrote that the commander was quick to praise, and slow to criticize. Little America always had its share of "troublemakers . . . soreheads and the disappointed." Byrd handled matters "by taking them on long walks, while he discoursed on philosophy, politics, people, or whatever else might be on his mind. After he had chilled and generalized the recalcitrants into submission, he would then approach their faults in the manner of an understanding schoolmaster." Charles Passel, who went south with the 1940–1941 United States Antarctic Service expedition, concurred:

> The Admiral never criticized anybody in front of anybody else. He did not belittle the men. If he had something to say, he'd say, "Charles let's go for a walk around the deck." I'd get up and we'd just start walking and he would tell me that "I am pleased at what you're doing on the expedition and I am happy that you are successful." My association with him was that he was a good leader and an excellent person to have as an expedition leader or person in charge of the overall operation of the expedition. I cannot fault him

at all. He was very understanding. You could go to him with a trouble and he would talk to you about it and he would come up with a solution that would make sense and help the success of the expedition.[51]

Norman Vaughan saw how Richard handled photographer Ashley McKinley, a good friend before and after the expedition, who threatened to go to pieces once winter came because he had nothing to do. Richard noticed his deepening depression, took him aside, and claimed that he needed someone he could trust absolutely to dig a deep hole in the barrier where the commander could bury a secret cache that no one else must know about. McKinley fell for the bait and spent much of the winter digging a separate, entirely useless, extra tunnel. "A miracle took place before our eyes," Vaughan recalled. "McKinley stopped being morose." Every morning he awoke in the icy darkness of the Little America sleeping quarters, happily pulled on his clothes and boots in the frigid barracks, "ate three meals a day, worked all day, slept well at night, and stopped his maudlin talk about home."[52] Another time, Byrd raised morale by a calculated act. A month after the sun disappeared, he suddenly ordered the supply officer to break open several cartons that contained fresh shirts for each of the men.

Byrd constantly reminded his men of Little America's isolation. Before 1950 no airplane possessed the range to fly the forty-six hundred miles back and forth to New Zealand. Ships were the only way in or out of Antarctic encampments, and prior to World War II they were so fragile as to make their arrivals—and departures—always problematic. Uncertainty about the duration of their ordeal added a further substantial burden to the already overstressed psyches of Antarctic explorers.

His "crusaders" were themselves an often difficult and contentious lot despite the lavish praise he heaped on them both before and after an expedition. Creative and often professionally driven, the scientists possessed greater resources of thought and meditation than the pilots, machinists, dog-team drivers, mechanics, and cooks who supported them. Yet the "'ologists" became as easily bored and readily frustrated with the endless monotony of daily life as anyone else, and their academic backgrounds and minds inclined them to suspicion and intrigue. Friendships and alliances were ever shifting—forged, then often bitterly broken, only to be reforged or eternally rejected.[53]

Byrd's exploitation of his position to advance his own personal interests has been a source of continuous and contentious debate within the relatively small polar community. Pilot Dean Smith is the major source of the most notorious allegations, and Smith was one of the few "Byrd men"—along with Balchen, Finn Ronne, and Alan Innes Taylor—who came to harbor a bitter dislike of his commander. Smith may well have been aggrieved not to have been given the chief pilot's slot, especially since Byrd had originally agreed to pay Smith more than either Balchen or June. In later years Smith became incensed at charges that he was a less than brilliant pilot.[54] If Smith's account of the Owen incident is correct, Byrd was surely guilty of shabby conduct, and he served neither the interests of the *New York Times* (who was paying part of his salary) nor the cause of historical truth. But no one denied that Owen was quite ill, and Byrd on at least one occasion felt fully justified in filing the reporter's daily dispatch to New York. As expedition leader, Byrd would naturally have been the one to write the account if Owen could not, and the fact that he was also being paid directly by the paper meant that if he had not done the writing, he might well have been accused of breach of contract. In his wretched state—and viral flu leaves one feeling wretched—Owen could well have "gone to pieces" for a time and said things he did not mean and later regretted. Byrd was obviously upset with the reporter, accusing him of harboring a hatred complex. But the commander proved as willing as Owen to let the matter drop once the man recovered, and there was no further talk of sending him out with the last ship at the end of the austral summer.

The allegation that Byrd cheated fliers out of their own discoveries is also a product of Smith's pen. According to the pilot, one day shortly before Byrd closed down the first season's flying, he gave Smith and Ashley McKinley permission to fly eastward over what would soon be named Marie Byrd Land. The mission proved rather dull, so Smith radioed Little America to request permission to fly into an area that Byrd had just visited but found fogbound. The commander radioed a reluctant okay, and Smith and McKinley soon found themselves in clear air near a magnificent Matterhorn-like peak rising in solitary grandeur eight to ten thousand feet above the Antarctic floor. Returning to base, they excitedly recounted their dramatic find, only to have Byrd insist that he had seen the peak first on his own recent flight. To prove his point, the commander produced a flight chart that Smith later wrote had been shabbily altered and thanked the flabbergasted pilot and photographer for confirming his own find. As the two men walked away, McKinley allegedly exclaimed sardonically, "You and I will never be great explorers." McKinley would work closely with Byrd after World War II, cowriting an elaborate cold war policy paper on the importance of Greenland, and never seems to have related the incident.[55]

Those who accepted Byrd's leadership and decisions uncritically tended to adore him. Those who comprehended the enormous pressures and burdens of command understood him. It was the men whose egos and agendas matched or approached his own who clashed with Byrd either on the ice or later at home.

Balchen certainly had no reason to view his commander uncritically. Neither did Smith. Another who ran afoul of Byrd was Larry Gould.

By early February the weather at the Bay of Whales was alternately calm and clear or stormy and windy. *Bolling* and *City of New York* were forced to constantly unmoor and maneuver in the tight confines of the ice-filled bay. Melville's seamanship was usually clumsy and often dangerous. Byrd concluded that the man was simply "dumb" and should never be hired on another Antarctic expedition. Under the circumstances it was essential to take advantage of every reasonable break in the weather to get the last supplies off the ships and ice and up to Little America before the looming polar night took hold. Byrd lashed his men to "make hay while the sun shines." His earlier concern for the dogs' welfare was a necessary casualty of his concern for the overall mission.

But Gould, in charge of putting the finishing touches on Little America while Byrd stayed aboard ship, proved timid. He "babies the boys as much as I drive them," Byrd recorded on February 10. "It makes it thoroughly difficult for me." At the first sign of bad weather, the second in command would order the dog teams and drivers to remain at the station rather than return to the anchorages to pick up more supplies. Another storm blew up on the evening of the tenth, but by morning it had subsided. Melville brought his ship alongside the barrier once again, and Byrd sent orders over to Little America to get the dog teams started. "It was in my opinion feasible for the dog teams to come out on the bay ice. Gould thought differently, but I ordered him just the same to send the teams in. I am tired of this babying business." He well knew the risks being run, Byrd added, but "we've got a job to do and we can't do it by stopping every time the wind blows." The commander evidently made his point clear, for thereafter the teams ran as often as Byrd wished. By the middle of the month he recorded that the teams were now "going full speed ahead. . . . We should completely finish up in several days now."[56]

Just as Byrd was resolving his flare-up with Gould, the Brophy affair reached a climax. Begging Byrd for a chance to at least visit the ice, Brophy had come down on *Bolling*'s second voyage just before the onset of winter. But the ship had not been able to penetrate the thickening pack and turned back. In a bizarre gesture, Brophy wired the *New York Times* that he had taken command and would conduct his own expedition. The *Times* ignored the absurd cable, but word naturally got back to the ice. On February 12, after repeatedly warning the man to stop criticizing him in daily radio messages, Richard formally fired Brophy. "I am convinced that he is still in a very nervous condition, and I have tried to make allowances for it. But I have reached the end of my rope. I am harassed enough by the elements down here," Byrd added from his desk aboard the storm-tossed *City of New York.* He did not have to endure "my Second in Command snapping at my heels." Given the financial straits of the expedition, Byrd offered Brophy a very generous severance package. After informing his disgraced colleague by cable that "your radios show an attitude of mind that is too unjust ever to be rectified," Byrd told him that his salary would be continued indefinitely and that all expenses to the States would be paid "if you are going back." Byrd thought he had finally resolved a problem that should have been taken care of long before. In fact, he was creating an even bigger headache for himself and especially his associates at home.[57]

As polar night began to creep over the Bay of Whales, Smith alleged one final incident that presumably proved that Richard Byrd was not only deceitful but a coward as well. Early in March, not long after Smith and McKinley's flight to the "Matterhorn," Gould, June, and Balchen took off in the big Fokker trimotor named *Virginia* for the Rockefeller Mountains to do some exploration. Little America had been largely constructed, all three aircraft had been brought down to the ice, and the two ships were at last nestled in New Zealand for the winter season. Byrd had sent several sledging parties out to mark trails and lay supplies for the next austral summer's major expeditions to the south, east, and west. The moment seemed right to get in some quick geological work before the onset of darkness. Byrd was initially hesitant about sending the Fokker far out from base so late in the season, but Gould had become obsessed by the low line of snow-covered hills after seeing them from aloft, and his commander eventually gave in. After takeoff, Balchen flew briefly southward to report on the trail parties' progress, then turned the Fokker north to the Rockefellers. There the three men landed safely, but almost immediately a blizzard blew in that lasted for days. Despite their most desperate efforts to lash the plane down, the howling winds picked up and tossed the Fokker about so badly that it was fatally damaged, and the men were stranded in their tent 135 miles from Little America. Hunkering down, they endured until the tempest at last subsided, then waited long days before they could make contact with camp and several more days before the weather both at the base and in the mountains permitted a rescue plane to come out.

Byrd took personal charge of the mission. At first he refused to countenance a flight, dispatching a dog team instead. Dean Smith found this "incomprehensible," as the polar night was fast approaching. Even now, there were far more hours of darkness than of twilight. Smith later alleged that he pleaded with his commander for the chance to go out alone and bring back the stranded party. Byrd eventually concurred with the need for an aerial rescue but according to Smith "would not permit such an important flight without his presence and also insisted on a radio operator." This was a no-win situation, since overcrowding of the aircraft dictated at least two men would have to stay at the crash site, necessitating a second rescue flight.[58] Nonetheless, Byrd prevailed in his determination to fly to the mountains in the Fairchild with Smith piloting and Malcolm Hanson manning the radio.

According to Smith, just before takeoff of the rescue plane from Little America, scheduled for 8:30 in the morning, Owen found Byrd in his room, swinging his leather helmet in his hands, staring at the floor. Smith had been warming up the Fairchild but at Owen's request came off the ice runway to knock on the commander's door on three separate occasions, trying to get him out. Owen told Smith that Byrd was praying, and each time Smith knocked the commander said that he would be right out. Smith later wrote that "it was nearly four o'clock"—seven and one-half hours after scheduled flight time—"when Byrd finally put in an appearance." In subsequent correspondence Smith hammered at the theme that he had waited all "day with my engine ticking over" for his commander to appear. "There were thirty odd witnesses," he later asserted to Bernt Balchen. Later, he amplified his remarks to the Canadian Aviation Historical Society: there had been forty witnesses to Byrd's alleged cowardice. When the commander at last emerged from his quarters, "his face was white as the snow under foot," and Smith concluded that Byrd feared he was about to perish on the forthcoming flight.

Out on the runway, Byrd ordered Smith to cancel the flight because of the rough condition of the ice, though Smith eventually talked him into a takeoff. But Byrd had already compromised flight safety enough, Smith later contended. "Instead of taking off in the early morning with many hours of bright sunlight ahead, by the time we got away the sun was already low in the west, we were flying directly into the gloom of dusk, compounded by a cloud deck moving in from the east." Once aloft, the commander seemed to regain his composure, but when the Gould party was at last spotted in the gloom and Smith prepared to set down, Byrd allegedly went completely to pieces. Screaming hysterically, "You're going to hit the mountain, you're going to hit the mountain!" he tried to take the controls from Smith, who had to wrestle him back into the cabin with Hanson's help. As the Fairchild landed with a slap of skis, Byrd cried out, "You've cracked us up! You've cracked us up!" When he alit, Byrd walked about ten feet, threw down a sleeping bag from the plane, and knelt on it for some time with his head bowed.[59] Such was Smith's story, and it was and is widely believed.

In fact, it beggars belief. Smith himself stressed that the polar night was fast approaching, with only a few hours of twilight remaining. "The long [South Polar] night was coming fast," historian Eugene Rodgers adds. "That weekend [March 15–17] the sky lit up with the season's first aurora, advertising the arrival of winter." The fast-closing night was the reason that Byrd initially chose to employ dog teams to rescue Gould and his companions. The fact that darkness was rapidly approaching, and that the precise location of the lost party was unknown, finally led the commander to scrap his plans and go with a chancy search and rescue by air. Yet Smith would have us believe that Byrd then kept everyone waiting seven-plus hours through the daylight hours before he eventually appeared. If Byrd stayed in his quarters praying—or not—for that long, or even some hours less, the entire mission out to the Rockefellers would have had to have been flown in total darkness. No man ostensibly terrified of flying would have countenanced such a mission in the early days of Antarctic aviation. Indeed, night flying in Antarctica was never undertaken until a new generation of explorers thirty years later in Operation Deepfreeze II discovered the cost of such folly for any but the most dire emergencies. Not until sufficient navigational aids were developed in the late 1970s did U.S. Antarctic Research Program directors permit one midwinter flight—"Winfly"—onto the continent each year from New Zealand.[60] If Byrd kept Smith and the others waiting while he gathered himself together in his room, he took far less time than Smith's story would have one believe.

Byrd's alleged hysteria at Smith's approach to the rescue site has universally been ascribed to his fear of flying. But another, more plausible, explanation is that he was reacting to the loss of the Fokker. The whole affair proved a nightmare to the commander, who was presented with yet another graphic example of how quickly and savagely Antarctic weather could damage if not destroy the expedition's fortunes. With the big plane gone, the next season's aerial operations, including the climactic flight up to the pole, were abruptly compromised. Only the Ford trimotor remained for long-distance mapping and exploring, and if the Fairchild, too, was lost in the Gould rescue attempt, Byrd would be reduced to just one primary long-range aircraft. Moreover, the Fokker's destruction ended Byrd's cherished dream of actually landing at the pole and spending a day or two there to make scientific observations. With the Fokker trimotor as a backup—or the primary aircraft, with the Ford trimotor as backup—the polar party could have suffered a mishap at the pole and still been rescued by the second big plane. But now there was no second big plane. To attempt a landing at the pole would be literally courting suicide if the aircraft cracked up or its engine froze after a few hours—or minutes—on the icy surface, forcing the party to walk the eight hundred miles back across the polar plateau, down one of the icy, crevasse-scoured glaciers, and out along the Ross Ice Shelf. Scott had perished that way with far better equipment than could be crammed into a single aircraft limited in weight by a lengthy flight. Gould's insistence on exploring the Rockefellers had cost Byrd dearly.

The pressures on Byrd at this moment were inhuman: the expedition was running ever deeper into debt, personnel problems were becoming acute, and now one of his two biggest, best, and most dependable aircraft had been destroyed. Byrd never publicly chided Gould or Balchen, and indeed there was no reason to. But he might have had a hard time taming his anger, for against his better judgment Gould had pressured him into permitting the late-season flight out to the mountains. Now he would have to confront Gould, not an attractive prospect for a man who occasionally "bawled out" incapable or "dumb" subordinates. This could well explain his reluctance even to undertake the flight. Once in the air and over a landing site that might prove treacherous, Byrd may have given in to momentary panic at the prospect of losing a second plane. But all we have is Smith's word that he panicked at all. Loss of another aircraft, even if no one were hurt, would necessitate calling in and possibly losing a third aircraft, which would cause termination of the expedition's aviation program—and for all practical purposes the expedition itself—then and there.

Byrd clearly missed Bennett. He never completely trusted another pilot to fly him safely, as Bennett had done on several occasions in the Arctic. Evidence suggests his skepticism was soundly based. Balchen was a consistently reliable flier—indeed, a superb airman. But he had proved personally antagonistic before and perhaps during the transatlantic flight; Dean Smith would prove incompetent on at least one future occasion. To calm his apprehensions, Byrd drank on at least some of his flights. Who knows if others did not as well? Richard Black, who commanded East Base during the 1939–1941 United States Antarctic Service expedition, once told me that the admiral liked to stash a brandy flask in his parka and take nips while in the air or on landing approaches. But Black never mentioned the man going to pieces in the way Smith would claim, nor did Owen in his admittedly brief account of the expedition. Wendell Summers, who flew with Byrd during Operation Highjump in 1947, saw a man aloof from his fellow fliers—he was, after all, a rear admiral—but far from fearful. Byrd did his own navigation and functioned normally. He was clearly able to suppress whatever terrors may have momentarily seized him.[61]

Whether in fact Byrd broke down out in the Rockefeller Mountains that day and prayed for long moments, kneeling on a sleeping bag, is yet another matter of debate. Gould did not relate the story in his 1931 account of the expedition, nor did anyone else at the time. Owen, who, of course, remained at Little America, said nothing about such an incident when writing his account of the expedition in his justly celebrated *The Antarctic Ocean,* published in 1941. The journalist waited until the year of his death, 1952, to state in a book about polar explorers aimed at the young-adult market that Byrd had indeed knelt briefly in prayer, then had radioed Owen not to mention the incident in his daily dispatch to the *New York Times.* Balchen supported Smith's story that Byrd got out of the plane and knelt silently for a time on a sleeping bag. But when Balchen informed Gould years later that he hoped to publish the account as part of his memoirs, Gould replied, "I look at my diary, Bernt, and I can find no reference to this at all."[62]

If Byrd *did* kneel in some sort of prayer, it was momentary, and he quickly regained enough self-command to take charge. He ordered Balchen and June back to Little America with Smith while he remained with Hanson and Gould in the mountains until the Fairchild could come back and take them to Little America. The three men then had to wait four days before the weather cleared sufficiently for the Fairchild to return. Gould, Byrd, and Hanson wedged themselves tightly into the little plane behind pilots Smith and June. The overloaded aircraft took off safely and arrived at Little America without incident. Byrd was quiet throughout the flight. Although he may have momentarily given in to terror, he did accept significant risk in flying in overloaded aircraft and living in a frozen tent for several days at a remote polar site, something his critics were loath to admit he would ever willingly do. Larry Gould defined Byrd's leadership qualities succinctly in giving his own account of the crisis. "I think Commander Byrd's most outstanding characteristic is his concern for the safety of his men. . . . The whole matter of coming to our rescue and of preparing people in the States for a possible catastrophe could not have been handled more intelligently."[63]

The Fokker's last flight and the return of the four trail parties marked the end of the first austral season for the expedition. Little America had been stoutly built on its "beautiful and eerie location." Out beyond the orange-painted shacks, the tall and spidery radio antennae, and the "spectral shapes of the anchored planes" stretched the vast Ross Ice Shelf. "Overwhelming solitude and a terrible stillness brooded over that immobile frozen scene," Byrd wrote. "Often we were shrouded in snow; soon we would be cloaked in a long darkness."[64] The first exploratory flights had yielded exciting and important new discoveries, and the first trails were marked out for the following year. Now each day the sun sank lower and lower in the horizon over the huge chunk of ice called Roosevelt Island just south of Little America. The cold intensified; thermometers were registering nearly fifty degrees below zero. It was time to go into the buildings, huts, and connecting tunnels heavily drifted over with snow.

Chapter 9

Zenith

As the 1929 Antarctic winter clamped down on Little America, men tried to keep as busy as possible. The meteorologists slipped briefly out into the dark several times each day to read the instruments measuring temperature, barometric pressure, wind direction, and velocity. "We made observations of ice conditions and posted a night watchman to record that weird spectacle, the aurora australis, which corresponds to the aurora borealis in the Arctic." Physicist Frank Davies conducted magnetic assessments. Radioman Malcolm Hanson conducted communication tests with New Zealand, went ten miles out on the dark and frigid barrier with Norman Vaughan for a week to conduct experiments on the ionosphere, kept the circuits open to radio stations KDKA and WGY in the States, and managed to link up with a University of Michigan observation post in Greenland that was measuring the aurora borealis. Comparing the two auroras kept the scientists excited, while the radio stations beamed news and programming directly to Little America, which not only entertained the Byrd expedition but kept it in public view as well. "Saturday night's broadcast by WGY, KDKA have given the expedition more publicity than any other means," one of Byrd's contacts in the radio world cabled in early September. All the Gannett and Hearst papers gave daily space to forthcoming broadcasts to Antarctica, and the *New York Times* usually devoted two columns on its front page the morning after. Radio remained a primitive and exciting medium in 1929, and when the stations contacted Little America directly and spoke with Byrd or Hanson, it caused a worldwide sensation. KDKA "receive[d] thousands [of] letters from all parts of the world," Byrd's radio representative told him at one point, "and desire repeat [broadcast] on Sept 14, with me at the microphone asking you a few questions."[1]

Russell Owen sent daily dispatches to the *New York Times* after Byrd reviewed them. The explorer later wrote deadpan that Owen "did a splendid job on a unique assignment. For the first time a day-by-day account of an Antarctic expedition was 'covered' like any other news event." This was exactly what Byrd wanted, of course: to be seen and to have his expedition seen as a seamless part of the daily life and experiences of the American public. Byrd later professed delight in Owen's Pulitzer Prize for the most outstanding news reporting of the year, "an award his accuracy, diligence, and alertness so richly deserve." In practice, however, he remained suspicious of Owen and kept a close eye on him. "Owen's right knee is swelling," Byrd recorded near the end of April as Little America went into "winter routine." "He said that fixing the fires wore him out, so he has now been relieved from all duties and he is doing nothing." Several days later, the commander cabled Hilton Howell Railey, requesting that he "make strong suggestion to Sulzberger or Birchall that they have some of the other people down here write stories such as Doctor Coman, Charlie Lofgren, McKinley . . . Physicist Davies," and others in order to "give a more comprehensive picture of expedition."[2]

Byrd and his colleagues also kept the Paramount movie cameramen busy. Joe Rucker and Will Van der Veer had proved themselves up to their assignment from the start. Bracing themselves on swaying, spray-filled decks, they had filmed the storm that struck *Bolling* and *City of New York* on the way down from New Zealand. They went up into *City*'s rigging and down onto the ice to record from often ingenious angles the ships' tedious, jarring journey through the pack. On one occasion they caught the image of *City*'s heavily smoking funnel reflected back from a sun-splashed ice floe. The men also managed to film part of the dramatic rescue on January 31 of several men pitched from *Bolling*'s deck into the water when the barrier gave way. The now dimly flickering images recorded nearly eighty years ago reflect the general panic as *City*'s overloaded lifeboat hit the water, its men rowing frantically toward their struggling mates. Rucker and Van der Veer later filmed the sledge trips that were ferrying supplies and aircraft parts from the ships to Little America, several aerial flights, and instrument readings both by daylight and by flares in the midst of the Antarctic night. Byrd once radioed Emanuel Cohen of Paramount News that "Joe and Van" were "on the job every minute," and had gotten "some remarkable shots containing both comedy and drama." Like the rest of the expedition, Rucker and Van der Veer necessarily curtailed their work during the winter but did make obligatory records of various "social events." The Paramount cameramen tried to cover incidents as they happened, but many had to be restaged because they happened too quickly or occurred without sufficient lighting, a common occurrence in the early days of cinema news when cameras remained big, bulky, and difficult to carry.[3]

Despite the cold and the dark, men soon discovered various ways to keep depression at bay. Byrd, who was a fanatic about exercise, had brought a fairly comprehensive gymnasium that he set up in what dog driver Eddie Goodale called the commander's "private cabin." Bernt Balchen noted that the commander also boxed and lifted weights with the men out in their quarters, and there were the nightly auction bridge games in Byrd's cabin. The four players were Byrd, Goodale, Rucker, and Ashley McKinley. Byrd partnered with Goodale for four months, thereafter with McKinley. Assistant meteorologist Henry Harrison apparently substituted from time to time. The men "came to know the commander fairly well," and Goodale found him to be "a most pleasant person to be with."[4]

Using flares or even a powerful flashlight, one could walk a "considerable distance" from Little America without great discomfort if the temperature did not exceed fifty below and the wind velocity twenty miles per hour. Byrd took frequent walks and often used these occasions to talk to his men. Some later maintained that he used the walks to extort information about possible disloyalty and to plant false stories about those he had come to dislike. The great majority, however, insisted that his purpose was to boost morale. Though some found Byrd's conversation at once opaque and pretentious, many others were mesmerized. "He was very aware of his impact on others," Wendell Summers, the veteran of Operation Highjump, recalled. "His looks, stature, bearing and speech begot respect, regardless of his rank." At the same time, Byrd was always approachable. No one hesitated to talk to him "almost anytime or anywhere." "When you conversed with" Byrd, "you learned about life, about emotions, about history, about values."[5]

Balchen spent hours reading in aerodynamics and math, discussing his ideas with Frank Davis and Henry Harrison. The forthcoming exploration season required much time-consuming planning. Byrd wanted to include more aerial missions to map as much of Antarctica as possible, in addition to the polar flight and Larry Gould's prolonged sledge trip to study the geological structure of the Queen Maud range. The details seemed endless and involved almost daily discussion between Gould, Byrd, the pilots, and the Little America support staff. One day during the course of discussing with Byrd computations for a flight, Balchen hinted at a question that had been preoccupying him for the past three years: had the *Josephine Ford* actually reached the North Pole? "B reaction to my mentioning the poss computation of the Jo Ford" was all that Balchen wrote in his diary. But years later, after Balchen and Byrd were both dead, adventure writer David Roberts published an article in *Outside* magazine titled "Heroes and Hoaxers: Commander Byrd's Flight of Fancy." Claiming to rely on an excised portion of Balchen's *Come North with Me*, Roberts wrote that Balchen promised Byrd that day on the ice to "go over the whole engine installation thoroughly" to make sure his computations were correct. Taking out the same slide rule he had used on the 1927 transatlantic flight, Balchen assured Byrd that "I've been keeping very careful figures on mileage and fuel consumption, just as I did on the *Josephine Ford*" during its trip around the country following the North Polar flight. Byrd allegedly interrupted at that point, "his eyes full of cold fire. 'Forget about that slide rule. From now on you stick to flying. I'll do the figuring.'"[6] Whether or not the incident took place as Roberts described, Balchen viewed his commander with deepening contempt as the expedition progressed.

Gould's forthcoming sled journey south across the Ross Ice Shelf to the trans-Antarctic mountains required an advance party to establish supply caches at fifty-mile intervals out to four hundred miles. "These depots were not only for the use of the geological party on the way back to Little America," Gould later wrote, "but for emergency use by the polar flight party." Depot 8, the farthest south, at the foot of the mountains, would be the base for the polar flight. Before starting their own work in the mountains, Gould and his men would locate a good landing field there and would stand by with a radio direction finder until the flight ended. The geologists would then move on to their own work.[7] Such an epic journey required as much advance planning as the forthcoming exploratory aviation flights. Meetings in the library of the executive building below the long Antarctic night went on for hours.

Despite occasional quick trips out into the South Polar darkness, the men of the Byrd Antarctic expedition soon "became a family of moles," scuttling through glistening snow tunnels with lanterns and flashlights. Byrd insisted on maintaining a rigid daily routine that revolved around a steady schedule of sleep and wakefulness. "Routine is vitally important during the winter months to prevent nervous collapse," he told himself in a diary entry just after the sun had disappeared. Meals were reduced to twice a day to compensate for the "let-up on exercise." No one would be allowed to "bunk in" late, for therein lay the way to declining morale. "Our major winter job is to be happy," Byrd preached. The only way to maintain such an attitude was to keep busy, not to brood and drowse in one's bunk. There was no way to fight off the cold entirely in the days before modern science brought central heating to the Antarctic, and coal stoves were the only source of tepid warmth. Temperatures in the sleeping quarters—only partially insulated against the frigid outdoors by drifted snow—were often no more than thirty to forty degrees warmer than outside, which meant that men routinely bundled into their sleeping bags when it was ten to twenty degrees below zero around them.

One o'clock, any morning, the watchman, in furs, his parka hood over his head, throws more coal in the library stove, the only stove kept going during the sleeping hours. In the other room is a row of double wooden bunks, each holding a huddled figure in a sleeping bag, head drawn under like that of a turtle.

Every half hour the lone watchman must duck out into the bitter cold. The aurora is painting its freakish, gyrating pictures across a dead sky. He notes the clouds, he checks each thermometer and thermograph to make sure the cold has not stopped the recording mechanisms. At 6 o'clock he makes the fire in the kitchen stove, which is on one side of the mess hall, opposite the bunks.

The clock strikes a high-pitched note, for the cold affects the bell, and the watchman "signs off" by calling Larry Gould. Gould's job is to get everyone up for breakfast. The men call him Simon Legree.[8]

As the first days passed, men became increasingly depressed, just as Byrd had been warned by veteran Antarctic explorers that they would be. Home was far away, and even though America's most popular entertainers—Ruth Etting, Fred Allen, Frances Upton, Bugs Baer, Jimmy Durante, Phil Baker—lined up to broadcast through often heavy static and fading signals down to the ice via WGY,[9] it was not enough. Despite Byrd's strictures, men took to their bunks, especially on weekends, for long hours at a stretch. The commander himself began to brood increasingly on the meaning of life and the universe as seen from the dark, frigid immensity of Antarctica.

Byrd was busy not only with managing matters at Little America but also with the expedition's business up in New York. The inevitable press of business was, in a way, healthy, for it kept the commander busier than his men. There were daily questions—on June 1 alone, for example, about the two ships up in New Zealand, about the maps that would emerge from the expedition, and about releasing Byrd's most recent report to the secretary of the navy. Byrd also sent a number of personal messages to Arthur Sulzberger and Fred Birchall of the *New York Times,* to Dudley Diggs of General Electric, and to Irving Berlin, thanking him for sending a personal message "in song." Three days later, the explorer sent out messages to such worthies as Isaiah Bowman, Harry Guggenheim, Raymond Fosdick, Judge Carter (Byrd's old benefactor from Philippine days and later), David Rockefeller, and Jack LaGorce (his longtime editor at *National Geographic Magazine*), informing each that Byrd had not forgotten them and that a trail or a part of the Little America complex was being named in their honor.

Later there were radio exchanges with Harold Tapley, who had replaced Brophy in Dunedin, about getting the two ships ready for the next season, when Byrd expected they would have "pretty hard duty" to perform, and other exchanges about getting mail down to Little America as soon as possible.[10] Money remained the most pressing need. On April 2 Byrd sent a rather frantic cable to New Zealand. Port costs to keep *Eleanor Bolling* and *City of New York* maintained through the austral winter were much higher (two thousand dollars per month) than he had budgeted for, and on top of that, he would have to pay the skeleton crews something. Fortunately, Byrd was blessed with an aggressive agent at home. Two days later, Railey wrote a soothing letter to Marie, stating that he had gone to her husband's old friend and benefactor Raymond Fosdick regarding the question "of total payment of Dick's obligations before he returns to the United States." Fosdick told Railey not to worry, assuring him "in unmistakable terms that every penny owed by the expedition will be paid in full before Dick returned from the Antarctic." The pledge covered every conceivable creditor. "It may take months. It may take a year. But it will be done." Byrd would presumably not have to confront unpaid bills on his return.[11]

There were a few pleasant responsibilities. One was to see that Captain Nilsen and the men of the *Larsen* were properly wined and dined when they passed through New York on the way home to Scandinavia. Railey laid on a party and some entertainments for them, and Byrd sent a telegram from Little America. Showing genuine appreciation to men for a job well done was a trait that endeared Dick Byrd to many.

Family matters continued to burden Richard's conscience. He and Marie maintained their intensely affectionate correspondence, but a letter sent off in March from Boston or the ice would not reach its recipient for at least six months. This did not stop young Dickie from writing occasionally. "I did not want you to go a way [*sic*] but you did," the boy told his father at some point during Byrd's stay on the ice. "I am very sorry you did." The eight and nine year old was always eager to press money on his parent, to let his father know that he understood the tribulations that "Daddy" was enduring and wanted in some way to share them. With a bit more time on his hands, Dick tried to stay in touch with his son. "I have named a big new land after mommie," he wrote soon after he reached the ice, "because mommie is the sweetest, finest and nicest and best person in the whole world." Dick urged his son to "take good care of her and be awfully sweet to her while I'm away," adding, "I love you my dear boy." In another letter he assured his son that he had kept all his letters and that "I read them all two or three times and during the winter which is six months of total darkness I will read them many times more because I always enjoy your letters." He wrote that he had used the five dollars Dickie had sent him to buy supplies "which will be necessary for the expedition." Marie was "the most unselfish person in the world," he told the boy, "and you are next to her."[12]

Brophy became a problem that would not go away. At the end of February, Railey learned that Byrd contemplated rehiring him in several months. Railey hit the roof. He wrote Marie an uncharacteristically frank letter in which he, in effect, told the Byrds to choose him or Brophy. After all that had happened, Byrd simply could not afford to keep Brophy with him. "It would cost him much, much more than the loss of my services. Believe me, I know that." Moreover, the commander was too far away to assess the Brophy mess in its fullest context. Only he, Railey, supported always by Marie's "sound judgment," was in a position to do so. Finally, "Dick should put these matters up to me directly. How can I function if I do not know what is going on in his mind and am constantly getting information second handedly?" Richard cabled Railey on April 2, urging "you do nothing unfair to Brophy. If he is capable of carrying on business we must not take away his opportunity to do so." And he sent an encouraging cable to Brophy himself after that luckless man said he was leaving a New Zealand hospital and heading home via Australia. "Remember," Byrd wrote, "no matter what hard luck you had we can work things out if you will continue to have faith in me." Byrd added personal best wishes from "Your friend." At the same time, the explorer radioed Railey "to investigate the circumstances surrounding Brophy's separation from the Chamber of Commerce at Muncie, Indiana, three years ago, and to get all the dope . . . on Brophy's background, with particular emphasis on his physical history."

Railey soon learned that whatever problems and peccadilloes Brophy might have been involved with in the past paled before the fact that he had just been hospitalized at Dunedin "for mental diseases" and faced deportation. "Mrs. Brophy is almost uncontrollable," he told Marie. Moreover, Brophy had gotten hold of pictures from the Antarctic and had peddled them to the New Zealand press, in violation of Byrd's contracts. Railey complained to Marie of "Dick's great hesitancy to take decisive action" against Brophy. As a result, "Brophy has the upper hand. His wife threatens suicide one day, retaliation the next. His father and mother are enroute to New Zealand and that is a major complication for reasons I do not care to put down here."[13]

Marie now began to step into the picture decisively, encouraging Railey to stand fast and letting him know that she was behind him in all he did. Together, they would shield Richard as much as possible from pressures at home. They would use radio contact with Little America to calm and reassure the explorer, not add to his burdens.

Those burdens soon increased. Mrs. Brophy walked out of the mental ward at Lenox Hill Hospital only to show up at Railey's door. He thought her "somewhat improved." But several days later, the woman relapsed. "One doctor," Railey informed Marie, "refused to handle the case because she refused to cooperate." A second doctor placed her in Murray Hill Sanitarium.[14]

Brophy reached New York the first week in June. Railey persuaded him to see Dr. Gregory, the "noted alienist" at Bellevue Hospital. Brophy was not dangerous, Railey maintained, only pathetic. The man's "family affairs," he wrote Marie, were "so frightfully involved" that it would be useless to press expedition matters on him, although it appeared that he had misappropriated a large amount of funds. Brophy told Railey his only desire was to "straighten out his domestic situation in order that he may make amends," and Railey was impressed by "Brophy's obvious and, I sometimes think, sincere humility." He radioed Little America on June 12 that he had attended Brophy's preliminary examination "by noted alienist" who had found the man calm and rational. Railey told Byrd he believed Brophy's problems revolved around his wife, with whom he was having "Hell's own time." Byrd had already reached other conclusions. He radioed Railey from the Antarctic on June 7, asking him to query Brophy closely about a number of alleged shortfalls on the New Zealand books, including sixty-five hundred dollars "from expedition personal expenses." Byrd resumed the dialogue two days later. Railey was to "speak frankly" to Brophy "and give me detailed report [on] whole matter." Railey should tell Brophy "carefully" that Byrd was not the source of the man's disturbed state, that Byrd had been loyal to Brophy and wished to remain so. "If he still claims that he has had no mental derangement, he must understand that his position is a serious one." Byrd doubted if Brophy had been faking insanity, "as he showed undoubted evidence of it two days prior to our departure [from] New Zealand."[15]

The Brophy mess weighed on Byrd throughout the long polar night. Railey continued to keep a close eye on Brophy, who soon went to Canada, but then returned. Not until early September, with a low sun back in the Antarctic sky, did the affair play out to its bizarre conclusion: Brophy faked suicide after leaving suggestive letters in his New York hotel room and his clothes at a Coney Island bathhouse. To Marie's nearly inexpressible relief, and that of Railey as well, the incident elicited little press interest. "Story . . . broke beautifully," Marie cabled her husband on September 8. The few news items, buried on the back pages of the nation's papers, emphasized that Brophy had resigned from the expedition months earlier and had returned to the States to take up other business interests. Marie and Railey had learned of two secret forwarding addresses that Brophy had arranged before his disappearance, and the two were convinced that Brophy was alive and well somewhere. Richard was not to worry further about the matter. Three weeks later, Byrd received a cable from Brophy's parents, finally released from being stranded in New Zealand, thanking him for all his help "during these days of trying anxiety." Richard, gracious to the end, replied that he would never forget the "wonderful job" their son "did for me in New York" and asked the senior Brophy to "consider me your sincere friend and allow me to do whatever is in my power to be of service to you."[16]

Railey screened Marie and the children from public engagements, including an invitation to be present at a tribute to Charles Lindbergh. Marie wanted to attend, but Railey counseled her that any breech of her desire to remain completely out of the public limelight would irretrievably compromise her position. In the gentlest terms, using the most circumspect language, he informed Marie that she must either maintain the seclusion from public life that she had hitherto chosen or jump with both feet into the middle of her husband's ongoing publicity circus; there was no third choice. She chose to continue her seclusion while taking an increasingly active role in shaping expedition matters from Boston and New York, often employing the tone of seemingly helpless confusion employed by southern belles of the day when they sought either favors or power. Railey seemed to "know just what to do" about the Brophy matter, she wrote at one point during that crisis. "You certainly handled our friend and his affairs in a 'masterly way.'" She also asked of Railey, "Do help me out in this old Hyams matter," complaining that the Walter Hyams clipping service Richard had engaged the year before was using the explorer's name "unscrupulously." When Railey promptly did so, she gushed, "I can never thank you enough for your attending to that Hyams matter for me. I hope it isn't going to be disagreeable to you."[17]

It was. The clipping service accused Railey himself of scuttling a perfectly legitimate business contract and trying to blacken the Hyams Agency in the process. The company asked, not unreasonably, what complaints Commander or Mrs. Byrd had with its service and demanded not only what it claimed was an outstanding bill of $150 but also a return of the clippings furnished since the previous autumn. Hapless in the face of this counterattack, Railey asked Marie to enumerate her complaints, which, she replied, involved the lack of magazine articles and editorials. She confessed that her complaints lacked focus and were rather confusing, "but I am poor at writing clearly." After a final exchange of correspondence that lasted into mid-September, Railey was forced to pay the $150 to terminate the affair.[18]

Marie's power grew steadily. She would do anything for Richard, and everyone knew it. On their wedding anniversary she wrote her husband a lengthy letter that might not reach him for a year. "I wish I could tell you how happy the last fourteen years have been for me. I can't realize it has been so long. I wish I could be with you to-day, Darling. There is so much that I want to tell you—about how happy I have been and am, and how much I miss you and love you. More than ever Dick—much more." She and Richard had a secret code that they used in cables back and forth between the States and the ice. Marie occasionally forgot it and was furious with herself, revealing the kind of temper she possessed if she cared to use it. "If I am not the biggest, most hopeless damn fool! And I was so sure I was right about that code," she wrote on one occasion early in 1929. "I didn't take it with me, as it never occurred to me I would need it in n.y. And when I found I did, I was equally sure I remembered it perfectly. Instead I added in an extra word to one sentence which of course balled everything up."

Such a lady was not to be trifled with, and she wasn't. Railey never made a decision, large or small, without consulting her and winning her permission. That July, for example, his secretary wrote, asking Marie's reaction to a proposal for "an all-scientific broadcasting program, led by Mr. Edison," wherein "six or eight of the most noted scientists in the United States" would "speak to Commander Byrd" not through a microphone but by a "movie-tone machine." Railey's objective was to "strengthen the scientific status of the expedition." He had already asked Richard and was waiting for a reply from Little America, but he wanted Marie's approval also.[19]

As the summer of 1929 passed, Railey became very close to the Byrd family. Marie invited him and his wife up to their temporary summer place at Rye Beach, and Railey discussed every aspect of expedition business with her. He planned to approach Van Lear Black, a mutual friend of Richard and Franklin Roosevelt, for additional funds; he would override Richard's insistence that he did not want another Fairchild aircraft unless it was donated; he had been tempted by an offer from ace newsman and adventurer Floyd Gibbons to go to Antarctica on an expedition in late 1930 after Richard returned home, and he bitterly regretted the temptation when it became public by means of a news conference Gibbons called in Washington. He had just been to the White House where he had been petted and photographed as Richard Byrd's chief representative. Marie's replies were infrequent, usually supportive, but occasionally sharp. She began one letter, "Please don't approach Van Lear Black. I know I can always say 'don't' so easily that it must be discouraging to you, but there is a good reason for not doing so that I am not at liberty to tell you. It is mighty wise of you," she warned, "to ask me first." "I shall be so interested," she purred another time, "in learning the news about the f.g. [Floyd Gibbons] Expedition after the conference in Washington. Have you sent Dick a message and if not, why not! I'll also radio him." A chastened Railey assured his patron that he had no intention of signing on with Floyd Gibbons or anyone else so long as the Byrds needed him.[20]

Marie made certain that he understood her concern, and also her expertise. She asked intelligent questions about dispatching new motors for the planes at Little America; she wondered about Richard's financial patrons, what they were up to that might harm or compromise her beloved husband in any way; she thanked Railey for smartly handling rude letters to her husband. In mid-November, shortly before the polar flight, Railey told Marie that he was beginning to be pressed to accept speaking engagements to talk about the expedition. Such pressures would surely increase. Should he accept the invitations? "What do you think?" As the 1929 holiday season approached, it was time to get out the apple list. Dick wanted to know if Tom or Harry could help. Would Marie find out? She sent the apples out herself and received the usual grateful notes from such notables as Admiral Moffett and Adolph Ochs of the *New York Times*.[21]

Down on the ice, Byrd and his men, crammed together in the dark, tense and stressed out, found little relief in cards or exercise. Liquor was another matter. Excessive drinking was the greatest problem that Byrd had to confront on both of his private expeditions, and he never handled the problem well. The United States was, of course, "dry" during the twenties and early thirties, and drinking, along with smoking, became a widely respected badge of rebellion. During the Greenland expedition in 1925, Byrd had issued a warning to his men against violating federal Prohibition laws, and he noted primly in his diary on Christmas Day 1928 that he had taken only a sip of champagne during the festivities, in part as an example to others. Nonetheless, the crew of *Bolling* had been drinking heavily just before the ship struck the Atlantic hurricane, and the men of both *Bolling* and *City of New York* had binged at Tahiti on their way to New Zealand. When the expedition reached Dunedin, nearly everyone went on a buying spree for booze, which Byrd did little to prevent. Once on the ice, the men began drinking in lulls between hauling supplies to the Little America site. Byrd and Gould joined them on several occasions.[22] As winter set in with increasing cold and total darkness, the drinking intensified.

The first party occurred on May 9 to celebrate the third anniversary of Byrd's North Polar flight, and thereafter the drinking never really stopped. Byrd's initial strategy was to stay aloof from the partying, though on one memorable occasion he was roped in and, after forcing drinks on several people, started to drink so heavily that he collapsed. As he was being hauled to his room, the commander begged his helpers not to tell Owen, nor even his little dog, Igloo. Drinking, suffocating confinement, and barely suppressed rage at certain colleagues inevitably led to practical jokes, some of them innocent and amusing, others less so, as when Pete Demas conspired with a few others—including Byrd—to wake everyone in the middle of the night with bloodcurdling screams that the barrier was breaking up and the camp was about to float off into the Ross Sea. As the calendar staggered toward August and the sun's reappearance, the drinking continued sporadically, leading to increasingly ugly confrontations, a few fistfights, and the isolation of the weakest members of the expedition. Eugene Rodgers's account of Little America in the polar winter of 1929, derived from a wide variety of accounts, suggests nothing less than a perpetual nightly uproar in the confined, freezing underground rooms of the camp.[23]

In mid-July Byrd at last confronted the growing problem when Jack O'Brien, a tough thirty-two-year-old surveyor who had played professional football, refused his commander's request to stop drinking after lights out. Byrd immediately ordered a general curfew, to be enforced by Demas, the night watchman, who had asked for the duty in order to have quiet hours to study for his forthcoming college years. The next morning at breakfast O'Brien tried to enlist at least one supporter, and Byrd jumped to the conclusion that he might be facing the initial stages of a general mutiny.[24]

Acutely aware of the limited leadership tools he had at his disposal, yet determined not to follow the disastrous course of assuming the role of martinet, Byrd chose several paths to defuse a possibly fatal crisis. First, he continued to encourage the classes that Gould and others held in the camp library every evening. Gould's class in geology was especially well attended by those who would be going out on the "Southern Part[ies]" once the sun returned. In his abortive polar dash twenty years earlier, Shackleton had managed to bring back coal, fossil plants, and petrified wood from the trans-Antarctic mountains, and Gould was anxious to confirm and amplify his predecessor's "proof of a temperate past." Harold June conducted a ground school in aviation, and Hanson a radio class. Unfortunately, the classes could not last until Taps at ten, and so there was always an hour or more to drink before lights out.[25]

Second, Byrd made crude attempts to stimulate camaraderie through the formation of various committees and groups, by far the most prominent of which was the "78 Club," which referred to the approximate latitudes, north and south, at which Byrd had established his polar bases. The club's objective was so transparent as to be almost insulting, for on the one hand it represented a plea for understanding by a beleaguered leader and on the other Byrd's ham-handed and very probably uncomfortable attempt to become one of the boys. All members accepted the proposition that "their leader's daily example of understanding, sympathy, unswerving courage, self-forgetting manhood, and productive energy . . . has made him at once foremost in the conquest of earth's unknown places whether land, sea, or air, and foremost in the hearts of all peoples, and . . . has inspired in his followers ideals as lofty as those for which their late comrade Floyd Bennett unhesitatingly gave his life."

Bad as was the justification for forming the club, Byrd's remarks upon assuming the presidency were worse. He told his listeners that the common values uniting club members were "character and loyalty to each other, as man to man," which all knew to be "the only thing that really counts." Dick Byrd was "simply one of 42 men." Money, influence, social position, and fame might all be important in the far distant world. But down here at Little America all knew "that what is important is how a fellow stands on his feet as a shipmate and a man." He wanted no politics in the club, nor would he accept "bossing" by himself or anyone else. Expanding unnecessarily on his earlier comments, Byrd stated with feigned humility that he harbored "a sneaking position that I really rank among the least of you." This wasn't false modesty, Byrd continued; he didn't mean to "knock" himself. But his highest aspiration was to be one of the boys. "I tell you frankly that if I can go along with you as one of you, and hold my own as a shipmate, I shall be very pleased with myself. And I shall be content if you all can say of me that I am your friend and worthy of your friendship." Indulging in modesty even further, Byrd said that Bennett "deserved far more credit" for the success of the Greenland expedition than anyone else. The same could be true of the North Polar flight, but fifty-two others had made that flight possible, and the "best of the fifty-two" were members of the 78 Club, including Balchen, Demas, Hanson, Owen, Alton Parker, and Van der Veer. As for the transatlantic flight, "Balchen did more for its success than I did."[26] Perhaps in that time and that place Byrd's posturing was not as transparent as it is to those reading his words while sitting comfortably in a warm room nearly eighty years later. But it was undoubtedly an embarrassment to the reasonably self-confident and self-sufficient explorers and aviators who lived through that long, dark austral winter at Little America I.

Byrd's third response to what perhaps was a growing social crisis within the camp centered on Russell Owen. Byrd simply did not like him, nor did others. It is a regrettable fact of human nature that groups under continuous stress quickly find a target and a scapegoat for their fears or frustrations, someone who is inevitably perceived as a misfit, and thus outside the group. Indeed, in extreme cases the group will take its very identity from the persecution of one or two hapless souls in its midst. Owen was openly fearful, verbalizing his worries about disaster. But his besetting sin was that he would not work. Demas characterized Owen as "small in stature and weak physically (the weakest here)." The former characteristic was acceptable, perhaps even beneficial. The latter was intolerable. Owen had "not participated in any of the work of the expedition other than his line to any extent," Demas wrote. The reporter always seemed to be sick or ailing in some way.

At first, Owen was not the only one to attract general enmity. Tom Mulroy, a fuel and water mechanic, exhibited a deadly combination of haughtiness and incompetence from the start of the expedition. One night he also lied about membership in an exclusive aviation fraternity and was found out. Embarrassed and

enraged, he turned on Ashley McKinley and slugged him, earning a general beating from his enraged colleagues, then a more specific one later from George Black,
the heavy-drinking supply officer, who decided Mulroy had not been punished
enough. Mulroy was understandably terrified by the whole incident and thereafter
behaved himself. Slowly, painfully, he ingratiated himself at least in part. Owen
did not, at least not with Richard Byrd.[27]

On July 20, eight days after his run-in with O'Brien, Byrd showed to a favored
few what Eugene Rodgers rightly calls an "extraordinary document," intended to
be read by those closest to him in case of his death. The fourteen-page memorandum was an extended diatribe against Owen, summarizing everything that Byrd
disliked or suspected about him. As long ago as the voyage down to New Zealand,
Owen had "boasted" that he could "make or break" any and every man on the expedition through his daily dispatches while deriding "any ideals connected with
the expedition" as "simply bunk." Everyone, Owen continued, was along for "selfish personal gain or adventure." He had "vilified Amundsen" while in Spitsbergen
to cover the Norwegian and his North Polar flight, and he returned from an interview with the world's greatest aviator "saying he hated Lindbergh's eyes." Surely, Dr. Dana Coman was right: Owen suffered from a "hatred complex." If Owen
was ever shown the memo, his response went unrecorded.[28]

Not even the formation of the 78 Club or the venting of his frustrations by
picking on Owen was enough to calm the demon of apprehension that clearly possessed Dick Byrd as the polar winter began to wane. The day after he wrote his
anti-Owen memo, Byrd invited Paul Siple, the not-so-young Boy Scout, out on
the dark ice shelf around the camp for a walk and a talk. It was the first he would
have with a small number of those he considered most dependable.

Byrd's objective was nothing less than the formation of a "Loyal Legion"—a
cadre of devoted followers who would help the commander quell any disturbances.
Byrd's motives can be interpreted as paranoid, or as common sense. Violence
seemed to be brimming just below the surface of the often uproarious little camp;
the Mulroy incident had demonstrated that. It was Dick Byrd's job to quell it any
way he could or see the expedition and his future go down in disgrace, if not worse.

Walking along the dark polar terrain with the younger men of Little America,
Siple, Vaughan, and others, booted feet crunching on the snow, Byrd, torch or
flashlight in hand, read from a five-page, twenty-nine-paragraph script that began,
"As I understand it, you came on this expedition to serve it by serving me, its leader.
You would not have signed up had you not determined to give me your loyalty. I
believe that because I believe in you." It was a "big moment for me," Byrd continued, when he could tell young Siple, Vaughan, and the others all that they had
meant to the expedition during the "dreaded monotony" of the long winter night,

a monotony that "in many other expeditions has affected the reason and hearts of men so that their loyalty has failed their leaders." But Siple, Vaughan, and the handful of others whom Byrd would anoint had "been as true as steel and honorable and noble in your loyalty."

Having said all this, Byrd interrupted to inquire whether his listener questioned his sincerity and whether the listener believed Byrd had been loyal to him. Since the commander had maneuvered his subordinate into an impossible position, there could be no question of returning an ambiguous answer. Moreover, some of the men, Vaughan among them, had quietly endured crises of their own—in Vaughan's case, the almost murderous dislike of his nominal superior, Arthur Walden. Since the expedition had arrived on the ice, the older man had seen his position as head of the dog-team drivers undermined by Vaughan's sunny, stubborn competence, and Vaughan had been told that Walden was out to get him, perhaps to murder him with a gun. Now Byrd was confirming Vaughan's sense of his own worth. In earning Walden's hatred the young man had been neither a fool nor a traitor to the expedition but, rather, a great benefactor.

There is "something very deep in human nature," Byrd continued, "that admires above everything, a record of manly friendship that remains true and loyal through all manner of vicissitudes." That was what Byrd wanted to conclude with Vaughan, Siple, and the others, a pact of firm friendship out of which would emerge a fraternity, "the purpose of which is to ensure, as far as possible, that neither now nor in civilization any person or persons in the expedition be permitted to be disloyal or mutinous." Only those whom Byrd could accept as friends "without reservation and with all the deep sincerity of the word friendship" could be accepted. And, of course, "for reasons which are obvious," no one but Richard Byrd would know who the others were "until we return to civilization." The leader had no doubts about Vaughan or Siple or whomever he was talking to; did that individual have any doubts about him? Whatever some may have thought, no one expressed any reservations, and the bargain was struck.

Then came the lengthy oath, summarized in the first sentence. Siple, Vaughan, and the others solemnly swore on their word of honor "and by all that I reverence and hold sacred, and without hesitation or mental reservation, that I will divulge to no one in any way and in no manner, anything whatever in connection with the LOYAL LEGION" unless Byrd's permission was first granted. Moreover, "in case of disloyalty displayed in a crowd when you are present," the Legionnaire would act "in response to a pre-determined signal and pre-determined course of action." The oath concluded with the remarkable pledge that the apprentice Legionnaire "as one of the embodiments of the spirit of this expedition will protect it against traitors from within. To all of this I swear, so Help Me God." Byrd then faced his listener and swore that he would hold the man's "pledged loyalty as a most sacred trust" and would return it with his own unshakable loyalty. Rodgers believes the Loyal Legion was basically a reflection of Byrd's waning confidence in his ability to control the expedition—and thus his "overwhelming insecurity." Vaughan's impression was that Byrd was really concerned with the expedition's return to "civilization" when others beyond the group would seek to deny the commander's achievements or "disregard the data he had collected."[29] Doubtless, Byrd's motives included both considerations.

Not even formation of the Loyal Legion, which included Vaughan, Siple, Demas, Fred Crockett, and Joe DeGanahl, could calm Byrd's nerves, and it seemed to Gould, Balchen, and others that the man was losing his grip. Someone, perhaps Balchen or Black, or even Byrd himself, suggested an official pledge of loyalty, and on August 1 it was duly delivered to the commander in the form of a handsome plaque made by Balchen and signed by all hands. Charlie Lofgren saw that it was transmitted to the States in the form of a testimonial. Byrd should have been happy, and mostly he was, but he wired Railey on the fifth that since "Owen has given this no publicity therefore no one should make it public as it would be breaking contract with the Times." However, the *Times* editorial staff—Sulzberger, Ochs, and Birchall—could be informed. Railey promptly sent a copy to Marie and told her several days later that he had arranged with the paper to publish the testimonial, "and they did it in such a way that the item did not appear to have been inspired by Dick himself or by any member of his expedition." Down in Little America, Gould followed up the testimonial with a little massaging of his own, telling his commander, "Of course you must understand that it is impossible for any of us to visualize or appreciate the battle you had in preparation for the expedition."

Unfortunately, poor Owen put his foot in his mouth once again, casually informing Byrd one day that "he didn't like dogs." Everyone knew of Byrd's fondness for the species. He saw to it that the pathetic death in harness of an old husky named Spy was prominently featured in the Paramount film of the expedition, and he had brought down to the ice his own fox terrier, Igloo, who had been with him in Spitsbergen. Owen's gaffe was inexplicable. He "is perhaps the only one in camp who doesn't like Igloo," Byrd marveled. "It is astonishing that he could have written such good articles about Iggie and old Spy. He got more commendation from the former over almost any story he has ever written." But for the moment Byrd's anxieties were tamed by the "spontaneous" tribute and other appreciative comments he received. He made no further efforts to impose loyalty.[30]

When the sun at last reappeared, the men, led by Gould with Byrd's indulgence, held another wild party, climaxing in a "football game" in the mess hall. Furniture and blackboards were broken amid the steady consumption of alcohol. "As might have been anticipated," Rodgers remarks, half a dozen members of the expedition kept on drinking and "kept at it on and off for days." At last, Gould summoned the problem drinkers to the library and ordered them to calm down. If they did not, they would be sent back home as passengers once *Bolling* and *City of New York* returned. Byrd was there and seconded his executive officer. The drinkers had already alienated their more sober and responsible colleagues and were sufficiently chastened to stay at least reasonably sober from then on.[31]

Just as the sun was poised to return in a glorious dawn and the camp began settling down with the prospect of the vigorous field season to come, the worst possible news arrived in a series of cables from the outer world. Wilkins, the only other man so far to fly in the Antarctic, was coming back, and for many long weeks it appeared from his cryptic comments that he would try to beat Byrd to the pole. Here was a crisis that at once depressed Richard and brought Little America together in a sense of competitive outrage. Wilkins was even cheeky enough to state that during the course of his infuriatingly vague set of flights he would come to Little America for Christmas dinner, and could Byrd please arrange to have some fuel cached to send Wilkins on his way? It all sounded as if Wilkins might try for the pole as early as the coming November; Byrd had not planned on making his trip until December.

"Wilkins is out to lick us," Byrd cabled Railey in evident gloom. "He is flying over the area [the peninsula to the Ross Sea] we are most anxious to explore and which is most important to science. I wish to impress upon you that the flight he proposes is even more important than a flight to the South Pole." Wilkins would enjoy a "big advantage" because his equipment "comes fresh from the States." Could Richard even assume a successful flight season aboard an aircraft—the Ford trimotor—that had been cooped up in an icy snow hangar for months? Moreover, starting much farther north, Wilkins could begin flying earlier. Byrd reiterated that the Australian "is going to make every effort to beat us to it. Don't forget that he was offered fifty thousand dollars by Hearst to beat me to the South Pole and that he will now possibly fly here by way of the South Pole." In spite of everything, Byrd told Railey, "we have got to be sports and have got to be square with" Wilkins, though this did not extend to revealing when the Byrd expedition would begin its own flight season.

For more than a month, neither Byrd nor Railey could get any information about Wilkins's plans or schedule. At last, on September 24, Hearst's *San Francisco Examiner* provided some details, though they remained infuriatingly imprecise. Wilkins was leaving New York City the next day aboard the steamer *Northern Prince* for Buenos Aires, where he would board the whaler *Melville* for the peninsula. He planned to fly "much further into the depths of the great white South than last Winter in his trail blazing expedition to lands never before trod by man." He would visit "the camp of Commander Byrd at the Bay of Whales" and hoped through the use of aircraft to determine if the Ross and Weddell Seas were connected at any point. This sketchy outline frustrated Byrd still further, and he promptly cabled Railey to tell Wilkins, "Have sent you three messages requesting your plans." Just in case Wilkins had missed all three, "I am having this message delivered by my representative Hilton Railey." Byrd did not disguise either his feelings or his objectives: "This is to force you to reveal your plans," not to thwart them, but "simply to be sure that you receive my requests. Again I want to wish you good luck."[32]

The definitive word on Wilkins's plan, or as close to it as Wilkins cared to make it, came the next day, not from Railey but from Owen's boss at the *New York Times*, Fred Birchall. One of the paper's reporters had interviewed Wilkins, who remained irritatingly coy about his schedule but quite forthcoming about his crew and objectives. The Australian did not mention the South Pole but did talk about a nonstop flight from either Deception Island or Marguerite Bay to Little America, a distance of about 2,500 miles. Wilkins seemed well equipped. His aircraft were the latest Lockheed Vegas, very reliable planes that Wiley Post would use three years later to fly around the world in record time. Wilkins's pilots left something to be desired, but the man had confidence. He planned to fly to Little America, board his whaler (which would have steamed down from the peninsula), and head back north "in time for the [German dirigible] Graf Zeppelin expedition over the North Pole next year."[33]

As the sun rose higher in the South Polar sky, flooding the vast shelf with light, Richard began to throw off his winter garments of anxiety and uncertainty. Reports that the world press was full of accounts of the resumption of expedition activities buoyed his spirits. Good news also came from brother Harry, who wrote Marie at the end of July that he was hearing "the most splendid reports about Dick. His Expedition is creating a great interest and has attracted the admiration of millions of people." Public interest was nice enough, but it did not pay the bills. When Harry Guggenheim said, however, that "when Dick returns . . . he will be the real hero of the world," it counted for something. Harry had other intriguing news for his brother. John D. Rockefeller Jr. and his family had been in Winchester for a visit. The young multimillionaire had expressed deep interest in Richard Byrd "and I think would be glad to help out in any way that would be necessary. The Rockefellers are most anxious for you to stay with them when you come to New York." Harry added the completely gratuitous advice that "it would be a splendid idea for you to do this."[34]

With Wilkins heading for the peninsula, Byrd's polar flight had to get under way as soon as possible. But some at Little America believed Gould's long-projected multimonth research trip to study the Queen Maud Mountains was of equal, if not greater, importance than a stunt flight to the bottom of the earth, which Amundsen and Scott had demonstrated was a bare plain of icy nothingness. The missions were, in fact, interrelated. The polar flight could not take place until Gould reached the foot of the Queen Mauds, laid several fuel depots, and stood by to rescue the fliers if necessary. But Gould and his five companions could not depart until the support team had sledged out to lay the four (not eight, as originally planned) supply depots at 50-mile intervals that would provide the final vital component Gould would need in his distant mission. Hanson was slow in preparing the radios for the field parties, and the cold remained so severe (down to sixty-below Fahrenheit) that the sledge drivers did not want to take their dogs out until it moderated.

Byrd pushed them all. He wanted to get going, to get the season started and completed. Who knew what heroics Wilkins and others yet unknown might accomplish? He broke up a bridge game one night in anger at Henry Harrison and called meetings to beg the sledge drivers to get out on the trail. They went, but soon returned without finishing their mission. The "snowmobile," a Ford Model A with skis and Caterpillar treads, broke down 80 miles out on the southern trail. The disconsolate crew walked back to base, eliciting little sympathy from their traditionalist colleagues, who looked askance at anything other than dog power. Byrd's response was mild and generous. He sensed the technology was as yet too crude for harsh Antarctic conditions. He would try again. Meantime, the crew had given their all.

But he was adamant on another point. As September passed into October and the support parties still struggled to complete their depot-laying missions, Gould, Pete Smith, and the others pressed Byrd to use the Fairchild or the Ford to lay the depots. The dog teams had not proved to be of the highest quality, and many of the animals were becoming exhausted pulling the heavy sledges through the cold and around the fearsome crevasse fields that stretched across the shelf, roughly 50 miles south of Little America.[35] But Byrd needed the smaller plane for possible rescue work on the polar flight, and the aviation gas supply was low. Gould later wrote mildly that he and the others could not move their commander, but in private the scientists were furious that Byrd seemed willing to sacrifice critical geological research to the polar flight.[36]

In fact, he was not, as he made very clear in several messages to Gould. The geologist and his party were also out on the trail by mid-October, traveling south for a time with the support party to test equipment, try out the dog teams, and just get a feel for trail life. The "geological party" was also carrying some of the supplies for deposit at the trail depots. But Gould's confidence in handling his dog teams, under admittedly harsh conditions, was no greater than the year before, when he had exasperated Byrd with his timidity during the building of Little America. Art Walden and the other members of the support party seemed no less hesitant. When Gould radioed Byrd that he wished to return to the camp to revise his plans, Byrd urged him to do so out on the trail and offered to send support. Gould promptly replied that he "was not prepared to continue as you suggest." The trail stove was proving very difficult and was impossible to repair. Byrd then sent a message to the support party, sympathizing with its "hard going" but begging leader Walden not to be discouraged. "Our thoughts are with you fellows and we know you will do as well as anyone could."[37]

When Gould returned, he and the other members of the geological party held a conference to modify their plans. The sledge loads had proved much too heavy, but even with a radical change the success of the geological mission seemed "most doubtful" to the geologists. Their commander sought to brace them. He read, then left with them, a rather lengthy memo in which he flatly stated that the accomplishment of the geological work "is of such transcendent importance that I will do anything within my power to make it possible for you to succeed." Byrd then proposed discarding "any idea" of using the geological party either to make a staging base for the polar flight at the foot of the Queen Maud mountain range or to act as a rescue party from that base. Moreover, Byrd pledged to postpone the departure of *City of New York* until February 10, "so as to give you many more weeks to accomplish your mission." If even this postponement were not enough, the commander would arrange to have a small "chaser" from one of the big whalers in the area (presumably *Larsen*) call at Little America, "probably as late as Feb. 20th or 25th," to pick up the geological party. In that case, Byrd would transfer from *City of New York* to the whaler, then to its chaser, and "come down on here" to Little America "to get the geological party." While Gould remained at Little America digesting his commander's pledge, Norman Vaughan and several others went back out on the trail within forty-eight hours, hauling their loads under Gould's modified plan "with a preliminary trip to the 100 mile base." Soon Vaughan was radioing that the dogs were giving out after only 16 miles. The animals required immediate rest "if they are to serve us later." Vaughan also reported "important deficiencies . . . in gear." This time Gould, stiffened by his commander's commitment to the project, hung tough. Stay out on the trail, he told the twenty-two-year-old Harvard man, lighten the loads somehow, stay off the sledges yourselves, and "let [the] poor dogs run." Later Gould advised Vaughan to take a rest for a day or two "and see if situation doesn't look better for dogs."[38]

Conditions were undeniably hellish. While weather at Little America remained heavily overcast with occasional flurries, there were storms down south, with heavy winds and snowfall as close as the 44-mile depot, where Walden's support party was holed up all of October 20. Three days later, Byrd radioed Vaughan not to kill any of the increasingly exhausted dogs without informing Little America, which could "use here any dogs that give out on the trail."

At last things began to come together. Vaughan radioed that he had not been racing the dogs too hard, in order to spare them for the long trip down to the mountains. On the twenty-sixth he radioed Little America triumphantly that the geological party had reached its objective, the 100-mile depot, on the previous day, Byrd's forty-first birthday. Soon after, the worn-out dogs and drivers of the supporting party completed the depot-laying missions.[39] Gould and his five companions left Little America on November 4, 1929, for the 400-mile trip down the Ross Ice Shelf to the Queen Maud Mountains.

Byrd was not altogether happy with the geological party as it prepared to depart. Gould and his boys were clearly inexperienced, worried unnecessarily about heavy sledge loads, and displayed a distressing tendency to give up. If their defeatism "should get around the camp it would undoubtedly be very tough on them with their shipmates," Byrd confided to his diary. "I feel I must protect them in this matter," which was why the trail parties' daily progress reports, pinned to the camp bulletin board, contained no disheartening messages. In fact, "the situation was nothing like as black as it seemed to be" because the dogs soon got into shape and began pulling well.[40]

Gould, Vaughan, Freddie Crockett, Mike Thorne, and Eddie Goodale were gone two and a half months, returning on January 18, 1930. The geological party covered 1,525 miles and got within 350 miles of the pole. Gould and his colleagues provided radio, radio direction finding, and potential rescue support for Byrd's polar flight; discovered sandstone and coal deposits in the Queen Maud Mountains; guessed correctly that the range might extend all the way to the Weddell Sea; speculated that the Weddell and Ross Seas were not connected; confirmed Byrd's earlier conclusion that Amundsen's "Carmen Land" did not exist; and exhausted most of their dogs to death in the process. Even as they started homeward, Gould's colleagues in the international geological and geophysical communities admitted with more or less grudging admiration that the Byrd Antarctic expedition was providing the world some excellent, indeed priceless, science. Some on the expedition, including Byrd's nightly bridge partner, assistant meteorologist Henry Harrison, believed that Gould's journey alone justified the entire enterprise. Certainly, it was a great polar epic and one that contained undeniably dangerous moments. At one point on the return journey, Gould fell several feet down a crevasse before his skis caught on the walls. Climbing carefully out, he "turned and stared down at the blue-black depth of death." But it was also a trek blessed with undeniable good fortune. The men journeyed during Antarctica's optimum weather season and encountered no prolonged bad weather. Many days were remarkably clear and even warm. At one point, Vaughan traveled along stark naked except for a pair of socks and boots. The greatest problems lay in crossing the vast crevasse field that stretched across the shelf south of Little America, and in sledging through chilly days filled with hoar frost that kept the trail as hard and gritty as sand, wearing out the hardworking huskies that pulled heavy sledges filled with several hundred pounds of gear.[41]

If scientists were impressed with the expedition's work, the American public was as enthralled with the South Polar flight as Byrd had hoped, even though the destruction of the Fokker had already cheated the explorer out of his dream of actually landing at the pole and spending a day or two there.[42] Setting aside his apprehensions, Byrd concluded that it was necessary to undertake one heavy-lift depot-laying trip by air to place a vitally needed cache of gasoline at the foot of the Queen Mauds just before the polar flight. This required test flights around Little America in the Ford trimotor, laden with 13,000 pounds of snow blocks to simulate the freight that would be needed on the long flight south. All three pilots took turns climbing to 10,000 feet, then struggling to reach higher altitude. It proved impossible with the load. The plane would have to get over the Axel Heiberg glacier—its planned route—at 10,000 feet or else. Balchen noted in his diary, "Trouble with REB interfering with my mech[anic]s."[43] Bad weather and equipment repair kept the big plane grounded until November 18, when with Dean Smith at the controls, Byrd, assistant pilot Harold June, and photographer Ashley McKinley took off for the mountains to lay their cache of food and fuel for the polar flight.

The journey did not prove to be one of Dean Smith's finer moments. "The previous flights out over the ice had not concerned me in the least, but there seemed something particularly redoubtable about heading into the heart of this desolate, lifeless continent," Smith later wrote. He "could not shake an illogical expectancy that it would in some venturous way be different 'down there,' so near to the end of south." Smith struggled to define his feelings, which were not those of fear exactly, but a sense of being keyed up. "Life processes speeded, senses inflated, awareness heightened: this, I presume, was the thrill one seeks in adventure."[44]

The clear day and visibility allowed Byrd to plot the awful crevasse field with precision. After passing over Gould's party starting out along the shelf 300 feet below, Smith took the plane up several thousand feet on a steady course. Several hours later, the awesome black peaks of the Queen Mauds began to come into view in the blue sky. Continually glancing to his left, Byrd saw nothing but the ice shelf stretching eastward before him. There was no mountainous "Carmen Land," as Amundsen had insisted after returning from his polar dash seventeen years before. The shelf apparently stretched seamlessly into what the American expedition had already named Marie Byrd Land. Should the Americans ever make an Antarctic claim based on accurate exploration, it would be immense.

Reaching what they thought was the Heiberg Glacier, Smith and Byrd found a decent landing space to the east. In fact, the plane had arrived some 25 miles to the northwest, next to Liv Glacier. Smith set the ski-equipped trimotor down carefully in a rough but acceptable field of ice. Swiftly, the men set up the cache and sped north following a jolting takeoff. But 150 miles short of Little America, the engines began to sputter. Copilot June, using the crude dipstick that was their only measure, found the fuel level frighteningly low. Smith later concluded that because of the enormous disparity between the big central motor and the two smaller wing motors, his tachometer did not give him accurate readings of the amount of power, and thus of fuel, that the central engine was consuming. The tachometer had been balky at takeoff, but Smith had made the decision not to inform Byrd, who, Smith later insisted, seemed white-faced with the fear of flying.

This was Smith's major error of the mission. The second error was June's, since he discovered a fuel leak while troubleshooting the declining fuel reserves yet did not tell Byrd. June was forced to cut off the two wing engines, which immediately stopped radio transmissions to Little America. Smith thought he could fly the plane with the single nose engine back another 70 miles or so to the expedition's previously abandoned snowmobile—still half full of gasoline—which had been spotted 80 miles south of Little America on the outward flight. This was the third major mistake of the mission, for soon the nose engine died completely as well, and Smith was forced to make a hasty and very risky dead-stick landing on the ice. The party was still 100 miles short of Little America.

The men frantically raced out of the downed plane to drain the warm oil out of the aircraft and keep it from freezing. Smith claimed that Byrd helped in this strenuous task for a time, but then put up a small tent and, claiming exhaustion, climbed in and went to sleep while McKinley cranked away on the emergency radio to summon help. Soon Balchen landed in the Fairchild with 100 pounds of spare fuel. The chief pilot had suspected that the Byrd party was down and started a rescue flight following the rough course he thought that Byrd and his colleagues had taken. Had Balchen not been able to home in on McKinley's signal, he might never have found the stranded aircraft in the vast immensity of the Ross Ice Shelf. The men quickly began refueling the big Ford as Balchen took off. But they could not get the engine started. As they cranked away, Byrd again dropped out, complaining of a bad back. McKinley was forced to radio Little America once more to have Balchen return. This time the rescue plane crew stayed until Smith and the others could successfully crank the Ford's engines into action. Eventually, the Ford was started, took off, and landed routinely at Little America.

But why had the plane run out of fuel in the first place? Byrd queried the experienced Balchen intensively as to "why the consumption had been so high and why they had not been able to start the engines." Demas and his fellow mechanics quickly found that a broken fitting and excessively high pressure created leaks in the gas pump and the fuel lines. They attributed these breakdowns to the faulty tachometer and an inexplicable carburetor malfunction. It was all quite depressing.[45]

So was the lack of coordination among the two pilots and Byrd while aloft. Why had not Smith and June alerted their commander (and McKinley) to the crisis before the sudden emergency landing? Why did Smith risk everyone's life trying for the snowmobile when a landing with one engine would have been far safer and the call to Little America for help no less risky? Was Smith telling the truth about Byrd's slack behavior after the emergency landing? Or was he merely trying to cover his own nearly fatal mistakes by deflecting criticism to his commander? Smith emphasized Byrd's fear of flying, then admitted that he, too, harbored some serious apprehensions while soaring above the Antarctic. And his failure to keep his commander apprised of potentially fatal problems would neither alleviate Byrd's ostensible fear of flying nor enhance his confidence in this particular pilot.[46]

A week after the flight, while Byrd was contemplating another cache-laying mission, the denizens of Little America learned that Wilkins had just made his first flight of the year from the peninsula. Would the Australian's next effort be a try for the pole? Byrd radioed the Wright engine company for advice on how to fix the fuel-consumption problem, and the aviation mechanics assured their commander that the Ford was good to go for a polar mission. Byrd abandoned any thought of another cache-laying flight. It was time to go for broke. At noon on November 28, Thanksgiving Day, Gould reported from his position at the base of the Heiberg Glacier that the last of the clouds over the mountains had blown away. The weather was fine and clear as far as he and his companions could see.

The following afternoon, shortly after three local time, Byrd, Balchen, June, and McKinley, all clad in reindeer-fur parkas with large hoods lined with wolverine or wolf hair, climbed aboard the Ford and lifted off from Little America. Balchen was at the controls, June in the right seat, and Byrd and McKinley in the cabin crowded with gear and emergency supplies, including skis, ropes, and a dismantled sled. The Fairchild had taken off first and for a time flew close escort, taking pictures of its big brother before turning back. The four men aboard the *Floyd Bennett* were committed. At the last moment, Byrd had insisted on adding more fuel, which made the plane quite heavy, but he trusted Balchen's flying abilities. Harrison had placed instruments in the plane's tail to measure various weather phenomena by the minute all the way to the pole and back. McKinley's motion picture camera would record the entire flight and what was seen and mapped along the way.

An angry Dean Smith remained behind at Little America. According to Balchen, Byrd told him on the day after Smith's controversial flight that "I was to be the pilot on the SP flt." Later that afternoon "Smith told me that I would not have been on the flight had not the incident happened on the return of the base flight."[47] Balchen added that Smith admitted the Norwegian's skiing and camping abilities were superior to his own. But however much Smith may have desired to stay on Balchen's good side, his hatred of Byrd grew from that moment. In 1972, fifteen years after Byrd's death, while Balchen was in the midst of his own campaign to discredit his former employer, Smith wrote to him that in his memoirs, "I cut out much material damaging to Byrd." Perhaps, Smith added, out of Balchen's own efforts, "the public will come to know that Byrd was a master of public relations, public image, and little else. A flier that did not fly, a navigator who did not navigate, a leader who did not lead and a Virginia officer and gentleman who could look you in the eye, give you a direct lie and his oath that it was the truth."

Three years later, Smith amplified his pique to Fred Hotson of the Canadian Aviation Historical Society, who promptly disseminated the charges without investigation. Alden Hatch, a mildly popular writer of the time, had just written an adulatory biography of the Byrds in which he labeled Smith a daredevil pilot of limited competence. Smith erupted. There was nothing in print anywhere about the real Dick Byrd: "Nothing, for instance, about Byrd's habit of stowing medicine bottles full of cognac on his person with which to bolster his courage on long flights over the polar ice from which he got so drunk on both the polar flight and the base laying flight [Smith's own] that when the plane landed at the gas cache at the foot of the Queen Maude [*sic*] range he was unable to walk straight or talk coherently. Nor about the eastern flight with Alton Parker as pilot" in early December, some three weeks after the polar achievement, "when he drank so much he went berserk and McKinley and June had to sit on him to keep him restrained until he passed out, completely helpless, and be dumped in his bunk to sleep it off. Quite a sight for the men of the expedition, who had all lined up to watch the triumphant return of the only flight that was made over unknown territory." Balchen, who became close to Smith in their mutual campaign to discredit Byrd, never mentioned his commander's drinking on BAE I, calling Parker's flight "the most important . . . in my opinion, of the expedition."[48] Such was the effect of Dick Byrd's considered decision not to trust his fate to Dean Smith.

Over the years the ballyhoo surrounding the South Polar flight has tended to obscure its genuine danger and boldness.[49] Once again, Byrd, with three companions now instead of one, would be flying hundreds of miles through an empty polar wasteland in an aircraft that, in this instance, had proved less reliable than the *Josephine Ford.* There were no emergency airfields within thousands of miles, no search facilities should the plane go down, no rescue ships or vehicles. The four men were on their own should the power fail or should the benign Antarctic sky turn treacherous and pitiless, as it so often did in an instant.

But Byrd and his men enjoyed one advantage that was absent on the North Polar flight. The topography of Antarctica was far from monotonous. Except on the largely flat, featureless polar plateau, navigation marks were everywhere. The great ice shelf was ruffled with crevasse fields, and the trans-Antarctic mountain range toward which Balchen aimed the plane provided a superb midflight reference point.

Below them as they labored on minute by minute lay only thousands of square miles of ice. Five men, five sledges, and perhaps fifty dogs lay somewhere in that vacant, frozen wilderness, but it would be virtually impossible to reach them or to land sufficiently close for survival. Otherwise, the interior of the continent was devoid of humanity. The stoutest heart would quail at the prospect of such a journey, and many did. Even Dean Smith acknowledged the courage it took for Balchen, June, McKinley, and Byrd to climb into the slow, heavy, bulky, underpowered short-range Ford aircraft and soar upward and out toward the very bottom of the earth.[50]

The four experienced only one bad moment, but it was terrifying. With Ashley McKinley cranking away at the motion picture camera, pausing only occasionally to change film, Balchen flew down the shelf without incident and approached Heiberg Glacier. But clouds obscured its top, whereas Liv Glacier, twenty-five miles away, was clear. After a brief discussion, Balchen headed for and up Liv, "a Niagric torrent" that Byrd and the others saw "in its full sweeping entirety . . . doomed to rigidity, with frozen whirlpools and waterfalls." Slowly, with infinite care, gaining altitude to stay above the rising, deeply pitted, and gouged icefall below, Balchen brought the heavy plane up the glacier. "Far ahead it bent in a wide curve to the west of south. About thirty-five miles away it disappeared into a vague white surface—could it be the plateau?" At ninety-six hundred feet, as the plane rose toward the polar plateau, it began to buck violently, falling off in the heavy winds spilling down from the plateau. The glacier steadily narrowed, the tall mountains on both sides hemming the aircraft in. Before him Balchen saw a tall peak of rock splitting the glacier in two. He would have to rise above it or crash. Byrd was transfixed by the scene, watching the nose of the airplane "bob up and down across the face of that lone chunk of ice." Balchen shouted orders to lighten the plane. June went back to help Byrd and McKinley throw out heavy bundles of food and empty 5-gallon gas tanks. The plane rose a bit, but not enough. Balchen shouted, "More!" At Byrd's order McKinley sent another 125-pound bag of food sailing out. The men watched as it shattered silently on the glacier below. But now the plane was bouncing and lurching in the winds that were whipping around the peak and racing over and under the aircraft. A crash was imminent. Balchen figured there might be a backwash of rising air on the right side of the peak. Banking the plane carefully, he moved over in that direction. With the wingtip seemingly brushing the rock of the mountainside, Balchen found his rising current and rode it upward between the peak and the mountainside and beyond onto the polar plateau. Euphoric with relief, the four men turned their attention to the pole ahead.[51]

At one point the engine backfired. June lurched forward to release all the plane's fuel in case of a crash, but Balchen yelled that he had just made the fuel mixture too lean. Making adjustments, he soon had the plane purring along once more.

By one in the morning, local time, on November 30, 1929, Byrd calculated that the geographical spot known as the South Pole was in sight on the featureless white plain below. Soon he announced that the *Floyd Bennett* and its passengers had reached the exact bottom of the earth.[52] Balchen believed they were close, within five miles, perhaps, but not at the pole itself. Already skeptical of Byrd's North Polar claim, the Norwegian now felt his suspicion of the man's competence and, perhaps, honesty vindicated. Nothing could be seen below, of course, but the same vast, monotonous ice field the plane had flown over since reaching the plateau. The tent and cairn Amundsen had left for Scott were either buried beneath the snow or blown away by polar gales. Byrd included a picture of the South Pole, or what his navigation said was the South Pole, in his *National Geographic Magazine* article. Many a reader must have wondered why the explorer had sweated and struggled so for this moment. But he had struggled, and here he was at last, the world's first person to have flown over—or very close to—both the top and the bottom of the world. His reputation as one of history's great explorers was confirmed.

The flight back was routine, though again there were stories of Byrd's alleged instability. Shortly after leaving the pole he allegedly pulled a pint bottle of cognac out of his bag and began drinking, crying over and over, "We made it! We made it!" If Byrd's exultation and relief lacked the laconic grandeur of, say, Edmund Hillary's return to Everest base camp with the words, "Well, we knocked the bastard off," his reaction was nonetheless understandable. The success or failure of the expedition was on his shoulders alone. He had seen to that by his ready assumption of a leadership role that not even his bitterest critics could deny. Moreover, this expedition was well on its way to becoming a smashing success, which could not be said of many recent polar expeditions. Men would not perish on the ice like Scott and his companions, nor disappear for months or forever like Shackleton, or Nobile and Amundsen in the Arctic.

Once back down the Heiberg Glacier, Balchen understandably had difficulty finding the supply cache since it was twenty-five miles away, so June took over, found it, and landed the aircraft. While Byrd kept drinking—according to Balchen and June—they and McKinley wearily hoisted 75-gallon gas drums up to the aircraft and refueled. Four and a half hours later they returned to a jubilant reception at Little America. They had been in the air eighteen hours and had flown sixteen hundred miles. Balchen had done nearly all the flying and had demonstrated once again that he was not only a master pilot with inhuman stamina but also a man of rare courage. Together the four had banished the specter of Hubert Wilkins, who never seriously contemplated a polar flight and six weeks later abandoned his plans to fly to Little America as well.[53]

Later that day, back in his quarters at Little America, Byrd wrote a handsome tribute to his colleagues that he later published in his semiofficial account of the expedition.

> Well, it's done. We have seen the Pole and the American flag has been advanced to the South Pole. McKinley, Balchen and June have delivered the goods. They took the Pole in their stride, neatly expeditiously, and undismayed. If I had searched the world I doubt if I could have found a better team. Theirs was the actual doing. But there is not a man in this camp who did not assist in the preparations for the flight. Whatever merit accrues to the accomplishment must be shared with them. They are splendid.

The Paramount film released within the year was a virtual silent movie with a music track but no voice-over narration—"talkies" were only three years old—until the South Polar flight. Then Floyd Gibbons came on to give a staccato, over-the-top narrative that is either annoying or amusing ("Out in the mess hall the men wait for hours, their faces framed in anxiety, their lips tense in suspense . . . that magnetic desert that has lured many men to their death . . . easy on the stick, old scout! . . . Dick Byrd, you're the kind of Byrd I like and I'm not talking feathers, either!"). Seventy years later the filmed record of the flight can still arouse awe.[54]

In New York and Boston, Railey and Marie had waited with the rest of the country—and much of the world—for news of the flight. Their nerves were further stretched by the loss of shortwave contact with Little America that extended from early morning to late afternoon. At last, the long-awaited signal was received with joy and relief. Brother Harry cabled a message from the governor's mansion in Richmond, ranking Richard's achievement "with the great events of the world." The rest of the country would confirm the elder Byrd's conclusion as soon as the expedition returned. Only the *National Geographic*'s John LaGorce introduced an unwelcome theme into the celebrations, passing on his concern through Railey that overcommercialization of the entire expedition might "tarnish Byrd's public image, painting him as the 'advertised and advertising explorer,'" a theme that Frederick Lewis Allen and other commentators and pundits were already broadcasting.[55]

There were a few more things to do. On December 5 Byrd climbed back aboard the Ford trimotor for a long mapping trip to the east. Alton Parker, who had not flown much, was pilot. June and McKinley came along as copilot and cameraman. The men traveled more than three hundred miles along the coast and into what would soon appear on the maps as Marie Byrd Land, discovering new archipelagoes in the sea and mountain ranges ashore, together with several lakes of open, deep water in the inland ice.

Seven weeks later, to break the tedium and apprehension of waiting for evacuation, Smith took Byrd aloft for a relatively short triangular flight over the Ross Ice Shelf to the west, soaring along the edge of the barrier, then swerving south for perhaps a hundred miles. Richard was anxious to find something more than simply miles and miles of white plain. He obviously wanted to find higher ice that might indicate land beneath. According to Smith, he at one point simply pronounced that he had found it. The disgusted pilot "barrel[ed] down" until the aircraft's skis were just a few feet above the surface. "I pointed to the altimeter's needle. It stood practically at zero. The Admiral [*sic*] glared."[56]

Byrd's frustration may have lain in the fact that although he and his colleagues had seen far more of Antarctica than anyone else, many secrets remained to tantalize. Most of the questions that had required answers back in 1928 were still unresolved. Gould later wrote of the expedition, "We always come up against the same question—we don't know—we don't know. And is not this after all the most vital reason why Antarctic exploration must go on?"[57]

A few more survey parties continued to map and chart the immediate area around the Bay of Whales, and there remained the constant recording of scientific data on the ice and in the atmosphere. The two meteorologists, Bill Haines and Henry Harrison, continued to send weather balloons aloft while taking various other readings. But once word was received that Gould and his party had left the mountains and were running for home, a holiday mood began to grip most of the camp. Much like "short-timers" anywhere, men began to lose their commitment and to fall away from the crowd. A pattern familiar to later sociologists began to appear—group death.

By this time the Richard Byrd political machine was well oiled. Brother Harry and Senator Swanson, chairman of the Senate Naval Affairs Committee, swiftly got together after the polar flight and drafted the legislation promoting Richard to flag rank. Eight days after Harry first contacted Railey on the matter, Richard radioed from Little America that he was pleased with the text and the men should proceed. Within forty-eight hours the legislation had passed both houses. Fred Britten, Swanson's opposite in the House, wrote Harry Byrd, "It was a real plea-sure to serve Dick in expediting the passage of the Swanson Bill and I am only sor-ry that I could not have arranged to make him the Chief of Operations of the Navy Department." Later Harry Byrd cabled the ice that he, Swanson, and Britten had been merely conduits. Without saying just how, the governor told his brother that "Captain Railey and Marie contributed more than any one else to the working out of your bill before Congress."[58] The news did not arrest the steady decline in morale at Little America, though most expedition personnel were sincerely glad for their pleased leader, and some must have felt, understandably, that it reflected well on the expedition as a whole.

Railey was not always so successful when it came to the by now perpetual cri-sis over money. Richard's Los Angeles business friend Robert Breyer passed through Boston briefly in the middle of January 1930, and though he did not have time to see Marie, he telephoned her to say that "there are very good possibilities in California" in terms of fund-raising "and that he will do everything in his pow-er to help." As he left the city, Breyer sent Mrs. Byrd a dozen roses. Funding short-falls evidently became acute shortly thereafter, and Marie rushed down to the ex-pedition's Biltmore Hotel headquarters in New York City to help. Railey took off to find money, and on January 30 while Railey was in New Orleans, Marie wired "Office Okay. Go California," adding that she would remain at the Biltmore to handle expedition business.

Railey arrived in Los Angeles a week later. Believing his obvious contact was Jesse Lasky, Railey hurried out to Paramount, where the studio chief told him that despite Byrd's exclusive contract with his studio, he thought "the [motion picture] industry will do its part if Los Angeles is organized on behalf of the expedition." Lasky called in popular actor Wallace Beery, who promptly offered to raise fifty thousand dollars through a benefit aviation meet at Mines Field (now Los Ange-les International Airport) if the Chamber of Commerce concurred. The proposed aviation meet, Railey cabled Marie, would be a "ballyhoo proposition involving leading stars Hollywood with much publicity." But Railey should have gone to Breyer first. When at last he did so, the car dealer was cool to the idea, either because he was hurt at not being initially consulted or because he was unable to persuade friends in the Chamber of Commerce to go along. Breyer, whom Railey characterized as "a real [guy] person," could devote only an hour a day out of a busy schedule trying to arrange an alternative "ballyhoo." As a result nothing happened, and Railey found himself midmonth on a Ford trimotor passenger plane heading east. "You see," he wrote Marie, "without ballyhoo only one method is open to us—man to man solicitation up and down the street." He had tried that approach also in Los Angeles and found it discouraging. "The expedition's background" there was "not too well established," nor was Byrd's reputation that firm, "except sentimentally, and that stuff, as you know, is so frail, so often hypocritical."[59] One of Richard's first orders of business upon returning from the ice was to concentrate on raising his visibility in southern California, including an assiduous cultivation of the always admiring Breyer. Railey, for the moment, was left to slog on in his ceaseless "man to man" search for funds while the expedition sank deeper into debt.

As the men awaited evacuation with growing impatience, drinking began again, sporadic at first, then heavier. According to Eddie Goodale, Byrd had tried to limit drinking earlier because of sensitivity to his own and the expedition's reputation during a time when "Prohibition was in full sway across the nation." But in these final months when many men in the party had finished their work, a group of dissidents calling themselves the "Bay of Whales Harbor Board" began meeting almost nightly in one of the living quarters to "let off steam." Jim Feury and Joe Rucker became "a committee of two to raid Dr. Coman's department of the necessary rations of pure grain alcohol." According to Smith, these eight to ten individuals even sought to "censor all radio messages. . . . For several weeks we had an undeclared mutiny; the atmosphere in camp was tense and ugly." Perhaps it was to dispel this tension that Byrd himself appeared one night "at the peak of the guzzling." The drinkers heard a knock on the door, "and a voice was heard, 'Let me in, fellows, I am a paid up member.'" Goodale was delighted. "No one can get mad at a man like that."[60]

Byrd never mentioned these incidents in his personal diary. But he did admit later that at least a few of his crusaders had had it with Antarctica. "I admit frankly that no situation—not even the struggle up the pass of Liv's Glacier—brought the worry this one did. For we were anxious to get home. Our work was done, and waiting was trying after months of great activity." The camp was on tenterhooks as *City of New York,* sailing down from Dunedin, met "one storm after another, advancing to the greatest battle of her always rugged life."[61] Eventually, young Siple and the handful of secret Byrd loyalists began to quietly monitor the Harbor Board group and reported to their commander, who was increasingly distracted by preliminary preparations for the reloading of goods and equipment. The men were invited to take home a pet from among the dogs. But problems of oversupply continued. The expedition had simply brought too much with it, and now food and gear and perhaps some young husky pups would have to remain on the ice forever.

As 1930 began, disquieting rumors circulated that *City* might not get through to rescue the expedition, stranding the men for another twelve months, including the fearsome polar winter. The barque radioed that it was trying to batter its way toward Little America through what the Norwegian whalers claimed was the worst ice pack in living memory. Captain Brown of *Bolling* briefly thought of crashing through to take the men home, but Byrd strictly forbade it. The ship's steel hull was simply too thin and fragile. Soon Byrd sent distress signals to the Norwegian whalers in the region, begging one of the big factory ships to break though to Little America. He also urged the State Department in Washington to put pressure on the Norwegian government for action. A query to the U.S. Navy for assistance brought the reply that the nearest warship or Coast Guard vessel was eight thousand miles away.

Railey placed pressure on the New York office of the Rosshavet Company, which owned *Larsen* and a sister ship, to see if one of them could be ordered into the pack to reach Little America. Byrd told Railey that five members of the expedition were so ill as to require hospitalization, which some in the expedition thought an exaggeration; indeed, they concluded that Byrd was deliberately exaggerating to gain even more attention in the world press. After hard negotiations the Norwegians promised finally to send in one of their big factory ships if absolutely necessary.[62]

The whalers' hesitation was understandable. *Larsen* or its sister probably could bash through all but the thickest ice, but to do so they would have to suspend whaling for a time and would risk suffering structural damage. The maritime insurance policies taken out with British, German, and Norwegian underwriters did not cover humanitarian activities. Torger Moe, Rosshavet's managing director, carefully "laid out" the situation for Railey, including the policy schedule covering every ship in the Rosshavet fleet. The Americans must make available to Rosshavet a letter of credit for three hundred thousand dollars "supported by the signatures of the responsible backers of the Expedition" and make immediately available an additional three hundred thousand dollars to cover the insurance of *Larsen* in advance for any rescue work the vessel might be called upon to undertake. Furthermore, *Larsen*'s whaling catch was insured for one million dollars; the Byrd expedition might be liable for that amount if *Larsen* or another large whaler was forced to spend most of the time smashing through the pack to rescue the party. Railey was outraged, venting his spleen to both Marie and Harry Byrd. Nonetheless, with characteristic energy he had already contacted Charles Bob, members of the Harvard and Yale committee, and others who pledged whatever necessary to rescue the expedition. Six hundred thousand to a million dollars, he assured Harry and Marie, was "available on an hour's notice if we have to have it."[63]

Down in Little America, Richard called more than a score of colleagues into his personal quarters for discussion, assessing whom would be loyal and whom he might have to confront back home. He gave the impression of wanting to learn frankly from his subordinates how he had performed as a leader. It was a wise move. Byrd had never before commanded a large group of men, but he would soon again, for he had committed himself to an early return to Antarctica. He needed to know what had worked and what had not, where he had been strong as well as where he had been weak.

Everyone was worn down by this time. "Personal jealousies and grouses showed up only after the South Pole flight when the majority of our gang was idle," easy-going Fred "Taffy" Davies recalled forty-five years later. Byrd, he added, "was quite jealous of the degree of affection shown by nearly all of us to Larry and Bernt, both for their efficiency and friendly personality." Nonetheless, "grouses" always occurred with idleness, and "this is not the same as disloyalty."

But some during those frustrating times took account of Dick Byrd and found him wanting. Sitting off by himself, the perpetually suspicious and critical Balchen wrote, "The leader of the expedition now just promoted to the rank of Rear Admiral US Navy (Ret) whom I have come to know quite well since I met him in Spitsbergen nearly four years ago has more than once puzzled me with his Dr. Jekyl [*sic*] Mr. Hyde appearances." Like Dean Smith and, later, Finn Ronne, Balchen concluded that Byrd was not only a poseur but an ignoramus. His North Polar flight, whatever its result, had given him a wholly undeserved reputation as "the greatest expert on Arctic aviation," and it "many times caused me difficulties when we were planning for this trip to smooth out some inane statements made by him in front of other people about the cold weather operations which we were facing down here." The man was a victim, his own witting victim, in fact, of "public adulation and undeserved know how," which in a number of instances that Balchen chose not to discuss allegedly placed BAE I in jeopardy.

Like Ronne and Smith, Balchen expressed unstinting praise for Byrd's promotional and even administrative abilities, commenting, "I have never known anyone who could equal him there." But Dick Byrd "was not an outdoor man,"

Balchen sniffed. "He had no interest in hunting, fishing and camping, skiing. He was one of our most consistent visitors to the gymnasium," working out assiduously, especially on sit-up exercises, but "his slight build and muscular structure indicated a man not used to the outdoors." The only motives that Balchen could find driving this weakling to the polar wastes were "publicity and notoriety." Perhaps the admiral's most infuriating trait was his irrepressible need for one-upmanship. "There was never a situation unless he had experienced it before 'on one of my previous trips to the Arctic,'" Balchen wrote. Finally, Dick Byrd was no navigator. "In all the years that I was together with him on board ships and down in the Antarctic I never saw him practice shooting the sun or take celestial observations."[64]

But after the South Polar flight, almost everyone wanted a piece of Dick Byrd, wanted to congratulate him and to honor him. Cable traffic to the ice in December was filled with notifications of this or that award. As always on such occasions Byrd was at his best, charming, gracious, and generous. When Isaiah Bowman of the American Geographical Society wired that he had been awarded the society's David Livingstone Century Gold Medal, the delighted admiral promptly replied, "Dear Isaiah. You're a trump old fellow and I think more than generous." Notified by Fred Birchall of the *New York Times* that the Smithsonian Institution had awarded him the coveted Langley Medal, Byrd wired back that all his aviation exploits had rested on a team effort and asked that the fifteen men who had been associated with him in one way or another in Greenland and Spitsbergen as well as Antarctica be acknowledged as well. The list he cabled north included Haines, Hanson, the now rehabilitated Mulroy, Demas, Parker, and Balchen, together with Van der Veer, the Paramount cameraman who had earlier been with Pathé News, and Russell Owen.[65]

With the nation's scientific and business organizations keen to associate themselves with Byrd and a highly successful expedition, conflicts were inevitable. At one point Railey wrote Harry Byrd that he was "sweating green paint . . . over a snarl in Dick's relationships with the American and National Geographic Societies." The two had become locked in battle over division of the expedition's materials. Railey spent Christmas week in intense negotiations with Jack LaGorce, the *National Geographic Magazine*'s editor in Washington, and Fosdick and Bowman in New York. Working until one in the morning the last day, Railey "solved the problem—to the complete satisfaction and great relief of Dick." Railey begged Harry Byrd not to disclose to his brother how frantic and occasionally even unpleasant discussions had been.[66]

At last, in early February, *City of New York,* after maneuvering outside the pack ice for some days, found a wedge and shouldered its way swiftly into the Ross Sea.

Although Byrd had told Captain Melville to break through the pack east of the 180th meridian to avoid the bad weather known to afflict the western areas of the Ross Sea, *City* actually arrived off McMurdo Sound, far to the west of the meridian. The captain, it was alleged, had always wanted to see Mount Erebus. For a time it appeared that the barque might be forced by bad storms to race back north through the pack without reaching the Bay of Whales. The tiny camp of Americans was under almost unbearable tension when on the evening of February 7, 1930, with most of the camp's population down on the barrier, the ship slowly materialized through the fog and haze. Thirty-six hours later, after a frantic round of hauling materials across the ice to the ship, Byrd and Haines walked out of Little America and headed down toward *City of New York*. "We'll be back, Bill," Byrd promised. "Not me," Haines replied. "Once is quite enough." As Byrd got off the sled that carried him to the ship's side, he looked at Vaughan and said to the young driver, "It's over, Norman." He walked a few paces toward the waiting barque, turned, and added, "We did it. Now we must celebrate our victory."[67]

Chapter 10

Politico

Word of the expedition's deliverance from the Antarctic pack ice reached the States by radio within hours, and while Byrd stopped briefly in Tahiti and then in Panama to write a formal report to the National Geographic Society, his friends and backers in the States prepared a series of lavish receptions. There would be the ticker-tape parade down Broadway, of course. Railey had approached mutual friends of the explorer and Franklin Roosevelt to see if the New York governor could host a reception. FDR expressed delight, and wouldn't it be splendid if the navy brought his good friend Dick and the entire expedition up the Hudson to Albany in a destroyer? The Navy Department was more than willing to oblige its most famous sailor and one of its most illustrious assistant secretaries.[1]

And so the festivities began in a steadily mounting crescendo. Byrd's ice-battered ships sailed into New York Harbor on Thursday morning, June 19, 1930. Mayor Walker and the usual dignitaries sailed out to meet the vessels and escort them to the pier. There Byrd leaped ashore to greet Marie with a manly handshake and for young Dick a restrained hug. Whatever passion and intimacies might exist between husband and wife would have to await suitable moments behind closed doors. Then came the motorcade driving slowly through a blizzard of ticker tape to city hall, the radio microphones awaiting the explorer's first words, the banquets and the awards, and all the rest. Next day it was on to Washington, D.C., and an afternoon reception for the entire expedition in the Rose Garden of the White House with President Hoover, followed by another formal dinner for everyone that evening and a presentation by the president to Byrd of the National Geographic Society Special Medal of Honor.

With his men looking on, Byrd spoke proudly but with modest demeanor of the expedition's achievements. It had carried the American flag a thousand miles farther south than ever before. The science had been brilliant. Such triumphs satisfied the mind. But what satisfied the heart, the youthful-looking explorer emphasized, was "that we left not a single man on the ice; that everyone is here tonight."

Somewhat surprisingly, however, it was the increasingly taciturn president, laboring under the first burdens of a gathering economic depression, who was most eloquent. The Byrd expedition had enriched humanity by expanding knowledge, Hoover said, which was a priceless boon for mankind, for whereas money was made and spent, "knowledge remains always with the race." The spectacular discoveries and science had all been due to Byrd's "painstaking preparation," his "foreknowledge of the special problems to be solved," and his "thoughtful plans to meet them," together with an infinite patience in execution. The gentleman explorer had demonstrated the traits of the born commander: "boldness at the right time, comradeship, those heroic qualities that endear the captain to his men." They had placed him at the forefront of national accomplishment. Little wonder that he was "beloved by the American people." But it was the "human values" Byrd had brought to his enterprise that most touched the public heart and fired its mind. "Every hidden spot of the earth's surface remains a challenge to man's will and ingenuity until it has been conquered. Every conquest of such a difficult goal adds permanently to mankind's sense of power and security. Great explorers, therefore, do not merely add to the sum of human knowledge, but also they add immensely to the sum of human inspiration."[2]

Early on June 24, Byrd and his men boarded the destroyer USS *Bainbridge,* which lay alongside the Hudson River pier at Ninety-seventh Street in upper Manhattan, for the trip to Albany. At four thirty that afternoon, they stepped off the warship to be greeted by FDR, who proceeded to orchestrate another round of "impressive and colorful ceremonies" at the state capitol. The next morning, Byrd and his men returned to the city by train. Two weeks later, back in his office at the Biltmore Hotel, Byrd wrote "dear Franklin" that "we are all still tingling with that great reception we got in Albany. Every one of my shipmates thought you were the greatest fellow they ever met. I have been bragging about you to them for two years and I am mighty glad that they got together with you."[3]

Only Dean Smith felt out of place. Governor and Mrs. Roosevelt's charm and graciousness and the impressive setting of the mansion served only to give him a sense of strangeness, wonder, and, above all, futility. Making his apologies to Eleanor Roosevelt, he walked into town, found a restaurant, and ate alone. Then he caught a train for New York. "It was time to take leave of pomp and circumstance. I was going home."[4]

At age forty-one, Dick Byrd was at the apex of his life. In five years he had vaulted from obscurity to worldwide fame by living "as dangerously as any modern man."[5] He had capped a series of aviation spectaculars with a smashingly successful, privately financed South Polar expedition that for eighteen months had dwelt on the edge of the Antarctic wilderness in a fabricated town dedicated to scientific research across a wide range of disciplines, from oceanography to geology, glaciology, and meteorology. He and his fliers had mapped more than 160,000 square miles of a largely unknown continent, and he had capped the expedition's broad scientific triumph by bringing everyone safely home.

In all of these endeavors, Dick Byrd had matured. The reckless, impulsive youth with the flare of anger, who wanted to fight everyone when his brother was injured with a rock, who would do anything to maintain the leadership of his gang, who threw himself foolishly at the big Princeton line and at gymnastic rings too far to reach, had become the prudent, restrained commander of men who cushioned the risks inherent in polar exploring with careful planning. He had generally responded well, and occasionally with real grace, to the intense pressures of organizing and carrying out a huge polar expedition.

He had not mastered all his weaknesses. In Russell Owen's remarkably measured assessment, Byrd's motivating forces remained ambition and vanity, but as Owen reminded his readers, ambition gets the world's work done, and who among us is free of vanity? Byrd was "imaginative, impulsive, and yet cautious, somewhat secretive and suspicious." The latter quality rubbed some the wrong way. But those who proved mentally and emotionally tough enough to thrive amid the many rigors of Antarctica did not take offense. At one point during the expedition, Byrd decided he wanted to catch some penguins and keep them alive to bring back to various zoos in the United States. He assigned the job of penguin maintenance to young Siple. But what to feed them? "Get in touch with zoos," Byrd told his young Boy Scout. Back came the word to feed the animals fish and cod-liver oil. But there were no fish immediately at hand, so the penguins predictably began to die. When Siple told Byrd, the commander asked him if he had contacted zoos. "Yes, I tried everything," Siple responded, mentioning zoos in Philadelphia, St. Louis, Washington, D.C., and the Bronx. Byrd looked at the youngster coldly: "Did you try Edinburgh and Hamburg?" No, the abashed Siple responded. "But you told me you tried everything," Byrd "hammered at me." Siple walked away embarrassed and angered, but determined never to do a job halfway again. The remaining penguins survived, and "years later when a problem seemingly stumped me, Byrd's voice and words would suddenly appear: *Did you try Edinburgh or Hamburg?* And I would continue on to a solution."[6]

Whatever his strengths and weaknesses, no one could deny Dick Byrd his triumph. Yet he enjoyed more adulation than any person should attain. It imprisoned him in a time, the 1920s, and a place, Antarctica, that he never escaped. If he had mastered the white continent, it had also mastered him, shaping his imagination and defining the dimensions of his ambition. After the first Antarctic expedition, his life would be a constant struggle to replicate and expand on his earlier heroics. He became a man trapped inside his own image of the great polar explorer. He came to believe that he alone held the keys to anyone's success in that perilous profession; anyone who wished to prosper would have to come through him and acknowledge him, and when they did not he became querulous, suspicious, even choleric. Antarctica was his, he insisted; he was mayor of the place. That conceit became his curse and his burden.

Some glimpsed this increasingly unhappy truth, and their voices reflected the first loosening of the grip that Dick Byrd had on public affection. To many sophisticates in the second year of the Great Depression, America's greatest explorer had become a bit of a bore. True, Middletown and village America still adored him, as did the people of Virginia who voted him number twelve in the list of all-time greatest Virginians (Washington, Jefferson, and Lee topped the list; Byrd was just behind Walter Reed and just ahead of Cyrus McCormick and Pocahontas).[7] Paramount's film *With Byrd at the South Pole* did well at the box office, and when the admiral's faithful dog, Igloo, passed away suddenly, it was a national story. "But in the larger centers of population," wrote Frederick Lewis Allen in one of the most popular books of 1931, "there was manifest a slight tendency to yawn: his [South Polar] exploit had been over-publicized, and heroism, however gallant, lost something of its spontaneous charm when it was subjected to scientific management and syndicated in daily dispatches." Allen's "larger centers of population" were undoubtedly confined to Manhattan Island, the Bronx, and the better parts of Long Island and Bucks County. In Los Angeles the admiral attracted six thousand people to the Shrine Auditorium even as Allen was completing his manuscript.[8] But Byrd had clearly lost the sophisticates and would never regain them. As the Great Depression took hold, he would lose even more of his public. "That he is, with Colonel Lindbergh, an international symbol of the undaunted man of action is not to be denied," Charlie Murphy would write in 1939. "Neither is the fact that many people, for reasons they find hard to define, do not altogether like him."[9]

In December 1930 Morris Markey, who had originated the *New Yorker's* famous "Reporter at Large" department, wrote a brief piece about the admiral for *Vanity Fair*. It was very much in the smart-aleck style then—as now—in vogue among the Manhattan intelligentsia. But it did catch the more dubious side of Richard Byrd and his pretensions. Markey maintained that America's preeminent polar hero was "the Tex Rickard of exploration rather than its Amundsen." Furthermore,

Byrd was honest enough to know that he resembled the famous boxing promoter of the twenties far more than he did a genuine explorer. "Deep in the breast of this charming and courteous Virginia gentleman there lives a little imp of the perverse which insistently tells him that his stirring exploits have a cheerful deal of nonsense about them."

During the Great War Byrd had first perceived "with the fine sensitiveness of a virtuoso that for a few years at least the mob would get its vicarious romance from aviation." Frustrated as he had been by the navy's later unwillingness to underwrite or include him in its most famous aerial stunts, Byrd had successfully dunned congressional committees into the appropriation of a million dollars for the 1919 seaplane flight to Europe, and this, as the future explorer realized, required a man of exceptional talent. "And he recognized his talent for what it was: the mystic flair of the born promoter." His flight to the North Pole confirmed his ability as a huckster, "an organization expert, and as a courageous fellow tested." But it was not until he had returned from the North Polar expedition and began to read the newspapers that the key to all his future technique was discovered. That key was science, the "pretty thing we worship" in "this happy half of the twentieth century." Science was to the "dim dreams of Manny Katz and Pat McCarthy what honor was to older cavaliers from Virginia, or the white cross to those Catholic knights who stormed the Bishop's Tower at Carcassone when death was riding hard." By 1930, Markey added, anyone could do almost anything "as long as he makes the sacred sign and hoists the *panache* of science. This was not lost upon the stunning intuition of our hero."

The North Polar and transatlantic flights were just Byrd's "fancy gestures toward immortality . . . only saluting pieces as it were." His South Polar expedition and flight were the apotheosis, wherein he expended hundreds of thousands of dollars and the substantial exertions of more than fifty men to support one flight to a geographical abstraction with no practical use whatever. "He flung an expedition toward the South Pole that flew the banner of Midas rather than Hannibal." Perhaps the scientists were toiling away in the long interval between arrival in the Antarctic, the flight, and departure, "but the radio dispatches so carefully edited by the Commander did not bother much with them." As for the million-dollar flight, it was good, but "a thousand fellows that haul your mail across the mountains every night could do it just as well." However, the daring airmail pilots who were falling to winter blizzards and summer storms in alarming numbers "couldn't make you groan with hope and terror while they fled across that icy wilderness. Byrd can. Furthermore, lest the point elude us, he can make you believe it is all for science—for that vague encyclopedia which somehow, you believe, will make living a simpler and a sweeter thing." So the country proclaimed the admiral a hero, just as he shrewdly expected that it would. "It was his triumph of promotion, and the good old U.S.A. fell tumbling to the call quite as wholeheartedly as the walls of Jericho succumbed to the persuasive influence of Joshua's trumpets."

So let us, Markey concluded, call Byrd "a wise and competent leader of men" and the best promoter of his time. He should be saluted as an appealing fellow, filled with a kind of perverse charm "for the reason that he knows his own tricks by their proper names. Let us wink (because we have seen him wink) at his dreadful pomposity and his pretentious gravity. Even in his cool and gentlemanly aplomb," Markey maintained, he often seemed a bit bewildered, and the mob liked that, for the mob, indeed everyone, was often bewildered by the pace and content of modern life. In the end, Markey proclaimed, Richard Evelyn Byrd was nothing more or less than a pole sitter in the grand manner, and so long as pole sitting was in fashion in a confusing world falling headlong into economic ruin and widespread personal anguish and even terror, he should be cheered as one who performed his task with supreme style and grace.[10]

Style and grace were not conspicuously part of Richard Byrd's makeup once his first Antarctic expedition became history. He became even more sensitive to slights, criticisms, and what he considered disloyalty. Perhaps it was simple fatigue from an unremitting schedule that would exhaust any man of any age. En route to St. Louis in early February 1931, Dick let his hair down to brother Harry. "The sophisticated gang who live by tearing down and making fun of others are after my scalp or rather they are after a few pieces of silver by scalping me." Pathos then swept over the country's youngest admiral. "I have not now or never had any help whatever in a positive way." Railey had been a disaster: he "has never made a positive move and I have cut loose from him now anyway."

Apparently, Marie had been the first to be disaffected, for shortly after Richard returned, she urged him not to leave the New York headquarters "until the business of the expedition is finished." Marie had concluded that, like Brophy, Railey was beginning to buckle under the strain. The Byrds did have legitimate complaints against the man. His travel and salary expenses had come to seventy-five thousand dollars, a huge sum for the mid-Depression era, "and it was only part time work. When he left me to go with Charlie Bob he put the whole burden on my shoulders." But Railey had placed his loyalty, energy, and not inconsiderable talents at Dick and Marie's disposal, and they rewarded him shabbily.

The poor man never grasped what happened. Four months before he had written rather forlornly to Marie that "I have missed, and often very greatly missed, the conversations we used to have before the Expedition returned to the United States." His wife, Julia, and he hoped that the Byrds "will not fail to let us know the next time you are in New York for we are eager to have you come out to Scarsdale and spend the night or weekend." No reply has been found. Railey soon burned all his bridges to the Byrds by becoming business manager for Wilkins and Lincoln Ellsworth, who were briefly contemplating the harebrained scheme of sending a submarine underneath the North Pole, a project far beyond the technological capabilities of the day.[11]

The seeds of Byrd's suspicion of his former Antarctic colleagues may have begun even before the expedition arrived home, when James Pond wrote Railey that "unless there is some definite contract arrangement prohibiting lecturing, many of the members of the Expedition are going to go on lecture tours. Some of the bigger men by getting into districts ahead of Dick might upset our own plans." Pond remembered that "when the crowd came back from the North Pole, everyone of them was lecturing." Floyd Bennett had gone to another promoter "and proved to be quite a bit of competition." The way to control matters was to sign up Byrd's people, then schedule them to avoid "duplicating any cities" where their admiral might be speaking. Gould was obviously "the first man to be considered." After that, matters grew murky. Owen would be fine, but only if he were "persona grata."[12] In the event, neither Gould nor Russell nor anyone else was willing to compete with their former commander until Pond, with Byrd's consent, summoned them.

Books were a different matter. Charlie Murphy helped Byrd crank out *Little America* in four months. Byrd signed the preface in his Chicago hotel room at two in the morning on November 16, 1930. His list of acknowledgments reads like a who's who of the American business, media, political, and philanthropic establishments: in addition to the old standbys, Ford, Rockefeller Jr., and Raymond Fosdick, he included Ochs, Sulzberger, and Birchall of the *New York Times;* the Daniel Guggenheim Fund; Justice Charles Evans Hughes; Joseph Pulitzer; national columnist David Lawrence; and many others, including Robert Breyer. He dedicated the book to his mother.[13]

Putnam signed Siple up, too, probably at Byrd's urging, and *A Boy Scout with Byrd,* like *Little America,* was written, published, and marketed in record time. Putnam tied its promotional campaign directly to *Little America* ("We believe that the success of LITTLE AMERICA opened up for the booksellers of this country an opportunity to sell in an extraordinarily big way a book for boys that will be read and enjoyed by the 800,000 Boy Scouts . . . and thousands upon thousands of boys and men in every town and hamlet of the country"), and directed Siple's subsequent lecture tour around the eastern United States. By the first week in March 1931, Putnam informed its young author that his first run of fifteen thousand copies had been sold and a second printing was under way.[14]

Gould was a competitor. *Cold: The Record of an Antarctic Sledge Journey,* which in fact covered the entire expedition, was published by Brewer, Warren, and Putnam in early June 1931, just seven or eight months after *Little America* and much under the two-year restriction that all expedition members had contractually accepted. Gould quite properly identified himself on the title page as "Second in Command, Byrd Antarctic Expedition." The book rivaled but did not contradict the admiral's account. Like *Little America* and *A Boy Scout with Byrd, Cold* either ignored or drastically attenuated any evidence of discord on the expedition. Ashley McKinley (who identified himself as "Third-in-Command") and Harry Adams (who claimed to be "Chief Officer and Navigator on the Expedition") also appear to have published at this time or soon after, although their books carry no publication date. McKinley's picture book seems to have been designed as a souvenir for expedition members. Adams's book is more substantive. In both accounts, Byrd is depicted as a strong and wise leader.[15]

Perhaps *Cold* had something to do with the fact that by early November 1931, relations between Byrd and Gould reached the point of rupture after months of misunderstanding and mutually hurt feelings, punctuated by exchanges of recriminatory correspondence. During the course of increasingly testy exchanges with his former second in command, Byrd alleged that Gould was more or less secretly plotting to mount his own Antarctic expedition out of Little America during the next austral season. Richard claimed to have no objections, but would have to consult his backers first, since they had obviously contributed substantially both in money and in goods to the camp's construction.

In fact, Richard's suspicions were accurate. Gould in 1931 did want to go south again, and the people he wanted to go with, and contacted about the matter, were Paul Siple and Bernt Balchen. In July 1980 Gould, then an aged emeritus professor at the University of Arizona, denied rumors that he had thought about or planned an expedition of his own to Little America. "I do not remember a letter from Paul Siple about it. It could hardly have been serious. It seems to me now that it would have been folly to have projected such an expedition with Adm. Byrd already in the field." Gould added that in 1931 he had just married and wished to return to his academic career, "which I did in 1932."

On April 24, 1931, however, Gould wrote what must have seemed to Siple a very flattering letter, taking the young man fully into the elder's confidence. Gould was delighted that Siple "repose[d] so much confidence in me." He had written to Byrd to ask him about his plans, Gould continued, "and he declined to tell me anything about them. I wanted to know for I hope that some time we shall be able to announce the Gould-Balchen Antarctic Expedition and we did not want to trespass in any way on the Admiral." Gould admitted that "when or even whether our expedition is going to materialize" was an open question. He stated, "We are both" (that is, he and Balchen) "still on the search for contributions with which to get started but these are frightfully hard days in which to raise moneys." Young Siple was obviously weighing his own chances in the bargain. Should he stay with Byrd or go with a man—or men—for whom he evidently felt great admiration and respect? Gould settled it for him. He urged the youngster to "not in any way jeopardize your interests by waiting for us."[16] Siple did not. By Christmas 1931 he was back in the Byrd fold, from which he would never again stray.

The hoopla surrounding his expedition and the upheavals caused by deepening economic depression kindled Dick Byrd's ambition to cut a prominent national and even international political figure. Throughout the turbulent months surrounding the 1932 presidential election, his voice was constantly heard throughout the land as head of the National Economy League. The league was formed in the summer of 1932, shortly after the Democratic National Convention in Chicago, when New York lawyer Grenville Clark, Byrd's friend from the war years, gathered several "old Plattsburg comrades" (Plattsburg was the army's major training camp in 1917–1918) and circulated a petition to Congress aimed "at the elimination of all expenditures for veterans who had not suffered disability as the result of war service." According to press reports, the movement immediately mushroomed "into a countrywide demand for economy in government generally." By late July conservative circles in New England were ready to organize in anticipation of the league's inaugural meeting in New York City. And the man they wanted to head the New England district on a "non-political, non-partisan"—and non-salaried—basis was Richard E. Byrd.

Breaking off his vacation and leaving the family behind at Latty Cove on the Maine coast, the admiral returned to Brimmer Street, where he told colleagues and the newspapers of his readiness to lead the crusade for a leaner, more efficient, and just government. Byrd emphasized that he had not given up or slowed down his plans for another Antarctic expedition, arguing that the work of the league would consume at most a few months. But it was work critical to the national interest. The country needed an unbiased "citizens' organization for national service," he told the receptive Boston press.[17] In fact, the nascent league served Dick's interests perfectly, providing him with the pretext for delaying his next expedition for another year while he continued to look for money. Within a week the national organizing convention nominated him chairman of the entire league.

By this time, the drama of the "Bonus Army" was reaching its climax in Washington, focusing the attention of the country on precisely those issues that the league wished to emphasize. Years before, Congress had voted the veterans of the Great War a bonus to be paid in 1945. But as the Great Depression fastened its grip on the land, many veterans concluded that if Congress could be induced to grant the bonus immediately, the plight of several million citizens would be eased. Men desperate for work and bread came together throughout the countryside during the spring of 1932 and began a "march" on Washington to pressure the national legislature into voting them their money now. Not only was the nation experiencing its greatest crisis since the Civil War, but it seemed to be in civil war once more. Hoover ordered the White House gates padlocked and the streets around the executive mansion cleared of pedestrians. For a long month, the Bonus Army remained encamped around Washington, while its spokesmen tried to get a hearing on Capitol Hill and movements such as the National Economy League emerged in reaction. Congress finally turned down the bonus petition, but many men and their families, with nowhere else to go, stayed on. After some hesitation, Hoover ordered the district police against them. The veterans resisted, giving the president a pretext to order in the army under Chief of Staff General Douglas MacArthur to clear the ragged, pathetic host from the city. On July 28, "four troops of cavalry with drawn sabers, six tanks, and a column of steel-helmeted infantry with fixed bayonets entered downtown Washington. After clearing the buildings on Pennsylvania Avenue, they crossed the Anacostia Bridge, thousands of veterans and their wives and children fleeing before them, routed the bonusers from their crude homes, hurled tear gas bombs into the colony, and set the shacks afire with their torches. That night, Washington was lit by the burning camps of Anacostia Flats."[18]

Although Hoover's action undoubtedly outraged a substantial segment of public opinion, conservative America rallied to his side. Who were these "bonusers" anyway but representatives of the undeserving jobless who had hoped to get rich quick without earning it and now wanted Congress to solve their problems? The only way out of the Depression, conservatives reiterated, was for government to cut spending and balance its budget. The veterans of '98 and 1917–1918 were costing the country huge sums in pensions and medical expenses. How many of them had actually been permanently disabled fighting for their country? If they had, they deserved support, but if they returned unscathed (and many had not even seen combat in Cuba, the Philippines, or the western front), they did not deserve government largesse. It was the selfish veterans and veterans' groups who were strangling the country and preventing economic retreat from being turned into victory. They were the ones whom the country must repudiate.

This was the essence of Dick Byrd's message to the nation. The average wage earner, though he might not know it, was the real victim of the organized "minorities"—disaffected veterans and unskilled laborers, together with the thousands of bureaucrats who bloated federal, state, and local government payrolls. These parasites were directly or indirectly taxing everyone for their own selfish interests. The league, said Byrd in brief remarks to its New England chapter, must be as inclusive as possible, and rigidly nonpartisan, but its agenda was clear: "We shall attempt to act with exact justice to all groups. But we will battle with all our strength to destroy those [government] abuses and inefficiencies which have created a chronic depression." The economic crisis had reached a point where the country must "present a war time front. Our enemies are ourselves with our wild city, state and federal extravagances; and the organized minorities who shout loud enough to get special privileges." As with other politicians seeking to invoke favor from the general public, Byrd called on "the too often inarticulate citizen . . . to protect the country from gross inefficiency in government and raids on the treasury by organized minorities."[19]

In early August the intrepid admiral stuck his head in the lion's mouth by addressing the resolutions committee of the Massachusetts American Legion during its annual convention at Lawrence. Richard "could not believe" that his "fellow Legionnaires" would repudiate the league and its platform. According to the text he released later that day, he first reiterated the league's objectives, which he insisted the legion could and should share. He then told his fellow veterans in unvarnished language that "in the minds of millions of our citizens the sins of all the veterans legislation, and that includes the civil war and Spanish American war, are charged against the American Legion," and that was why "the feeling against the legion has become considerable throughout the country." The resolutions committee was not impressed. "Summarily" rejecting Byrd's "plea," the committee sent to the floor the usual resolutions protesting against any reduction or curtailment of existing benefits and supporting the late Bonus Army's demands for government rescue immediately. A presumably chastened Byrd announced he would not seek to address the full convention but rather would return briefly to Brimmer Street before setting off for Plymouth, Vermont, to take counsel with Calvin Coolidge.[20] After that it was back to the lecture circuit to talk, not of blizzards and penguins, but of inefficiency and waste in government.

Despite subsequent neglect by historians, the league became a major force in national political life during the pivotal weeks and months of the 1932 national campaign and beyond. As he rushed about the country, Byrd made no further mention of going south; the league consumed him. He told Rockefeller in mid-December that he had "been going so fast and far" that communication even with old friends had been impossible. Forty-two states had either formed or were forming league chapters, and he had visited thirty-five cities and found "a wonderful response."

Once again Byrd hinted at deeper considerations that framed his work for the league. The organization promoted good government, for it was "founded on the philosophy that government in a democracy is what the voters who participate in elections make it." If those voters could be energized to support the league's ideals, "we can eventually (after we finish our present job) undertake to make the people of the country internationally minded in the right direction, in the same way that we are now undertaking to make the people tax conscious and tax minded." Byrd had great plans for the league, returning in his letter to Rockefeller to themes that he had first expressed to the press following his transatlantic flight five years before. He was "very anxious," he wrote,

> to guide this movement in the proper direction because it can be a force for unity in the country for some years to come. I say this because our biggest job is to show the interdependence of our human relationship which has grown from necessity from the direction our civilization is traveling. When we can show different groups and sections how dependent they are upon one another, we can be sure then that the efforts of the League will not have been in vain from that standpoint alone. The teachings of Christ were never more vital to our progress than they are now.

Once the league got its message across "in this country," Byrd went on, "we can then go to work . . . among nations." He urged his friend to read an article in the forthcoming *Saturday Evening Post* calling attention to "our ignorance and inexcusable indifference towards our problems with the Western European countries."

Regrettably, Byrd continued, the illimitable promise of the National Economy League was threatened by "a very effective under-ground attack going on against me on the part of the minorities who have a death grip on the throat of this country." He did not worry personally because he had expected attacks. "My philosophy in the matter is this. I should use my name and prestige while it is worth something. If I lose it all in this fight, then I won't worry too much about it because it has been well worth-while."[21]

For several months after the formation of the league, Byrd had it all his own way. In October he was welcomed with banner headlines in Wilmington, Delaware; Detroit; and Springfield, Illinois. In November he carried his message to Pittsburgh, where he spoke to eighteen hundred at Carnegie Hall, and to Winston-Salem, North Carolina, where twenty-one hundred members of the National Grange heard him make a "solemn plea" to the farm group to support "a curtailment of governmental expenditures and thereby afford an opportunity for the reduction of taxes." At every stop in every city he hammered at the twin themes of reducing costs and taxes, insisting that he was a friend, not an enemy, of the American worker, of the veteran, of Mr. and Mrs. Average Citizen. "Admiral Richard E. Byrd, a great favorite in Springfield," ran a typical newspaper editorial of the day, "is now exploring new fields where his difficulties will probably be much greater than those with which he has had to contend on his polar expedition. He has tackled the American tax monster!" By taking on this "monster," the editor of the *Illinois State Register* added, the admiral "is rendering a service far greater than that of a victorious general in time of war."[22]

The American Legion and other veterans' groups flailed away at the formidable hero. Louis Johnson, the legion's national commander, charged that Byrd was simply "unwittingly and unintentionally" the "stalking horse for the one person out of 3,000 of our population who is against the veterans of America." Byrd turned the attack aside contemptuously. He was only a stalking horse for millions of properly aroused and concerned Americans who feared the "hundred minorities" who held "a death grip on the throat of this country" and should not be allowed to feed at the public trough. His response was widely applauded. "Admiral Byrd . . . continues to have all the better of it in exchanges with his legionary critics," one prominent midwestern newspaper concluded.[23]

But the strain was telling. Richard and his family, along with the Lindberghs, could not escape the growing dangers that confronted celebrities as the Great Depression deepened. Byrd and Lindbergh maintained a distant and somewhat strained relationship. They both, of course, belonged to New York's exclusive Explorers Club (as did Ellsworth, MacMillan, and the other active polar men). They would occasionally meet there or on some public occasion when both were on the road. While governor in the late twenties and early thirties, Harry Byrd once invited Lindbergh to Virginia along with other prominent Americans, and he wrote his younger brother about the occasion. The Lone Eagle had received "a splendid reception," but Harry was glad his brother had not come. Dick's many admirers concluded that he had stayed away so as not to steal any limelight from the Lone Eagle, and that was fine with Harry. Lucky Lindy had given two speeches in which he did not once mention his benefactor, Richard Byrd, though he did tell a reporter he had "great admiration" for the explorer. "Guggenheim and all other speakers gave you full mention," Harry concluded with satisfaction. "I can only account for Lindbergh's lack of courtesy by the fact that he has no conception of the finer niceties of good fellowship."[24]

Despite the tensions, the two men remained publicly affable. In late June 1930 a press photographer posed the two in New York City. The much taller Lindbergh, dressed in a business suit, bent down slightly to grasp the hand of Dick Byrd in congratulations for his successful Antarctic expedition. Byrd, in navy whites, standing back a bit so he need not lift his head too high to gaze into Lindbergh's eyes, was congratulating the "colonel on his new son."[25] Nineteen months later, on the night of March 1, 1932, someone kidnapped that son from the Lindbergh home in rural New Jersey. After ten weeks of frantic search and tantalizing, frustrating correspondence with the kidnappers, the little boy's badly battered body was discovered in a shallow grave in a nearby patch of woods. Richard and Marie had four children of their own, the youngest only six. What could they do? The problem became especially acute when Byrd boldly confronted the nation's angry veterans' groups.

He would soon claim that his own "life was threatened time and time again, as well as that of my family. Depredations were committed around my place. I had to have a guard for my family . . . at Mt. Desert Island." The Maine State Police stayed with the family at Latty Cove throughout the summer of 1932 while Richard traveled extensively on league business. When the Byrds returned to Brimmer Street in the autumn, Boston's finest took up the job of protection. Bolling remembered "a policeman stood guard . . . as we walked to school."[26]

The family obviously needed a place where it could relax and play with at least some security, far from the limelight. In earlier years Marie and the children had often summered in various spots around Boston and elsewhere on the East Coast. But now privacy and seclusion were paramount. Richard wanted something else as well: a touch—or more than a touch—of luxury that befitted his newly exalted rank and status. In 1931 the Byrds began summering at a compound at Latty Cove on the remote southern side of Maine's Mount Desert Island near the village of West Tremont, thirty-five minutes by auto from Bar Harbor and twenty-six miles from the nearest railroad station at Ellsworth. For five years they rented the property from Robert Winsor Jr. and his wife, Susan. Robert was Byrd's agent at Kidder, Peabody, and Company, Boston's preeminent brokerage house. The Byrds were demanding tenants: Marie insisted each year that the Winsors see to it that new flowers were planted around the compound and that a gardener be secured to keep the foliage in good shape. But they were also responsible people; Winsor once told the admiral that he and his wife would rather have the Byrds in residence than anyone else.

The facility consisted of 170 acres, with nearly a half mile of frontage on Bluehill Bay. It contained two saltwater swimming pools (one a shallow-water wading pool for children, the other a deep pool with a diving board and chutes), a tennis court, a large dock complex, a generally unused white farmhouse at the entrance to the property with a garage for two autos, and the centerpiece, twelve log cabins. It was a grand place to swim and play in the cold waters of the Atlantic or to hike around the compound. The family enjoyed it thoroughly. It was the only place they could really be alone. In August 1936 Richard at last purchased the property for $17,500; the Winsors' original asking price had been $25,000. Ten years later Richard would sell it for $18,500.[27]

In May 1933 Richard wrote Eleanor Roosevelt, trying to entice her and the president to stop at the cove during their annual summer yacht cruise up the coast (1933 would prove the last time that Roosevelt had the leisure to sail Maine waters). "I don't know whether or not you have a swimming pool at Campobello," Byrd wrote. "Anyhow, we have two at Latty Cove," which was "very much secluded in the woods," with a "wonderful dock" on the water side "that a sea-going yacht can come alongside." The nearest summer residence "is over a mile away. There is one log cabin with four bedrooms and a big living room. There is another log cabin with four bedrooms right by the swimming pool. There are five additional log cabins so that there is room enough for a regiment. A special telephone line has been run into the camp, but it can be cut off if necessary." Although Richard invited the rich and powerful to Latty Cove (Roosevelt came in the summer of 1936 and Edsel Ford the following year), the "camp" was above all Byrd's hideaway from the constant pressures of a life of planning, correspondence, lecturing, travel, and travail on the distant southern ice. Here at the cove, in the days when he was not entertaining, he could relax with Marie and the children. Those times were all too infrequent and all too short, but he did his best, and to the family they were priceless.[28]

By this time the Byrds were well settled into 9 Brimmer Street as their permanent residence. The address was an old-fashioned five-story brick house on the correct, "water," side of fashionable Beacon Hill. There Marie took charge, and while her husband was off in the Antarctic, she renovated the place substantially. "As you know," she wrote at one point, "we haven't room enough. I want a great big library and study for you with built in bookcases and paneled walls, all comfortable and *sit*able. I also want a nice room for little old Dick and a gymnasium & playroom combined for all *five* of my precious children." Since No. 9 was insufficient, Marie proposed assuming the lease on adjacent No. 7, which the Ames family also owned. Paying half-rent on the dwelling would cost only $1,800 a year, or it might be possible to buy out the family's share of the trust. "I think it would be *marvelous*," she continued, "and by that time money will be available again and why not do it? At all events, No. 11 is not on the market and Mr. Bowditch will hold on like grim death knowing we want it. We could stand plenty of extra room besides the most important things I mentioned." Not only did the Byrds acquire No. 7 and Richard get his big library and office, but he also hired a series of private secretaries and staff over the years, beginning with the always efficient Hazel McKercher, to handle his usually heavy speaking schedules and substantial flow of correspondence. At one point he would write deprecatingly of the "ruinous" chaos that his "footless" habits brought home to his family.

An explorer's home is his office, recruiting station, headquarters, and main cache. Mine was the mobilization and demobilization point of all my expeditions. The telephone used to ring at all hours. People tramped in and out as if it were a public place. Mukluks and sleeping bags and pemmican samples and sun compasses cluttered up the living room, the bedrooms, the closets—every nook, in fact, where I could find room to dump them. And meals were never on time because Daddy was (1) on the long-distance telephone; or (2) spinning yarns with an old shipmate; or (3) preparing a talk; or (4) getting ready to go off somewhere.[29]

Marie coped with it all, whether her husband was present or not. "Everything runs happily and smoothly," she assured Dick in the same letter in which she proposed expansion through acquisition of No. 7. "A peaceful serene household thanks to loyal and thoughtful maids. There never seems to be upsets and disputes over nothing." The children, as so often the case, grew up in quiet revolt, being neat, tidy, and on time. On the road Richard tried to maintain ties with short notes to his son and the girls. At one point he wrote "Dicky" from Rochester, New York, asking how the boy was getting along in school, if he liked games and his teachers. He told the ten year old that his tent was warm enough to put up even in a Boston winter. It was obviously late, and Richard was tired, fumbling for thoughts and words. At one point, young Dickie wrote his chronically absent father forlornly that he would undoubtedly be doing better in school if his dad were there.[30]

Bolling Byrd Clarke recalled years later that her father loved being with his small children, who were enraptured by his wonderful stories and beguiled by his ideas of things to do. In her midtwenties, Katherine, whom Byrd called "Taff," fondly remembered "the glorious Easters you used to have for us kids years & years ago with eggs & presents & Easter dinner." Like her siblings, Bolling adored her father and missed him terribly when he was gone. When she saw him walk carefully down the gangplank from his second Antarctic expedition in 1935, shattered in body if not in spirit from his ordeal alone at Advance Base, she rushed to him. But his friend and president was waiting to greet him, to say nothing of the press and the newsreel cameras. He pushed her away with the words, "Not here dear. Later, when we are alone." The child was devastated.[31]

In mid-November 1932 foes of the National Economy League discovered (it was not hard, given the glare of publicity that had surrounded Byrd for nearly a decade) that the explorer himself was receiving a rather fat pension for what were certainly non-combat-connected disabilities—roughly four thousand dollars per annum, in fact, a princely sum in the brutally deflationary years of the Great Depression. The first person to speak out was Brigadier General Milton A. Reckford, commander of the Maryland Department of the American Legion and the state's adjutant general. In a speech at Baltimore Reckford attacked Byrd as a prime "beneficiary of the Government's system of paying pensions and compensations to able-bodied men." How could a man who was "physically able to explore the Arctic" be a pensioner since 1916 in various naval grades up to rear admiral? According to one reputable newspaper, legion officials spread the story around the country that Byrd was receiving a federal pension for a football injury, not a wartime injury. "Soon the story confronted Admiral Byrd wherever he appeared."

Congress decided to appoint a joint committee to look into the matter. National Economy League members learned that several congressmen had "dug up Admiral Byrd's record in the Navy Department showing the sums he received in pensions and that these congressmen told their friends among the veterans that they were 'all set for Admiral Byrd' when he appeared" before the joint committee to urge reduction or elimination of veterans' payments. Moving swiftly, the league replaced Byrd as spokesman.[32]

Richard fought back as well as he could, lobbying a divided Navy Department for an official letter of explanation and defense, but the American Legion and others refused to put the issue to rest.[33] They contacted the editor of the Fleet Reserve newspaper, *Naval Affairs,* about the story, which prompted Byrd to write directly to the highest-ranking officer in the service, Chief of Naval Operations William Pratt. Pratt replied that until reading the explorer's letter, "I had no idea that there had been the slightest bit of criticism of your work with the National Economy League from any service people. I assure you that the Navy can have no possible attitude antagonistic to the purpose of the organization in which you are officiating and in which you are doing excellent work. Indeed, far from being critical of you and your mission, the Navy is for you and your mission."

Pratt soon backed his words with action. Joint congressional committee member Louis Ludlow, who would soon become known as the sponsor of an antiwar amendment narrowly defeated by the House, wrote a letter of inquiry to the navy's Bureau of Personnel about the Byrd pension matter. He received in reply a detailed, carefully written, two-page, single-spaced letter from Admiral Alfred W. Johnson, chief of the bureau setting out precisely why Byrd was entitled to the pension benefits he was receiving. Richard was dissatisfied with even this gesture of unequivocal support. Two weeks after the navy's reply to Ludlow, he was badgering Johnson again to make some further changes and clarifications to the official statement. "Calvin Coolidge, with whom I have talked several times, says that the fact that I am subject to call to duty should answer all the criticisms that have been made. That is why I am suggesting that this be included in your statement."[34]

By the end of 1932 Richard's opponents, though comparatively few in number, had him on the run. Early in the new year he offered to quit the navy in response to criticism in both the House and the Senate. Byrd's many congressional supporters, led by Claude Swanson in the upper chamber and including joint congressional committee chairman McDuffie and Republican congressmen Chiperfield and Taber, expressed outrage that Byrd's opponents would be so underhanded as to link his personal behavior to the idealism of his cause or the sterling nature of his character. But Senator Robinson of Indiana was unmoved. Byrd's prominent affiliation with the league was "thoroughly inconsistent" with his willing acceptance of forty-two hundred dollars a year from the government. "He is a young man. I don't suppose any one would say he is in dire stress or needs the pension particularly. To be entirely sincere, it seems to me Admiral Byrd should come to the government and say 'I don't need the $4,200. Here it is.'"

Robinson was joined by the formidable congressman Wright Patman of Texas, a prominent defender of veterans' rights who stormed that the league was "an outlaw organization" and that Byrd should return his pension. These were devastating criticisms, and the admiral met them the only way he could. In a formal statement issued from Brimmer Street, Byrd said he would "give up my status in the navy and all that goes with it if the American Legion, which the Senator represents, will favor before Congress the repeal of that dangerous, costly law which grants pensions to veterans of all our wars who received no injury or disability from war service."[35] It was a weak riposte (he did not promise to return his accumulated pension, for example), and though he continued to receive strong support in the nation's press the fact that he had been displaced as league spokesman before Congress gravely compromised his usefulness.

The one man who might have helped chose not to. Franklin Roosevelt stood aloof both from the organization and from his old friend. He had good reason. Immersed in a bitter presidential campaign, FDR watched while his erstwhile ally allowed himself, with stunning naïveté, to become affiliated with an organization loaded with the candidate's enemies, most notably Al Smith, who had bitterly fought Roosevelt for the Democratic nomination just weeks before the National Economy League was born. Smith was joined on the league's advisory committee by such Republican stalwarts as Calvin Coolidge and Elihu Root, together with world war heroes General John Pershing and Admiral William Sims.

Byrd's first effort to enlist FDR's help came in mid-September 1932, when he sent a cable to the candidate proposing to release a statement designed to force Roosevelt to embrace the league. Byrd promised not to release the statement until FDR could approve it, and apparently the matter died with Roosevelt's silence. A week later Byrd reluctantly refused a request by Eleanor Roosevelt and Louis

Howe to accept the honorary chairmanship of the Young Men's Democratic Club, stating that he had become too great a target of wrathful veterans' groups so far pledged to support the Democratic standard-bearer. Byrd could not resist lecturing his old friend: "Frankly, Eleanor, I think that Franklin will make a great mistake if he does as has been suggested, i.e. gives the bonus to those [veterans] who are destitute. There are a great many reasons why this should not be done. This is my honest and best opinion and I know a great deal about the matter." Byrd insisted, with some accuracy, that there was a popular reaction in the land "against the veterans' abuse." Since FDR was going to get the veteran vote anyway, why did he not chide the Hoover administration for not putting aside moneys over the previous year to pay for the bonus? Eleanor replied rather coolly, "I quite understand your position and, on the whole, both Louis and I think that you had better not take the Chairmanship." She also promised to see that FDR got Byrd's ideas on the bonus issue.[36]

Whether or not he knew it—and he never acknowledged or commented on the matter—Richard was getting the Roosevelt treatment from his old friends. Eleanor was, and would continue to be, the admiral's conduit to her husband. But her influence was always uncertain. FDR would remain aloof, the genial friend when possible, silent when necessary to protect his own interests and preserve his options. This strategy left Byrd, along with many others, permanently bewildered and frustrated, and FDR always in control.[37]

The following spring Richard unburdened himself to John D. Rockefeller Jr. For nearly a year, he wrote, "I was the target for all the veterans' organizations and a million or so veterans. They vilified me throughout the land." After mentioning threats to his family, he added, "I was lied about most shamelessly in every veteran's magazine in the country." But the ordeal was worth it, Richard insisted. He and the league had made the country "economy minded." But, of course, the National Economy League was only a small part of Byrd's eventual dream, "that is," he reminded Rockefeller, "my desire to devote myself ultimately to international amity and coordination. My method," Byrd continued, "has been apparently a very indirect one. That is, I have been working away from the center in order to make my work in the center more productive when I finally reach that stage of my plan. It is like going away from the charmed circle, which is the home, in order to make more certain the security that is there."[38]

Then with a single masterful stroke on the eve of Roosevelt's inauguration, Richard suddenly recouped his fortunes and regained much, if by no means all, of his stature in the public mind. The vigor and energy were his; the idea belonged to Harry, who suggested that one way the beleaguered league could finish its work "with great credit" was to get behind FDR "and start a national campaign that he be given the power to reduce expenses." Since Richard and the league had been bedeviled by details, avoid them and say simply that at this moment of almost unparalleled crisis in American history, "the nation looks to the President and the President should have this power, and that the League is working to sustain the President." Once the league had helped Roosevelt obtain the power he needed, Harry added, Richard "should retire from the picture."[39] The implacable hatred of the American Legion and the Veterans of Foreign Wars prevented both agricultural and labor organizations from working within the league structure, but Richard brought them into a "Coalition Committee" that he hastily put together during the final days of the Hoover administration and the first hours of the New Deal.

The committee included Newton D. Baker, Woodrow Wilson's secretary of war; Nicholas Murray Butler, the outspoken president of Columbia University; Harry Emerson Fosdick, the prominent religious philosopher; William Green, president of the American Federation of Labor; H. G. Harriman, president of the U.S. Chamber of Commerce; Edward A. O'Neal, president of the American Farm Bureau Federation; Walter Lippmann, the most prominent journalist, columnist, and public philosopher of his day; Al Smith; and, of course, Richard E. Byrd, chairman. In a statement to the new president issued on March 7, 1933, the committee announced that it had petitioned the governors of each of the forty-eight states to issue a proclamation to their congressional delegations, asking them "to support you, our chosen leader, at this time of great crisis." The committee "respectfully submit[ted]" for Roosevelt's "consideration that the dire need of the hour calls for national unity in support of our President—a unity even more complete and unselfish than that necessary in war."[40]

The following day, forty-four governors and the District of Columbia duly issued their proclamations to widespread public acclaim. Governors of the other four states were prevented from doing so by existing law. It seemed that Richard Byrd had singlehandedly brought a bitterly divided country together to support a new, untested, but clearly determined leader.[41]

Twenty-four hours later, Byrd was on national radio both before and after the reading of FDR's message to the opening session of the Seventy-third Congress. In the course of his remarks, Byrd disclosed that the Coalition Committee had enlisted the cooperation of the Federal Council of Churches in Christ, the National Catholic Welfare Council, the Central Council of American Rabbis, and the Union of Orthodox Rabbis to have each governor's proclamation read in as many pulpits as possible in each state. For the past three years, the explorer-turned-politician told his radio audience, the country had fought "one of the most baffling battles of its history. In the twinkling of an eye the material paradise of gigantic production, swift commerce and huge profits vanished. All about us tumbled the edifice of the so-called new economic era." But a new day was about to emerge. The storm that seemed in retrospect so necessary had, thankfully, broken, and the skies were clearing. United behind a new president, the nation would rebuild itself. "Victory lies ahead."[42]

In a sense, it was all show, puffery with no substance, exhortation without direction. But the work of the Coalition Committee was as instrumental in its way as the national banking crisis in helping FDR obtain from a panicked country the unity upon which the revolutionary first hundred days of the New Deal rested. Byrd had become a political force in the country, and he was elated, writing exultantly to young Rockefeller on the day of FDR's inauguration that the "federal objectives" of the National Economy League had been achieved. The immediate payment of the veterans' bonus had been prevented, payments to veterans for injuries received in civil life had been cut, and various government departments had been reorganized to avoid waste and costly duplication. The last two, Byrd noted, were powers that Hoover had requested and Congress had provided. "You can see," Richard added, "how the objective of the Coalition Committee worked in very nicely with the National Economy League." Byrd wrote another letter to his wealthy young patron later that same day. It was "a very beautiful thing" to see labor leader Bill Green working with the heads of the farm organizations and the governors in their request to Congress to give FDR the power he would need to balance the budget. "They did it absolutely unselfishly without the knowledge of exactly what the President was going to ask for. They knew that the President would ask for some powers that would be unpopular with their followers. These men, as you know, have a big task in holding their leadership." But Richard had whipped them into line and in so doing glimpsed a bigger task ahead that needed doing and that he could do. "Anyhow, the unity, which at times I have discussed with you, has turned out to be not just a useless dream. It is not only possible to achieve something of it in this country but also internationally. It is certainly needed internationally." He enjoyed the "entire confidence" of the country's agricultural and labor leaders, Byrd added. "This I value more than I can tell you," for these were the people who had to prevent "serious class trouble throughout the nation."[43]

Byrd also owed an enormous debt to Rockefeller himself, and, characteristically whenever and wherever money was concerned, he spelled it out in detail to Arthur Packard, the young philanthropist's financial counselor. The bulk of Rockefeller's sizable donation, Byrd said, was expended by the Coalition Committee during its few frantic weeks of existence. "Because of the limitation of time and the necessity for immediate action," most correspondence with the nation's governors and their staff "was by telephone and telegraph. The total sum devoted to Coalition activity was $1280.21."[44]

Ignoring his brother's sage advice to have done with the organization and its crusade, Byrd told audiences that the league's job "had just begun. . . . We must continue in action behind the President, with a sustained effort. Let me repeat that—sustained effort." The league was organizing in forty states, congressional district by district, city by city, town by town. "That is the way the minorities organize, and that is the way the people must organize."[45] During those turbulent early weeks and months of the New Deal, a number of prominent demagogues and panacea peddlers were abroad in the land: Huey Long, Father Coughlin, and Francis Townsend, to name but a few. To distracted and overworked people in the White House, Byrd may have seemed, at least marginally, another. Perhaps it was time to get him back to the ice.

The prospect of another Antarctic expedition had never been far from Byrd's mind. The lure of South Polar adventure was attracting many able men. Gould and Siple had toyed with the notion; Lincoln Ellsworth, Wilkins, and Balchen never abandoned the idea. Ellsworth was another major polar explorer of the early aviation age who, like Wilkins, has largely disappeared from view. A Chicago-born (1880) engineer who amassed a fortune, then took to a life of professional adventuring, including the North Polar expeditions of 1925 and '26 with Amundsen, Ellsworth, along with Wilkins, had by 1932 become a formidable polar flier. Between them Ellsworth and Wilkins forced Byrd to acknowledge that he could never claim a monopoly over Antarctic exploration.

Edsel Ford and Rockefeller came to Latty Cove during the summer of 1931, and Byrd no doubt sounded them out then on prospects of funding for another expedition. He had already enlisted Marie and Hazel McKercher to get things rolling. In early January, Marie had sent a telegram to "Kerch" that could have been drafted by a navy supply officer: "Have free storage space Navy Yard (Boston). Am informed Navy supply ship Vega reaches Brooklyn Navy Yard February 10 leaving there February fourteen and arrives Boston sixteen. Can have free transportation aboard also unloading facilities here. Must however know approximate cubic footage of space needed on ship. Would it be better and cheaper to cart stuff to Brooklyn Navy Yard to Vega or send by truck. Do what you think best. Let me know so can make definite arrangements here. M. A. Byrd." Several months later Richard, then on the lecture circuit, actually dispatched a "Memorandum to Mrs. Byrd," requesting information on the first expedition's payroll.[46]

By October 1931, Richard was "simply swamped with work" getting the new expedition, BAE II, under way. Early the following January, he wrote Breyer that an unnamed friend had promised use of a ship, and that he himself had managed to gather about forty thousand dollars' worth of supplies and material. The navy had put a marine officer on duty as expedition supply officer. Five days later, on January 16, 1932, Byrd formally announced he was going back to Little America, "with the principal objective," he would later claim, being a flight to the Weddell Sea.[47] Unfortunately, Ellsworth had the same idea and, after unsuccessfully sounding out Wilkins, turned to Balchen to go with him.

Throughout the first four months of 1932, Byrd and Ellsworth circled each other warily. Both, it would seem, clearly desired to maintain a friendship always strained by competition. In January Byrd sent Ellsworth a flag that he had taken with him over the South Pole. Two days later he informed Ellsworth that he had named a mountain in Antarctica for him. Ellsworth replied with fulsome thanks. Over the next several months the two men tried to arrange a meeting to sort out their developing plans, but it never took place. Finally, on March 24, 1932, Ellsworth cabled Byrd, asking the admiral to "write me confidentially if you expect to return to Little America this coming season." Ellsworth prefaced his request with the comment that he had "possible plans" to be in the Antarctic also. In fact, Ellsworth, Wilkins, and Balchen had already agreed "to go down to Bay of Whales and camp somewhere in neighborhood of Amundsen's and Byrd's bases, assemble the plane and fly across to the Weddell Sea." Balchen wrote in his diary that the plane would be an advanced Lockheed Special Transport with a cruising speed of up to 180 miles per hour. Byrd was on tour and so did not reply immediately to Ellsworth's query.

Sometime in early April the two men got together, but it must have been a brief and noncommittal meeting. On the sixteenth, Byrd wrote the millionaire sportsman and explorer, "Will you please let me know what you decide to do?" The admiral enclosed some brief advice and information on ice-pack conditions. The following day the New York Times announced an Ellsworth-Balchen South Polar "trip" that would reach the Ross Sea in September 1933, with the chief objective of a flight to the Weddell Sea. Two days later Byrd dashed off a cable to Ellsworth: was the Times quoting correctly "in all particulars" the date of his proposed expedition and "routes to be flown?" The admiral signed the cable, "Kindest regards & good luck, R. E. Byrd." Ellsworth shot back an immediate, laconic reply. The Times was correct; "Regards."[48]

Byrd waited nearly two weeks, then sent one of the most remarkable letters he ever wrote. "I am asking you to keep this matter absolutely confidential. This letter is for you alone." Byrd wanted to keep his friendship with Ellsworth absolutely above reproach, he said, and so candor and frankness were required. He also assumed that his friendship meant as much to Ellsworth. Byrd then reminded Ellsworth (and sent two press clippings in support) that back on January 16 he had told five hundred people at the Explorers Club of his "principal objective to fly to the Weddell Sea." Yet here was Ellsworth announcing the same goal. And he was taking Balchen with him.

Now, of course, Ellsworth had "talked it over with me, but what has transpired since then has me worried considerably." Several dozen "sources" had informed the admiral of the "bad feelings" generated by Ellsworth's announcement. "People" just did not understand why Ellsworth was, in effect, out to undercut Dick Byrd. "On top of that you are taking Balchen, who got his Antarctic knowledge with me." The article in the *Times* concentrated on Ellsworth's proposed journey and a probable British expedition "but did not even mention mine, although mine was announced before either yours or the British and had been tentatively announced many months before January." A "number of people" had written Byrd expressing certainty that Ellsworth was not planning to go south next year "and that the idea is to lull me to sleep so that your expedition could get down there ahead of mine."

Richard hastened to assure his colleague that "in every case where possible I have defended you," adding that he would continue to defend his friend wherever and whenever possible. "I just want to tell you that my confidence in you is absolute. You and I simply must not allow any bitter, ambitious, envious, jealous, money-mad human nature on the part of others to cause a controversy and public scandal that will mess everything up." There were some, Byrd hinted darkly, "who would be very glad to cause a controversy." Who were they?

They were Bernt Balchen's partisans. Returning from the Antarctic eighteen months before, Byrd had publicly lauded the man who had flown him to the South Pole as not only a great pilot but also "an excellent mechanic and aircraft engineer and constructor." Moreover, "when Bennett and I went up" to Spitsbergen "to attempt the flight to the North Pole . . . we knew almost nothing about flying a large three-engined plane from the snow with skis, and we had considerable difficulty in starting with heavy loads on the snow and from breaking skis." Balchen "saw our difficulties" and showed the ignorant Americans how the Norwegians burned a mixture of tar and resin into the skis to "greatly increase their efficiency." For these and many other reasons, "Balchen was a hundred percent in every respect, but above all," this "gentleman, friend, athlete and leader" had "always played the game."

But in going with Ellsworth without Byrd's permission, Balchen had clearly broken the rules—Dick Byrd's rules on loyalty and friendship. "A great many people . . . have been attempting to make Balchen the hero of everything I have ever attempted to do" and were delighted to learn "when they saw your announcement that he was not to go with me again." Of course, such folk did not know, Byrd added, that he had encouraged Ellsworth to take Balchen. But Balchen did not even communicate with his patron and benefactor, Richard Byrd, about going with Ellsworth, "and yet I have always played the game with him one hundred percent when we were friends during the expedition. I don't know why he could not have at least told me about going with you."

Certainly, Byrd had always given Balchen full credit for everything he had ever done, "not only in my writings but verbally in my lectures." It was Byrd who brought Balchen to the States, Byrd who called public attention to the man, Byrd who was nothing but delighted whenever Balchen got credit and recognition. His friends were on the "wrong track," Byrd added, "by trying to help him by downing me."

The problem was not just Balchen but competition itself in this black moment in American history. Byrd claimed to have received a long and "solemn" letter "from one of the greatest organizations in the country and signed by one of the most brilliant men I know warning" that if he and Ellsworth both went south, "competing in exploration," it would be a public disaster that would ruin both men. It was essential to meet and resolve any difficulties. It was also essential that Ellsworth not make any more rash pronouncements before such a meeting could occur. "All during the Winter night the members of my expedition knew that I was going back and that my main objective was the flight to the Weddell Sea from Little America, and this fact became very widespread." There were rocks and shoals ahead, Byrd warned. "Let's try to miss them." In closing, he wished Ellsworth the very best. "It is my fervent prayer that you will understand this letter," just as Byrd would trust Ellsworth to keep it "sacred between us" as the only two survivors of the "Polar Legion."[49]

Byrd could not leave the matter alone. Nine days later another lengthy, heavily annotated letter issued from 9 Brimmer Street. "Regardless of the way other explorers have hated each other, cut each other's throats and messed up each other's lives, let's you and I play the game," he begged Ellsworth. Byrd confessed feeling that his very future depended on "my finishing up my job from Little America." If he did not believe this, he would "step aside, regardless of everything," and let Ellsworth "go ahead without any competition from me." The two men must meet so Byrd could explain "just why it all depends upon my doing my job from Little America." Ellsworth must understand that Dick Byrd was not trying to "beat anybody else to it" or trying to "obtain new glory." But Little America was "an absolute necessity for the success of my future and for my men who have been working so hard and sacrificing so much for me." "Lincoln, old fellow," he continued, "my plans are just as definite as yours and the date is just as definite," although, he admitted, he could not say for certain if he would be able to get under way for the Bay of Whales in 1932 or the following year. He warned Ellsworth that even if he took "just a few men" south, the expense would be astronomical. Ships, in particular, "cost like the very dickens."

Byrd's tone changed to pathos and defensiveness. The Antarctic was not big enough for two costly expeditions. "If someone goes in ahead of me and does the only spectacular thing there is to do," it would bankrupt Richard Byrd, because it would be impossible to realize enough money from movie rights, writing, and lecturing to pay off the costs of his own endeavor. And the only spectacular thing left to do from Little America was the flight to the Weddell Sea, which Byrd had been the first to announce. Byrd urged Ellsworth to resist talk that "I am a bloated bond holder because it is not true." Outstanding bills from his first expedition exceeded one hundred thousand dollars.

The admiral next returned to his growing obsession with Bernt Balchen. "There has been a decided movement among many in New York to glorify Balchen." Someone had even written a play with him as hero. That was fine; after all, Byrd had made the man by giving him "every bit of credit he deserves in every possible way." Balchen had a "nice personality," and Byrd was "devoted" to him "on the expedition." But the flier headed up only one department and "did not do it all by a long shot as a lot of those people would like the world to think." The problem was loyalty. "Balchen has apparently not been entirely loyal," or, rather, Byrd wrote in the margin, he had been loyal, but other people had "turned his head some or rather affected him in some way because we were the closest friends possible on the expedition." History was full of examples "where a man who has been helped by another one, forgetting all about the things that have been done for him, becomes antagonistic to the man that gave him the ladder to success." Balchen was given that ladder when Byrd took him south, where "he obtained the knowledge that will simplify his going back there to do this job." In a passage that must have caused Ellsworth to shudder, Byrd closed by writing that he had to break off, but "perhaps I will write some more tomorrow." Byrd handwrote a postscript: "Lincoln I am deeply moved by your suggestion that you and I stick together."[50]

Ellsworth's reply, which crossed Byrd's second letter, was masterful. The explorer-sportsman cabled that he had not replied to Byrd because he had been in the hospital with ptomaine poisoning. Ellsworth mildly observed that Byrd had not said he was definitely going to the Antarctic this year, whereas he, Ellsworth, now definitely planned to do so. Therefore, when Byrd's plans solidified, "why not get together and discuss possibility of mutual cooperation. How reasonable that seems," Ellsworth added, twisting the knife a bit, "considering the objective and the money and effort required" to attempt the fifteen hundred–mile or so flight between the Bay of Whales and the Weddell Sea. "I can assure you of both frankness and unselfishness in suggesting this." Ellsworth added that he would be sailing within the week to Europe, where he maintained a home in Switzerland much of the year.[51]

Thereafter, Byrd's messages to Ellsworth declined in length but not in fervor. "It goes mightily against the grain to be in this competition with you," the admiral wrote in late May. "I have racked my mind to find some way out of it but so far without success." By this time Byrd had recruited Siple, Victor Czegka (an "outstanding mechanical engineer" and carpenter), and a few others from the first expedition to make initial plans for BAE II. He told Ellsworth, however, that "our going is most doubtful" in the current year. In a burst of uncharacteristic candor, he admitted that he had not even selected an airplane, and "the value of a dollar is so great now it seems a pity to have to spend money on this expedition at this time."[52]

Byrd may well have been playing a game of his own. Three weeks earlier he had written to his de facto West Coast representative, Robert Breyer, "Ellsworth is going down to Little America with my permission. He is a friend of mine. I could not very well deny him permission since he has set his heart on going." Friend or no, Ellsworth had stolen Balchen because he could afford to pay the flier seven hundred dollars a month and Byrd could not. "This is the sort of thing that was going on that I told you about. . . . [T]he result . . . makes it pretty tough competition for us at a time when money is scarce. Ellsworth, of course, is a millionaire and has the money in his own name." The "depression may lick us but not if our friends, like yourself, that the expedition has, will stick by us." On May 20 Byrd wrote Breyer again, begging for immediate help. Byrd had secured the old ice ship and former revenue cutter *Bear of Oakland* for a dollar a year, but it needed to be completely outfitted. "We simply cannot spend a lot of money on equipment such as crockery, cooking utensils, mattresses, etc." If Breyer could get up to the U.S. Army Supply Base in Oakland and see Byrd's old confederate Salah Chamberlain, he might be able to talk the army out of some essential equipment to complete furnishing the cutter before it set sail for New Zealand and the ice.[53]

At the end of May Ellsworth stunned Byrd with a short cable. "Confidentially," there seemed to be a "bare possibility of my equipment being ready this year." Could Byrd reveal anything more of his plans? Byrd replied on June 11 that a recent newspaper report of his imminent departure for the Ross Sea was incorrect. "Prepared discuss with you agreement not to go down Antarctic this year. Cannot bind myself until talk over some details with you." Clearly, it was time to talk, if not on Byrd's terms, then about some terms. The following day, Ellsworth cabled from his home in Lenzburg, Switzerland, that he would be "perfectly willing" to discuss an agreement whereby neither expedition would depart for the ice that year. He would be back in the States in about a month, he added.[54]

By this time Czegka was immersed in his job as "supply officer BAE II." In early March, the U.S. Marine Corps warrant officer had confirmed to potential donors that "Rear Admiral Byrd is now making plans for a Second Expedition to the Antarctic." Czegka had begun the previous year by drawing up a list of needed materials, goods, and services from memory and experience of BAE I. Then he "painstakingly traveled through the encyclopedic Manufacturer's Catalogue, item by item, just to make sure nothing was left out."[55]

Shortly thereafter, Byrd himself told Breyer that he was "going ahead with my plans to return to Antarctica next fall," though in reality 1933 seemed a more realistic target date. The admiral had already set Czegka and Siple to work "up here at the Boston Navy Yard getting together material." Soon Norman Vaughan joined them. Breyer had already begun "soliciting some subscriptions here for the expedition." He was upset by news that Balchen and Ellsworth were planning an early flight from the Bay of Whales to the Weddell Sea. That was Byrd's objective. Should the Ellsworth expedition have free use of Byrd's Little America camp in the bargain?[56]

As Richard's anxiety reached a peak, Ellsworth suddenly backed off, cabling that "the only condition upon which I can agree absolutely to defer my expedition until next year is that you give me your promise without reservations not to go yourself this year." Four days later Dick replied from the Democratic National Convention in Chicago, telling Ellsworth he felt a "deep responsibility" to "play game squarely with you." As a "patriotic duty" he had just accepted the chairmanship of a "national organization to fight Depression. Will give entire time next several months this project." Though he would continue to accumulate provisions, "my departure very uncertain." Dick refused to give Ellsworth his categorical word of honor that he would not head south in 1932, but "apart from everything else starving people growing more numerous so that public opinion may halt expedition." Ellsworth got the message. Sometime later he cabled from Switzerland: "I am taking it for granted you will not go south this year so shall remain at my home . . . until September first then sail [to] America."[57] In October Byrd reminded "My dear Lincoln" of an informal arrangement that all three fliers had apparently forged. "Wilkins agreed with me that neither of us should leave until next year." Dick clearly assumed that Ellsworth bought into the bargain as well, for he begged his competitor not to be bothered by any dispute, "since I don't think anyone is paying attention to it." He had seen a picture of the plane Ellsworth planned to take to the ice in 1933: "It looks like a splendid one."[58]

Richard had already decided to choose surrender over confrontation if Ellsworth engaged in double dealing. In September he told Ellsworth that should he decide to stop in New Zealand on the way south, H. L. Tapley and Company could be of great service. "They acted as my representative . . . on my last expedition and were of inestimable service to me." Byrd went so far as to inform Tapley that Ellsworth might be heading his way.

Early in 1933, Ellsworth became engaged to Mary Louise Ulmer, and the couple married in late May. Richard and Marie apparently met the pair on several occasions, and Ellsworth invited the Byrds to the wedding. Although they did not attend, Richard and Marie sent an impressive gift. Just before the wedding Ellsworth wrote "Dear Dick," asking "if I could borrow from you that pair of ten power Bush field glasses that I gave you in Spitzbergen." Byrd sent them off the next day. As Ellsworth's preparations rapidly matured in the summer of 1933, Byrd wrote Norman Vaughan that his competitor was "inadequately equipped for ski boots. Let's supply him with a set for the trail." At the same time he instructed Czegka to send Ellsworth a two-man cooker that Ellsworth "wants."[59] Finally, on June 22, 1933, just three weeks before Ellsworth planned to sail south from Los Angeles, Byrd wrote that "I am rushing the boots through. . . . I sincerely hope you have a sketch of Little America. Balchen, of course, knows where most of the stuff is, and you are welcome to anything we have there." Byrd told Ellsworth whom he could contact in New Zealand regarding messages from and to the ice on behalf of his bride, adding that when he reached Dunedin he planned to engage for BAE II "a fellow by the name of Brusted" who was an expert dog-team handler. "You see, Lincoln, if either one of us has a forced landing, I believe my 150 dogs can do the rescue work. I will be depending, of course, upon Brusted to help us out, since every man who goes on the trail in an emergency should be an expert on skis, and Brusted is that." Byrd closed by wishing Ellsworth "a wonderful voyage and all the luck in the world."[60]

Richard ultimately mastered a painful incident by allowing cold realism to overcome outrage. Since Ellsworth and Balchen could be neither stopped nor dissuaded, they should be helped. If anything happened to the pair, Dick Byrd was not going to place himself in a position to be accused of contributing to their fate by sins of either commission or omission. Moreover, he had developed his own winning hand for keeping himself at the forefront of Antarctic adventure—one that could not be trumped: "Advance Base."

Chapter 11

Jeopardy

y the late summer of 1933, as the country strove to grasp the audacious dimensions of Franklin Roosevelt's New Deal, the Second Byrd Antarctic Expedition rapidly took shape. Amid the usual uproar and uncertainty of trying to get another large polar expedition under way with the "shouting confusion of telephones and telegrams, hammers banging, hand trucks rumbling, orders and counter-orders, wild goose chases," Richard received an invitation from Eleanor Roosevelt. Could he and Marie have dinner at the White House and spend the night of September 6? The day after their gathering, FDR sent a long note to "my dear Dick." The president was "delighted that you have had the faith to go ahead with this scientific expedition to the antarctic continent and that you have definitely set the date of departure for September 25. It is because you and I are such old friends," Roosevelt continued, "and because I have followed so closely your three previous expeditions, that I expect to keep in close touch with your new expedition." The president was "especially interested in the exhaustive study of weather on the antarctic," that "weather maker for the greater part of the South American continent." Byrd should know that he and his colleagues had the "full support of the United States Government and that you can call on the Government in case of need or emergency," a welcome pledge in view of Byrd's problems getting out of the Bay of Whales three years before.[1]

There may have been more to the dinner gathering. Years later, in the midst of an unsuccessful attempt to rescue Operation Highjump II from presidential cancellation, Richard told President Truman's secretary of defense, Louis Johnson, that "in 1933, preceding the 1933–35 expedition," a comprehensive aerial mapping and claims project for Antarctica "was discussed with President Roosevelt, and approved by him." Only the lack of suitable aircraft at that early date made such a mission impossible. If Richard remembered matters correctly, it was the first time—though far from the last—that anyone of importance in Washington openly raised the notion of making U.S. territorial claims in the Antarctic based largely on Byrd's own extensive explorations.[2]

Whatever was discussed that September evening in 1933, FDR's relief was palpable. His friend and possible rival was going into a deep freeze for at least eighteen months, and the president hurried him on his way by applauding the explorer's decision to leave early. That proved impossible. *Bear of Oakland* was able to clear Boston Harbor on time, but the main supply vessel, *Jacob Ruppert,* did not depart until October 11. Still, Byrd could be of use to the New Deal before he sailed. On October 2 the admiral signed a reemployment agreement as part of the National Recovery Act's industrial codes of conduct, thus carrying "the blue eagle of recovery to the southernmost limits of the earth."[3] With that act his career as a public political figure came to a temporary close.

No excursion ever headed south to the ice burdened with more goals, objectives, and agendas—open and hidden—than did Richard Byrd's second Antarctic expedition of 1933–1935 (BAE II). Byrd told people the white continent lured him back by its "intangible attraction," then proceeded to enumerate several tangibles, including "the pull of discovery, of seeing new lands, and fitting into the jig-saw of geography the missing pieces beyond the horizon."[4]

Indeed, he planned to pull off the greatest polar coup of all, placing in eclipse any and every one of the comparative handful of people who had ever been to Antarctica. Who had ever lived alone, or even with a companion or two, amid the dark, howling, frigid South Polar wasteland, hundreds of miles beyond the barrier, for the four to six months of its dreadful winter? No one. But Dick Byrd would. Should he survive, he would have a tale to tell greater than any yet told. An Antarctic winter hermitage would solidify beyond all question his status as one of the greatest polar explorers, if not the preeminent.

Exactly when and how Byrd hit upon and matured his plan for an advance base is nearly impossible to determine. According to Charles Murphy, Byrd first mentioned the project as early as 1930, immediately upon the return of BAE I.[5] "He remarked, then, that he had been thinking it over for some time." Murphy remained close to the admiral after collaborating on the 1928 biography, and Byrd would appoint the writer chief publicist for BAE II, taking him down to Little America essentially as Russell Owen's replacement. Though a flight between the Ross and Weddell Seas would certainly be spectacular, the establishment of an advanced weather station high up on the polar plateau for occupation during the dreadful Antarctic winter night would be even more so. Only heavy aircraft and tracked vehicles, working in tandem, could carry the requisite materials and supplies down the Ross Ice Shelf. Only the biggest aircraft could lift them up over the Axel Heiberg or Liv Glaciers to the plateau. A successful advance-base project to measure polar weather from deep within the Antarctic continent would ratify Byrd's reputation as the most innovative and effective pioneer on the polar frontier.

Economy, Byrd said, "was to be the controlling element in the drafting of all specifications." The centerpiece would be a "shack," or "mountain hut," as it was variously called—a little prefabricated house on the Antarctic ice prairie—weighing at most fifteen hundred pounds, portable, capable of being assembled rapidly and easily, "staunch enough to withstand rough handling and, besides, winds up to 150 miles per hour; and as warm as ingenuity could make it." Victor Czegka designed the shack, and Ivor Tingloff, a Massachusetts master carpenter, built it during the last weeks before BAE II sailed south.[6] Tingloff made the walls four inches thick and sheathed the inside panels with a special metal insulation that he covered with a layer of heavy fireproof canvas painted green from the floor halfway up and then silver to the ceiling. He agreed with Byrd and Czegka that the shack should be sunk into a pit dug out of the Antarctic snow in order to keep it out of reach of the worst winds and blizzards and to benefit from the warmer winter temperature "that always prevails beneath the snow." A "narrow porch-like roof" extended from the front of the house to serve as a food storeroom in its own right and as a vestibule for several further tunnels that the inhabitants would dig out from it for further storage. "Cut into this porch-like extension, and directly over the door, is a trap-door which will serve as an entrance to the shack. There is a ladder for it." Tingloff built the little house in his workshop; Siple and Czegka oversaw its dismantlement and transportation to *Jacob Ruppert,* where it was carried to Little America.

How many people would occupy the shack and where, exactly, it would be were also unclear. But from the outset, Byrd seems to have rejected as impossible placing the shack up on the polar plateau. The aircraft of the day simply did not possess either the weight or the power to transport it there. Byrd told Norman Vaughan that four men would inhabit the advance base from April to October "at the foot of the Queen Maud Mountains four hundred miles away from all the others." The four would "know the joy and terror of six months of utter isolation, "and Norman, of course I would like you to be one of the four men." Vaughan, his recent marriage already unraveling, reacted joyfully. Byrd found it hard to contain his own emotions. "No one in the world has ever done this before," he told Vaughan. "Imagine what it will be like, living in the interior of the Antarctic continent. We shall prove that the human spirit can withstand every impediment."[7]

It was not to be. Instead, if Vaughan is to be believed, Dick Byrd broke his heart one spring morning in 1933, walking along the esplanade that borders Boston's Charles River. Keeping "his eyes straight ahead," the admiral told his admiring acolyte that he had decided there would not be enough time after unloading supplies and building Little America II to make the shack suitable for a group of four. "I've had to revise my plans," Byrd said. He would not take anyone out to the Queen Mauds. Only he would go to man Advance Base.[8] After mulling the matter over for a time and seeking his father's advice, Vaughan decided not to go south with Byrd. He saw a side of his beloved mentor—an overweening desire for personal glory and acclaim—that he understood but could not, in the end, condone.

Although there is little reason to doubt Vaughan's story, he must have been a man of great discretion, for no one else seems to have caught on to Byrd's intentions before he sailed. As the admiral reluctantly severed his affiliation with the National Economy League, Czegka and the others continued to obtain the needed gear for another massive assault on Antarctica. Like its predecessor, BAE II would combine exploration and serious science with entertainment. Byrd shamelessly wrote at one point, "We also had another asset—a story to sell."

By the summer of 1933, "nearly 100 people, mostly volunteers, were . . . struggling to get us ready." Czegka was a tireless solicitor and an equally impressive administrator and innovator. At one point, the admiral wrote tersely, "Get all your heads together and lick this steering proposition for me in some way." Czegka and his people did. Working with Czegka and newly appointed supply officer Stevenson Corey, Byrd managed to acquire a thirteen hundred–mile-range Curtiss-Condor transport that he named for William Horlick, who supplied money for its purchase, and two smaller aircraft, a single-engine Fokker (loaned by Alfred P. Sloan of General Motors and named *Blue Blade*) and a twin-engine Pilgrim monoplane that Byrd christened *Miss American Airways.* "We picked up tractors, snowmobiles, and other vehicles, food and clothing, tools, rope, nails, telephones, radios and an unbelievable amount of electrical equipment," Vaughan recalled. But he, Czegka, and the others "made our own tents and some specialized clothing."

Byrd obtained only $150,000 in cash, "a meager war chest for an expedition with a million dollar task," so materials and stores "either given outright or loaned" proved essential. Times were hard, and cadging for support was even more exhausting than before. Byrd, Czegka, Siple, Vaughan, and others wrote nearly 30,000 letters to prospective donors. Czegka himself wrote 127 letters, trying to persuade various manufacturers to donate overalls; "in the end we had to buy them." Roosevelt and Secretary Claude Swanson may have helped Byrd obtain the World War I–era steam freighter *Pacific Fir* from the U.S. Shipping Board for a dollar a year; they may have pressured the city of Oakland to part with the capable old wooden-hulled ice ship *Bear* on the same extraordinarily favorable terms. But it was Dick's brother Harry, now ensconced in the upper chamber of Congress, who directly pressed Commerce Secretary Roper (whose department oversaw the Shipping Board) to secure the "rusty old oil burner" for Richard, who promptly renamed the vessel in honor of his patron Jacob Ruppert.

Ruppert, Rockefeller, Edsel Ford, Horlick, and the National Geographic Society rallied around the explorer once again. They were joined by such new contributors as General Foods (which agreed to underwrite the weekly broadcasts from Little America on CBS Radio while providing the expedition thousands of boxes of Grape-Nuts cereal), the Mackay Radio and Telegraph Company, Tidewater Oil Company, and Thomas Watson of IBM.

Byrd also mended broken fences with Paramount Pictures after having been wined and dined by Louis Mayer. Dick wrote Emanuel Cohen in June that he would go to "infinite pains" to get "the proper kind of a movie" this time around. It was the only way "to keep from going bankrupt." He had not really understood the technique or impact of motion pictures in 1928 or 1930, Richard stated. Now he did, and he assured Cohen "that the second expedition would face more ice, do more flying, and create more news than the first expedition." But there was more. He told Cohen that he had "a dramatic secret plan which he could not put down on paper," but did reveal that "two men will spend the winter night at the foot of the mountains only 300 miles from the Pole where temperatures will be as low as 90 degrees" below zero. If there was not drama in this exploit, drama did not exist. In the theatrical way he had come to employ when seeking to engage the attention of the wealthy or powerful, Byrd swore Cohen to secrecy about everything. His ploy worked, and Paramount assigned John Herrmann and another cameraman to the expedition. Working through Harry, Richard also contracted with the U.S. Postal Department to establish an official office at Little America II from which he could sell postal covers and even issue an expedition stamp, both of which proved lucrative sources of income.[9]

The expedition's oddest acquisition was undoubtedly the "autogiro," a crude rotorcraft precursor of the helicopter. The man selected to fly it was little more than a boy, age eighteen at the time of recruitment. Bill McCormick had lost his father when he was four, and his older brother, Joe, had assumed the role. Lindbergh's heroics had inspired Joe to become a flier, and when Bill graduated from high school Joe was ready to play mentor. The two young men spent several summers flying out of Atlantic City, dropping daredevil parachute jumpers in the waters off the big steel pier. At that time manufacturers Harold Pitcairn and the Kellett Company had become interested in "autogiros," which they believed could be made safer than the aircraft that seemed to be crashing every day or night somewhere in the country. The McCormick brothers contracted to obtain one of the new vehicles from Pitcairn for their summer 1933 Atlantic City air show, but the manufacturer suddenly went out of business. The boys turned to Kellett, who supplied them with a vehicle and recommended Bill to Richard Byrd when the explorer—ever eager to try out new aviation technology—decided to take an autogiro to the ice.

Byrd had no money to purchase a vehicle, but Pep Boys, then as now an auto accessory firm based in Pennsylvania, bought one for him from Kellett "and, of course, left it up to the factory to select the pilot." Like so many others, McCormick thus achieved his boyhood dream by a circuitous route. So wrapped up in flying had he been that he had not even known Byrd was preparing another expedition. But in his recent boyhood McCormick had been enthralled with the admiral, following his North Polar and transatlantic flights closely. When Byrd subsequently said he was going south and would take a Boy Scout with him, thirteen-year-old Bill McCormick was determined to be the one. Only later did he realize that the incredible requirements were far beyond his reach. Now he and his untested autogiro were going to be part of polar history.[10]

BAE II set up formal headquarters at the Beverly Hotel on East Fiftieth Street in Manhattan. Byrd's personal representative this time was John McNeil, a rather shadowy figure whose postexpedition tenure would be as brief as Hilton Railey's had been following BAE I. Although there is comparatively little documentation for the activities of the New York City headquarters during the 1933–1935 venture in the Byrd Papers, what little remains suggests that from the outset Marie and the ever faithful "Kerchie" made certain that McNeil enjoyed far less discretionary power and authority than had Railey four years before.

Experts in no fewer than twenty-two "divisions and sub-divisions" of scientific research, including meteorology, glaciology, botany, biology, zoology, astronomy, physics, geography, terrestrial magnetism, and oceanography, sailed with Byrd. The government and various universities, themselves badly strapped for money, loaned the expedition nearly one hundred thousand dollars worth of scientific equipment.[11] Richard would willingly take novices, but he wanted fellows he could trust from BAE I to form the core of his second expedition. As sailing drew near he was pleased to see that "the clans began to gather": June, Noville, Quin Blackburn, and Finn Ronne (whose father, Martin, had been a valuable member of BAE I) from Norway. Alan Innes Taylor, a former Canadian mounted policeman, and expert dog handler, was a valued newcomer.

Not everyone was available, and Dick pulled every wire he could to get the men he wanted. Because of repeated budget cuts, the Weather Bureau was particularly loath to release anyone, especially an already reluctant Bill Haines. As he had days earlier when searching for a suitable big ship, Dick instinctively turned to Harry, who gladly pulled every wire and placed every pressure he could on the bureau and its parent department, Agriculture, to obtain Haines's services. "I drove through the Shenandoah National Park with the President on Saturday," Harry informed his younger brother in mid-August. "I took the liberty of mentioning to him your desire to have a weather man accompany you. He said that he would be delighted to see that this is done." Harold Ickes's Department of the Interior would be taking over the Weather Bureau from Agriculture under a new government reorganization, and Harry made sure that FDR's chief confidant, Louis Howe, "would cooperate" with Ickes in seeing that Dick not only got a weatherman for BAE II but got the weatherman he wanted.[12]

Still, Byrd was always a bit of a soft touch for those who not only yearned to go south but also demonstrated it by stubborn application. Al Wade was a young professor of geology at the University of Delaware when he wrote Byrd in early 1933 to apply for the expedition. Unfortunately, the admiral replied, his scientific department was already full. As the country was in the depths of the Great Depression, faculty salaries were at the poverty level, so in order to supplement his income Wade headed for Maine that summer to work as a counselor at a boys' camp. Since he had to drive through Boston, he stopped at 9 Brimmer Street to press his cause in person. Ringing the bell, Wade found himself facing the admiral, who invited him in for tea and cake but remained adamant that there was simply no room. Wade drove on to Maine, but returning just before the fall semester he decided to drop in on Byrd one more time to press his case. Again, the admiral answered the door, laughed, and said, "'Come on in, we'll have some tea or something.'" Once settled, Byrd was quiet for a long moment, then told Wade that he would need help loading and unloading supplies both in New Zealand and on the ice. He could not promise that Wade would "make" the winter-over party, but "at least you'll get on the expedition and get down there."

Wade jumped at the chance. A few days later, aboard the *Jacob Ruppert* at pier side in Boston, he found himself stripped to the waist and filthy, part of a working party bagging soft coal meant for the winter party. "Pretty soon one of the other fellows introduced himself," saying, "'I'm Professor Earl Perkins, I'm from Rutgers University,'" and Wade replied, "'Well, I'm Professor Al Wade, I'm from Delaware.'" Byrd took both men to the ice and kept them for the winter-over. Wade made one trip east to the Edsel Ford Ranges that proved a major boost to his career.[13]

Gordon Fountain was another eager youngster who found his way into BAE II. His father was a friend of Norman Vaughan, who late in 1932 offered to show young Fountain around *Bear of Oakland* (usually referred to simply as *Bear*), which had just arrived from the West Coast. Ike Schlossbach, preparing for his first expedition with Byrd, was aboard the filthy ship, trying to make sense of the clutter. Fountain asked him how he could apply. Well, the brawny man replied, the boy could "turn to and see what happens. None of us know whether we're going to make it or not." Fountain worked like a Trojan that day and for many weeks thereafter, but in the end he was left on the dock. Months later, he received a radiogram from the ship's captain, Robert English. *Bear* had just returned from taking the expedition to the ice but was short several crewmen; if Fountain could find passage to New Zealand, he would find a berth. The youngster managed to work passage on a British "motor vessel" heading for the South Pacific. Within weeks he was a member of *Bear*'s company, and although he did not winter over, he made every voyage to the ice save the first.[14]

Schlossbach had already had a varied career before he wound up on BAE II. A pilot, he claimed to and probably had commanded surface vessels, submarines, and a flight squadron. He had been part of Wilkins's ill-fated effort to take a submarine under the Arctic ice pack. He eventually lost an eye, but this did not prevent him from a prominent career in Antarctic exploration with Byrd in 1933 and 1939, Finn Ronne in 1946–1947, and on Operation Deepfreeze twenty years later. Donald McLean, a doctor with the Ronne expedition, recalled meeting Schlossbach for the first time. Coming aboard ship in Beaumont, Texas, he could not find Captain Schlossbach until somebody told him that the commanding officer was down in the hold. McLean "found a guy who was throwing 100 lb bags of anthracite coal into the prow of the boat and so I asked him where the Skipper was and he stood back and stuck up his hand and said, 'Good to meet you. That's me.'" Schlossbach was nearing sixty at the time.

Ronne's wife, Edith, or "Jackie," as she preferred to be called, found Schlossbach "funny. He was a riot." She also discovered that he was something of "an expedition hobo." Schlossbach had a "miracle cup," which at once attracted and repelled his fellow expeditioners. Arising in the morning, Ike would pour hot water into it. Jackie and others on the expedition swore that if he then turned the cup in one direction it would be coffee, in the other, it would be soup. "You know, it was just a filthy, dirty cup and he never washed it, but that was Ike."[15]

On Saturday, October 21, 1933, "with a cheerful good-bye to his native Virginia," Dick Byrd "pointed the prow of his flagship Jacob Ruppert toward the bottom of the earth." Byrd had briefly docked the vessel at Newport News in order to install a heavy boom for loading and unloading his big Condor biplane onto land, ice, or water. *Bear* had departed Boston almost a month earlier, on September 25, because of slower speed. *Ruppert* left the New England port on October 11. But *Bear* soon ran into the same kind of devastating Atlantic weather that had initially crippled *Eleanor Bolling* on BAE I, and with the same result. The barque was forced to put into Newport News for caulking, and *Ruppert* followed.

Byrd was exhausted. He had been on the go—frantically so—since arriving home with BAE I three and a half years earlier. In the last hectic weeks and days of preparation, his determinedly calm and genial manner began to crack, and the expedition's doctor scolded him firmly. Dick must "haul in your sails a bit—and take it easier from here on out." He owed it not only to the expedition but also to "your family to do it." The admiral had been "harassed daily with the same continuous grind seeing the *same faces*—not much rest." Dick had to "shut most of us out at a set time each day and pull up with the family, or eat Friday night chicken with me—or any other night." Dr. Shirey saw a control freak who could not delegate enough work to others, not even Czegka, Siple, or Corey. "Outline what you want done," Shirey added. "It'll be done & you'll be in better shape for the big stuff." Dick had not been "so taut" three months before, but now "you are tired & don't know it." But Byrd pressed on, his cares seemingly endless. Inevitably, as had happened five years before in California, he came down with a debilitating malady during his last days in the States. This time a throat infection kept him confined to a Norfolk hotel room for several days. Apparently, he had said his family farewells in Boston, for news accounts give no indication that Marie was present to nurse her husband on this occasion. But brother Harry was there after performing one last task—obtaining a suitable "loan" of coal for the expedition from the Pocahontas Fuel Company in New York City.[16]

Ruppert sailed on its own for New Zealand and the ice, leaving the smaller, slower *Bear* to follow ten days later. Fortunately, the old freighter's voyage down to Panama and along the upper west coast of South America was a tonic for all hands. One bright day and clear night followed another, and there was little for Byrd to do, though observations of marine life and land bird migrations "began as soon as we set off."[17]

Richard planned to venture into Antarctica's Pacific Quadrant between the base of the peninsula and the Bay of Whales, making landfall at tiny Peter I Island, lying within the Antarctic Circle south and west of Cape Horn. "In that locality Charcot, Wilkins and de Gerlache had made substantial penetrations" of the ice pack "without raising the continent." All hoped *Ruppert* could do better. After it attained "the deepest southing," the admiral would not only find the coast by aircraft but also, "if possible," make "a non-stop flight westward to Little America" with the powerful medium-range Curtis-Wright Condor "fitted with skis and floats, and wonderfully handy for exploring." *Ruppert,* with the men and supplies for Little America II, would follow. Such an aviation spectacular might well trump whatever ideas Ellsworth harbored.

Shortly after clearing the canal, however, Richard received devastating news from Washington that forced him to revise his ambitious plans. Despite prior assurances from "the best counsel" that the Condor's new variable-pitch propellers were perfectly safe, Richard was now told by the War Department that subsequent testing indicated that structural weaknesses developed at high vibration. Since the props would need to run at maximum revolution to gain the height necessary for prolonged flight, "that finished the matter, so far as we were concerned." Not only would Byrd not countenance serious risk to the flight crews, "but a failure of the initial flight operation might completely wreck the whole program." The admiral had to abandon not only the propellers (he had taken conventional fixed-pitch propellers along as a precaution) but also any notion of extended flights. On November 8, five hundred miles west of Callao, Peru, Byrd diverted *Ruppert* to Wellington, New Zealand. The next day Ellsworth's *Wyatt Earp* docked at Dunedin, and its crew immediately began assembling their own long-range aircraft, which Ellsworth planned to take into the ice as soon as possible.[18]

Byrd's new plan was to refuel at Wellington, then strike out for the Pacific Quadrant "on a southeasterly slant, ultimately steaming eastward along the front of the pack and making a series of direct thrusts toward the coast by ship and plane." Sailing through an empty ocean toward New Zealand, *Ruppert* made a brief call at Easter Island, where a gale marooned some of the crew and scientists for an uncomfortable twenty-four hours. Before the storm hit, however, most of the expedition members rode out to "look at the huge grotesque images" that made the island famous. It was a brutally hot day, and some of the men, including Bill McCormick, the autogiro pilot, had literally had to barter their shirts for a horse. Sweaty, itchy, and miserable, the men came across a crystal-clear little lagoon. "You could see the bottom and no waves, just ripples. And everybody sat there on their horses and somebody said 'Doesn't that look inviting?' Without saying a word, Byrd slipped off his horse, went over the edge, stripped down stark naked and said 'Come on, what are you waiting for?' and jumped in." McCormick would tell the story often in later years as a reminder that Richard Byrd "was just a regular guy after all." Stuart Paine also discovered his commander's humanity at about this time. "The Admiral as yet hasn't the slightest idea who I am & I haven't exchanged more than two words with him," the young radioman and dog-team driver wrote mournfully in early December. The following evening, however, he found himself next to Byrd at the Saturday-night movie shown on deck. While watching *42nd Street* with Ruby Keeler, "the Admiral talked about his visit to Hollywood & the feminine charms who roam its streets."[19]

The men were somewhat fooled, for Dick Byrd had decided to change drastically his leadership pattern. On this expedition, unlike the last, there would be no bridge games in his "private cabin," no joining in the boxing matches in the commons area or suddenly knocking on the door of a party to be let in as a member in good standing. BAE I had toughened and matured the Admiral of the Antarctic. Siple later alleged that his friend and captain's new mood had come about when an unnamed pilot from BAE I upon returning home had dressed himself in poor clothing, donned his medals, and arranged to be found, ostensibly destitute, on a park bench. Byrd—and the many admirers among his men—never forgave or forgot the unnamed individual. Byrd concluded from this incident that "an easy relaxed style of leadership as 'one of the boys' . . . tended to undermine respect."

On BAE II, whether aboard *Ruppert* or *Bear,* Byrd ate not in the wardroom "but in his own quarters on the bridge." Ashore while at Little America II, "he did not eat with the gang in the Mess Hall . . . not even at Christmas or Midwinter night, nor watch movies with us . . . except one time when the movie of BAE I was shown and he gave a running commentary." Instead, the admiral "maintained a businesslike, no nonsense manner . . . with the general run of his men. . . . He was not prickly, surly, or conceited-acting," Alton Lindsey remembered. "He had confidence in his men, perhaps over-confidence," but he would not be one of them. He conspicuously exempted the veterans of his first Antarctic trip, Bill Haines, Paul Siple, and Quin Blackburn, who remained physically and socially close to their commander.[20]

Ruppert reached Wellington on December 8 and anchored just behind Ellsworth's ship while its fuel bunkers were quickly refilled. The old freighter departed four days later on Ellsworth's tail, for that explorer had consumed a full month at Dunedin, loading supplies and preparing his aircraft, and did not sail until the tenth. While in port at least some of Byrd's boys continued the heavy drinking that had marred the expedition since departure. Stuart Paine and a colleague went to Wellington's Grand Hotel for a long talk during "which we both got quite drunk." The two inebriates agreed that there were only "about 12 men on board who are worth a damn & that the Admiral knows exactly what is what." Paine had already gotten angry with Stevenson Corey, who "has shown his double face, as was expected, & is holding out because of some personal grudge or dislike. We can't figure it out." Another expedition member had just emerged from a sustained three-week "drunk," and two others "did not show up til three this afternoon very drunk. They are at it again + both are making damn fools of themselves." Another day in port Paine wrote disgustedly, "[Harold] June threatens to quit + the expedition seems to have developed into a circus."[21] The "crusaders" on Byrd's second expedition were proving even more fractious than those of 1928–1930. Clearly, it was time to get back to sea.

Ruppert carried some bizarre cargo into the ice. In addition to 95 men, 135 dogs, a few husky pups, and "all materials and goods necessary to comprise a polar village and sustain its inhabitants for a year and a half" (including a raft of "talkie" motion pictures courtesy of Will Hays and Paramount Pictures), Byrd had also secured three cows, one of whom was discovered to be quite pregnant. The Guernseys had been "loaned" by farmers apparently on the condition that "we could get them through alive." The provision of fresh milk for however long the cattle lived would be a major morale booster for everyone who chose to be marooned on the ice.[22]

As the old freighter plowed south toward Antarctica and a new year, Byrd let his excitement show. *Ruppert* "was headed for a great adventure. Instead of going straight to the Bay of Whales, we were bound for the unknown." He informed the world through the weekly radio broadcasts that were beginning from the ship (and would continue at Little America II) of his firm belief "that in that lost world" at the bottom of the earth, "aviation will find something of value to humanity." Not even a "terrific gale" near the southern end of the "shrieking Sixties" (that is, the 60th latitude) dampened the admiral's confidence, and on December 19, a week out of Wellington, as day broke in "a lovely golden panel of light pushing through softly furred, gray cumulous clouds," Richard Byrd returned to Antarctica. High in the rigging, Dick Russell caught sight of the first iceberg. "A moment later half a dozen more lifted frosted domes above the horizon. Soon the sea was crowded with them." At that moment the pregnant cow, "Klondike" (the others were named Southern Girl and Deerfoot), decided it was time to give birth, even though the Antarctic Circle remained a few degrees to the south. Although the bovine's agricultural sponsors nearly thirteen thousand miles away were disappointed that one of their products did not enter the world within the actual confines of Antarctica, they were pleased to learn through Murphy's regular radio broadcast that the newborn was a bull calf. According to Byrd, "by unanimous consent he was called 'Iceberg.'"[23]

Byrd decided to devote the early part of the first summer season to making "aerial thrusts" from *Ruppert* toward the unknown coastline of newly named Marie Byrd Land using the suspect Condor seaplane. Earlier expeditions had found several places in the area where "curious indentations" persisted in the ice pack, suggesting the existence of nearby land "damming or deflecting the ice." Following the 150th meridian south of the Antarctic Circle, Byrd found to his "astonishment" nothing but open sea until he reached 67 degrees, 9 minutes south, where the pack ice at last appeared in concentrations thick enough to threaten *Ruppert*. But this year, for the moment at least, Antarctica appeared benign. There were twenty-four hours of daylight, a good bit of sun, and no fog, which was fortunate because of the hundreds of icebergs. A lead opened up, and Captain William Verleger, a retired navy lieutenant, sent the freighter into the ice farther south than any freely navigating ship had yet gone. When the pack began to close in once more, Byrd ordered Verleger to stop the ship and "with some difficulty and risk" dropped the Condor over the side into a patch of clear water. Byrd eagerly got aboard the plane, and it took off, flying directly south for more than two hundred miles. As the minutes passed the pack ice below grew thicker, "more ominous," but no land appeared. Disappointed, Byrd returned to *Ruppert* and ordered Verleger to steam eastward toward the 120th meridian, where Charcot had earlier made a deep penetration of the pack without sighting land. Byrd was convinced that if *Ruppert* could penetrate as deeply as the Charcot expedition, the Condor seaplane would find the elusive coast.[24]

Moving eastward, however, proved dangerous. The pack closed in again, and as Verleger with difficulty extricated his ship from its clutches and headed for open water to the north, the expedition found itself in the midst of the "Devil's Graveyard," the "greatest ice-berg producing region in the world." Maneuvering in clear weather among the monstrous blocks of floating ice was a challenge to any seaman, but now fog clamped down, and "for days we never saw the sun." Then the wind blew up, compounding the difficulties of navigation. Radar was nearly a decade away; only the human eye could detect the awful dangers that lay all about the ship. As the old freighter wrestled against the forces of wind and tide, all aboard were aware that the thin-skinned vessel could directly strike or be struck by a berg at any moment, or it could snag its hull on an ice spur, as had *Titanic* barely twenty years before. Should *Ruppert* go down, even if all the crew managed to get off into boats, the men of BAE II would be marooned in the watery, windy wastes of Antarctica, hundreds of miles beyond help. *Bear* was still up in the South Pacific, weeks behind as a result of its encounter with the Atlantic hurricane. One day the fog lifted long enough for Byrd and scientist Tom Poulter to count several hundred bergs, but then murk descended once more.

As Verleger struggled to control his vessel in the windy, choppy seas, he was assisted by Commander Hjalmar Gjertsen, a renowned ice seaman whom Byrd had temporarily hired away from the Norwegian Navy. "Enormous ghostly ice castles would suddenly loom ominously in the gray mist and every few hundred yards gained by the *Ruppert* raised a new flotilla with spray dashing up their icy green bulwarks." At one point seawater got into the ship's oil supply, dropping steam pressure so precipitously that Gjertsen could not keep the ship's bow to the wind. "*Ruppert* rolled heavily in the trough of the sea with spray sloshing across her decks." Bits of sharp ice called growlers "passed perilously near." Slaving away, the engineers managed to purge the oil and get pressure back in the boilers, but on Christmas Day, as Gjertsen slowed the vessel down in the fog, "a big iceberg appeared dead ahead." The helmsman slammed the wheel hard over and barely missed the monster. Gjertsen later admitted that this was his narrowest escape in a long career as a polar navigator. All the while, *Ruppert* pushed doggedly along a zigzag course "over a thousand miles along the edge of the unknown."[25]

Byrd began to worry. All the maneuvering had so far produced only one frustrating flight, and time was getting short if Little America II was to be built at the Bay of Whales before the winter night descended. Near longitude 116 degrees, *Ruppert* moved south into the ice pack again, reaching 72.5 degrees, where clear water permitted another flight by the Condor seaplane on January 3, 1934. Once again Antarctica frustrated the dogged admiral. A gray mist closed in soon after takeoff, and the ice pack ran to the limit of visibility whenever the weather cleared briefly. Pilots Harold June and William Bowlin soon encountered thick fog and found themselves flying blind over an iceberg-choked pack for much of the mission. At one point, "about 110 miles south we cut across an enormous stretch of ice. At first it had the appearance of shelf ice, anchored, perhaps, to [the] continental Barrier. In the mist we couldn't tell what lay beyond." Crossing at about three hundred feet over "that immense slab on which an army could have maneuvered without being cramped," the fliers glimpsed "two huge Emperor penguins, the only living things we saw. They must have heard our engines, because, after glancing wildly around, they dropped to their bellies and scuttled off. Probably it never occurred to them to look up." Byrd thought the poor, frightened creatures were "the loneliest couple on the face of the Earth."[26]

Byrd had directed Haines to radio weather reports to the aircraft every fifteen minutes; so far there was no cause to abort the mission. But soon after flying over the penguins, June beckoned Byrd forward to the cockpit and pointed to a southern horizon "black with snow squalls." It was time to turn and run for home. Bowlin took the controls and brought the Condor up into higher, calmer air. But the airspeed indicator froze, and the Condor began to ice up. Bowlin took the plane back to one hundred feet. "Sodden clouds pressed down. A brace of snow squalls swelled darkly across our course." Great "blobs" of mist flowed past the cockpit windows while the gently rocking wings "wallowed" in them. Byrd feared flying directly into an iceberg, for several that had been briefly glimpsed on the flight south seemed well over one hundred feet high. Everyone peered through the gloom. "Flying quite low, we twice burst over huge bergs with barely 50 feet of clearance." Dodging snow squalls, Byrd and his colleagues groped for the *Ruppert* in the murk and wind and cold. The men were doubtless guided by radio beam back to safety, though Byrd never mentioned it. Once the plane touched down next to its mother ship and was hoisted aboard, "we started the long voyage back to the west" and the Bay of Whales. "You fellows stole one that time," Haines remarked as the flight crew tramped wearily into the mess hall.

Fortunately, wind and current had dispersed much of the pack, and *Ruppert* experienced little difficulty during the long voyage to the Ross Ice Shelf. Six days after the second flight, with *Ruppert* as far south as 69 degrees, 50 minutes, Byrd ordered the ship stopped and the Condor lifted over the side for a third flight along the 150th meridian. The flight proved short and as unrewarding as the others. Dick Byrd had still not found, much less traced, the coast of Antarctica along the Pacific Quadrant. Still, he claimed, he and his fliers had driven "quite a substantial wedge into this unknown area." The best strategy would be to build Little America II, wait for *Bear,* then use that ice-capable vessel "to get in through the back door," running directly along the coast east of Little America through what was hoped would be a continued weak and dispersed late-summer ice pack.[27]

Ruppert reached the Bay of Whales on the morning of January 18, 1934. Byrd could not have been especially pleased. An undated memorandum in his BAE II files set down the dates when ships of earlier expeditions had gotten through the ice. January 14 had been the latest. But, of course, *Ruppert* had been attempting, and in a measure had achieved, some serious exploration. BAE II arrived at the Bay of Whales accompanied by upsetting news from Lincoln Ellsworth. Just days before, his own expedition had occupied the original Little America site as a base for his own flight, only to be thrown out by "a great upheaval in the bay" so severe that it damaged his plane beyond repair. He had been forced to return to the States.[28] Thus, BAE II arrived with some trepidation. How solid and reliable was the edge of the Ross Ice Shelf? Perched precariously not far from the edge of the barrier, might Little America II become untenable? And what would happen should a crisis strike in the middle of the polar night?

Even before *Ruppert* departed Wellington, CBS in New York was badgering Charlie Murphy about how the broadcasts from BAE II should be presented. According to the breathless CBS introduction, broadcasts to and from the expedition constituted "the most remarkable feat in the history of radio," and the company was determined that they go smoothly. The company insisted that Murphy and his "guests" confine themselves to simple narration involving "human interest stories and ships doings." "On no account" should one of the more obscure members of the expedition sing a song because of the "probability of distortion and fading making vocal solo reception very bad." Using the expedition's newly formed "glee club" and various instrumentalists, on the other hand, was "okay." And CBS wanted to know why Murphy planned to "save ship's bell for ice pack, why not make it part of standard opening and closing of program until expedition dissembles at Barrier?"[29]

Richard allowed at least one old and staunch supporter, George Noville, to sign up with press services, and Noville's agent soon reported that "story series going swell. Starting publication this week in five hundred papers including fifty college papers." Additional requests to sign on were "arriving daily."[30] Calculation as well as friendship doubtless influenced the admiral's decision. By diffusing accounts of BAE II, Byrd doubtless hoped to calm fears and jealousies, especially during the harsh and stressful winter months when the men of BAE II, most of them new to Antarctica, would be cooped up for weeks on end.

As Christmas approached, the Byrd husband-and-wife team moved smoothly into high gear. At home, Marie took charge of filling the apple list and received a number of flattering acknowledgments. Richard was undoubtedly delighted to learn that the expedition was receiving very favorable press.[31] Christmas 1933, "a long way from home & those I love so much," was nonetheless "jolly . . . aboard ship, even though it is foggy, wet & cold outside." Stuart Paine noted in his diary that "last night we sang carols and drank [Charlie] Murphy's brandy. We ate & ate & ate & stuffed & drank [photographer John] Herrmann's whiskey. There has been plenty of Christmas spirit aboard." Far too much, it would prove, for the expedition's well-being. A week later, Paine noted that the coming of 1934 was celebrated aboard *Ruppert* with whiskey and "the rapid ringing of the ship's bell."

The holiday season proved something of an ordeal for Murphy. On the twenty-seventh, a senior CBS executive sent a cable to the ice, ripping Byrd's public relations officer. "Client agency [General Foods, the Grape-Nuts cereal maker] and Columbia [Broadcasting Company] people all complaining you failing precisely carry out orders there-by hampering program success" and technical operations. "Program control must remain this end and instructions must be carried out." According to CBS, Murphy had badly muffed the precise timing schedule while inserting his "personal participation" at the expense of his commander. Granted, Murphy was "master of ceremonies," but that did not give him license to hog the show. "You should be . . . only speaking as little as possible and only in brief bits." It was "highly important" that not only Murphy but also "admiral and others enunciate each word crisply, separately, and distinctly." In a follow-up cable CBS told Murphy that the "following routine must be followed each week until instructions." The program must be opened with three blasts from *Ruppert*'s whistle. Then the slowly, carefully enunciated words "Hello, America, Byrd Expedition calling," a pause, and then a repeat: "Hello, America, Byrd Expedition calling." Murphy was then to give *Ruppert*'s position, the weather, temperature, and any other pertinent data, followed by a musical number (presumably from the studio in New York), the introduction of Byrd, his talk, another musical number, and sign-off—all not to exceed seven minutes![32]

Richard appeared strangely unmoved by Murphy's indiscretions, which were not dissimilar to those for which he had condemned Owen on BAE I. The admiral's restraint may well have been due to a number of factors, most important of which was the prospect of more than adequate supplies. During his abortive stay at abandoned Little America I, Ellsworth and his men had determined that "everything is intact including the radio masts" and the airplane. The huts were, of course, "completely covered with snow, but it is safe to assume they are intact, too. This news means a great deal to us," Paine wrote in his diary. "More room, larger quarters, perhaps some privacy, good library, supplies, food etc." With the supply and housing problems solved, Byrd could anticipate with ever greater relish the surprise he was about to unleash on the world once *Ruppert* and the late-arriving *Bear* had been unloaded at the Ross Barrier, the agonies of "Misery Trail" had been overcome, and Little America II was a reality.[33]

Misery Trail. No one who participated in BAE II would ever forget its agonies. "I hope never to go through such an experience again," Paine wrote. Five hundred tons of supplies and building materials had to be hauled across "a glorious mass of crushed + twisted" bay ice that in most places jammed tightly against the barrier, then along the barrier to the Little America base site. Byrd quickly deployed his men and cracked the whip. "Worked ten hours out there without a respite. Cold + tired," Paine wrote in late January.[34] Perhaps he was too tough, Byrd later admitted, "but I had been through the mill before, and I knew something about the job of getting a polar expedition started off on the right foot." Conditions in the Bay of Whales permitted *Ruppert* to get within two miles of Little America, but impassable pressure ridges barred a direct approach. The men had first to hack a snaking trail through the ridges. A ten-foot gap of open water was bridged with telephone poles, but the ice moved constantly under the influence of wave and wind: "every day or so we would have to bridge a fresh crevasse."

The job would have been impossible without the advanced technologies that Byrd had brought with him from civilization. Intrigued by the possibility of tractor transportation on the ice, yet strapped for cash, he had been rescued in part by his admiring French friend André Citroën, who was in the process of sponsoring a tractor exploration to the Gobi Desert. Citroën learned of Byrd's needs through a mutual friend and promptly sent off to New Zealand three of his "light and fast" half-track cars designed "for long range exploration." They arrived just in time to be loaded aboard *Bear* for the Bay of Whales. Edsel Ford contributed two light "snowmobiles," and the Cleveland Tractor Company "presented a marvelous vehicle, a Cletrac, which was virtually a snow dreadnought, with a load capacity of 20,000 pounds." Byrd promptly put these vehicles to work along with the usual dog teams and even, on occasion, the airplanes to haul the hundreds of tons of material to the base site.

"Thursday afternoon, January 18, was the beginning of the nightmare," he later wrote. "The end didn't come until the cold and darkness of May. Long cruel days, unnumbered days, days of aching effort, dragging from one task to the next" under alternately sunny and sullen skies. And always the ever deepening cold that enveloped and defined every moment. "Time was everything, time was nothing, time was something that ran on and on, lacing the dissolving hours with the blinding pain of fatigue; there was no end to it, only a terrible penalty if you allowed it to get the upper hand."[35]

"The dogs were badly out of condition," Byrd wrote, "and as wild as March Hares to boot." Drivers soon discovered that their animals had peculiar social relationships that derived from the "ancestral wolf pack." Although the dogs quickly developed a "tremendous amount of affection" for their drivers, they never seemed to settle the question of rank—of superiority and subordination—among themselves. They easily became insanely jealous. Their drivers were inexperienced and had to learn how to handle the unstable animals on the job. Even the few experienced handlers easily got into trouble. On the first "practice run" from the ship to Little America, young Finn Ronne, an alleged expert, allowed the two teams under his control to cross paths, "triggering in seconds one of the worst dog fights I had ever seen." The snarling animals tore into each other, yelping and screaming, maiming and ripping open their mates. All Ronne and his two companions could do was use the butt end of their whips to slowly break the infuriated animals apart. The Norwegian skied back to *Ruppert,* summoning his boss, Innes Taylor, with a first-aid pack. By now the ice was covered with lame, frightened huskies who promptly tore their dressings off. "It took us an hour to get the mess straightened out."

According to Byrd the dogfights went on for several days, at the end of which "there were few drivers with voice enough left to speak above a whisper." Back at the bay, heavy seas forced *Ruppert* and *Bear* (which finally arrived on January 30) to shift moorings several times. This was an effort in itself since each change required new "dead men" (long, thick pieces of wood, usually telephone poles) to be driven horizontally into deep holes in the ice to which the lines from the ship could be securely fastened. At one point early on, Byrd concluded that unloading could best be done directly onto the barrier if a suitable low point could be found. Cruising slowly along the barrier wall in *Ruppert,* Byrd found what he was looking for, a place where the barrier dropped to within forty or fifty feet of the water. Haines was with Byrd on the bridge, and the admiral had just turned to ask his meteorologist what he thought of the place when "there was a sound like a skyscraper collapsing" and a quarter mile of barrier came loose, "streaming downward, spilling and tumbling into the sea," where it fanned outward, covering the water. The savagely rocking vessel managed to maneuver out of harm's way, but enough ice had fallen "to sink a whole fleet of warships." Haines calmly offered that this was not a good place to moor.[36]

The next day the expedition almost lost its best aircraft when the Condor, now configured with land skis, "rose smartly into the air" from the barrier and headed off to the base site with a load of supplies. Observers on board *Ruppert* were horrified to see that the plane's two big skis had broken from their horizontal position. The preventer wire that kept them in a horizontal position had snapped. Any landing would have been "a frightful crash." Bowlin, flying as copilot, gamely opened his cockpit window and crawled out on the wing as June, flying the aircraft, kept it at the lowest possible speed to remain airborne. Out in the freezing slipstream Bowlin reached down and made "a valiant" effort to somehow push the skis back in place. He could not do it and carefully crawled back along the wing and into the cockpit. Now it was up to June to somehow get the plane down safely. Descending in a "long, curving glide," June in one smooth act leveled the plane off just above the ground and pulled its nose up to the stalling angle. "The sudden decrease of air speed threw the skis into a horizontal position" just as the plane touched down.[37] In terms of sheer skill, Byrd had chosen his chief pilot wisely.

As January passed into February and February into March, a new city slowly emerged around old Little America as prefabricated buildings were brought from *Ruppert* and reassembled. Electrical wires and power and telephone lines were strung inside and out; a modern science lab and weather observation station were built along with the "Adolph Ochs radio station and broadcasting plant." Sophisticated machine and carpenter shops went up, along with a medical facility, a dairy barn housing the three cows and the bull, snow hangars for the aircraft and snow garages for the vehicles, and, finally, sleeping and eating quarters for fifty-six men who would winter over. Little America I was used to the utmost, and connecting tunnels and passageways were dug from above into the original facility.[38] As with its predecessor, Little America II was not the work of trained construction battalions or workers, as would be the case with the big expeditions after World War II. It was put together by cooks, pilots, dog-team and tractor drivers, seamen from the ships anchored to the ice, and scientists.

Paine took the agonies of Misery Trail in stride. Early on he wrote, "Plenty to eat, lots of exercise + immensely healthy."[39] But not all was well with the men of BAE II. Friction grew steadily, and tempers frayed on Misery Trail between the dog-team and tractor drivers, "as a few of the tractor drivers, sitting in warm cabs and throwing chocolate wrappers out into the snow would refuse to yield to the forty-foot-long trains of harnessed dogs careening precariously while hauling a ton of supplies."

Unfortunately, Byrd himself contributed to the mounting stress and tension. He had placed Noville in charge of unloading the ship and June in charge of operations on the ice as well as in the air. He made Innes Taylor responsible for transport and Demas for the operation of the tractors. Tom Poulter, whom he named chief scientist, monitored construction of Little America II. These were all wise appointments, but Byrd blundered badly in creating a command structure for the wintering-over party.

As *Ruppert* approached the Bay of Whales, Richard called Poulter to the bridge, chatted with him briefly, then offered him the position of second in command. Poulter demurred. This was his first trip to Antarctica in an expedition filled with veterans. Surely, Harold June or Paul Siple were far more experienced than he. No, Byrd replied. Siple was too young, and "he wouldn't consider June because he liked his liquor too much." According to Poulter, Byrd forbade liquor on the ice except small amounts for medicinal purposes.

Pondering his commander's comments, Poulter at last reluctantly agreed to become Byrd's executive officer, leaving June, who had expected the position, bitterly—and openly—angry. Instead of facing June down, Richard caved in to his old comrade (who had been at his side since Spitsbergen), and in an act of incredible folly appointed his chief pilot head of an expedition staff whose role would be to establish, by majority vote, "any rules and regulations for the operation of the Expedition and with a two-thirds vote could over-rule the order of any officer in camp."[40]

June was not the only one becoming estranged from the expedition and its commander. Young Finn Ronne was embarrassed for being "screamed" at by other expedition personnel for inadvertently getting out of the boat ahead of Byrd when the advance party reached the Bay of Whales, thus becoming the first BAE II member to set foot on Antarctica. Later he was disgusted to find that Byrd's first act in establishing Little America II was to send onto the ice the bags of mail to be canceled and sent home to their senders, who would then pay a special fee to the expedition to help defray expenses. "The ship[s] would leave within a couple of weeks and the cancelled mail had to be on board." Ronne was gleeful when a blizzard struck the camp, burying the sacks under ten feet of snow. The sacks were not discovered until Edgar Cox stumbled over them in midwinter while digging a pit outside the cow barn. Ronne was amused that "none of the recipients ever knew why it took more than a year for their letters to reach them."[41]

When *Bear* arrived at the end of January, Richard compounded his earlier mistakes. Waiting impatiently for a week while the barque was hastily unloaded, he abandoned his command and leaped aboard, ordering *Bear* out of the bay on a cruise eastward to fulfill his obsessive determination to explore the adjacent coastline. Earlier voyages by Scott in 1902 and the Japanese naval lieutenant Choku Shirase ten years later suggested that an archipelago might exist beyond Cape Colbeck. Even if such a feature could not be found or did not exist, a line of sonic soundings that oceanographer S. Edward Roos wanted to make would be sufficient justification for the cruise.

To some, the hasty voyage smacked of abandonment. "I can't understand how the Admiral could leave even before his base was established," Paine confided to his diary, "but he did. He never visited the [temporary] Pressure Camp [established as a Misery Trail way station] once during the stay of 42 of his men there though he drove through several times between L. A. and the ship." Paine lost respect for his commander that he never fully regained. "I have just about reached the conclusion he is a publicity seeker + nothing else." The barque was back in the Bay of Whales within six days, Richard's quest for new discoveries largely frustrated. But it had been fun. "There was a joy and spirit to the *Bear*'s attack" on the pack ice that "were lacking in *Ruppert*'s." *Bear* was wooden hulled and built for ice operations. "She could hit with both hands where the flimsy *Ruppert* had to wheedle and cajole: she could lower her head and bore in where the *Ruppert* had to turn tail and seek a better 'ole."[42]

When Byrd returned, Dr. Shirey, the expedition's physician who had earlier warned his admiral against overwork, asked to be relieved and sent home with the ships before winter. Displaying the dogged loyalty he always extended to those who were consistently loyal to him, Richard would ever after claim that Shirey diagnosed himself with high blood pressure, and that such "poor health" convinced this most responsible of men that he must surrender his duties before he became an unconscionable burden. Shirey added to the impression by cabling his wife that if no replacement could be found, the "Old Guy," as he characterized himself, would remain on the ice and "do my duty regardless [how] things will break."[43]

Long after Byrd's death, Poulter provided a different explanation. Shirey had no health problems except an excessive love of the bottle. The admiral had discovered that his dedicated doctor in fact "was apparently more interested in the liquor supply than he was in the expedition." This had gotten Shirey in trouble as early as Wellington. "Byrd is peeved with Shirey," Paine noted, "as he should be, that so many men were taken aboard here. Shirey has blundered enough with the personnel I wonder he continues on the job." Several weeks later in the ice, Paine added that "the more I see of Shirey, the less I think of him." Such a man could not remain in Antarctica. Murphy prepared a news release emphasizing Shirey's "own diagnosis" of ill health and his unwillingness to jeopardize the project.

But the doctor's impending departure left BAE II without a physician on the eve of the polar winter. Byrd later wrote that he felt he had let his men down, and the "terror" of wintering over without medical support was suddenly dramatized when *Ruppert*'s skipper fell ill with pneumonia. Byrd was forced to call in all his favors to obtain a replacement in time. Through "regular channels," presumably the State Department, he forwarded a request for a physician to the New Zealand government. Soon word came back from Wellington that a plethora of doctors were volunteering to join the Yanks on the ice. Louis H. Potaka, a Maori, was quickly chosen, and His Majesty's Government in London gladly made available the British exploration ship *Discovery II,* then at Auckland, to transport the doctor southward. *Bear* raced out of the Bay of Whales and through the ice, fog, and gales of the southern seas to meet the British vessel north of the pack and bring Potaka back to Little America.

Antarctica refused to cooperate. *Bear* could not break back through the ice pack, and a frustrated Captain English pondered sailing back to New Zealand. As always in a crisis, Byrd acted with decisiveness. He ordered English to hold fast and called young Bill McCormick to his quarters. The autogiro pilot was astounded when his commander told him what had been done. Dick Byrd never "ordered" anyone to do anything. "He . . . always discussed things with you and would tell you what he wanted and then you would do it. But this time he actually gave an order [to English] to stand by." Byrd told McCormick that he wanted to go aloft in the autogiro to inspect the ice pack around the Bay of Whales. No problem, McCormick replied. The craft would be ready to go after an hour's warmup. Fine, Byrd replied. "Give me a call." Rising aloft in the fragile and unstable little whirlybird, the two "flew for three or four hours," exposed to freezing cold in the 'giro's open cockpit. So much for Byrd's fear of flying! The bay had begun to slick over with pancake ice, but the admiral wasn't worried. "Oh, that won't be a problem," he yelled to McCormick over the blades whomping and beating the frosty air overhead. "That's only thin ice. The *Bear* can get through that." Only the ice pack remained a danger.

When Byrd landed, Haines told him he could not fly again for at least twenty-four to forty-eight hours. A heavy storm was on its way. The next day when McCormick dashed to his admiral's quarters through wind and blowing snow he found a happy man. "It's been blowing like hell here hasn't it Mac?" Byrd told the mystified pilot, who agreed that it certainly had. Well, Byrd replied, those heavy winds had created the heavy seas necessary to loosen and scatter the pack. *Bear* with Dr. Potaka and needed supplies should be in the bay shortly. And so it was. By the end of February both ships had finished unloading and gone north for the year, leaving the men of BAE II to confront a series of supply caches on the ice that had to be manhandled onto sleds for the trip to Little America by tractor or dog team.[44]

While most of the men concentrated on getting the supplies into buildings and tunnels, Byrd ordered the dog-team and tractor drivers to head south down the broad Ross Ice Shelf to establish supply caches for the forthcoming summer season's exploration work. But before much could be done, an incident on March 4 brought Byrd's own plans to the fore. That day the unstable ice shelf off the much greater chunk of ice that supported the Little America I and II base sites began to crack under the constant surge of water beneath. Poulter measured the widening cracks around Little America, and Byrd called a hasty meeting of his veterans from the first expedition. Clearly, some sort of emergency "Retreat Camp" had to be hastily built on the stable high barrier behind the island if the expedition was not to come to grief.[45] This decision set the entire schedule back a full month and precluded any idea of establishing an advance base sufficiently large and sophisticated to support Byrd and two others.

Richard would have to go it alone at Advance Base, and as poor weather at Little America began to clear, Byrd directed Siple to "cut all the food supplies" for the advance base "down to that required for *one* man. Reduce all weight to a minimum. Take the canned food out of their boxes, and arrange them in 1,000 pound shipments ready to put into the planes as soon as they are conditioned for flight." Unfortunately, the heavier Fokker had just been wrecked in a short test flight. The Pilgrim would have to carry all the food supplies.[46]

Byrd would later go to great lengths to emphasize that he had brought to Antarctica "a hard-bitten crew who were well-able to take care of themselves." Demas and Haines were serving on their third polar expedition, Siple on his second. Noville had enjoyed various responsibilities in civil life as well as having accompanied Byrd on both his North Polar "affair" and transatlantic flight. Innes Taylor "had dueled with Zeppelins in London's wartime skies and had trekked the Yukon for the Royal Canadian Police." June, "whom I appointed Chief of Staff [*sic*]," had flown down to the South Pole scant years before. "To these men I could entrust the winter destinies of Little America without fear." After all, the long polar night would be "tranquil." No parties would be out on the trails, and "secure from the blizzards and cold life finds new and easy ruts underground." The admiral may have been deceiving the public, but surely after his tense experiences on BAE I he could not have been fooling himself. His omission of Poulter and of Poulter's ostensible command position in this context was at once striking and disturbing.[47]

Thomas Poulter is a relatively obscure figure, though he made substantial contributions to American science. At the time Byrd appointed him to the expedition, Poulter was teaching at Iowa Wesleyan University in Mount Pleasant, which like all small institutions of education in the depths of the Great Depression was clinging to existence by an eyelash. It did boast one distinguished graduate, James A. Van Allen, whose future work in particle physics and space science uncovered the radiation belt that circles the earth and bears his name. In the early thirties, Van Allen paid forty-five dollars a semester to attend Wesleyan and lived at home. Drawn to science, he found that "Professor Thomas Poulter in physics and Professor Delbert Wobbe in chemistry were my principal inspirations. Each was a one man faculty of his respective department." Van Allen decided to major in physics after Poulter offered him a part-time student assistantship. The young man "came to have an almost worshipful regard" for Poulter's "mechanical ingenuity, his intuitive use of physics and chemistry as a way of life, and his devotion to experimental research." Poulter was already preparing for his role in BAE II, and in the summer of 1932, following his freshman year, Van Allen helped the professor build a simple seismograph while checking out a field magnetometer on loan from the Carnegie Institution of Washington, D.C., that was one of the most elegant instruments Van Allen ever saw.[48]

Poulter was a man whom almost everyone instinctively liked. A big bear of a fellow like Siple, he was always "right there, doing all the hard work."[49] But, to some, this amiable mechanical wizard was incapable of leading men. "Poulter has shown himself quite incompetent to direct this end of the expedition," Paine concluded in late February, not long before Byrd headed out to Advance Base. June, in contrast, "has remained calm + quiet + has accomplished more than all the others put together."[50]

Clearly, Byrd undercut his second in command, leaving him bereft of any effective *means* to exercise command. The men of BAE II had begun heavy boozing in New Zealand, and it did not stop once in the ice. Serious trouble arose as soon as Byrd departed to explore the adjacent eastern coast. Stevenson Corey, the expedition's supply officer, noticed a sled being loaded with liquor and decided to tell Poulter. Before he could, June and his helpers brought the sled into the camp about two o'clock one morning. Poulter said nothing as he watched the men hide the supply down in the ruins of Little America I. Every time June and "his collaborators" came back, they quietly checked to make sure the booze supply had been untouched, "and each time," Poulter later wrote, "I would recheck to make sure they hadn't moved it." Poulter concluded with undoubted correctness that the soon-to-depart Dr. Shirey had turned over what had become a substantial medicinal supply to his friends and fellow imbibers. "I felt sure," Poulter added, "that if I moved the supply they would get another from Dr. Shirey and I wouldn't know its location."[51]

It seems that Poulter did not tell his commander of the incident; he should have. Byrd had foolishly given the jealous June a position from which to formally challenge Poulter's leadership, and now the unhappy pilot was obviously laying down an informal challenge as well. There were other signs of discontent at Little America II on the eve of Byrd's departure for Advance Base. Ronne and a young radio operator had already chosen to live apart, constructing their own quarters out of a "room-sized aviation crate." Ronne called the hideaway—which contained bunks, a stove, a working table, and a radio—"Blubberheim," and it became his haven from the stresses and tensions of group living.[52] Byrd had preached the centrality of community in the harsh polar environment and had imposed such a spirit on BAE I with initially mixed results that in the end proved generally positive. Now he was letting BAE II fray at the edges while he went off, first on *Bear,* then down to Advance Base, to follow his own inclinations.

On March 16 Byrd dispatched a nine-man party south in several of the little red-and-black Citroën half-tracks with material for "Bolling Advance Base." Every resource was thrown into the effort: the Pilgrim monoplane, dog teams and sledges, the Citroëns, and the big Cletrac tractor, which pulled four sledges. Much to Ronne's disgust, Byrd recalled the Innes Taylor party from where it had been laying a trail and depositing food at the 155-mile depot. Advance Base would not be established at the foot of the mountains after all; given the uncertain state of radio communications over long distances and the possible requirement for emergency rescue, to say nothing of the possibility of an emergency evacuation of Little America II, 400 miles was simply too distant. Byrd settled for a spot 23 miles beyond the 100-mile depot. "Preparations had to be thorough but expeditious," Ronne recalled, "for when the four-month-long winter night closed in, travel would be impossible. Already the sun was almost parallel with the horizon; soon it would not rise at all."[53]

The dog-team and tractor parties laying down markers or setting food caches found trail life both grim and monotonous. The Antarctic "snow" was often resistant both to dog's feet and sled runners. The great crevasse field still lay roughly 50 miles south of Little America, ready to swallow men, animals, and sleds. Farther on, crevasses masked by bridges of snow posed an even more terrible danger. Drivers feared constantly that they and their animals might find the trail abruptly giving way beneath their feet, pitching them down deep into the ice sheet to a frigid, painful death. On normal days the teams and their dogs slogged southward hour after hour on a flat white landscape (except for occasional pressure ridges) toward a horizon already darkening alarmingly toward winter. Cold defined every moment, every action, as temperatures plummeted to sixty-five degrees below zero. Frequent blizzards added to the misery. The slightest wind caused the cold to cut through the heaviest clothing, and men's bodies became icy while their faces and extremities were frostbitten. Everything froze and had to be thawed: liquids, skin, equipment, zippers. Climbing in and out of snowy sleeping bags was an ordeal; so was cooking (a laborious process) and putting up and striking tents. Food was limited by weight, and thus monotonous and bland; washing dishes consumed more time that might have been spent moving south and returning home. The dogs were always unreliable. Skittish, vicious, or hysterically angry, they needed constant attention, and their frequent fights taxed the patience and competence of the finest drivers, of whom Byrd had precious few. Radios broke down frequently, which prompted the admiral to cable home for advice and for new equipment to be sent to the ice with the ships when they returned the next year. "On this trip," the troublesome but undeniably gallant Ronne wrote, "I learned first hand how much punishment the human body could endure."[54]

The Citroën half-tracks and the big Cletrac tractor had their own set of problems: nearly frozen fuel and lubricants, machinery parts that broke and snapped in the dreadful cold, occasional breakdowns. But until time came to establish Advance Base, the vehicles performed well, justifying Byrd's guess that motorized transportation as a complement to aviation was the key to wide-ranging Antarctic exploration.

Establishing Advance Base proved as difficult and exhausting as the construction of Little America II. At one point the Pilgrim aircraft, "yo-yoing back and forth carrying materials and supplies and anything else they needed out there," was forced down by fog and a whiteout while on a delivery mission to Innes Taylor's dog team at the 100-mile marker. Byrd went aloft in the little autogiro with Bill McCormick to find the downed plane. As a freezing slipstream blew over the open cockpit, McCormick flew the fragile, shaking little craft low over the ice shelf some 60 miles to the spot where the Pilgrim ought to have been. There was no sign of the plane, but McCormick remembered pilot Bill Bowlin complaining that his directional gyrocompass was drifting him off to the east of the southern trail. Heading in that direction, McCormick and Byrd soon spotted the downed aircraft and, returning to the trail, found a dog team with a radio and landed beside it. McCormick then took off with one of the dog-team members back to the downed aircraft to show him where it was. Upon landing back on the southern trail, however, McCormick cracked a cylinder head on the autogiro, so it was down also.

Byrd raced back to Little America by dog team and promptly dispatched another group of men and dogs with fifty gallons of gasoline and a new cylinder head to ensure that the Pilgrim and the autogiro could get safely aloft. It was just another day at the South Polar office, and McCormick felt vindicated. From the beginning his little eggbeater had been the butt of jokes. The autogiro was variously described as "the whirligig, the infuriated palm tree, the palm tree with the DT's," and so on. Pilgrim pilot Bowlin had been one of the worst offenders, and he was not altogether happy to be found by the 'giro rather than by dogs and men. A day or so later the tractor party came to grief just south of the 50-mile depot. The Citroëns and the big Cletrac had been performing admirably from the start in transporting vast amounts of goods and supplies, and the Citroëns had followed Innes Taylor's dog teams out on the trail southward, helping with the caching of food before returning to Little America to load up materials and goods (including Byrd's "shack") for Advance Base.

Now, however, while making a trail through the pressure ridges, a Citroën driven by June and Bernie Skinner lodged in a crevasse. The two drivers managed to extricate their vehicle just as the big Cletrac and the two other Citroëns arrived. The following morning the Cletrac stalled fatally when a pin sheared off the crank, undoubtedly because of the extreme cold. The vehicle had to be abandoned with its sledges until the Citroëns reached the Advance Base location, off-loaded their own sledges, then returned to pick up the materials from the stalled Cletrac. Weary, frozen men labored in the bitter cold of a darkening Antarctic autumn to load and off-load tons of supplies both at Advance Base and at the site of the stalled Cletrac. At last, on March 21, a frost-covered Innes Taylor and his colleagues coming up from the southern trail with their dog teams met the tractors and their shivering drivers coming down from Little America at "one hundred mile depot" (actually 123 miles from base) in temperatures ranging from thirty-five to fifty degrees below zero Fahrenheit. The next morning all hands turned to the construction of Byrd's hermitage.[55]

Meanwhile, a number of scary incidents had occurred at Little America. Chief radio engineer John Dyer fell from the top of an antenna pole 45 feet to the ice. Incredibly, he suffered only a barked shin (heavy clothing undoubtedly cushioned the impact). Next, the newly arrived doctor, Louis Potaka, had to operate on a navigator suffering from strep throat. Then Pelter, the aerial photographer, suffered an attack of appendicitis. As Byrd assisted Potaka in the cramped operating quarters, the doctor knocked over a lamp, setting fire to the bag containing the surgical instruments and threatening the whole camp with disaster. All this happened, Byrd recorded, "just a day or so after the Fokker *[Blue Blade]* had crashed in full view of the camp, and four men, stunned but otherwise unhurt, had crawled out from the wreckage."[56]

One hundred twenty-three miles south, the vast ice shelf was now lit for only a few hours each day, and men worked hastily, bolting Byrd's modest little shack together, digging the adjacent storage tunnels, and covering them with burlap or tarpaulin roofs. As the sun dipped below the horizon and the temperature dropped to sixty below, the men brought out pressure lanterns and blowtorches so that the work could be finished. Up at Little America, Dick Byrd prepared to depart while Charlie Murphy sent out a lengthy message from the radio room: "Rear Admiral Richard E. Byrd will be the sole occupant of the expedition's winter advance base on the Ross Ice Barrier. It is his decision to spend the winter night there, alone, in a one-room shack not much larger than is required for elbow room. . . . It is unlikely that he shall return before the end of October," because "the excessive temperatures of the winter night, the darkness, the suddenly striking storms, and the hazards of navigating the crevasses along the trail make a winter journey of that length a formidable undertaking."

Advance Base lay at a point where "the rolling Barrier has flattened out until the sky fully claims vision." The shack had been sunk beneath the "snow surface," and soon snowdrift would "obliterate all but the radio antennae, the spinning anemometer cups and the mast of the silver weather vane marking it as the world's southernmost meteorological station." The explorer wished the world to know that his heroics were strictly routine. "Before flying to advance base, Admiral Byrd said: 'I hope that no one will make anything of what I am about to do. I am doing it because I am anxious to do it and am making no sacrifice of any kind whatsoever.'" No one should worry if the radio went out. "I am not a radio operator so the radio will probably fail. This should be no cause for concern." The admiral had never been more clever: he not only told people not to worry but also told them what not to worry about. It was a masterful example of self-promotion.[57]

He had already written the children. "Dickie" had just turned fourteen, Bolling was eleven, Katherine was about to celebrate her tenth birthday, and Helen was now seven. All were old enough to understand what Dad was doing. "I really should have written more letters to you," their father wrote from Little America near the end of February, just before *Bear* departed for New Zealand, "but I have been terribly busy trying to get my two ships safely to the Bay of Whales and my men and material to Little America." By the time they received his letter, Richard added, Antarctica's "long winter night will have begun, and we will then be living practically entirely under the snow." During the long days and weeks of darkness, he promised his children, "I am going to plan a lot of things we can do together that will be the greatest possible fun, and I am never going to leave you again." He wanted "you all to know" how much he thought of them and how "tremendously" he missed them, "more than you can possibly realize." They must take care of Mommy and "be good to her" while he was away.[58]

Marie was stunned by her husband's decision, of which she had known nothing. In a typically coded (and undated) cable from the ice Richard assured her that he had "planned the whole thing," and she should not worry. "I swear to you that I will be more careful than I have ever been, as careful as it is humanly possible. It is my faith in your poise and great strength that makes it possible for me to do this thing." Marie "was extremely unhappy about Advance Base," Bolling recalled. "However, knowing how important it was to Dad, she went along with it." Bolling speculates that her mother "MUST HAVE often GONE through . . . terrible anxieties . . . though she never spoke of them to me—nor, I think, to any of her children not wanting to cause us any worries."

Investors, too, were greatly concerned. Should Byrd perish alone out there on the ice, how would they recoup their losses? Bereft of the one man who could make the expedition sound dramatic on film, in lectures, and at personal appearances, the National Geographic Society, the *New York Times,* General Foods, Paramount Pictures, and numerous other backers would be forced to swallow thousands of dollars in losses at the very depth of a prolonged and apparently endless depression. They made their concerns known, but Richard Byrd had gone too far to be stopped.

The precise nature of Marie's and the investors' alarm can be gleaned from a cable Richard sent his wife three days before he left for Advance Base. Most of the message was in code, but he began "in the clear" by saying rather laconically that it "seems to be my duty to go to mountain house. It will be only about a hundred miles from Little America and can easily be reached during winter night if necessary by tractors." The shack was fireproof, Dick added, "and I am using safe kind of fuel which will keep house very warm also using automatic fire extinguishers." In fact, Richard had experienced problems with his shack from the moment he moved into it upon return from *Bear's* eastern cruise in early February. On March 28, as Byrd began his first week's residence out on the ice, Murphy admitted in a message to the States that the admiral "had his troubles" with the new home. "Put up in a hurry" at Little America by Ivor Tingloff, who was deeply engaged in other essential duties, the shack was far from airtight, and as a consequence a "fine drift" of snow and "cold droughts" of air sifted "into the place whenever the wind blew." The stove was a source of deeper concern. The first one gave off such powerful whiffs of kerosene that Murphy, who stated that he also lived in the shack for a time, "finally fled." Siple, "who was heart and soul" in seeing to the perfection of the shack, "never would admit there was anything wrong with the stove; not even after the fumes had made him ill for a day." Instead, the young scientist insisted that he gotten a cold. Byrd prudently ordered a new stove installed, a small coal-burning device that machinist Vernon Boyd converted to kerosene. Byrd tested the new facility for several weeks, fiddling with the burners, "trying to determine how the stove could be made to yield the most heat with the least consumption of fuel. In the camp there was some doubt as to which would prevail—Admiral Byrd or the stove." With the temperature in the shack hovering around zero degrees Fahrenheit and the pitcher of water frozen hard as a rock, Richard at last claimed success, and as the shack warmed he professed himself satisfied with his only source of heat, though in the final days before departure he moved back into his old quarters off the library in the "Administration building."[59]

As Tingloff, Siple, and others began putting together the shack at Little America, a "tawny," injured husky named Carlos and an abandoned "fox-like white

Siberian" named Nome became agitated. Byrd had taken the dogs in because he felt sorry for them. Now they "prowled around, sniffing at things, doubtful, interrogating." The next morning, at Retreat Camp where the tractors stopped to top off their tanks, the dogs had to be driven back. They came home to Little America restless and anxious. Disdaining the comfortable crates in the tunnels at Dog Town, they raced inside any building whenever a door opened.[60]

Byrd's exit from Little America at midmorning on March 22, 1934, was dramatically undramatic. In his quarters at the administration building he dictated a few last messages and a simple set of instructions. "Several friends of long standing chatted with him" as he looked about for "desirable things" that might have escaped the packers' attention. A strap on his fur mukluk broke as he pulled it on, and he asked someone to take it to the tailor for a quick repair job. Tom Poulter wrote on the flyleaf of the "auroral notebook" that Byrd was carrying south to mark down observations and impressions: "The best of luck to you until we meet again. (in the morning)." Then one of the aviation mechanics came below to say that Bill Bowlin was ready to go in the Pilgrim and did not want to wait and have the oil freeze up. Byrd shook hands with everyone, mounted the ladder up the vertical shaft that served as an entrance to the building, and walked out to the plane. "Only a handful of men were there. The rest were working in the dog tunnels. Few knew he was leaving." The admiral stopped briefly to talk. "Please tell the other men that I have not said goodbye to them individually because I never say goodbye." Then he was gone, ducking through the freezing propeller slipstream and slamming the door shut. A few minutes later the Pilgrim was airborne. As it cleared the low ridge to the south, Bill Haines "came flying into the radio shack." He had Byrd's fur mukluk. "My God, he's gone off without this," the meteorologist groaned. "It will take me seven months to deliver it."[61]

Chapter 12

Breakdown

ittle more than an hour after soaring aloft from Little America, the admiral landed at Advance Base, bundled warmly in a fur parka. The following day dog-team drivers Stuart Paine and Finn Ronne joined Richard Black from Little America in digging supply tunnels for Byrd's dwelling, and stretching tarpaulin over the roof. "Black doesn't seem to be able to take it," Paine grumped, "[and] is getting on all our nerves." Finally, it was time to set up the admiral's bunk and "fire up the potbellied stove." Up to then, Paine added, "Byrd hasn't been feeling well, but today he was out with us." The shack assumed a "homelike character," and Byrd turned in for a good night's sleep. "So did some of the men," Ronne recalled, who stretched out on the floor in their sleeping bags. But the shack was too small to accommodate everyone, and so "we dog drivers shivered in our tents on top-side as the temperature plummeted to 65 below zero." The next morning a warm and rested admiral told Ronne, whose lips were cracked and bleeding from the cold and whose beard was covered with ice, that he had taken a midnight stroll and had found Ronne "snoring like a good Norwegian . . . so I knew you were still alive." As the dog teams prepared to head north to Little America, Paine noted that "REB was very appreciative of what we had done + came to call me Stu before we left."[1] At last the tractor parties started for home, leaving Richard Byrd alone on the ice.

Charlie Murphy had already informed Hazel McKercher up in Boston that the admiral had asked him "to act as his personal representative" while he was away. Murphy had always enjoyed Byrd's confidence, so the message he sent to the world on March 28 surely had the admiral's approval. In it Murphy dilated at length on his commander's forthcoming ordeal.

Whatever its inner or outer implications, these things are at least apparent. It will be isolation. He will be on his own as few men have been. And all the decorations he has won, the honors he has been given, the urbane existence he has travelled in civilization, aren't going to help him start a fire at 70° or 80° below zero; keep blizzards from overwhelming his sunken shack; keep drift from choking delicate instruments, ice from collecting in the gasoline driven generator of his radio transmitter; cook three meals a day, or mend or wash clothes; or contrive a substitute for this missing thing or that; or help him find this buried shack if a swiftly striking storm should overtake him on one of the daily walks that are his habit, no matter how cold it may be.

So perhaps this isolation can scarcely be called splendid. The notion of Admiral Byrd presiding in a sort of lordly exclusiveness at the southernmost frontier of human activity can hardly be sustained. What it will probably amount to is a continuous struggle for existence, and an unrelaxing vigilance against fire, cold, and illness. Very likely this is what has drawn him. The scientific considerations, which are important, are secondary.[2]

Byrd's decision to abandon his men and live in solitude throughout the austral winter of 1934 fundamentally changed the structure of his second expedition. This time he would not be present to manipulate, adjudicate, or suffer the behavior of colleagues too long cooped up in a polar winter camp with little real work to occupy them more than a few hours a day. He washed his hands of the day-to-day stress of managing fifty-odd men, choosing to winter over ostentatiously alone. Many of the men came to bitterly resent his decision. "I wonder now whether REB will make out this winter," Stuart Paine wrote as his dog team headed back to Little America. "He isn't a practical man at all + hasn't the faintest idea of how to use his hands. He cooked Jello the other night + it was the first bit of cooking he has ever done. The radio he doesn't know a thing about, not even the code. Suppose something gets out of adjustment or breaks. His communications are completely shut off." Still, Paine rather envied his admiral's "staying out there in a way, away from people, cares + worries. He plans to write a book on philosophy which will take up much of his time."

Once Paine, Innes Taylor, and the other dog-team drivers reached Little America, however, generous feelings toward Byrd swiftly dissipated. "Am a bit, in fact very disappointed + hurt about our whole [southern cache-laying] trip + the expedition as a whole," Paine added. "As far as I can see, our whole trip was futile + in vain. We are merely tools for the Admiral's ambitions. . . . To struggle + work for something worthwhile is one thing, to do that for nothing is all too disheartening. . . . My nose frostbitten, both cheeks swollen with [dog] bites + my fingers + toes numb from having frozen, I find it has all been rather useless."[3]

Byrd later told the public that getting away from it all was a driving objective of his sojourn at Advance Base, and along with his ever present desire to cut a dramatic figure by some bold, unforeseen act (that in this instance would undercut any similar action by Ellsworth), it undoubtedly was. Moreover, because he was largely unreachable, Marie and his New York representative, John McNeil, could not pester him with daily problems and crises. Nor could troublesome characters like Brophy expect to elicit the same prolonged and often confused attention.

In the end, one is left with the conclusion that Dick Byrd's decision to spend the austral winter of his second Antarctic expedition alone was very much in character. He had always been most comfortable when flying high by himself, whether on the trapeze far above the gymnasium floor at Annapolis or with the only other man he completely trusted in the air, Floyd Bennett, as they winged their way to the top of the world and glory. His subordination to MacMillan and McDonald in Greenland had been an ordeal, and the same might well be said of the tense times before and during his Atlantic flight with Balchen and the others, or of his command during the long winter months of BAE I. Alone on the ice 123 miles from anyone else, he would, indisputably, be his own man, beholden to no one. And as Professor Matouzzi has observed, such a stunt was expected to be at once newsworthy and lucrative.[4]

What he later chose to tell—eloquently, to be sure—about his time alone at Advance Base constitutes most but not all of what we can now glean of Richard Byrd's ordeal on the Antarctic ice sheet that austral winter of 1934. Byrd's "Auroral Notebook" and his messages to Little America fill in the story. At first, all went well. Upon his return he wrote that March, April, and May 1934 constituted "one of the greatest and most satisfying periods of my life."[5] His days were surprisingly full. The eight weather instruments required constant attention. Twice a day, early morning and midevening, he opened the trapdoor and in his heavy foul-weather clothing stood outside reading the various instruments by flashlight or magnesium torch; then he glanced at the perpetual night sky to record the general weather conditions. Dropping back down into the warmth and security of his hut, he painstakingly recorded his observations on U.S. Weather Bureau Form no. 1083. While outside he also spent long moments closely watching the aurora, whose pulsating beauty moved him deeply. The auroral observations went into columns of his own notebook, wherein he recorded date, time, auroral intensity and length, and altitude above the horizon.

Keeping in touch with Little America by radio consumed more time. The gasoline generator that powered the transmitter gave off fumes, so Byrd kept it in an alcove halfway down the food tunnel, bringing it into the shack about an hour before transmission to warm it to the point that it could be cranked up. He spent more time reviewing Morse code, with which he should have already been familiar through his naval service. News that the trail parties had all returned to Little America and that the camp was tightly secured for the winter relieved him of the last of his anxieties about his men.

He soon discovered that his shack could be a trap were he not careful. In their haste to build the site and be gone, Ronne, Siple, and the others had not sunk the dwelling deep enough. (Nor had they stored the food supplies carefully. Byrd spent hours that first month rearranging the contents of the food tunnel to his satisfaction.) A raging blizzard that came on several days after he began living alone so covered the exposed roof with ice as well as drift snow that Byrd found it almost impossible to open the trapdoor and get out. Locating a piece of two-by-four timber he battered the door open with his good arm, then spent the better part of April 5 and 6 cutting, hacking, and shoveling a new escape tunnel and hatch through the heavy Antarctic "snow."

The aurora enthralled him with its brilliance and the pulsations of its cosmic rays. "Distinct at first," he wrote of the aurora in early April, then it "gradually" faded. The light waves moved rapidly, Byrd added, "most intense at center fading out at each end." On the thirteenth he noted a "brilliant display at . . . across sky to Eastward." Two days later: "At 8. The aurora extended across the Eastern Sky. Over and curtains at 9." In early May he watched the aurora for an hour as it extended across the sky, measuring its "ray structure" and observing its shape. "It disappeared at 5:30 and returned at 5:45" with a reduced intensity. At one point he made a crude drawing of the aurora stretching across the black horizon from 45 to 145 degrees. "No rays at first," he wrote, "no waves."[6] Byrd's notes give no hint of depression or despair. On the contrary they suggest a man doing what he wished and fulfilling a deep personal yearning—to be alone yet at one with nature and the cosmos.

Later he would recall and write of the never-ending cold that surrounded him like a freezing shroud, defining his every experience, his every waking moment. He slept with the trapdoor open, doubtless terrified of being imprisoned again under a blanket of ice and snow. But this meant the temperature in the shack each morning hovered between ten and forty degrees below zero as Byrd struggled out of a sleeping bag that was frost-encrusted by his breath. "My socks and boots, when I picked them up, were so stiff with frozen sweat that I had to first work them between" stinging hands. The novocaine in his medical kit froze and shattered, as did the chemicals in the firebombs. "Two cases of tomato juice shattered in their bottles." He ate little at breakfast or lunch; dinner was the high point of the day. For a week or so, it was a "fiasco" until he more or less mastered the rudiments of cooking. Whether he realized then that he had sentenced himself to an act of bravado beyond his capacity to implement, or whether he reached the conclusion years later at his writing table amid the warm embrace of civilization is unclear.[7]

Certainly, he would remember and record "the best times" at Advance Base, "the times when neglected senses expand to an exquisite sensitivity." He claimed that his spirit found peace in the "unfathomable, tantalizing" fogs and in an afternoon so clear that "you dare not make a sound, lest it fall in pieces." One day in mid-April, Byrd took his daily stroll near the shack.

> The sun had dropped below the horizon, and a blue—of a richness I've never seen anywhere else—flooded in, extinguishing all but the dying embers of the sunset.
>
> Due east, halfway to the zenith, Venus was an unblinking diamond; and opposite her, in the eastern sky, was a brilliant twinkling star set off exquisitely, as was Venus, in a sea of blue. In the northeast a silver-green serpentine aurora pulsed and quivered gently. In places the Barrier's whiteness had the appearance of dull platinum. It was all delicate and illusive.

Byrd "paused to listen to the silence," his crystallized breath "drifted on a breeze gentler than a whisper" that pointed southward toward the pole. Once again a day was dying, but this time not in melancholy, but "in great peace," and "harmony." Out of the eternal stillness there came to the solitary figure standing alone on the ice more than a hundred miles from anyone else

> a gentle rhythm, the strain of a perfect chord, the music of the spheres, perhaps. The conviction came that that rhythm was too orderly, too harmonious, too perfect to be a product of blind chance—that, therefore, there must be a purpose in the whole and that man was a part of that whole and not an accidental offshoot. It was a feeling that transcended reason; that went to the heart of a man's despair and found it groundless. The universe was a cosmos, not a chaos; man was as rightfully a part of that cosmos as were the day and night.[8]

There was little serenity or harmony 123 miles to the north. With no legal structure to fall back on, with no sanctions at his disposal, and with a divided structure of decision making sanctioned by Byrd himself before his departure, Tom Poulter attempted to carry out his duties with fidelity and fairness.

Himself a teetotaler, Poulter was determined to end the liquor problem before it began, and he thought he knew how. A half-mile tunnel was being dug from camp to the magnetic observatory, and at one point about 50 feet from its source the shovelers had cut through an old tunnel from Little America I which extended another 50 feet. Poulter had "kept this old tunnel in mind for future reference." June happened to be out on the ice shelf with the trail parties, and as soon as Byrd pulled away from the barrier aboard *Bear* for his eastern cruise, Poulter ordered two men to bring the chief pilot's liquor cases to him.

Descending alone into the tunnel system where the others could not see him, he buried the cases at the far end of the old Little America tunnel, then used snow blocks that had been dug out of the new tunnel to wall up the cache. "Shav[ing] those blocks off flush with the new tunnel wall," Poulter concluded that they matched perfectly. The whole business "was completed long before June returned to camp." When he did, he promptly sent a message to his commander aboard *Bear,* complaining about the lost liquor. Byrd should have chastised his pilot then and there. Instead, according to Poulter, he told June that "such matters" were Poulter's responsibility, "and to take it up with me." June never did.[9]

Having hidden June's liquor supply, Poulter proceeded to bury the rest of Dr. Shirey's cache. Leaving camp by himself "during the wee hours of the morning," he quietly dug a pit close alongside the tunnel leading to the magnetic observatory. "I would put a number of cases of liquor in this pit and cover it with snow. By morning this would usually be drifted over and all traces of activity obliterated." Poulter knew he could find the supply anytime he wished simply by going into the tunnel with a wire probe. "Only Charley [*sic*] Murphy knew what I had done with the confiscated supply."[10]

Then Poulter made a mistake. On April 1, just after June and most of the trail party returned from settling Byrd in at Advance Base, the new commander of Little America told George Noville he could serve some spiked punch after dinner. The results were disastrous. "Haines didn't even get out of the Science Lab last night. . . . June fell off the ladder to his bunk. Morgan and Russell were both in a bad way." Sterrett, a young medical student, "got drunk and departed, supposedly headed for the Ad Building." Someone found him a short while later "in a pile of snow." Another few moments and the young man, drunk as he was, would have begun to freeze to death. A man determined to impose authority would have ordered all liquor supplies brought out and destroyed. Instead, Poulter decided to dump "most" of the liquor "we have on hand and then hope that the private supplies are soon exhausted."[11]

Two days later Poulter noticed "some drinking . . . but no one drunk." However, June now began to move against him, for on the fourth the base commander wrote that he had appointed Dr. Perkins and pilot Bill Bowlin "assistant executive officers" to George Noville in an effort to forestall any effort by June to form his executive committee from among the rest of the scientific and support staffs. Events spun out of Poulter's control on the ninth as June ordered Tingloff to work on a sledge instead of helping Poulter, then got the carpenter drunk. "June, Ting-loff, and Haines all got tight. June can stand more than the others and he was on his feet today, but Tingloff was still out."[12]

Poulter was beset by other problems as well. "There seems to be considerable consternation in the States about REB occupying Advance Base alone." Marie and the admiral's friends flooded the Little America radio shack with messages imploring Byrd to reconsider and return to base. The senders invariably directed Murphy to pass them on to Advance Base without fail. Poulter and Murphy considered the requests, but decided to ignore them. It was too late to bring the admiral back, and even if it were not, "he wouldn't even consider it." On April 7 Ashley McKinley, Byrd's old comrade from BAE I, cabled Poulter directly, asking him to see that messages got through to the admiral "about his leaving Advance Base at once." Again, Poulter ignored the request, "still thoroughly convinced" that Byrd would not return.

Another crisis emerged a few days later. Up in New Zealand, *Ruppert*'s crewmen "were stealing everything loose on the ship," including several drums of gasoline, and selling the commodities. The two night watchmen aboard were wholly ineffectual. The expedition's agent at Dunedin, Jim Duncan of H. L. Tapley and Company, had hired two "shoremen" to watch the vessel on a temporary basis. The matter seemed to require "some action" on Poulter's part, but he was uncertain what to do. In fact, there was little or nothing he could do. Byrd had given him a position but little authority, either over the men at Little America or over the expedition as a whole. While the Admiral of the Antarctic listened blissfully to the music of the spheres far out on the Ross Ice Shelf, his expedition slowly went to pieces at Little America and in New Zealand.[13]

As the cold and the darkness deepened over Antarctica, June continued his mischief. One day he told Dr. Perkins that tractor fuel was very low, a falsehood, according to Poulter. "He also said there would be no support to the scientific program from the planes by instructions from Admiral Byrd." Indeed, the admiral was not interested in the scientific programs at all, June continued, "except as a means to an end; namely exploration." On the twenty-sixth there was another "party" after dinner. "June seems to have quite a supply" of liquor, Poulter noted gloomily. According to Poulter, the chief pilot began openly soliciting supporters and told one "that he was going to 'get TCP' if he had to wreck the Expedition to do it."

Some of the men began getting completely out of hand, probing the snows with six-foot-long steel rods, trying to locate the cache. Poulter was disturbed to learn that a few of them believed they had found it and were planning "to 'get it that night.'" The base commander with two "trusted helpers" again went out onto the dark, frozen landscape, working "all night" to move the entire liquor cache into Poulter's personal quarters. But a few days later, Poulter again gave Noville "a few bottles to spike some punch after dinner." The commander never explained his action, which he inevitably came to rue. It may well have been that his abstemiousness invited derision and cries of hypocrisy among the more raucous members of the expedition that Poulter found unendurable at times. In any case, the fearfully cold night of April 28, 1934, was a particularly poor time to permit a bacchanal.

Poulter designated two others to help him monitor the party and make sure everyone got safely to their bunks. But they failed. Two of the partygoers passed out in the dog tunnel, where the temperature was fifty below. Another man went "topside," attempting to go from one building to another, and collapsed in a small depression. Fortunately, all three were found in time, and at last Poulter had had enough. Over the next few days, by his own estimate, he poured some five hundred fifths of "Golden Wedding" whiskey into the snow through a hole that he drilled in the floor of his meteorological observation platform. He masked the odor by periodically dumping chlorinated lime into the space created by the dumped alcohol and by burning wood in the nearby tunnel. But what to do with the bottles that took up as much space empty as full? Poulter wrote that he "knew how a murderer felt when he hadn't figured out ahead of time what he was going to do with the body." The commander wisely decided to bury them in four five-foot, eighteen-inch diameter holes in the floor of the tunnel next to his shack. He knew that as the bottles inevitably broke in the deep cold, the snow would insulate the sound. Poulter told only the faithful Charlie Murphy what he had done. Both men later wrote that throughout the remainder of the expedition's stay in Antarctica, "many hours" were spent "by various members" looking for the liquor cache.

Murphy later claimed that the drinking had begun even before the last of the hastily deposited stores had been moved from the ice to the camp. "Winter darkness had fallen, the stores were still scattered over the Barrier, and much work remained to be done. But it was hard to keep men slaving in the cold and drift as long as the songs and laughter of good fellowship welled up through the crust from the celebrants in the shacks underneath." Murphy's brief 1939 account differs slightly from Poulter's memoir twenty-four years later. According to Murphy, the base commander poured out twenty cases of rye and bourbon, then smashed the bottles in a burlap bag to deaden the sound before scattering the fragments over the barrier. But Murphy agreed that "all winter long" the thirsty men of BAE II, "supposing that the liquor had been moved to a new hiding place," spent most if not all of their spare time "prodding the Barrier with long brass rods, chanting: "Little Rod, won't you call / When you've found the alcohol!" Murphy believed Poulter's impulsive decision was "tragic," even though he never betrayed his supe-

rior. Nor did he ever tell Byrd during their months-long exchange of messages between Little America and Advance Base. But he concluded that Poulter's "destruction of the whiskey" constituted "the most serious internal situation to vex
any" of Byrd's "expeditions."[14]

Poulter's failure lay not in destroying the whiskey but in his inability to exert
strong leadership over a polar winter camp seething with stress and tension. He
did little to quell the bouts of heavy drinking that continued to erupt sporadically throughout the month of May. Nor did he try to curb June's rebelliousness, even
when June "said that he told REB that he did not like me, didn't trust me, etc., all
of which I knew from REB." The fault lay not with Poulter, however, but with
Byrd. Given clear authority, Poulter would have had a chance to exercise firm authority. The divided command structure Byrd had devised left his nominal number two practically powerless.

Meanwhile, the situation with *Ruppert* up in Dunedin continued to deteriorate.
Tapley and Company had induced the New Zealand Customs Service to seal the
ship, but the seals had been broken and the ship looted again. The disgusted Jim
Duncan threatened to resign. Poulter at last called a meeting with Noville, Murphy, June, and Haines to discuss the matter, and in a surprising act of unanimity
the five "decided to ask Captain Verleger for his resignation." Once more, Byrd,
rusticating in his polar hermitage, was apparently not consulted.[15]

As Poulter struggled with discipline and morale, Murphy spent hours each week
writing his weekly radio script and "cajoling" members of the expedition to participate. Dr. Gil Morgan, the seismologist, put together a singing and instrumental group called the Knights of the Grey Underwear, and one evening the ensem-
ble performed their own skit called *Penguin Parade*. Others formed a "female"
chorus line and danced. In Boston, Marie got the children out of bed and they
trooped down to their parents' big Italian bed and curled up to listen to the
voices coming through the scratchy static from ten thousand miles away. The
Antarctic show quickly became a favorite of the trendy New York City glamour
set who flocked to the CBS studios after dinner in their tuxedos and evening gowns
to listen to twenty-odd minutes of live entertainment and seven of foolishness
coming through big speakers before going off to the opera or the night clubs.
Corny as they were, the broadcasts kept the frozen hermits at Little America in
contact with home while Grape-Nuts cereal sales multiplied and General Foods,
together with CBS, made a lot of money.

Not everyone on the ice was happy with the arrangement. Byrd could not flack
the cereal without using it, and so hundreds if not thousands of boxes were taken
south as what today would be euphemistically called a "free gift." For Steve Corey
the gift was less than appreciated. The supply officer did not like the cereal to

begin with; eating it half-frozen after the boxes had been chipped out of their niches in the food tunnel was intolerable.[16]

Boozing did not prevent June or the other members of his aviation unit from making "desperate efforts" to get the expedition's aircraft under cover for the winter. The planes stood wing to wing out on the barrier, and twenty men were drafted to build hangars around each of them out of huge blocks of stacked snow. The work was brutal and backbreaking, especially around the big Condor, which stood more than sixteen feet from skis to upper wing with an overall length of just under forty-nine feet. June and his men sawed and fitted snow blocks into a wall six feet above the barrier, then dug a pit below. The plane was then gently lowered onto skis inside the pit until the upper wing sank beneath the snow-block wall. The hangar was then roofed over with tarpaulin. Each of the snow hangars "will be large enough to enable aviation gang to make complete overhaul of planes and engines during winter," Murphy told the world in a radio message toward the end of April.[17]

Out at Advance Base, Byrd later wrote, adventure had begun to pall. Less than a month into his vigil he began to appreciate "the brain-cracking loneliness of solitary confinement . . . the loneliness of a futile routine." Mornings were especially hard, rising alone in the dark. "One may be a long time realizing it, but cold and darkness deplete the body gradually; the mind turns sluggish; and the nervous system slows up its responses. . . . Try as I may," he recalled years later, "I find I can't take my loneliness casually; it is too big." The eternal silence depressed him, and he soon came to dread getting up each morning for the eight o'clock weather observations. Lying abed listening to the steady, reassuring ticktock of his clock was infinitely preferable.

Still, he was able to do some of what he liked between the constant "watchfulness for signs of trouble" and the "rituals" of carefully recording weather data, keeping his shack somewhat tidy, maintaining scheduled radio contact with Little America, cooking slowly (and poorly), and keeping the trapdoor area free of drifting snow. He dipped into the works of Somerset Maugham and George Santayana, as well as Yule's *Travels of Marco Polo*. He listened to some music and dreamed often of his boyhood building and manning forts with brothers Tom and Harry, "not just 'pretend' forts . . . but elaborate earthworks and bastions which transformed the Byrd grounds into an armed city and kept Mother wavering between indignation and terror, since her gardens were ruined, and an innocent step at any instant might bring a bone-chilling imitation of musketry from an unseen ambuscade."[18]

Most important, he exercised. Mornings in his bunk before arising he did fifteen minutes of muscle-stretching contortions. In the afternoon or evening he walked for as much as an hour or two, driving a series of split-bamboo sticks into the snow every thirty yards or so from the shack's trapdoor as a precaution. The walks were essential, he believed, to maintain calm and perspective, but one polar night he became too immersed in his thoughts and awoke to a nightmare. Somehow, he had wandered far beyond the last stick. Where was he? Which way led back? The suddenly terror-stricken man paused to compose himself. The overcast had cleared, and he found two stars to use as reference points; then he made a little marker of snow and started off in one direction, his flashlight faintly illuminating the gloom. After 100 paces he stopped and swung the flashlight around in an arc. No sticks. Carefully, he retraced his steps. The only living being in more than 100 miles of polar wilderness continued to search for his only source of warmth and shelter buried beneath the ice. Returning the 100 paces he saw nothing; worse, he had lost his snow marker. Quelling panic, he again swung the flashlight; its beam picked up the marker about 20 feet to the left. Byrd walked to it, swung himself 30 degrees, and stepped off another 100 paces. Once more, he saw nothing but the dark plain of white stretching endlessly. *"You're lost now,"* the "appalled" man told himself. He would have to lengthen his walk from the beacon, but in so doing he might never find it again. One can only guess at the demons of fear that must have consumed him in that awful moment and the self-discipline required to beat them back. He decided to lengthen his radius from the snow beacon from 100 to 130 paces. On the 129th step, his flashlight picked up one of the bamboo sticks "not thirty feet away."[19]

On April 27 Murphy informed the world that Byrd had completed his first month of isolation. Things seemed to be going well, and the admiral "maintains the impact of his leadership at Little America," directing Poulter "to have the full resources of the expedition ready for an early start in the extensive scientific and exploratory projects planned for the spring and summer seasons," and ordering June to overhaul and make available the two aircraft left near the base from BAE I. Tractors and aircraft were to be "thoroughly overhauled" during the winter night and the dogs exercised. The men were to keep themselves fit.[20]

At Advance Base, May passed without incident. Byrd later claimed that by the third week of the month, the eighth week of his sentence, he had perfected his psychological defenses. "I feel able now to withstand any assaults the beleaguering night may launch." He looked forward to the rest of his stay with pleasure and spent several hundred words describing his notion of man and the cosmos, which amounted to the dual propositions that "For those who seek it there is inexhaustible evidence of an all-pervading intelligence" and "The human race . . . is not outside the cosmic process and is not an accident."[21] Then disaster struck.

The admiral later wrote that he awoke on the morning of May 31 with the calendar warning: radio schedule. He breakfasted, then went about preparations "methodically." When Little America came online he sent several messages that he had prepared, including one to Marie and McNeil about various "ways and means" by which the expedition's expenses could be reduced. He then communicated at length to both Poulter and Murphy. At his desk in the shack, Byrd could hear the engine in the tunnel clacking away as it provided the power for transmission. Suddenly, it seemed to skip, and Byrd excused himself and, unhooking the lantern, went into the tunnel, where the air hung thick with exhaust gases. "Thinking the mixture was at fault, I bent over the carburetor and tinkered with the needle valve." He started to straighten up. The next thing he knew he was on his hands and knees, dreadfully confused, and "helpless to do anything about it." He managed to struggle back to his desk and terminate contact with Little America. Later, hearing the engine still skipping, he staggered into the tunnel to shut it off before he asphyxiated. "Dizziness seized me, and my heart turned fantastic somersaults."[22] It was the beginning of a nightmare that would go on for weeks.

He lay in his sleeping bag as hours turned to days, head and eyes aching and pounding with pain, heart racing, mind wandering. His initial feeling was one of humiliation. He had never been sick since youth. The puny boy who had built himself up with a strict and harsh regimen of physical exercise now lay in semi-consciousness hour after hour, unable to do anything for himself in the freezing shack that had become a prison.

Exactly what felled the admiral became a matter of some debate over the following years, and his own contemporary record indicates that he may not have been dramatically cut down so much as slowly worn down. Some (including Byrd, his son, and this writer) long assumed that the culprit in Byrd's poisoning was not the gasoline engine but the stove over which he had labored and struggled in Little America. Lying stuporous in his bunk the admiral gradually reached the same conclusion. Of course, "the engine dealt the blow that knocked me down," but Byrd now recalled that "long before" he had felt a kind of weakness; he remembered the notches he had taken up in his belt, "the headaches and hurt in my eyes earlier in the month." Perhaps his lungs had frosted in the cold, or there was something "organically" wrong with him. But surely, the stove had been and certainly now was the prime suspect.

However, Poulter, Waite, and Demas, who came to rescue Byrd, subsequently lived in the shack with no ill effects for fifty-nine days. It had to be the generator out in the tunnel. Poulter discovered that the men who hastily installed the machine had failed to include a tight-fitting exhaust pipe that would carry the generators' fumes above the snow's surface. Instead, they "merely made about a six inch diameter opening in the snow up to the surface. When the engine was in place the exhaust pipe pointed straight up toward this opening which was more than a foot above the end of the exhaust pipe." With temperatures ranging from sixty to seventy degrees below zero Fahrenheit, "very few of the exhaust fumes ever got out of the tunnel." Byrd poisoned himself with carbon monoxide each time he entered the tunnel and turned the generator on and off for his scheduled broadcasts.[23]

Sick with shame as well as fumes, Byrd convinced himself that "my stupidity was to blame." He was Rear Admiral Richard Evelyn Byrd, United States Navy, retired, "and not worth a damn to myself or anyone else." He decided his chances of recovery were slim, his ability to take care of himself nil. Nonetheless, he determined to tough it out. He had repeatedly told the men at Little America that *no* attempts should be made to traverse the broad Ross Ice Shelf during the winter night; any such journey could lead to catastrophe, and, like Shackleton, Dick Byrd was determined not to lose a man in Antarctica. If anyone were to die, it would be he. So he must have faith that he could weather the awful sickness that had overcome him. But despair brought him low; he lashed himself unmercifully. His fears echoed those of Scott and the other doomed polar explorers: what would happen to loved ones should he perish, as seemed all too likely?

In those hours of "bitterness," he later wrote, his entire life passed in review as an exercise in futility. His sense of values had been totally wrong; he had blinded himself to the truth "that the simple, homely unpretentious things of life are the most important." He was no martyr to science, but merely a monument to self ishness. He had come to Advance Base looking for peace and enlightenment so he could become "a more useful man." Perhaps he had found what he was looking for, but then he had mucked the whole thing up. The notion that his observations could advance the cause of science was merely a "romantic delusion." He was filled with "gall and wormwood." His anguish pitched his thoughts back onto those same deep grooves they had followed in earlier times of crisis during the Greenland expedition when he had feuded with MacMillan and on the way to Spitsbergen with the dangerous North Polar flight looming before him—love of Marie together with a rather maudlin celebration of the family he so often neglected. "At the end only two things really matter to a man, regardless of who he is; and they are the affection and understanding of his family. Anything and everything else he creates are insubstantial," merely "ships given over to the mercy of the winds and tides of prejudice."[24]

The "Auroral Notebook" and the few scraps of paper with scrawled words and messages that he brought out of Advance Base at the end of his ordeal suggest that what he set down for public consumption in 1938 faithfully reflected what he felt and experienced four years before. "My physical condition has been very desperate," he scrawled in his "Auroral Notebook" under a heading: "may 30 to june 4th inclusive." In those first awful days he used deteriorating weather as an excuse not to make extended impressions of the aurora: "the weather has been overcast most of the time. Once for a few minutes in the afternoon (the Second) there was aurora for a few minutes. There probably would have been aurora if it had not been cloudy." Soon after his first seizure he found himself "rang[ing over] the whole broad reaches of hell before finding sleep." Perhaps it was that night if not later when he awoke to scrawl on a sheet of paper from the Beverly Wilshire Hotel in Los Angeles: "and so ended the Battle of the Dead."[25]

Somehow, in some way, he managed to pull through the first half of June without going totally mad. His heroism was striking. Twice and sometimes more each day he pushed his way up through the trapdoor and out into the dark, icy wilderness to make his observations. He may have gone partially blind. Certainly, his writing deteriorated along with his ability to observe. "If aurora in the northwest," he wrote rather confusingly in early June "but so vague cannot be certain. So have not recorded." Later he or someone at his direction typed out the scrawled notes, giving him a chance to make them more coherent and understandable. He tried to meet every responsibility to his people up in Little America ("Important radio schedule," he wrote in his "Auroral Notebook" on June 7), and to maintain a sense of routine in his transmissions so as not to alarm radioman John Dyer, Charlie Murphy, and the others in Little America. He repeatedly repoisoned himself in the process. On the fourteenth he radioed Poulter, asking if moisture had any effect on carbon monoxide. "Please," he begged in quiet desperation, "make exhaustive recommendations for keeping down carbon monoxide fumes." His next line was at once garbled and alarming: "The one thing above all others for the trail work next summer is to save train [presumably "have terrain"] well marked please put down more markers even than you think necessary."

Was this an implicit cry for help? Poulter and Murphy could not see their commander; only infrequently did they hear him. Their only real clue to his condition was in the content of his messages; they began to think he was in trouble. Eight days later, on the eighteenth, Poulter sent a long, considered reply to Byrd's request. He and Murphy then put their heads together and hatched a scheme to fetch their leader.[26]

Poulter had signed on as an astronomer. One of his objectives was to make meteor observations from the bottom of the earth, and as the polar night came on he had achieved some "phenomenal results" at Little America. He wanted to establish an advance base of his own south of camp, but had been frustrated for reasons he never fully explained. When he contacted Byrd on June 21, Poulter described the results he had so far obtained, and "I told him that since we had been forced to cancel my proposed trips out 30 miles, I would like to come to Advance Base for a few days for these observations." Citroën no. 1 had been overhauled and would be ready for a test run shortly; surely, the 123-mile "base line" would be far better for observation than a hastily rigged facility just 30 miles from Little America. And perhaps, Poulter added, Byrd might want to return with him upon completion of the initial observations, leaving two or three chaps at Advance Base to finish the job.[27]

It was a delicate moment; not only might Byrd's life be hanging in the balance, but so might his always shaky personal finances and the fiscal integrity of the expedition itself. Byrd's increasingly desperate situation from June to August 1934 "figured heavily" in ongoing negotiations between Little America and CBS– General Foods. The initial contract between the expedition and two of its key sponsors was up for renewal on June 20, just as Byrd's situation began to become alarmingly clear to Murphy. Should Byrd perish, or come back an invalid or near invalid, the media contract would be imperiled, if not void. On the other hand, "the radio story" of Byrd's "experiences will be a news event of the first importance," as Murphy cautiously cabled Marie on June 2, before her husband's growing crisis had become clear.

Obviously hoping to turn the growing crisis to maximum advantage, Murphy suggested that CBS–General Foods might be approached for even larger funding for the last half of the contract period. Mindful, however, of the ignorance of everyone off the ice (and most of those at Little America as well), Murphy concluded with admirable caution that the negotiations would "probably have to be handled tactfully." By late June, however, Murphy clearly felt it impossible to disguise the crisis at Advance Base, and the *New York Times* was reporting that a rescue mission would undoubtedly have to be mounted. Murphy used the mission to "pitch . . . Byrd's upcoming rescue as a 'news event of the first importance.'"[28]

Byrd replied cautiously to Poulter's June 21 message, indicating that the poison had not yet wiped out his mental faculties. The idea might be a good one, but he would not approve such a trip "until after we had completed the trial run and reported on it." His next lines betrayed his condition. The man who had sharply impressed on everyone his desire to complete the mission and not hazard lives in an abortive rescue attempt now told Poulter he was "very anxious" to get back to Little America "in time to take up many things in States and New Zealand in connection with ship departure." "Money matters" were also "terribly serious," and the admiral wanted to take a direct role in shaping "spring operations plans." Byrd then directed Poulter to "please start making preparations and plans for trip here with tractors." He proceeded to remind his subordinate how important it was to pay attention to details. The engines must be prepped for cold running; the trail must be carefully marked; the men must be insulated from extreme cold ("Siple can help with this"), and so on.

Then the admiral changed course. No matter what was done or not done, "don't want you to send for me until sufficient light and men can make trip without risk or undue hardship. Please give me plans next broadcast." However ill he might be, Byrd was clearly determined to keep the pace of events in his own hands. "Sufficient light" would not return to the vast Antarctic ice sheet until mid-August. Shortly after the exchange with Little America, Byrd scribbled in his diary with a fairly steady hand: "Though I was not proud of myself for doing so I okayed [Poulter's] project but laid down certain safety precautions and made the stipulation that if they should miss the trail they must return to Little America." But he added in evident relief, "Poulter is getting the tractors ready for the trip."[29]

Like the Kennedy brothers in a much greater crisis a quarter century later, Poulter and Murphy decided to ignore the second part of Byrd's message and act on the first. He had given—or seemed to give—permission for an early tractor trip to Advance Base. So it would be done.

But not everyone in Little America agreed. Once more, Poulter handled a critical matter clumsily. He should have revealed his plans to the entire camp immediately. Instead, he waited three weeks while suspicion gradually developed that he was hiding something important. On the twenty-sixth, Poulter sent a memo to Haines, Murphy, and Innes Taylor, announcing that he was going out on the trail "this afternoon" with Pete Demas, Bernard Skinner, and Bud Waite. The four men would test the rebuilt Citroën and determine whether the trail flags leading south could be seen with the tractor headlights and a special small searchlight that Poulter had developed. Suspended from a cord around the neck, the light could be swung in a 360-degree arc. The party would be fully equipped with trail rations and equipment and would not go far. It would proceed "cautiously and take no chances." But if things went well and the lights of Little America's towers could be seen, "we may remain out there a while so as to get some calibrations on the radio compass."

The trip proved something of an ordeal, but also a great success. No one knew exactly where the trail lay, so the men had to probe with the lights from the vehicle and on foot through the nighttime gloom. Once the flags were found, everyone had to be wary of crevasses, but they went about 25 miles down the trail southward without mishap and returned about ten that "night." Thirty-six hours later, Poulter informed Byrd during their next regularly scheduled radio contact "that on our test run we found the trail relatively easy to follow." Once again, Poulter believed Byrd gave tentative approval to the trip, but the admiral continued to obscure his thoughts "with some long messages."[30]

Down at Advance Base, Byrd suffered through days of unending pain, cold, and despair. At one point he took down his shaving mirror (which he had not used for some time) and looked into it: "The face that looked back at me was that of an old and feeble man. The cheeks were sunken and scabrous from frostbite, and the bloodshot eyes were those of a man who has been on a prolonged debauch. Something broke inside me then." But he endured, fighting to maintain his simple schedules: the periodic radio broadcasts to Little America, the weather and auroral observations. Climbing out of the shack onto the immensity of the often windswept barrier cleared his mind and body with fresh air, and gave him back the broad perspective that his poison-filled prison shack denied him. In mid-June he recorded excitedly a "great Ellipse in the Eastern sky, the upper edge broken for a little distance in the northeast." But the bitter cold always drove him back quickly into his hell once more with frosty skin and beard.

In the shack conditions were often not that much better. He later told Poulter that because he tried to keep his stove off as much as possible (up to fourteen hours a day), temperatures reached incredible lows inside as well as out. "The temperature was once eighty degrees below zero and often ran twenty degrees colder than at Little America." He tried to rise above his persistent melancholy, but the plummeting midwinter temperatures and sporadic ingestions of poison every time he went into the tunnel to start the generator to transmit messages to Little America bore him down. Each exchange forced him back into his bunk, newly asphyxiated and convinced "that Murphy was always studying me in his cynical, penetrating fashion" for signs of weakness that would bring the premature rescue attempt Byrd dreaded. His few scrawled notes written in preparation for the exchanges with Little America were undated, but it may well have been at this time that he scribbled angrily: "Dyer insists that I am interfering. I will not interfere. Do you have to test all the afternoon and night. Can't you squeeze in a time for me." His suspicions of Dyer and Murphy peaked shortly thereafter, when he transmitted: "Monday 2 P.M. Pse [Please] ask marie not to worry about fumes." Had the two men at Little America told Mrs. Byrd about her husband's ordeal? If so, she maintained an inhuman silence then and later. Whatever the facts, Richard was clearly terrified that his self-imposed ordeal and possible death would sully his reputation and deeply wound his loved ones.[31]

On June 18, as Poulter and Murphy discussed and planned up in Little America, Byrd suffered a relapse. In the preceding days he had slowly begun to gain a little ground, his melancholy receding ever so slightly. The generator had been running badly during the previous radio schedule, so Byrd spent an extra twenty minutes tinkering with it and clearing ice out of the ventilator shaft above. Inevitably, the fumes overcame him again, and he collapsed and crawled to his bunk. All his energies were consumed in getting through the exchanges with Dyer and Murphy; then he went back into his sleeping bag. Too weak to move, he could not climb up the ladder and out onto the barrier to take his evening weather observations.

"That night I scarcely slept at all, but tossed instead in my sleeping bag racked by pain and literally shaken by the thumping in my heart." Curled in his bunk, "I mumbled like a monk fingering his beads."[32]

Then, at last, the tide began to turn. Struggling through to June 21, Byrd began to dream of the sun's return. The event was still two months away, but with the austral winter solstice he had reached the depths of winter; from now on every moment, every hour, every day was a step nearer home. On the twenty-second, the stricken explorer roused himself sufficiently to write of "a sight magnificent beyond description. A river of silver across my zenith from north to south. The movement caused the aurora to appear as if it were flowing toward the North Pole." For a brief time, too, "a very bright moon" provided comfort and delight. Poulter's proposal to come with the sun was an added tonic; no need now to fight through till October. Poulter might even come earlier, and in his stubborn illness Byrd slowly warmed to the idea. But most important was the deliverance wrapped within a seeming disaster.

On July 5 the generator broke down. Byrd saw it as the last straw in a series of catastrophes that had brought him to the brink of death and madness. Frantically, he took the machine apart, praying that it was reparable. It was not. "The fault was fatal. The lug on the generator drive shaft had sheared off," doubtless due to the cold. "Bent over with weariness and despair, I concluded finally that my world was falling to pieces." Now, he would have to rely on the emergency hand-powered radio to communicate with Little America. "Cranking a hand-crank generator with one hand and keying with the other would be a difficult job for a well man," Poulter later commented, "and now his responses were naturally slow and labored." Byrd doubted his strength. In fact, the poisoning stopped, for he now had no further need to enter the fume-filled tunnel, and his stove, though he did not realize it, was perfectly safe.[33] If Poulter could dispatch a rescue party, the admiral might yet survive.

But Little America was bitterly divided over the proposal. Poulter's secrecy had backfired. Vernon Boyd and others had brought radios to the ice. Despite notification to keep them off during confidential contacts with Advance Base, Vernon Boyd and an unknown number of colleagues, referred to derisively by some as "the sewing circle," listened in. Murphy several times begged the men to desist, but they refused. "Whenever he would send anyone over to tell them to turn off their sets, we could hear the sets go off about the time the person approached and resume soon after he departed." Murphy was not popular with many of the men, for unlike everyone else on the expedition he was not only Byrd's close friend but also the only salaried member, being paid a handsome sum by CBS. Poulter, of course, had become anathema to many because of his antiliquor policy.

On June 30, Poulter posted a notice on the camp bulletin board that brought matters to a head. In seven short paragraphs he informed the expedition that "the Admiral will likely be back to Little America in about a month." Trail operations would be starting "as soon thereafter as possible." Under the circumstances, excessive drinking was simply out of the question. It had continued sporadically, and Poulter did not know the source. Presumably, some if not most of the men had bought copious amounts of liquor in New Zealand and stashed it among their personal belongings. In any case, those working out on the barrier and ice shelf simply could not drink "unless specifically order[ed] to the contrary" by Dr. Potaka. "So strongly do I feel this that if this is not observed, I plan to either replace" the miscreants "with other men, or even drop the proposed work from the program, regardless of how great its importance." No project, Poulter concluded, was worth an "undue risk" to individuals. Al Lindsey paraphrased this into "lips that touch hootch shall never touch hoosh," a reference to trail food. Richard Black promptly tacked the "adage" on the galley door, and Lindsey just as promptly removed it since "it wouldn't help" Poulter's "state of mind."[34]

Innes Taylor replied to Poulter's notice that same day. In a memo sent not only to his chief but also to Haines, Noville, June, Murphy, and Potaka, the trail boss stated flatly that no winter journey by tractor to Advance Base should be undertaken "prior to the latter part of August unless absolutely necessary." The waning polar night provided only "bad light" at best; following the flagged trail south was thus an "impossibility." Mechanical breakdowns were all too possible in the "killing temperatures," and new crevasses could well have developed. Innes Taylor reminded his colleagues, "Luck played a very large part in the tractor operations last fall." Several vehicles fell into crevasses that "the dogs had safely traversed." Such factors had to be carefully weighed, and having weighed them himself, Innes Taylor concluded that a successful effort to rescue Byrd "in July" was "a twenty five to one shot."

This time Poulter did not retreat. On July 3 he posted another notice on the camp bulletin board, stating that it was "quite likely" a tractor party would be sent to rescue the admiral. He emphasized that such an expedition would also exploit the opportunities for research in auroral photography, pilot balloon observations, and the like. Poulter also wished to "obtain moving pictures" of Advance Base and of Admiral Byrd "required by Paramount." He closed by stating that he hoped to pick men for the tractor party as soon as possible. He also replied to Innes Taylor that in "my judgement it will be feasible to make a trip to the Advance Base and return with tractors between July 18th and 29th." Moonlight would be continuous at that time, and as for crevasses, the snow bridges over them had certainly frozen hard and solid during the icy weeks and months of the polar winter. They should pose no hazard.[35]

Poulter's messages immediately divided Little America and led to extensive discussions and exchanges of messages.[36] Stuart Paine, editor of Little America's weekly news sheet, the "Barrier Bull," urged his fellow explorers to consider "very seriously" what would happen if the rescue mission failed. The loss of one or especially two tractors in a feckless effort to save Byrd would "wipe out" field operations for the coming austral summer and destroy the expedition.[37] June immediately called a meeting of the executive staff, which drafted a three-page, single-spaced "composite report" that it hoped to send down to Byrd, rejecting the idea of a mid- or late-winter tractor journey to Advance Base. Noville, Pete Demas, Innes Taylor, and Ken Rawson, a twenty-three-year-old aerial navigator for whom Byrd came to hold a very high regard, joined June in forming the core of opposition to Poulter's project.

The five rejected Poulter's contention that a single Citroën would be sufficient to get through. The probability of mechanical failure made a two-tractor trip imperative. They emphasized the "remote" possibility of following the flagged trail south in the poor visibility of the polar night, especially during times of fog or storm. They denied Poulter's contention that sufficiently firm snow bridges could be found over crevasses, and told Byrd in conclusion that he was the "only person who can possibly bear responsibility for ordering the trip." The five assured their admiral that "the thought uppermost in our minds has been your welfare and that of the expedition." But, of course, Byrd had divorced his welfare from that of the others the moment the last tractor left him alone out on the ice. His emergency had created a situation in which it was *either* his welfare *or* that of the expedition.[38]

Poulter sat on the executive staff report for several days, then informed its members that he had decided "not to read it to the admiral." The matter would be reconsidered while "we . . . go full speed ahead on the preparations so as to be ready for whatever the Admiral designates." Poulter wrote in his memoir that although "a concerted and organized effort continued to try every means possible to prevent a winter journey to Advance Base," he "was just as determined that it had to be made." On July 13 June, in his capacity as "chief" of the executive staff, called a meeting at the Little America Science Lab. Not only were Poulter and his five opponents present, but so were Charlie Murphy, topographer-geologist Quin Blackburn, Finn Ronne, Ike Schlossbach, Paul Siple, Innes Taylor, and a few others. June gave a lengthy recapitulation of his objections, then requested to be relieved of any responsibility for what might happen if Poulter's proposed tractor trip came to grief. Realizing the implications of June's request, Murphy, seconded by Blackburn, made an immediate motion to grant it, which passed unanimously. Too late, the chief of the executive staff realized that he—and his four companions—had been effectively shorn of further influence over matters.

Murphy then took the offensive on behalf of Poulter. He asked those present if they would "care to hear how the notion of the proposed trip developed," and at once he received unanimous assent. Without dwelling on the alarming aspects of Byrd's behavior over the radio waves, Murphy emphasized that Byrd himself had stated "the advantages offered by the tractors for an early start" on the spring scientific program. Byrd had *not* called for help, and he had repeatedly emphasized "that the trip if undertaken must be surrounded by every possible precaution." Nonetheless, "in view of the background of the affair," Murphy believed that Poulter had no choice but to undertake a rescue attempt. Moreover, the scientific aspects of the proposed journey were promising. Meteor observations from far out on the ice shelf would surely advance the cause of science, Murphy continued, "and it would not be in keeping with the high ideals of the expedition not to accept some risk where scientific results seemed to justify." Finally, Murphy called on Poulter, who strongly insinuated that the chief purpose of the journey would be scientific, not humanitarian. Byrd had given no conclusive signs that he was in distress.[39]

June and his cohorts would not let matters rest. Many radio listeners had drawn their own conclusions about the admiral's condition and had developed strong feelings about the feasibility of saving him. Some of June's colleagues, including Innes Taylor and Gil Morgan, promptly petitioned June (who passed the petition on to Poulter) to call another meeting for the express purpose of allowing individual members of the executive staff the opportunity to register their position regarding the rescue mission. Poulter rejected any effort to force him to abandon his plans, but he told the petitioners that he would be pleased to call another get-together to review plans and preparations.

After the nightly movie on July 14, Murphy called the meeting to order in the science lab. Debate was raucous from the beginning. Although no coherent minutes were taken, and we have only Poulter's summary to rely on, Lindsey, who was not there, wrote in his diary that "the rulers of destiny of L.A. staff convened to cuss each other out." Immediately, June or one of his followers introduced a motion "to the effect that there be no trip made to Advance Base before November." For the next three hours "heated arguments raged pro and con with comparatively little controlled order." Finally, at eleven o' clock everyone realized no vote had been taken on any motion, "and everyone was ready to call it quits." June immediately called for a vote on his motion and got an approval and a second. Leroy Clark, the navy chief yeoman and secretary who had been Byrd's unofficial correspondent during *Bear*'s trip eastward, was instructed to read the motion. When he called out the name of the man who seconded it, that individual immediately protested, "saying that wasn't the motion that he seconded." Murphy leaped up, declaring that there had not, in fact, been a motion before the meeting all evening.

"Someone" then called for adjournment, someone else seconded, "and it passed overwhelmingly." At last, opposition to the tractor trip collapsed.[40]

As the meeting broke up the night watchman rushed in to report a light on the barrier to the south near Retreat Camp. Several individuals immediately leaped to the conclusion that Admiral Byrd was walking in from Advance Base. Poulter was skeptical. A quick check of the base indicated that "Rip" Skinner was missing, and everyone knew he liked a practical joke. Nonetheless, when the search party scoured the camp, they found a man dressed in furs and about Byrd's size and shape lying face down in the snow. Convinced it was he, the men rushed the unconscious form back to Little America. "When they took him into Noville's shack for the first time and got enough light to see it was Skinner, he had to run." The following day, several outraged members of the expedition called on Poulter, demanding that Skinner be disciplined, though in fact the fraud had been concocted by Al Lindsey and a few others. Poulter, who had been under enough stress himself, chose to see the admittedly obscure humor in the prank and did nothing.[41]

Free of opposition at last, Poulter hastened his preparations, while Murphy alerted the New York office to the media possibilities—and pitfalls—inherent in the rescue. On the sixteenth, he wired northward: "The preparations of the tractors for the coming winter trip to Bolling Advance Base is the project of major importance at the present time. This trip is the first of its kind ever attempted and is both formidable and hazardous. . . . If the trip fails, or if anything serious occurs during the trip please kill the story immediately."[42]

Down at Advance Base Byrd kept up his struggle to survive. Although he took no aurora observations between July 17 and July 30, and not again until August 3, in "outline" notes dictated later (which may have been part of the "diary" he kept while at Advance Base), he proudly stated that he was mostly able to maintain his rigid schedule of weather recording, though "occasionally, it was impossible for me to open the trap door." As soon after the morning eight o'clock observations as possible he completed "the necessary duties to keep me alive" (which mainly involved putting out the stove), then got back into his sleeping bag, climbing out ten hours later, at 6:30 P.M. to light the stove for his evening meal. Byrd claimed that he restricted his cooking largely to meat and soft foods: rice, cream of wheat, lima beans, cornmeal, fried eggs, and broiled seal with an occasional steak if he felt well enough. He also ate canned goods, turnip tops, corn, and peas and developed a passion for canned figs. "Eating was terribly difficult—had to force things down my throat and to do that, successfully, practically chewed everything until it disappeared." He tried to read Emil Ludwig's *Napoleon* and one of John P. Marquand's more obscure novels, but often the pages blurred after a moment or two and his headache either returned or intensified. Music was better. One evening he played "In a Monastery Garden," "Tales from the Vienna Woods," and other selections on his phonograph machine that, incredibly, had not frozen up. When he could not read, he played solitaire, but "much of the time my arms got very tired just dealing the cards."

Next came the evening observations. Years later, Al Lindsey would marvel at Byrd's commitment and dedication, "which fails to impress most movie-makers and journalists—the permanent value of finding basic scientific knowledge." No one had manned an inland Antarctic outpost throughout a polar winter: the unbroken, unprecedented, day-to-day weather observations that Byrd recorded in those awful months in 1934 proved an invaluable foundation for understanding Antarctic, and thus global, weather. In the end, they justified whatever folly attached to his lonely sojourn.[43]

Bundling himself up even more, Richard would painfully climb the few steps of his ladder, push open the trapdoor, and step out onto the vast ice shelf, where he checked all the instruments by flashlight, kept them free of clogging snow, inked the register, and changed the register sheets. Returning below, he heated up the register's batteries, which he kept under the table, by placing a lantern under them. "This would prevent them from stopping from the cold before I got up." He then tried to wash up and "always" filled lanterns with kerosene just before turning in. "Even turning over in bed produced considerable fatigue in my muscles—my shoulders were apparently full of poison and made sleep difficult because I couldn't sleep on my back." He feared taking sedatives in his weakened condition because he might never wake up. "I had to train my mind and control it to the utmost in order to get to sleep at all." An hour or two later he was wide awake, "and there would be another struggle to get to sleep." Toward morning he would feel himself falling into a semicomatose state and subconsciously fought against it, fearing that death would come if he allowed himself to sleep much longer. He awoke, bleary-eyed and aching, to another "day."

But as his deliverers commenced their journey, Byrd roused himself again to shape and mold his unfolding tale. His hand was shaky, his writing almost indecipherable. "[Poulter?] didn't realize that I was [taken?] down with carbon monoxide when he radioed me that he would like to make the attempt," Byrd scrawled one day on a sheet of lined notepaper. "I was surprised of course but it was great news, for it was a glimmer of hope." Soon after he scrawled a message to Murphy on an undated sheet of paper he would use in his next communication with Little America: "We must not create the wrong impression. I suggest news story something like following: Sun starts back now [alternatively might back soon] moonlight soon twilight. Has been discovered that tractors can follow trail in moonlight and twilight therefore will start soon for Byrds base will lay supplies at bases." He added a poignant personal note: "Do you realize Charlie that aside from times at l.a. [Little America] and on Bear I have eaten alone for about 8 months. Living in this shack now over 4 months. What I miss most is light as I can only use lanterns on account of fumes. Mighty glad sun has started back."[44]

At two-thirty in the morning of July 20, 1934, a single Citroën half-track, painted orange, "resembling an awkward moving van" and hauling a sledge of supplies, left Little America for Advance Base on what would prove to be the first of "the three coldest trips ever made in history in a vehicle." Aboard were Poulter, the leader; "Rip" Skinner, driver; an "especially nervous" Amory H. "Bud" Waite, radio operator; and Carl O. Peterson and Bernard Flemming, who would take over the scientific observations from Byrd at his shack 123 miles away.[45] "With its two headlights glowing in the dark and its engine "purring softly," the vehicle "was reminiscent of a fiery mouthed dragon," Stuart Paine wrote that night in his diary. Poulter left behind notes of appreciation to Murphy, Innes Taylor, and others who had worked unstintingly to get the expedition under way. Despite Haines's prior problems with drink, Poulter left him in charge of the camp with Murphy as "Fourth-in-Command . . . in accordance with Admiral Byrd's instructions."[46]

Four miles out they lost the trail and had to retrace their steps to find the flags. It was snowy and foggy; the temperature hovered around seventy degrees below zero Fahrenheit. There was no wind as the men groped their way, "bounding over the sastrugi at 1½ miles per hour." At 6.5 miles they encountered their first crevasse and pressure ridges. Peterson began taking eerie motion pictures of the pitch-black surroundings, using magnesium flares for illumination. Flemming rode the sledge to add weight and balance. Shortly before seven, just 11 miles out, the Citroën's fan belt came off, and the men lost the trail. Putting the belt back on, the men retraced the trail to the nearest beacon and located it just as the fan belt came off again. This time it was replaced. Proceeding slowly south again as the wind picked up, the men often lost the trail in the dark and had to retrace their line of advance to find it. By eleven that evening the moon was "visible," but snow and frost crystals in the air badly dimmed its luminosity. Soon there were no stars or moon, and they steered by compass. At one in the morning on the twenty-first, Little America passed a message to Waite: Byrd was reporting clear weather at Advance Base "and urges us to fight through." Murphy added, "Keep your heads up and best of luck." In partially clearing weather the men picked up the pace. By eight o'clock they were 31 miles out. Ten and a half hours later, they arrived at 50-mile beacon, which sat in "a maelstrom of crevasses." They had actually traveled 135 miles.

Then the radio went out, and the trail around the crevassed area disappeared. Heavy snows had completely obscured the flags. With the wind again "picking up" and no radio contact possible with either Byrd or Little America, Poulter decided to return. Waite and Peterson agreed with their commander; Skinner and Flemming voted futilely to press on. A blizzard struck soon after as the men struggled sometimes on and sometimes off the trail. Reaching what they thought was the 28-mile marker "but more likely 30," in temperatures close to eighty degrees below and with a 60-mile-per-hour gale blowing them about, the five stopped again as they once more lost the trail. Utterly spent, they bundled into the tractor and had their first food in fifty-one hours: oatmeal and a lukewarm cup of chocolate. (Lindsey would later note that imbibing truly hot drinks in the Antarctic cold "would cause metal fillings in our teeth to contract and fall out," so drinks were always kept cool. In fact, hot drinks would expand metal fillings relative to the surrounding teeth and crack them.) Peterson and Flemming then pitched a tent and went to sleep while the others cramped themselves in the tractor. The tent mates awoke after four hours to find themselves completely snowed in, while the three in the tractor slept the day away. Bestirring themselves at last, the five headed back toward Little America and after six hours picked up a light on the horizon. It was the 100-watt-light that Poulter had asked be placed atop the radio tower at Little America. Soon the men were home again.[47]

Byrd was devastated. Once he had learned that the rescue operation was under way, his anxiety escalated. "No doomed man pacing a cell in the hope of an eleventh-hour reprieve can possibly have endured more than I endured; for, besides my own skin to think about, I had the lives of five other men on my conscience." He had not been able to get through to Little America for hours once he learned of the trail party's departure and became "nearly frantic with anxiety about the tractor men." He took the radio receiver apart but found nothing wrong. The airwaves remained silent. He raised the trapdoor several times, peering out onto the frozen ice shelf, deceived that lights on the horizon might be the tractor, only to realize they were the winking of far-distant stars on the horizon. When at last his receiver came alive with news, his "hopes died" and with them the brief "emotional lift" from knowing that rescue might be at hand. "I was all hollow inside. Everything that was reasonable had been tried, and it all added up to nothing."[48]

Back at Little America, even supporters of the rescue operation were becoming thoroughly disgusted. Paine had already concluded that his nominal commander was a glory hound. "I have lost all respect + confidence in REB as a leader, dubbing him a marvelous promoter, but lacking in the qualities of leadership and justice." Now Paine wrote of "the monotony, the pathos, the struggle of a group of foolish men gathered here to satisfy an already satiated leader's publicity complex. That's pretty strong, but time will test it to find out whether it's true." Poulter, however, refused to concede and became convinced that because the trail south was serpentine, especially around the notorious crevasse area 50 miles out, adequate illumination was the key to a successful mission. Losing the trail ahead, one needed only to glance back at the nearest light, rather than struggling to find a trail flag that might be partially obscured by snow. A fully lighted trail would, of course, make the return journey that much easier.

Poulter, Waite, and the others pondered the problem. "The source of light that proved to be most satisfactory was a candle mounted in the top of a snow beacon about four feet high." The candle would be enclosed in snow on all but one side and on that side "we used a thin sheet of pyralin to transmit the light and yet keep the wind from blowing out the candle." But how could these beacons be lined up on the trail? Returning to his shack, Poulter picked through the array of instruments that the spring field parties planned to employ. He concluded that a geologist's compass that Siple was planning to use on his expedition into adjacent Marie Byrd Land was just perfect; Poulter could use it and return it long before Siple departed. The compass would be "set up on a Jacob's staff and be lined up ready to use in about fifteen seconds, and I felt it should give us the necessary accuracy." The solution in hand, Poulter and his men prepared for another rescue attempt, but the weather turned bad, and for the next week they were confined to camp. One day the Paramount cameramen, John Herrmann and J. A. Pelter, begged Poulter to take both still and moving pictures of Advance Base "while the Admiral is there." Poulter evidently agreed, for the expedition movie contained scenes taken by magnesium flares of Byrd working outside and reading his instruments. The movie audiences of 1935 never guessed the admiral was deathly ill.[49]

But in the austral winter of 1934 the men at Little America, and especially Dyer, the radioman, guessed it. Byrd's insistence that he was experiencing trouble with his radio set was beginning to wear thin. When he did broadcast his messages were "slow and dragged. . . . [T]hey filtered through in groups of three or four words, then he would spell out 'wait,' and minutes would elapse before he continued." When queried, the admiral replied laconically, "bad arm." By the end of July when Poulter again set out, no one was fooled. As the astronomer waited with growing impatience for the weather to lift he experienced a "ghastly feeling" looking south into the "blackness of the Antarctic night." His friend Dick Byrd was out there in distress yet refusing to call for help. Poulter decided this time he would "make a dash" for Advance Base and to hell with the flagged trail. Peterson, Flemming, and Skinner would be left behind; only he, Demas, and Waite would go.

Suddenly, out of the darkness Dick Byrd was calling again, broadcasting over and over again: "Where is tractor, I have heard nothing for days." Dyer broke in and reestablished contact. Poulter came on to tell his commander that help was on the way as soon as the weather cleared. "Can only hear a few words," Byrd replied. "I have lights outside from 3:00 to 8:00 AM, everything O.K. Sorry to be so much trouble. Good luck."[50]

By August 4 Poulter could wait no longer. A "hint of dawn" lightly illuminated the barrier around noon, and so he, Demas, and Waite started out shortly before then to take maximum advantage of whatever light there might be to get them through the pressure ice and crevasses that dotted the Amundsen Arm of the Bay of Whales. Recent blizzards had obscured the flagged trail south, but Poulter pressed on, skiing ahead of the tractor whenever danger loomed. A crevasse suddenly yawned ahead, and Poulter directed Demas to drive west around it. That proved impossible, and the men had to backtrack 2 miles before starting south again. An hour or so later, as Poulter rode atop the half-track's cab, illuminating the way ahead with the portable searchlight around his neck, all three men heard a boom behind them, and Demas at the controls felt the Citroën begin to slip backward. He gunned the throttles, and the half-track and the first sled it was pulling gained traction and got away. But the second and last sled snapped its lines and with its two-ton load fell about 10 feet onto a snow block in the 35-foot crevasse. The three men were forced to stop, go down into the crevasse, and unload the sled by hand, "with battery acid dripping down on us as we hung there." The men then pulled the sled out and reloaded it in the Antarctic darkness. The temperature had warmed to fifty-six degrees below.

After eight hours of backbreaking work the men pushed on in deteriorating weather. Poulter abandoned his perch on the cab roof and skied ahead. "In a short time a blinding" snowstorm "made it impossible to travel and we made camp, and left the engine idling to keep it warm." Ahead lay the first great pressure ridge, and as the storm subsided Poulter skied out and found the passage through it and, incidentally, the trail south. After getting through, Poulter paused and built the first candle beacon. A quarter mile farther on, he built the second. Four miles ahead there should be a sharp incline up to 200 feet. Near the top of the slope there should be a bamboo pole marker in the snow with two five-gallon oil cans on it. Demas drove on, and as expected the incline came into view, and shortly the pole marker. Suddenly, the men felt vindicated; their mood lightened. They were traveling faster than at any time "on night travel." But soon they were slowed, as Poulter paused every mile to establish another candle beacon. Then the uneven terrain dictated that the candle beacons be set closer together, for otherwise they disappeared whenever "the tractor would strike low surface." On the evening of the fifth, thirty-six hours after leaving Little America, the Citroën had traveled only 20 miles down the trail. A blizzard struck, and the men were forced to make camp. Twelve hours later they started again.

Once more disaster struck. The half-track's clutch began to slip. Waite later guessed that the clutch plate had blown back at the crevasse in the attempt to get clear. There was no alternative but to return home. Poulter notified Haines he was dropping the sleds at 23 miles and returning with the crippled vehicle. It was hoped it could be repaired quickly while the three men rested, and then they could set out again. It was not to be. Soon after turning homeward, the Citroën's clutch began to slip repeatedly. Demas nursed the vehicle for 13 miles. Ten miles short of camp the engine began to overheat, despite the intense cold. The fan belt had broken, "and that lost us all ignition," together with most of the radiator coolant. Poulter had included only one spare, badly worn, belt. Demas put it on and stuffed snow into the steaming radiator (luckily not cracking the block in the process), and the men went on. Within a mile the second belt broke. For the next ten hours or so, Poulter fabricated one makeshift belt after another out of the cotton alpine rope someone had brought along. No belt lasted more than a mile. "Then to make matters worse the gas line clogged with ice crystals and we were delayed more than an hour with it." The men staggered into Little America at three in the morning on August 7, "half frozen, covered with grease and oil, too weary and disgruntled to relate our troubles."

While Demas and Waite went to bed, Poulter ordered a new clutch installed in Car no. 1. Car no. 2 had not completed overhaul, and no. 3 had caught fire and burned during unloading operations. Its engine had been repaired, but "the cab was far from windproof, there were boards in the doors instead of glass, it had no headlights, and no instrument board." Although the upholstery had been repaired, "all the temper had been taken out of the springs by the fire." Unfortunately, the clutch from a spare engine would not fit Car no. 1, but it did no. 3. So while one crew of men shifted the personal gear from no. 1 to no. 3, another transferred the headlights, installed a "makeshift" instrument panel, wind- and waterproofed the cab, checked the ignition, and put in a new battery. Then the men set out again early in the morning of August 8.[51]

Byrd was hanging on by instinct now, and he ceased all auroral observations. Hope was gone, but "the animal tenacity in me, as in every man, would not let me give up." At long last, it would be rewarded. A mile south of Little America, Demas's oil gauge showed no pressure. He promptly hauled Car no. 3 back to base, where troubleshooting determined that the gauge on the hastily installed instrument panel was itself faulty. "So we headed south again with the temperature $-44°$ and the sky overcast beneath the ink-black dome of a sky whose horizon was only faintly lit at noon by a brief, grayish blush."

Guided by the candle beacons, the trail party traveled quickly. In a matter of hours the men reached mile 23, where they picked up the abandoned sledges. In poor visibility, the men carefully marked their trail and reached 30 miles south by noon the first day before being stopped by bad weather, which forced them to camp until eight o'clock the following morning, August 9.

Byrd, meanwhile, had apparently become frantic. "The Admiral calls for help,"

Lindsey recorded in his diary. "Message radioed by the Admiral pleading 'Come at once!' He gives the impression of being in dire straits, getting weaker, can't crank [the generator] for more than a word or two at a time, in the contacts." Years later, Waite recalled that the message he received from Little America shortly thereafter stated that Byrd had cried, "Get them here fast! We found out later, that he had found out a storm was coming and wanted us to get to the shelter of the 'shack' before it hit." Waite added that even a modest 50-mile-per-hour blow could generate 20-foot drifts that would make sighting Byrd's little hut impossible.[52] Whatever the admiral's motive, the tractor party of three pressed on toward Advance Base with renewed urgency.

Navigating by means of their candle beacons and geologist's compass, Poulter, Demas, and Waite "hit the row" of trail pennants indicating they were slightly left of the 50-mile marker. "In closing one candle atop the beacon we set our course for the first leg of the detour around the valley of crevasses." Swiveling this way and that, detouring around one obstacle after another, the men moved generally south. A shirtsleeved Pete Demas drove inside the now tightly enclosed and overheated tractor cab "all those miserable hours, unable to see through his scratched plastic windshield," while Poulter and Waite, bundled up against the brutal cold, took turns on the roof, "pounding one for, 'Go Right,' and two for 'Go Left.'" The men were forced to change the carbon brushes on the generator every four hours, as they vaporized in the icy cold, "and having long since run out of spares, [we] were using shaped bits of battery carbons with the pig-tail soldered back in them, with wooden match sticks under the springs to hold 'em down." The generator had become the critical item once the batteries froze solid since it was essential to keep the headlights burning.

Poulter feared they were nowhere near the trail. Then early on the morning of the tenth, the men stumbled across the giant Cletrac tractor that had been abandoned as it was returning from its abortive mission to Advance Base months before. "This was the most welcome sight we had seen since leaving LA," Poulter would remember. They were on the trail. Following its supposed course and correcting for changing compass deviations brought them to the 75-mile depot. Poulter and his gallant companions could at last feel "that we were on the last lap of our most frustrating journey." Soon the men reached 81 miles south, just 42 miles from Advance Base. They had been on the trail for nearly two days without eating or sleeping.

In his hut, Dick Byrd had erupted in a dither of activity. Murphy's messages indicated that Little America at least realized his plight, and was coming for him, Poulter's polite fiction about a scientific mission to study meteors notwithstanding. How soon might Poulter arrive? And if he came close, could he find the speck of Advance Base buried in the vast emptiness of the Ross Ice Shelf? Byrd began eating better as his stomach settled, and he started making plans. He could certainly set off gasoline pots as Poulter came closer, but could he do more? At one point he decided to set fire to a gasoline-soaked kite and exhausted himself running some 200 yards along the shelf getting the burning piece of paper aloft. Poulter may or may not have seen it, for he noticed a quick blue flare in the southern sky that convinced him Byrd was waiting. But the radio to Little America went out, and both rescuers and their object groped blindly for each other through an often howling polar night.

Around noon on August 10, opening his trapdoor after an hour of restless reading, Byrd at long last saw a light rising and dipping on the vast, silent terrain to the north. Now all he had to do was prepare and wait. Some dozen miles away, Poulter saw a point of light and directed Demas to steer for it. After half an hour he concluded that he was seeing a steadily glowing star that had pulled the half-track about 10 degrees off course. Ordering Demas to tack back to the right, Poulter "reestablished our candle beacon navigating." Roughly 10 miles from where Advance Base should be, Poulter picked up a flickering light, "which we were able to follow the rest of the way." It came from one of Byrd's gallon cans that he had filled with gasoline and ignited, as he had promised Little America he would do. Slowly, his trapdoor opened, and Poulter saw a little old man tottering toward him, "Emaciated, hollow-cheeked, weak and haggard." "Come on down," Byrd said, "I have some hot soup for you."[53]

It would be two months before he was in shape to be moved back to a camp riven by drink and discord. Before leaving Little America, Richard had concluded erroneously that he suffered from diabetes, "so he had taken a large supply of insulin" to Advance Base. It lay untouched. Waite discovered "also a large untouched liquor cache." The admiral had not been drinking after all.[54]

The first thing was to get him "on a good diet," which he had not been able to sustain because serious cooking wore him out. Next came daily rubdowns and massages, then, after a week or so, short walks out on the vast ice shelf now brightening with the return of the sun, though temperatures continued to hover around sixty below. As the weeks passed and a tepid light and warmth returned to the Antarctic, Poulter got Richard to increase his exercise both inside the shack and out. Byrd's recovery was only part of Poulter's workday. The astronomer carried out daily meteor and aurora observations both on his own and with scientists at Little America via radio. "We also continued the weather observations which the Admiral had carried on even through his most trying days in late June and July."[55]

Through it all, Dick Byrd said little. He had left a note for Poulter on top of his briefcase in case he should perish, instructing the second in command to send all papers, photos, and other documents to Marie. "If anything happen[s] to her destroy them all. I trust you." Beyond that, for the two months that Demas, Waite, and Poulter lived with their commander, "jammed together in his nine-by-thirteen room, we learned next to nothing of his experience." Byrd "told us no more than bare courtesy required." Was he humbled, humiliated by failure, or what he perceived to be failure? Yes, and no. At the time and in memory he battled himself over the meaning of his ordeal. After four further years of life and reflection, he wrote that he probably could have "stuck it out alone" until the sun and a rescue plane arrived, "had it not been for that damnable hand generator" needed to crank up for radio contact with Little America.

Yet he also admitted "that I needed help badly." During the first days and weeks of his rescue he gladly let the others take charge, and as they did so "the darkness lifted from my heart, just as it presently did from the Barrier." Still, he sought to "conceal" from the others the extent of his "weakness." "I never mentioned and, therefore, never acknowledged it." What weakness did he mean? Physical? Moral? Both? The others never pressed him.[56]

In early October he was deemed fit enough to return to Little America. Wind and clouds kept the planes grounded until midmonth, when on the twelfth (Byrd erroneously claimed the fourteenth), Bill Bowlin, Clay Bailey, and Ike Schlossbach flew down in the Pilgrim. The sky was still overcast, but Waite was able to contact the aircraft and "talk it down." The great ice shelf was flooded with light now, and the first sledging parties were already out on the trail. Poulter would fly back; the others would remain behind long enough to close Advance Base and return in the Citroën. "I climbed the hatch" into the plane "and never looked back," Byrd later wrote. Perhaps he could not. Richard had surely left what remained of his youth if not his life at Advance Base. Perhaps he left his vanity and certainly his skepticism as well. He carried off within him a humbler perspective and a deep appreciation of the beauty of life—or so he said.[57]

Stuart Paine, now a lukewarm supporter at best of the admiral, wrote that Byrd was "rocky when he got here. Came to about supper time. He does not look so bad, perhaps this is the first time he has been sober." Al Lindsey's initial impression was of a tired and prematurely old man who nonetheless recognized him and thus retained his wits. In fact, Byrd was just totally exhausted. Shortly after landing, the "haggard and grey haired" commander insisted on touring the entire camp, talking with everyone, and bringing himself up to speed on developments since his departure four months before. Out of concern for his sensibilities, his unidentified "guide" steered him away from the "Sealarium" where Lindsey and others did their animal dissections. To Lindsey's eternal gratitude, however, Byrd quietly returned on his own later in the day to inspect the little facility and ask pertinent questions.[58]

Richard "caught the brunt of the after-effects" of the winter's drinking spree as "his hardier explorers, after draining the compasses of alcohol, were then running mouth wash and a patent medicine called Dr. Baxter's Lung Preserver through a home-made still." The by-product produced the desirable numbness, Charles Murphy added, but also "left tempers vile." Haines had been in command during Poulter's absence. "Up to several days ago," Paine wrote on August 18, Haines had "refrained from liquor. Today he broke down, and now orders Perkins, who has charge of the liquor cache, to deliver so many pints a day to him. Consequently, he is enormously plastered." That morning, a Saturday, Haines had ordered everyone back to bed. At supper, some wag "fed him a toasted sandwich filled with leather." The sun returned on August 23. It should have been a happy holiday. Instead, the temperature plummeted to seventy-one below Fahrenheit, while Little America celebrated with a rather frantic and decidedly boozy party that created "rather a pitiable" environment, "with some people drunk, most of the others sober and disgusted + disappointed at the whole business." Paine took the opportunity to corner Murphy at dinner to tell the publicist of his growing unpopularity among the men because of excessive secrecy regarding Byrd and his condition. Murphy "finally conceded to post all dispatches concerning the Admiral as soon as received," which would subdue somewhat the criticism. Two weeks later Paine found himself "kind of depressed all day," and he soon wrote of the deep "monotony of our existence" that "has become increasingly trying. Everything," washing, bathing, even brushing one's teeth, required such effort as to "become a trial. It is not really worth the effort. Our personal habits have slipped," and hygiene soon followed.[59]

In September Bill McCormick's little autogiro crashed. Haines was employing the craft for upper air temperature observations. With equipment aboard, the tiny machine could hold only one man, so McCormick flew with a weather recording device. He and Haines discovered that temperatures often rose dramatically for a few thousand feet above the surface of the ice. Eager to gather more information, McCormick pushed his luck too far. Spinning aloft one day, the autogiro suddenly became "unmanageable," and McCormick rode it upside down 150 feet to a spine-jolting crash. As he saw the snow "coming up pretty fast" the pilot reached over to cut the ignition switch in order to avoid a fire upon impact. His left arm out-stretched at the moment of impact snapped above the elbow. "Fortunately, it was only a simple fracture, not compound," but he was flat on his back for six weeks. The shocked ground crew discovered that the machine had cracked up because "snow had collected in its fuselage, making it tail heavy."[60]

Little America remained riven with bitterness as Dick Byrd returned. Several hours after his plane set down someone placed the frozen remains of a husky dog (which had dropped dead on the trail) head up in the snow with a sign around its neck that read, "I died for Byrd; Why don't you?"[61]

Fortunately, the mood soon lifted. Like their equally high-strung colleagues on BAE I, the scientists, pilots, and support personnel of the Second Byrd Expedition craved work and movement. Just as the drinking and low morale on BAE I subsided significantly with the return of the sun, so it did on BAE II. Responding to purposeful work, men threw off their winter garments of repentance and misery. Paine, who in the course of the winter night had trashed just about every one of his colleagues—most notably Poulter, Innes Taylor, June, Clark, and Siple—for shirking, incompetence, ill temper, or some other personal flaw suddenly found that "a new happiness has come over all of us." The work in and out of doors preparing for the austral summer research program took men out of themselves and "has brightened our outlook considerably. Healthy exercise has done a lot," the returning sun "a great deal," and "the approaching trips" have "spurred us to greater efforts + we are happier because of this." By October 1 dog teams, tractors, and aircraft were leaping away from Little America, fanning out over the continent on a multitude of missions.[62]

Byrd's role in these bursts of creative scientific activity was influential but not decisive. Although he had given his blessing to the general plans and overall objectives of the expedition's science program, the individual dog-team and tractor parties had worked out specifics of each exploratory thrust under the general direction of Poulter and Innes Taylor as Byrd sat or lay huddled at Advance Base. When the admiral returned, Ronne saw a "pale and thin" man walk from the plane to Noville's shack, and Byrd himself admitted that although he was "eager" to step back into his various leadership roles, "I was not long in discovering that a few were beyond me." (With the artless curiosity of the twenty-four year old, Siple asked his admiral if the experience at Advance Base had been worth it. "Yes," Byrd told him, "I learned much, but I never want to go through that experience again.")

Dr. Potaka specifically warned the admiral against flying long missions. Byrd was "still in bad condition from my Advance Base experience." Suppose one of his flights was forced down a few hundred miles or even less from Little America? "I should be a drag on my companions when they would start walking back." But the admiral was keen to get aloft and impatiently awaited his chance.

Before his departure for Advance Base, Byrd had agreed to Siple's request to lead a summer trail party "into the virgin east." Siple's party, including geologist Alton Wade, together with supply officer Stevenson Corey acting as radioman and photographer Olin Stancliffe, traveled by dog team. On September 27 June, Ken Rawson, driver John H. Von der Wall, and radio operator Carl Peterson set out with one of the Citroëns, towing two sledges loaded with thirty-six hundred pounds of supplies to lay advance supply depots for Siple. "Rawson kept the compass free from the magnetic disturbances of the tractor by lying with his compass on one of the trailer sleds from which all iron had been excluded." Day after day the sturdy little half-track ground on as the men dropped off supply caches from the sledges every 35 miles. The designers at Citroën had added small removable cabins to the back of the vehicles built for exploring the Gobi. The same accommodations were obviously suitable for Antarctic travel as well, and the "cars" that the Byrd expedition employed for exploring on the ice in 1933–1934 resembled those "camper trucks" that began appearing on American highways a quarter century later. June and his colleagues thus enjoyed a warm haven with bunks, a stove, and a radio as they traversed the South Polar wilderness.

After 150 miles the surface became increasingly rough and began to rise. For a time the men thought they might have to abandon part of the load, but the Citroën proved reliable even in the roughest terrain. By the time they dropped off a cache at mile 173, they estimated their position to be above 3,000 feet, higher than some of the peaks of the Rockefeller Mountains only 45 miles away. At mile 207, a blizzard socked them in for a week, and they needed another twenty-four hours to dig themselves out. The half-track and its sledges eventually reached the base of Mount Grace McKinley, and the men climbed higher to discover peaks not visible five years before when Byrd, Gould, and the others had first overflown the region. Rawson took both solar and star observations before the party headed back to Little America, having covered more than 530 miles without mishap. Tracked vehicles, like the airplane, were proving invaluable tools of Antarctic exploration and research.[63]

Siple and his team followed June's path a month later, enduring blizzards of their own to attain the northern section of the Edsel Ford Ranges, and striking deep into the formerly unknown reaches of Marie Byrd Land. Siple, a fine dog-team leader, fell hopelessly in love with Antarctica as he skied out ahead of the teams on the good days to encourage the dogs and mark the trail. Hour after hour he was by himself in the deep, bone-chilling stillness of the South Polar continent. His thoughts and his life were his own, and like so many others who would come to that secret land, he returned to civilization forever changed. He and the others got back to Little America after seventy-seven days of hard travel with "a wealth of geological and biological specimens." Wade concluded on the basis of his geological studies that the mountains and vast ice sheet of Marie Byrd Land formed a distinct part of Antarctica.[64]

Thus ended the first great penetration of the West Antarctic Ice Sheet. Veteran Antarctic scientist John Behrendt asserts that nothing "comparable was done until the IGY [International Geophysical Year of 1957–1958]. Merely flying over in a plane, while useful, doesn't tell much about the ice sheet," Behrendt adds, "or geology/glaciology," given the "poor air navigation and lack of aerogeophysical tools available in the 1930s–'40s." As is so often the case in science, however,

Wade's conjectures did not stand the test of subsequent research. IGY scientists seemed to confirm his hypothesis of a "subglacial connection" between the Ross and Weddell Seas, but it was finally disproved years later through ongoing field evaluations that uncovered "the complexities of the subglacial topography."[65]

The two southern trail parties did equally remarkable work. The "geological party" led by Quin Blackburn and including navigator Stuart Paine and dog-team driver Richard Russell (a veteran of the 1925 Greenland expedition) was to extend Larry Gould's work on BAE I in the Queen Maud Mountains. For young Paine, it would be "probably the most enjoyable summer I shall ever have spent."[66] The second party, including Demas, physicist Ervin Bramhall, geologist Gil Morgan, and Bud Waite, hoped to drive to the foot of one of the great mountain glaciers at the base of the Ross Ice Shelf and, with heavy seismological equipment, climb up the glacier and out onto the polar plateau itself to measure the thickness of the ice. This "plateau party," however, soon came to grief. The vast crevasse field that gave Gould such trouble four years before stymied the Citroëns that carried all of the heavy equipment and most of the food and supplies. "We had believed," Byrd later wrote, "that a trail for the tractors lay to the eastward, but after several days of search both east and west no safe path could be found." Without the tractors, dog teams hauling the heavy seismic equipment could not reach the mountains.

It was up to Byrd back at Little America to decide what to do. He ordered the geological and plateau parties to amalgamate, diverting the plateau party into Marie Byrd Land to attempt an assault on the polar highland from that area. With the dog teams driven by Finn Ronne and Albert Eilefsen now under his control, Blackburn made rapid progress southward, despite their heavy loads. "Tied together in tandem," the three dog teams pushed south into a fresh crevasse field 400 miles out. Soon a snow bridge, weakened by the crossing of the lead team, gave way as the second crossed. As Blackburn felt his feet give way, he threw himself forward and found himself hanging on the edge of a deep crevasse with his dogs who, "bellies down in the snow," scrabbled frantically with their fore- and then hind legs to gain enough traction against the weight of the dangling sledges to get out. Neither human nor animal was lost, but all the geological and navigational instruments and most of the food and clothing were on the sledges. For the next seven hours, Blackburn and his men dangled over the crevasse, laboriously unloading the sledges until they were light enough to be pulled up, and the advance continued. According to one polar historian, "All three of the long range trail parties," including Siple's, "had similar experiences." Byrd later told his readers that he got "gray hair" from "constantly hearing of such things over the radio from five or six separate parties in the field."

Reaching the base of the Queen Mauds, the two parties split, and Blackburn decided to ascend Thorne (now called Scott) Glacier, 50 miles west of the vast Axel Heiberg. He, Paine, and Dick Russell donned crampons to obtain the necessary purchase, but the dogs easily took the ice in stride, neither falling nor stumbling. Toiling up the 120 miles of blue ice amid "a splendor of mt. Scenery" that comprised Scott Glacier and its environs, the three men began to go hungry, and the dogs became sick on pemmican. Soldiering on, Paine was thunderstruck by the 13,000- and 14,000-foot mountains towering all around the vast glacier. "A grander evidence of the overwhelming natural forces at work in this region is nowhere to be seen," he wrote with freezing fingers on December 2. "It makes our petty cares + ceremonies + don'ts seem pretty trivial to the powers in motion here."

Throughout the traverse he and Blackburn triangulated positions in order to generate a map of the massive glacier and the far (polar) side of the Queen Maud range. Reaching the top of the glacier at last, the three men found a naked peak, which they named Mount Weaver, rising before them. They promptly climbed its 2,000 feet in three hours. "We are most southern mt. climbers in the world," Paine wrote exultantly later that day, "having climbed mt. further south—Looked to South + all but saw the pole—only three small mts to south of us." The three moved out onto the plateau itself, establishing more ground-truth navigational stations. Gazing back toward the top of glacier and the surrounding mountains— many of which he or Blackburn had named, Paine saw the most spectacular and beautiful "setting . . . I have ever seen. It is almost as though we are among friends—friends of radical different personalities, some big, some small, some fat, some lean, but friendly all the same. . . . [W]e feel truly like gods." Russell's discovery of lichens—living organisms—at the foot of the Organ Pipes and Mount Scudder constituted another southernmost "first" for the geology party. These finds remain the southernmost traces of prehistoric and contemporary plant life, for there is no exposed land south of Mount Weaver. Paine believed he and his colleagues had left Little America "without the faith of most of our fellows." Obviously, "we have accomplished as much if not more than any party in the field."

They were but 210 miles from the bottom of the earth, and there was "needless to say an urge to go on to the Pole itself, which they could have done had they prepared for it." But, as Byrd concluded, "their work lay in the mountains which, scientifically speaking, were more important than reaching the Pole." Paine was thrilled nonetheless. "We are in pretty select company now—Byrd, June, McKinley, Balchen are the only Americans ever gone further south than we. But we are the first Americans to set foot on land this far South. That's quite a feather in our cap." So were the discoveries on Mount Weaver that proved a geologist's dream, with a dozen clearly defined seams of coal and a "profusion" of fossils, including fragments of tree trunks, in nearby moraines.

On the rush home Paine successfully fought off snow blindness much of the way. At one point, he and Russell took advantage of "incessant" southern winds by splitting the black emergency tent in half to rig as sails to speed the sledges along the Ross Ice Shelf. On January 11, "tired but happy," the three men together with the last of their gallant animals were back in Little America to broad acclaim.[67]

Meanwhile, the original plateau party, burdened by heavy gear but still in possession of tractor power, "swung east to probe the thickness of the Marie Byrd Land plateau." Employing dynamite charges to make seismic soundings, Morgan and Bramhall determined "that when they were camped at from 2,000 to 3,000 feet above sea level the ice beneath them was roughly 1,000 to 2,000 feet thick." After traveling some 850 miles, the plateau party returned to Little America.[68]

Byrd himself was determined to resolve one of the great nagging questions in Antarctic research: was the "continent" truly a single landmass or two or more big islands? One way to find out if the Ross and Weddell Seas were connected by a body of frozen water—a "transcontinental strait" beneath the ice sheet—was by aerial instrument measurement. On November 15 Byrd took advantage of the first good day of flying weather to go aloft ("rightly or wrongly") with June, Bowlin, Rawson, and radio operator Clay Bailey. Flying southeast, the Condor passed over a belt of crevasses at what appeared to be the foot of a plateau wherein the snow-field was cut by a definite depression. Turning northward above the plateau, the Condor encountered a rising snow surface, and Byrd concluded that the plane was flying over the plateau earlier found by June when he led the tractor party toward the Edsel Ford Ranges. Coming up on Mount Grace McKinley, Byrd was thunderstruck to discover that the mountains ran east and west, not north and south, as he had thought when he first saw them in 1929. "In other words, we had seen the mountain range from its end and not along its length. Now we should have to make a flight to the eastward to check this trend." Such a flight was too much for the weakened admiral, who had already given over aerial navigation responsibilities to the "competent and cool" twenty-three-year-old Rawson.

Three days later he dispatched the same flight crew, minus himself, back to Mount Grace McKinley, where June and the others traced the Edsel Ford Ranges eastward "as far as gasoline supply and weather would permit." Byrd waited impatiently in the control shack at Little America while Rawson flashed position reports back from the plane. As the *William Horlick* flew east down the range, which soon "narrowed down to a single line heading slightly northeast," then bending east and southeast, the flight crew looking north over the line of peaks "could see dark water sky, indicating that the coast line parallels in general the axis of the mountains." But what about the great depression in the ice field farther south? The day after June's latest flight, Blackburn's geological party reached that area and reported sighting high land to the east, which seemed to negate the idea of a vast strait connecting the two Antarctic seas. After another three days during which the weather cleared at Little America, Byrd dispatched June and his boys out to check Blackburn's observation. The flight was a smashing success, for not only did the men find Blackburn's plateau "rising to a considerable altitude and rolling unbrokenly to the point" where new peaks were sighted, but on the way out, around latitude 85 and the 110th and 115th meridians, "a cluster of ice-ridden peaks" emerged on the horizon that suggested a farther eastward extension of the Queen Mauds. Swinging toward home, June encountered a solid "mass of low-lying clouds as far as the eye could reach in every direction." Slamming the throttles forward, the pilot raced the clouds to Little America and ducked in under them just as foul weather closed down the base.[69]

Byrd wanted to see for himself. On November 22, twenty-four hours after June's latest flight, the admiral joined his fliers on one last trip back to the plateau area. "Again I fear I gave Dr. Pohaka [sic] some concern." Finding the depression area, Byrd ordered the Condor to turn eastward while sounding the elevation of the ice below with an altimeter. Several times June brought the aircraft to within a few feet of the snow to get the most accurate readings, which indicated a steadily rising ground elevation. "To the south and east the plateau extended unbrokenly . . . rising in altitude." To Byrd's mind, "the results were conclusive. The long-sought strait was non-existent." His theory was destroyed. "Correlating our flight data with the Geological party's discovery . . . we can now say that the plateau of Marie Byrd Land probably rolls unbrokenly from the South Pacific Ocean to that geographical point we call the South Pole. It extends at least 1,000 miles north and south and probably many hundreds of miles further." (Byrd's conclusion was, of course, overturned by later research.) Thereafter, he ordered his fliers to concentrate on mapping the coastline of Marie Byrd Land, but the area proved to be "one of the cloudiest in the whole of Antarctica"—at least in Byrd's experience of the continent. "Every attempt we made was defeated," and by mid-January it was time to go home.[70]

While the fliers were making some spectacular discoveries and disproving attractive theories, Poulter, with his assistant, Richard Black, had shifted to a seismological study of the Bay of Whales area. Poulter first had to devise a portable station that could be moved quickly and often to obtain the widely spaced measurements he desired. Using two dog teams in tandem, Poulter and Black devised means of carrying explosives, navigational instruments, radio, and camping equipment on one sledge, the seismograph with geophones and a reel carrying five cables on the second. Equipment for no fewer than 25 sites could be carried in one 950-pound load.

Poulter and his four-man team set to work in late October, after the field parties had left Little America, and by the end of November the team had made 78 test shots and were ready for "more distant journeys." Byrd lent his senior scientist an airplane whenever feasible, enabling Poulter to shoot from a series of seven stations in a radius of approximately 35 miles around Little America. Poulter flew briefly to Advance Base as well as to a new site 75 miles south of Little America. He completed his work in January after some 510 seismic soundings. He and his team had materially advanced understanding of the dynamics of the Ross Ice Shelf and in the process discovered a major island, for the great rising ice chunk just south of the Bay of Whales proved to be encrusted land—an island that Byrd promptly named for President Roosevelt.[71]

By December the men of BAE II were waiting impatiently to go home; not even the traditional Christmas feast and presents saved for a year could boost morale for long. Ronne, who had managed to stay out of the shenanigans of the previous winter, once more removed himself to "Blubberheim," refusing, he later wrote, "to engage in petty squabbles, common in a polar camp."[72] As 1935 came to the Bay of Whales, Byrd ordered the men to start laying trails down to the bay ice so that when the ships arrived, they could be loaded and the expedition depart as quickly as possible. He also sent Demas, Skinner, and three others back to Advance Base to take down and bring back the shack for return to the States and to tow the abandoned Cletrac tractor back to the Bay of Whales for use in loading supplies for the homeward trip.

Whatever social crises might have dogged the expedition while most of the men waited for the ships was forestalled by Antarctica's sudden benignity. The ice pack proved no problem for *Bear,* and only a temporary one for *Ruppert* and its new captain, Gjertsen, who had replaced the disgraced Verleger. At midmorning on January 19, 1935, *Bear* steamed around the point and into the bay; *Ruppert* arrived a week later. The next ten days were filled with hectic loading of men and supplies (including the Ford trimotor in which Byrd had flown to the pole in 1929 but could not bring back from BAE I). *Ruppert* proved spacious enough to carry all the dismantled aircraft, the entire complement of dogs, the four cows, and two of the three invaluable Citroëns. Only one of the Citroëns (Car no. 2) and the Cletrac had to be left behind. Some men willingly went three days without sleep to get everyone and everything aboard. The always unstable ice conditions in and at the mouth of the bay hampered loading and maneuvering, at one point threatening to trap *Ruppert.* But everything essential had been loaded by the afternoon of February 5, and when *Bear*'s captain suggested that they "go back and try to get the rest of the things," Byrd said no; BAE II had pushed its luck long enough: "Let's shove off." The ships quickly steamed away, and Little America II lay alone and abandoned in the deepening gloom of an Antarctic autumn. Stopping briefly to pick up twenty-five penguins at Discovery Inlet, the vessels set course for Dunedin in dense fog but through scattered ice. Byrd "drew a measure of happiness" from the departure. He was once more leaving Antarctica without having lost a man.[73]

Despite its many follies, BAE II proved as successful as its predecessor. Although heavy drinking doubtless compromised safety and June's rebelliousness added to the natural tensions of an Antarctic winter camp, the scientists nonetheless carried on their work with dedication and discipline. Throughout the polar night—and, indeed, during the two austral summers that BAE II spent on the ice—men tended their instruments, made their daily observations, and spent long hours in labs and observatories, teasing out nature's many South Polar secrets. Despite the irritations that could erupt into sudden anger, despite the loneliness and sense of isolation, there was, for most, great fun and deep pleasure in it all.

In July 1939 Poulter published an article in the *Scientific Monthly* titled "The Scientific Work of the Second Byrd Antarctic Expedition" that summarized research and key findings in oceanography, cosmic ray studies, glaciology, ornithology (including "one hundred and seventeen skins, chiefly of the larger oceanic birds"); the "examination of various bacteria, plankton, mosses, and algae collected in Antarctica"; meteorology and astronomy; terrestrial magnetism, geophysics; geology; and, not least, the study of radio communications to and from this most remote and hostile corner of the earth. Poulter added a bibliography of some seventy articles and papers that had emerged from BAE II in the four years since its close. He also included a number of photos showing the expedition's several well-equipped labs and observation posts.[74]

All of this resulted from the initiative of one man—Richard Byrd. On two occasions, using his own intelligence, wit, borrowed finances, and talents, Byrd created, equipped, transported, and ran large, sophisticated scientific stations on the edge of the South Polar wilderness thousands of miles from anywhere. June's contentions notwithstanding, the purpose and basis of those stations *was* the advancement of earth science and research. Byrd not only raised the money to support these enterprises but also made the decisions regarding who would go south with him, and thus what kind of work would be done. He may have been a "daredevil adventurer" in the public mind, but he was also dedicated and committed to science. Although his interests centered around aviation, navigation, and communications, he was bright enough to appreciate in the most general terms much of the scientific inquiry of his day. In his two private expeditions, Dick Byrd and his "boys" materially advanced both polar and earth science, a substantial achievement in human inquiry that built upon the foundations laid by Scott, Mawson, and others of the pioneering Antarctic generation. Byrd's scientists confirmed the orientation of the expedition and justified their leader's faith in picking and supporting them. Whatever character weaknesses emerged during the long winter night at Little America II were effaced by the sheer amount of good fieldwork accomplished over a period of a little more than one hundred days. Even Byrd himself could take a measure of satisfaction from the sojourn at Advance Base. If he had inexcusably jeopardized the expedition by removing himself so dramatically and foolishly from it, his daily observations constituted the first coherent record of the weather of interior Antarctica. In the end, he proved as dedicated a scientist as any of his colleagues. But as he headed north toward home, he doubtless entertained other, and in his mind loftier, thoughts.

Chapter 13

Stumbling

He was never the same again, though he stayed firmly fixed in the public mind to the end of his days.

There were no ticker-tape parades when he returned this time; 1935 America was too impoverished for lavish spectacle. Although his old friend the president greeted him personally at dockside, Richard, always slender, now looked dangerously thin as he tottered down *Ruppert*'s gangplank at the Washington Navy Yard. Asked by a reporter about his next trip south, the admiral replied, "I won't talk about going back now. I've got enough of it for awhile."[1]

His health would remain poor for several years. Some months after his return, he took the family to Latty Cove, and Harry begged his younger brother to either write or ask Marie to do so about "how you are." Richard replied shortly that he was "making some progress" in getting rest, "but am still harassed with a thousand and one things."[2] But millions still loved him, and he needed both their money and their applause. Barely pausing to recuperate, he let the remorseless tasks of book writing, filmmaking, and lecturing engulf him once more, for the inevitable expedition debts had to be whittled down if not paid off entirely, and there was always the comfortable lifestyle to be maintained. Richard returned to the lecture circuit in September 1935 for a tour that would not end until the following May. At one point, he broke off to participate in the seventy-six-minute film about BAE II that Paramount Pictures rushed to completion. The studio hyped it shamelessly: "This Was a Voyage of Death . . . In All Nature There Was Nothing Like It! The Ice Swallowed the Land . . . But American Courage Returned It to the World . . . Admiral Richard E. Byrd Presents His Thrilling Adventure Film DIS-COVERY as Mighty in Its Glory as America Itself. SEE Killer Whales the White

Nightmare! The GREAT ALONE ON A DEAD PLANET The Devil's Playground! A Lost World. The Furies! Antarctica!" If Richard was embarrassed by the hoopla, he never let on. Instead, he complained to Harry that "I have had to work much too hard." He strove "with all that is in me to simplify my living."[3] It was a theme that he would set forth with increasing urgency and poignancy over the coming years, but "simplicity" would always elude him.

By early December he had given 120 talks; most went well. "People are apparently as interested as they were in 1930. I am talking to as many people as I did in the boom time." Richard was pleased that his brother liked *Discovery*, the hastily compiled account of the recent expedition. "Now that the book and the geographical article are out of the way, I will be able to lead a more normal life." "I continue to hear the finest possible things about your lecture, your moving pictures and your book," Harry replied.[4] By the end of Richard's second lecture tour early in 1937, *Time* magazine reported that "the Admiral, who, while changing trains in his blue uniform has sometimes been mistaken for a porter or stationmaster, will have told 1,250,000 people in 250 cities about the South Pole.[5]

Richard needed good and reliable friends more than ever, and his appreciation of his informal West Coast agent, Robert Breyer, steadily deepened. "Bonnie" not only kept an eye on former expedition members such as George Noville, who continued to have a drinking problem, but also introduced himself to Lincoln Ellsworth when the explorer came to Los Angeles. "You will remember our conversation with Bernt Balchen at the California Club and Wilkins' statements abut our expedition not cooperating?" Breyer wrote proprietarily at one point. "Thought there might be some thought of this in Ellsworth's mind and I want to do everything to dissipate this because I realize your friendship for him." Richard was delighted with Bonnie's tactful handling of the situation, but not with Balchen—or June. In early April 1936 he wrote Harry, thanking his brother for acting on behalf of Ashley McKinley who "flew to the pole with me and made all the other flights. I think a lot of him and want to do anything for him that is within my power." Balchen who also "flew to the pole with me has been quite selfish about things and now June is pretty well off the track." Normally loyal to his men to a fault, Richard may have discovered June's openly expressed skepticism back in 1934 about rescuing him in the midst of the South Polar night. The apostasy of men like June and Balchen was all the more reason, Richard added, to keep friendships with those like McKinley who had been "so absolutely loyal to me through thick and thin."[6] Richard's dark mood was surely due, in part, to poor health. He would not quit lecturing; a series of short forays into the South and Midwest that spring left him at one point "down and out for ten days." When the ordeal at last ended he complained to Harry that the pace had been "so fast and furious I wasn't able to keep up with matters," and told cousin Harold that he was "mighty glad" the "very strenuous tour" was at last behind him.[7]

But the lectures continued to be a lucrative source of income for the chronically strapped explorer. For the 1935–1936 season he charged 60 percent of the box-office gross, with a fifteen hundred–dollar guarantee. For a one-day stand in Los Angeles, in 1935, he was paid sixty-one hundred dollars, and his estimated net earnings for the entire tour came to nearly two hundred thousand. The Hollywood films that dramatized his South Polar adventures always did well, and the titans of industry still loved him. But as the Great Depression continued to grip the nation, power flowed steadily away from commerce toward politics, away from Wall Street and Manhattan's executive suites and into the offices and bureaucratic warrens 240 miles south in Washington, D.C., where "hard-boiled" government officials and military people paid scant if any attention to Richard Byrd. If the cheering had not stopped, it had become muffled.

Then, late in the spring of 1936, the admiral's admirers in the business community suddenly lifted his heart. "The great industries of the country that contributed material to my expedition are giving me an enormous dinner on June 5th," he told Harold. Nearly fifteen hundred organizations were sponsoring the banquet, Byrd continued, which "puts the stamp of approval on my expedition by the great group of the country that bears the burden of the country."[8]

Tom Watson of IBM arranged it. He had contributed more than twenty thousand dollars to BAE II on the condition that Byrd take to the ice IBM's first "Radiotype Equipment" that, as described, was clearly an initial version of what would soon come to be known in America as a teletype machine. A tangled skein of scheduling, technical, and legal problems prevented the gadget from being effectively employed, but Watson remained grateful for Dick Byrd's strenuous efforts to have it tested at the end of the expedition.[9]

Dick had been good to his new friend, thanking Watson effusively for his support of BAE II and writing acquaintances in England, including the Duchess of Westminster and General Sir Alex Gedley, asking them to provide the businessman and his daughter with "some hospitality." Moreover, he had concluded that the president of IBM was "one of the greatest minds in the country." Now Watson would repay the favor in full. The man conformed perfectly to Byrd's concept of a great American—a driven social climber and creative businessman determined to leave his mark on the world. Watson had begun his adulthood with the fledgling National Cash Register Company back in 1895 when the country was in its last great depression. Fired nearly twenty years later, he promptly founded the Computing-Tabulating-Recording Corporation in April 1914 and proved to be an effective and ruthless competitor. In the early thirties, with International Business Machines well under way, Watson and his wife moved to New York City from their home in the suburbs and immersed themselves in society. Their son recalled that "during the social season from October to May, their lives became a regular round-robin: Monday night at the opera with a few other couples, maybe two dinner parties and a charity banquet during the week, and then, every few weeks, an IBM dinner. Father wanted to know everyone important in New York, and eventually he succeeded."

Watson bulldozed his way to the presidency of the city's Merchants' Association "and began socializing with people like John D. Rockefeller, Jr. and Henry Luce." He also joined the Explorers Club and so came to cultivate not only Richard Byrd but also Lowell Thomas, the famed radio personality, newsman, and international adventurer. Watson was a compulsive award gatherer as well, accumulating honorary degrees from modest academic institutions in California, New England, France, Canada, Belgium, and even Peru.[10]

It is not difficult to see why Watson was attracted to Byrd. Like so many others the businessman was impressed by the explorer's ability to organize and manage big private enterprises; to take them to the farthest, most bitterly hostile corners of the earth with no loss of life; and with skillfully managed publicity to turn each endeavor into an unqualified, heroic success.

Yet there was something more—and less—to Watson. The man was a committed internationalist, but for reasons that have been interpreted as sinisterly self-interested. Trustee of the Carnegie Endowment and member of the Foreign Policy Association and the Council on Foreign Relations, Watson became "the most determined business advocate" of Secretary of State Cordell Hull's trade reciprocity program and FDR's New Deal. Prominently identified with Coolidge- and Hoover-style conservatism during the twenties, Watson was, by 1935–1936, "Roosevelt's favorite spokesman in the industrial and financial communities."[11] At the same time he was cozying up to Adolf Hitler to advance IBM's interests abroad.

Watson put together an impressive committee to organize the Byrd banquet. The presidents of Armour and Company, Coca-Cola, General Foods, and the *New York Sun* agreed to serve, as did Edsel Ford, Walter Chrysler, William Horlick, Walter Kohler, Jacob Ruppert, and the already legendary Alfred P. Sloan of General Motors. Most of these men had steadfastly supported Byrd's expeditions from the prosperous twenties onward. Myron C. Taylor, president of United States Steel, agreed to serve on the banquet committee, as did Owen Young, head of General Electric. Young John Rockefeller was also a member, along with Arthur Hays Sulzberger of the *New York Times*. On May 29 Watson tendered Byrd a preliminary luncheon at New York's Waldorf-Astoria Hotel that was attended by most of the organization committee as well as others who had supported the admiral over the years. Nicholas Murray Butler, the brilliant, opinionated, and erratic president of Columbia University and a leading figure in the American peace movement, was also present. Director of the Carnegie Endowment, he had recently established the National Peace Conference and was widely considered "the most influential conservative internationalist of his time." He was also a firm Republican who stood bitterly opposed to the New Deal.[12]

Shortly before the luncheon Byrd wrote Watson that he was thinking seriously whether or not to announce his future plans at the June 5 dinner. His doctors had ordered the explorer "to get rested up," but thereafter, Byrd said, he was keen "to devote the rest of my life to international coordination of effort and friendship." He would return to exploration for two years "sometime in the future." But from now on his life of adventure would be subordinate to philanthropy. "For years I have been interested in this matter" of world peace, he continued, "in fact ever since I was a boy, and I have received considerable encouragement from some great industrialists and men like Mr. Rockefeller."

Clearly, the time seemed ripe for some sort of general peace initiative. The revised version of the First World War, depicting the former crusade of nations and alliances as in fact a ghastly blunder and meaningless bloodletting, had taken deep root in the public minds on both sides of the Atlantic. After 1936 no one could doubt that Hitler and Mussolini, whether separately (as seemed likely prior to 1938) or in tandem, were militarizing and brutalizing their peoples and that another "Great War" on the scale of 1914–1918 or even larger was in the offing. Sophisticated observers, including Richard Byrd, also understood the menace of Japan. Men and women of goodwill across the entire spectrum of the peace movement sought with ever growing urgency for an effective farewell to arms, but none seemed to exist.[13]

Byrd had first revealed his interest to Rockefeller on Astor's yacht back in 1926. But Japan's invasion of Manchuria five years later sealed his commitment. Toward the end of February 1932, as Japan completed a conquest that then as now was widely perceived as inaugurating a second world war, Rockefeller wrote Byrd, "This Oriental situation is distressing in the extreme, is it not? What the outcome will be one finds it difficult to prophesy. There ought to be some way of settling conditions of this kind, other than the terrible method now being employed. Whoever can point out that way and get it adopted will be rendering to civilization perhaps the greatest service that any individual could possibly render." Byrd replied a week later from Indiana, where he was lecturing in preparation for BAE II. "The situation in the Orient has crystallized to a degree my thoughts about international amity. I am more anxious than ever to get the job I have started thoroughly finished so that I can devote my energies to the matters which you know I am so interested in." When Byrd met Butler at the luncheon in late May 1936, "he was obviously and profoundly impressed by" an influential public figure "whose internationalism he took as a model for his own."[14]

Watson's banquet was the apex of Dick Byrd's public life as a professional hero. That warm New York late-spring evening, limousines deposited America's industrial, scientific, professional, educational, and cultural elite and their gowned, coiffed, and jeweled ladies to gather as a brightly chatting crowd in the Grand Ballroom of the Waldorf-Astoria Hotel, ready to toast the great Antarctic explorer. Young Rockefeller was present, of course, as were Edsel Ford, Chrysler, and Sloan. Jacob Ruppert, whose New York Yankees would win another World Series that autumn with a youngster named Joe DiMaggio, shared the dais with the admiral and these worthies along with Owen Young of General Electric, Myron Taylor of United States Steel, and Walter Kohler, the Wisconsin kitchen and bath manufacturer. Down on the floor among several hundred other invited guests sat George Abbott, the Broadway impresario, at table 32; Mr. and Mrs. Lee Eastman of Eastman Kodak Company at table 10; and boxer Gene Tunney at table 2. Marie and young Richard were at table 3.

After the crowd devoured chilled honeydew melon with limes, *comsommé double viveur au legumes,* cold filet of Kennebec salmon Romanoff ("well decorated in jelly"), breast of chicken *en casserole,* and various other delights, concluding with frozen bombe Andalouse and petits fours, Dr. William Mather Lewis, president of Lafayette College and a leading after-dinner speaker, rose to deliver the keynote address, after which Colonel Henry Breckinridge, Woodrow Wilson's undersecretary of war and now attorney and adviser to Charles Lindbergh, presented Byrd with a medallion. Lewis's remarks are lost to the record, but the medallion was reproduced in the handsome program. One side depicted a long-haired, fur- and boot-clad admiral by his crude radio at Advance Base. On the back was a dedication to "Dick Byrd. Gallant Gentleman" who, "due to a combination of unforeseen circumstances," shouldered "the duty, as he saw it to keep, Alone, a six months vigil for meteorological observation at the world's southernmost outpost. Before the middle of the long Antarctic night he was stricken desperately ill" but "chose to deliberately die rather than tap out an s.o.s. on his radio" and "further squandered" chances at survival by hand-cranking his set to "keep his schedule and report 'All's well' to Little America," lest his comrades suspect the truth. "For months of the bitterest average cold ever endured he hung precariously on the edge of the abyss, untold suffering did not compel him to alter his decision. By a miracle he was spared."

In his response, Byrd managed to surpass such colossal puffery. He told the enraptured audience and an enthralled media that he was turning his life around. He was done, through, finished, with polar exploration for the foreseeable future. His ordeal at Advance Base had seen to that. "Much of the time during the dark months and sleepless hours when I lay on the edge of life" in "the shadow of the South Pole . . . I could not read, so that thought was my only companion." He recorded his musings in a diary, and proceeded to read excerpts to the audience.

He discovered that he had to take charge of his dimming, poisoned mind or it would take charge of him, and out of his ordeal came "the crystallization of plans" that he had long pondered. Despite his agony he forced his thoughts toward "an unprejudiced mental picture of civilization" that he had first presented to the French press nearly a decade before. The great nations of the world, steeped in fear, folly, antagonisms, and reprisals, were "20,000 years behind the individual civilized citizen in his conduct toward his neighbor. . . . In fact, international relations are often highly primitive." When he left for the ice, Richard continued, the country was gripped by economic, social, and psychological depression. Two years later he returned to a world "that is again threatened with war. The great lesson had not been learned. I find a growing mass fear. Nations everywhere have been swept by a nightmare" and in their mutual terror were "arming to the teeth against the day when the nightmare will come true."

Byrd's own beloved science, "with so many opportunities . . . to push out the boundaries of the unknown and build fairer and better life for human beings," was being perverted "to prepare a cataclysm which will bring to final ruin all we have achieved in the last three hundred years." Even aviation, "which was a gift that would tie us together as members of the same human race in knowledge, understanding, and friendship," was being "perverted to uses that were never dreamed of." Indeed, "the threat of the airplane" formed the base of the present world terror, for aviation-become-airpower "made possible the extension of warfare to every city and hamlet of the world." What was the use of new inventions and knowledge "if they lead us only to a Dark Age? Surely there must be some way out of this blind alley into which we have driven ourselves," and he pledged to devote much of his remaining life to finding the exit. "I shall start my work for international amity, though I realize only too well that my part will be an extremely humble one, for my experience lies in far different fields."

"Hundreds of millions" must share his fears and his dream. The scourge of war had to be banished. That meant that the reactionary, anachronistic nation-state itself had to bridge the vast gulf between itself and its progressive citizens. Once true international peace was achieved, the road to a "fairer and better life" for all mankind could be built. Richard expressed great faith that people in general do not choose the wrong roads and that goodwill itself could be "an effective bond" of international union.[15]

In the days that followed, Richard was pleased, then delighted, and finally awed by the public response to his pledge. The flood of correspondence in and out of Latty Cove and Brimmer Street was so great that Richard was forced to hire an additional secretary. From Maine he wrote Rockefeller of "the hundreds of organizations I have heard from." The enormous public response was "encouraging," Richard added, "because it indicates that the great mass of the people can be organized so that they can become vocal and effective." He had made the same comments four years before in connection with the National Economy League.[16]

But the Great Depression continued to grip the nation, and power continued to flow steadily away from Richard's kind of businesspeople. It was time to cultivate others. That summer Franklin and Eleanor Roosevelt dropped by the Maine retreat for a brief visit. The president was in the midst of an intense reelection campaign, and his ultimately smashing victory over Alf Landon, "the careful Kansan," was by no means clear at the time. Whether the two men—and their wives—discussed world affairs and the need for a peace initiative is unclear, but several weeks later FDR gave a campaign speech at Chautauqua, New York, in which he both declared his opposition to war and questioned the inflexible isolationism mandated by current neutrality legislation. Shortly thereafter, the president raised a trial balloon in an interview with the well-known journalist Arthur Krock. Might world tensions be eased by a great power conference devoted to airing grievances and securing reforms?

Byrd was initially, and properly, cautious. When at the end of the year he was asked to join the Emergency Peace Campaign (EPC) being developed by the American Friends Service Committee, he wrote a nearly sycophantic letter to young Rockefeller, wondering if it was all right to do so. The EPC, Richard wrote, would be a "campaign to keep us out of a possible war . . . carried on next spring in 150 cities." He added that he was "more determined than ever to devote my time to working for peace." But two full years after his ordeal at Advance Base, "I find that I have not entirely recovered from that fume poisoning." He would require another year to mend. Rockefeller's reply was prompt but noncommittal. Three days before Christmas, Richard wrote Watson that he had signed on with Clarence Pickett "in the Emergency Peace Campaign," designed "to provide some antidote to the war fever that would strike this country in case of a general war in Europe."[17]

As Richard's remarks to Watson suggest, the "emergency peace" impulse reflected the confusion of the time. Was it designed to keep the United States out of a

European war, to mitigate the effects of such a war (should it occur) on domestic opinion, or some combination of both objectives? Or something else entirely? That incoherence together with Richard's own political naïveté doomed whatever possibilities he may have had to make a substantial contribution to both American foreign policy and public life. He plunged headlong into the vortex of late-1930s national politics with little idea of the dangers involved. As with the National Economy League he felt all that was needed to set things right were large doses of compassion and empathy administered by men and women of goodwill. "Intelligent thought put into intelligent action can solve any of the problems that are irritating the nations of Europe and Asia," he wrote to Nicholas Murray Butler the next month. "Friendly discussions around a table are infinitely more efficient than discussions with cannon, which solve nothing."

But the American peace movement was badly divided. The American Friends Service Committee was determinedly pacifist, which Richard proved in the event not to be. Left-wing radicals in the peace movement "went their own way from the beginning" and offered the admiral little in the way of interest or encouragement. Internationalists championed collective security, whose implications they seldom explored, placing them at odds with the American Friends Service Committee, which roundly rejected such a policy as justifying the use of force. The government, too, was split over the issue. Whereas Roosevelt moved generally in the direction of collective security—a political solution to the world's troubles—his secretary of state, Cordell Hull, preached the virtues of international free trade, and Eleanor Roosevelt dallied with the pacifists. Richard never clearly grasped either the subtleties or the intensity of the conflict and over the coming months and years veered erratically from one position to another without understanding how or why he antagonized those he sought to woo and serve.[18] Clearly confused by the currents swirling about him, Richard as early as the end of 1936 "begged" Henry Haskell, a prominent member of the Carnegie Endowment, to "please straighten me out" regarding the numerous and conflicting peace societies with similar names. He had been contacted by so many organizations, Richard added, "it is only natural I should get balled up."[19]

His one clear directive came from Eleanor Roosevelt, who late in 1936 publicly invited him to help inaugurate the No Foreign War Crusade. He had no choice but to accept. Eleanor and Franklin were old friends, and through them, as no one else, he could exercise his yearned-for influence over public opinion. He never seems to have realized that the nation's first couple were often deeply divided over public policy and that the doughty Eleanor matched her husband in fighting ability; unlike Franklin, however, she wielded no legal powers. On April 6, 1937, the twentieth anniversary of Woodrow Wilson's signature of the joint congressional declaration of war, Richard and Marie Byrd went to the White House, where that evening the nation's first lady and most glamorous admiral spoke to a national radio audience on behalf of peace.

Richard declared that "the most important piece of unfinished business" from the war was the establishment of an "effective international organization" that could suppress future conflicts. He reiterated his by now well-known belief that technology had so shrunk the world that no nation or group of nations could afford to pursue a policy of isolationism. Those preaching such a policy were at best "misguided idealists." Each and every country had the right to protest the waging of war anywhere in the world. The No Foreign War Crusade would provide the antidote to the swelling war fever of the time. "The serum to be used is education which this month will be carried on in thousands of cities of this country."

The crusade was but one of two elements of the Emergency Peace Campaign. The other object of the campaign, Byrd declared, was "to try to call a halt on the great armaments race." Once again Byrd pointed to the evils inherent in human flight. "Airplanes, which I had hoped would be the instruments of good-will, have become flying cannons of destruction, utilized only too often to kill the sick and the women and children." Twenty days later, the Nazi bombing of Guernica would provide a haunting punctuation to Byrd's assertion. Richard closed with the reminder that "the intolerance of the world is contrary to the teachings of Christ," and he appealed particularly to the women in his audience, "who really bear the brunt of war and its sorrow," and to the young people upon whom the burden of conflict would fall to take up the cause of peace. "Is it not high time for the great masses of the people of the world who suffer in war to rise up in righteous wrath and demand that nations stop their quarreling?"[20]

The speech attracted wide attention, and had Richard left matters there his ancient friendship with Franklin Roosevelt would probably have remained intact. But sixteen days after the speech, he was lured into a blunder from which he never recovered.

The next big event on the EPC calendar was to be a "great mass meeting" on April 22 at Convention Hall in Philadelphia. Sometime in the interim, O. K. Armstrong, a leading pacifist, called Henry Haskell at the Carnegie Endowment "to discuss the admiral's forthcoming speech." Armstrong "deduced" that both Haskell and Nicholas Murray Butler, two staunch internationalists, could support the notion "that a national referendum should be required before the United States could go to war." Somehow, the Admiral of the Antarctic was persuaded to support the idea, clearly missing or ignoring its profoundly disturbing implications. Perhaps yet another lavish, nationally broadcast testimonial dinner on his behalf at the Explorers Club in New York just two days before his Philadelphia speech distracted him. Buoyed by praise and his steady fame, Byrd in his remarks at Philadelphia "went the whole way to endorse the war referendum proposal."

FDR promptly cut him off. The proposal, which soon made its way to Congress in the form of the Ludlow Amendment, represented a blatant assault on executive power—and, indeed, of legislative prerogatives as well—in the field of foreign policy making. It is difficult to imagine that the amendment (which in early 1938 failed by but a single vote in House committee) would have been upheld even by the anti-FDR Supreme Court. Byrd should have recognized this immediately. The man had been in and around the Washington political scene for twenty years. According to one close student of the EPC, Byrd had no idea that he would alienate the internationalists. These sophisticates immediately realized, however, that "plebiscites," such as the war referendum proposal, had become "the 'ready tool[s]' of dictators." The reaction of the internationalist community to his Philadelphia speech "came as a terrible shock" to the admiral. It should not have. In addition to its profound domestic implications, the war referendum proposal would have destroyed any possibility of U.S. participation in any current or future collective-security arrangement. Richard scrambled to undo the damage, pleading with Haskell for an explanation of the problem and for some guidance in dealing with the wave of invitations he received to speak to peace societies "whose positions he did not know." Byrd also "promptly terminated" his relationship with Armstrong.[21]

The admiral was able to repair relations with Butler and some of the other internationalists, but he never won back his president. In fact, he soon compounded the Philadelphia blunder by appearing as an errand boy for Tom Watson. While in Washington Byrd was approached by an IBM vice president "in connection with talking to President Roosevelt about getting permission to use a certain short wave." Byrd proved amenable, and the company promptly set to work "with care and thoroughness," as Watson's assistant soon wrote the admiral, "so that when you are pleased to extend your help to us, you will be armed with a fully substantiated story." Watson had already provided Byrd with a large check to cover all expenses for a European peace mission. Richard returned the money in a "Dear Tom" letter in early June in which he told the industrialist that after "doing considerable studying" and holding many discussions "(which have been very illuminating)" with the president, Hull, Butler, and others, "I was given some confidential information which caused me to conclude that it was better to delay my trip" for at least a month, perhaps longer. But "confidentially" he informed Watson that "I am planning a very interesting good-will flight which includes Germany, Japan, and Italy."[22]

A month later, having accumulated and digested the materials that IBM sent along, Richard at last approached FDR. But a covering letter to Eleanor conveyed his sense of isolation and distress. Both she and Franklin had encouraged him to contact them both directly "instead of through the various offices." But "I find it impossible to phone him or see him," Richard continued. "Those who surround him invariably say he is too busy." A tone of self-pity crept into the letter: "Please don't concern yourself with this," he assured Eleanor. "It is not my object to complain. I am puzzled but I guess the answer is that what I have tried to do is of no importance." Still, Richard was clearly hurt. The last several times he had tried to see "Franklin I could not avoid the feeling that I was not only intruding, but making a nuisance of myself." Perhaps it was time to give up "peace work." But he had decided "that as long as you stick with me I will keep going." With FDR unavailable, Byrd had turned to Cordell Hull, who "has been very splendid and had given me all the time I need to insure my not advocating any foolish peace plans that might handicap the efforts of the Administration." He had recently been to Grand Rapids where he had addressed "10,000 young people." Had Eleanor seen the speech? And "I am getting some encouragement from other countries. Last month there was formed in France the Byrd Foundation, the purpose of which is to strive for peace in Europe. . . . I have received resolutions offering support from countries as far away as Australia."

It would take "very hard work and a very long time for me, in my unofficial capacity, to be able to accomplish the slightest effective thing for peace." Was he suggesting that the White House make him a roving ambassador or bestow some sort of official position to promote his peace efforts? Eleanor was left to wonder, for her friend immediately veered into his request for Tom Watson. Since Richard could not get Watson's request into "Franklin's" hands, could Eleanor do it for him?

In his letter to FDR, Richard urged the president to allocate one shortwave radio band to Watson "that he needs for the establishment of his international broadcasts." Richard implied that the contents of those broadcasts would promote international peace and goodwill, and in a confidential aside to Eleanor he had noted "some opposition in Congress and elsewhere about certain wave lengths being used by the Administration." But "should Watson have one of these wave lengths, he could say, unofficially, a great many things, it would not be possible to say officially." Watson was no "fair weather friend and supporter of the Administration," Richard assured FDR. The admiral had recently spent much time with the industrialist (who was traveling in Europe, including Nazi Germany, at the time) and had been impressed once more by the man's "courage of his convictions and his sympathies." Moreover, Watson "doesn't hold his punch because there may be those present who don't agree with him." "I have a very wide acquaintance in this country," Richard reminded Roosevelt in conclusion, "and I know of no one who, from the standpoint of unselfishness and the big outlook, can handle this international radio station as effectively as could Mr. Watson."[23]

When the letter at last reached his desk sometime in early August, Roosevelt could only have been stunned once again by his friend's artless approach to politics. Granting the newly elected president of the International Chamber of Commerce (ICC) his own powerful shortwave radio station would have been a stunning giveaway of governmental power. And Watson by this time was involved in some very dubious activities on behalf of Nazi Germany. Invoking his power and prestige as incoming president of the International Chamber of Commerce, Watson arranged to have the 1937 ICC conference—"the world's commercial summit"—meet in Berlin. "Working with [Joseph] Goebbels as stage manager, Watson would make" the conference "a commercial homage to Germany. Hitler, in turn, would make that event a national homage to Thomas Watson." The führer bestowed upon the president of IBM the "Merit Cross of the German Eagle with Star," a specially created honor to "'foreign nationals who made themselves deserving of the German Reich.'" The award "ranked second in prestige only to Hitler's German Grand Cross." According to one bitter critic, "Thomas Watson was more than just a businessman selling boxes to the Third Reich. For his Promethean gift of punch card technology . . . enabled the Reich to achieve undreamed of efficiencies both in its rearmament program and its war against the Jews."[24] Although this sweeping indictment may or may not stand the test of rigorous scholarly inquiry, Byrd's close identification with Watson at a time when the businessman's moral sensitivities were at best blunted was not wise.

Indeed, Richard's affiliation with the nation's unpopular business elite had become so pronounced by the summer of 1937 as to seriously compromise his public influence and his insistence that he represented no special interests or interest groups. Not only had he fallen into Watson's orbit, but he also continued to embrace Edsel Ford as well. The first six months of 1937 were the seedtime of labor militancy, as walkouts and sit-down strikes struck every corner of industrial America. Ford Motor Company, "with [its] ugly crew of strikebreaking hoodlums," led a handful of stubborn corporate holdouts, most concentrated in the steel and meatpacking industries. Kohler Industries, which provided key support for all of Byrd's private and semiprivate expeditions, would remain unorganized for decades.

Throughout the spring and summer, as labor unrest swept the country, Henry Ford and his son remained defiant, sending the company goons out to enforce discipline at all Ford plants. Edsel partially broke under the strain and rushed away from Detroit for weeks of rest and recuperation. He found both at Latty Cove. "Edsel came up here completely worn out," Richard told cousin Harold in Texas. "You know what he and his father are going through with the labor situation."

With Byrd's affiliations visible to all, Roosevelt felt no impulse to rush a reply to his request that Watson be granted his own personal radio band. When the president finally responded, "he did not commit himself," Byrd told Watson, "though he is much interested in this whole radio idea." Since Watson was not returning from Europe until November, the two men agreed that the matter should not be pressed until then; it was never revived.[25]

Rebuffed by FDR, uncertain of Eleanor's support, and instinctively comfortable with the most conservative, if not reactionary, business interests in the country, Richard cast about for new ways to fund his work. He quickly settled on the idea of his own personal organization. He told Watson that he needed a "group of prominent men behind me . . . some of my best friends who are leaders in industry," adding that he "sincerely and earnestly" hoped Watson would head it. "I would suggest some such title as Byrd Associates organized to help me in my work for the advancement of science and a better international organization." Byrd reminded his friend that he had gotten Charles Evans Hughes to head a similarly titled group back in 1927 "to help me in my work for the advancement of science and aviation. This group disbanded at my own request after Mr. Hughes became Chief Justice" of the Supreme Court. The committee should include Rockefeller, Ford, Clarence Francis (president of General Foods), Owen Young of General Electric, and others unmentioned. If Watson was too busy to help, Richard concluded, he would fully understand.[26]

The admiral quickly stumbled on a way to keep Watson in his debt. Three days later he informed the industrialist that while in Washington, "I learned of a movement to have the I.B.M. investigated by Congress" for price gouging federal agencies "in connection with the enormous rental costs of machines." Richard expressed pious horror. "This sort of thing is outrageous. To investigate a concern that is one hundred per cent. ethical in every way is absolutely unfair." Richard assured his friend that "the investigation has been temporarily stopped by a friend of mine," presumably brother Harry or one of his allies. "I hesitated to bother you with this while you were in Europe," Richard added, "but I have finally concluded that you would want to know what is going on." Watson most certainly did. He put his vice president and general manager, F. L. Nichol, on the matter immediately. Nichol contacted Byrd, got the particulars, and got to work squelching the inquiry.

Six weeks later, Watson wrote Byrd from the ICC conference in Berlin about the admiral's personal peace organization. "I cannot tell you how much I appreciate your interest and help in this matter and I believe that if it goes through, a small, carefully selected group can do a world job that will be worthwhile." Watson found Nazi Germany "a delightful country," filled with "interesting people from different parts of the world." FDR's mother was spending time at the hotel, which "keeps the American flag flying daily in her honor." The thoughtful gesture "gives the place a touch of the United States."[27]

Byrd continued to cultivate Cordell Hull, whose idea of world peace through world trade many American industrialists—Watson included—found most congenial. In mid-June Richard went to the State Department for daylong talks with the secretary "and some of his specialists in international matters." Byrd discovered that "the department seems much interested in the Antarctic situation." So was he. Several days before his visit with Hull, Richard asked brother Harry to have his "assistant look into the matter of making a formal claim for the land I discovered and claimed in Antarctica. Something really should be done about this," he added. "It's a great pity if it isn't." At the bottom of the letter, Richard scrawled, "Since writing this I note the British are bringing up the matter of their claim." When Richard finished speaking with Hull, the secretary insisted that he also talk with counselor R. Walton Moore, who had taken the lead in defining U.S. policy in the South Polar region. Later Richard told brother Harry that "I recommended to the Secretary of State, and very strongly to" Moore, "that we claim the areas east of the 150th meridian that we discovered and mapped. There cannot possibly be any controversy because no English expedition has been in that part of Antarctica. I am beginning to think that it is very important that we claim this territory," Richard continued, "and it is only fair to me, after all my work, that the government do so." Tired, semi-ill, and distracted as Byrd was, Antarctica was beginning to exert its pull once more. Writing to cousin Harold some weeks later, he stressed how hard he had worked that summer at Latty Cove, then scrawled a postscript: "Will probably go to the Antarctic again next year."[28]

By this time, after the inevitable stresses and uncertainties inherent in creating a new organization, Byrd Associates had come into existence with an impressive cast of business and political figures. Carter Glass, Virginia's venerable senior senator, was chairman. The Advisory Council comprised Nicholas Murray Butler, Herbert Hoover, Arthur Sulzberger of the *New York Times,* former secretary of state (and future secretary of war) Henry L. Stimson, Admiral Cary Grayson (Woodrow Wilson's former physician and now chairman of the American Red Cross), and Watson. The Steering Committee included Clarence Francis of General Foods and eight other men and women of somewhat lesser prestige but no lesser importance.[29]

In October 1937, Richard published in the *Christian Herald* the speech he had delivered the previous July to the Christian Endeavor Convention in Grand Rapids. The article demonstrated how completely he had absorbed the hard lessons of the previous spring. There was no mention of a war referendum. He sneered equally at the "peace-at-any-price" groups and the "adamants" who clung rigidly to one formula. There was no one formula for world peace, he asserted, beyond "the one Christ gave us," and no one was paying attention to the Savior at this stage in international history. Global harmony, Richard concluded, "must be striven for, as I have said, on a thousand fronts." Somehow, in some way, the effort would yield the result. Richard also drafted an article sharply opposing the idea of a war referendum. Adopting the internationalists' position, he claimed that such a "plebiscite" could be too often turned to sinister uses, whereas modern warfare was such that hostilities could mushroom to catastrophic proportions within hours, rendering the cumbersome referendum process not only moot but dangerous as well. For some reason the article was never published.[30]

Byrd Associates got off to a rousing start, with membership on the Advisory Council and Steering Committees attracting wide and favorable notice. "I do not know of *anyone, anywhere* who could possibly get this group with their very divergent political views, together on the same enterprise and at the same time get them to work cooperatively," Breyer wrote from Los Angeles. He was naive. Byrd's business and political "associates" all favored Hull's reciprocal trade program that also attracted a substantial body of supporters within the peace movement; all were Republicans with the exception of the staunchly conservative Virginia Democrat Carter Glass. As 1938 began, Byrd continued to pick up various awards for international cooperation, while Watson himself took to the national airways on behalf of the associates to preach Cordell Hull's gospel of world peace through world trade.[31]

There proved little for Richard to do. Individual members of Byrd Associates kept the organization in the public eye. In January Watson invited Butler to help open IBM's new corporate headquarters in a lavish ceremony that attracted wide public attention. In April the Foreign Policy Association teamed with the National Peace Conference to publish a pamphlet titled *The Hull Trade Program and the American System* by Raymond Buell, who was also identified with the Byrd group. The previous month Hull and the by now familiar "committee of educators, scientists, publishers, and cultural leaders" feted Byrd again at a testimonial dinner in Atlantic City. Finally, in May, Pierre Benazet, the French senator and head of the Byrd Foundation in Paris, "proclaimed triumphantly . . . that he had established the Universal Union for International Law and Safeguarding Peace at the Hague."[32]

Back in December Richard had informed Harry that he had sold all his stocks "and have no income." Therefore, "I must cut my expenses as drastically as possible," which meant that "I will have to discontinue my payments to the Byrds. . . . Let's see if the other Byrds can't help for awhile," Richard added. In a postscript he railed against his federal income tax burdens, some of which he clearly believed were of a dubious nature and all of which were ruining him. "They have been after me just as they were after you," he told his brother. "If I am able to lick them in the Courts, it will cost me a whole lot." Surely, Harry could understand why Richard had cut expenses "ruthlessly and drastically" until he could regain financial equilibrium. In fact, Richard had not sold all his stock, for in April 1938 he and Breyer exchanged correspondence in which Byrd asked if "it would be humanly possible to sell my stock" in light of "some very bad losses recently." Richard had already turned to wealthy friends for money. Replying in early May to the receipt of a five hundred–dollar check from Watson, he wrote, "This is the third time you have come to my assistance in a time of emergency." It would not happen again, Richard assured the businessman; Watson had already done too much on his behalf.[33]

At this moment of apparent crisis, Richard, by a stroke of good fortune, expanded his property holdings in Maine dramatically. There had been increasing trouble at Latty Cove over the past several years, with people breaking into the cabins and looking through closets and bureau drawers. The place was simply too accessible both by land and by water. In early 1938 Marie stumbled onto "Wickyup," a large property on the mainland near East Sullivan that lay at the end of two miles of dirt road. The "camp," which consisted of a big log cabin on the edge of Tunk Lake with mountains visible from the back patio, "was practically given to our family," Bolling recalled. It had been built rather recently by a group of businessmen for their family vacations, but the Depression had killed that dream, and the place had remained unused for a number of years. Marie acquired the property complete with furnishings, rugs, curtains, silverware, and kitchen tools. Even here, the Byrds were occasionally bothered by "strangers walking around," but there were far fewer of them.

"Wickyup was our one family place where we could be a close family surrounded by the peace and quiet of nature and enjoying each other's company without the interruption . . . and curiosity of strangers," Bolling recalled. Her sister Katherine wrote their father near the end of the war that she was "dieing [*sic*]" to get some leave from her job at an army base in New York City and "go up to Wickyup. . . . That is one place I will *always* want to go to. Boy what a swell spot that is!" Distracted by Antarctic business and then the war, Richard hung on to Latty Cove until 1946, when he sold it for a modest gain on the purchase price. "Confidentially," he told a Maine acquaintance, "the taxes on it were far too high, something like 4% or 5% on the investment, which is terrific, you know." Richard thought about buying another piece of property as a replacement, but never did.[34]

Hitler's bloodless conquest of Austria in March 1938 followed by the Sudeten crisis and Munich the following autumn practically destroyed the world-peace-through-world-trade foundation upon which Byrd Associates rested, and the organization began a rapid decline. Its woes were accentuated that summer when Benazet brazenly solicited financial contributions directly from members of the association ostensibly in Richard's name. Byrd immediately disavowed the Frenchman, emphasizing, quite rightly, that he and Benazet had had very little direct contact and that the Frenchman knew few Americans and had not coordinated his efforts in Europe closely with the associates. Byrd admitted that he knew very little about the inner workings of the Paris organization that bore his name. Benazet soon disappeared from the scene in the growing war scare that gripped all Europe after Munich.[35]

Increasingly bereft of personal political influence, Richard turned to supporting and stiffening brother Harry in his bitter personal and ideological fights with Franklin Roosevelt and the New Deal. Out on the lecture circuit part of the year and at home much of it, the younger brother steadily assured his elder that he was pursuing the right course, that the president was treating him shabbily, and that support for a Harry Byrd presidential candidacy was widespread and growing. The latter was an assertion that Richard would continue to make—often vociferously—to the end of his days. "The country is headed toward ruin," Richard wrote in one typical jeremiad in mid-August. "But God knows if the masses of the people will ever realize what made that ruin. I think these contests held by various institutions regarding the President's popularity are damnable things and doing a great deal of harm." The senator, in turn, kept his younger brother supplied with articles and pamphlets explaining his various anti–New Deal positions and policies. Occasionally, he solicited Richard's advice.[36]

Antarctica, as always, was a constant companion. Richard's return to the lecture circuit in the autumn of 1936 had prompted the first of a flood of queries and requests about his next expedition. One writer in Bloomington, Illinois, claimed that during his presentation the night before, the admiral had "made a few statements that suggested he might return to the Antarctic." Hazel McKercher drafted dozens, then scores, of replies during the next two years, turning away potential applicants with variations of the same message: the admiral would not be returning to Antarctica for years, if at all.[37]

Then in the spring of 1938 Richard's attitude suddenly changed. He began responding directly to applicants, telling them that he would be going to Antarctica the following year, though "this expedition will be of much smaller scope than my previous one." Still, he hesitated. In a revealing note to Breyer he said that he was "not going to the South Pole this year because I am not entirely over the fume poisoning and because I think it is bad judgment to start out during a depression. I had a very tough time on the last expedition getting my supplies together."[38]

But Antarctica continued to preoccupy Richard in another way during that summer and autumn. He had at last succumbed to the blandishments of friends and had begun to write a book about his ordeal at Advance Base four years before. Previously, he had gotten substantial help from ghostwriters Fitzhugh Green, Howard Mingos, and especially Charles Murphy. He probably wrote none of his earlier books by himself. *Alone* was a somewhat different matter. Although Murphy wrote the published product, it emerged from "an original manuscript" that was the exclusive product of Byrd's mind and pen. The duo exchanged a series of letters throughout the summer of 1938 in which Murphy both urged and showed his colleague how to "organize your ideas and impressions." Richard worked on his own draft well into the fall. He first mentioned the project to brother Harry in mid-July. The family had just moved into Wickyup. "Down from the patio and through some pines," Bolling recalled, "Dad had a wharf which jutted out over rocks to the lake." It was there, with the help of Hazel McKercher, that "he spent many hours writing, putting the final touches on Alone." He toiled through August, telling Harry, "I am still desperately busy with my book. . . . I will be at least another month," he added, for "writing a book is not an easy job. It is much harder even than most speeches because it is a permanent record. I work every night until 1:00 o'clock including Sundays and holidays." Finally, after keeping applicants for the next enterprise at bay ("My plans are rather uncertain and I cannot say when I will start on another expedition. I could not give encouragement to any one at this time"), he informed Harry on October 17 with palpable relief: "I have finished my book and will be able now to do some other things."[39]

Alone appeared at the end of 1938 and proved to be a masterpiece wrung out of folly. Seventy years on, it stands at the apex of polar literature and remains a distinguished contribution to American letters. *Alone* became an immediate and long-lasting best-seller, reconfirming for many years to come Richard's stature as a polar hero and literary figure. For the most part, it roughly followed and lavishly amplified the notes and observations he had set down at Advance Base. The only fresh element was his profound skepticism over the role of science and the scientist. He went to Advance Base "armed with the justifications of a scientific mission," which under the dreadful blows of his illness and frigid isolation had become "a dead-end street. . . . The one aspiration I still had was to be vindicated by the tiny heap of data collected on the shelf in the Escape Tunnel. But even as I seized upon this, I recognized its flimsiness; a romanticized rationalism, as are most of the things which men are anxious to be judged by." Scientists, he concluded, "are nothing more than glamorous middlemen between theory and fact, material- ists jobbing in the substance of universal truths."[40] He included himself in that assessment.

"As you probably know better than anyone outside of my family," he told Brey- er several weeks after the book's appearance, *Alone* "is far more to me than just an- other book." He was delighted with its initial sales, as they were "far better, in fact, than I ever expected." He hoped it would "solve the public relations problem which you and I have so often discussed." When the book did not appear to be selling as well in California as he wished, Richard leaped to his typewriter and sent off several anguished notes to Breyer. Could he help stimulate sales in this way or that? What was wrong out there in Los Angeles—was his personal unpopularity crippling sales? After canvassing several stores and sellers, Breyer tried to soothe his friend. The book was doing as well in the Golden State as elsewhere, and Richard should not worry. If there was a problem, one bookseller said, it may have been due to a perceived lack of action in the book in comparison to the explorer's ear- lier tomes. The woman was a fool, Richard shot back in reply. But what about Breyer himself? Did he dislike the book? Breyer sought to mollify his friend by mailing his own freshly bought copy to Boston for Byrd's autograph.[41]

Byrd may have been politically naive, but he was no fool, and when war came in 1939 his instinctive loyalties went not to the isolationists but to those who would revise current neutrality laws by ending embargoes on arms exports to Britain and France. The awkwardly named Non-Partisan Committee for Peace through Revision of the Neutrality Law was formed as the chief lobbying group, and Byrd promptly became a member. The one man whom Dick and Harry Byrd came to mistrust above all others was Charles Lindbergh. "Lucky Lindy" had vis- ited Nazi Germany in 1937 with his wife, had been decorated by the Nazi hierar- chy, and had been shown Germany's latest frontline aircraft. Lindbergh returned deeply smitten with the apparently hyperefficient Nazi state. Critics such as play- wright Robert E. Sherwood concluded that the aviator not only was impressed with Nazi "technological achievements" but had also given up on democracy, which seemed "hopelessly inefficient" in contrast. To men like Lindbergh, fascism was the wave of the future. Harry Byrd at first thought Lindbergh shared his con- servative views and was photographed with the hero when Lindbergh came up to the Hill to testify. But Dick was suspicious of his longtime rival for public affec- tion. At the end of September 1939 he warned his brother to "consider matters very carefully before you join up in any way with Lindbergh. There are millions of people who think he is pro-Nazi and, therefore, anti-English. I cannot believe it, but that is the impression that has gotten abroad. Also he is a died-in-the-wool Republican." However, Dick added, Harry surely knew what he was doing, and in a letter three days later the elder brother insisted that he had not been taken in by Lindbergh, adding "strictly confidentially" his belief that the aviator in fact "favors the revision of the present" hyperrestrictive "neutrality laws" in order to help England and France.[42]

Three weeks later Harry had to admit he had been duped. Lindbergh's most recent speech "was a great mistake from every standpoint." Dick agreed, noting that "Lindbergh has come in for some tremendous criticism" in New England. "I cannot understand his viewpoint." But Dick reminded his older brother that his hands had been tied since early July when FDR placed him on active duty to lead the brand-new United States Antarctic Service.[43]

Chapter 14

Recovery

As Byrd's disillusion with the peace crusade deepened during the latter half of 1938, his thoughts again turned southward. Replying near the end of August to an offer of dogs for his next adventure, he admitted that "I have plans for another expedition but they are somewhat immature so that I am not in a position to tell you anything definite."[1] Another season on the ice, however, was beyond him; he no longer possessed either the physical stamina or the emotional capability to command an Antarctic winter camp. Instead, he contemplated making "a flight from the United States to Australia via Antarctica." When in the following summer his maturing plans for an aviation expedition at last coincided with government imperatives, he informed Harry that "I am going down to the Antarctic this year," but, "of course, I do not intend to spend the winter." He had already publicly committed himself to a privately sponsored endeavor "to map out, survey and claim territory definitely for the United States." But he expressed hope to lead "a government-sponsored expedition." As he told Harry, "I expect that I would be a good deal better off with several Government ships there."[2]

The United States had not sponsored an Antarctic expedition since the days of Charles Wilkes nearly a century before. But the darkening world scene prompted Washington policy makers to consider the possible strategic and economic importance of the white continent. Cruising through the Pacific equatorial islands in November 1937, Richard Black, civil engineer on BAE II and now a field representative in the Department of the Interior's Division of Territories and Island Possessions, discussed with his division director, Ernest Gruening, the possibility of a modest government expedition to the Antarctic that Black would lead. Finn

Ronne was also interested in leading a five-man party to the island archipelago off the Antarctic (then called Palmer) Peninsula from which the men would travel, presumably by dog power, down the coast to the Bay of Whales, where the ship that had dropped them off would pick them up.

Before Ronne could complete negotiations with a Norwegian whaling vessel, Black had submitted a formal memorandum to Gruening, detailing his ideas. According to one account, Gruening was aware "of certain vague requirements of the Government for an official American venture into the Antarctic regions and he became active in encouraging such an enterprise." "Before I knew what was happening," Ronne recalled, at least four federal agencies "had leaped into action and blown up my modest little plan into a much vaster Government expedition under Byrd, which duly took place."[3]

Black's initiative coincided with growing international interest in Antarctica, including, most disturbingly, the proclamation or reconfirmation of extravagant national claims. By the eve of World War II, France, Norway, and Argentina had announced sweeping rights of sovereignty to 290 degrees of the Antarctic Continent. None of these nations, however, had conducted extensive inland exploration. Nonetheless, Paris and Oslo joined the British, Australian, and New Zealand governments in 1938 to announce an agreement on "aerial rights" over the white continent, and the British ostentatiously dispatched a research vessel to study and chart South Polar waters. Following long-established policy, Washington rejected all explicit and implicit territorial claims to Antarctica, while quietly encouraging Lincoln Ellsworth to make personal claims of his own during the American aviator-explorer's last and greatest journey south. Ellsworth duly claimed an area still known as the "American Highland" on the Indian Ocean side of the continent.[4]

And then there was Adolf Hitler. Late in the autumn of 1938, Berlin stunned the international diplomatic and polar communities with the announcement that Nazi Germany was immediately dispatching an expedition to claim a large swatch of the Antarctic continent. The official motive, which limited historical research has largely confirmed, was to shoulder Germany's way into international whaling in the far southern seas. Whale sperm oil was essential not only for a variety of peacetime uses such as the production of margarine and soaps but also as a source of glycerine, "essential for explosives and precision instrument lubricants." The chief promoter of the expedition was Hermann Göring, Hitler's number-two man and director of a four-year plan designed to effect Germany's immediate economic recovery and self-sufficiency. "To guarantee future whaling rights in rich Antarctic waters, Germany needed a foothold on the southern continent," and its sailors and fliers undertook to do so with Teutonic thoroughness.

No fewer than eighty-six scientists and seamen sailed from Hamburg just before Christmas 1938 in the powerful, well-appointed, and well-stocked eighty-two hundred–ton steamer *Schwabenland.* Also on board were several highly experienced airmen from the German national airline Lufthansa, who would, in three short weeks of flying, pilot their two sturdy ten-ton Dornier Wal seaplanes over much of the Antarctic continent that lay directly south of the Atlantic Ocean between the African and South American continents. When the expedition returned to a noisy celebration in Hamburg the following April, *Schwabenland*'s skipper, Alfred Ritscher, an experienced polar explorer, claimed to have surveyed more than 230,000 square miles. Although at least one later account whittled the figure down to 135,000, the Germans had certainly explored an area nearly as large as—perhaps larger than—the state of California, returning home with more than eleven thousand mostly high-quality aerial photos to prove it. *Schwabenland* also carried five hundred–pound steel javelins with Nazi flags designed to be dropped every 15 miles during each flight. Flying over and around the spectacular mountains of the area proved so hazardous, however, that on each flight to the range the German airmen simply dumped the heavy javelins out of the plane as soon as it was out of sight of the mother ship. Still, the expedition had achieved every goal that Göring had set, including the establishment of a broad claim to coastal Antarctica, essential to the future establishment of one or more whaling stations and processing facilities. Norway was so angered that its government announced a rival claim to the region the day before *Schwabenland* reached it. Undeterred, Hitler proclaimed that area "Neue Schwabenland" and thus the first portion of a new German empire outside of Europe. Hitler's Antarctic coup became front-page news in the increasingly tense spring of 1939.[5]

Washington's hand was clearly being forced on the issue of territorial claims to Antarctica, and when Gruening approached the State Department with Black's memorandum late in 1938, he found a ready reception. The departure of the Nazi expedition provided the department with the necessary excuse to take the matter of U.S. occupancy in and claims to Antarctica straight to FDR, who instinctively turned to his old friend Dick Byrd for advice and support.

Just when Byrd became involved in plans for a government-sponsored Antarctic expedition is unclear. One source suggests the latter half of 1938; Byrd himself always claimed that he knew nothing until January 1939, when two State Department officials, Hugh Cumming and "Geographer Boggs," suddenly and secretly appeared at 9 Brimmer Street. According to Byrd they carried a letter from FDR, "suggesting that the State Department converse with me concerning claims of territory in Antarctica." Byrd ostensibly "had no idea" of any official interest in the white continent, nor did the State Department supposedly have any inkling of his slowly maturing plans for a long-range flight over the South Pole. "I told

Mr. Cumming that I would gladly abandon any undertaking if the Government needed my services." Byrd also agreed either then or very shortly thereafter to make available *Bear of Oakland,* which he had recently purchased for a nominal sum, then placed under Marie's ownership, undoubtedly for tax purposes.[6]

After the Cumming-Byrd meeting, matters moved swiftly—in fact, much too swiftly. Black was promptly summoned to Washington, where he began active planning within the Division of Territories for an expedition designed to "fly the American flag officially in the Antarctic for the first time" since Wilkes. State remained cautious, however. Officially flying the flag did not necessarily mean the making of claims. Secretary Hull subsequently wrote "that as a matter of ordinary prudence it would be inadvisable to take any positive action toward the assertion of United States sovereignty claims in the Antarctic pending an examination on the spot of the value of the areas to which the United States might possess the basis of a claim." He added primly that international law demanded "some form of occupation of the areas mentioned as a condition incident to the exercise of sovereignty over them should it be determined that such action was in the best interests of this country."[7]

Even before Black was well settled in at Interior, Byrd himself became involved in the planning and organization process, advising State on "estimated annual costs." FDR invited the admiral down for a noontime chat—undoubtedly one of those flattering "lunch-on-a-tray-with-Roosevelt-at-the-White-House" affairs that became such a symbol of in-crowd political status during the New Deal and war years. FDR told his old friend and recent thorn in the side that he wanted to establish at least two bases and, Byrd later wrote coyly, "gave several reasons for his interest in substantiating whatever claims this country had a right to make to the South Polar territory." From February to August 1939, Dick added, he gave his time, "without compensation, to the Government's contemplated project." Only then was he placed on active-duty status, but never, he claimed, did he "receive active duty pay for my services."[8]

Nonetheless, the administration did give Byrd all the help it could. Roosevelt had already directed the State, War, Navy, and Interior Departments to commence cooperative planning for the expedition. The president went so far as to suggest annual American colonization of Antarctica "at Little America and at the region South of the Cape of Good Hope." The colonies should be evacuated each austral autumn to avoid the rigors and costs of wintering over. Hull immediately invited his colleagues in the other three departments to appoint representatives to an interagency committee. Following a period of intense consultations, the four departments in late July 1939 established a formal executive committee to oversee ongoing preparations for the expedition. On November 25 FDR formalized the committee's existence and made it the directing body of the United States Antarctic Service. Five days earlier Byrd stepped aboard the small Interior Department motor ship *North Star* and headed for the Bay of Whales.[9]

Ideally, the USAS should not have sent its first ships south until the autumn of 1940; Byrd's experience had been that adequate preparation for an Antarctic expedition consumed at least eighteen months. But FDR was impatient. Europe was going to war at last, and what the future might bring was anyone's guess. Press reports surrounding extravagant Argentine claims to the South Polar region during the summer of 1939 indicated that Norway and other South Polar claimants anticipated resolving the entire issue at an international conference to be convened at Oslo the following year. No one could then guess that Norway and nearly all of western Europe would be under Nazi or Fascist boots by that time. Roosevelt was determined that Antarctic "colonization" must begin that year, which meant the ships must depart for the South no later than October or November.

For long weeks in the winter and early spring of 1939 the administration tried to keep the whole enterprise a secret. At the end of April, Paul Siple congratulated an old friend, Louis Quam, of the University of Colorado for his "ability to put two and two together. You hit the nail on the head but I don't dare admit it because at the moment everything is supposed to be confidential, even though some news did leak out as you have seen." By that time, Siple was already at the Boston Navy Yard and "tremendously rushed trying to both finish my [doctoral] Thesis and taking over this present job of equipment organization."[10]

A rather reluctant Congress passed an initial $10,000 funding bill on May 2, 1939, but as late as the end of June Siple was writing fellow BAE veteran Vernon Boyd that conditions remained decidedly unsettled. The expedition was now public knowledge. Nonetheless, "one day it looks as though everything will go through all right and the next day things are not so good, but at present there seems to be an upswing of spirit to indicate that the big Government project may go through." If by any chance it did not, Siple added, "it appears almost definite that the Admiral will try to get away in October using a large plane and the 'Bear,'"[11] presumably for a brief aerial survey of western Antarctica or perhaps for a flight across the continent to Australia. Congress at last voted a $340,000 appropriation in July that everyone recognized "was inadequate for a unilateral operation of the magnitude proposed." So the legislators agreed that the USAS should be a "combined governmental and private enterprise," which practically allowed the government to raid the "equipment and many supplies which had been assembled for" Byrd's "proposed private venture." It was tacitly, then formally, accepted that further private donations to the expedition might be made through Byrd under rigorous terms and conditions. The prize among the materials donated by Byrd himself was *Bear of Oakland,* which the navy took over and formally renamed USS *Bear.*[12]

Willing as he was to be looted, Byrd soon concluded the whole enterprise was too little and too late. Siple agreed. By late July, the admiral was "so swamped with expedition details," Siple wrote, "that he has had to delegate problems to many of us," the "us" comprising both old Antarctic colleagues and new recruits. The former Eagle Scout, now married and with a geography Ph.D. from Clark University in hand, was designated "field representative" of the expedition "and "technical supervisor of equipment." He soon began handling an incredible range of administrative, fiscal, personnel, and procurement problems with an aplomb and competence found in very few individuals, especially one barely thirty years old.

When dealing with the public, press, and fellow bureaucrats, Byrd—and his boys—could and did make a strong and effective case for national interest. Sometime in the late summer of 1939, Siple drafted a brief message regarding the expedition for Byrd to use on a national radio broadcast, though it is clear from media silence then and later that he never did so. The purpose of the USAS "project," "probably the most important with which I have ever been connected," was "to claim for the United States large areas of territory that have previously been discovered by Americans." Byrd and his men also hoped to explore "areas which no human eye has yet seen, as well as carry out a comprehensive program of scientific research" in the fields of meteorology, geography, oceanography, biology, and geology.

Plans called for the biggest expedition ever sent to Antarctica: three ships—he would soon lose the splendid steel and motor vessel *Northland* to the navy's wartime demands—150 men, 180 dogs, two light army tanks, "a huge snow cruiser designed specifically for this expedition by Dr. Thos. C. Poulter who was chief scientist and second in command on my last expedition," four airplanes, "and many other items." Byrd elaborated and embellished these themes in numerous letters to prospective donors and benefactors including the Navy Department. Begging one of its big, new long-range PBY patrol planes, Byrd reminded the chief of naval operations that at one time Washington could have laid plausible claim to at least a part of Greenland through "right of discovery and occupation." Now that frigid island, which lay as a natural stepping-stone between the United States and a Europe on the brink of war, was in other hands. "Our Government" was not about to make the same mistake in Antarctica, which suddenly loomed as perhaps equally important strategically. The loan of a single PBY "is a cheap method for the Government to achieve this end."[13]

Byrd was most explicit in a June 21 letter to the president of the Firestone Footware Company: "Several nations have already claimed territory" in Antarctica, "which should rightfully belong to the United States," he wrote, "and reliable rumors have it that Germany, following her surprise move in the Antarctic of this year, is to return with an effort to establish claim to the coastline of American areas in the Pacific Quadrant," that is, between the Bay of Whales and the Antarctic Peninsula. "I would like to try once again to add more of this territory by aerial reconnaissance and mapping to the territory of the United States before it is too late."[14]

But the expedition soon attracted a vociferous group of skeptics, scoffers, and critics. Gone now were the earlier cheers for a youthful admiral's "contagious enthusiasm," his "distinguished achievements" on behalf of exploration and "scientific flight." A St. Louis editorial summed up their thinking perfectly: "Does the country want to foot the bill for another Antarctic expedition to glorify Richard E. Byrd?" A Major Al Williams, writing in the *Washington [D.C.] News,* condemned Byrd's publicly financed "'Pole Vault'" as a "Dopey Project." "I didn't think any group—not even politicians—would appropriate" a hefty sum "of the taxpayers' money to finance that silly Byrd expedition to the Antarctic. . . . Admiral Byrd's aerial circuses, when carried on as private profit-making ventures, were Byrd's personal business. But having apparently exhausted the advertising sponsorships of every conceivable commercial article from mattresses to candies, . . . the Admiral's business becomes public business." Byrd, "a nice fellow personally," had become "the greatest American showman up to and including Barnum," employing "aviation as a stepping stone to wealth and popular acclaim." No one should begrudge him his skills or his success so long as the public pocketbook was not affected. Was it more than a "sad coincidence" that Byrd should have "launched" his "scheme in the face of his senatorial brother's stand against wild spending"? There might be some use in sending the admiral up to the Arctic "in the hope of some day flying an air route via the North Pole to Europe," but the Russians had recently "exploded that racket. And racket it is, because ice, snow and Arctic weather do bear a relationship to safe air transport." Byrd's expedition southward, "exposing our poor Monroe Doctrine to pneumonia in the Antarctic," was nothing less than "a crisis in asininity beyond the wildest winged imagination."[15]

In a way, Byrd asked for what he got because whether for money or glory the explorer would not or could not cease his endless self-promotion. Having mounted a financially unsuccessful exhibit of his polar artifacts at the Texas Centennial back in 1936–1937, he allowed lecture manager Leo McDonald to create "Admiral Byrd's Penguin Island" at the fabulous New York World's Fair three years later. Byrd spent as much time at his exhibit as an overcrowded and stressful schedule—

including initial preparations for the new Antarctic expedition—permitted. But it did his waning reputation no good. Whereas General Motors' Futurama (a fanciful look at American life in 1960) and the various European pavilions were tasteful and exciting, an acerbic young reporter for the *New Yorker* named Brendan Gill found a "woebegone Admiral Byrd seated among a few equally woebegone Antarctic penguins at a concession he had opened in the so-called Amusement Area." Nearby, and far more popular, was "a hapless nudie show, sneaked into the fair under the sacred name of education." The bare-breasted girls had supposedly been taught the customs of ancient Amazon warriors, thus giving credulous patrons an ostensible look into a lost classic world. "From time to time, one or another of the girls would lift a silvery paper-maché spear and toss it listlessly at some enemy offstage," while the crowd watched "her rosy nipples rise and fall," sighing "with gratitude at having our minds so much improved."[16]

Slowly but surely, the United States Antarctic Service took shape during the summer and autumn of 1939, despite the outbreak of world war in early September, which caused the armed services to renege on offers of long-range aircraft and other equipment. Byrd's usual cast of private donors took up the slack handsomely. A scientific program led by Alton Wade was cobbled together, and the executive board decided on establishment of two semipermanent U.S. bases. For Dick Byrd it would all be different this time. He had the help of two emotionally strong and administratively capable people—Siple and Black—who took over much of the day-to-day supervision of the expedition at home, en route, and as base commanders in Antarctica (Siple at Little America, Black at the peninsula), which would free their nominal commander to do what he did best: broad aerial exploration. The ships—two rather than the hoped-for three—were better, too. The tough, modern diesel-engined thirty-five hundred–ton *North Star* was the finest vessel he had had to date.

At the same time this was a government expedition, and one that might be expected to deglamorize Antarctica through routine, long-term occupation by scientist-bureaucrats. A corner was being turned in South Polar research. The days of daring adventure by a handful of men wintering over in fragile camps beneath black, blizzard-filled skies were giving way to more mundane adventures. Dick Byrd had overseen the last of the old; now he was commanding the first wave of a potentially new era. Press and public reacted accordingly. When *North Star* departed Boston on November 15, it merited only a picture and a half-column story on page 48 of the *New York Times*. Leaving Philadelphia in a snow squall six days later after hauling aboard the expedition's refurbished Beechcraft airplane (it sat next to Poulter's Snow Cruiser on the forward deck), the crew found that most of the reporters who had earlier been milling around had left. "There were only a few people around to see us off besides the fellows' wives and friends," young Charlie Passel noted in his diary that evening, "and they were mostly gobs [sailors] and men working around the [ship]yard."[17]

Richard stayed behind to complete *Bear*'s outfitting and loading, telling reporters as *North Star* pulled away from its dock that the United States might occupy Antarctica continuously for "possibly five or six" years, "depending on the wishes of Congress." Most of the explorers heading for the ice would be relieved by others after thirteen months, he added. "Although some of the first might remain down there, once is enough for most men." The admiral announced two major goals for the expedition he commanded: strengthening (though *not* necessarily announcement) of U.S. claims to the white continent and further exploration by the "giant snowmobile [snow cruiser] of some 675,000 square miles of unknown territory." When Dick at last left on November 26, he flew to Miami, then Havana on the way to Panama to join *North Star*. His departure and arrival in Cuba merited just a dozen lines in the *New York Times,* buried at the bottom of page 38.[18]

As the ships sailed down the Pacific, Byrd had time to read and digest FDR's official orders, which he had not received until he reached Panama. The president began his nine-page letter by telling Byrd that his appointment as commanding officer of the United States Antarctic Service was the result "of your experience and brilliant achievements in polar exploration and because of the confidence the people of the United States have in you and your qualities of leadership." Roosevelt then got down to cases. Reminding his old friend that the United States had never recognized any foreign claims to sovereignty over Antarctica, Roosevelt sternly directed that no member of the service "shall take any action or make any statements tending to compromise this position." FDR authorized members of the expedition to take "appropriate steps such as dropping written claims from airplanes" or "depositing such writings in cairns, etc. etc." that "might assist in supporting a sovereignty claim by the United States Government," and Byrd was directed to keep a careful written record of all such acts. The scientists and sailors who went to the ice were encouraged to record their experiences on film, in writing, even in paintings. But no one outside the Antarctic Service must gain access to such materials. Finally, Roosevelt ordered Byrd to return to the United States directly after "completion of your duties in the Antarctic during the spring of 1940 . . . as your presence in this country at that time is essential for other duties in connection with the administration of the United States Antarctic Service."[19] Whether the explorer ever asked his president to include such language so as to avoid any conceivable charges of cowardice or faintheartedness or whether FDR honestly believed that his friend could not and should not command the ambitious expedition from the field is not known. In any case, Dick Byrd would not be wintering over—nor would he ever again.

Christmas 1939 was spent at sea, and *North Star* entered Wellington Harbor forty-eight hours later for a three-day visit, then dropped down to Dunedin for the usual frantic loading of last-minute supplies. By January 3 the motor ship was under way for the ice. Six days later the first bergs and pack were encountered, and on January 11 young Charlie Passel awoke to find "the barrier staring me in the face." Antarctica had been benign this time, and Dick Byrd was back home. *Bear* had cleared Panama on December 6 with a big Barkley Grow amphibian aircraft aboard and was making directly for the Bay of Whales.[20] By mid-January Byrd was up and flying around the area, while off-loading and building efforts to establish Little America III before the onset of the polar night continued smoothly in exhausting twelve-hour shifts that left many wondering what time or even day it was.[21]

On January 19 Byrd boarded the newly arrived *Bear* and set out for a series of sea and aerial investigations northeastward along the coast of Marie Byrd Land toward the peninsula. Returning briefly to Little America, he set out again on February 1 on a long exploring excursion toward the peninsula where East Base would be established. For six weeks Byrd and his colleagues fought violent winds and often foggy, stormy iceberg-choked seas. To the tense and stressed men aboard *Bear* the Admiral of the Antarctic was serenity itself. During one of the frequent times that the ship was "locked" in the ice amid growlers and bergs, young naval navigator George Dufek heard Byrd, "pac[ing] the bridge around the tiny pilot house," mutter to himself, "Patience is what you need in the Antarctic. Wait—give wind and tide a chance to change. It will loosen the ice and allow us to go on." Then warming to his subject, Byrd turned to Dufek and said, "Remember that George. It applies to life, too. When you get stuck—don't give up. Be patient. Wait. Hold what you have. Circumstances will change and let you go on again." Nearly twenty years later, shortly after Byrd's death, Dufek remembered those words.[22]

As *Bear* bucked and pranced through stormy seas, there was no Russell Owen or Charles Murphy aboard to record the ordeal. The dramatic prose with which it was described to the Navy Department and the USAS Executive Committee was doubtless composed by Dick Byrd himself. At one point the little vessel rolled in fifty-degree arcs that sent men and furniture "careening across the officers' wardroom." Byrd's cabin was drenched by boarding seas that poured into his quarters through a ventilator shaft. What meals could be prepared under such conditions were eaten standing up. At one point *Bear's* young skipper, Lieutenant Richard Cruzen, ordered the upper and lower topsails set in an attempt to clear the pack.

"Bluejackets going aloft to furl or set canvas" found the sleet-stiffened material tearing at their hands or flapping wildly in the wind. "Lines eluded their grasp and the foot ropes, uncertain support at best, gave slippery footing. Decks were constantly awash as green seas broke over the bow and weather-rail." As late as the nineteenth, nearly three weeks into the voyage, "snow, darkness, and ice—the tireless watchdogs of [the] south polar sea," prevented Byrd and his men from getting *Bear* close enough to reach the coast by plane. The growing darkness was especially disturbing, cutting down what flight time might become available if and when the foul weather lifted.[23]

The weather at last slowly cleared during the final week of February. Byrd and Dufek raced aloft with the flight crew to be thrilled by thousands of square miles of new discoveries. *Bear* pushed through the pack and occasional snow squalls to reach the farthest point of any American vessel in the area. Once it achieved the record, however, the barque had to run for its life. "Turned back by solid pack, icebergs, and poor visibility, she found retreat virtually impossible. As far as one could see from the crow's nest lay a billowing ice-sheet. Wind had jammed loose floes so tightly behind the vessel that further navigation seemed impossible. Encouraged only by sea-sky [that is, skies reflecting open seawater], dark, low-hanging clouds, toward the northeast," Cruzen with infinite care conned his little ship slowly through the ice field, "winding a tortuous channel or carving a new one whenever necessary. Several times, when *Bear* was brought to a sudden jarring stop, she had to back astern and ram the floes." Propeller flashing wildly, "it was nip and tuck." Ice pilot Johannsen told Byrd and Cruzen that if the vessel had remained in the pack another hour, it might have been caught and frozen fast for at least a year.[24]

But at last, their fortune changed. Winds moderated, skies cleared, and on February 24 *Bear's* radio shack informed the world that "triumphing over fog, gales, and pack ice, Rear Admiral Richard E. Byrd . . . Commander of the United States Antarctic Service, today reached and photographed the long-sought south Pacific coast of Antarctica, 1,200 miles east of Little America." The goal of explorers for the past 166 years had been finally attained. In addition to filling in 200 miles of coast, Byrd also "discovered a vast mountain range to southward, rearing thousands of feet above sea level, an ice-covered island 80 miles offshore, mountains to the southeastward, and a great pack-enclosed sea." Characteristically, Byrd included in his triumphant dispatch the names of the flight crew, chief machinist's mate Ash Snow, pilot, and Earle Perce, radioman first class, the copilot.

On a total of three flights between the twenty-fourth and twenty-ninth, the three men and George Dufek (who replaced his admiral on one flight) found and roughly sketched in 800 miles of what is now the Eights and Walgreen Coasts, including mountains, islands, bays, and other features, discovering in the process that Thurston Peninsula was really an island.[25]

It was grand adventure, good science, and perhaps the happiest, if not the most carefree, time that Dick Byrd ever spent in Antarctica, apart from the first weeks at Advance Base. Behind him, the hyperefficient Paul Siple and his men were going about the business of constructing West Base–Little America III with energy and dispatch. East Base would soon be built. If there were to be crises over liquor, Siple or Black would have to resolve them. If personal animosities had to be soothed or manipulated, they would be responsible. The task of planning and carrying out intricate programs of fieldwork and study, including long, dangerous flights deep into the interior, and seeing it all through to a successful conclusion would be theirs. Byrd's area of responsibility was confined to *Bear* and to flying, and he found himself surrounded by competent subordinates in each sphere. There was the simple challenge of confronting Antarctica's always formidable forces. The tense competition with the ever shifting, always potentially deadly ice pack was a game whose enjoyment can be understood only by those who have played it. When the game was won, the pack mastered, and the skies opened for flight, challenge gave way to sheer beauty. Floating aloft for hours at a time in their fragile, vibrating box, Byrd and his colleagues viewed a majestic polar landscape of gray, blue, white, and black never before seen by human eyes. Byrd was reclaiming his position as the preeminent explorer of his age.

By March 3 *Bear* had reached the mouth of Marguerite Bay on the peninsula, and Dufek was on the bridge charting small islands and a reef. Within twenty-four hours *North Star* steamed in from a hasty trip to Valparaiso, and by the fifth the ships, their motor launches, and at least one plane were actively searching the big bay for a suitable base site. Heavy swells and limited maneuvering room kept both vessels in constant peril.[26]

Byrd and Black had actually spotted what would become the base site as early as the sixth on a flight toward Red Rock Ridge. East Base would be on "a small rocky island in Marguerite Bay in the vicinity of Neny Island . . . south of a camp established by John Rymill, an English explorer, in 1936." Swooping low in their aircraft, Byrd and Black spotted the Rymill cabin "free of snow and apparently intact." Beside it was a cache of neatly stacked boxes. From *North Star* that evening a party of seven, including Black and Ronne, "tramped across a mile of thin bay ice to make a preliminary survey of the site." But winds that blew steadily down the big bay at more than 70 miles per hour and spiked 20 to 30 miles per hour higher, together with heavy swells, prevented *North Star* from moving in to discharge its cargo until the eleventh. And even then the vessel "reached the island only after its launch found a narrow channel between Neny Island and one of the many icebergs which block the entrance to the bay." Getting men out of East Base promised to be as difficult and hazardous as getting them in.[27]

East Base was a "low, rocky islet . . . one side of which supported the chin of a stagnant glacier that could provide a highway to the interior of the peninsula." Byrd would have preferred basing at Charcot Island, but ice conditions had prevented the ships from getting in. "Stonington Island," as the East Base perch was named (in honor of the Connecticut seaport from which America's first Antarctic explorer, Nathaniel Palmer, had sailed), would have to do. There was no room for an airfield, but the top of the nearby glacier provided a sufficiently broad, level stretch, and soon one of the artillery tractors was chugging up and down the icy incline hauling supplies while the East Base party rushed to get their five prefabricated dwellings up before bad weather set in.[28] Soon enough, it was time to go and leave the wintering-over party to its own devices. Byrd was back in the States at the end of the month.

By the following spring it had become clear that the looming war emergency had transformed the United States Antarctic Service into an unwanted luxury. East and West Bases were abandoned, the men brought home. Byrd continued to chair the Executive Committee of the service, but his thoughts were straying elsewhere. The country was locked in a bitter struggle between the isolationists and those who either favored outright intervention or, at the very least, defending America by aiding the British ally. Byrd was determined to get into the struggle. "Ever since you have been President," he wrote FDR in early June 1941, "the people around you have under estimated my ability to help you. . . . However, I have always done, and will continue to do, the best I can." He had decided, Richard told FDR, "to take to the stump to refute Lindbergh and the rest of the America First Committee." To do this, he would have to go on inactive duty for several months, and with the United States Antarctic Service winding down he assumed that the navy's Bureau of Navigation would have no objection. Unspoken was the request that if it did, he could count on his old friend at the presidential desk to intercede on his behalf. What he planned, Byrd continued, was the same kind of campaign of national unity he had waged in 1933 that had resulted in the telegram of support from the state governors just before Roosevelt's first message to Congress. After several unctuous paragraphs lauding the president's magnificent this and superb that, he concluded, "Good luck, Franklin! I know what a terrible problem you have in your deep desire to avoid war, alongside the fact that probably England cannot survive without the active help of our fleet."[29]

Byrd then traveled out to the Midwest, where he found the isolationist America First Committee, headed by Lindbergh, and Senators Burton K. Wheeler and

Gerald P. Nye, among others, to have "a big following." By late July he was in Maine, "working up here for national unity. The country is not together as it should be," he told an old navy friend. "I expect to give some talks at mass meetings."[30] Although Byrd's dream of igniting a national unity crusade never got off the ground, he was the keynote speaker at a National Emergency Rally sponsored by the Council for Democracy that filled Madison Square Garden in mid-August 1941. He used the occasion to make his "first public declaration on the war."[31]

He told the packed Garden and a nationwide radio audience that World War II, "the age-old struggle between democracy and tyranny, between freedom and slavery, between good and evil," was "everybody's war. This time the fight is to the death. And, so far, as we all know, tyranny has won." Hitler believed, wrongly, that the "easy-going" peoples of a democracy could not match his disciplined, efficient hordes, and there were others (he did not name Lindbergh or anyone else specifically) who believed it, too. The second even more powerful truth that Americans could not avoid was that the world had shrunk dramatically in size. Many people still failed to grasp "what . . . high speed transportation and communications mean. . . . They believe we can hide in our own little cabin in the wilderness and let the forest fires rage around us. They do not face the truth that the Atlantic ocean, even with Hitler bitterly engaged, is not wide enough to isolate the Nazi fifth column from South America." In these circumstances, what would the world be like should England fall? "Even when Hitler loses this war," Byrd pressed on, the American people would "have to face this great and solemn fact: That the United States is an integral and responsible part of the entire world and that we can never again shirk our duty as inhabitants of this planet."

In measured, stately cadences, Richard asserted that the country had ineluctably become one under tyranny's fearful threat. "Be you an interventionist or a non-interventionist: be you for peace or for war; be you of English descent, or German or Italian or French or Irish; be you a Republican or a Democrat; a Catholic or Jew or Protestant or non-believer; a rich man or a poor man; whether you like Roosevelt or whether you don't; whether you are a farmer, laborer, or businessman; whether you are a white man or a Negro you are, if you still think freedom is better than slavery, if you still believe in our way of life, an American first."

To those who cried that in seeking to preserve democracy through the inevitable regimentation of war we would lose it, Byrd replied that democracy was a spirit and that the "institutional gadgets" by which it was maintained and expressed were "elastic enough" for an innovative and free-spirited people to "adjust to fit the crisis."

Roosevelt had recently proclaimed the Four Freedoms—freedom of speech, religion, and assembly and freedom from want—as the cornerstone of national life, and popular artist Norman Rockwell would soon begin to express them eloquently on the cover of the *Saturday Evening Post,* the country's most popular weekly. Byrd concluded:

> Here at Madison Square Garden tonight, we are enjoying the four freedoms of our Bill of Rights. Here is your free press. Here on this platform is your free speech. You who listen to me worship as you please. And here, in this meeting place, is your freedom of assembly. What are we going to do to re-pay Democracy for these freedoms? Are we going to sit back and enjoy them as though no one had ever fought and died for them?—or are we going to make our personal sacrifice every day so that our defense effort may be fur-thered? Are we going to divide our national house against itself through dis-sension—or are we going to stand united behind the President as if at war with an unconquerable morale? Americans, what is your answer?

If today the speech seems a bit melodramatic, a bit over the top, the times were, in fact, melodramatic. Western Europe had fallen, Hitler's troops and tanks were racing across Russia, Japan was in the process of dismembering China. Richard would publicly support FDR's increasingly interventionist policies until Pearl Harbor resolved all doubts.

Once war came in December 1941, Byrd promptly returned to active duty. The precise nature and dimensions of his wartime work are often difficult to determine, since much of it was highly classified, and for security reasons he said and wrote comparatively little about it. Obviously, any sort of fleet command was out of the question; he would have been the first to admit he had no background for it, and he was too senior to command either a capital ship or an aircraft squadron, which was also beyond his experience. Back in 1930 he had wisely turned down the op-portunity to head the navy's Bureau of Aeronautics, realizing how antagonistic such an action would be. His political instincts were still sound; he would not lob-by for a wartime billet that would bring his name into controversy or his reputa-tion into question. He wound up having a busy war, moving back and forth be-tween Washington and the Pacific and European battle fronts, making substantial if relatively obscure contributions to victory while playing the bureaucratic battle of Washington with zest.

Richard's first wartime assignment may have been his most important, tackling the formidable problem of expanding naval aviation to war-winning dimensions. In a crisply written and argued paper that he submitted to higher authority in ear-ly May 1942, Byrd stated that the navy would require a half-million pilots and support personnel. They should be acquired from a half-dozen sources: American citizens flying abroad (most with the RAF), a "V-5" program for aviation cadets in college, flight training for selected naval officers out of the fleet, "citizens" who could qualify for aircraft delivery units "and duty with utility units," a more rapid advancement in grade for "naval officers now qualified and available," and, finally, promotion to officer pilot status of qualified men from the enlisted and warrant ranks. Byrd then suggested in some detail how each of the source programs should work. He then left the project to others as he took up other missions. But he left behind the foundation for resolving one of the nation's most pressing wartime problems.[32]

During the following forty months of war, Byrd led two important if not especially daring reconnaissance missions to the South Pacific, seeking out the best spots for advance bases to wage war against Japan. He traveled to France and Belgium in late 1944 to observe and report on close ground-support operations by the U.S. Army Air Force and finally went back to the Pacific near war's end to help plan the anticipated invasion of Japan and to serve on the Strategic Bombing Survey's assessment of the vast air raids against Tokyo and other Japanese cities. In 1943 he traveled to California to rally war-plant workers and, during brief stints in Washington, successfully pushed for the creation of a supreme five-star command—general of the armies and fleet admiral. Through his friendship with FDR and other close contacts in the White House, Richard saw to it that the navy got its share of the spoils. Whatever resentment he may have generated in the service by his earlier ballyhoo behavior and his flag rank without command experience was substantially softened by his dogged bureaucratic work on behalf of navy objectives.

Throughout his life Dick Byrd tried to keep any hint of illness or injury out of public and, if possible, family view. Late in 1943, just days after returning from the Pacific, he was injured in a plane crash. How badly is unclear. The only evidence is an anxious query from nephew Harry Byrd Jr. and Dick's own admission to FDR at the end of January 1944 that "I am feeling better all the time, and will return to Washington soon," with a completed report on his trip to the Galápagos and Marquesas Islands. Three weeks later he still had not finished the report; it finally cleared the Navy Department in early April.[33]

The report, stamped "Secret," ran to six volumes. Byrd concentrated on "Book VI," his own "Senior Member's Review." Regrettably, no complete texts of the report, including Book VI, are readily available. But Byrd retained enough materials in his private papers to indicate its thrust. For the first, but not last, time he exploited an opportunity to portray himself as a strategic thinker of global vision. He and his team took "it for granted that the broad purpose of the Government is to ascertain as soon as practicable just what islands or areas" in the South Pacific "should be neutralized or controlled (wholly or in part) by this nation in the post-war era to fill the combined needs of diplomacy (used in the broad sense), commerce, and national security." But government planners could not ascertain in a vacuum. Some set of guiding ideas about the nature and structure of the post-war world (which would come into being after a "confused and possibly even a dangerous period . . . which may easily last for years") would have to be developed. Richard Byrd set himself that task.

There could be no doubt of the "world wide will for peace," he began. But the war's "devastating aftermath" would be a "severe test" for the democratic process. "Democracy is still up for trial." Should the Allies lose World War II to Hitler and the Japanese, it "would be democracy's funeral." But even victory would bring great problems because the increasingly close and intimate "contact of men and nations" emphasized man's "amazing selfishness" that in itself threatened "the functioning of democracy." Science and technology were not answers but rather posed threats: "The more science shrinks the world, makes the land more productive, and increases the population, the more difficult it would be for democracy to survive in the midst of anti-democratic governments. . . . [T]he more the human race, by means of science, shrinks the world and overcrowds it, the more individual liberties will have to be curtailed and the more individual license taken in the name of liberty will have to be eradicated from our system." And "if nations and men do not voluntarily collaborate" to achieve scientific and material progress, "they will eventually be made to do so by a dictator."

It was essential that the American people and government "be honest enough to face that fact that the defeat of our most powerful enemy," presumably Nazi Germany, "will not necessarily have been a victory for democracy and its processes." Byrd was even more pessimistic: democracy had "not yet proved that it can compete successfully in war with dictatorships." Looming on everyone's horizon, of course, was the Soviet Union. To the harder heads in Washington—most emphatically including Richard Byrd—"Russia" was a looming problem of uncertain dimensions. "At some period before Japan surrenders," the Kremlin would "either seek or secure" a substantial territorial adjustment in East Asia and the Pacific at Tokyo's expense. Should diplomacy fail, Stalin would gain his way by war. Byrd assumed a perhaps prolonged postwar period of uneasy peace between Russia and the West, which would be strengthened by the welcome resurgence of France. As Russia grew in power, "it will be the policy of this Nation to attempt to understand her" in order to retain the friendliest possible relations. Byrd implicitly admitted that Stalin's government might be "drifting" toward greater democracy, but "whatever may be the shape into which evolution moulds the Russian form of government, it will affect powerfully the shape of the governments of many other nations of Eurasia, and, in fact, the whole world."

Byrd was a southerner, born less than a quarter century after the convulsive struggle of slave states to maintain their way of life through independence. No doubt he shared the instinctive racism of his generation. But he was no fool. "We know that it is folly to underestimate the courage and potentialities of alien or colored races," he wrote, and so the possible forthcoming struggle between Russia and the West for the minds and hearts of Eurasians—and by implication and extension those inhabiting Africa and Latin America—could be neither dismissed nor ignored. Indeed, in Eurasia "there are six men for every man in the Western Hemisphere and ten men for every man in North America. Will the vast hordes of" a "Eurasia" dominated by the Soviet Union "tend as a whole away from democracy?" If so, the results would be catastrophic, for "the physical power of these nigh two billion of people (or a majority of them) united with a common ideology would be militarily irresistible should Eurasia be industrialized and mechanized as we are."[34]

The report, together with Byrd's pessimistic assessment, received instant praise from the handful initially cleared to read it. Admiral Yarnell called the effort "masterly," and urged Navy Secretary Knox to read key passages. Richard was eager that his friend in the White House see it, and its author, immediately. "Send me a telegram," he wrote William Leahy, "and I will come shooting down. I guarantee to be easy on the President because I know he must be greatly in need of a let-up from things and people." Leahy's reply was frosty. FDR was about to leave for another conference with Churchill at Quebec. In a brief "Dear Byrd" letter the chief of staff said Roosevelt had received both the report and Byrd's covering letter. "He asked me to inform you that he will not have time to talk to you about your report . . . until after his return to Washington." Roosevelt cleared the report in mid-June and permitted "distribution in a confidential status to the State, War, and Navy Departments" as well as the Joint Chiefs.[35] Richard had to be satisfied with that.

The following April, nine days after Roosevelt's death and shortly before the German surrender, Richard told nephew Harry that he was "continually being held up on urgent jobs. . . . Just the other day I got a new job that has to do with working out the coup de grace to Japan."[36] His task was to outline the organization of Okinawa—which finally fell to American forces on June 1—as an advance staging base for the invasion of Kyushu, tentatively set for November 1. Richard went out to Guam, then on to Okinawa, which he left "about the time the Japs surrendered" the island to join Admiral William Halsey's fleet, where he remained riding aircraft carriers and battleships until the atomic bombs and Soviet entry into the war abruptly brought hostilities to an end. On September 2, 1945, he stood on *Missouri*'s quarterdeck and witnessed the formal end of mankind's most cata-clysmic war.[37] By this time his Okinawa report, dated July 1, had been at Admi-ral Chester Nimitz's headquarters on Guam for several weeks.

The document marked a turn in Richard Byrd's life. From the beginning he had tested and pushed himself, always active, never at rest, pursuing an existence of constant challenge and struggle. Probably he had never wholly overcome the lin-gering effects of his prolonged poisoning at Advance Base a decade before. Then came the wartime plane crash, undoubtedly traumatic emotionally if not physi-cally. The cumulative effect on his mental faculties first revealed itself in this re-port. Gone were the clear prose and crisp sentences that marked his earlier writ-ings. Richard correctly emphasized to Nimitz that every aspect of Operation OLYMPIC, the prospective invasion of Kyushu on November 1, was at least 30 to 50 percent behind schedule. But he then expended ten pages reviewing well-known strategic timetables and shortfalls in leadership, construction schedules, in-terservice cooperation and coordination, and morale. The writing was repetitive, tedious, and vague. The only substantive recommendation exhorted his superiors to get on the ball and appoint a "tough two-star admiral" (himself?) as island deputy commander "to sort things out." Byrd missed the point—as he later would when polar affairs officer in the Pentagon—that his superiors already knew what the problems were; what they needed were imaginative and practical solutions. Byrd, supposedly a master administrator and logistician, failed to provide them; it was the first time he had really failed the navy in World War II, and it would not be forgotten.[38]

Moreover, he would have to confront the brutal fact that the war had forever destroyed his world. New standards and criteria of heroism had emerged from the forty-four months of sustained combat. Thousands of men (and a handful of women) had exemplified them. His valuable contributions to victory were lost in the flood of national achievement. But much worse, he began to lose the modest influence that he had had on national affairs since the midtwenties.

Early in the postwar world, Richard began building up trouble for himself at the White House. He and Harry Truman were not strangers. Over the past two years they had cooperated closely in the moral rearmament movement. Despite his busy wartime schedule, Richard retained a passion for ideological crusades, and as and when he could he helped reshape moral rearmament from a pacifist to an anti-Axis campaign, emphasizing industrial harmony and production for victory. He and Truman had a "good talk" in June 1943 about the movement's new spirit, and the senator promised to get behind Richard's latest petition for harmony in wartime industries. A year later moral rearmament was in trouble. Several of its young leaders had been drafted, and the movement threatened to collapse. Truman leaped into the breach, releasing a pamphlet titled *The Fight to Serve* that heralded "Moral Re-Armament's contribution to the war effort" and its "fight to secure industrial production." The young leaders could best serve the country by continuing their work, not reaching for a rifle and going to the front. According to a press release from the senator's office, twenty-one prominent congressional, business, and labor leaders signed the foreword to the pamphlet. Heading the list was Rear Admiral Richard E. Byrd. A month later Richard addressed a Washington crowd following the premiere of moral rearmament's latest "industrial drama," *The Forgotten Factor.* The theme of the play, and of Richard's remarks, was the overwhelming need for teamwork in every aspect of life, from waging war to making and sustaining peace. Teamwork had to be the guiding force from factory floors to international negotiating tables if the new and frighteningly complex industrial world were not to crush man and his fragile civilization. Truman cochaired the Committee of Invitation; Richard was prominently listed as a sponsor.[39]

A year later the camaraderie abruptly dissipated. As president Truman was now concerned with world power politics, not idealistic crusades. Dick Byrd's fawning letters to Franklin and Eleanor Roosevelt in the late thirties had clearly put off the scion of Hyde Park. But Roosevelt was self-assured and shrewd enough to know when to use and exploit an old friend, when to selectively reward him, and when to ignore him. Harry Truman was made of less confident, more suspicious clay. The peppery little man from Missouri had no use for sycophants, and Dick Byrd presented himself as one of the finest. By the end of 1945 Truman was in deep trouble with millions of consumers, workers, and businessmen over economic reconversion; with powerful elements in the Pentagon over the issue of military unification; and with soldiers and sailors infuriated with what they considered the slow pace of demobilization. The new and uncertain president didn't need oily courtiers cloaking their own ambitions and agendas—or those of close family members—under cover of condescending lectures on the difficulties of democratic government together with servile protestations of loyalty.

But that was precisely the impression Dick Byrd imparted in a letter to the new president in December 1945.

> What I want to tell you is that I wish every American could understand the incredible complications of your job and the little time you have to handle the infinitely difficult problems resulting therefrom. . . . President Roosevelt was an intimate friend of mine of years' standing, and I got a good idea of the burdens he shouldered, which were greater than those of any president before him. But yours are even greater, because you must relinquish dictatorial powers (we know that it would be dangerous not to do so) and bring or-

der into the great confusion by cumbersome democratic processes. . . . It is my opinion this war has disrupted things, national and international, far more than most people realize. It is much too soon for politicians to play politics as usual and criticize you unfairly and for minorities to threaten you when you, working for the good of the whole country, refuse to yield to their selfish demands. . . . The attitude the people should have toward your task is, as I see it, quite different from the one they actually have at present. In my small way I will do all I can to help. I want to repeat what I said when I saw you last—that I want to do all I can to back you up, and if I see anything going wrong I will bring it to you and not to your enemies. Count on me for anything I can possibly do for you.

Truman's brief reply was perfunctory: it was hard to get good help these days, he admitted, and he greatly appreciated the admiral's offer of assistance. "I hope I can take advantage of it."[40]

But as he sought to get close to Truman personally, Richard took positions and became identified with policies that in time made him anathema to the administration. His contempt for American foreign policy in general and Washington's approach to the United Nations in particular was withering. "Every day," he railed to brother Harry (who needed no encouragement), "I find myself appalled at the weak stand free men take in backing up right in the face of evil." He and Harry, still a major player in the U.S. Senate, obsessed over the UN, and at one point Richard lost his head completely, condemning his old Hyde Park friend in the cruelest and bitterest tones. The men of Yalta who "were a party to the agreements on the veto formula" had "committed treason against the people of the United States."

At one point late in 1945 he unwisely vented to Senator Burton K. Wheeler, the arch isolationist who had also come out against the veto power in the UN Security Council. Wheeler had "hit the nail on the head where our pusillaneous [sic] attitude towards Russia is concerned." Still, "I guess I made a mistake in writing him." Fortunately, brother Harry was able to suppress the letter, though his own standing at the White House was in rapid decline. Richard would not give up. Early in 1946 he was at his brother again: "This nation [is] still bungling in our international affairs. . . . I can find no statesman either in this Administration or among those in Congress on the Foreign Relations Committee. . . . It almost seems as if we are doing all we can to encourage Russianism throughout the world" by recognizing "forcibly communized" nations while casting adrift potential democratic allies. "We are discouraging the forces that hold in check extreme Leftism and encouraging the forces that assist the world tendency toward Leftism. This nation has been doing that ever since the trouble started in Europe." And now, even Douglas MacArthur, "who feels very strongly with me" and doubtless knew

better, was "using his influence to make Japan the fertile soil for this extreme liberalism under which so many are hiding to disguise their extreme Leftist tenden-
cies." When the Soviets first invoked their UN veto power in early February 1946,
Richard erupted again: "Why in the name of Hell our leaders should feel surprised
is a great mystery to me. It was perfectly evident from the beginning that Russia
would take every possible advantage of the veto formula."[41]

Such thinking—which neither Richard nor Harry chose to disguise—did not
endear the Byrds to the White House. Years later Truman returned Richard's file
to Defense Secretary Louis Johnson with the comment, "I think I have always had
his number, and that was one of the reasons why I could see no reason for building him up further. He is running true to the Byrd pattern."[42]

Antarctica remained Richard's chief preoccupation. As the war roared to its violent climax in the summer of 1945, he took time from arduous travels and a busy
schedule to draft two papers about future U.S. interests in the white continent.
Hitler's U-boats had cruised near the Antarctic Circle, and his armed merchant
cruisers had on several occasions preyed on Allied whaling fleets. Hard-pressed
wartime Britain had nonetheless sent a small, secret expedition to the Antarctic in
1943 (Operation Tabarin) to contest "Nazi-leaning" Argentina's claim to the
peninsula. It was therefore more than possible that as technology steadily advanced, unfriendly nations might build "arsenals" on the vast ice shelves and use
them as bases. Unless Washington kept a close eye on the South Polar regions, "we
may some day be surprised by a coup from an unbelievable direction."

Moreover, Antarctica was the size of the United States and Mexico combined,
and no comparably sized landmass was devoid of valuable natural resources. It was
thus "folly" to assume that the South Polar wastes were without potential value.
Geological reconnaissance, touching only a tiny fraction of the continent, had
nonetheless discovered "traces of many minerals." Fuel and energy sources appeared to be abundant there, and as he contemplated the prospects, Richard's mind
soared into the realm of fantasy. Antarctica was a livable environment with the materials men brought with them. "With ingenuity" it could be possible for men to
live there permanently while "less dependent upon the outside world. Greenhouses
could be constructed for production of fresh vegetables. Stone is available for
building and coal is available for fuel." Within the United Nations' "new World
Peace structure" Antarctica might even become a test case in international cooperation and harmony through a "world condominium." No nations had yet
claimed parts of the continent on the basis of permanent occupation. "There are
no racial problems involved," while "outside the whaling industry" (still "dormant"
in the wake of the war), "there are no economic complications at present. Such a
condominium could offer equal rights to all nations for exploitation under control of the World Government."

If such a pleasing prospect were to be realized, the United States would have to hustle to establish bargaining chips to make an Antarctic condominium a reality. This meant staking claims and establishing at least semipermanent base sites. "Now is the time to act," he wrote from Tokyo just eight days after Japan's formal surrender, "while we have trained manpower and excess equipment. It is proposed," he continued, "that we use aircraft carriers and long-range planes to make a complete survey of the continent. Map its coasts and interior. Rejuvenate the U.S. Antarctic Service and use the Antarctic as a polar scientific laboratory." Washington must "not lose sight of the future in the smugness of our immediate victory and hope of world security." If the United States did not act "now," its citizens might regret their sloth "in our lifetime." Richard's blunt recommendation: "a full scale reconnaissance of Antarctica . . . during 1945."[43]

The navy had practical and immediate interests of its own that might be fulfilled by a massive postwar Antarctic expedition. As the shortest route between the Soviet and U.S. landmasses, the Arctic would inevitably play a major role in any World War III. The armed forces, the navy not least among them, needed to develop and demonstrate cold-weather capabilities. It took time to organize suitable operations, but in the summer of 1946 carrier task forces began maneuvering in Davis Strait ("Operation Nanook"). However, with army fliers impatiently demanding an independent air force and once more deriding the navy as obsolete, "Nanook"-style operations were not enough. The sailors needed a really major military show to retrieve their waning fortunes. The dead of winter was no time for naval maneuvers in the Arctic. But December to March was summer in Antarctica, and a massive expedition there would maintain the momentum of cold-weather training. Precisely how Dick Byrd got his memoranda—or the ideas therein—before the navy brass is unclear. Certainly, he knew all the right people, who owed him—often personally—for his work in successfully lobbying Congress and the White House to establish the rank of fleet admiral. And, as he had first demonstrated twenty years before, he knew how to get their attention and engage their interest. In August 1946 Vice Chief of Naval Operations D. C. Ramsey issued orders to the commanders of the Atlantic and Pacific fleets, formally setting in motion the Antarctic Development Project, unofficially known as "Operation Highjump." It would be carried out during the forthcoming austral summer by a dozen warships and twice as many aircraft, divided into three task groups, whose mission was to see and map as much of Antarctica as possible in at most six to seven weeks of flying. Dick Byrd would be going home once again.[44]

In some ways it was like old times. The navy would provide extensive film documentation of the expedition, and Metro-Goldwyn-Mayer immediately agreed to produce and distribute a commercial film. There was no question but that the Admiral of the Antarctic would command.

But command structures are always tricky, and in this case Richard was, in effect, kicked upstairs. Ramsey designated him "officer in charge." Richard would coordinate overall planning and would be at least in part responsible for the project's success—or failure. But effective day-to-day command of ships and men was subsequently bestowed by Atlantic-fleet commander Marc Mitscher on Richard Cruzen, who had commanded *Bear* in 1939–1941 and, after distinguished wartime experience, Operation Nanook. Cruzen's navigator on *Bear*, George Dufek, had enjoyed an equally distinguished war record and rapid promotion. He would now command the exploratory Eastern Group. Captain George Bond would command the Western Group, whereas Cruzen himself would take charge of getting the Central Group through the ice to the Bay of Whales—and home again.[45] Once Little America IV was established, Byrd would fly into the Bay of Whales from the fleet carrier *Philippine Sea* to oversee the aerial-mapping activities of the Central Group. Although he was clearly meant to exercise distant command at best, Byrd wound up saving the expedition, though it has never been acknowledged or even widely known to this day.

Dick Cruzen's Central Group—two big, fragile cargo ships and an equally brittle command ship together with a submarine and a single icebreaker for assistance—found the Ross Sea ice pack nearly impenetrable. Hour after hour, day after day, the ships slammed and maneuvered their way through pack, ridges, and hummocks of unprecedented thickness. The submarine had to turn back to open water. At last, on January 12, the pack loosened and lightened. Three days later the icebreaker *Northwind* broke into the ice-choked Bay of Whales. The three bigger vessels, at least one with a badly leaking hull, followed meekly behind. Byrd was to arrive off the ice pack in *Philippine Sea* in about ten days, ready to fly into what he hoped and assumed would be an open and operating Little America IV. But Cruzen lost his head. He cabled Byrd aboard the carrier that the entire enterprise was so far behind schedule, and the ice so terrible, that the entire operation should be wound up no later than February 5, three weeks away and a full month before Byrd had any expectation of leaving.

Larry Gould had sent a roughly similar "can't do" message to his commander eighteen years before, and Byrd had encouraged him to go out on the trail and get working, resulting in one of the great all-time treks in South Polar history. Now Byrd, the commander, ordered his troops out once more. In a longish reply he told Cruzen that he had been following the ordeal "throughout and have been with you and behind you every mile of the way. Thus reasoning behind your momentous conclusion is understood and your purpose respected." But this was no time to quit. A February 5 departure from the ice would result in "nearly one hundred percent of the most important phases of the mission uncompleted." The navy would be devastated, its international prestige in shambles. Congress and the rest of the government might never fund another polar expedition, "thus delaying the conquering by our nation of the elements in polar regions which is so important to our national security." The strategically and economically critical South Polar region, with all its many and varied resources, would be abandoned to other nations.

Byrd then entered a caveat. In a time of peace, hazarding men's lives unwarrantedly was unacceptable. If Cruzen truly thought he would lose hundreds of men by tarrying overlong amid Antarctic ice and storms, Byrd would not only respect the decision but also support it. "A number of alternative plans" might be carried out. One involved rushing the transports to safety outside the pack. *Northwind* and its soon-to-be-arriving sister ship, *Burton Island,* could do the job, then return to the Bay of Whales to evacuate the Little America contingent. "But this very radical change in plans presents so many new angles that it is impossible to give you a clear picture of my ideas by radio." Byrd then urged Cruzen to maintain a maximum flexibility of thought until the officer in charge reached the ice in a few days to view the situation and discuss matters.

Drawing on his years of experience and wide reading in Antarctic literature, Byrd hypothesized that the great concentration of ice "filling the Ross Sea to the westward may possibly [leave] some open ice free areas to the eastward" that the task force could use as a bolt-hole. Moreover, "a fair chance" existed that the entire Ross Sea might be entirely ice free by mid-February. If Cruzen could remain of good cheer, his superior would soon be present to support and help him. So far as known, Cruzen never made such a radical suggestion again. Working like Trojans, the Seabees and sailors of the Central Group hastily erected the tent city called Little America IV, and Operation Highjump proceeded to its scheduled and relatively successful close.[46]

On the evening of January 29, 1947, Dick Byrd led the six DC-4 transport planes that would do the aerial mapping from Little America off the flight deck of *Philippine Sea* with a roar and blast from jet-assisted takeoff bottles strapped to each wing. Like so many of the admiral's flights since Pensacola thirty years before, it was a risky enterprise. The island superstructures of the World War II *Essex*-class fleet carriers did not permit launch of aircraft with as wide a wingspan as the R4D's. They would have to be launched in the several hundred feet forward of the ship's island. Moreover, the clearance between the flight deck and each aircraft's set of skis was only three inches. "Rightly concerned," Richard invited the chief pilot with whom he would ride, Conrad "Gus" Shinn, to his stateroom for dinner, anxiously asking, "You really think you're going to get off? You really think so?" Shinn said yes.[47]

The flight into Little America was a nail-biting, white-knuckle affair, as bad weather threatened to close the airstrip down before the six aircraft could land. All made it, although the last two depended on the homing signal from the command ship *Mount Olympus* to land through rapidly lowering clouds and murk. Bad weather closed down Little America IV soon after the planes arrived, preventing any flying for a week. During that time, the thin-skinned cargo and communication ships departed through loosening pack ice, leaving the fliers, scientists, and support personnel alone. Over 144 hours between February 7 and 20, Byrd and his pilots—assisted by ground-support personnel working to the edge of exhaustion and beyond—made some remarkable flights as they fanned out east, west, and south from the Bay of Whales, comprehensively photomapping the eastern curve of the Ross Ice Shelf, tracing the "west coast" ranges of Victoria Land and the Queen Maud escarpment, and proving at last that a single trans-Antarctic mountain range did indeed exist, bending around from Victoria Land to the Horlick Mountains and on eastward to the Thiel Range.

A return flight to the pole by the Admiral of the Antarctic was, of course, obligatory. It proved to be a frigid but relatively routine experience. Then the new icebreaker *Burton Island* crunched through the thickening pack ice to bring everyone safely home, leaving the tents, aircraft, and equipment of Little America IV huddled on the ice shelf with its earlier sister sites. Byrd and Metro-Goldwyn-Mayer later decided for reasons lost to record to hoke up the South Polar flight by making it seem a replay of 1929. The mission was obviously re-created months later on one of Metro's back lots, and the admiral looks a bit the abashed fool as he jettisons huge packages clearly marked with red crosses out of an airplane window to unseen ground below. Perhaps he realized that among other things he was at once parodying and trivializing Bernt Balchen's earlier display of matchless airmanship.

Following months of production problems that vexed and irritated Byrd (the studio shamelessly juxtaposed events for dramatic effect), Metro at last released *The Secret Land* in early 1948, and the film won that year's Academy Award for technical excellence. Richard at first expressed pleasure with the movie, then carped bitterly and quite unfairly to incredibly patient and understanding studio officials that the film downplayed his role as supreme mission commander.[48]

Nonetheless, he had been the first to oversee the maneuver of a modern fighting fleet in Antarctic waters and its safe return. He had restored his image in the public mind as Admiral of the Antarctic and America's greatest explorer. Coming home in the late spring of 1947, he had every reason to believe that his reputation remained impregnable.

Chapter 15

"Ever a Fighter So"

Harry Truman broke his heart. A planned Highjump II never jumped. Beset by sudden controversy, Dick Byrd, a prematurely aged sixty, found himself sinking into irrelevance.

The year 1948 was too soon for another massive naval expedition to the South, and by 1949 the Byrd brothers were anathema to the White House. Harry, along with Strom Thurmond of South Carolina, had become a leading critic of Fair Deal policies within the Democratic Party, whereas Richard had become identified with the navy's unpopular and bitter opposition to an armed forces "merger." To many, World War II had demonstrated beyond question the need to unify the services for the sake of efficiency and greater mission clarification. The navy soon realized it could not defeat the unification impulse; it could only hope to shape the legislation in such a way as to defend its interests. With his history of successfully fighting airpower zealots like Billy Mitchell, and his direct entrée to the innermost circles on the Hill, Richard soon found himself in the middle of a cluster of very nasty fights. From the end of the war to midcentury, the brothers worked pretty much in tandem to define and defend the navy's position and sustain its entrenched administrative rights and prerogatives.

Richard also pressed for the promotion of friends and colleagues whom he believed had served the nation well, got Harry to secure a West Point appointment for Admiral William Leahy's son, and worked hard to see that favorable navy pay legislation was passed. Just before departing for Antarctica in mid-December 1946 he supplied his older brother with a very detailed account of "how the Republican leaders felt about the Merger." "While I am away," he added ten days later, "please help the Navy Harry old fellow all you possibly can—the good Lord knows they are going to need it. Those in authority and my great friends are Admirals Nimitz, Ramsey, Denfeld, Sherman, Radford, Robbins. I hope you will counsel with these officers whenever they want to see you."[1]

By the summer of 1949 planning for Operation Highjump II had reached the advanced stages. Ships (including the huge "battle carrier" *Franklin D. Roosevelt*), men, planes, and equipment had all been earmarked for a further massive aerial and ground assault to unlock the last secrets of the southern continent. Then, in mid-August, Navy Secretary Dan Kimball, at the behest of Defense Secretary Louis Johnson, abruptly canceled the expedition. Stung, outraged, disheartened, Byrd promptly told Kimball "just what I thought of what he had done." For a moment, Richard believed he had gotten away with it; Kimball had not seemed "very offended." The admiral soon learned differently. In the days and weeks after the decision he found that his "strong statements to top officials have only resulted in my humiliation and degradation." Senator Ed Robertson, Harry's colleague from Virginia, wrote Richard that he was "sick at heart to read the news of the cancellation of the Antarctic Expedition. I know how you had set your heart on trying to round out and complete, as far as possible, the wonderful work you had already accomplished on the Antarctic Continent." Robertson had no doubt where the blame lay. "Truman has all the publicity angles and Johnson is trying to get as many as possible away from him for [a presidential run of his own in] 1952."

The Byrd brothers seized on every rumor and tale to fix responsibility for the awful deed. "I hear Walter Winchell made a statement that Truman had a fit after my success in Virginia in the primary," Harry wrote, "and, by reason of that, he cancelled your expedition." He had not heard the broadcast himself, Harry added, "but several people called me up." Other elements of the conservative press took up the cry. "Obviously, the Navy is not abandoning the expedition because it wishes to," George E. Sokolsky charged. "It has been ordered to give it up by the President of the United States who dislikes Byrds. The expedition would have been in charge of Admiral Richard E. Byrd, our greatest explorer and brother of Senator Harry Byrd. Enough said!" Jack Lait bemoaned "The Sinking of Task Force 66." "Reports" indicated "that the President killed the project in a spirit of schoolboy pique against the admiral's brother, Senator Harry F. Byrd, who routed the ticket Truman was backing in the Virginia State elections." The president, Lait added, "is as bitter an enemy as he is a loyal friend." Lait, a sensational journalist at best, admitted that the "tale as it buzzed about the Capitol, cannot be riveted down."[2]

Dick Byrd never recovered personally or professionally from the cancellation. He remained in the Pentagon as its chief polar affairs officer and turned his attention to strategic planning for the Arctic and especially Greenland. But his health, never robust after the ordeal at Advance Base, began to fail again, and rivals old and new openly harassed and challenged him.

In August 1947 he went into the Johns Hopkins University Hospital in Baltimore "because of a flare-up from the injury I got during the war," an apparent allusion to the 1944 plane crash. He told business patron John Reeves that "I entered with a temperature of 105, but it soon got normal again, and I was told by the doctors I was fairly tough." The following year, however, he was dogged by "a very bad bronchial infection" throughout the autumn. Truman's astounding re-election that November depressed him further. "The New Deal is basically unsound and immoral," he wrote Harry in December, neglecting or forgetting that his old friend, the squire of Hyde Park, had been its chief architect. "It is built upon the idea that the money of those who have been successful is used to buy the votes of those who haven't been successful. It's a racket and has produced a 'pauper mentality' in millions of our citizens." The nation's "publishers" were the chief culprits behind the public decline, for "they have failed most miserably in their duty to the free enterprise system. They have allowed their commentators to help us to the Left," which was dominated by "visionary professors" running the government.

Truman's inaugural prompted another burst of spleen from 9 Brimmer Street.

> A reactionary politician today is a man who fights for the principles on which this nation was based and who tells the people the truth instead of telling them lies to get their votes. . . . [W]e are already a socialist nation. I find myself these days in a constant state of amazement that this nation would so enthusiastically and emotionally glorify the man who is taking us along the road that leads to disaster. . . . And on top of all this, we witness an Inaugural that is the most enthusiastic one we have ever had. I imagine the crowd down there was made up of Communists (who are glad to see our country on the road to ruin), and liberals and many good citizens who are simply jumping on the bandwagon.

"I agree with every word you say," Harry replied.[3]

Richard's poor health continued into 1949. He and Marie had planned to go to southern California to see daughter Katherine and her husband, Bob Breyer Jr., the son of his old Los Angeles friend and associate. They never made it. "I could kick myself from here to China for cutting Marie and me out the trip," Richard wrote his old friend "Bonnie" Breyer. "I got knocked for a loop because I got up after eight days of pneumonia and started working. The relapse was worse than the original attack." He promised as he had, and would, so many times that he planned to "ease up." He never did. Ten days later he wrote Harry, "This last business brought me up with a 'round turn.'" One senses a bit of panic as he added that usually "it takes one Hell of a wallop to bring me to my senses." He admitted to several "handicaps" in fighting to retain good health. "One was the carbon monoxide at the Advance Base, and the other was that injury I got during the war." Marie finally made the trip to California alone.[4]

Richard's frustration over the stall in his own career was compounded by the successes and attacks of his enemies. Between 1944 and 1953, Bernt Balchen was the subject of a number of flattering articles in national magazines that not only emphasized his undoubted wartime heroics in the Arctic and Greenland but also insisted that he had been the "guiding genius" of both the first Byrd Expedition and the transatlantic flight and had saved Byrd's North Polar flight by repairing *Ford*'s damaged skis and waxing them properly. A number of Antarctic veterans leaped to Richard's defense.[5]

But Greenland, not history, was the catalyst that sent the Byrd-Balchen feud into orbit. In May 1951 Richard submitted to the Joint Strategic Survey Committee of the Joint Chiefs of Staff a sweeping report on polar strategy and in particular the need to focus on the importance of Greenland. The report was based on an initial August 1950 document together with photographs, a map of Greenland graphically depicting the information provided in the body of the report, a "strategic map of the Arctic," and various climate and temperature statistics. Most important, Richard included in his presentation a verbal "discussion of Polar strategy." A month later, on June 8, he received a formal commendation from Chief of Naval Operations Forrest Sherman for his "energy, skill, unremitting effort, and superior performance of duty in making this valuable contribution to the art of naval warfare."

Thereafter, both the air force and the navy moved swiftly under Byrd's overall direction to implement plans to establish both strategic air bases and weather stations in Greenland. The focus of operations was the establishment of a strategic air base well within range of targets in European Russia, including Moscow. Navy and coast guard icebreakers escorted several cargo ships and LSTs to a point of windswept tundra in far northwestern Greenland, just south of the 1925 MacMillan-Byrd operating base at Etah, and established a major aviation facility at Thule. At the high point of the cold war several years later, no fewer than fourteen thousand air force mechanics, machinists, radarmen, weathermen, and B-52 flight crews manned or used Thule Air Force Base with its several long runways.[6]

Who determined the base site would all too soon become a matter of jealous debate. But there can be no doubt that Bernt Balchen, now a reserve colonel in the U.S. Air Force, was primarily responsible for willing Thule into existence.

Balchen had supplemented his invaluable wartime work in Greenland with later experiences there and in Alaska to become probably the most accomplished and knowledgeable polar aviator America possessed. In September 1949, while commanding the Tenth Search and Rescue group in Alaska, he made the first nonstop flight to Norway in a C-54. Balchen asserted that the operation was personally approved by Air Force Chief of Staff General Hoyt Vandenberg. By this time, Air Force Secretary W. Stuart Symington and others were testifying before Congress on behalf of personal legislation that would give Balchen a regular, permanent commission. The legislation did not pass until 1951 despite repeated testimony and heavy lobbying by the air force.

Balchen was ordered to Washington almost as soon as his big air force cargo plane touched down in Norway after the flight from Alaska. "All publicity" about the triumph suddenly "stopped" while a "press conference [was] arranged," presumably to publicize the achievement properly and carefully. Just as he arrived, Balchen later wrote, he received a telephone call from Admiral Byrd, "who asked me to come and see him immediately. I left the conference and met him. He asked about the flight and about my general work in Alaska. He also asked about my flying. I took out my green instrument card and showed him. He then asked me who had given me permission to make this flight. This I told him. He then turned around and looked angrily at me and said, 'If you think that you will get a promotion to general in the Air Force, just forget about it. Not over my dead body. I will see to that.'"[7]

Whether this incident took place, or can be characterized as Balchen reported it, is highly questionable. The "Revolt of the Admirals" against armed-forces unification was well under way at this time, with Dick Byrd clearly identified as a partisan. The navy and air force were locked in venomous debate over the relative merits of the B-36 strategic bomber versus "super" aircraft carriers. Only the most foolish naval officer could wish or hope to influence the air force promotion process, and when it came to bureaucratic politics Dick Byrd was no fool. But there was no doubt that two men of towering egos and ambitions, each of whom was suspicious (and in Balchen's case contemptuous) of the other, had both reached the conclusion that their lifework was now central to American strategic calculations, and they were determined to have a major say in how those calculations were shaped. Early in 1951 the air force ordered Balchen to the Pentagon to become its liaison on all Arctic matters, then promptly dispatched him to Greenland as construction project officer for Thule air base.

Whatever Balchen's problems with Byrd, he was magnificent in ramrodding Thule through to completion. In a single year, thirteen thousand men and more than three hundred thousand tons of equipment were dedicated to building a modern air base in the most hostile environment in record time. Preparatory work got under way in March when the first men and matériel were airlifted in by the Military Air Transport Service. But heavy equipment and materials could only be sealifted in. The year 1951 proved to be "a late ice year," and the navy experienced problems with both the pack and bergs as it tried to get its ships north, and then keep them safe while unloading. Byrd was at Brimmer Street much of that summer, but his assistants kept him closely apprised of developments. As everyone worried about apparently impossible schedules and a short operating season, J. M. Tully wrote Byrd in late July that "Colonel Balchen is, as always, the optimist and the navy operations people complete pessimists and Colonel McKinley and I believe the true facts lie about half way in between." But Balchen held everyone to their tasks, and a month later, McKinley wrote, "the situation has changed completely as regards optimism and even the Navy's reports are quite exuberant now." The ships at Thule had completed unloading, and the two more on their way to the site would doubtless discharge their cargoes and be gone before the waters froze. McKinley called Balchen to congratulate the man whose exuberance had been fully vindicated.[8]

Dick Byrd's political antennae were always sensitive, and in the autumn of 1951 he sensed that elements in the Pentagon, perhaps even in the navy itself, wanted to shunt him aside. Late in September Admiral Duncan, the vice chief of naval operations, congratulated him on having passed his yearly physical exam. "I don't know anybody here that had any idea of washing you out on that score," Duncan added. The blow fell two months later. On November 28 the Joint Strategic Survey Committee shot down Byrd's report on the usefulness of Greenland for military operations. "Information on the Arctic regions is incomplete," the committee determined, "and what is now available would in all probability be inadequate to serve as a basis for the conduct of effective joint operations on short notice." Moreover, Byrd's request that a separate Arctic affairs section staffed by all three services be established within the Department of Defense was rejected as wholly unnecessary. Essentially, the committee argued that Byrd and his planners had made the Arctic too important. There were other strategically critical areas of the world requiring greater attention.[9]

These conclusions left the air force in effective control of Arctic policy and operations. Thule was now complete, and farther down Greenland's west coast another base was being developed at Sondrestrom, the famous "Bluie West Eight" World War II staging facility for B-17 flights from North America to Europe. The air force also took the lead role in establishing an elaborate distant-early-warning line of sophisticated radar stations stretching across the Arctic from Alaska to the east coast of Greenland to detect sudden, Pearl Harbor–like bomber or (later) missile attacks from the Soviet Union. Once again, the navy played the handmaid's role, providing the cargo vessels and icebreakers required to hastily construct coastal and near-coastal sites during the short summer seasons of 1955 and 1956. Balchen anticipated being project manager for the Canadian portion of the enterprise until he was suddenly relieved in July of 1953 and assigned recruiting duties in Ohio. Angry and bewildered, he wondered who had sabotaged his career.[10]

A week after the committee rejected his report, Byrd asked to be relieved from active duty. There were nearly five thousand more or less experienced polar hands available now, he wrote the chief of naval operations, many, if not most, of whom had acquired their expertise on one or more of his own expeditions. Let them handle things from now on. The office of technical assistant for polar operations had been created to make policy recommendations. If those recommendations failed to meet approval, what was the use of the office? He was evidently induced to stay on, however, for by mid-December he had submitted another proposal to accomplish what the committee had asked for, namely, creation of a much stronger informational and data base on Greenland. But early in 1952 the Joint Chiefs themselves rejected the whole exercise. The admiral's Greenland report would be distributed "to appropriate agencies within the Services" for whatever use they might make of it. Richard did not renew his application to be relieved of active duty, continuing to work, collecting data from around the federal government on Arctic conditions in order "to suggest remedies" for "Russia's great preeminence in cold weather and arctic fighting." In August 1952 he received another, informal, commendation addressed by the chief of naval operations but signed by his deputy. Richard was praised for his "continued keen interest in the Cold Weather problem" and for the fact that his technical office remained "a valuable source of vital Arctic and Antarctic information."[11]

But Richard was well over sixty now. He had reached the point of average longevity for men of his time with a history of strenuous exertion, frequent tension and strain, and at least two major medical crises. Complaints of feeling poorly began to creep into his correspondence. Early in 1949 he complained to daughter Katherine about "this confounded relapse I had this time from pneumonia," adding that it had "taught me a good lesson" about letting up on work. A year later, he assured a business associate that columnist Walter Winchell's report of his ill health was unfounded. "I broke a blood vessel, exercising, and had to have the bleeding stopped. It took several days but I am o.k." In January 1951 one of his "lower starboard teeth" began to "kick-up like hell," and he requested immediate attention at Bethesda Naval Hospital. In September he mentioned casually to John Rockefeller that "my convalescence is over successfully and I am now on my way back to duty." He never revealed the nature of his malady.

In the spring of 1953 he told Harry that he was resigning from "all the ex-
tracurricular things I am doing" and mentioned that he was a member of more
than two hundred organizations, many, if not most (like the Boy Scouts), eager to
have his active participation. An obviously relieved older brother replied, "You
have been under a terrible strain for a number of years," and Harry reminded Dick
that "both you and I have reached the age where we should not try to do as much
as we have in the past." Wise words, but soon Richard was writing his brother that
"it is now 9:30 P.M." in Boston, "and I am leaving at 10:30 for Maine. I am going
to have a few days with Marie. I am rather desperately in need of a let-up. Damn
fool am I for attempting to do so much!" Within a month Richard informed his
brothers that he was "out here among the doctors" at the Mayo Clinic in Rochester,
Minnesota, for an unspecified malady. He was on his feet again in October, but
the next month he informed cousin Harold he was back in Boston with "a pretty
bad bug and I am still in bed," dictating all his correspondence to Marie.[12]

Finn Ronne suddenly emerged as a further source of irritation. The Norwegian
came out of modest wartime service determined to carve his own niche in Antarctic exploration.[13] Like Balchen, he fancied that Dick Byrd was out to block him,
though, in fact, Richard firmly supported Ronne's plans and requests for government funding on no fewer than three occasions if for no other reason than they
did not clash with his own. Ronne became firmly convinced that the only good
polar science was the "small" science of modest, one-or-two-ship, thirty-person expeditions. Operation Highjump—"big" science conducted with a score of planes
and ships together with several thousand men—struck Ronne as quintessential
Byrd foolishness. When a government review board rejected Ronne's proposal to
establish small, permanent base camps in Antarctica, he apparently attributed the
rebuke to Dick Byrd, and thereafter his references to the Admiral of the Antarctic
and close associates such as Paul Siple were invariably venomous.[14]

Ronne spent part of 1947 and early 1948 under the banner of "the American
Antarctic Association," using the United States Antarctic Service's East Base on
the peninsula. The Americans were cheek by jowl with the British, who had returned to the area to reconfirm their historic claim. The two communities cooperated to an extent both scientifically and logistically. Ronne led his small band
of scientists in not only exploring the peninsular area but also mapping by aerial
photography the front of the Filchner Ice Shelf as far east as Gould Bay (which
Ronne named). As a consequence, the massive shelf ultimately received its present name, the Filchner-Ronne Ice Shelf. Ronne and his people did some good
science, though two navy icebreakers, *Burton Island* and *Edisto,* had to cut their
small icebound ship, *Port of Beaumont,* out of Marguerite Bay in order to get them
home, where they received a modest welcome that included a "very nice message"

from Dick Byrd that was subsequently read at the American Geographical Society banquet honoring the expedition.

Ronne let loose his spite late in the year. "It may amuse you to know," he wrote Larry Gould, "that reb [*sic*] has called" several members of the Ronne expedition

> long distance twice in one week, and the substance of the ranting and raving seems to have been to try to get me back in his folds. reb claims he could have stopped me in getting the ship, and because he didn't, I should have named a major feature after him. My not doing so, *he thinks,* leads the public to think we are on the outs, etc.—that I am blackening his character, and that he will not stand for it—in no uncertain terms. The reality of the situation is becoming extremely funny. With all his popular prestige, influence and power, he worries about an unknown struggling competitor—imagine.

Ronne had learned from one of his colleagues that Byrd's "plans for this year to fly from New Zealand and over to Chile have been canceled and all fireworks are being organized and concentrated for an all out attack on the Continent by plane next year." A small but "well organized joint British-Norwegian-Swedish Expedition to Queen Maud Land" would doubtless do "excellent work. Too bad this country can't enter into this field the way other interested parties are doing—perhaps one day we will wake up."[15]

In the spring of 1949, Ronne approached the Joint Research and Development Board with a proposal for another wintering-over expedition to Gould Bay. "It will interest you to know," he wrote Gould, "that 'my friend' has squelched my plan in which I hoped to operate under the Navy." In fact, according to Ronne himself, the board had not "squelched" his plan at all. It merely asked for "a more detailed scientific" proposal and invited him to present it the next month. Gould replied that he was "distressed but not surprised at the manner in which your plan to operate under the Navy has been squelched. It is impossible to understand the selfishness of some people."[16]

Ronne was also convinced that Byrd had urged or ordered his friends at the *National Geographic Magazine* not to publish Ronne's article on his recent expedition to the Antarctic Peninsula. In early April Edward Sweeney, a professor of law at Northwestern who had met Ronne while on temporary duty with Byrd at the Navy Department after the war, wrote Gilbert Grosvenor, requesting the society's president to reconsider. "I am told by Commander Ronne that the Society has rejected his proffer of an article." Given the immense space devoted to Highjump, Sweeney continued, it was a shame that the "significant gap in the Society's coverage" of Antarctic research could not be closed with a lavish pictorial article on the accomplishments of Ronne and his men. "I have recently corresponded with

Admiral Byrd about the Ronne article, believing that there might be a misunderstanding, and he has just written: 'I would be very glad to see the Geographic publish an article by Ronne, and I will be glad to even go so far as to tell the Geographic that I think an article from Ronne would be a fine thing. I would myself enjoy reading it.'" Ronne's frustrations grew when not only did he fail to obtain research-board support for another expedition, but sales of his book remained below two thousand copies "in spite of all the efforts."[17]

Richard was understandably angered by Ronne's behavior. When Ronne sought to mount another modest expedition in 1954, engaging the enthusiastic support of both Larry Gould and Bernt Balchen, Richard wrote Harry to warn him: "The two Norwegians whom I told you about who have been trying to discredit me have a Bill up in Congress introduced by Congressman Tollefson and Senator Case to put Ronne in charge of an Antarctic expedition."[18]

Though he denied it, Ronne clearly conceived his enterprise as the opening round—the pathbreaking, foundation-laying effort—for the forthcoming International Geophysical Year whose members were already well advanced in planning a concerted, synergistic international effort to understand the earth through a series of scientific programs in which Antarctic research would play a central part.[19] Ronne was shrewd, telling Gould that, in effect, the IGY people had spurned him. Early in 1953, Ronne recounted, he had been approached by various U.S. scientists about possible participation in IGY planning. He had even attended a meeting or two. But at the last one, "I was amazed to see Paul Siple walk in. I told Wally [Atwood] then and there that I wanted nothing further to do with it if Paul was going to be connected with this sub-committee, of which he was not a member, since he was merely an earpiece for the Admiral." According to Ronne, Atwood gave him assurances that he would talk to Siple "and see that such was not the case." "Pacified" and "somewhat naively," Ronne added, he turned all his plans over to Atwood, who never contacted him again.

Ronne insisted that he did not feel welcome with the IGY crowd and that all he wanted to do was to establish a small, permanent base in "Gould Bay" where he could conduct various photographic flights to complete the aerial-mapping program begun at East Base in 1947–1948. But he had already planted in Gould's mind the notion that from his base the three U.S. IGY stations then contemplated could be "flown out in the field." When Ronne presented his plan to Gould at the end of May 1954, he emphasized that his contemplated aviation photographic unit could "fit in with the IGY." Moreover, since the navy had indicated that it would not support his expedition (though other federal agencies would), passage of the Ronne bill by Congress would send a message to the sailors that they had better get in line and support Antarctic research across the board, including the

IGY. In other words, Ronne was mounting a preemptive strike. By getting to the ice first, he would control the flow of men, supplies, and scientific work for the IGY.[20]

Gould was already immersed in preliminary planning for the American contribution to IGY, but Byrd proved slow to grasp the implications of the program and its impact on his own future. Early in June 1954 Richard wrote Gould that he had learned of the proposed Ronne expedition "when I received copies of the bill printed in the House and Senate. The newspaper items stated that you and Ronne and Balchen were members of the American [Antarctica] Association and that Ronne would be the leader and Balchen would run the aviation end." Byrd undoubtedly guessed if he did not already know that Gould was well aware of his active dislike of the two Norwegians, so he probed carefully for information about connections. "I am deeply interested in I.G.Y., though no official has contacted me about it." He had learned of the program in the newspapers, "long before I heard of the Ronne-Balchen expedition," and had "called up a man at Tech [presumably Massachusetts Institute of Technology] who had been connected" with IGY. Since that time, "Paul Siple has kept me somewhat informed. Naturally," the program and those connected with it "will have my complete cooperation and good wishes," though whether Ronne and his partners were "hitched up to the I.G.Y. I don't know." Gould did not enlighten him, and so Richard and his always loyal brother reacted to the Ronne expedition viscerally, working closely to see that Ronne's legislation never reached the floor. Richard lobbied the Defense Department and the old Byrd hands to oppose Ronne, which led to one of the very few criticisms Byrd ever made about Paul Siple. The always loyal right-hand man, "as usual, is more or less straddling the fence and comes out with no firm stand of any kind." Harry kept assuring his brother that no action would be taken, but the bill did come up before the Armed Services Committee, where navy representatives, undoubtedly at Richard's prompting, successfully sniped at it for its cost. Harry apologized for allowing the measure to get that far. The anti-Ronne forces would be better organized at the next congressional session, he promised, should the proposal reappear.[21]

When the bill reached committee, Richard wrote his brother that he "wanted to be very sure not to do anything that would not be on a proper plane of conduct. I do not want to do anything or say anything that would not be right and just," and Harry should follow similar deportment. He had given the matter a great deal of thought, Richard added, and had concluded that perhaps "such things as government expeditions should" not "be ordered by Act of Congress." But he could not conceal his real objection. "Ronne and Balchen certainly have little respect for the truth. Many people acquainted with them are aware of this fact."

Ronne had given "a wrong impression of what his position really was" during the recent hearings when he claimed to be second in command at East Base back in 1940–1941. That position really meant very little in the overall scheme of things. "I dislike the gentleman in question very considerably; because he deliberately told lies about me, just as Balchen did, to get sympathy and help. And further, he disregarded orders in the Antarctic; and I should have been much harder on him than I was."

With the legislation dead for 1954, as promised, Richard wrote young Harry Jr., who had taken over management of the *Winchester Star.* "There are a couple of Norwegians that I brought over to this Country and took down to the South Pole who have been very disloyal to me; and they got Senator Case (who is a good man and a friend of Harry's) to present a bill in Congress forcing the Government to send Ronne down to the Antarctic on a big expedition. This bill, if passed, would have knocked out any other expeditions, such as the one I am trying to organize." Fortunately, Richard added, John Stennis, the Mississippi Democrat who chaired the Senate Armed Services Committee and Richard's friend and political ally since the 1920s, "stuck by me throughout as my best backer (next to Harry, of course)."[22]

While Richard's status began to fray within the polar community, his constant need for money kept him in the public eye. The children were grown, but 7–9 Brimmer Street and the Maine vacation property remained expensive, and the Byrds had always lived well. In the late twenties, Richard and a good friend, Harris Thurston, had developed a lightweight clothing fabric "with breather characteristics" called Byrd Cloth, which was meant to replace heavy fur parkas. Byrd Cloth was windproof yet not so tightly woven that a little air could not get through to prevent sweating that would eventually turn to ice against the body. Byrd and others wore the material during BAE II, and a decade later the explorer had a contract with Borman Sheep Lined Coat Company. Late in 1943 Reeves Brothers clothiers approached Byrd with a proposal: it could perfect Byrd Cloth to the point that the material could ward off "icy winds, sleet, and snow. Yet when worn over inner garments, it kept the body warm without the chill dampness" of furs and other types of polar gear.[23]

Richard jumped at the chance to affiliate with one of the country's leading clothiers. He wrote to John Reeves in early January 1944, baiting the hook with a "strictly confidential" disclosure. "When the war is over I expect to take a flight from Pole to Pole, and in doing so hope to explore several hundred thousand square miles of new discoveries. . . . I am telling you this because I believe such a flight would not hurt the promotion of the Byrd cloth." As for the Borman people, Reeves was not to worry. Neither Byrd nor Thurston "took this matter seriously." Borman's was small, and though it had taken advantage of the inventors contractually, "they are extremely friendly and would not want to injure me in any way. They deal mostly in sheep-lined coats."

Not until late September 1947, however, was Richard able at last to wriggle out of the final commitments he had to Borman and Thurston, joining Reeves Brothers as a full-time consultant at a guaranteed annual income of ten thousand dollars to be paid in quarterly installments. Reeves knew, or soon guessed, that Richard was chronically pressed for cash. Soon Reeves Brothers began providing Richard with extra funds. "I want to thank you for the good news you gave me at lunch," Richard wrote his provider in late June 1948. "I had no idea that such good fortune was in store for me. I am sure you can realize what it meant to me when I tell you that I went in the red last year." "To put it mildly," Richard told Reeves a year later, "I am deeply grateful to you for the bonus. You couldn't possibly have selected a time when its arrival would have been more welcome." Gratitude was invariably accompanied by ostentatious expressions of unworthiness. Richard had not worked hard enough to earn such beneficence from his employer, but he would in future "prove my gratitude by doing everything I can to deserve such very friendly consideration." Richard traveled to Spartanburg and Bishopville, South Carolina, to help John Reeves open a new plant. The forty-seven hundred Reeves employees in the area took out a full-page ad in the *Spartanburg Herald-Journal* to welcome the admiral, and the newspaper expected ten thousand people to greet him during his two-day stay, which included the usual speeches and banquets.[24]

Reeves worked his man hard, and Richard responded. He was expected to appear and to speak at every major textile-industry function that Reeves thought important. The admiral remained a highly visible and popular public figure, and his presence could make or break a dinner or a conference, especially if he showed and narrated one of the many films he had patched together himself. As time went on, Richard was not so subtly pressured to endorse other lines of Reeves clothing products. In exchange, he received high-quality clothing, especially Byrd Cloth shirts, specially made for him.

Dick Byrd clearly relished his association with Reeves Brothers, for it not only brought in a guaranteed income—and then some—but also maintained his stature as a revered figure in national life. As the years passed, Byrd not only shilled hard for Reeves Brothers but also began sending his "boss" little tidbits of Washington gossip and analysis. In June 1948 Reeves thanked the admiral for "certainly being a great help to us in our meeting, particularly in the discussion of the future probable Government budget, etc." A year later, Richard pronounced "the drift toward Socialism" in Washington at an end (he would soon change his mind), reporting "confidentially" that famed financier and informal government adviser Bernard Baruch "called up my brother last night (while I was dining with him) and said that he felt strongly that a ten percent reduction should be made in the money being given to the western European nations" under the Marshall Plan. "The senators" had at last come to the realization that "the immediate danger was nothing as great as they had originally thought," and Richard reminded Reeves that "a year ago" he had concluded "there was no possible chance of war with Russia for many months. As a matter of fact Russia has not yet recovered enough to fight."[25]

Richard was as intemperate with Reeves in condemning Truman and the Fair Deal as he was with everyone else in his close circle. Expressing delight with the 1949 off-year elections in Virginia, Richard told Reeves that the election "became a national issue" because "the Communists, the Leftists, and other extreme Liberalists saw an opportunity to do injury to my brother." Reeves hastily replied that the result "pleases me no end."[26]

As Highjump II loomed, Richard hastened to assure Reeves that he was keeping the navy's judge advocate general apprised of his business connections "so that everything will be on the table." In anticipation of several months on the ice, Richard had asked Reeves if he could receive the following year's consultant fee in a lump sum, and Reeves had hastened to comply. Later Richard offered to return the check, but Reeves refused. Richard shared his despair fully with the clothier, telling him at one point that if Highjump II was well and truly canceled, "I will borrow the planes we have conditioned and an icebreaker and do the job myself."[27]

With the outbreak of the Korean War, Richard's indiscreet leaks to Reeves became indefensible. "I thought it might be of real interest to you to know that the Joint Chiefs of Staff think there is only a 50–50 chance of our holding Korea," he wrote during that first desperate summer of the war. "In fact, General Bradley so informed the Armed Services Committee. Please keep this confidential." Richard added that he had developed "a national policy from my long study" of the Arctic, "which I shall in several days present to the Department of Defense and the National Security Council, and perhaps the President. . . . If you would like to see this study I have made, I'll be glad to bring it up to you." To hand a copy of a document that would surely be classified "Secret" if not higher to a private businessman with no known ties to the federal government undoubtedly constituted a court-martial offense. Reeves expressed interest in seeing the study, but fortunately for Byrd it was rejected so soon and decisively thereafter that his indiscretion went unnoticed.[28]

As his influence and power in the Pentagon steadily drained away in the early fifties Richard clung ever more tightly to Reeves, bombarding him with gushy notes. "As 1950 draws to a close," Richard wrote pompously, "I think I should very briefly sum up for you my efforts for Uncle Sam during the year." But before plunging into a mercifully brief account of why his national defense paper failed to gain even a minimal clearance for circulation, Byrd asked Reeves "if you realize you are the closest approach to a Boss that I have ever had in civil life. . . . And right here and now I would like to say that I am sure, as sure as I can be of anything, that I could not have picked a Boss that I would think more of or under whom I would rather serve than one John M. Reeves. As you know, I have done so little for you in the past year that it has been on my conscience."[29] That would change however, for late in 1951 the clothier enticed his distinguished colleague to participate in a rather bizarre charade.

The event was "the first ever of its kind, mammoth Fashion Panorama" at Madison Square Garden. On the evening of November 8, New York's fashion industry—buyers and merchandise executives—together with the interested public, would gather for a gala show: "a coordinated preview" and "A Dramatic Showing with Entertaining Interludes" of spring fashions to an audience of fourteen thousand. The affair would benefit "Interfaith Brotherhood House," a project designed by "Interfaith in Action" to draw the spiritually disparate New York City garment industry "into a closer understanding by supplying this busy community with a 'Town Hall,'" including a gym and swimming pool "for young people and underprivileged youth."

Richard may have been sucked into the affair on false pretenses. Six weeks earlier he agreed to appear as an "honorary guest speaker" and also to appear at a number of related events, including a television program and a recording to be broadcast the same day as the Panorama, perhaps as part of it. But Reeves had other ideas and inveigled Richard into appearing not as an "honored speaker" but as part of the show itself.

The program began with various salutes to Interfaith in Action. At last the Honorable Judge George J. Beldock, justice of the New York State Supreme Court, cried out from his box, "And now, on with the show!" A "newsboy" promptly appeared, shouting, "Extra! Extra! In the next few seconds, 17,000 men and women will leave Madison Square Garden in a supersonic jet, which at this very second, is warming up to send them on the first flight of fashion in the rarified stratosphere of the Fashion World." And where best send these good folk first but the North Pole? And who would be there to greet them but Richard E. Byrd, rear admiral, United States Navy (retired). Richard had already been closely questioned "about type of fur worn by" Arctic native peoples; "how often they change clothes"; what men, women, and children wore; questions about hairdos; and so on.

Now, to the accompaniment of "Baby It's Cold Outside," singer Michael Brown appeared to warble a tune about furs. Otto Grosse, owner of Northwest Fur Farms, the world's largest producer of fine mink, then strolled onstage together with four inevitably "lovely" fur-clad models to tell people what "the American Fur Farmer has done for the most beautiful women in the world—the American women." Grosse proceeded to dilate at some length on ten mink furs modeled by slender, pretty young ladies, and suddenly there was Dick Byrd to extend "greetings and welcome to the Land of the Midnight Sun."

After making a safe, lame joke about the lack of women at the South Pole, he spoke of a "young lady" who had just emerged from eleven years in a Soviet slave labor camp to report that women had "much more endurance against the cold" and experienced far less "nervous strain" in frigid temperatures than their apparently less hardy male counterparts. Richard had wanted to plug the "Iron Curtain Refugee Committee" with which he had recently become associated, but the textile people evidently thought pushing any other product—however worthy—was unseemly. After praising the impending Interfaith Brotherhood House, Richard proceeded to describe what Arctic "Eskimos" wore. "Mrs. Eskimo's fashions seldom change," Richard concluded. "However, here in civilization, we know that ladies' styles are constantly changing. Tonight you will see next year's fashions in this remarkable Fashion Panorama. On with the show!"[30]

If Richard had not exactly sold his soul, he had certainly tarnished his reputation. Sardonic critics beginning with Morris Markey back in 1930 had accused him of frivolous self-promotion. With the Fashion Panorama, he at long last proved them right. He reopened himself to charges of being a lightweight, a panderer to the worst as well as the best in public taste who, under sufficient provocation, might succumb to temptation and claim to have done things—flying to the North Pole, for example, or discovering an Antarctic mountain—that in fact he had never accomplished. Richard never saw himself that way: he took obvious pride in his participation in the Fashion Panorama, directing a secretary to secure for him one of the hard-to-obtain programs from the affair. In later years he would flack "Tidykins" children's snowsuits, made of "Nylon Byrd Cloth," posing with tots in full-color ads in the Sunday *New York Times* while clad in his own polar furs. He traveled with Reeves to various parts of the South for the opening of Sears-Roebuck outlets, and kept his employer apprised of various legislation affecting the textile and clothing industries.[31]

His respect, even awe, for John Reeves as a successful captain of industry was genuine and refreshed by continual loans over and above his annual retainer and by occasional expense-paid trips for himself and Marie to the Reeves Brothers factories that dotted the South Carolina and Georgia countrysides. John Reeves and others like him were Fighters for the American Way of Life, bulwarks against the ever present, ever growing Communist Menace. Moreover, the clothier intuitively understood and graciously responded to Richard's constant need for money to sustain a lifestyle grounded not so much in fine homes and goods—though these were obvious accouterments of the successful life—but in an insatiable love of public relations and communications that required highly skilled (and paid) secretaries and expensive office space. Reeves not only loaned Richard money but also made "no objection" when his admiral sought business opportunities elsewhere.[32]

Richard's chronic financial needs grew more acute during the last years of his life. "I made a few minutes' appearance on television in order to help my depleted exchequer," he wrote Harry in the spring of 1954. "It was a show called 'Masquerade.' Just before going on, I felt the whole thing was going to be very undignified; but I guess it came out O.K." He also made other television appearances at that time, and maintained a heavy lecture schedule. A year later Richard complained yet again of being terribly overworked, "trying to do things for Uncle Sam to the point where it is absolutely essential that I get help."

He wrote Texas cousin Harold Byrd that "except for official matters," the navy gave him no assistance as he began to arrange another Antarctic expedition. "I have a list of about a hundred" other efforts he was making to aid his country that "stem directly from my enormous activity in the past in connection with exploration." He had decided this spring of 1955 to establish "some sort of an organization as suggested by Coleman Andrews, the Tax Commissioner." The result was Antarctic Associates. By the time the organization materialized he had enlisted the invaluable assistance of David Martin, who had come over from the International Refugee Committee to be his personal secretary. Martin subsequently wrote that Richard's many "friends and admirers" had "prevailed upon the Admiral to permit the establishment of a non-profit organization known as 'Antarctica Associates, Inc.,'" to collect tax deductible contributions to Richard's many causes. Martin went so far in the summer of 1955 as to propose to cousin Harold that he bring together "20 or 25 leading Texans" at a Dallas dinner to present Richard "with a purse of 25 to 50 thousand dollars" prior to the admiral's impending departure for the ice. "Of course," Martin added, the money would not be for Byrd's personal use, "but to assist him in rendering his continuing services to our nation in the realm of polar exploration." Such a lofty objective would crumble in the face of Richard's declining health. In one of the last letters he wrote, Richard told Harold (who had just contributed a thousand dollars to the organization), "If it weren't for the Antarctic Associates, I would be completely sunk."[33]

By midcentury Richard was devoting an increasing portion of his always crowded schedule to international philanthropy. During and after the war years he devoted considerable energy to the moral rearmament movement while decrying the growing communist menace to all who would listen. These preoccupations soon melded into a single cause: the plight of displaced persons and political refugees fleeing from behind Stalin's Iron Curtain. In the late forties Richard became honorary chairman of the International Rescue Committee (occasionally referred to as the International Relief and Rescue Committee), originally founded in 1933 to assist escapees from Nazi Germany. He also chaired its offshoot, the Iron Curtain Refugee Campaign (ICRC), formed in 1945 to send emergency food and clothing aid "to people who have fled from Russia and her satellite states." By 1949 the International Rescue Committee was dedicated to "political rescue work" of "antitotalitarian democrats from the secret police of Europe" and included among the list of those saved artist Marc Chagall, musician Wanda Landowska, and writers Franz Werfel and Hans Habe. Nearly one hundred thousand "escapees" from Communist eastern Europe were in West Germany, the Allied zones of Austria, France, and Turkey.

Among the fifty-one ICRC field-workers scattered across eight European countries from Turkey to Sweden were six Americans. "Professionally trained, politically educated, personally dedicated," the primary task of these field-workers "is the rescue and relief of the most valuable elements among the anti-Communist refugees, the potential leaders of a liberated Eastern Europe." But once they were rescued and their immediate needs met, they were often adrift. The task of the Iron Curtain Refugee Committee was to get the best or most promising of these people into the United States and to care for them while they got their feet on the ground.

Richard's letters inviting various prominent Americans to become affiliated with his campaign boiled with enthusiasm. "During the last decade we have succeeded in crushing one totalitarian evil. Now the Soviet police state rises to enslave men and nations under the banners of another totalitarianism. Before the march of this Eastern scourge, hundreds of thousands of men, women, and children are escaping from behind the Iron Curtain because they will not live in bondage. They come to us confident the free West will aid them."

Once again, Richard displayed a flair for attracting to his banner people with whom he was deeply at odds philosophically. Among the prominent state governors whose name appeared on the campaign masthead were such liberal luminaries as Adlai Stevenson of Illinois and the prominent New Dealer Chester Bowles of Connecticut. California's Earl Warren was also listed, but Warren's liberalism would not be clearly evident for another decade. The sponsoring committee included such other prominent liberals as A. A. Berle, Eleanor Roosevelt, Helen Gahagan Douglas (soon to be smeared by young Richard Nixon as "the Pink Lady"), and the ubiquitous Arthur Schlesinger Jr. Moderates and conservatives were represented by former New York governor and two-time Republican presidential nominee Thomas E. Dewey and New Hampshire governor Sherman Adams, who would become President Eisenhower's chief of staff. Prominent writers and intellectuals of a moderately leftist bent included poet and author Archibald MacLeish, critic Henry Seidel Canby, and librettist Oscar Hammerstein Jr.[34]

As with all else he did, Richard threw himself energetically into the campaign, speaking, signing letters of invitation to join the campaign as well as newspaper advertisements, and doubtless spending long hours on the telephone networking to bring one more vibrant organization into being. He infused his speeches on behalf of the campaign with the vague rhetoric of moral rearmament: mankind must somehow unite behind the golden rule, the basis of all religions and philosophies, to bring about a peaceful and prosperous world. His letters of invitation to the powerful and famous invoked "this new terror" of communism and its "revival," in even more all-pervading form, of the concentration-camp system. Refugees from and brave agents throughout Eastern Europe were providing documentary evidence of "the rise of organized terror equivalent to that of Nazi Germany."[35]

Richard terminated his duties with the Iron Curtain Refugee Campaign late in June 1950 once its initial program was complete. But he continued to work hard almost to the day of his death for the parent International Rescue Committee despite his ostensible figurehead status as honorary chairman. In the spring of 1950 the campaign and committee, apparently under Byrd's leadership, sent at least one and perhaps several large shipments of food, clothing, and bedding to the citizens of Berlin just struggling upward from the terrible effects of the yearlong Soviet blockade of the city. Three years later Byrd was prominently featured in a gala dinner in honor of West Berlin mayor Ernst Reuter. Within weeks the workers of East Berlin would stage the first of several abortive East European uprisings against communist rule, and in a brief welcoming essay published as part of the dinner program, Richard wrote that free men believed in individual rights that "no power should curtail. Today we see these rights flouted with bestial contempt" in East Berlin and elsewhere throughout the communist bloc.[36]

The International Rescue Committee was far more politically aggressive and conservative in makeup than the Iron Curtain Refugee Campaign. Leo Cherne and Joseph Buttinger, both professional anticommunists, headed the organization as chairmen and cochairmen, while retired diplomat and international troubleshooter Angier Biddle Duke was president. The board of directors was generally undistinguished with the exception of movie mogul Samuel Goldwyn and critic Henry Canby. One name that appeared on both the campaign and committee letterheads, however, was General William J. ("Wild Bill") Donovan, wartime head of the Office of Strategic Services, the precursor to the CIA. By the midfifties, Donovan and the International Rescue Committee had become actively involved in combating a Soviet "come home" drive to lure defectors back to their Eastern European and Russian homelands, and had also expanded its activities to Southeast Asia.

"Free South Vietnam, Asia's Rice Bowl," had become, in the committee's words, "A Sanctuary of Freedom." The Geneva Accords of 1954 provided for division of Vietnam at the seventeenth parallel on May 19, 1955. Prior to that time, peoples would be free to move either south or north at their discretion. According to a committee report published in late 1955, thousands of refugees poured into the South, threatening to overwhelm the fragile new government. Swiftly, "a voluntary mobilization of the free world took shape spearheaded" by young business and professional people in the Philippines, soon joined by the International Junior Chamber of Commerce and the International Rescue Committee. The mobilization effort soon picked up a name, "Operation Brotherhood," and a cochairman, Richard Byrd. In July 1955, when Angier Biddle Duke prepared to leave for Southeast Asia to oversee the operation, Richard sent him on his way with a letter to South Vietnam's embattled prime minister, a young, rather strange chap named Ngo Dinh Diem. Richard praised Diem for his struggle "against heavy odds" to keep South Vietnam a sanctuary for freedom-loving Vietnamese. In a lengthy letter Richard indicated that he knew something about events on the ground in Vietnam. He had read the reports of the field representative, had spoken at length to Duke, and begged Diem to provide the committee's envoy with all necessary information together with "your frank opinions" so that Operation Brotherhood could continue to be an effective agent of assimilation.[37]

Richard's longtime prominence guaranteed that his refugee work would be noticed; the public mood guaranteed that it would be praised. Sometime around 1950 a national magazine provided a flattering thumbnail sketch of Byrd's leadership of the Iron Curtain Refugee Campaign, and in the summer of 1954 President Eisenhower wrote an informal note to Byrd bestowing "my personal appreciation of your services to our country—services in a wide variety of fields and covering a span of many years," most recently with respect to "escapees from the iron curtain countries." Ike also thanked the admiral for supporting the administration's "philosophy and legislative programs." In fact, both Richard and Harry were becoming resigned to "Eisenhower Republicanism" as perhaps the best they could hope for in the foreseeable future.[38]

Richard received one last acknowledgment of his continued public stature in the spring of 1956, when famed newsman Edward R. Murrow profiled him and Marie on *Person-to-Person,* a program that combined celebrity gazing with tasteful restraint in a combination rarely again seen on popular television. A pleased Richard grumbled to Harry that "I couldn't see Ed Murrow. He was in New York and I was in Boston. If I get a passing mark [Harry had praised his appearance enthusiastically] that is all I expect on my speeches, etc."[39]

By this time Richard was fully involved in the International Geophysical Year, that all-consuming monster that sucked every Antarctic penny and program into its maw. Clearly, bureaucratic and professional careers and empires would be forged within IGY confines, and ambitious individuals were already maneuvering for choice positions. It was no place for a sixty-five-year-old man of lingering will but faltering powers.

Richard had gone to Panama late in 1953 in connection with one of his many duties and projects, in this case a dollar-a-year job as director of the Panama Canal Company. He picked up a virus there and when he returned home the following February soon fell violently ill with a "bug" and a stubborn high fever that gripped him for many months while he struggled to piece together the implications of the forthcoming IGY. At one point in June he suffered a serious attack of the hiccups and spent the summer of 1954 in and out of the hospital while some of the best medical specialists in Boston and New England tried to isolate and kill the "bug." In September he went back to the hospital with a prolonged temperature of 104 degrees, and alarmed doctors injected him with "massive doses of penicillin," which finally did the trick. By the end of September his fever was at last gone, leaving him weak and debilitated, weighing no more than 130 pounds. He admitted to Harry that Dr. Chester Keefer of Massachusetts Memorial Hospital "might have saved my life!" Even then, Richard's driven personality allowed him no rest. "I never stayed in bed. I had too much energy to do that and they allowed me to walk up and down the corridors of the hospital, which I did after the fashion of a caged lion." He had always been slim, but from now on he would be gaunt, and a bit shaky. At one point a visiting nurse nicked a blood vessel while administering a shot, and he had to be rushed back to the hospital, where he bled internally for more than seven hours while staff began arranging an emergency operation. The artery stopped bleeding on its own; no one knew why. "Please keep it confidential about my being in the hospital," Richard begged Harry. "Washington is a terrible place for gossip where sickness is concerned. Besides, I hate like hell to admit that I have been sick. I am only telling you about my condition because I told you that I would."[40]

As he fought to regain his health, the IGY swept past him, and only a modest initiative by the National Security Council provided an opportunity to clutch a handhold. A U.S. National Committee on the IGY headed by Dr. Joseph Kaplan of the University of California–Los Angeles had been formed as early as March

1953 to plan the American contribution to this multipronged international program, and Byrd's old Antarctic hands Paul Siple and Lloyd Berkner were soon appointed to it. As the pace of preparation speeded up in the autumn of 1954, Detlev Bronk, president of the National Academy of Sciences, asked Larry Gould to form an Antarctic subcommittee "in order to plan more carefully the scientific activities in that region and to deal with the related logistics problems." Anticipating the subcommittee's formation, Bronk had asked Byrd the previous June to become the expert consultant to the Gould subcommittee. Richard struggled to remain aloof. "I have, as perhaps you know, long been interested in organizing another expedition to the Antarctic and in developing more interest on the part of our government in the scientific investigation of Antarctica." But he would, Richard told Bronk, accept the consultant's job with the understanding that "I would like to see any undertaking with which I might be connected cooperate 100% with the International Geophysical Year."[41]

The National Security Council had naturally become interested in the political, diplomatic, and military ramifications of the IGY and formed a committee to investigate the nature and extent of formal U.S. government participation. Richard told Gould "in the strictest confidence" that he had been asked to chair the NSC Working Committee, "but I couldn't give the time that would be required in that job." But it may well have been Richard who suggested to the NSC committee that an icebreaker be sent south a year early to scout out possible U.S. IGY sites and also determine if any facilities from Highjump eight years before remained for possible use by the IGY.[42]

By the end of November 1954 Richard finally began to move, taking matters into his hands in a rapid "evolution of polar matters." He had gotten Ashley McKinley and George Dufek deeply involved in the government planning process and had pushed himself and Dufek (who was chairman of an Antarctic-policy group in the Pentagon) to the head of the queue of those about to say formal good-bye to the icebreaker *Atka* as it departed for Antarctic waters. Gould (whom he had just successfully recommended for membership to the prestigious Century Club in New York City) asked him to move from expert adviser to honorary chairman of the IGY Antarctic Committee, which he graciously accepted. At last, in the spring of 1955, the White House announced that "the United States will send an expedition to the Antarctic next November to begin work on three observation sites needed in connection with the . . . International Geophysical Year. Rear Admiral Richard E. Byrd . . . will be designated . . . officer in charge, the same title he held on the last Navy Antarctic expedition in 1946–47."

The appointment elicited "many favorable editorials" and one substantial puff piece in the *Washington Star,* depicting him as adventurous as always, poised to "command the U.S. International Geophysical year expeditions to the Antarctic . . . next November" and determined to unlock the final secrets still shrouded behind the South Pole. Richard was pleased but wary. "It would seem that the people of the country favored my selection," he wrote nephew Harry, but there were "enemies in Washington who want my job. Strangely enough, they were born in Norway. I brought them over here and helped them for years. I guess that's the way of life." But for a time, even the Norwegian threat faded. As officer in charge Richard possessed power to approve or veto assignments. He told Gould in May that he was "fathering a bill that would enable Dufek to be Task Force Commander. He is a splendid man." In fact, the navy had already promoted Dufek from captain to rear admiral in order to become commander, U.S. Naval Support Force, Antarctica (Task Force 43). Richard's intervention simply ensured ratification by a Congress and White House already more than a little bewitched by the whole concept of an International Geophysical Year. "In January 1955, proud of his creativity, Dufek proposed the code name Operation Deepfreeze for the Navy's IGY role. (The name would be changed to Deep Freeze in late 1956 when the Amana food-freezer complained of copyright infringement.)"

In August Ronne wrote a rather cringing letter, begging the admiral to know that he had nothing to do with yet another incendiary column by the mischievous Drew Pearson charging that unnamed "government officials" were scheming "to undermine" Byrd's leadership of the IGY in favor of Ronne. Ronne begged Byrd to understand that he was as badly hurt as anyone since he wanted assignment to the Weddell Sea area "and hope that something for me can be included in the overall IGY plans for both this year and the coming years." Byrd had already favorably mentioned Ronne's work in a recent Sunday *American Weekly* article for which Ronne expressed deep appreciation. Ronne, too, got his wish, and before he sailed south in early November 1956 (aboard the icebreaker *Staten Island* that included the author among its crew) he wrote the patron he would never see again "to express to you again my pleasure with my assignment to the Weddell Station and my appreciation of your good efforts in my behalf."[43]

But behind the influence and the laudatory articles and editorials lurked a cruel reality. Scientists and sailors were circling each other warily, each side determined to shape and control the IGY enterprise. The scientists had correctly concluded early on that Dufek and his naval superiors had their own agenda to subvert IGY scientific programs to the navy's interest in "arriv[ing] at a dependable appraisal of [Antarctica's] military worth," including "yet undiscovered strategic materials." Many observers, including veteran Antarctic correspondent Walter Sullivan, interpreted Byrd's command responsibility narrowly; the admiral would simply "monitor policy" that others both forged and implemented. Even that narrow mandate, however, placed a tired and worn-out man in a bind, for it left open exactly who would make policy and whose needs and agendas would drive the IGY. Would it be the navy and Defense Department with their strategic interests in further mapping and exploration or the civilian scientific component with its interest in observation and analysis?[44]

Throughout the summer and fall of 1955, as the IGY took shape, Richard spent several weeks in Washington, talking to congressmen and responsible officials in the various executive departments. He wrote Hugh Odishaw, the executive secretary of the U.S. IGY national committee, that although collaboration between the navy's latent Task Force 43 and the scientific programs and personnel of the IGY were generally proceeding at "an outstandingly happy and productive" pace, "there are several points at which improvement might be possible." Alarmed scientists saw matters in a much blacker hue. A full year earlier, Balchen, who was briefly assigned to the National Science Foundation in 1954–1955 to work on initial IGY planning, fueled Gould's growing concerns about the navy's real agenda. "Odishaw had a conference with Dick Black the other day and Black told him that he had asked Karl Eklund if he would be willing to take command of the [impending] South Pole station. Black figures on taking charge of the Main Base. This, in addition to what Capt. Dufek told us at the briefing on the 13th of October, leads me to conclude that it is the Navy's intent to take over the whole operation of the Antarctic program for the IGY."[45] Balchen created, stimulated, or reflected the central anxiety that would dog the Antarctic community for years to come.

With his great moral authority, Byrd might have resolved the scientist-sailor impasse at the outset. He chose not to try during the critical early months of IGY planning. His health remained poor, but he also insisted on remaining active with refugee work while incessantly reworking and revising his thoughts on the proper path to world peace and understanding. Gould tried to bring him along, passing on critical information ("the whole matter of logistics for the International Geophysical Year is now in the hands of the committee headed by Dufek, and I judge he is doing a very good job of it"), notifying him of every important meeting of the Antarctic Committee, and receiving in return the admiral's regrets that he could not attend this time, but would Larry like to know what he was doing to stop the drift toward socialism at home and war abroad?[46] More vigorous and committed people began stepping into a leadership vacuum made acute by both personal and institutional rivalries.

Richard at last glimpsed the ground shifting, and did the sensible thing: he reached for more power, rushing to the one man in authority who owed him a number of favors. Chief of Naval Operations Arthur Radford pressed officials in the defense secretary's office to issue a statement, which Richard believed both clarified and amplified his responsibilities as officer in charge. In fact, it did no such thing. The directive issued by acting defense secretary Reuben B. Robertson on October 21, 1955, directed Richard to work through the secretary of defense and the department's Operations Coordinating Board "on matters pertaining to the U.S. Antarctic Program." But the statement employed terms such as *advise, assist,* and *recommend* at every point where an officer truly in charge would have been given the authority to *direct* and to *order.* Moreover, the directive now firmly tied Richard to the navy and the Defense Department—agencies that the scientific community argued should play subordinate roles in implementing the IGY. It was a recipe for incessant conflict. The position was no place for an exhausted man. Richard, however, chose to interpret the directive positively. He told Harry that it showed "what a tremendous task I have. . . . Harry, old fellow, I have had a terrific battle for two years. The . . . directive marks the end of it." He had waged a lonely struggle, Richard added, with only Radford and Harry to help him "nullify to a degree inordinately ambitious men who wanted my job and a certain officer's great effort to humiliate me."[47]

In the meantime, no officer in charge could be kept out of Antarctica. Moreover, Odishaw, fearing the navy would overwhelm IGY scientific activities with its own strategic agendas, wanted Byrd and several civilian scientists to accompany the ships and men of Deep Freeze I whose mission was to establish the first three American scientific stations at McMurdo Sound, Kainan Bay, and the South Pole. Odishaw evidently thought Byrd to be sufficiently detached and evenhanded as to keep his old subordinate George Dufek in line. Late in November 1955 Richard flew off to New Zealand, where he won wide praise, thanking the Kiwis for use of Christchurch as an essential aerial staging point for U.S. Antarctic operations and for deferring to the existence of the developing U.S. base at McMurdo Sound within the New Zealand Antarctic claim.[48] December 15 found the Admiral of the Antarctic on the bridge of the navy's newest and most powerful icebreaker, *Glacier,* as it first encountered the South Polar ice pack. Strung out behind the mighty icebreaker were several smaller sisters of the "Wind" class, escorting three cargo ships.

Richard had never seen anything like it. Twenty-seven years earlier the first hardy band of Byrd men had wedged and pushed their way through the pack aboard the 502-ton, 200-horsepower *City of New York* with only the sound of a wooden hull against ice and the occasional cry of a bird or penguin or seal to break the silence. Now the 8,625-ton steel-girt *Glacier* crunched and smashed its way along, while sky and sea were blasted by the noise of big reconnaissance helicopters gliding and hovering overhead. Byrd would have witnessed a roughly similar scene back in 1947 had he gone into the Bay of Whales with the Highjump Central Group. But he had chosen a risky flight instead.

With both Byrd and Dufek aboard, flag quarters on the icebreaker were cramped. Richard deferred to Dufek and took the smaller cabin so that the task force commander would have sufficient room to conduct daily staff meetings. The two men prowled around each other carefully. Richard was keen to stop from time to time to establish oceanographic observation stations; an increasingly impatient Dufek, tasked with the enormous responsibility of establishing a permanent American presence on the white continent, usually deferred with greater or lesser grace.

Antarctica by now was so familiar to the old explorer, yet so eternally fascinating. "Seals dotted the ice," Richard later wrote; "a few fat, lazy Weddells, many slimmer, more agile crabeaters, and the occasional voracious sea leopard and rare Ross seal. Adélie penguins, Antarctica's perennial welcoming committee, tobogganed on their stomachs across the ice to escape the onrushing ship." *Glacier* first went to McMurdo Sound on the far southern edge of the Ross Sea. As the great ship's motors died out, an awed crew stood amid a sudden silence, mesmerized by towering Mount Erebus that lay before them. Following a quick reconnaissance and a "photo op" with Byrd on the ice (which confirmed a U.S. right of occupancy), *Glacier* and a small convoy of cargo ships and icebreakers moved along the massive ice barrier to Kainan Bay, thirty-five miles east of what was left of the Bay of Whales, and established Little America V. By now, this part of the massive Ross Barrier was becoming progressively unstable, and after serving through the International Geophysical Year, Little America V would be abandoned in the austral summer of 1959–1960.[49]

Once on the ice there was little for Byrd to do. Dufek, Major Murray Weiner (the air force adviser), Bill Hawkes (the chief pilot), and Siple (director of scientific projects) knew what flights and tractor journeys they wanted made. For the first time, aircraft would deploy to Antarctica direct from another landmass, New Zealand. So Richard, an old man now in his late sixties, desperately tired and frail, had his picture taken with Siple, Weiner (on his third Byrd expedition), Eddie Goodale (of BAE I fame), and young Dickie, still, as in 1947, a navy lieutenant. He willed himself to tramp around the remnants of the Bay of Whales, looking at the remains of his earlier Little Americas, and visited the ships off-loading cargo along the low Kainan Bay ice tongue.

The old magic was still there. Young Cliff Bekkedahl, navigator of the navy cargo ship *Arneb,* was in the wardroom when "the Virginia gentleman of just never-to-be-seen-again presence" walked in.

> The place just went silent in respect . . . clearly there was a presence in the room—a slight, handsome, distinguished looking gentleman, probably in his 70s at the time [Richard was sixty-six]. . . . A living hero. Someone I had read about in elementary school. And as he worked his way around the wardroom

and came to the junior officers and it was my turn to say hello, and you know he just had this way of making you feel like you were the only person in the room and the only reason he came to the Antarctic was to have a conversation with you. He asked exactly the right questions and would listen, and of course, in my role as navigator, he instantly had some very kind, generous words to say about the challenge and responsibility. . . . A slight, not very firm handshake, but again, he was an older man.

Bekkedahl noticed "a rather short, dark-haired, stocky full lieutenant" with the caduceus of a medical doctor on his collar standing nearby. Edging over to the "not . . . very happy looking young man," Bekkedahl asked if he was enjoying his Antarctic adventure. Not in the least! the man replied. In fact, he was hating every moment of it. "I'm here to make sure the Admiral doesn't die. If the Admiral dies, my Navy career is gone, shot, they told me that. That I was not to let the Admiral," who insisted on "going up and down ladders, going in and out of helicopters and that sort of thing," die "while he was down in the Antarctic." Many who saw him up close wondered if he might not die before he got home. But in a way he was home. "I am mayor of this place," he joked to the cameramen, and his comment was quickly picked up and sent around the world.

But there were heartbreaking moments, too, reminders that for all the magic and the reputation, the Admiral or Mayor of Antarctica no longer wielded power and influence or even generated much respect among the careless and thoughtless. Byrd's old comrade "Bud" Waite was still a vigorous and active player on the South Polar stage, and he recalled years later that "one of Dufek's LCDRs [lieutenant commanders] actually refused Byrd the use of a plane one day in the early Deep-freezes. I wasn't there but the old man, very weak and sometimes even pitiful in his thinking in that modern fleet was badly upset for days." Richard Conger, Byrd's personal photographic assistant, told the author that soon after the old man had come back from the ice, he broke down and wept, "They don't want me anymore, Dick. They don't want me anymore."[50]

Between the third and fourteenth of January 1956, the fliers of Deep Freeze I in their R5D "workhorses" fanned out over much of Antarctica, concentrating on the South Pole area and the "pole of inaccessibility" beyond that had beckoned Richard nearly a decade before. One day Richard himself climbed into a plane, tightly bundled in heavy clothing and blankets, and flew to the pole—now a relatively brief three-to-four-hour journey. Once again, there could be no thought of a landing. Richard could claim to have been to the bottom of the earth three times without ever having set foot on it.

There were reasons for this frenetic activity. Washington wanted to stake out the politically and scientifically most important base sites for itself, especially at the South Pole itself, and the United States was the first member to go to Antarctica in strength. Byrd's mere presence imparted a stronger legitimacy to the quest, though the insistence of friends and family that he was instrumental in "locat[ing] and establish[ing] sites for other bases" seems a bit extreme, given the breadth and many interests of the polar scientific community by that time. Pictures show the admiral thin almost to the point of emaciation, and though Dufek could not keep him from the polar flight, he doubtless would have overruled his superior's wish to attempt other adventures. Byrd's chief actions were to dispatch a note to the Soviet IGY party, welcoming it to Antarctica and informing its members exactly where U.S. aircraft had flown and explored (according to Sullivan a kind of "we got here first" initiative), and to recommend that the IGY parties active in Antarctica form some sort of permanent compact beyond rather than within the confines of the United Nations. One subordinate would recall "many truly wonderful chats" with the old man. "At the time he was being harassed by a lot of needless maneuvers on the part of certain junior officers," said Robert Hendrickson, "and I shall always like to think that in some measure I was able to ease his burdens on this phase of his operations in Antarctica." A number of youngsters, especially enlisted men, would recall decades later that meeting or seeing the Admiral of the Antarctic was one of their great moments on the ice.[51]

By February 1, after only a month at Little America, Richard headed home aboard *Arneb*. Whether it entered his mind that he might be seeing the last of this horrid, enthralling land he loved so much and had done so much to explore and to publicize, he never said. Three weeks later he was back in Boston.

He fought to the end. As final planning for the IGY swung into high gear in the summer of 1956, Larry Gould, always sympathetic to "the Norwegians" and sharing their assessment of Richard's character, sought to ensure that the U.S. contribution to the IGY would not become just another Byrd expedition. In March 1956, Gould wrote Balchen that "there seem to have been major differences of opinion between REB and the naval commanders in Deepfreeze #1. I predict there will be a big row, and I am keeping my fingers crossed." Gould was aware that Balchen proposed to make a dramatic Scandinavia-to-Antarctica, or perhaps even pole-to-pole, flight as part of the IGY. The Norwegian had recently been home talking the matter over with friends, and had also raised the matter with Joseph Kaplan and Hugh Odishaw, the leading scientific figures in the American IGY. Now the Norwegian government was ready to formally approach the United States about the scheme and naturally planned to contact and work through Dick Byrd as officer in charge of the U.S. Antarctic Program. Balchen was aghast, "as it might kill the whole thing even before we get a chance to get it out. The only chance for

them to get this through with REB in the picture, is if I pull out of it entirely."
Balchen added that he was strengthened in this belief "by information I gathered
about REB's and his henchmen's doings in IGY and Deepfreeze." Balchen told
Gould that he had informed the Norwegian government and scientific community that they could, in effect, work with IGY or "REB" but not both. Gould
agreed. "Nothing could be worse than to have this thing funneled" through Dick
Byrd. "If REB gets involved, it might turn into a publicity stunt for him." The
matter was apparently never pursued.[52]

Although Gould clearly mistrusted and disliked Byrd, he needed him—everyone in the Antarctic community did. With the IGY commitment to build four
more Antarctic scientific stations during Deep Freeze II close at hand, command
relationships had to be clarified, and Byrd at least had to formally ratify whatever
decisions were reached. Gould's motives at this point are obscure, but he may well
have hoped to exploit real or potential divisions between Byrd and his "henchmen"
on the one hand and the navy on the other to gain dominance or at least autono-
my for the scientists. In late July 1956 he submitted a proposal titled "Antarctic
Operational Command Relationships" to Byrd and the Navy Department for their
comment. Richard replied immediately that he had "gone over" the paper but
wished to defer a final opinion until Siple returned from the ice "and we can discuss the matter thoroughly." Gould wanted Siple to command the South Pole Station. "Of all Antarctic IGY assignments this is the 'plum' and Paul is the man for
it," Gould told Byrd. "Everyone is in agreement about this. . . . I do greatly hope
that it will be possible for you to take such action as is necessary as soon as possible for Paul to take on this assignment."

But Byrd—and Siple—saw complications. As chief scientist, Siple was also
Byrd's de facto deputy, and in a position to oversee activities at all seven of the proposed U.S. IGY stations that would dot the Antarctic landscape. Moreover, he was
in a prime position to help Gould plot the course of the U.S. Antarctic Research
Program. Siple rather liked his current role; so did Byrd. "Paul and I both realize
that you have to make a decision in a hurry on the South Pole base," Richard wrote
Gould on August 17, "and I just want to assure you that we have been giving this
matter a lot of thought." Siple would make a decision within a fortnight, and
Richard told Gould that it properly was his to make. He hoped that, as South Pole
base commander, Siple could still "spend part of his time in the IGY office, so that
he could coordinate plans with you and help in the selection of personnel." Siple
was unquestionably the best man for the South Pole job, "but the whole situation
has become so complicated that Paul has been having a devil of a time trying to
make up his mind."[53]

Nine days later Richard sent a four-page memorandum to the chief of naval operations, Arleigh Burke, commenting on Gould's proposed Antarctic operational command relationships. Like so many of his productions since 1945 it was often rambling and verbose. Nor did it address the question as to whether Siple could be both South Pole base commander and IGY chief scientist. But Richard got his idea of command firmly across. Leadership, not structure, was what counted in Antarctica. Gould's paper "is a meticulously worded compendium to satisfy differences of opinion at staff levels between designated agencies." It evidently concluded that the only way to solve the desires of both the IGY scientists and the navy for command responsibility was to share authority. But such a solution "fails completely to fix local responsibility for the essential ingredients of harmony such as morale . . . and communal cooperation." Defense and the scientific community together should find, identify, and choose the best people.

> I would place the stations under single, clearly defined leadership acceptable to [both] the Department of Defense and IGY, regardless of whether it is military or civilian. If any individual assigned to a base objects to the leader because of his being a military man or a civilian, transfer him to a place where he will be satisfied. The men going to a base must as fully accept the assigned leader as the leader is willing to accept the men. The best way to safeguard minority interests if the base has either civilian or military leadership is to establish an executive officer under the leader to handle military base functions on the one hand, or the science program on the other.

Having cut right to the point, Richard proceeded to elaborate. He had been requested, he told Burke, to assign "my Deputy, Dr. Paul Siple, to the position of scientific leader of the South Polar base." This would not do. Under Gould's proposed command relations, this uniquely experienced and qualified Antarctic veteran would have to "make known" his logistic needs "to some junior officer or noncom logistician over whom he would have no authority and who could not possibly have the polar living experience of Dr. Siple." Presumably, "a capable leader" could "make a go of any situation," Richard continued, but the U.S. program should strive for something better at all seven of his Antarctic research stations: leadership that was "simple, straightforward, and without strings attached." In Siple's case, "if assigned complete charge of the South Polar Base," he "could make a vital contribution in an area where the attention of the scientists is focused." But Richard extrapolated in ways that could only have been disturbing to the navy and heartening to the scientists, if they had known about it. "The station leaders being assigned by the IGY [that is, Gould and the other senior scientists] are senior, mature men, leaders not only in their fields, but leaders of men. I can not believe that the proposed dual command" suggested in the Gould paper "presents a framework for their satisfactory working out [of] their responsibilities."

Richard concluded with a peroration: "If we don't maintain an all-out first team effort, the IGY, Department of Defense, Navy, U.S. Air Force—in short, the nation—will become embarrassed."[54]

Richard got his way, at least with regard to Siple and the South Pole Station. Gould, who had kept out of the fight by taking a two-month fishing vacation at Jackson Hole, thanked him handsomely: "I think your memorandum of August 20 in answer to the one over my signature is a superb statement. I think back to my various experiences in exploration, and I am sure you are right about keeping the command single rather than split." By mid-September Siple was packing his bags to go back to the ice and to the most awful spot on earth.[55]

But Richard paid heavily for his success. Dufek by this time utterly mistrusted him and in a fit of pique kept Siple off the first flight to actually land at the South Pole on the last day of October 1956. According to Deep Freeze historian Dian Olson Belanger, Dufek "'emphatically stated' that only Navy personnel" would be on the flight whose departure was revealed to the flight crew at the last moment. Pilot Gus Shinn would later "suggest" that Dufek's "motive for secrecy was that he did not want Siple, of the 'Byrd faction,' on that plane to share the glory."[56]

Two months later *Time* magazine's last issue for 1956 featured Siple on its cover and in a long accompanying article on the building of South Pole Station (soon to be renamed Scott-Amundsen South Pole Station at Byrd's own urging) quite dismissed Dick Byrd as a has-been. His title of officer in charge was "largely honorary," the article said, adding, quite cruelly, that "some senior officers" on Operation Deep Freeze II "have found the aging Byrd a difficult man to deal with, and as a 'Byrd man' Siple has inherited some of their antagonism." Since George Dufek commanded Deep Freeze II there was no question where the navy's opposition to Byrd's leadership—and Siple's—lay. The article proceeded to laud Siple's ability to shrug off conflict by carrying "the buddy-system philosophy even to these austere levels of disagreement. 'Intolerance,'" he was quoted as saying in an obvious dig at Dufek, "'is a symptom of someone's inability to adjust to the next guy's faults,'" a perfect comment on how Antarctica had taught one man to live a gracious and productive life.[57]

By now, Richard was utterly spent, confined to Brimmer Street. Old friends came one last time. "In mid-February [1957] things began to add up that he was not long for this world," Richard Black told Siple months later.[58] Byrd's friends in the Defense Department thought a "high honor might cheer him and possibly prolong his life." Perhaps President Eisenhower could bestow a Freedom Award. But that would take months and a congressional approval that not even Harry Byrd could rush through. On the other hand, the secretary of defense could award Richard a Medal of Freedom—the highest civilian award—as soon as he wished.

Black and the navy got things moving, and very early on the morning of Feb-

ruary 21, 1957, Arleigh Burke "and about ten of us," including Black and Harry
Byrd, climbed into Burke's R4D (the same type of aircraft used in Operations
Highjump and Deep Freeze) and flew up to Boston. Navy Public Affairs got the
word: no photographers or press either on landing or at 9 Brimmer Street. Marie
and Dickie were expecting them at eleven o'clock, and they were prompt. The party was ushered into the downstairs library, where coffee and sandwiches waited.
After a moment Marie and Dickie appeared with "the doctors." There would be a
little delay, the party was told as Marie departed. Later Black learned that it was
due to Richard's difficulty in dressing; he had to take "frequent and long" applications of oxygen, twenty minutes' worth, then a trouser leg; another twenty minutes, the other trouser leg; and so on. The admiral would be in full dress uniform;
nothing less would do. And he would be in the upstairs office, sitting in his favorite chair, from which he had planned and directed the very greatest efforts and
moments of his—and of many other peoples'—lives.

Shortly after noon Marie came down to announce "very cheerfully" that all was
ready. Someone else told the party how the ceremony would be carried out: when
to speak and break away and so on. They climbed the stairs and entered Richard's
office. Black was horrified. He had not seen the admiral since August—six
months. The man now weighed eighty-nine pounds. "His blue uniform looked
like it was on a coat hanger, and his face was the mask of death—but he was erect
and smiling and his eyes were clear and good. Harry walked over first and in old
Virginia style kissed him on the cheek." Richard spotted Burke. "Hello, Arleigh!"
Burke walked over to his side. Then Richard called out each person by name, and
one by one they went over and shook his hand. When about half had been called,
Richard paused and looked at Burke a moment. The chief of naval operations
cleared his throat and began his preamble, but Richard held up his hand and then
greeted the remainder of the party. Burke then read out the citation, stumbling a
bit with emotion. Black saw that Richard had trouble concentrating. He picked
up a stray paper here, another there, once a pencil, "as though about to make some
changes" in the citation perhaps, or to draft "a press release of the event."

At last Burke finished the reading, stepped up to shake Richard's hand, then
turned away. It was the signal for everyone to leave. But as the party started for the
door, Richard held up his hand again, and as all turned and waited expectantly, he
joked softly, "You people are lucky. I don't have to make a speech." Two weeks later, in the midst of a deep sleep, Richard Evelyn Byrd slipped away into that eternity of which the Antarctic winter night that he came to know so well is perhaps
our best metaphor.

Notes

Abbreviations

Byrd Collection	Richard E. Byrd Collection, Handley Regional Library, Winchester, Virginia
Byrd Papers	Admiral Richard E. Byrd Papers, Record Group 56.1, Byrd Polar Research Center Archives, The Ohio State University Archives, Columbus
EBB	Eleanor Bolling Byrd
HFB	Harry F. Byrd
HFB Jr.	Harry F. Byrd Jr.
MAB	Marie Ames Byrd
NARA	National Archives and Records Administration, Suitland, Maryland
REB	Robert E. Byrd
RG	Record Group
USAS	United States Antarctic Service

Introduction

1. "The Spirit of Adventure," undated editorial, folder 43, Byrd Papers.

2. Charles J. V. Murphy, "Admiral Byrd: Greatest Polar Adventurer Goes to Claim Antarctica," 27, 29, 37; Robert N. Matouzzi, "Richard Byrd, Polar Exploration, and the Media," 210.

3. Alton A. Lindsey, "Inside Byrd's Second Antarctic Expedition," p. 13, accession 19935, folder 15, "Publications by Lindsey," Lindsey Papers.

4. Edward Goodale, "Admiral Richard Evelyn Byrd and His Place in History: Nineteen Twenties and Thirties," p. 4, Goodale Papers.

5. Lindsey, "Inside Byrd's Second Antarctic Expedition," 3, 7.

6. Lindsey, "Admiral Richard E. Byrd's Two Approaches to Leadership," p. 3, accession 199815, folder 2, "Byrd and BAE II," Lindsey Papers.

7. Frederick Lewis Allen, *Only Yesterday* (1931; reprint, New York: Bantam, 1957), 252.

8. REB to Rodman Wanamaker, May 23, 1927, folder 4344, Byrd Papers; Byrd, "The First Flight to the North Pole," folder 4272, ibid.

Chapter 1. "Danger Was All That Thrilled Him"

1. Byrd, *Alone* (New York: Kodansha International, 1995), 36, 49–51. This facsimile edition of the 1938 publication issued by G. P. Putnam's Sons of New York contains slightly different pagination than the original. All citations are to this edition.

2. Typescript copy of an untitled article from the *Alexandria (Va.) Gazette,* September 16, 1886, in folder 32, Byrd Papers. Eleanor Bolling's distinguished family line was remembered at her death in 1957, just six months after that of her illustrious son, in an article titled "Mrs. Byrd, Mother of Tom, Dick and Harry, Dies at Home," *Winchester Evening Star,* September 18, 1957, folder 33, ibid.

3. Charles J. V. Murphy, *Struggle: The Life and Exploits of Commander Richard E. Byrd,* 3.

4. Ibid. The quote and related material is from "Virginia Byrds Again to Fore," *New York Times,* February 14, 1926, sec. 9, p. 6.

5. William Byrd II is quoted in Thomas J. Wertenbaker, *The Golden Age of Colonial Culture* (1949; reprint, Ithaca: Cornell University Press, 1961), 125. See also Carl Bridenbaugh, *Myths and Realities: Societies of the Colonial South* (1952; reprint, New York: Atheneum, 1966), 13–193; and Bernard Bailyn, *The Origins of American Politics* (New York: Alfred A. Knopf, 1968), 139. Dick and Harry Byrd's angry reaction to publication of their ancestor's diary is in many letters in folders 45, 47, and 117 in the Byrd Papers. See especially REB to Otway Byrd, February 25, 1942, folder 117; to HFB, March 9, 1942, folder 45; and to HFB, March 20, 24, April 20, 1942, folder 47. Harry's own anger is conveyed in HFB to REB, March 3, 1942, folder 117.

6. John H. Crown, a Baltimore journalist, went to Winchester shortly after Richard Byrd's flight to the North Pole in 1926 and did a thorough study of the town and the Byrd family ("Hometown Bursting with Pride over 'Dick' Byrd," *Baltimore Sun,* May 26, 1926, copy in Byrd Collection). Byrd's comments on Winchester's Civil War experience are in the unpublished portion of his manuscript for *Skyward,* p. 13, folder 3876, Byrd Papers (hereafter cited as *Skyward* manuscript). Maude Ludwig's letter to REB, January 19, 1950, is in folder 33, ibid. Harry Flood Byrd remembered taking his grandmother to the cinema and her teary reaction to the flag (telephone interview with author, November 1, 2001).

7. "Byrd's Rising Star," clipping in folder 41, Byrd Papers.

8. See REB to HFB, April 5, 1950, folder 51, ibid. Douglas Southall Freeman's letter to HFB, May 2, 1951, is in ibid. and quoted in part in Ronald L. Heineman, *Harry Byrd of Virginia* (Charlottesville: University Press of Virginia, 1996), 3. Richard Evelyn's encouragement of young men is recounted by Fred Kosslow to HFB, March 12, 1957, folder 57, Byrd Papers. His insistence on being informally addressed as Dick is in Crown, "Hometown Bursting with Pride."

9. Quoted in Crown, "Hometown Bursting with Pride."

10. Byrd's political philosophy and influence are emphasized in ibid., which also contains the quote about his skills as Virginia House Speaker. He set forth his uncompromising racism in a June 1907 address to the alumni of the College of William and Mary titled "What Have the Public Schools Done for the Negro and What Can They Do?" which was published as a pamphlet, a copy of which is in the Byrd Collection. "My own belief," Byrd told his audience, "is that the negro must be placed in a condition of absolute and unquestioned subordination. The subordination must pertain to every point of contact with the white race. This is not only essential to the stability and prosperity of society, but it is essential not only to the well being but the very continued existence of the black race."

11. Murphy, *Struggle,* 11. The distant blood ties between the two Bolling women were confirmed by Senator Harry Flood Byrd (interview by author, October 25, 2001). His father, Harry Flood Byrd Sr., was usually known as Harry F. Byrd, whereas Harry Flood Byrd Jr. has used all three names. To avoid confusion, I have identified him as HFB Jr. The interview is hereafter cited as HFB Jr. interview, October 25, 2001.

12. Heineman, *Harry Bird of Virginia,* 3.

13. Byrd's comment on his father is in the *Skyward* manuscript, 13. See also Crown, "Hometown Bursting with Pride"; and HFB Jr. interview, October 25, 2001.

14. REB to EBB, December 13, 1949, August 21, 1950, April 8, 1953, folder 33, Byrd Papers. FDR's comparison of Eleanor Byrd and Sara Delano was related in HFB Jr. interview, October 25, 2001.

15. The characterization of Eleanor Byrd is by Murphy, "Admiral Byrd," 29. Murphy was for many years a close friend and chief publicist for Dick Byrd. Dick's recollection is in REB to EBB, June 24, 1952, folder 33, Byrd Papers.

16. REB to EBB, June 24, 1952, December 22, 1954, ibid. Eleanor's disinclination to daughters is in REB to EBB, January 19, 1955, ibid.

17. Crown, "Hometown Bursting with Pride."

18. William C. Alexander to HFB, March 13, 1957, folder 57, Byrd Papers; REB to EBB, July 19, 1952, July 9, 1955, December 22, 1954, folder 33, ibid.

19. Quotes are from Crown, "Hometown Bursting with Pride."

20. Byrd's boyhood recollections are in the *Skyward* manuscript, 12–13. See also Crown, "Hometown Bursting with Pride." Her comments about her son's daring are in Heineman, *Harry Byrd of Virginia,* 5; "'Dick' Byrd as a Mercury of Modern Flying Science," *Literary Digest* 94, no. 9 (July 23, 1927): 40; and HFB Jr. interview, October 25, 2001. The "Western Gang" episode is in Heineman, *Harry Byrd of Virginia,* 5. Dick's recollections about brother Tom's temper are in REB to HFB, November 19, 1948, folder 33, Byrd Papers, as well as the *Skyward* manuscript, 13. Swanson's recollections are in the introduction to *Discovery: The Story of the Second Byrd Antarctic Expedition,* by Byrd, vii.

21. Murphy, *Struggle,* 12–14. Crown describes the Clarke County farm in "Hometown Bursting with Pride."

22. Whether Robert Peary or Frederick Cook did in fact ever reach the North Pole has become a matter of bitter contention and jealous scholarship. The clearest, most measured, and most compelling evaluation I have found is in Pierre Berton, *The Arctic Grail: The*

Quest for the Northwest Passage and the North Pole, 1818–1909 (New York: Viking Penguin, 1988), 553–631.

23. Byrd, *Skyward* manuscript, 4, 13. For Byrd's youthful determination to be the first to reach the North Pole, see Edwin P. Hoyt, *The Last Explorer: The Adventures of Admiral Byrd,* 21.

24. "Virginia Byrds Again to Fore"; REB to Mrs. Harry F. Byrd, August 2, 1948, folder 49, Byrd Papers; to EBB, August 29, 1950, July 29, 1952, December 22, 1954, folder 33, ibid.

25. Harry Flood Byrd told the author the story of his father and the Antietam Paper Company (interview with HFB Jr., October 25, 2001). Heineman also gives the story prominence in *Harry Byrd of Virginia,* 6–7. See also "Introduction of Senator Harry F. Byrd," folder 33, Byrd Papers; Fred Kosslow to HFB, March 12, 1957, folder 57, ibid.; L. Ferdinand Zerkel to HFB, March 12, 1957, folder 58, ibid.; and Heineman, *Harry Byrd of Virginia,* 5–6.

26. REB to EBB, March 17, 1950, folder 33, Byrd Papers.

27. Bertram Wyatt-Brown, *Southern Honor: Ethics and Behavior in the Old South* (New York: Oxford University Press, 1982), 14–15; Wendell Summers, "Diary and Comments: Operation Highjump with Admiral Byrd, January 2–April 14, 1947," enclosure to letter from Summers to author, August 19, 1998.

28. Byrd, *Skyward* manuscript, 17; REB to EBB, March 17, 1950, folder 33, Byrd Papers. "Youngest Globe Trotter Starts," *Winchester Star,* August 9, 1902, stated that Dick was eleven years old on the day he departed (photocopy in Byrd Collection). John Crown later emphasized Carson's political influence and also stated that young Dick set off for the Far East when he was eleven ("Hometown Bursting with Pride").

29. Mrs. Wendall is referenced in "Youngest Globe Trotter Starts"; and Byrd, *Skyward* manuscript, 15. Byrd's first public reference to traveling around the world at age twelve seems to have been in 1928 in Murphy, *Struggle,* 27. Twenty years later, in 1948, he emphasized the fact again in an official biographical sketch that he prepared for the navy following Operation Highjump (folder 4005, Byrd Papers). In March 1950 he again recalled his trip around the world at age twelve to his mother, who never disputed the assertion (REB to EBB, March 17, 1950, folder 33, ibid.).

30. Typescript copies of the four newspaper articles dated January 26, February 11, March 19, 27, 1903, are in folder 8, Byrd Papers. Photocopies are in the Byrd Collection.

31. Byrd, *Skyward* manuscript, 14–17.

32. Murphy, *Struggle,* 27–33; Swanson, introduction to *Discovery,* by Byrd, vii.

33. Raimund E. Goerler, ed., *To the Pole: The Diary and Notebook of Richard E. Byrd, 1925–1927,* 40.

34. Hoyt, *Last Explorer,* 18.

35. L. Ferdinand Zerkel to HFB, March 12, 1957, folder 58, Byrd Papers; REB to HFB Jr., September 17, 1931, folder 37, ibid.; REB to EBB, January 17, 1950, June 11, 1952, folder 33, ibid.

36. Crown, "Hometown Bursting with Pride."

37. REB diary, January 1, 1925, quoted in Goerler, *To the Pole,* 28.

38. Byrd, *Skyward: Man's Mastery of the Air as Shown by the Brilliant Flights of America's Leading Air Explorer, His Life, His Thrilling Adventures, His North Pole and Trans-Atlantic Flight, Together with His Plans for Conquering the Antarctic by Air* (New York: Jeremy P. Tarcher / Putnam, 2000, a reprint of the 1928 ed. published by G. P. Putnam's Sons), 23–24 (all subsequent citations of this work are from this edition); Hoyt, *Last Explorer,* 23.

39. Murphy, "Admiral Byrd," 29; Swanson, introduction to *Discovery,* by Byrd, viii.

40. *The Lucky Bag, 1912,* 74, copy in Special Collections and Archives Division, Nimitz Library, United States Naval Academy, Annapolis, Maryland. A slightly different text is also in folder 4005, Byrd Papers. Also quoted in part in Swanson, introduction to *Discovery,* by Byrd, ix; and Hoyt, *Last Explorer,* 25–26.

41. "Biography," folder 4005, Byrd Papers; Hoyt, *Last Explorer,* 27–28; Byrd, *Skyward,* 24–25.

42. Roy A. Grossnick et al., *United States Naval Aviation, 1910–1995* (Washington, D.C.: Naval Historical Center, n.d.), 14–15; Hoyt, *Last Explorer,* 29.

43. Hoyt, *Last Explorer,* 29–30.

44. Goerler, *To the Pole,* 10.

45. Murphy, "Admiral Byrd," 30; anonymous to MAB, March 22, 1962, folder 1, Byrd Papers; MAB to REB, n.d., folder 65, ibid.; Bolling Byrd Clark e-mail to the author, September 29, 2001; REB to EBB, June 24, 1952, folder 33, Byrd Papers; "Young Naval Officer Wins Pretty Bride," *Winchester Evening Star,* January 21, 1915, photocopy in Byrd Collection.

46. Joseph B. Ames to Lilla [?], May 9, 1898, folder 1, Byrd Papers.

47. REB to MAB, January 16, [1927], folder 69, ibid.; William D. Leahy to Richard E. Byrd Jr., September 30, 1957, folder 2119, ibid.

48. "Young Naval Officer Wins Pretty Bride."

49. REB to Gladys F. Wood, April 21, 1945, folder 8, Byrd Papers. FDR's comment about the nimble moose is in Arthur M. Schlesinger Jr., *The Crisis of the Old Order, 1919–1933* (Boston: Houghton Mifflin Sentry, 1964), 372.

Chapter 2. Reaching for the Skies

1. Byrd's observation is in Byrd, *Skyward,* 25 (see chap. 1, n. 38). Franklin Roosevelt to REB, n.d., folder 4126, Byrd Papers. Unless otherwise noted, Byrd's postings while on active naval service are set forth in his official biography, "Rear Admiral Richard Evelyn Byrd, Jr., United States Navy Retired," Navy Biographies Branch, OI-450, March 8, 1957, Special Collections and Archives Division, Nimitz Library, United States Naval Academy, Annapolis, Maryland.

2. Copies of Byrd's orders to and instructions regarding command of the Rhode Island

militia, together with his appointment by Governor Beekman to the Promotion Board, are in folders 4126 and 4127, Byrd Papers; "Mattie" to REB, April 16, 1917; Frank S. Livingston to REB, June 1, 1917, folder 4127, ibid.

3. E. G. Blakeslee to REB, January 29, 1917; BuNav to REB, February 6, 1917; Charles W. Abbot [?] Jr. to William S. Sims, April 4, 1917; R. Livingston Beekman to Secretary of the Navy, June 28, 1917, ibid.

4. Undated memorandum from the Navy Department, Bureau of Navigation; Claude Swanson to REB, June 6, 1917, ibid.

5. Byrd, *Skyward,* 25.

6. Josephus Daniels to REB, July 20, 1917; "Navy Department, Commission on Training Camp Activities," undated memorandum; W. G. Isaacs to REB, February 4, 1918; Walter Camp to REB, February 5, 1918; James J. Ewing to REB, February 18, 1918; "Sailors' Recreations," *Baltimore Star,* January 11, 1919, all in folder 4127, Byrd Papers.

7. Byrd, *Skyward,* 25–26. Byrd was able to obtain preliminary orders as early as August 31, 1917, but was apparently held on the commission for some months thereafter, for his orders indicate that he did not report to Pensacola until February 9, 1918. See Navy Department Order no. 791864 to Lieutenant (jg) Richard E. Byrd, USN, Ret., folder 4126, Byrd Papers.

8. Grossnick et al., *United States Naval Aviation,* 12–13; George F. Pearce, *The U.S. Navy in Pensacola: From Sailing Ships to Naval Aviation (1825–1930)* (Pensacola: University Presses of Florida, 1980), 121.

9. Pearce, *U.S. Navy in Pensacola,* 148, 156, 158.

10. In May 1955, Byrd identified as "girls" and "hefty girls" the thousand-odd cattle that the navy contemplated taking to the Antarctic in support of the several scientific stations to be established there. A year later, he inquired of a Texas cousin, "What's become of the girls that picketted [*sic*] me? They were beauties; especially the ones who carried the placards that said: 'Admiral Byrd, Try Me' and 'Admiral Byrd Is Down on Women.' There was another one of the young ladies whose placard said, 'Admiral Byrd, I have a Parka and I am Ready To Go!'" (REB to Colonel Harold D. Byrd, United States Air Force, May 18, 1955, June 8, 1956, folder 31, Byrd Papers).

11. Byrd, *Skyward,* 27–47 (quotes on 43, 45).

12. Ibid., 31–32.

13. Pearce, *U.S. Navy in Pensacola,* 155.

14. Byrd, *Skyward,* 50.

15. Richard K. Smith, *First Across! The U.S. Navy's Transatlantic Flight of 1919* (Annapolis: Naval Institute Press, 1973), 16–20; Goerler, *To the Pole,* 98.

16. Byrd later published his letter without the marginal notes (*Skyward,* 53–54). The original letter, dated May 13, 1918, is in folder 4126, Byrd Papers.

17. Byrd, *Skyward,* 55; REB to Chief of Naval Operations (Aviation), July 9, 1918, with endorsement; REB agreement with H. E. Adams and with T. Bolan, August 2, 1918; Commandant U.S. Naval Air Station, Pensacola, Florida, to REB, August 2, 1918, folders 4126 and 4127, Byrd Papers.

18. Byrd, *Skyward,* 57–62.

19. Ibid., 72.

20. Commanding Officer, U.S. Naval Air Forces, Canada, to Administrator of the Government, St. John's, Newfoundland, October 9, 1918; Josephus Daniels to REB, October 14, 1918; Commanding Officer, U.S. Naval Air Forces, Canada, to Commanding Officer, U.S. Naval Air Station, Halifax, Nova Scotia, October 18, 1918; REB to J. H. Towers, October 26, 1918; Commanding Officer, U.S. Naval Air Forces, Canada, to Chief of Naval Operations, October 26, 1918, folder 4126, Byrd Papers; C. F. Bennett to REB, December 20, 1918; "Statement of the Contribution of Lieut. Commander Richard E. Byrd, U.S.N to the Success of the Recent Trans-Atlantic Flight," folder 4127, ibid.; REB to Joseph R. Anderson, December 16, 1924, folder 4130, ibid.

21. H. K. Hines to the Chief of the Bureau of Navigation, n.d.; W. T. Grant to Josephus Daniels, December 20, 1918; Daniels to Grant, December 23, 1918, folder 4127, ibid.

22. Basic information on the navy's transatlantic flight of 1919 has been derived from Smith, *First Across!* The origins and content of Daniels's February 4, 1919, directive are discussed on pp. 37–39.

23. Commanding Officer, U.S. Naval Hospital, Washington, D.C., to REB, January 22, 1919, folder 4126, Byrd Papers; Byrd, *Skyward,* 69–70.

24. Percy Rowe, *The Great Atlantic Air Race* (Toronto: McClelland and Stewart, 1977), 18–21, 23–24, 34; Edward Jablonski, *Atlantic Fever: The Great Transatlantic Aerial Adventure* (New York: Macmillan, 1972), 1–2.

25. "Statement of the Contribution"; Byrd, *Skyward,* 71.

26. Smith, *First Across!* 49.

27. "Statement of the Contribution." Byrd's remark about his hobby is from Byrd, "Don't Let Them Die," 13.

28. Byrd, *Skyward,* 75–80; Rowe, *Great Atlantic Air Race,* 95.

29. Byrd, *Skyward,* 80–83; Grossnick, *United States Naval Aviation,* 39, 46.

30. Rowe, *Great Atlantic Air Race,* provides the most detailed and authoritative account of the Alcock-Brown flight. Jablonski, *Atlantic Fever,* 35–52, is concise.

31. P. W. L. Bellinger to the Bureau of Navigation, May 14, 1919; H. K. Hines to the Bureau of Navigation, June 11, 1919; Augustus Post to REB, July 15, 1919, folder 4127, Byrd Papers; Acting Secretary of the Navy to REB, August 22, 1919, copies in folders 2894 and 2900, ibid.

32. Telegram from Glenn Curtiss to REB, July 7, 1919; Navy Department, Bureau of Navigation, to REB, August 13, 1919; various letters to W. B. Miller, President, Norwalk Tire Company, August 13, 14, 15, 1919, folder 4127, ibid.

33. William F. Trimble, *Admiral William A. Moffett: Architect of Naval Aviation* (Washington, D.C.: Smithsonian Institution Press, 1994), 7 (quote), 71–72, 75; Byrd, introduction to *From Frigates to Flat-tops: The Story of the Life and Achievement of Rear Admiral William Adger Moffett, U.S.N., the Father of Naval Aviation,* by Edward Arpee (privately printed, 1953), xix; Byrd, *Skyward,* 102–3.

34. Byrd's memorandum is discussed in Trimble, *Admiral Moffett,* 76.

35. William A. Moffett to Thomas R. Ryan, February 22, 1922, folder 4126, Byrd Papers.

36. Byrd's comments about his relationship with Moffett are in Byrd, introduction to *From Frigates to Flat-tops,* by Arpee, xviii. The efficiency reports are quoted in Claude A. Swanson, introduction to *Discovery: The Story of the Second Byrd Antarctic Expedition,* by Byrd, ix–x.

37. Byrd, *Skyward,* 91–97; Trimble, *Admiral Moffett,* 137.

38. REB to Frank W. Mondell, July 1, 1921; Mondell to REB, July 5, 1921, folder 4127, Byrd Papers; Rear Admiral L. R. de Steiguer to REB, October 28, 1924, folder 4130, ibid.

39. Rowe, *Great Atlantic Air Race,* 175.

40. REB to Ralph Wood, August 5, 1921, folder 4130, Byrd Papers; Bureau of Navigation to REB, August 6, 1921, folder 4126, ibid.

41. Byrd, *Skyward,* 100.

42. The reports to Moffett, dated August 27 and September 2, 1921, are in folder 161, Byrd Papers. Additional material, including Byrd's various travel orders and his August 25 report to Commander Pence, are in folder 4126, ibid.

43. A. V. Vyvyan to REB, September 2, 1921, folder 161, ibid.

44. F. J. Merkling to REB, August 6, 1921; REB to Merkling, January 23, 1922; REB, fragment of undated letter, folder 4127, ibid.; REB to HFB, April 7, 1925, folder 4235, ibid.

45. Graphic accounts of the disaster may be found in the *Washington Post,* January 29, 30, 31, 1922. REB to Surgeon General, February 21, 1922; J. T. Moore to Surgeon General, March 6, 1922, folder 4235, Byrd Papers.

46. Byrd, *Skyward,* 123–24.

47. Bureau of Navigation to REB, March 6, May 17, 1923, folder 4126, Byrd Papers; Bolling Byrd Clarke, e-mail to the author, September 29, 2001; Murphy, "Admiral Byrd," 38.

48. REB to Mrs. Bryan Conrad, April 5, 1932, folder 70, Byrd Papers; to Charles J. Faulker, January 21, 1925; to Thomas K. Byrd, January 21, 23, 1925; to E. O. McDonnell, February 12, May 6, 28, 1925, folder 4235, ibid.

49. REB to REB Jr., February 18, 1925; to George W. Linkins, April 14, 1925, folder 4235, ibid.

50. Copies of REB's orders from the Bureau of Navigation from November 1923 to July 1924, with travel endorsements, are in folder 4127, ibid., as is the letter from the assistant secretary of the navy to REB, December 13, 1923. REB's account of his successful lobbying for naval aviation reserve appropriations is in Byrd, *Skyward,* 124–25.

51. The above-cited materials relating to REB's effort to obtain restoration of rank in May–June 1924 are in folder 4126, Byrd Papers; REB to FDR, December 20, 1924, folder 4130, ibid.

52. REB to Rear Admiral L. R. de Steiguer, November 1, 1924; Theodore Roosevelt to

REB, October 1, 1924, ibid. An excellent account of the Roosevelt family rift is Linda Donn, *The Roosevelt Cousins: Growing Up Together, 1884–1924* (New York: Alfred A. Knopf, 2001).

53. Copies of REB's orders from August to November 1924, folder 4126, Byrd Papers; cable, folder 4235, ibid.

54. The bulk of the correspondence detailing REB's struggle in 1924–1925 to regain his lost rank is in folders 4126 and 4130, ibid. Specific correspondence is Claude Swanson to Julian L. Latimer, December 19, 1924; FDR to REB, December 29, 1924, folder 4126, ibid.; REB to HFB, December 11, 1924, with enclosures; to FDR, December 20, 1924, with enclosures; to Tom Byrd, December 16, 1924, folder 4130, ibid.; to Tom Byrd, January 3, 1925, folder 4235, ibid.; "Apples List—1937," folder 171, ibid.; REB to HFB, December 9, 1947, folder 49, ibid.

55. REB to FDR, December 20, 1924, folder 4130, ibid.

56. Copy of the *Congressional Record* for January 22, 1925 (concerning REB's legislation), folder 4126, ibid.; Edwin S. Broussard to FDR, January 31, 1925; REB to Carl Vinson, January 23, 1925, folder 4235, ibid.

57. Goerler, *To the Pole,* 16.

Chapter 3. Breakthrough

1. Goerler, *To the Pole,* 20; Grover Loening, *Amphibian: The Story of the Loening Biplane* (Greenwich, Conn.: New York Graphic Society, 1975), 33. Bartlett's decadelong career with Peary is traced in Berton, *Arctic Grail,* 523–630 (see chap. 1, n. 22). Fitzhugh Green's Arctic experience and renown and Coolidge's role in establishing the Moffett Commission are in Byrd, *Skyward,* 125 (see chap. 1, n. 38).

2. MacMillan's sterling character and his contributions to Arctic exploration in general and the development of the 1925 Greenland expedition in particular are recounted in John H. Bryant and Harold N. Cones's highly partisan *Dangerous Crossings: The First Modern Polar Expedition, 1925* (Annapolis: Naval Institute Press, 2000), 8–10, 26–29.

3. Ibid., 27.

4. REB diary entry, January 1, 1925, quoted in Goerler, *To the Pole,* 28; REB to R. A. Bartlett; to C. E. Bauch, February 24, 1925, folder 4235, Byrd Papers.

5. William A. Moffett to Henry Ford; to P. W. Litchfield, March 9, 1925, folder 4235, Byrd Papers.

6. Bryant and Cones, *Dangerous Crossings,* 31–32; Donald B. MacMillan, "The MacMillan Arctic Expedition Returns," *National Geographic Magazine* 48, no. 5 (November 1925): 477–78.

7. REB to Bauch, March 7, 13, 1925, folder 4235, Byrd Papers.

8. REB to Litchfield; Moffett to Litchfield (letter and cable); Moffett to William C. Young, March 13, 1925, ibid.

9. REB to Gilbert Grosvenor, March 16, 1925, ibid.

10. Moffett to Grosvenor, March 17, 1925; REB to Litchfield; REB to Young, March 18, 1925; Grosvenor to Moffett, March 19, 1925, ibid.

11. Moffett to Edsel Ford, March 19, 1925; to Raymond Fosdick, March 21, 1925; Louis McHenry Howe to Fosdick, March 21, 1925; REB to Fosdick, March 21, 1925; Ford to John D. Rockefeller Jr., March 23, 1925; Rockefeller to Ford, March 24, 1925, ibid.

12. REB to Litchfield; to Young, March 24, 1925; Litchfield to REB, March 24, 1925, ibid.

13. REB to Ford; to Fitzhugh Green, March 26, 1925, ibid.

14. Byrant and Cones, *Dangerous Crossings,* 26, 34, back flyleaf.

15. REB to Green; to Fosdick; to Theodore Roosevelt, March 27, 1925; to the Chief of the Bureaus of Aeronautics and Navigation; to the Secretary of the Navy, March 28, 1925, folder 4235, Byrd Papers; Bryant and Cones, *Dangerous Crossings,* 34–36.

16. REB to Moffett, March 28, 1925; to Robert Bartlett, March 30, 1925, folder 4235, Byrd Papers.

17. Bryant and Cones, *Dangerous Crossings,* 37–40 (quote on 40).

18. "Wilbur Names Byrd to Head Polar Flight," *New York Times,* April 9, 1925, 15. Byrd's account of his successful lobbying campaign is in Byrd, "The X in Exploration," 34.

19. REB to A. C. Carson, March 31, April 11, 1925; to MAB, April 4, 1925; Carson to REB, April 8, 1925, folder 4235, Byrd Papers.

20. REB to Green, April 10, 1925, ibid.

21. REB to HFB; to Louis McHenry Howe, March 31, 1925; to Ford, April 4, 1925, ibid.

22. Bryant and Cones, *Dangerous Crossings,* 46, 49.

23. Loening, *Amphibian,* 34–35.

24. "Planes Hop Off, One Commanded by Amundsen, the Other by L. Ellsworth," *New York Times,* May 21, 1925, 1; "Planes Overdue at Spitsbergen Base: Dangers of Expedition," *New York Times,* May 23, 1925, 1; Thomas L. Vince, "The Polar Passion of Lincoln Ellsworth," p. 40, undated, unidentified article, copy in accession 199815, folder 5, Lindsey Papers.

25. Loening, *Amphibian,* 36–37; Bureau of Navigation to REB, May 11, 21, 23, June 3, 1925, folder 4127, Byrd Papers; REB to P. L. Bellinger, May 11, 1925, folder 4235, ibid.; anonymous to REB, Naval Aircraft Factory, Philadelphia, June 12, 1925, folder 4233, ibid.

26. John O. LaGorce to REB, May 29, 1925; E. O. McDonnell to REB, May 29, 1925; REB to LaGorce, June 1, 1925; to McDonnell, June 1, 1925; to H. A. Baldridge, June 2, 1925; to Godfrey L. Cabot, June 3, 1925, folder 4235, Byrd Papers.

27. The following account of the meeting is from "Naval Conferences on Amundsen Relief," *New York Times,* May 28, 1925, 1–2.

28. "MacMillan Ready to Go on Double Quest," *New York Times,* June 14, 1925, sec. 9, p. 1.

29. Ibid.

30. "Back Safe on Spitsbergen," *New York Times,* June 19, 1925, 1; Vince, "Polar Passion of Ellsworth," 41.

31. REB to Chief of Naval Operations, June 17, 1925; Moffett to REB, June 17, 1925; A. W. Johnson to REB, June 18, 1925, folder 4233, Byrd Papers; REB diary entry, June 20, 1925, quoted in Goerler, *To the Pole,* 29–30.

32. MacMillan, "MacMillan Expedition Returns," 486.

33. Commanding Officer, Naval Aviation Unit, USS *Peary* to Secretary of the Navy, June 29, 1925; Navy Department press release, Sunday, July 19, 1925; "Geographic News Bulletin . . . The National Geographic Society Release Not before July 19," folder 4234, Byrd Papers. REB to Lieutenant Schur, Chief Boatswain Reber, et al., July 10, 1925, folder 4232, ibid.

34. MacMillan, "MacMillan Expedition Returns," 486.

35. Ibid., 486–87.

36. REB diary entry, July 8, 1925, quoted in Goerler, *To the Pole,* 30–31.

37. REB diary entry, July 12, 1925, quoted in ibid., 31.

38. REB to D. B. MacMillan, July 8, 1925; to E. F. McDonald, July 9, 10, 1925; McDonald to REB, July 11, 1925, folder 4232, Byrd Papers.

39. REB diary entry, July 12, 15, 1925, quoted in Goerler, *To the Pole,* 31, 32; REB to MacMillan, July 22, 1925, folder 4233, Byrd Papers; MacMillan, "MacMillan Expedition Returns," 495.

40. REB to the Secretary of the Navy, July 17, 18, 20, 1925; to Governor Philip Rosendahl, July 23, 1925, folder 4236, Byrd Papers; to Rosendahl, July 24, 1925, folder 4232, ibid.; to Secretary of the Navy, July 25, 1925, folder 4233, ibid.; REB diary entry, July 27, 1925, quoted in Goerler, *To the Pole,* 33.

41. REB to MacMillan, July 28, 1925, folder 4233, Byrd Papers; REB diary entries, July 29, 30, 1925, quoted in Goerler, *To the Pole,* 34–36.

42. Navy Department press releases, July 28, 29, 1925, folder 4234, Byrd Papers; REB cables to Ford, to Fosdick, to Navy Department, to Eleanor Bolling Byrd, to HFB, July 29, 1925; to Navy Department, July 31, 1925, folder 4236, ibid.; MacMillan, "MacMillan Expedition Returns," 500.

43. The extensive correspondence and cable traffic between Byrd, his wife, the Navy Department, and Zenith Radio Corporation may be found throughout in folders 4233, 4234, and 4236, Byrd Papers.

44. REB to Secretary of the Navy; to Carl Vinson; to Frederick Hale; to HFB, August 2, 1925, folder 4236, ibid.; Byrd, "Flying over the Arctic," 519.

45. Bryant and Cones, *Dangerous Crossings,* 100–105; Navy Department press releases, August 4, 6, 1925, folder 4234, Byrd Papers; Commanding Officer to Personnel of Polar Unit, July 19, 1925, folder 4232, ibid.

46. REB diary entry, August 16, 1925, quoted in Goerler, *To the Pole,* 37. Byrd's account of poor flying conditions is in Byrd, "Flying over the Arctic," 520. Peter Freuchen's recollection is in his *Vagrant Viking: My Life and Adventures,* trans. Johan Hambro (New York: Julian Messner, 1953), 135.

47. Byrd, "Flying over the Arctic," 531.

48. Unsigned paper titled "Flight to Ellesmere Island on August 8, 1925," folder 4229, Byrd Papers.

49. Ibid.; Byrd, "Flying over the Arctic," 524–26; Navy Department press release, "Messages from Lieut. Comdr. R. E. Byrd with MacMillan Arctic Expedition," August 7, 8, 9, 1925, folder 4234, Byrd Papers.

50. Byrd, "Flying over the Arctic," 525.

51. Ibid., 519–20; MacMillan to REB, August 10, 1925, folder 4232, Byrd Papers; National Geographic Society press release, August 13, 1925, folder 4234, ibid.; Goerler, *To the Pole,* 36.

52. MacMillan's and Byrd's daily accounts of the flights during the 1925 Greenland expedition are often confused and contradictory, especially Byrd's reports to the Navy Department. For example, he reported a single flight to Beitstad and Hayes Fjords three times in three days, and it is impossible to determine whether "last night" refers to the evenings of August 10, 11, or 12. Byrd prepared an official report on his way home that is much more coherent; unfortunately, only a fragment has survived. I have generally followed Byrd's published account, adding, where pertinent, materials from his report, his daily messages to Washington, MacMillan's article, and his own contacts with the National Geographic Society. See Byrd, "Flying over the Arctic," 527–32; and MacMillan, "MacMillan Expedition Returns," 502–10. Several of Byrd's dispatches to Washington are in folder 4229 of the Byrd Papers, the remainder in folder 4234. His fragmentary official report is in folder 4231. A number of MacMillan's reports to the National Geographic are in folder 4236. Despite their animus toward Byrd, Bryant and Cones provide a generally accurate account (*Dangerous Crossings,* 106–27).

53. "Landing on Ellesmere Island," folder 4229, Byrd Papers.

54. "Release from the National Geographic Society, dated 8–13–25," folder 4234, Byrd Papers; Byrd undated and fragmentary "Report of Activities," folder 4231, p. 18, ibid.

55. "Navy Department Immediate Release, 17 August 1925," folder 4234, ibid.

56. Byrd, "Report of Activities," folder 4231, pp. 20, 22, ibid.; MacMillan to REB (twice), August 17, 1925, folders 4232 and 4233, ibid.; REB to MacMillan, August 17, 1925, folder 4232, ibid.; National Geographic Society release, August 19, 1925, folder 4234, ibid.; "Polar Sea Fight May Be Abandoned," *New York Times,* August 19, 1925, 1; Bryant and Cones, *Dangerous Crossings,* 117; "MacMillan Gives Up Polar Sea Flight," *New York Times,* August 20, 1925, 8.

57. Byrd, "Report of Activities," 26; Byrd, "Flying over the Arctic," 532.

58. REB diary entries, August 17, 22, 23, 1925, quoted in Goerler, *To the Pole,* 37–38; REB to MacMillan, August 20, 1925; Navy Department press release, August 20, 1925; MacMillan to National Geographic Society, August 20, 1925, folder 4234, Byrd Papers.

59. Byrd, "Report of Activities," 26; Byrd, "Flying over the Arctic," 532.

60. John A. Stabler to MAB, September 16, 1925, folder 4224, Byrd Papers; Commanding Officer Naval Arctic Unit to Personnel Naval Arctic Unit, September 20, 1925, folder 4233, ibid.

61. REB to Grover Loening, undated, folder 4233, ibid. Mitchell is quoted in Roger Burlingame, *General Billy Mitchell, Champion of Air Defense* (New York: McGraw-Hill, 1952), 152; and Ruth Mitchell, *My Brother Bill: The Life of General "Billy" Mitchell* (New York: Harcourt Brace, 1954), 309–10. See also Bryant and Cones, *Dangerous Crossings,* 185–89.

62. MacMillan to REB, September 22, 1925; REB to MAB, September 23, 1925, folder 4233, Byrd Papers; REB to Secretary of the Navy, September 22, 26, 1925, folder 4236, ibid.

63. REB to Secretary of the Navy, September 26, 1925, ibid.; REB, "Memorandum, Bonne Bay, Newfoundland, September 27, 1925," folder 4232, ibid.; McDonald to REB, September 27, 1925, folder 4233, ibid.

64. McDonald to REB, October 1, 3, 1925; REB to McDonald, October 2, 1925; "U.S. Naval Unit, S.S. *Peary,* En Route Nova Scotia," October 2, 1925, folder 4233, ibid.

65. "Maine Welcomes MacMillan Home," *New York Times,* October 13, 1925, 25; "MacMillan Ship Hit Reef," *New York Times,* October 17, 1925, 17; "Canadians Hint MacMillan Clash," *New York Times,* October 18, 1925, 21; Bryant and Cones, *Dangerous Crossings,* 151, 166.

66. Bryant and Cones, *Dangerous Crossings,* 166.

67. REB to J. S. Kean, November 20, 1925; to Thomas B. Byrd, December 3, 1925, folder 4237, Byrd Papers; Bryant and Cones, *Dangerous Crossings,* 186–88; Byrd, *Skyward,* 102–3.

68. T. Arthur Smith to REB, October 20, 1925; William Comstock, J. M. Odea, John W. Smith, and J. C. Mcleod to REB, October 27, 1925; LaGorce to REB, October 30, 1925, folder 4237, Byrd Papers.

69. REB to Mason M. Patrick, December 3, 1925, folder 4237, Byrd Papers; Byrd, "Flying over the Arctic," 519.

Chapter 4. Triumph

1. "Byrd to Explore Arctic from Air," *New York Times,* January 31, 1926, 1.

2. REB to Robert H. Clancy, November 16, 1925, folder 4237, Byrd Papers.

3. Albert Francis to REB, November 11, 1925; REB to Clancy, November 16, 1925; to Grosvenor, November 17, 1925, to Anita M. Boggs, November 18, 1925; to R. S. Robertson, January 20, 1926, ibid.

4. "Virginia Byrds to Fore, *New York Times,* February 14, 1926, sec. 9, p. 6.

5. REB to W. H. Hobbs, December 6, 1925, January 18, 1926; to David Lawrence, January 20, 1926; to George Hubert Wilkins, January 22, 1926; Lawrence to REB, December 21, 1925, folder 4237, Byrd Papers. Byrd's dislike of the *New York Times* is in REB to HFB, November 11, 1938, folder 42, ibid. Freuchen, *Vagrant Viking,* 209–10 (see chap. 3, n. 46); Goerler, *To the Pole,* 41–42.

6. "Against Joint Pole Trip," *New York Times,* July 19, 1925, 1.

7. Quoted in Goerler, *To the Pole,* 44.

8. REB to A. J. Lepine, November 19, December 3, 1925, folder 4237, Byrd Papers; to Ford, January 27, February 6, 1926; Lepine to REB, February 6, 1926, folder 4269, ibid.; Byrd, "The X in Exploration," 34; "Fly On! Fly On! Edsel Ford Talks about Aviation to Commander Richard E. Byrd," *Colliers* 81, no. 19 (May 12, 1928): 8–9, 55; Goerler, *To the Pole*, 41–50. Information on Anthony Fokker is in Carroll V. Glines, *Bernt Balchen, Polar Aviator*, 4.

9. Byrd, "The X in Exploration," 34; Grosvenor to MAB, July 16, 1925, folder 4234, Byrd Papers.

10. "Virginia Byrds to Fore," 6.

11. Matouzzi, "Richard Byrd," 219.

12. Ibid., 220; Goerler, *To the Pole*, 46.

13. Byrd's discussion of the forthcoming North Polar flight is in Byrd, "Byrd Outlines Plan to Reach the Pole," *New York Times,* March 28, 1926, sec. 9, p. 6.

14. REB to W. E. Hocking, November 3, 1925; Howard H. Cox to REB, October 4, 1925; REB to Cox, November 14, 1925; to Gertrude Lane, December 12, 1925, folder 4237, Byrd Papers; to Rockefeller, September 28, 1933, folder 2877, ibid.

15. Byrd, "Byrd Outlines Plan"; REB diary entry, April 5, 1926, central file, Byrd Papers, also quoted in Goerler, *To the Pole*, 60. Byrd quoted the young lady's letter in Byrd, "The First Flight to the North Pole" (in the *National Geographic Magazine*), 358.

16. REB diary entries, April 8, 10, 11, 14, 15, 16, 17, 21, 24, 1926, quoted in Goerler, *To the Pole*, 64–65, 67–71. Spitsbergen is often misspelled as "Spitzbergen."

17. REB diary entries, April 25, 28, 1926, quoted in ibid., 72–73.

18. See http://www.svalbard.com/infosvalbard.html.

19. Bernt Balchen, *Come North with Me: An Autobiography,* 16–17. Further autobiographical material is in box 1, folder 2; box 5, folder 9; and box 6, folder 1, Bernt Balchen Collection.

20. Balchen, *Come North with Me,* 23–26 (quote on 26); REB diary, April 29, 1926, central file, Byrd Papers, also quoted in Goerler, *To the Pole*, 73; Balchen diary and biographical summary, "29/4/26," box 1, folder 2, Balchen Collection.

21. The following account of Byrd's difficulties in establishing his crude air base on Spitsbergen is from REB diary entries, April 29, 30, May 1, 1926, quoted in Goerler, *To the Pole*, 73–76; Byrd, "First Flight" (in the *National Geographic Magazine*), 360, 363; Balchen, *Come North with Me,* 26–28; Balchen diary, "May 1–5," 1926, box 1, folder 2, Balchen Collection; and Floyd Bennett, "Our Flight over the North Pole," 175–76.

22. Balchen, *Come North with Me,* 27.

23. Byrd, "First Flight" (in the *National Geographic Magazine*), 360.

24. The account of the journalistic wars on Spitsbergen and final preparations for the American polar flight are from Balchen, *Come North with Me,* 36–42, Balchen diary, "3/ 5," "8/5," and "9/5," 1926, box, folder 2, Balchen Collection; Bennett, "Our Flight," 176–77, 261; and Richard Montague, *Oceans, Poles, and Airmen: The First Flights over Wide Waters and Desolate Ice,* 9–10. Bennett's account diverges sharply in both chronolo-

gy and emphasis from those of Balchen and Montague. Byrd makes no diary entries beyond Monday, May 3. His own brief accounts in *Skyward,* 163–65 (see chap. 1, n. 38), and "First Flight" (in the *National Geographic Magazine*), 363, make no mention of Balchen's critical help and observations. According to Byrd, the only problem was that the Fokker was overloaded and that by a judicious reduction in load Bennett was able to get off without troubles. Byrd failed to mention the earlier problems with the ski wax. Bennett did not mention Balchen at all.

25. Balchen diary, "5/7," 1926, box 1, folder 2, Balchen Collection.

26. Byrd, "First Flight" (in the *National Geographic Magazine*), 363.

27. Bennett states that Byrd impulsively decided to go while heading toward *Chantier* for a brief pretakeoff sleep ("Our Flight," 261).

28. I have taken the account of the flight from Byrd, "First Flight" (in the *National Geographic Magazine*), 365–76; Byrd's official "Navigation Report" to the National Geographic upon his return to the United States reprinted in Goerler, *To the Pole,* 148–57; and Bennett, "Our Flight," 261–64. The description of *Josephine Ford* is taken from a two-page brochure produced by the staff of the John Wanamaker department store in Philadelphia where the plane was briefly exhibited in the grand court after its return from the Arctic. See John Wanamaker, *Conquerors of the North Pole: A Brief Story of This Epoch Making Flight, with a Description of the Airplane Which Made Possible the First Carrying of the United States Flag to the North Pole by Air,* copy in the Byrd Collection.

29. Balchen, *Come North with Me,* 45, recalls Amundsen's emotional response but not Byrd's alleged reply.

30. Balchen diary and biographical summary, "11/5" [1926], box 1, folder 2, Balchen Collection. Balchen tells a slightly different story in *Come North with Me,* 47–49.

31. See Balchen to Laurence M. Gould, April 2, 1958, box 3, Laurence McKinley Gould Papers.

32. Montague, *Oceans, Poles, and Airmen,* 11–15, 188–89, 281–300. The suggestion that Balchen virtually coauthored Montague's startling book is in "Did Peary or Byrd See the North Pole? Debate Heats Up," an article released by the New York Times Service and appearing in the *Detroit Free Press,* December 21, 1971, copy in box 6, folder 5, Balchen Collection. The veracity of the assertion is found in Montague to Balchen, March 30, 1967, box 10, folder 1, ibid. Montague to Balchen, January 5, 1972, box 6, folder 6, ibid.

33. Montague to Balchen, March 30, 1967, box 10, folder 1, Balchen Collection.

34. Montague to Boyer, January 8, 1972, in response to Boyer letter of January 3. Montague's letter, "The Byrd Polar Controversy," is in the *Washington Post,* January 5, 1972. All three documents are in box 10, folder 1, ibid. Montague to Balchen, January 5, 1972, is in box 6, folder 6, ibid.

35. Balchen's physical condition was related by Mrs. Balchen to Gould, December 13, 1976, box 6, folder 2, ibid. Vern Haugland, "Was Byrd Trip a Flight of Fancy?" *New York Times,* December 14, 1971, copy in box 6, folder 5, ibid. The same source contains copies of Haugland's AP story that appeared more or less complete in the *Los Angeles Times, De-*

troit Free Press, and the *White Plains (N.Y.) Reporter Dispatch* under various titles. Balchen's "Statement to Associated Press re N.Y. Times story" dated December 15, 1971, on Balchen's personal letterhead is in box 10, folder 1, ibid.

36. Balchen's remorse is in an undated article by Elizabeth Simonoff, "Byrd Did Not Fly over Pole Says Balchen," copy in box 6, folder 5, ibid. Audrey Balchen's denial that her ex-husband, Bernt, said what he clearly did say to Haugland and the *New York Times* is in Audrey Balchen to editor, *New York Times,* May 12, 1996, box 10, folder 1, ibid.

37. Dennis Rawlins, *Peary at the North Pole: Fact or Fiction?* 262–72; Finn Ronne, *Antarctica, My Destiny: A Personal History by the Last of the Great Polar Explorers* (New York: Hastings House Publishers, 1979), 188–89; Bess Balchen Urbahn interview in Nancy Porter Productions, *Alone on the Ice: The Story of Admiral Richard Byrd,* WGBH Boston production for the *American Experience* television series; Boyce Rensberger, "Diary Disputes Byrd's Polar Claim," *Washington Post,* May 9, 1996, A2–3; Goerler, *To the Pole,* 52–53. Balchen may well have found or been given a copy of Byrd's official report, for among his papers is an eight-and-a-half-page undated "Navigation Report of Flight to Pole" signed "Respectfully R. E. Byrd" (box 6, folder 7, Balchen Collection). Rawlins's assertion that Byrd discovered nearly seven hours into his flight that the aircraft was being dramatically slowed by headwind and doctored the record in a frantic effort to prove otherwise takes up the entire issue of *DIO: The International Journal of Scientific History* 10 (January 2000). See esp. pp. 7–8, 30, 33 (captions to charts) and p. 44 from which the quotes in the text are taken.

38. Montague letter published under title "The Byrd Polar Controversy," *Washington Post,* January 5, 1972, copy in box 10, folder 1, Balchen Collection; Vern Haugland to Balchen, January 3, 1972, ibid.; Barry Goldwater to Mrs. Harold E. Isakson, April 26, 1973, box 9, folder 2, ibid.

39. Murphy first made his charge against Balchen in a letter to Amory H. ("Bud") Waite dated February 6, 1972, just as Montague's book reached print. He amplified the observations quoted above in a subsequent undated letter to Waite. "General Spaatz liked Balchen's bluff heartiness. [Balchen] saved airmen on the Greenland ice cap" during World War II, "& Spaatz admired him for that. After the war, the Scandinavian countries formed their air line under a financial & political consortium. Balchen was given the title of Chief Executive, in the expectation that his American reputation would clear the path for essential technical and political arrangements on the American side of the Atlantic. He bungled the job so badly that he was shunted aside. He returned to the Air Force and was assigned to the building of the great base at Thule" on the Arctic west coast of Greenland "as an overseer for operations. Finletter, then Secretary of the Air Force, wanted Balchen promoted. The Air Force was anxious to establish forward bases in Norway, and to have authority to stockpile nuclear weapons there. The Norwegians wanted neither. Finletter decided that one way around the opposition was to promote Balchen to Brigadier and send him to Norway to negotiate the desired leases. He was taken aback to find that the Air Force High Command was resisting the idea. At that stage, I was simultaneously on the staffs of both Finletter and General Vandenberg, with the title of Special Assistant. Finlet-

ter asked me to find out where the block was and the reason for it. I had the answer quick-ly, being familiar with the Air Force high command structure. Balchen's foe was the Deputy Vice-Chief of Staff for Operations, Lieutenant [General?] Roger Ramey, my friend. Ramey told me that Balchen would be promoted over his dead body. He had no use for Balchen. The Thule operation had been bungled. Balchen had shown himself to be both inept and irresponsible. Worse still, the Central Intelligence Agency had registered a stern warning that Balchen had been indiscreet in his discussion of U.S. plans, and that the information had reached the Soviets. Finletter sighed when I so reported to him, and that ended Balchen's hopes for a star" (Charles J. V. Murphy to Amory H. Waite, February 6, 1972, "Correspondence—Byrd N.P. Flight, letters concerning controversy over, 1971–72," Amory H. Waite Papers; Murphy to Waite, April 18, 1982, and n.d., "Correspondence—Murphy, Charles J. V.," in ibid.).

　　40. Bernt Balchen manuscript, "The Strange Enigma of Admiral Byrd," p. 1, copy in accession 199815, folder 14, "Diary, Lindsey's from BAE II," Lindsey Papers.

　　41. Stuart D. Paine, diary entry, July 29, 1934, in *Footsteps on the Ice: The Antarctic Di-aries of Stuart D. Paine, Second Byrd Expedition,* ed. M. L. Paine, 161; Charles F. Passel, *Ice: The Antarctic Diary of Charles F. Passel,* 52–53; Finn Ronne, *Antarctic Command;* Dian Ol-son Belanger, *Deep Freeze: The United States, the International Geophysical Year, and the Ori-gins of Antarctica's Age of Science* (Boulder: University Press of Colorado, 2006), 299–300, 336–37, 339–45. According to numerous diary and other contemporary accounts un-earthed by Belanger, Ronne, among other things, examined and, when he desired, cen-sored all personal as well as official outgoing communications from Ellsworth Station and "punished" several station personnel by refusing to let them send any outgoing commu-nications whatever. Ronne refused to equip a field party with essential radio equipment, arguing that it belonged to the air force and that the navy had not given permission to use it. He demoted junior scientists to the status of navy enlisted personnel, assigning them menial duties that clearly interfered with their scientific work. See John C. Behrendt, *In-nocents on the Ice: A Memoir of Antarctic Exploration, 1957* (Boulder: University Press of Colorado, 1998). According to Behrendt, then a twenty-four-year-old graduate student working at Ellsworth Station, Ronne at one point "even went into the past and told how Byrd always tried to block him. The idea of what later became the East Base of the U.S. Antarctic Service Expedition [1939–41] was his originally, but [President] Roosevelt didn't know of him when he heard about it and called Byrd in, and Byrd took it over" (142).

　　42. Goerler, *To the Pole,* 151, 156; Wanamaker, *Conquerors of the North Pole;* Balchen, *Come North with Me,* 43, 45; "He [Demas] Defends Admiral Byrd's Record," *Oakland Tri-bune,* December 27, 1971, 17; Dennis Rawlins to "Pete" Demas, December 20, 1973, box 6, folder 2, Balchen Collection.

　　43. Sverre Petterssen to Bernt Balchen, September 2, 1958, box 6, folder 6, Balchen Collection; Marvin Miles, "Study Supports Byrd's Polar Flight Story," *Los Angeles Times,* February 22, 1973, copy in box 9, folder 2, ibid.

　　44. Summers to author, July 3, 2001.

45. Paul Lashmar, *Spy Flights of the Cold War* (Annapolis: Naval Institute Press, 1996), 26.

46. See Keith A. Pickering, review of *To the Pole,* by Goerler, in *Polar Record* 36, no. 197 (April 2000): 158–59.

47. Leslie Reade, *The Ship That Stood Still: The* Californian *and Her Mysterious Role in the* Titanic *Disaster* (New York: W. W. Norton, 1993), 144; comment by John Rose, quartermaster second class, United States Naval Reserve, February 15, 2007.

48. Colonel William Molett, "Yes, Richard E. Byrd Made the North Pole," unpublished paper supplied to the author by Brian Shoemaker, p. 2.

49. From Byrd's formal "Navigation Report" to the National Geographic Society, quoted in Goerler, *To the Pole,* 156.

50. Ibid.

51. A summary of the 1927 *Jane's* performance information on the Fokker is in box 6, folder 7, Balchen Collection. I also checked the specifications in a telephone conversation with the National Air and Space Museum's librarian-archivist in Washington, D.C., on May 16, 2007. See also Fokker technical data base–Record 8 of 43: Fokker FVIIa-3m at http://library.thinkquest.org/c002752/fokker.cgi?page=bwar2; and Wanamaker, *Conquerors of the North Pole.* Balchen's assertion that *Ford* was in fact underpowered by the Wright Whirlwind engines is in Balchen to Miss Evelyn Moore, October 12, 1956, box 6, folder 6, ibid. Charles Froesch's gentle rebuttal is in Froesch to Balchen, March 18, 1958, ibid. Professor Liljequist's article is "Did the 'Josephine Ford' Reach the North Pole?" *Interavia,* no. 5 (1960) is in box 6, folder 4, ibid.

52. Ronne, *Antarctica, My Destiny,* 186; Summers, telephone conversation with author, March 16, 2002.

53. Rawlins, *DIO: The International Journal of Scientific History* (January 2002): 30.

54. Rawlins to Ohio State University Archives, May 4, 1996, with May 6, 17, 1996, addenda, pp. 4, 11, copy in Byrd Papers, no folder given.

55. Respected Byrd scholar Sheldon Mark has noted "that airplanes are not like cars. Pilots and flight engineers can change the configuration of their plane. They can choose to fly economically, using a low power setting, getting more miles per gallon and flying at a low airspeed. Or they can choose a higher-power or full-power configuration, burning more fuel but getting higher airspeed." Mark adds that "three months before Byrd bought Fokker Trimotor No. 1 and renamed it the Josephine Ford, the same airplane was tested by the Army Air Service. The engines were the same type as used on the North Pole flight: Wright Whirlwind J-4Bs. The Army loaded the plane with 4000 lbs worth of passengers and baggage. The plane weighed 4000 pounds empty. So the total weight was roughly equivalent to the weight of the plane after the first few hours of the North Pole flight. The Army set the engines at over 1700 rpm and got an airspeed of 117 mph. The Balchen flight log doesn't prove that the Jos. Ford didn't reach the Pole. It only proves that during the U.S. air tour, Bennett and Balchen weren't asking the plane to work too hard" (Mark to Raimond Goerler, n.d., "RAIS Files, Byrd Papers).

56. Molett, "Yes, Byrd Made the Pole," 4–5; emphasis added. The colonel's professional qualifications are set forth in a brief introduction to another unpublished paper ti-

tled "Analysis of Admiral Byrd's Erased Sextant Reading." A corroborative view is Brian Shoemaker, review of *To the Pole*, by Goerler, in *Polar Times* (Spring–Summer 1998): 21.

57. Byrd, "Arctic Exploration by Aircraft"; and Byrd, "The First Flight to the North Pole," folders 4271 and 4272, Byrd Papers.

58. See the excellent map in Bryant and Cones, *Dangerous Crossings,* 28 (see chap. 3, n. 2), which clearly delineates the vast unexplored area of the western Arctic and also clearly delineates the various exploratory routes by ice and air to and toward the pole prior to the Amundsen-Ellsworth flight of 1925. Byrd briefly discusses the search for land during the polar flight in "The First Flight to the North Pole," p. 28, folder 4272, Byrd Papers. Not until 1937 did the four-man team of a Soviet scientific drift station initially established quite near the North Pole exult that "we established beyond all doubt that there cannot be any land in the vicinity of the Pole" (Ivan Pannin quoted in William F. Althoff, *Drift Station: Arctic Outposts of Superpower Science* [Washington, D.C.: Potomac Books, 2007], 49).

59. Glines, *Bernt Balchen, Polar Aviator,* 11.

60. I came to this conclusion independently of and later than Ohio State University professor of astronomy Gerald H. Newsom, whose fifteen-page examination of the Byrd-Bennett flight vindicates Byrd on every point ("Comments of Admiral Byrd's Diary from his Presumed Flight to the North Pole, 7 July 1997," p. 1, copy in Byrd Papers). Rawlins does address this point, but dismissively. From 135 miles south of the pole, it was possible to see quite a distance. "So Byrd & Bennett very likely saw past 89°N—probably the first humans ever to see into the 90th degree of northerly latitude. Had there been mountainous land at the Pole, they should have spotted it" (Rawlins to Ohio State University Archives, May 5, 6, 17, 1996, 11). True, but they could not count on seeing much smaller geological features, or even substantial open water or other striking physical phenomena at or very near the pole. They had to fly to within at least twenty miles or less to fully satisfy themselves that they were not laying themselves open to charges of fraud by the Amundsen party, should it reach the top of the earth.

Chapter 5. Hero

1. The account of Byrd's arrival in New York is based on Byrd, *Skyward,* 188–90 (see chap. 1, n. 38); and Balchen, *Come North with Me,* 56–58.

2. "Commander Byrd Receives the Hubbard Gold Medal," *National Geographic Magazine* 50, no. 10 (October 1926): 377–83 (quotes on 378, 383).

3. Byrd, *Skyward,* 191, 193, 194, 195.

4. Allen, *Only Yesterday,* 134 (see introduction, n. 7); Rice's quote can be found in John Bartlett, *Familiar Quotations: A Collection of Passages, Phrases, and Proverbs Traced to Their Sources in Ancient and Modern Literature,* ed. Justin Kaplan, 16th ed. (Boston: Little, Brown, 1992), 643.

5. Byrd's remarks to Robert Davis were reprinted the following year in "'Dick' Byrd as a Mercury," 33, 36 (see chap. 1, n. 20).

6. For Rodman Wanamaker see the various entries in the "Yahoo" information service on the Internet. Bolling Byrd discussed her father's spirituality in a letter to the author, August 3, 2001; REB to Rockefeller, February 18, 1931, folder 2883, Byrd Papers.

7. REB to HFB, June 28, 1926, folder 34, Byrd Papers.

8. REB to HFB, February 8, July 3, 1926 (two letters), and two undated cables; HFB to REB, June 28 (cable), 30, July 7, 1926, ibid.

9. REB to HFB, July 24, August 2, October 9, 1926, ibid.

10. Byrd, *Skyward,* 213–15; Goerler, *To the Pole,* 98.

11. REB to HFB, July 2, 1926, folder 34, Byrd Papers; James B. Pond to REB, November 17, 1926, folder 491, ibid.; Balchen, *Come North with Me,* 59–61.

12. Byrd, *Skyward,* 201–5.

13. Byrd, "Don't Let Them Die," 13.

14. Kenneth S. Davis, *The Hero: Charles A. Lindbergh and the American Dream* (Garden City, N.Y.: Doubleday, 1959), 161; A. Scott Berg, *Lindbergh* (New York: G. P. Putnam's Sons, 1998), 100.

15. Byrd, "Don't Let Them Die," 186.

16. Byrd, *Skyward,* 205–8.

17. The exact date of the flight is in dispute. Byrd claimed it was April 20 (*Skyward,* 212); Scott Berg, Lindbergh's biographer, states it was April 16 (*Lindbergh,* 104).

18. Byrd, *Skyward,* 213–14; Eugene Rodgers, *Beyond the Barrier: The Story of Byrd's First Expedition to Antarctica* (Annapolis: Naval Institute Press, 1990), 10.

19. Balchen, *Come North with Me,* 89.

20. Byrd, "Don't Let Them Die," 186; Davis, *Hero,* 165–66, provides a splendid account of the Nungesser-Coli takeoff. The Lloyds of London estimate is from Berg, *Lindbergh,* 104.

21. Byrd, "Don't Let Them Die," 186.

22. Balchen, *Come North with Me,* 91–92.

23. Byrd, *Skyward,* 215–18; Balchen, *Come North with Me,* 90–98 (the quote referring to the *America's* rechristening is on 96); Berg, *Lindbergh,* 113–16 (quotes on 114, 116).

24. REB to Wanamaker, May 23, 1927, and n.d., folder 4344, Byrd Papers.

25. Byrd and Balchen generally agreed on the beginnings of the flight to Paris, though Byrd claimed the aircraft took off an hour earlier than it did. See Balchen, *Come North with Me,* 101–3; and Byrd, *Skyward,* 227–28. It is the last time the two agreed on anything.

26. Richard E. Byrd, "It's Safe to Fly," 7–8, 43.

27. Byrd, *Skyward,* 229–30; Murphy, "Admiral Byrd," 37; Goerler, *To the Pole,* 113.

28. Noville quoted in "The Air Not Yet Conquered," *Literary Digest* 94, no. 8 (July 16, 1927): 6.

29. Byrd, *Skyward,* 249.

30. Ibid., 228–48; Byrd, "Our Transatlantic Flight," 366–67; Goerler, *To the Pole,* 111–17; Balchen, *Come North with Me,* 102–21; Murphy, "Admiral Byrd," 37; Norman

Vaughan with Cecil B. Murphey, *With Byrd at the Bottom of the World: The South Pole Expedition of 1928–1930,* 88–90.

31. *New York Herald* (European edition of the *New York Herald Tribune*), June 30, July 1, 1927; *Paris Times,* June 30, 1927, original copies in Byrd Collection.

32. *New York Herald* (European edition of the *New York Herald Tribune*), July 1, 1927; *Chicago Tribune and the Daily News New York: Europe's American Newspaper,* July 1, 1927, in ibid.

33. Balchen, *Come North with Me,* 120–21; and Byrd, *Skyward,* 249–50, recount the stumbling trip from the plane to the village. *Chicago Tribune and the Daily News New York: Europe's American Newspaper,* July 2, 1927, Byrd Collection, contains front-page articles on popular reaction to news of the crew's safety on both sides of the ocean. The alleged discovery of Byrd asleep on the beach is in cable from "Roberts," folder 4360, Byrd Papers.

34. Quoted in "'Dick' Byrd as a Mercury," 34 (see chap. 1, n. 20).

35. Accounts and illustrations of the Paris crowds are in Byrd, *Skyward,* 250–51 and photo section between pp. 183 and 184. Ferdinand Foch to REB, undated message; Boris to REB, July 9, 1927, folder 4360, Byrd Papers; Glines, *Bernt Balchen, Polar Aviator,* 56 (see chap. 4, n. 8).

36. Calvin Coolidge to REB; Frank Kellogg to REB, June 30, 1927; Dwight F. Davis to REB, July 1, 1927; REB to Coolidge; to Kellogg; to Davis, July 2, 1927, folder 4360, Byrd Papers.

37. "'Dick' Byrd as a Mercury," 36, 38.

38. All quotes are from "Air Not Yet Conquered," 5.

39. Bill Gunston, ed., *Chronicle of Aviation* (London: JOL International Publishing, 1992), 247; Allen, *Only Yesterday,* 157–58.

40. Byrd, "Don't Let Them Die," 13, 186–90.

41. Herbert Adams Gibbons to REB, July 20, 1927, folder 4360, Byrd Papers.

42. Byrd, *Skyward,* 251.

Chapter 6. Celebrity

1. Bovard's and Gillespie's cables to REB in Paris and REB's messages to Whalen and Green from *Leviathan* are in folder 4360, Byrd Papers, together with other messages dealing with his homecoming celebrations.

2. Glines, *Bernt Balchen, Polar Aviator,* 57 (see chap. 4, n. 8).

3. "Public disillusion was never far from the surface when even the [1919] World Series and the two biggest prize fights of the time [Dempsey-Tunney] were fixed." The grand "fixer" was gambler Arnold Rothstein, who masterminded the Black Sox scandal (his biographer strongly suggests that the 1914 and 1916 World Series may have been thrown as well) and had his hand in every major shady deal from 1919 to his murder nine years later. See David Pietrusza, *Rothstein: The Life, Times, and Murder of the Criminal Genius Who Fixed the 1919 World Series* (New York: Carroll and Graff, 2003); and Warren G. Gold-

stein, review in *Washington Post Book World,* November 9, 2003, from which the quote is drawn.

4. McBain quoted in Lisle A. Rose, *Assault on Eternity: Richard E. Byrd and the Exploration of Antarctica, 1946–47* (Annapolis: Naval Institute Press, 1980), 20; F. Scott Fitzgerald, *The Great Gatsby* (New York: Macmillan/Collier, n.d.) 2.

5. Murphy, *Struggle,* 1.

6. Howard Mingos to REB, December 29, 1925, folder 4237, Byrd Papers.

7. REB to H. W. August, February 18, 1927, folder 490, ibid.; REB undated "Memorandum of Instructions . . . ," folder 486, ibid.; REB to the Pond Lecture Bureau, August 24, 1926, folder 456, ibid.; H. F. Truman to Charles Creasy, December 7, 1926, folder 491, ibid.

8. Pond to REB, November 17, 1926, folder 491, ibid.

9. REB to Ralf Earle, November 22, 1926; Pond to REB, November 27, 1926, REB to H. W. August, February 18, 1927, Ibid., folders 490 and 491.

10. "Lt. Commander [*sic*] Richard E. Byrd—Route"; "Commander Byrd's Lecture Engagements, 1927–28"; "Admiral Richard E. Byrd, Itinerary of American Lecture Tour from September 30th to December 31st . . . Revised to October 4, 1930"; REB to Mr. Robins, January 15, 1927; to Lincoln Ellsworth; to General Passenger Agent, Erie Railroad, March 1, 1927, folders 480, 489, 490, ibid.

11. Matouzzi, "Richard Byrd," 222–23.

12. Joseph Pulitzer to REB, February 28, 1927; REB to Pulitzer, March 7, 1927; Pond to Green, March 7, 1927, folders 490, 491, ibid.

13. REB to Pond, March 18, 1927; Pond to REB, March 21, 1927, folders 490, 491, ibid.

14. Elbert D. Wickes to REB, February 27, 1928; Louis J. Alber to REB, March 14, July 6, August 16 (cable), August 22, September 1, 1928; REB to Alber, March 22, September 10, 1928, folder 480, ibid.

15. REB to Twining Lynes, October 15, 1927, folder 480, ibid.; Byrd, "The X in Exploration," 36.

16. Byrd, "The X in Exploration," 36.

17. Ibid.; Murphy, "Admiral Byrd," 36; "Byrd to Receive Unique Tribute from School Children," *National Education Association Journal* 20, supp. no. 70 (March 1931); "Letters to Byrd," *National Education Association Journal* 20, nos. 151–52 (May 1931); "Admiral Byrd's acknowledgement of the National School Children's tribute at Detroit Convention," folder 4792, Byrd Papers; James E. West, "The Selection of a Boy Scout for the Byrd Antarctic Expedition," appx. to Paul Siple, *A Boy Scout with Byrd* (New York: G. P. Putnam's Sons, 1931), 153–55 (quotes on 153, 155).

18. REB to FDR, October 1, 4, 26, 1927; to E. Roosevelt, December 20, 1927, folder 2900, Byrd Papers.

19. Murphy, "Admiral Byrd," 27.

20. Quoted in Diana Preston, *A First Rate Tragedy: Robert Falcon Scott and the Race to the South Pole* (Boston: Houghton Mifflin, 1997), 225.

21. Berton, *Arctic Grail,* is a superlative account of its subject (see chap. 1, n. 22).

22. Amundsen is quoted in Francis Trevelyan Miller, *The World's Great Adventure: The Fight to Conquer the Ends of the Earth; One Thousand Years of Polar Exploration Including the Heroic Achievements of Admiral Richard Evelyn Byrd* (privately published, 1930), 346–47.

23. Murphy, "Admiral Byrd," 27; Byrd, "The X in Exploration," 34. Scott's last despairing plea is reprinted in Preston, *First Rate Tragedy,* 204; Walter Sullivan, *Quest for a Continent* (New York: McGraw-Hill, 1957), 56; and numerous other biographical and historical sources on Antarctica.

24. Hoover is quoted in Miller, *World's Great Adventure,* 4.

Chapter 7. The Secret Land

1. The quotes are from Richard E. Byrd, "Our Navy Explores Antarctica," 429 and, on the setting sun, from C. E. Borchgrevink, *First on the Antarctic Continent: Being an Account of the British Antarctic Expedition, 1898–1900* (London: George Newnes, 1901), 126. The rest of the paragraph relies heavily on the author's own South Polar impressions gained in 1956–1957 and 1978.

2. The word *Antarctica* is derived from the ancient Greek *anti* and *arktos,* meaning "opposite the Bear," or Arctic (*Polar Regions Atlas* [Washington, D.C.: Central Intelligence Agency, 1978], 40). This publication contains the best overview of South Polar journeys, flights, and scientific and political developments. The finest general history of Antarctica known to me is Walter Sullivan's excellent but badly dated summary *Quest for a Continent* (see chap. 6, n. 23). His discussion of Magellan's faulty identification is on p. 21. Russell Owen's *The Antarctic Ocean* is an often neglected classic that also contains a good, brief discussion of the South Polar continent in the minds of antiquity. For Magellan, see also Samuel Eliot Morison, *The Great Explorers: The European Discovery of America* (New York: Oxford, 1978), 600. Other useful histories of Antarctic exploration are Ian Cameron, *Antarctica: The Last Continent* (Boston: Little, Brown, 1974); and Frank Debenham, *Antarctica: The Story of a Continent* (London: Herbert Jenkins, 1959). Even more dated than Sullivan, Cameron, and Debenham but surprisingly complete and informative about the "heroic" and immediately postheroic age of Antarctic exploration is Lorene K. Fox, *Antarctic Icebreakers* (New York: Doubleday, Doran, 1937). Fox, who received help from such South Polar veterans as Laurence Gould, Byrd, Lincoln Ellsworth, George Hubert Wilkins, and Debenham himself, did her homework and read the documents, especially published diaries and memoirs of the participants, which she included at appropriate points throughout her text. A comprehensive though dry and narrow treatment of South Polar exploration is Kenneth J. Bertrand, *Americans in Antarctica, 1775–1948* (New York: American Geographic Society, 1971).

3. Quoted in Sullivan, *Quest for a Continent,* 35.

4. An excellent account of Mawson's ordeal is Leonard Bickel, *Mawson's Will* (New York: Stein and Day, 1977).

5. Sullivan, *Quest for a Continent,* 52–60.

6. Owen, *The Antarctic Ocean,* 4–5, 35; Byrd, "Our Navy Explores Antarctica," 429; S. Paine diary entry, December 15, 1933, in *Footsteps on the Ice,* ed. M. L. Paine, 46, 48.

7. Oceanographer Art DeVries defined Antarctica in this way to writer Michael Parfit during Operation Deepfreeze '84 (Parfit, *South Light: A Journey to the Last Continent* [New York: Macmillan, 1985], 120).

8. Frederick A. Cook, *Through the First Antarctic Night, 1898–1899* (New York: Doubleday and McClure, 1900), 289–91, 326; Alfred Lansing, *Endurance: Shackleton's Incredible Voyage* (New York: McGraw-Hill, 1959), 38.

9. Borchgrevink, *First on the Antarctic Continent,* 128–29, 135, 153–55.

10. Owen, *The Antarctic Ocean,* 3–4.

11. Shackleton is quoted in Fox, *Antarctic Icebreakers,* 186; his crewman, Frank Worsley, is quoted in Lansing, *Endurance: Shackleton's Incredible Voyage,* 53.

12. Byrd, "Our Navy Explores Antarctica," 521.

13. Laurence McKinley Gould, *Cold: The Record of an Antarctic Sledge Journey* (New York: Brewer, Warren, and Putnam, 1931), 266. The quotes regarding Amundsen and Scott are from "Scott 150 Miles from South Pole Jan 3: Will Stay in Antarctic Another Year," *New York Times,* January 18, 1912.

14. The quotes regarding Scott and Shackleton are in Fox, *Antarctic Icebreakers,* 158, 203. Byrd's quote is from "Our Navy Explores Antarctica," 522. See also Preston, *First Rate Tragedy,* 41, 229 (see chap. 6, n. 20).

15. Dr. Edward Todd, director, U.S. Antarctic Research Program, National Science Foundation, made this observation on several occasions to the author, then polar affairs officer, U.S. Department of State.

16. Byrd, *Little America: Aerial Exploration in the Antarctic; The Flight to the South Pole,* 311.

17. Siple's comments are from "Exploration: Compelling Continent," *Time* 68, no. 27 (December 31, 1956): 17.

Chapter 8. Southward

1. Typescript article "Why I Am Going to the South Pole," for December 1927 *World's Work,* folder 3877, Byrd Papers.

2. Nancy Porter Productions, *Alone on the Ice* (see chap. 4, n. 37).

3. Byrd, "The Conquest of Antarctica by Air," 127, 128.

4. Byrd, *Little America,* 3–4; Matouzzi, "Richard Byrd," 225.

5. Matouzzi, "Richard Byrd," 222.

6. REB to M. D. Clofine, August 2, 13, 1927; Clofine to REB, August 9, 1927, folder 2255, Byrd Papers; Rodgers, *Beyond the Barrier,* 22–23 (see chap. 5, n. 18); Murphy, "Admiral Byrd," 31, 37.

7. The map of the first Byrd Antarctic expedition's surface and aerial explorations, complete with geographic names, is in Byrd, "Conquest of Antarctica," 129. His desire to name

a mountain after Los Angeles hotel manager P. G. B. Morris is set forth in an unsigned letter (probably from his personal secretary, Hazel McKercher) to Commander H. S. Saunders, June 13, 1938, folder 7170, Byrd Papers. The folder also contains a comprehensive "List of Landmarks Discovered and Named by Byrd Antarctic Expeditions I and II . . . Revised to November 1941," plus several other pieces of correspondence attesting Byrd's near obsession with getting friends' and benefactors' names on the Antarctic map.

8. See, for example, "Cash Receipts—Byrd Expedition II, August 17, 1935, and related document "Refunds" in folder 7173, Byrd Papers.

9. Byrd, "How I Pick My Men," 12–13, 54, 58; Byrd, "Crusaders," 6–7, 169–70, 173–74, 177.

10. Quoted in Lawrence James, *Raj: The Making and Unmaking of British India* (New York: St. Martins Griffin, 1997), 155.

11. Quoted in Byrd, "How I Pick My Men," 12.

12. Ibid., 13.

13. Ibid., 54.

14. Ibid., 58.

15. Ibid., 58.

16. Byrd, "Crusaders," 6.

17. Dean C. Smith, *By the Seat of My Pants* (Boston: Little, Brown, 1961), 179, 191.

18. Byrd, "How I Pick My Men," 13, 54.

19. Agreement between REB and Paul Siple, signed August 24, 1928, folder 4793, Byrd Papers. This folder contains copies of all the agreements signed by REB with each member of the first Antarctic expedition.

20. Byrd, *Discovery,* 18.

21. Rodgers, *Beyond the Barrier,* 28, 30–31.

22. D. Smith, *By the Seat of My Pants,* 181–82.

23. Rodgers, *Beyond the Barrier,* 41.

24. Byrd, *Little America,* 5–6.

25. Ibid., 3–13 (quote on 9).

26. Rodgers, *Beyond the Barrier,* 31–32.

27. MAB to REB, n.d., folder 64, Byrd Papers.

28. Paul Siple, *90° South: The Story of the American South Pole Conquest,* 39.

29. H. H. Railey to MAB, December 22, 26 (cable), 27, 31, 1928, folder 69, Byrd Papers.

30. Byrd, *Little America,* 15; REB diary entry, December 2, 1928, folder 4561, Byrd Papers.

31. REB diary entries, December 2, 3, 5, 26, 1928, folder 4561, Byrd Papers; Rodgers, *Beyond the Barrier,* 55.

32. REB diary entry, December 8, 1928, folder 4561, Byrd Papers; Rodgers, *Beyond the Barrier,* 55.

33. REB diary, December 12, 1928, folder 4561, Byrd Papers.

34. REB diary entries, December 15–23, 1928, ibid.; Owen, *The Antarctic Ocean,* 228.

Byrd's criticism of Melville is from the December 23 entry; critical comments on his leadership from other members of the expedition are in Rodgers, *Beyond the Barrier,* 55.

35. REB diary entry (first one), December 25, 1928, and enclosure, "Annual Report of the Penguin Club—Xmas Jubilee—'City of N.Y.' Byrd Antarctic Expedition—1928," folder 4561, Byrd Papers.

36. REB diary entry (first one), December 25, 1928, ibid.

37. REB diary entries, December 26, 27, 1928, ibid.

38. Byrd, "Conquest of Antarctica," 145, 148; REB Expedition Order, December 27, 1928; diary entries, December 28–January 1, 1929, folder 4561, Byrd Papers.

39. Vaughan with Murphey, *With Byrd,* 41–42.

40. Richard B. Black, "Antarctic Wintering Over: The Expeditions of 1933–34 [*sic*] and 1939–41," 32, copy in folder 2, Lindsey Papers.

41. Vaughan with Murphey, *With Byrd,* 45–46, 49–50.

42. REB diary entries, January 2–8, 1929 (quote from January 5), folder 4561, Byrd Papers; Byrd, "Conquest of Antarctica," 149–51.

43. Vaughan and some others would dispute this. "A bright, highly energetic man," Vaughan has written, "Byrd never asked any of us to do anything he was not willing to do himself" (Vaughan with Murphey, *With Byrd,* 41). The record, unfortunately, speaks otherwise.

44. REB diary, January 12, 1929, folder 4561, Byrd Papers. The quote regarding REB's first flight are in Byrd, "Conquest of Antarctica," 154. The region from the Eights Coast to the foot of the Antarctic Peninsula and around to the Ronne Ice Shelf is called Ellsworth Land.

45. Byrd, "Conquest of Antarctica," 155–58 (quote about the barrier collapse is on 158); Byrd, *Little America,* 101–32 ("indescribable relief" is from 132).

46. REB diary, January 8, 1929, folder 4561, Byrd Papers; MAB to REB, January 9, [1929], folder 64, ibid.

47. MAB to REB, January 19 [1929], folder 64, Byrd Papers; Railey to MAB, January 30, 1929; MAB to Railey, February 1, 1929, folder 69, ibid.

48. Rodgers, *Beyond the Barrier,* 72–74, covers the incident in full and includes Byrd's comment to his wife. Byrd's relevant diary entries are December 31, 1928, and January 8, 1929, folder 4561, Byrd Papers.

49. In an interview sometime in the mid-1980s, Alton A. Lindsey, a prominent member of the second Byrd Antarctic Expedition, remarked that undoubtedly some members were delighted to see their commander go off for a proposed six-month stay alone on the ice. "I'm not talking of homosexuality—I'm practically certain there wasn't any, even any suggestions of that—I'm referring mainly to booze" (Bruce S. Young, "Byrd II and Other Polar Matters: An Interview with Alton A. Lindsey," p. 15, n.d., accession 19918, folder 7, Lindsey Papers). Byrd was aware of the issue. According to Lindsey, he at first told at least one financial backer that he would post "two men to the 'Mountain House'" in 1934 to spend the austral winter alone. But he held the idea "so briefly as to be practically nonexistent. Siple told me [Lindsey] one important reason, Byrd had explained to him what

he thought the 'smart-aleck New York writers' would have done with that arrangement" (Lindsey, "Inside Byrd's Second Antarctic Expedition," 5 [see introduction, n. 3]).

50. Rodgers, *Beyond the Barrier,* 236.

51. Ibid., 228–36; Murphy, "Admiral Byrd," 37; Raimond Goerler, oral history interview with Charles Passel, February 14, 2000, The Ohio State University Polar Archives, Columbus.

52. Vaughan with Murphey, *With Byrd,* 65–68.

53. Vaughan quote in Nancy Porter Productions, *Alone on the Ice.* See also Stuart Paine's numerous diary entries on this subject, in *Footsteps on the Ice,* ed. M. L. Paine.

54. See, for example, Dean C. Smith to Fred W. Hotson, June 24, 1974, and unsigned "A Case for Historians, 8/75," box 6, folder 2, Balchen Collection; Alan Innes Taylor to Balchen, April 24, 1972, March 1973, box 9, folder 1, ibid.

55. D. Smith, *By the Seat of My Pants,* 194–99 (McKinley is quoted on 199). Rawlins, *Peary at the North Pole,* 271, later picked up the story, claiming that Byrd's deception reflected a basic character trait.

56. REB diary, February 10, 11, 15, 1929, folder 4561, Byrd Papers.

57. REB diary, February 12, 1929, ibid.; Rodgers, *Beyond the Barrier,* 83–84.

58. Dean Smith letter to Canadian Aviation Historical Society, n.d., quoted in typed manuscript titled "A Case for Historians, 8/75," box 6, folder 2, p. 9, Balchen Collection.

59. Ibid. See also Rodgers, *Beyond the Barrier,* 105–7; D. Smith, *By the Seat of My Pants,* 200–208; D. Smith to Hotson, June 24, 1974, box 6, folder 2, Balchen Collection.

60. Veteran Antarctic explorer-scientist John Behrendt provided me with this information.

61. Richard Black and I discussed Byrd's drinking during a luncheon sometime in 1981. Summers discussed his flights with Byrd in a letter to the author, August 19, 1998. Owen briefly discusses the expedition in *The Antarctic Ocean,* 227–32.

62. Laurence M. Gould to Balchen, April 12, 1958, RG 401/59, box 3, Gould Papers; Rodgers, *Beyond the Barrier,* 103, 109.

63. Rodgers, *Beyond the Barrier,* 102–9; Gould, *Cold,* 7–34 (Gould's comment is on 31).

64. Byrd, "Conquest of Antarctica," 170.

Chapter 9. Zenith

1. Byrd, "Conquest of Antarctica," 175; Meinholtz to REB in REB diary entry, September 5, 1929, folder 4562, Byrd Papers.

2. Byrd, "Conquest of Antarctica," 172–73; REB diary entry, April 23, May 4, 1929, folders 4561, 4563, Byrd Papers.

3. REB diary entry, June 12, 1929, folder 4562, Byrd Papers; Alfred Zukor and Jesse Lasky, *With Byrd at the South Pole* (Paramount Publix Corporation, 1930). Rereleased in DVD format by Milestone Films and Video, n.d.

4. Goodale, "Admiral Byrd and His Place in History," 5 (see introduction, n. 4).

5. Byrd's observation on the safety of walking in low temperatures is in "Conquest of Antarctica," 175. Byrd's propensity for exercise and especially walking has been commented upon by many veterans of his expeditions. Wendell Summers stressed it to me in his letter of August 19, 1998.

6. Bernt Balchen, personal diary (typescript), "Antarctica . . . 1929, Life in Camp," box 1, folder 2, Balchen Collection (hereafter cited as Balchen personal diary and date or subject entry); Roberts, "Heroes and Hoaxers," p. 69, copy in box 6, folder 5, ibid.

7. Gould, *Cold*, 69–70.

8. Byrd, "Conquest of Antarctica," 174. See also Gould, *Cold*, 53–55. REB diary entry, April 23, 1929, folder 4563, Byrd Papers.

9. REB diary entry, June 1, 1929, folder 4562, ibid.

10. REB diary entries, June 1, 4, 10, 11, 1929, ibid.

11. REB diary entry, April 2, 1929, folder 4561, ibid.; Railey to MAB, April 4, 1929, folder 65, ibid.

12. REB diary entries, April 23, 25, 1929, folder 4563, ibid.; Richard Byrd Jr. to REB, n.d.; REB to Richard Byrd Jr., n.d., January 31, 1929, folder 97, ibid.

13. Railey to MAB, April 17, 1929, folder 65, ibid.

14. Railey to MAB, May 11, 21, 22, 1929, ibid.

15. Railey to MAB, June 15, 1929, ibid.; REB diary entries, June 7, 9, 14, 1929, folder 4562, ibid.

16. MAB to REB in REB diary entry, September 8, 1929; Brophy's cable to REB; REB reply in REB diary entry, September 25, 1929, ibid.

17. REB to Walter Hyams, April 16, 1928; Hazel McKercher to MAB (cable), April 9, 1929; Railey to MAB, April 17, 29, May 14, June 8 (two letters), 24, July 5, 1929; Carrie Waite to "Mrs. Commander E. Byrd" (cable), April 29, 1929; MAB to Railey (two letters), n.d.; REB diary entry, June 7, 1929, ibid.

18. See correspondence between Railey and Walter Hyams and Company between July 5 and September 17, 1929; Railey to MAB, July 30, August 3, 22, 1929; MAB to Railey, August 6, 1929, folder 65, ibid.

19. MAB to REB, January 14, 20, 1929, folder 64, ibid.; unsigned letter to MAB, July 8, 1929, ibid.

20. Railey to MAB, July 17, 18, 20, 22, 26, 1929; Marie Byrd to Railey (two letters), n.d., ibid.

21. MAB to Railey, n.d.; Railey to MAB, November 15, 27, 1929, ibid.; Moffett to MAB, December 27, 1929; Adolph Ochs to MAB, December 28, 1929, folder 168, ibid.

22. Rodgers, *Beyond the Barrier*, 81 (see chap. 5, n. 18).

23. Ibid., 131–39. See also REB diary, June 20, 1929, folder 4562, Byrd Papers.

24. REB diary entry, July 13, 1929, folder 4561, ibid.

25. REB diary entry, June 27, 1929, folder 4562, ibid.; Sullivan, *Quest for a Continent*, 48–49; Belanger, *Deep Freeze*, 29 (see chap. 4, n. 41).

26. REB diary entries, June 2, 16, 30, 1929, folder 4561–62, Byrd Papers.

27. Rodgers, *Beyond the Barrier*, 136–37, 143 (Demas quote on 143).

28. Ibid., 140–42 (quote on 140). A copy of the memorandum with the penciled heading "in Re Russell Owen" is in folder 6683, Byrd Papers.

29. The origin, purpose, and oath regarding the Loyal Legion are in an undated, untitled memorandum, folder 4792, Byrd Papers. Vaughan recounts his recruitment into the Loyal Legion in *With Byrd*, 85–87 (quote on 86). His troubles with Walden are recounted on 55–63. Rodgers, *Beyond the Barrier*, 146.

30. Rodgers, *Beyond the Barrier*, 148; REB diary entry, August 5, 1929, folder 4562, Byrd Papers; Railey to MAB, August 10, 1929, folder 32, ibid.; August 12, 1929, folder 65, ibid.

31. Rodgers, *Beyond the Barrier*, 153–54.

32. Summary of the *Examiner* article and Byrd's cable to Railey for Wilkins in REB diary entry, September 25, 1929, folder 4562, Byrd Papers.

33. REB diary entry, September 26, 1929, ibid.

34. REB diary entry, October 19, 1929, ibid.; HFB to MAB, July 31, 1929, folder 35, ibid.

35. Cold temperatures prevented the snow from softening into ice beneath the sledge runners. The dogs were thus pulling their loads over surfaces that had the consistency of dry sand.

36. Gould, *Cold*, 118; Rodgers, *Beyond the Barrier*, 162.

37. REB diary entry, October 17, 1929, folder 4562, Byrd Papers.

38. REB diary entries, October 18, 20, 23, 1929, ibid.

39. REB diary entries, October 20, 23, 26, 1929, ibid.

40. REB diary entries, October 27, 29, 1929, ibid.

41. Gould, *Cold*, 125–256; Vaughan with Murphey, *With Byrd*, 107–36 (quote regarding the crevasse is on 134); Byrd, *Little America*, 393–412; Rodgers, *Beyond the Barrier*, 211. Byrd also included in his personal diary many, though not all, of the daily radio messages that Gould sent from the field. See REB diary entries, December 1929–January 1930, folder 4563, Byrd Papers.

42. After the Gould-Balchen party crashed in the Rockefeller Mountains in March 1929, Byrd instructed Railey to approach Tony Fokker about "donating" a second trimotor that would be sent down to Little America with the relief ships that autumn. Presumably, the vessels could bash through the pack by the first week or so of December 1929, which would have met Byrd's original schedule for the South Polar flight. But Fokker refused to provide a second aircraft, and even if he had, Wilkins's sudden intrusion pushed the polar flight schedule up to November, and both *City* and *Eleanor Bolling* could not be gotten out of dry dock in New Zealand soon enough to race to the Bay of Whales even if the ice pack had been accommodatingly thin or scattered. See REB diary entries, June 4, 20, September 5, 1929, folder 4562, Byrd Papers.

43. Balchen personal diary, "16/11."

44. D. Smith, *By the Seat of My Pants*, 217 (see chap. 8, n. 17).

45. Balchen personal diary, "18/11."

46. Smith's accusations against Byrd came at a particularly bad time since four days be-

fore the flight Railey got Byrd's permission to bail the pilot out of financial difficulties with his broker to the amount of $1,250 (Railey to MAB, November 14, 1929, folder 65, Byrd Papers). Railey himself had borrowed money from Byrd, apparently to buy stock just as the market peaked in mid-October. A month later, with the market gyrating wildly, Railey bought even more stock to cover his indebtedness to his employer (Railey to MAB, November 15, 1929, ibid.).

47. In his 1958 memoirs, Balchen wrote of a walk-and-talk that he and Byrd had shortly before the flight. According to Balchen, Byrd told the Norwegian that he had been so right in so many ways so often that even though he did not wish to have Balchen pilot the South Polar flight, he had no choice. This egregiously self-serving statement, which no one else was around to hear, was later picked up by Byrd's critics and also by the historian of the expedition (Rodgers, *Beyond the Barrier*, 180–81). Balchen described the crew's apparel, the position of the men, and the crowded cabin in letters to Andrew Poggenpohl, art editor of the *National Geographic Magazine*, February 28, May 3, 1962, box 6, folder 2, Balchen Collection.

48. Balchen personal diary, "11/22" and "5/12"; Dean C. Smith to Balchen, January 4, 1972, box 6, folder 2, Balchen Collection; Smith to Canadian Aviation Historical Society, n.d., reprinted in "A Case for Historians, 8/75," p. 10, ibid.

49. Preparations for and the story of the polar flight have been described in a number of sources, including Byrd, *Little America*, 326–45; Byrd, "Conquest of Antarctica," 198–19; and Rodgers, *Beyond the Barrier*, 180–87.

50. D. Smith, *By the Seat of My Pants*, 225–26.

51. The quotes are from Byrd, *Little America*, 333, 335, 336.

52. Byrd's South Polar flight has also been enveloped in some controversy, though with Balchen along as chief pilot it has been less spectacular than the North Polar flight. No one aboard or elsewhere ever denied that the plane got within a few miles of the pole. Balchen states that he did his own calculations from dead reckoning and sent a message from the pilot's seat to Byrd in the fuselage when he estimated the aircraft was fourteen minutes from the bottom of the earth. Exactly fourteen minutes later, Byrd sent a message forward that by his calculations they were overflying the South Pole. Sixty years later, Eugene Rodgers discovered a letter of gentle complaint from McKinley to his commander soon after the expedition returned home "disput[ing] Byrd over using Antarctic flight data for making maps." The aerial photographer added: "Dick, without going too deep into either the polar or eastern flights, you know that my polar records, while kept with all possible precision, were asked to be destroyed and not used as they were, and that I was never furnished with complete navigational data." Unlike his North Polar flight, Byrd openly admitted that due to the aircraft's severe "rocking . . . I could not get accurate astronomical sights at the pole and had to go by dead reckoning." He therefore informed Railey soon after returning to Little America that he "bent over backwards" *not* to claim that *Floyd Bennett* had gotten to the precise geographic bottom of the earth, but close enough. A National Geographic Society committee in 1931 determined that he had flown within at least four miles of the objective. It should be noted that Byrd was quite candid on the matter,

possibly because his growing rival, Balchen, was with him, but possibly because he was an honest man who did not wish to claim too much. He had navigated as well as possible and could claim that he and the others had seen the actual bottom of the earth, which, of course, was—and remains—as Godforsaken as Scott described it. Balchen, *Come North with Me,* quoted in Glines, *Bernt Balchen, Polar Aviator,* 89–90 (see chap. 4, n. 8); Rodgers, *Beyond the Barrier,* 189–90.

53. Railey to MAB, January 9, 1930, folder 69, Byrd Papers.

54. Byrd, *Little America,* 345; *With Byrd at the South Pole.*

55. Railey to MAB, November 29, 1929, Byrd Papers, folder 65; HFB, to Railey, November 30, 1929, folder 36, ibid.; Matouzzi, "Richard Byrd," 219.

56. D. Smith, *By the Seat of My Pants,* 227–28.

57. Gould, *Cold,* 265.

58. See relevant cables and messages between HFB and Railey, December 13–21, 1929; Fred Britten to HFB, December 24, 1929; Railey to REB, January 6, 1930, folder 36, Byrd Papers.

59. MAB to REB, January 16, 1930, folder 64, ibid.; MAB to Railey, January 30, 1930; Railey to MAB, February 8 (two, one cable), 15, 1930, folder 69, ibid.

60. Goodale, "Admiral Byrd and His Place in History," 4; D. Smith, *By the Seat of My Pants,* 230.

61. Byrd, *Little America,* 365.

62. Railey to MAB, January 30, 1930 (two letters), folders 36 and 69; February 4, 1930, folder 32, Byrd Papers.

63. Railey to HFB; to MAB, February 13, 1930, folder 35, ibid.

64. "Taffy" Davies's remarks are in flysheet titled "Byrd Antarctic Exped I Newsletter—Nov 1975," box 6 folder 2, Balchen Collection. Balchen's own observations are in an untitled three-page paper in box 7, folder 7, ibid.

65. REB diary entries, December 12, 19, 20, 1929, folder 4563, Byrd Papers.

66. Railey to HFB, December 31, 1929, January 10, 1930, folder 36, ibid.

67. Rodgers, *Beyond the Barrier,* 241; Vaughan with Murphey, *With Byrd,* 241; Byrd, *Discovery,* 1.

Chapter 10. Politico

1. Railey seems to have set the ball rolling in early February, and by the fifteenth arrangements were well advanced. See Jerome D. Barnum to Railey, February 15, 1930, folder 2896, Byrd Papers.

2. "Admiral Byrd Receives the Society's Special Gold Medal of Honor," *National Geographic Magazine* 58, no. 2 (August 1930): 228–38 (Hoover's remarks quoted on 231–32).

3. Railey to Byrd (telegram), June 13, 1930; Rear Admiral W. B. Franklin to Byrd, June 25, 1930; to the Secretary of the Navy, June 25, 1930; Byrd to Franklin, June 30, 1930; Byrd to FDR, July 7, 1930, folder 2896, Byrd Papers.

4. D. Smith, *By the Seat of My Pants,* 234 (see chap. 8, n. 17).

5. Murphy, "Admiral Byrd," 37.

6. Owen, *The Antarctic Ocean,* 226; Siple, *90° South,* 47–48.

7. HFB to REB, June 15, 1931, with enclosure, folder 37, Byrd Papers.

8. Robert Breyer to REB (cable), January 7, 1931, folder 14, ibid.; Allen, *Only Yesterday,* 252 (see introduction, n. 7).

9. Murphy, "Admiral Byrd," 38.

10. Morris Markey, "The Admiral—Richard E. Byrd," *Vanity Fair,* December 1930, 45, 114. Biographical material on Markey is from the dust jacket of his later book, *Well Done! An Aircraft Carrier in Battle Action* (New York: D. Appleton-Century, 1944).

11. REB to HFB, February 8, 1931, folder 37, Byrd Papers; to MAB, n.d., folder 66, ibid.; Railey to MAB, September 30, 1930, folder 69, ibid. A good, brief summary of the Wilkins-Ellsworth proposal to sail a submarine under the North Pole is Stewart B. Nelson, "Rediscovering World's 1st Arctic Sub: NAUTILUS of 1931," *Polar Times* 3, no. 10 (January 2007): 35.

12. Pond to Railey, folder 484, Byrd Papers.

13. Byrd, *Little America,* vii–ix.

14. Sales promotion titled "Another Putnam Book with Extraordinary Sales Possibilities," January 22, 1931; Milville Morton to Siple, January 26, 1931; M. L. Dolan to Siple, March 6, 1931; "Doug" to Siple, March 30, 1931, "Letters Received, 1931," box 2, Siple Papers.

15. Harry Adams, *Beyond the Barrier with Byrd* (Chicago: Goldsmith Publishing, n.d.) (his praise of Byrd is on 31–34); Ashley McKinley, *The South Pole Picture Book* (New York: Samuel W. Miller, n.d.), no pagination, copies in Byrd Collection.

16. Rodgers, *Beyond the Barrier,* 276 (see chap. 5, n. 18), summarizes the exchanges between Byrd and Gould; Gould to "Gerry," July 5, 1980; to Siple, April 24, 1931, "Letters Received," box 2, Siple Papers.

17. "Extravagance Hit as N.E. Forms Economy League Branch," *Boston Herald,* July 22, 1932, copy in folder 8388, Byrd Papers.

18. William E. Leuchtenberg, *Franklin D. Roosevelt and the New Deal* (New York: Harper and Brothers, 1963), 15.

19. Quoted in "Byrd to Head Economy Drive: Accepts Chairmanship for N.E.," *Boston Herald,* July 22, 1932, folder 8388, Byrd Papers.

20. FDR to REB, July 24, 1932, folder 2897, ibid.; newspaper clippings, "Byrd and MacNider to Address Legion Convention at Lawrence," "Byrd Cannot Believe Legion Will Oppose Economy League," and "Veterans Reject Economy League Plea at Lawrence," both dateline Lawrence, Massachusetts, August 12, 1932, *Boston Herald,* folder 8387, ibid.

21. REB to Rockefeller, December 17, 1932, folder 2883, ibid.

22. "Byrd Defies Tax Monster," *Illinois State Register,* October 16, 1932, folder 8388, ibid. See also related clippings in this and folder 8386.

23. Clippings "Byrd Accepts Title of Stalking Horse," *New York Times,* November 28, 1932; "Byrd Calls Attack by Legion Chief a Grand Compliment," *Boston Herald,* No-

vember 28, 1932; "What We Pay," *St. Louis Post-Dispatch,* November 30, 1932, folder 8388, ibid.

24. HFB to REB, n.d., folder 35, Byrd Papers. At one point Harry Byrd mentioned his responsibilities in helping to prepare the budget, which would place the letter during his term of governorship between 1926 and 1932. Lindbergh, of course, had no prominence prior to 1927.

25. Photo caption, "Congratulations All Around," *Winchester Evening Star,* June 24, 1930, copy in Byrd Collection.

26. REB to Rockefeller, September 28, 1933, folder 2877, Byrd Papers; Bolling Byrd, e-mail to author, January 22, 2002.

27. See the correspondence between REB, MAB, and Robert Winsor Jr., between April 18, 1933, and August 18, 1936; also Winsor to Arthur Humill, April 17, 1935, folder 466, Byrd Papers. A formal description of the property together with the "Memorandum of Agreement" between Byrd and the purchasers, April 16, 1946, is in folder 465, ibid.

28. Byrd's comments to E. Roosevelt, May 3, 1933, and to FDR and his secretary Marguerite ("Missy") Lehand, both July 27, 1935, are in folders 2898 and 2899, respectively, ibid.

29. MAB to REB, n.d., folder 64, Byrd Papers; Byrd, *Alone,* 92–93 (see chap. 1, n. 1).

30. REB to Richard Byrd Jr., October 2, 1930, folder 98, ibid. Dickie's letter is quoted in Nancy Porter Productions, *Alone on the Ice* (see chap. 4, n. 37).

31. Bolling Byrd's recollections of her father and her reunion with him in 1935 is in Nancy Porter Productions, *Alone on the Ice.* Katherine Byrd Breyer to REB and MAB, April 6, 1950; REB to Robert and Katherine Breyer, March 28, 1951, folder 6, Byrd Papers.

32. "Byrd Superseded in Veterans' Fight," *Baltimore Sun,* December 20, 1932, clipping in folder 6, Byrd Papers.

33. A. W. Johnson to REB, November 16, 1932; REB to Johnson, November 28, 1932, folder 2859, ibid.

34. William V. Pratt to REB, December 6, 1932; F. B. Upham to Louis Ludlow, December 17, 1932; REB to Alfred Johnson, December 29, 1932, ibid.

35. "Byrd Ready to Quit Navy for Economy" and "Points to Record of Admiral Byrd," *New York Times,* January 4, 1933; "Declares Byrd's Critics Do Him Great Injustice," *Boston Transcript,* January 4, 1933, folder 8388, ibid.

36. REB draft cable to FDR, September 16, 1932, folder 2460, ibid.; REB to E. Roosevelt, September 22, 1932; E. Roosevelt to REB, October 4, 1932, folder 2897, ibid.

37. See, for example, REB to E. Roosevelt with enclosure, November 9, 1932; to FDR, November 10, 1932; to E. Roosevelt (cable), n.d.; to FDR, November 29, December 30, 1932, ibid.; to E. Roosevelt, January 32, 1933, folder 2898, ibid.

38. REB to Rockefeller, September 28, 1933, folder 2877, ibid.

39. HFB to REB, February 27, 1933, folder 39, ibid.

40. REB to Rockefeller, March 20, 1933, folder 2877, ibid.; a copy of the Petition from the Coalition Committee "To the Honorable Franklin D. Roosevelt President of the United States," folder 2900, ibid.

41. Jonathan Garland Pollard to REB, March 24, 1933, folder 2887; B. B. Moeur to REB, March 29, 1933, folder 2883, ibid.

42. Typescript copies of Byrd's radio speeches delivered over the National Broadcasting System before and following the president's message to Congress, March 9, 1933, folder 3500, ibid.

43. REB to Rockefeller, March 20, 1933 (two letters), folder 2877, ibid.

44. REB to Arthur W. Packard, May 23, 1933, ibid.

45. "Address Given by Rear Admiral Richard E. Byrd, National Chairman, National Economy League, under Its Auspices, at White Plains, N.Y., Tuesday Evening, March 21, 1933," folder 3500, ibid. See also "MS for 'The Rotarian' by Rear Admiral Richard E. Byrd, F.H. McAllister, 3/23/33," ibid.

46. REB to HFB, September 17, 1931, folder 37, ibid.; MAB to McKercher, January 10, 1931; "Memorandum to Mrs. Byrd," April 13, 1931, folder 69, ibid.

47. Breyer to REB, September 28, October 21, 1931; REB to Breyer, October 24, 1931, folder 14, ibid.; Breyer to REB, January 6, 1932; REB to Breyer, January 11, 1932, folder 15, ibid.; REB to Lincoln Ellsworth, May 2, 1932, folder 6345, ibid.

48. The exchange of correspondence and cables between REB and Ellsworth from January 7 to April 19, 1932, is in folder 6345, ibid. Balchen set forth Ellsworth's thinking in several personal diary entries for April 13, 16, 20, 1932, in notebook-diary subject "1933–35 Ellsworth Trans-Antarctic Expedition," in box 1, folder 4, Balchen Collection

49. REB to Ellsworth, May 2, 1932, folder 6345, Byrd Papers; "Message from Richard E. Byrd," read at the reception honoring Balchen at Teterboro, New Jersey, July 2, 1930, box 6, folder 2, Balchen Collection.

50. REB to Ellsworth, May 11, 1932, folder 6345, Byrd Papers.

51. Ellsworth to REB, May 11, 1932, ibid.

52. REB to Ellsworth, May 21, 1932, ibid.

53. REB to Breyer, May 4, 20, 1932, folder 15, ibid.

54. Ellsworth to REB, May 25, June 12, 1932; REB to Ellsworth, June 11, 1932, folder 6345, ibid.

55. Byrd, *Discovery*, 12; Victor H. Czegka to Loose Wiles Biscuit Co., March 4, 1932, folder 6084, Byrd Papers.

56. REB to Breyer, March 25, 1932; Breyer to REB, April 28, May 24, June 6, 1932, folder 15, Byrd Papers.

57. Ellsworth to REB (cable), June 18, date obscured (cable), 1932; REB to Ellsworth (cable), June 22, 1932, folder 6345, ibid.

58. REB to Ellsworth, October 31, 1932, ibid.

59. REB's extensive correspondence with Ellsworth from late 1932 to June 1933 is in ibid. Information regarding Tapley is in Tapley to REB, November 3, 1932, and REB to Ellsworth, December 19, 1932. REB's New Year's note to Ellsworth is dated December 30. Byrd again alludes to the "Polar Legion," stating that he and Ellsworth are the only two survivors. Ellsworth's request for binoculars is in his letter to REB, May 14, 1933; REB's reply is dated May 15. Byrd's provision of ski boots and cookware to Ellsworth is in

"Memo to Mr. [Norman] Vaughan," June 19, 1932; and undated memo and memo of June 23, 1933, to Czegka, folder 6084, ibid.

60. REB to Ellsworth, June 22, 1933, folder 6345, ibid.

Chapter 11. Jeopardy

1. The quote is from Byrd, *Discovery,* 18; Mrs. Roosevelt's invitation is in E. Roosevelt to MAB, August 26, 1933; FDR to REB, September 7, 1933, folder 2898, Byrd Papers.

2. REB to Louis Johnson, August 30, 1949, folder 7336, ibid. Throughout the New Deal years and beyond, FDR was both highly aware of Antarctica and its possible future strategic importance, and desirous of making extensive U.S. claims there. Thus, in his epic November 1935 flight from Dundee Island off the northern tip of the Antarctic Peninsula to Byrd's abandoned Little America II base at the Bay of Whales, Ellsworth dropped claim markers in the area south of the peninsula and north of Marie Byrd Land that subsequently became known as Ellsworth Land. He did the same in his 250-mile flight inland on January 11, 1939, from his ship off the Ingrid Christensen Coast. The region he overflew has been known since as the "American Highland." Although these U.S. claims were ostensibly secret, they were or became publicly known no later than the 1957–1958 International Geophysical Year when Sullivan revealed them in *Quest for a Continent,* 100–105 (see chap. 6, n. 23). Ellsworth's claims, however, were never recognized by international law, which insists that "'effective occupation' is the only reason for ownership" in the Antarctic—or anywhere else. The official U.S. position, stated by President Kennedy at the moment that the Antarctic Treaty (1961) came into force, was and remains that "nothing in the treaty shall be interpreted as either a renunciation or recognition of claims or bases of claims" (*Polar Regions Atlas,* 41, 43 [see chap. 7, n. 2]).

3. "Copy of Radio Talk Made by Mr. [Nicholas Murray] Butler on Monday Evening, October 2, 1933," folder 3500, Byrd Papers.

4. Undated and unsigned statement by REB, folder 3877, ibid.

5. Unless otherwise noted, the following account, including quotes, of the development of Advance Base with its singular "shack," is from Charles J. V. Murphy press release, Little America, March 28, 1934, pp. 3–4, in folder 6831, ibid.

6. Quote is in ibid. Byrd did not authorize construction until just seven weeks before *Bear of Oakland* was scheduled to sail (REB memo to Czegka and Siple, August 1, 1933, folder 6084, ibid.).

7. Vaughan with Murphey, *With Byrd,* 172.

8. Ibid., 176.

9. Matouzzi, "Richard Byrd," 228–31 (quote on p. 230). See also Lindsey, "Inside Byrd's Second Antarctic Expedition," 4 (see introduction, n. 3); Byrd, *Discovery,* 2, 9–18; Goerler, *To the Pole,* 123, 124. See also Goerler, "*Alone:* A Class of Polar Literature—Questions and Answers," in *Poles Apart—Poles-on-Line: Proceedings of the 19th Polar Libraries Colloquy, 17–21 June 2002, Copenhagen,* ed. Kirsten Canning and Vibke Sloth Jakobsen (Copenhagen: Danish Polar Center, 2002), 122. The characterization of *Pacific Fir/Jacob*

Ruppert is in Bertrand, *Americans in Antarctica,* 314 (see chap. 7, n. 2). REB's terse note to Czegka on the steering problem is dated August 1, 1933, folder 6084, Byrd Papers. For Harry Byrd's assistance in obtaining *Pacific Fir/Jacob Ruppert,* see Daniel C. Roper to HFB, August 17, 1933; HFB to REB, August 18, 1933, folder 39, Byrd Papers. For Harry's assistance in getting the U.S. Postal Department to issue an expedition stamp as REB requested, see HFB to REB, September 8, 1933, ibid. For IBM's "loan" of a "Radiotype" machine, see M. Y. Battin to John McNeil, October 2, 1933, folder 1938, ibid.

10. William S. McCormick interview, March 8, 2000, transcript pp. 1–5, 32, American Polar Society, Byrd Polar Archival Program oral history project, The Ohio State University, Columbus.

11. Byrd, *Discovery,* 2, 4, 6.

12. Gathering of the clans is in ibid., 13. The exchange of cables and letters between REB and HFB, July 28–August 14, 1933, regarding a weatherman for BAE II is in folder 39, Byrd Papers.

13. McCormick interview, March 8, 2000, transcript pp. 13–14. McCormick claims that Wade went to the Rockefeller Mountains, but a biographic sketch undoubtedly drafted by Wade accompanying one of his early postwar articles states that he traveled to the Edsel Ford Ranges. See F. Alton Wade, "Oil in Antarctica!" *Oil Weekly,* April 1, 1946, 4–7.

14. Gordon Fountain interview, October 19, 1996, transcript pp. 2–4, American Polar Society, Byrd Polar Archival Program oral history project.

15. Dr. Donald McLean interview, April 27, 1997, transcript pp. 1–2, ibid.; Jackie Ronne interview, July 20, 2000, transcript pp. 57–58, ibid.

16. "Byrd's Ship Heads for the Antarctic," *New York Times,* October 22, 1933; G. O. Shirey to REB, October [?], 1933, folder 149, Byrd Papers; REB to HFB (cable), October 12, 1933; HFB to REB, October 12, 1933, folder 39, ibid.

17. Young, "Byrd II," 4 (see chap. 8, n. 49).

18. Byrd, *Discovery,* 16, 20–21; Bertrand, *Americans in Antarctica,* 366.

19. McCormick interview, transcript pp. 32–33; S. Paine diary entry, December 4, 5, 1933, in *Footsteps on the Ice,* ed. M. L. Paine, 38.

20. Lindsey, "Byrd's Two Approaches to Leadership," 2 (see introduction, n. 6).

21. Byrd, *Discovery,* 21; Byrd, "Exploring the Ice Age in Antarctica," 410; Bertrand, *Americans in Antarctica,* 366; S. Paine diary entries, December 8, 9, 13, 1933, *Footsteps on the Ice,* ed. M. L. Paine, 40, 42.

22. Byrd, "Exploring the Ice Age," 410.

23. Ibid., 411, 414–15; Byrd, *Discovery,* 36–37. A portion of Byrd's radio broadcast is repeated in Nancy Porter Productions, *Alone on the Ice* (see chap. 4, n. 37).

24. Byrd, "Exploring the Ice Age," 411, 414–18.

25. Ibid., 419–20; Young, "Byrd II," 5.

26. Byrd, *Discovery,* 57.

27. Ibid., 58; Byrd, "Exploring the Ice Age," 421–23.

28. Byrd, "Exploring the Ice Age," 424. The undated memorandum is in folder 6345, Byrd Papers.

29. The numerous messages to and from *Ruppert* during late November and throughout December 1933 are in ibid. CBS's instructions to Murphy on broadcasting are in a cable to Murphy signed Ensign, December 1, 1:26 P.M., marked "Urgent." "The most remarkable feat in the history of radio" is taken directly from one of the broadcasts, as repeated in Nancy Porter Productions, *Alone on the Ice.*

30. G. Sutton to George O. Noville (cable), n.d., folder 6345, Byrd Papers.

31. Leo MacDonald to REB (cable), December 26, 1933, ibid.

32. CBS official Klauber to Murphy (cable), December 27, 1933, ibid.; S. Paine diary entries, Christmas 1933 and New Year 1934, in *Footsteps on the Ice,* ed. M. L. Paine, 49, 52.

33. S. Paine diary entries, January 8, 1934, in *Footsteps on the Ice,* ed. M. L. Paine, 55–56.

34. S. Paine diary entries, January 24, 25, July 17, 1934, in ibid., 64, 157.

35. Byrd, *Discovery,* 17, 79; Byrd, "Exploring the Ice Age," 425.

36. Young, "Byrd II," 7; Ronne, *Antarctica, My Destiny,* 20; Byrd, *Discovery,* 83–85, 88, 91; Byrd, "Exploring the Ice Age," 426–27.

37. Byrd, "Exploring the Ice Age," 427.

38. Ibid., 429; Ronne, *Antarctica, My Destiny,* 21.

39. S. Paine diary entry, January 26, 1934, in *Footsteps on the Ice,* ed. M. L. Paine, 68.

40. Thomas C. Poulter, *The Winter Night Trip to Advance Base: Byrd Antarctic Expedition II, 1933–35* (privately printed, 1973), 1–2, copy in author's possession. I am grateful to Thomas Poulter Jr. for permission to quote from this invaluable document. S. Paine diary entry, February 5, 1934, in *Footsteps on the Ice,* ed. M. L. Paine, 71n.

41. Ronne, *Antarctica, My Destiny,* 12, 21.

42. S. Paine diary entry, February 10, 1934, in *Footsteps on the Ice,* ed. M. L. Paine, 73. *Bear*'s brief voyage is recounted in Byrd, *Discovery,* 107, 111–12.

43. Byrd, *Discovery,* 101; Byrd, "Exploring the Ice Age," 427; Guy Shirey to Mrs. Guy Shirey (cable), n.d., folder 6831, Byrd Papers.

44. Byrd, *Discovery,* 101–4; Poulter, *Winter Night Trip to Advance Base,* 1; McCormick interview, transcript pp. 7–8; S. Paine diary entry, December 13, 1933, January 26–28, February 27, 1934, in *Footsteps on the Ice,* ed. M. L. Paine, 41–42, 67–68, 80.

45. Byrd, "Exploring the Ice Age," 425–26, 429.

46. Lindsey, "Inside Byrd's Second Antarctic Expedition," 5–6.

47. Byrd, *Alone,* 33–34 (see chap. 1, n. 1).

48. James A. Van Allen, "What Is a Space Scientist? An Autobiographical Example" (Iowa City: University of Iowa Department of Physics and Astronomy), an article originally published by Annual Reviews, Inc., appearing in the *Annual Review of Earth and Planetary Sciences* 1, no. 26 (1990), http://www-pi.physics.uiowa.edu/java/, chap. 3, "College and Graduate Work," 1.

49. Fountain interview, transcript pp. 8–9.

50. S. Paine diary entry, February 23, 1934, in *Footsteps on the Ice,* ed. M. L. Paine, 76.

51. Poulter, *Winter Night Trip to Advance Base,* 2.

52. Ronne, *Antarctica, My Destiny,* 43.

53. Poulter, *Winter Night Trip to Advance Base,* 6; Ronne, *Antarctica, My Destiny,* 30, 37; Bertrand, *Americans in Antarctica,* 327.

54. Ronne, *Antarctica, My Destiny,* 32; REB to McKercher (cable), March 21, 1934, folder 6831, Byrd Papers. See also S. Paine diary entries, March 1–23, 1934, regarding the "Journey of 'Seven Hells,'" in *Footsteps on the Ice,* ed. M. L. Paine, 82–98.

55. Bertrand, *Americans in Antarctica,* 327–29; McCormick interview, transcript pp. 9–11; S. Paine diary entries, March 21–23, 1934, in *Footsteps on the Ice,* ed. M. L. Paine, 98–99.

56. Byrd, *Alone,* 23–24; Byrd, "Exploring the Ice Age," 413, 444; BAE II press release, March 15, 1934, folder 6831, Byrd Papers; McCormick interview, transcript pp. 30–31, 33.

57. BAE II radio message/press release, "Little America, Antarctica, March 26, [1934]," folder 6831, Byrd Papers.

58. REB to children, February 26, 1934, folder 111, ibid.

59. REB's undated cable to his wife is quoted in Goerler, *Alone:* A Class of Polar Literature," 123. For a summary of investors' concerns, see ibid. BAE II radio message/press release, "Little America, March 28, [1934]," folder 6831, Byrd Papers; BAE II press release, March 26, 1934, ibid.; Bolling Byrd Clark to author, April 23, 2002.

60. BAE II radio message/press release, March 26, 1934, folder 6831, Byrd Papers.

61. Ibid.

Chapter 12. Breakdown

1. Ronne, *Antarctica, My Destiny,* 38; S. Paine, diary entries, March 22, 24, 25, 1934, in *Footsteps on the Ice,* ed. M. L. Paine, 98–101.

2. Murphy to McKercher, March 28, 1934; BAE II radio message/press release, March 28, 1934, folder 6831, Byrd Papers

3. S. Paine diary entries, March 26, April 1, 1934, in *Footsteps on the Ice,* ed. M. L. Paine, 102, 109.

4. See chap. 11, n. 9.

5. Byrd, "Exploring the Ice Age," 432.

6. "Remarks" n.d., "13th," "Apr 15," and following May 9 observations, "Auroral Notebook," folder 3685, Byrd Papers.

7. Byrd, *Alone,* 77–79 (see chap. 1, n. 1).

8. Ibid., 84–85.

9. Poulter, *Winter Night Trip to Advance Base,* 3 (see chap. 11, n. 40). Poulter's total abstinence was noted by Murphy ("Admiral Byrd," 37).

10. Poulter, *Winter Night Trip to Advance Base,* 3.

11. Ibid., 4–5.

12. Ibid., 5–6.

13. Ibid.

14. Ibid., 6–8; Murphy, "Admiral Byrd," 37–38.

15. Poulter, *Winter Night Trip to Advance Base,* 8.

16. Nancy Porter Productions, *Alone on the Ice* (see chap. 4, n. 37); Arts & Entertainment Network, "Richard E. Byrd: The Last Explorer," on *Biography This Week,* May 18, 1996.

17. BAE II radio message/press release, "Little America, Antarctica, April 26, [1934]," folder 6840, Byrd Papers.

18. Byrd, *Alone,* 93, 94, 96, 113.

19. Ibid., 117–18.

20. BAE II radio message/press release, "Little America, Antarctica, April 26, [1934]," folder 6840, Byrd papers.

21. Byrd, *Alone,* 160–61.

22. Ibid., 163–64.

23. Ibid., 171; Poulter, *Winter Night Trip to Advance Base,* 83.

24. Byrd, *Alone,* 177–79.

25. Ibid., 187. The scrawled note is in folder 6086, Byrd Papers. The "Auroral Notebook" with the May 30–June 4 entry is in folder 3685, ibid.

26. REB to Poulter, June 10, 1934, and Poulter's reply of June 18 are reprinted in Poulter, *Winter Night Trip to Advance Base,* 10–11. Byrd scribbled a draft message that differed in detail, asking Poulter to "find out from factory that made my stove burner whether or not solvents suitable to use in it from standpoint fumes." The draft is in folder 6086, Byrd Papers. Byrd's "Auroral Notebook" entries are in folder 3685, ibid.

27. Poulter, *Winter Night Trip to Advance Base,* 11–12.

28. Matouzzi, "Richard Byrd," 231–32.

29. Byrd's reply is partially summarized and partially reproduced in Poulter, *Winter Night Trip to Advance Base,* 12. His own diary comments are in folder 6086, Byrd Papers.

30. Poulter, *Winter Night Trip to Advance Base,* 13–15, contains a summary of the tractor trip and of the exchange of messages with Advance Base.

31. Byrd, *Alone,* 191, 198. The scrawled notes are in folder 6086, Byrd Papers. His observation of the great ellipse is in "Auroral Notebook," folder 3685, ibid. Byrd's comment to Poulter about the cold shack is in Poulter, "Admiral Byrd's Solitary Vigil," *Kappa Alpha Journal* (May 1935): 190, copy in folder 3945, ibid.

32. Byrd, *Alone,* 212–14.

33. Ibid., 215–33 (quote on 233); Poulter, *Winter Night Trip to Advance Base,* 15.

34. Poulter, *Winter Night Trip to Advance Base,* 15–17. The notice to the camp is reprinted on p. 17 and also in S. Paine, *Footsteps on the Ice,* ed. M. L. Paine, 149. Lindsey diary entries, June 30, July 1, 5, 1934, in "Lindsey Diary from BAE II," accession 199815, folder 14, Lindsey Papers.

35. Innes Taylor's memo is reprinted in Poulter, *Winter Night Trip to Advance Base,* 18–

19. Poulter reprinted his July 3 notice to the camp and his same-day memo to Innes Taylor in ibid., 22–23.

36. In early December 1956 Ronne told young scientist John Behrendt that Little America II "was split 27 to 26 as to whether to rescue Byrd" (Behrendt to author, April 9, 2007).

37. *Barrier Bull,* no. 8, July 7, 1934, folder "Byrd Antarctic Expedition II, Newsletter," Waite Papers.

38. The executive committee report is reprinted in Poulter, *Winter Night Trip to Advance Base,* 26–28.

39. Ibid., 35, 40–42.

40. Ibid., 43–46; Lindsey diary entry, July 14, 1934, "Lindsey Diary from BAE II," Lindsey Papers.

41. Poulter, *Winter Night Trip to Advance Base,* 47; Lindsey diary entry, July 14, 1934, "Lindsey Diary from BAE II," Lindsey Papers.

42. Quoted in Matouzzi, "Richard Byrd," 234.

43. Lindsey, "Inside Byrd's Second Antarctic Expedition," 6 (see introduction, n. 3).

44. Byrd's typed notes and his undated writings are in folder 6086, Byrd Papers.

45. Poulter, *Winter Night Trip to Advance Base,* 56–64; Waite to editor, "Hints and Klinks," August 10, 1982, folder, "Byrd Antarctic Expedition II: Correspondence, Writings and Illustrations," Waite Papers (hereafter cited as "Correspondence, Waite Papers").

46. S. Paine diary entry, July 20, 1934, in *Footsteps on the Ice,* ed. M. L. Paine, 158; Poulter, *Winter Night Trip to Advance Base,* 63.

47. Poulter reprinted a summary of the last portion of the tractor journey in *Winter Night Trip to Advance Base,* 65–67. Waite recalled the journey (the quotes are his) in his "Hints and Klinks" letter, Correspondence, Waite Papers. He also kept a detailed diary of this first, and the last, efforts to reach Byrd. The diaries are in folders "Diary of First Relief Trip to Bolling Advance Base, July 1934" and "Second Relief Trip to Bolling Advanced Base, Aug–Sept 1934," Waite Papers. See also S. Paine diary entry, July 24, 1934, in *Footsteps on the Ice,* ed. M. L. Paine, 158–59; and Lindsey diary entries, July 23, September 16, 1934, in "Lindsey Diary from BAE II," Lindsey Papers.

48. Byrd, *Alone,* 254, 261.

49. Poulter, *Winter Night Trip to Advance Base,* 68, 69, 74; S. Paine diary entries, April 9, July 24, 1934, in *Footsteps on the Ice,* ed. M. L. Paine, 117, 159.

50. Poulter, *Winter Night Trip to Advance Base,* 74–75.

51. Poulter's careful account of the abortive second trip and its heartbreaking aftermath is in ibid., 75–78. See also Waite, "Hints and Klinks" letter, Correspondence, Waite Papers.

52. Lindsey diary entry, August 9, 1934, "Lindsey Diary from BAE II," Lindsey Papers; Waite, "Life Story Rescue of Byrd," p. 16, folder "Biographical," Waite Papers.

53. Poulter, *Winter Night Trip to Advance Base,* 78–81; Byrd, *Alone,* 279, 283, 285–86, 288–93; Poulter, "Byrd's Solitary Vigil," 187; Goerler, "*Alone:* A Class of Polar Literature," 125 (see chap. 11, n. 9). Waite's recollections are in "Hints and Klinks" letter, Cor-

respondence, Waite Papers; and also in his "Flashes from the South; or, The Thirty Year Long Adventure of an Antarctic Radio Operator," pp. 23–24, folder, "Biographical," Waite Papers. See also Waite's diary, "Second Relief Trip," Waite Papers. Byrd's greeting is quoted in both Poulter, *Winter Night Trip to Advance Base,* 81; and Byrd, *Alone,* 293.

54. "Biographical—Life Story Rescue of Byrd," 17-page typescript draft for Ray Meyers, June 1979, folder with same title, Waite Papers.

55. Poulter, *Winter Night Trip to Advance Base,* 83.

56. Poulter, "Byrd's Solitary Vigil," 187; Byrd, *Alone,* 294–95.

57. Byrd, *Alone,* 295.

58. Poulter, *Winter Night Trip to Advance Base,* 83–84; S. Paine diary entry, October 13, 1934, in *Footsteps on the Ice,* ed. M. L. Paine, 176; Lindsey diary entry, October 12, 1934, "Lindsey Diary from BAE II," Lindsey Papers; Lindsey, "Inside Byrd's Second Antarctic Expedition," 9; Young, "Byrd II," 11 (see chap. 8, n. 49).

59. Murphy, "Admiral Byrd," 38; S. Paine diary entries, August 17, 23, September 5, 9, 1934, in *Footsteps on the Ice,* ed. M. L. Paine, 166, 167, 169–70.

60. McCormick interview, transcript pp. 30–31, 33 (see chap. 11, n. 10); S. Paine diary entry, September 27, 1934, in *Footsteps on the Ice,* ed. M. L. Paine, 175–76; Lindsey diary entry, September 28, 29, 1934, "Lindsey Diary From BAE II," Lindsey Papers. McCormick subsequently claimed that after eight weeks of inaction following the crash he was eager to get back to flying and quickly got into the air as Bowlin's copilot on one of the Condor aircraft's flights "east." McCormick accurately described the flight, but there is no indication that he in fact was on it. The man was recalling in the year 2000 events that took place sixty-six years earlier, in 1934. Such are the perils of even the most careful and responsible oral histories (ibid., 33–34).

61. Lindsey diary entry, October 12, 1934, "Lindsey Diary from BAE II," Lindsey Papers.

62. S. Paine diary entry, September 19, 1934, in *Footsteps on the Ice,* ed. M. L. Paine, 172–73. Byrd's detailed accounts of the autumn 1934 Antarctic research season are set forth in "Exploring the Ice Age," 445–74; and *Discovery,* 248–375. See also Bertrand, *Americans in Antarctica,* 337–53 (see chap. 7, n. 2). An excellent brief summary is Sullivan, *Quest for a Continent,* 96–99 (see chap. 6, n. 23). Finn Ronne and Paul Siple contributed brief accounts in *Antarctica, My Destiny,* 49–60; and *90° South,* 59–60, respectively. See the prolific Poulter's summary, "The Scientific Work of the Second Byrd Antarctic Expedition," *Scientific Monthly* 48 (July 1939): 5–20, typescript copy in folder 6753, Byrd Papers. Poulter appended a list of approximately seventy scientific reports that had been produced to that time from *both* Byrd expeditions.

63. Ronne, *Antarctica, My Destiny,* 48; Siple, *90° South,* 59; Byrd, *Alone,* 296; Byrd, "Exploring the Ice Age," 445–46, 462; Sullivan, *Quest for a Continent,* 96.

64. Siple, *90° South,* 59–60; Sullivan, *Quest for a Continent,* 96, 97–98.

65. Behrendt to author, April 9, 2007.

66. S. Paine diary entry, January 11, 1935, in *Footsteps on the Ice,* ed. M. L. Paine, 246.

67. Byrd, "Exploring the Ice Age," 454–57; Sullivan, *Quest for a Continent,* 96–97; S.

Paine diary entry, November 30, December 2, 3, 10, 17, 1934, January 11, 1935, in *Footsteps on the Ice,* ed. M. L. Paine, 218, 219, 220, 225, 230, 231, 246, 239 (photo caption).

68. Sullivan, *Quest for a Continent,* 97.

69. Byrd, "Exploring the Ice Age," 464–67.

70. Ibid., 469.

71. Bertrand, *Americans in Antarctica,* 353–54; Sullivan, *Quest for a Continent,* 97.

72. Ronne, *Antarctica, My Destiny,* 55. Ronne's ostentatious removal from his raucous colleagues and his holier-than-thou sobriety had been welcomed by Poulter, who wrote at the height of the earlier liquor crisis the previous May: "Today is a Norwegian National holiday. Ronne, Eilefsen, and Peterson all want to celebrate this national independence day with a little drink, so Noville and Murphy came to me for a pint of rum which I gave them as I knew they would not make a scene but would go down to Old Blubberheim and drink it quietly" (Poulter, *Winter Night Trip to Advance Base,* 9).

73. Byrd, *Discovery,* 375–83 (quote on 383); Bertrand, *Americans in Antarctica,* 356–57.

74. Poulter, "Scientific Work of the Second Byrd Expedition," 5–21, copy in folder 6753, Byrd Papers.

Chapter 13. Stumbling

1. *New York Times,* May 11, 1935. The Arts & Entertainment Network replayed newsreels of Byrd's descent down *Ruppert*'s gangway at the close of its program "Richard E. Byrd: The Last Explorer" (see chap. 12, n. 16).

2. The exchange of letters between the brothers during June and July 1935 is folder 40, Byrd Papers.

3. Theodore E. Ash to REB, May 5, 1935; REB to HFB, October 19, 1935, ibid.; to HFB, May 11, 1936, folder 125, ibid. A copy of the advertisement flier for the BAE II film *Discovery* is in the Byrd Collection.

4. REB to HFB, December 4, 7, 1935; HFB to REB, January 4, 1936, folder 40, Byrd Papers. In addition to the traditional book and article for the *National Geographic Magazine,* Richard wrote a short piece for the *Reader's Digest* and allowed Murphy to add substantial materials from the Little America perspective. The collective effort was published as "Antarctic Night," *Reader's Digest,* February 1936, 112–26.

5. "Byrd of Peace," *Time,* April 12, 1937, 61; Breyer to Editor, *Columbia (S.C.) State,* March 4, 1936; to REB, March 4, 1936, folder 19, Byrd Papers.

6. Breyer to REB, March 24, 1936; REB to Breyer, March 22, April 10, 1936, folder 19, Byrd Papers; to HFB, April 7, 1936, folder 125, ibid.

7. REB to Breyer, March 22, 1936, folder 19, ibid.; to HFB, May 11; to Harold Byrd, May 1, 1936, folder 125, ibid.

8. Byrd's lecture earnings were later revealed by Murphy ("Admiral Byrd," 30); REB to Harold Byrd, May 15, 1936, folder 125, Byrd Papers.

9. Walter S. Lemmon to McNeil, January 3, March 8, 1934; McNeil to Lemmon,

March 19, 1934; McNeil to Harold S. Garnes, July 14, 1934; exchange between REB and McNeil during January 1935 in folder 1938, Byrd Papers. In October 1935 A. Davis, advertising manager for IBM, wrote McNeil asking for permission to reprint the map of Antarctica accompanying Byrd's article for the *National Geographic Magazine* as it displayed prominently the "Thomas Watson Escarpment" (Davis to McNeil, October 14, 1935, ibid.).

10. REB to HFB, June 11, 1935, folder 40, ibid.; to Thomas J. Watson, August 1, 1935, folder 1938, ibid. Information on Watson is from Robert Sobel, *I.B.M.: Colossus in Transition* (New York: New York Times Books, 1981), 23, 32–47; Thomas Watson Jr. and Peter Petre, *Father Son & Co.: My Life at I.B.M. and Beyond* (New York: Bantam Books, 1990), 43–45; and Rex Malek, *And Tomorrow . . . the World? Inside I.B.M.* (London: Millington, 1975), 46–47.

11. Richard A. Harrison, "Paladin and Pawn: Admiral Richard E. Byrd and the Quagmire of Peace Politics in the 1930s," *Peace and Change: A Journal of Peace Research* (Winter 1984), 31. This article presents a superb overview of Byrd's fumbling, often foolish "peace" activities.

12. Ibid., 31–32. A list of the organizing committee for the Byrd dinner is included in the complete program for the banquet in folder 1942, Byrd Papers.

13. An excellent survey of the American peace movement between the wars is Charles Chatfield, *For Peace and Justice: Pacifism in America, 1914–1941* (Knoxville: University of Tennessee Press, 1971) (quote on 121).

14. REB to Watson, May 27, 1936, folder 1939, Byrd Papers; Rockefeller to REB, February 25, 1932; REB to Rockefeller, March 3, 1932, folder 2883, ibid.; Harrison, "Paladin and Pawn," 32.

15. "Thought Was My Only Companion by Rear Admiral Richard E. Byrd, U.S. Navy, Retired," typescript dated June 11, 1936, folder 1939, Byrd Papers. See also "The Daily News Record, Harrisonburg, Virginia," June 6, 1936, copy in folder 8391, ibid.

16. Watson to REB, May 28, 1936; Eugene F. Hartley to REB, July 6, 1936; REB to Hartley, June 29, 1936, folder 1939, ibid.; REB to Breyer, July 13, 1936, folder 19, ibid.; Rockefeller to REB, June 20, 1936; REB to Rockefeller, August 12, 1936, folder 2878, ibid.; Harrison, "Paladin and Pawn," 32.

17. REB to Rockefeller December 5, 1936; Rockefeller to REB, December 9, 1936, folder 2878, Byrd Papers; REB to Watson, December 22, 1936, folder 1939, ibid.

18. REB to Watson, May 27, 1936, folder 1939, ibid.; "Letter of Admiral Byrd to Dr. Nicholas Murray Butler," January 1937, printed as Appendix I in undated memorandum "To Show That Byrd's Efforts to Help Roosevelt Have Been of a Practical Nature," folder 813, ibid.; Harrison, "Paladin and Pawn," 30.

19. Harrison, "Paladin and Pawn," 34.

20. Chatfield, *For Peace and Justice*, 278. Byrd's speech was reprinted as part of an article titled "'No Foreign War' Cry New Crusaders," *New York Times*, April 7, 1937.

21. Harrison, "Paladin and Pawn," 36–37. Comments on the Explorers Club banquet are in Assistant in Special Educational Projects, Board of Education of the Methodist Epis-

copal Church to National Broadcasting Company, April 21, 1937, folder 1942, Byrd Papers. See also REB to Hartley, May 17, 1937, ibid.

22. REB to Hartley, May 17, 1937; Hartley to REB, May 21, 1937, L. S. Harrison to REB, May 24, 1937; REB to Watson, June 7, 1937, folder 1942, Byrd Papers.

23. REB to E. Roosevelt; to FDR, July 6, 1937, ibid.

24. Edwin Black, *IBM and the Holocaust: The Strategic Alliance between Nazi Germany and America's Most Powerful Corporation* (New York: Three Rivers Press, 2001), 131.

25. Melvin J. Sheider to McKercher, August 3, 1937; REB to Watson, August 28, 1937, folder 1942, Byrd Papers; to Harold Byrd, folder 26, ibid.; Leuchtenberg, *Roosevelt and the New Deal,* 240–41 (see chap. 10, n. 18).

26. REB to Watson, June 7, 1937, folder 1942, Byrd Papers.

27. REB's letter to Watson of June 18, 1937; Watson's reply of August 14; and the interim correspondence between REB and F. W. Nichol are all in ibid.

28. REB to HFB, June 8, 18, 1937, folder 41, ibid.; to Harold Byrd, August 10, 1939, folder 26, ibid.

29. Folder 41 of the Byrd Papers contains correspondence between the brothers regarding successful efforts to enlist Glass and Grayson. A list of Byrd Associates is in folder 4136, ibid.

30. A typescript copy of "The Path to Peace," is in folder 3875, ibid.; a draft copy of "War Referendum," is in folder 3877, ibid.

31. Harrison, "Paladin and Pawn," 42; Breyer to REB, January 14, 1938, folder 19, ibid.; Watson to REB, January 14, 1938; REB to Watson, January 22, 1938, folder 1940, ibid.

32. Harrison, "Paladin and Pawn," 42.

33. REB to HFB, December 21, 1937, folder 41, Byrd Papers; Breyer to REB, April 7, 1938; REB to Breyer, April 11, 1938, folder 19, ibid.; Watson to REB, April 26, 1938; REB to Watson, May 5, 1938, folder 1940, ibid.

34. Bolling Byrd Clark to author, November 27, 29, 2002; Katherine Byrd to REB, July 4, 1945, folder 5, Byrd Papers; REB to Phillip Currell, April 27, 1946; Percy T. Clarke to Jerome Knowles, June 12, 1946; "Memorandum of Agreement," April 16, 1946, folder 465, ibid.

35. Harrison, "Paladin and Pawn," 42.

36. The 1938 correspondence between REB and HFB is in folder 42, Byrd Papers. Richard's insistence that the country was going to ruin is in an August 11 letter to Harry.

37. John Meyer to Byrd Antarctic Expedition, October 21, 1936; [McKercher?] to Meyer, October 23, 1936, folder 7236, ibid. The exchange of correspondence between Byrd or McKercher and various applicants fills this and the immediately following folders in the Byrd Papers.

38. REB to Otto Hanschel, April 5, 1938, ibid.; to Breyer, April 12, 1938, folder 19, ibid.

39. REB to HFB July 13, August 11, October 17, 1938, folder 42, ibid.; REB to Joseph Tatornic, September 29, 1938, folder 7237, ibid.; Bolling Byrd Clark to author, Novem-

ber 29, 2002. The collaborative nature behind the book is emphasized in Goerler, *"Alone: A Class of Polar Literature,"* 127 (see chap. 11, n. 9).

40. Byrd, *Alone,* 178–79 (see chap. 1, n. 1).

41. REB to Breyer, December 7, 30, 1938, January 10, 1939; Breyer to REB, January 4, 18, 1939, folder 19, Byrd Papers.

42. REB to HFB, September 26, 1939; HFB to REB, September 29, 1939; clipping of undated *New York Herald Tribune* photo and caption "Lindbergh Visits Embargo Revisionists in Senate," ibid.; Robert E. Sherwood, *Roosevelt and Hopkins: An Intimate History* (New York: Harper and Row, 1948), 130.

43. HFB to REB, October 17, 1939; REB to HFB, October 18, 1939, folder 43, Byrd Papers.

Chapter 14. Recovery

1. REB to Mrs. Edward Clark, August 22, 1938, folder 7188, Byrd Papers.

2. REB to HFB, June 30, 1939, folder 43, ibid.; to Hon. Harry R. Sheppard, April 1, 1941, USAS, NARA, RG 126, General File I, 1939–1942, box 5, folder "Budget" (hereafter cited as USAS, NARA, topic, box, and folder); "Byrd Persists in Plan for Antarctic Trip," *New York Times,* June 24, 1939, 3.

3. Typescript titled "The United States Antarctic Service Expedition, 1939–1941," no author, dated April 27, 1954, p. 1, folder 7214, Byrd Papers; typescript "Introduction" to Records of the United States Antarctic Service," USAS, NARA, 1; typescript titled "Chapter XXI: The United States Antarctic Service Expedition, 1939–1941," folder 7215, p. 1, ibid. (hereafter cited as "Chapter XXI"); Ronne, *Antarctic Conquest,* 18–19.

4. *Foreign Relations of the United States: Diplomatic Papers, 1938,* 5 vols. (Washington, D.C.: U.S. Government Printing Office, 1955–1956), 1:972–75; *Foreign Relations of the United States: Diplomatic Papers, 1939,* 5 vols. (Washington, D.C.: U.S. Government Printing Office, 1955–1957), 2:1–6; "Discovery II: British Research Ship Sails from New Zealand for Study and Charting Voyage around South Pole," *New York Times,* February 8, 1938; "Argentina Claims Antarctic Land in Conflict with U.S. and Britain," *New York Times,* July 25, 1939; Cordell Hull to Representative A. Willis Robertson, March 26, 1940, USAS, NARA, General File I, 1939–1942, box 5, folder "Budget."

5. Very few published accounts exist of the 1938–1939 Nazi Antarctic expedition, due largely, it would seem, to the destruction of much documentation as a result of Allied bombing raids during World War II. Nearly all accounts are in German. An excellent brief English summary of the literature is Cornelia Lüdecke, "German South Polar (Schwabenland) Expedition (1938–1939)," in *Encyclopedia of the Antarctic,* ed. Beau Riffenburgh, 2 vols. (New York: Routledge, 2007), 1:456–57. I have relied heavily on an unpublished thirteen-page paper written in the early 1980s by a colleague in the U.S. State Department, Richard White, titled "New Schwabenland: Adolph Hitler's Claim to Antarctica," which the author generously shared with me. Both quotes are on p. 2. White's short but highly informative article deserves publication and wide readership. See also "Hitler's Polar Am-

bitions: Germany Plans to Annex an Antarctic Territory," in *Antarctica: The Extraordinary History of Man's Conquest of the Frozen Continent* (New York: Reader's Digest, 1990), 264–65.

6. REB to Sheppard, April 1, 1941; Hull to Robertson, March 26, 1940, USAS, NARA, General File I, 1939–1942, box 5, folder "Budget"; "Introduction" to "Records of the United States Antarctic Service," USAS, NARA. Marie Byrd's legal ownership of the barkentine *Bear of Oakland* is revealed in a memorandum from the secretary of the navy to the commandant, First Naval District (Boston), titled "Chartering and Commissioning S.S. BEAR," folder 7227, Byrd Papers. Byrd did not begin formal transfer proceedings until the end of May 1939 (REB to Captain C. C. Hartigan, May 29, 1939, ibid.).

7. Hull to Robertson, March 26, 1940, USAS, NARA, General File I, 1939–1942, box 5, folder "Budget."

8. REB to Sheppard, April 1, 1941, ibid.; "Chapter XXI," 2. Richard made the same complaint to his brother Harry (REB to HFB, October 18, 1939, folder 43, Byrd Papers).

9. "Introduction" to "Records of the United States Antarctic Service."

10. Siple to Quam, April 29, 1939, folder 7231, Byrd Papers.

11. Siple to Boyd, June 29, 1939, folder 7184, ibid.

12. Typescript, "The United States Antarctic Service Expedition, 1939–1941," dated April 27, 1954, pp. 3–4, folder 7214, ibid.

13. Untitled and undated typescript with the handwritten notation "Do for Admiral's Broadcast," folder 7287, ibid. See also REB to the Chief of Naval Operations, June 21, 1939, folder 7227, ibid.; to Harry L. Bailey, August 11, 1939, folder 7141, ibid.; and Paul Siple to Bruce Bliven, September 8, 1939, folder 7210, ibid.

14. REB to J. W. Thomas, June 21, 1939, folder 7186, ibid.

15. Clipping from *New York Times,* April 27, 1933, and related stories, folder 8389, ibid.; "Economy Boys at Work," *St. Louis Post-Dispatch,* July 6, 1939, typescript copy in folder 7284, ibid.; Major Al Williams, "Byrd's 'Pole Vault' Financed by U.S. Is Called 'Dopey Project,'" *Washington News,* July 24, 1939, typescript copy in folder 7230, ibid.

16. Leo McDonald to McKercher, July 7, 1939, folder 29, ibid.; Brendan Gill, *Here at the "New Yorker"* (New York: Random House, 1975), 141.

17. "North Star Starts for the Antarctic," *New York Times,* November 16, 1939; Passel, *Ice,* 3.

18. "North Star Starts for the Antarctic"; "Byrd Flies to Havana," *New York Times,* November 26, 1938.

19. Copies of the president's November 25, 1939, letter are in folders 2900 and 2901, Byrd Papers.

20. Passel, *Ice,* 39–41; Bertrand, *Americans in Antarctica,* 415–16 (see chap. 7, n. 2).

21. Bertrand, *Americans in Antarctica,* 416; Passel, *Ice,* 47–49.

22. Accounts of the voyage of and flight operations from *Bear* are based on the following sources: REB to Executive Committee, January 27, 29, 1940; enclosure to U.S. Department of the Interior, Office of the Secretary, to REB, August 2, 1940, folder 7265, Byrd Papers; and Navy Department press releases, January 26, 27, 1940, folder 7228, ibid.

These press releases are occasionally misleading. For example, the navy declared that *Bear* had actually moored inside Sulzberger Bay when, in fact, it lay far to the east. Balancing information in the releases against Kenneth Bertrand's scholarly reconstruction can be a chore. See Bertrand, *Americans in Antarctica,* 418–20, for a good summary of the flights, including the near collision with a mountain. Bertrand probably relied heavily on Roger Hawthorne's article "Exploratory Flights of Admiral Byrd (1940)," *Proceedings of the American Philosophical Society* 89, no. 4 (December 1945), 398a–e, copy in folder 7212, Byrd Papers. A typescript first draft is an enclosure to Hawthorne to REB, August 22, 1940, folder 7182, ibid. Clay Bailey to Ruth Hampton, January 23, 1940, folder 7262, ibid.; George J. Dufek, "Admiral Byrd's Greatest Discovery, *This Week: The National Sunday Magazine,* July 7, 1957, copy in folder 57, ibid.

23. Navy Department press releases, February 16, 17 (two letters), 21, 1940, folder 7228, Byrd Papers.

24. Ibid., February 23, 1940.

25. Ibid., February 26, 28, 1940; Dufek to REB, "Subject: Narrative of Airplane Flight Made on 25 February 1940," folder 7267, ibid.; Bertrand, *Americans in Antarctica,* 420–22.

26. Navy Department press releases, March 8, 9, 11, 1940, folder 7228, Byrd Papers.

27. Ibid., March 13, 1940.

28. Sullivan, *Quest for a Continent,* 159 (see chap. 6, n. 23).

29. REB to FDR, June 10, 1941, folder 2900, Byrd Papers.

30. REB to HFB, June 20, 1941, folder 45, ibid.; to Dewitt Ramsey, July 22, 1941, USAS, NARA, General File I, 1939–1942, box 4, folder "Aviation Reports."

31. Copies of Byrd's August 19, 1941, speech at the National Emergency Rally are in folders 2902 and 3509, Byrd Papers; the latter folder also contains a copy of the Council for Democracy's press release on the affair.

32. Byrd's memorandum of May 8, 1942, to the Assistant Chief of the Bureau of Aeronautics together with related documentation is in folder 4135, ibid.

33. HFB Jr. to REB, January 8, 1944, folder 62, ibid.; REB to FDR, January 25, February 18, 1944, folder 2900, ibid.; REB to William D. Leahy, April 14, 1944; Leahy to REB, April 18, 1944, folder 2118, ibid.

34. Materials relating to the Special Mission investigation of certain Pacific islands is in folder 4137, ibid.

35. REB to Leahy, April 14, 1944; Leahy to REB, April 18, 1944; to the Secretary of the Navy, June 22, 1944, folder 2118, ibid.; H. E. Yarnell to Secretary of the Navy, June 15, 1944, folder 4137, ibid.

36. REB to HFB Jr., April 21, 1945, folder 62, ibid.

37. Byrd's late wartime experiences aboard Halsey's Third Fleet are recounted in REB to J. M. Reeves, August 4, 1945, folder 2852, ibid.; and in an untitled manuscript fragment, folder 3879, ibid.

38. REB to Commander in Chief, U.S. Pacific Fleet and Pacific Ocean Areas, July 1, 1945, folder 4138, ibid.

39. Harry Truman to REB, June 3, 1943; "Advance Release from the Office of Senator Harry S. Truman, for Publication in Newspapers of Monday, April 12, [1944]"; "Remarks by Rear Admiral Richard E. Byrd following the Premier in Washington of 'The Forgotten Factor,' an Industrial Drama for National Teamwork, May 14, 1944"; "The Washington Premier of *The Forgotten Factor* . . . the National Theater, May 14, 1944," Senatorial and Vice Presidential Files, Harry S. Truman Papers.

40. REB to Truman, December 14, 1945; Truman to REB, December 19, 1945, President's Secretary's Files, Truman Papers.

41. REB to HFB, November 24, 26, December 6, 1945; HFB to REB, November 30, December 4, 1945, folder 49, Byrd Papers; January 2, February 6, 1946, folder 46, ibid.

42. Truman to Louis Johnson, April 7, 1950, President's General File, Truman Papers.

43. Undated, unsigned paper, and "Rough Draft, 9/10/45" in folder 7310, Byrd Papers; Belanger, *Deep Freeze,* 18 (see chap. 4, n. 41).

44. Accounts of Operation Highjump include Rose, *Assault on Eternity;* Sullivan, *Quest for a Continent,* 173–248; and Bertrand, *Americans in Antarctica,* 483–513.

45. Rose, *Assault on Eternity,* 35–37.

46. REB to Cruzen (cable from *Philippine Sea*), January 17, 1947, folder 7299, Byrd Papers.

47. Belanger, *Deep Freeze,* 21.

48. See the exchange of correspondence between REB and Louis B. Mayer, William C. Park, and an unnamed director of the Division of Public Information between December 2, 1947, and April 5, 1948, folder 2256, ibid.

Chapter 15. "Ever a Fighter So"

1. REB to HFB, May 6, 1947, folder 48, ibid.; to HFB, December 18, 28, 1946, May 29, 1947; HFB to REB, June 6, 13, 1947, folder 49, ibid.; REB to Leahy, July 11, 1946; Leahy to REB, July 19, 1946, folder 2118, ibid. For the King appointment, see REB to HFB, January 27, February 8, 1949; and HFB to REB (cable), February 4, 1949, folder 50, ibid.

2. "Naval Message: Addressees: CincLantFlt, CincPacFlt, et al.," August 16, 1949; REB to Louis Denfeld, August 16, 1949; to Breyer, August 19, 1949; folder 7229, ibid.; HFB to REB, August 26, 1949; REB to HFB August 27, 1949, folder 50, ibid.; George E. Sokolsky, "These Days" column, copy in folder 7330, ibid.; Jack Lait, "The Sinking of Task Force 66," copy in folder 7331, ibid.; Ed Robertson to REB, August 26, 1949, folder 7336, ibid.

3. REB to Reeves, September 10, 1947, folder 2852, ibid.; REB to HFB, "Dec. 1949 [1948 from context]," January 25, 1949; HFB to REB, January 31, 1949, folder 50, ibid.

4. REB to Breyer, February 4, June 9, 1949, folder 20, ibid.; to HFB, February 14, 1949, ibid., folder 50.

5. Bernt Balchen and Corey Ford, "War below Zero," *Colliers,* February 19, 1944, 11–12, 78ff (quotes on 11); February 26, 1944, 14–15, 76ff; March 4, 1944, 52–55, 58ff;

Reader's Digest, May 1944; John Hersey, "Three Airmen: Artist Tom Lea Finds in Them Characteristics of All Flyers," *Life* 16, no. 22 (May 29, 1944): 70–71; Bernt Balchen, "Our Secret War in Scandinavia," *Colliers,* March 9, 1946, 14–15, 56ff; March 16, 1946, 72–76; A. C. McKinley to DeWitt Wallace, February 18, 1953; Edward E. Goodale to Wallace, February 26, 1953; Francis Drake to McKinley; to Thomas L. Sullivan, February 25, 1953, folder 2338, Byrd Papers.

6. A copy of the May 11, 1951, memorandum submitting the Greenland report is in folder 4138.1, Byrd Papers; CNO Sherman's letter of commendation is in folder 33, ibid. Various documents relating to the increasingly intense U.S. activities in the Arctic in 1951 and beyond are in folder 4138.4, ibid.

7. Balchen's postwar Arctic career can be gleaned from an unsigned autobiographical sketch he left that is in box 6, folder 7, Belchen Papers. See also Lowell Thomas, "The Last of the Vikings," in box 6, folder 1, ibid.; and Glines, *Bernt Balchen: Polar Aviator,* 213–23 (see chap. 4, n. 8).

8. J. M. Tully to REB, July 27, 1951; McKinley to REB, August 22, 1951, folder 4138.3, Byrd Papers. Fragmentary, unattributable biographical sketch of Balchen in box 6, folder 2, Balchen Collection.

9. "Report by the Joint Strategic Survey Committee to the Joint Chiefs of Staff, 28 November 1951," folder 4138.3, Byrd Papers.

10. Glines, *Bernt Balchen, Polar Aviator,* 230–32.

11. The materials cited and quoted above are all in folder 4138.3, Byrd Papers.

12. REB to Mrs. Robert G. Breyer, February 11, 1949, folder 12, ibid.; to Graham Reeves, April 3, 1950, folder 2843, ibid.; to Arnold Court, January 29, 1951, folder 4138.3, ibid.; to Rockefeller, September 28, 1951, folder 2880, ibid.; to HFB, May 10, 1953; to HFB and Tom Byrd, August 10, 1953, folder 53, ibid.; to HFB, July 21, 1953, folder 54, ibid.; HFB to REB, June 4, 1953, ibid.; REB to Harold Byrd, November 27, 1953, folder 31, ibid.

13. Ronne, *Antarctic Command;* Behrendt, *Innocents on the Ice* (see chap. 4, n. 41).

14. John Hughes to James Forrestal, October 19, 1945, folder 2890, Byrd Paper; REB to Chairman of the House Naval Affairs Committee, n.d., copies in folders 2890 and 7295, ibid.; Ronne to REB, November 5, 1946; REB to the Chief of Naval Operations, November 8, 1946, folder 2890, ibid.; Wallace W. Atwood to REB, August 22, 1947, folder 7302, ibid.; to REB, October 21, 1947, folder 2890, ibid.; L. L. Davis Jr., "Memorandum for the Record, September 5, 1947," ibid.; Ronne to Gould, November 16, 1946, box 3, Gould Papers. Shortly after Byrd's death, Ronne told a colleague at Ellsworth Station that when Ronne "took his own expedition to East Base at Stonington Island . . . Byrd fought against his getting support in Washington" (Behrendt, *Innocents on the Ice,* 142).

15. Gould to Ronne, April 20, 1948; to Paul G. Schmidt, November 1, 1948; Ronne to Gould, November 2, 1948, box 3, Gould Papers; Ronne to REB, July 9, 1948, folder 2890, Byrd Papers; Sullivan, *Quest for a Continent,* 260 (see chap. 6, n. 23). The correct name of the joint European expedition was the "Norwegian-British-Swedish Expedition," and according to Behrendt, although losing three men in two and a half years, it "made

the first ice thickness soundings on the . . . East Antarctic Ice Sheet" while "set[ting] the standard and developed the techniques used for the IGY geophysical-glaciological programs" (Behrendt to author, April 9, 2007).

16. Ronne to Gould, March 1, 1949; Gould to Ronne, March 3, 1949, box 3, Gould Papers.

17. Edward C. Sweeney to Gilbert Grosvenor, April 4, 1949; Ronne to Gould, June 11, October 11, 1950, ibid.

18. REB to HFB, May 3, 1954, folder 54, Byrd Papers.

19. Belanger, *Deep Freeze,* 30–31 (see chap. 4, n. 41). The idea for an "International Geophysical Year" emerged from a dinner party that physicist James A. Van Allen gave for several colleagues at his home in Silver Spring, Maryland, on April 5, 1950. Van Allen later recalled the event in some detail. See his "Genesis of the International Geophysical Year," *Polar Times* 2, no. 11 (Spring–Summer 1998), 5.

20. Ronne to Gould, May 3, 10, 29, 1954; Gould to Balchen, May 5, 1954, box 3, Gould Papers.

21. REB to Gould, folder 7400, Byrd Papers; HFB to REB, June 30 (cable), July 1 (cable) July 6, 7, 15, 21, 1954, folder 54, ibid.; REB, "Memorandum—Ronne," July 2, 1954, folder 2890, ibid.

22. Ronne to Gould, July 13, 1954, box 3, Gould Papers; REB to HFB, July 7 (second letter), 1954, folder 54, Byrd Papers; to HFB Jr., September 9, 1954, folder 63, ibid.

23. "Script to Be Used as a Direct Quotation from Admiral Byrd," folder 2841, Byrd Papers.

24. Reeves to REB, September 11, 23, 1947; REB to Reeves, September 13, 1947, June 28, 1948, May 11, 1949, folder 2852, ibid.; Reeves to REB, September 22, 1947; Jack Flegle to REB, May 14, June 14, 1948; REB to Flegle, June 9, 1948, folder 2847, ibid.; "AGREEMENT made as of the 22nd day of September 1947, by and between RICHARD E. BYRD of Boston Massachusetts . . . REEVES, BROTHER, Inc. . . . and W. HARRIS THURSTON, INC."; J. Elin to REB, May 16, 1950; Charlie Schroeder to REB, July 12, 1950, folder 2843, ibid.; J. L. Miller to REB, August 31, 1948, folder 2850, ibid.; REB to Reeves, May 17, 1947, folder 2852, ibid. Materials relating to REB's visit to South Carolina are in ibid. and in folders 8378 and 8382.

25. Reeves to REB, June 7, 1948; REB to Reeves, April 5, 1949, folder 2852, ibid.

26. REB to Reeves, August 3, 1949; Reeves to REB, August 4, 1949, folder 2852, ibid.

27. See August–September 1949 exchange of correspondence between REB and Reeves in ibid.

28. REB to Reeves, July 13, 1950; Reeves to REB, July 17, 1950, folder 2843, ibid.

29. REB to Reeves, December 27, 1950, folder 2852, ibid.

30. Charles F. Schroeder to Claire Wolff, September 26, 1951; ? to REB, October 29, 1951, folder 2847, ibid.; G. F. Wood to Schroeder, November 1, 1951, "ANNOUNCING *Fashion Panorama,*" folder 2848, ibid.

31. Unnamed "secretary" to Schroeder, November 21, 1951, folder 2847, ibid.; Schroeder to REB, May 17, September 17, October 1, 1954, March 31, 1955; REB to

Schroeder, April 8, 1955, folder 2849, ibid.; REB to Reeves, April 22, 1955, folder 2854, ibid.

32. REB to Reeves, November 27, 1951, September 6, December 22, 1952, folder 2853, ibid.; Reeves to REB, April 2, 1953, folder 2845, ibid.

33. REB to HFB, March 9, 1954, folder 54, ibid.; REB to Harold Byrd, April 19, 1955, February 5, 1957, folder 31, ibid.

34. For information on the origins and objectives of the International Rescue Committee see typescript copy of the pamphlet "Assignment RESCUE" and "Program and Objectives of the International Rescue and Relief Committee," both in folder 4109, Byrd Papers. A brief summary of the Iron Curtain Refugee Campaign and its work is in "Richard E. Byrd," a brief sketch copied, it would appear, from either *Look* or *Colliers* magazines sometime in 1949, '50, or early '51 in folder 8382, ibid. Official sponsors of the Iron Curtain Refugee Campaign are listed in the letterhead of REB to Will Clayton, September 27, 1949, William L. Clayton Papers.

35. REB speech, "We Must Not Let Them Die," October 20, 1949, typescript copy in folder 4109, Byrd Papers; REB to Clayton, February 16, 1950, Clayton Papers.

36. REB to David Martin, June 27, 1950, folder 1945, Byrd Papers; Ernst Reuter to REB (cables), April 24, June 1, 1950, folder 2860, ibid.; Maxwell D. Taylor to REB, June 7, 1950, folder 3143, ibid.; "Dinner to Honor ERNST REUTER," folder 4109, ibid.

37. Information on the composition of the International Rescue Committee and on the origins of Operation Brotherhood is in "Assignment RESCUE," folder 4109, ibid.; "Red 'Come Home' Drive Gaining in Free World, Survey Reveals," *New York Times,* March 28, 1956, copy in folder 1945, ibid.; REB to Ngo Dinh Diem, July 7, 1955, ibid.

38. "Richard E. Byrd," folder 8382, ibid.; Dwight D. Eisenhower to REB, June 1, 1954, folder 4109, ibid. For Richard's generally favorable view of the early Eisenhower administration (when Ike gave the party's right wing rope enough to hang itself), see REB to Harold Byrd, May 1, 1953, July 6, 7, September 8, 1954, folder 31, ibid.

39. REB to HFB, March 26, 1956, folder 55, ibid.

40. REB to Rockefeller, January 22, 1954, folder 2880, ibid.; to Reeves, January 22, 1954, folder 2854, ibid.; to HFB, April 16, September 8, November 4, 1954, folder 54, ibid.; to HFB, June 4, 1954, folder 55, ibid.; to HFB, August 26, 1954, folder 63, ibid.; to Thomas B. Byrd, June 17, 1954, folder 109, ibid.; to "Bobbie," November 1, 1954, folder 13N, ibid.

41. Belanger, *Deep Freeze,* 33; Detlev W. Bronk to REB, June 21, 1954; REB to Bronk, June 29, 1954, folder 7400, Byrd Papers.

42. REB to Gould, October 4, 1954; Gould to REB, October 12, 1954, folder 7400, Byrd Papers; Sullivan, *Quest for a Continent,* 301.

43. REB to Commander Glen Jacobsen, November 24, 1954; to Gould, November 29, December 23, 1954, May 27, 1955; Gould to REB, December 12, 31, 1954; Joseph Kaplan to REB, February 8, 1955, folder 7400, Byrd Papers; White House press release, March 28, 1955, announcing REB's appointment, folder 4004, ibid.; HFB to REB, April 4, 1955, with enclosure, folder 56, ibid.; REB to HFB Jr., April 14, 1955, folder 63, ibid.; Ronne

to REB, August 3, 1955, October 29, 1956, folder 2890, ibid.; Belanger, *Deep Freeze,* 48–50.

44. Sullivan, *Quest for a Continent,* 342; Belanger, *Deep Freeze,* 50, 62.

45. REB to Hugh Odishaw, July 26, 1955; to Gould, August 20, 1944, folder 7400, Byrd Papers; Balchen to Gould, November 19, 1954, box 3, Gould Papers.

46. See REB correspondence with Gould and Odishaw between April and October 1955 in folder 7400, Byrd Papers. The quote is from Gould to REB, December 8, 1954, box 3, Gould Papers.

47. Deputy [Acting] Secretary of Defense to REB, October 21, 1955, folder 2865, Byrd Papers; REB to HFB, November 13, 1955, folder 56, ibid.

48. Belanger, *Deep Freeze,* 188.

49. Byrd, "All-Out Assault on Antarctica," 141, 146; Robert Newcomb oral history interview, March 17, 2000, pp. 7–8, Byrd Polar Research Center, The Ohio State University, Columbus; Belanger, *Deep Freeze,* 359.

50. Waite to Murphy, May 20, 1980, folder "Correspondence, Murphy, Charles J. V.," Waite Papers. Conger and I worked together in producing *Assault on Eternity.*

51. Sullivan, *Quest for a Continent,* 342–44; untitled memorandum, n.d., folder 4005, Byrd Papers; Robert C. Hendrickson to HFB, March 15, 1957, folder 58, ibid.; Cliff L. Bekkedahl oral history interview, May 17, 2001, pp. 46–47, Byrd Polar Research Center, The Ohio State University, Columbus; Brian Shoemaker, telephone conversation with author, January 16, 2003.

52. Balchen to Gould, March 5, April 2, 1956; Gould to Balchen, March 13, 1956, box 3, Gould Papers.

53. REB to Gould, August 3, 17, 1956; Gould to REB, August 7, 1956, ibid.

54. REB, "Memorandum for the Chief of Naval Operations, August 20, 1956," ibid.

55. Gould to REB, August 27, September 8, 1956, ibid.; REB to Gould, September 13, 15, 1956, folder 7400, Byrd Papers.

56. Belanger, *Deep Freeze,* 158, 159.

57. "Exploration: Compelling Continent," 13, 17 (see chap. 7, n. 17).

58. Richard Black to Siple, September 18, 1957, "Letters Received," box 12, Siple Papers.

Selected Bibliography

Manuscript Sources

The major source for this biography is the 495 boxes (523 cubic feet) of Richard Byrd's personal correspondence, official reports, and other documents together with photographs and maps that constitute the Admiral Richard E. Byrd Papers housed as Record Group 56.1 at the Byrd Polar Research Center Archives, The Ohio State University, Columbus. Other important sources on Byrd's life and times include the following:

Balchen, Bernt, Collection. Primarily personal correspondence, 11 boxes. Library of Congress, Washington, D.C.

Byrd, Richard E., Collection. Handley Regional Library, Winchester, Va.

Clayton, William L., Papers. Harry S. Truman Library, Independence, Mo.

Goodale, Edward, Papers. Accession 19975. Byrd Polar Research Center Archives, The Ohio State University, Columbus.

Gould, Laurence McKinley, Papers. National Archives Records Administration, Suitland, Md.

Konter, Richard W., Papers. Accession 19861. Byrd Polar Research Center Archives, The Ohio State University, Columbus.

Lindsey, Alton A., Papers. Various accession numbers. Byrd Polar Research Center Archives, The Ohio State University, Columbus.

Roos, A. Edward, Papers. Accession 199810. Byrd Polar Research Center Archives, The Ohio State University, Columbus.

Siple, Paul, Papers. National Archives Records Administration, Suitland, Md.

Truman, Harry S., Papers. President's General Files; President's Secretary's Files; Senatorial and Vice Presidential Files. Harry S. Truman Library, Independence, Mo.

Waite, Amory H., Papers. Accession 19851. Byrd Polar Research Center Archives, The Ohio State University, Columbus.

Oral History Collections

Raimund Goerler, Brian Shoemaker, and others have conducted numerous oral history interviews under the auspices of The Ohio State University's Polar Oral History Program administered jointly by the American Polar Society and the Byrd Polar Research Center, funded by the National Science Foundation. A list of all interviews conducted and those currently online is at the Polar Archives' Web site, http://library.osu.edu/sites/archives/polar. The following proved particularly useful:

Cliff Bekkedahl
Gordon Fountain
William S. McCormick
Donald McLean
Robert Newcomb
Jackie Ronne
James Van Allen

Unpublished Diaries, Recollections, and Papers

While researching the history of Operation Highjump, published as *Assault on Eternity: The Exploration of Antarctica, 1946–47* (1980), I spoke with a number of "Byrd's boys" who are no longer with us, most notably Amory "Bud" Waite, Richard B. Black, and Richard Conger. For this work, Wendell Summers, a pilot on Highjump, provided me with further insights about Admiral Byrd together with a copy of the diary Summers kept while on the expedition. I am indebted to Elgin Long and Colonel William Molett for their willingness to share unpublished research papers ("Flying to the Sun: Richard Byrd's Conquest of the North Pole" and "Yes, Richard Byrd Made It to the North Pole," respectively) concerning Byrd's controversial 1926 flight. Brian Shoemaker kindly placed me in contact with both highly experienced Arctic flyers. In addition, Mr. Summers provided invaluable information on the critical question of aircraft ski position and drag. I also remain deeply indebted to the individual, whose name I have inexcusably forgotten, who provided me with a copy of Thomas Poulter's riveting, unpublished account, "The Winter Trip to Advance Base," the fullest and frankest revelation of events, not only the daring attempts to rescue Byrd from his solitary 1934 vigil on the ice but also the tumultuous events at Little America II that preceded the efforts. Finally, I am deeply grateful to Bolling Byrd Clarke and to Senator Harry Flood Byrd Jr. for sharing their thoughts and memories about a remarkable father and uncle, and to Thomas Poulter Jr. for recollections of his father, the de facto commander at Little America during the critical portions of the second Byrd Antarctic expedition. Senator Byrd spoke to my wife and me for most of an October morning in 2001 at his office in Winchester, and followed up with a letter of clarification. Mrs. Clarke responded fulsomely to several e-mail queries during the course of my research. Mr. Poulter kindly granted permission to quote from his father's recollections.

Published Diaries

Paine, M. L., ed. *Footsteps on the Ice: The Antarctic Diaries of Stuart D. Paine, Second Byrd Expedition.* Columbia: University of Missouri Press, 2007. This diary is in a class by itself as an exciting and informative firsthand contemporary account of the joys and rigors of an early Antarctic expedition.
Passel, Charles F. *Ice: The Antarctic Diary of Charles F. Passel.* Ed. Tim Baughman. Lubbock: Texas Tech University Press, 1995. This source contains a wealth of material about the United States Antarctic Service expedition of 1939–1941.

Byrd's Own Writings

If read with caution and skepticism, Byrd's many magazine and book accounts of his aviation and polar exploits yield important information and insights into his character and its testing under stress. As with many autobiographers, it is not so much what Byrd wrote but what he omitted about himself and others that provides frequent fascination. The single exception is *Alone,* a frequently scorching and lacerating self-assessment of personality under assault by polar forces that remains unmatched in the literature. Among Byrd's most significant writings are the following:

"All-Out Assault on Antarctica." *National Geographic Magazine* 110, no. 2 (August 1956): 141ff.
Alone. New York: G. P. Putnam's Sons, 1938.
"The Conquest of Antarctica by Air." *National Geographic Magazine* 58, no. 2 (August 1930): 127ff.
"Crusaders." *Saturday Evening Post* 201, no. 12 (September 22, 1928): 6–7, 169ff.
Discovery: The Story of the Second Byrd Antarctic Expedition. New York: G. P. Putnam's Sons, 1935.
"Don't Let Them Die." *Saturday Evening Post* 200, no. 48 (May 26, 1928): 13, 186ff.
"Exploring the Ice Age in Antarctica." *National Geographic Magazine* 68, no. 4 (October 1935): 409ff.

"The First Flight to the North Pole." *National Geographic Magazine* 50, no. 3 (September 1926): 357ff.

"Flying over the Arctic." *National Geographic Magazine* 48, no. 5 (November 1925): 519ff.

"How I Pick My Men." *Saturday Evening Post* 200, no. 43 (April 21, 1928): 12–13, 54ff.

"It's Safe to Fly," *Colliers* 80, no. 10 (September 3, 1927): 7ff.

Little America: Aerial Exploration in the Antarctic; The Flight to the South Pole. New York: G. P. Putnam's Sons, 1930.

"Our Navy Explores Antarctica." *National Geographic Magazine* 92, no. 4 (October 1947): 429ff.

"Our Transatlantic Flight." *National Geographic Magazine* 52, no. 3 (September 1927): 366–67.

Skyward. New York: G. P. Putnam's Sons, 1928.

"The X in Exploration." *Saturday Evening Post* 200, no. 27 (December 31, 1927): 5, 34ff.

Critical and Laudatory Assessments of Byrd by His Colleagues

Balchen, Bernt. *Come North with Me: An Autobiography.* New York: E. P. Dutton, 1958.

Bennett, Floyd. "Our Flight over the North Pole." *Aero Digest,* September 1926, 175–77, 261–64.

Gould, Laurence McKinley. *Cold: The Record of an Antarctic Sledge Journey.* New York: Brewer, Warren, and Putnam, 1931.

Murphy, Charles J. V. "Admiral Byrd: Greatest Polar Adventurer Goes to Claim Antarctica." *Life* 7, no. 18 (October 30, 1939): 27–38.

Owen, Russell. *The Antarctic Ocean.* New York: Whittlesey House, 1941.

Ronne, Finn. *Antarctica, My Destiny: A Personal History by the Last of the Great Polar Explorers.* New York: Hastings House, 1979.

———. *Antarctic Command.* Indianapolis: Bobbs-Merrill, 1961.

———. *Antarctic Conquest.* New York: G. P. Putnam's Sons, 1949.

Siple, Paul. *A Boy Scout with Byrd.* New York: G. P. Putnam's Sons, 1931.

———. *90° South: The Story of the American South Pole Conquest.* New York: G. P. Putnam's Sons, 1959.

Smith, Dean C. *By the Seat of My Pants.* Boston: Little, Brown, 1961.

Vaughan, Norman D., with Cecil B. Murphey. *With Byrd at the Bottom of the World: The South Pole Expedition of 1928–1930.* Harrisburg, Pa.: Stackpole Books, 1990.

Secondary Works about Byrd and His Expeditions

Bertrand, Kenneth J. *Americans in Antarctica, 1778–1948.* New York: American Geographic Society, 1971.

Bryant, John H., and Harold N. Cones. *Dangerous Crossings: The First Modern Polar Expedition, 1925.* Annapolis: Naval Institute Press, 2000.

Cameron, Ian. *Antarctica: The Last Continent.* Boston: Little, Brown, 1974.

Debenham, Frank. *Antarctica: The Story of a Continent.* London: Herbert Jenkins, 1959.

Glines, Carroll V. *Bernt Balchen: Polar Aviator.* Washington, D.C.: Smithsonian Institution Press, 1999.

Goerler, Raimund E., ed. *To the Pole: The Diary and Notebook of Richard E. Byrd, 1925–1927.* Columbus: Ohio State University Press, 1998.

Heineman, Ronald L. *Harry Byrd of Virginia.* Charlottesville: University Press of Virginia, 1996.

Hoyt, Edward P. *The Last Explorer: The Adventures of Admiral Byrd.* New York: John Day, 1968.

Matouzzi, Robert N. "Richard Byrd, Polar Exploration, and the Media." *Virginia Magazine of History and Biography* 110, no. 2 (2002): 209–36.

Montague, Richard. *Oceans, Poles, and Airmen: The First Flights over Wide Waters and Desolate Ice.* New York: Random House, 1971.

Murphy, Charles J. V. *Struggle: The Life and Exploits of Commander Richard E. Byrd.* New York: Frederick A. Stokes, 1928.

Rawlins, Dennis. *DIO: The International Journal of Scientific History* 10 (January 2000).

———. *Peary at the North Pole: Fact or Fiction?* Washington, D.C.: Robert B. Luce, 1973.

Rodgers, Eugene. *Beyond the Barrier: The Story of Byrd's First Expedition to Antarctica.* Annapolis: Naval Institute Press, 1990.

Rose, Lisle A. *Assault on Eternity: Richard E. Byrd and the Exploration of Antarctica, 1946–47.* Annapolis: Naval Institute Press, 1980.

Sullivan, Walter. *Quest for a Continent.* New York: McGraw-Hill, 1957.

Index

Abbott, George, 389

Acosta, Bert: after the transatlantic flight, 163, 170; on *America*'s transatlantic flight, 156, 158–63, 161; incapable of instrument flying, 156, 160; setting flying endurance record, 155; transatlantic flight attempt, 153

Adams, Harry, 291

Adams, Sherman, 449

Advance Base, in BAE II: Auroral Notebook of wintering at, 345, 355–56, 390; Byrd forbidding rescue attempt from, 355, 359; Byrd leaving for, 342, 383, 488n49; Byrd not discussing beforehand, 316, 339–40; Byrd wintering alone at, 314–16, 335, 339–40, 343–45, 356; Byrd's evaluation of experience, 355, 375, 402; Byrd's illness at, 356, 368; Byrd's life at, 346–47, 364–65, 372–73; Byrd's long-term health effects from, 379–80, 423, 433–34; Byrd's recovery at, *206;* Byrd's requiring safety top concern in rescue from, 357, 363; Byrd's rescue from, 354–58, 370–73; commitment to work for peace reached at, 390–91; concerns about Byrd's plan to winter in, 340–41, 349; construction of shack at, 315, 339; dismantling, 381; location of, 337; meetings about rescue attempts from, 362–64; memorialized on medallion, 389; movies of Byrd and, 361, 368; opposition to rescue attempts from, 361–64, 502n36; problems at, 352–53, 360; radio communication from, 345–46,

358–60; rescue attempts from, 364, 366–67, 371–72; route for Byrd's rescue from, *207;* second rescue attempt from, 367–70; set up of, 337–39, 343, 346; shack at, *207,* 356; stove problems in shack, 341, 354–55, 359; third rescue attempt from, 370–72

Aero Club of America, 37–38, 150

Aero Club of Norway, 102

Aero Digest, 123–24, 126

Aircraft. *See also* Aviation; Dirigibles

Aircraft, for Amundsen and Ellsworth's Arctic expedition, 71–72, 74–75

Aircraft, for BAE I, 217, 224, 258, 265; BAE II retrieving, 381; loss of Fokker, 244, 246–47; pilots for, 222–23, 242; on South Polar flight, 271–72, 274; transportation of, 224–25, 235–36

Aircraft, for BAE II, 316, 321, 352; autogiros, 317–18, 334, 338, 374; Fokker wrecked, 335, 339, 491n42; problems with, 322, 331; transportation to Advance Base, 315, 337–38, 342

Aircraft, for Byrd's Arctic expedition, 64–67, 101, 112, 115; amphibious, 62–63, 66, 71–72, 74–75; for Antarctic exploration, 189–90, *208,* 314; choice of, 66, 106; heavier- *vs.* lighter-than-air, for polar flights, 62–63, 92, 97–100, 143; influences on fuel consumption in, 480n55; interest in, 50–52, 98–99; MacMillan preferring, 61, 92; multimotor, 104, 106, 154–56; planes *vs.* airships, 126–27; for polar expeditions, 60–61, 64, 103, 113; for polar flights,

103, 107, 118; problems launching, 117–18; single- *vs.* multiengine planes, 49–50, 154–56; USAS losing use of military equipment, 410, 412. *See also Josephine Ford*
Aircraft, for Deep Freeze I, 457
Aircraft, for Ellsworth's Antarctic expedition, 327
Aircraft, for German Antarctic expedition, 407
Aircraft, for MacMillan Arctic Expedition: Byrd and crew training on, 72–73; Byrd finding, 70–71; Byrd's defense of, 97–98; criticisms of, 93–94; damage to, 88–90, 95; loading, 83, 86; mechanical problems, 92; reassembly of, 74, 82; used as seaplanes, 82–83, 86
Aircraft, for Operation Highjump, 429
Aircraft, for transatlantic flight attempts, 44–45, 51–53, 151–53. *See also America*
Aircraft, for U.S. government expedition to Antarctica, 410, 412
Aircraft, for Wilkins's second expedition, 266
Air Force, U.S., 47, 434–37, 478n39
Alaska, 435; Amundsen taking *Norge* to, 123, 142; in Byrd's Arctic expedition plans, 64–65, 106; in MacMillan Arctic Expedition plans, 68, 74; in Wilkins and de Bayser's polar expedition plans, 102–3, 112
Alber, Louis, 175
Alcock, John, 41, 45, 152
Alcohol. *See* Drinking
Allen, Frederick Lewis, 5, 147, 166, 277, 287
Alone, 18, 402–3
America (airplane for Byrd's transatlantic flight), 158–63; crash of, 154, 224; crew for, 155–56; Fokker and, 152–54; ready to fly again, 156; test flights of, 154, 157
America First Committee, 417–19
American Antarctic Association, 438, 441
American Friends Service Committee, 391–92
American Geographical Society, 282
American Highland, Antarctica, 406, 497n2

American Legion, 294, 296, 300
Ames family, 26–27, 298
Amundsen, Roald, 2; Antarctic expeditions of, 183, 188–89, 234–35, 269, 271; Arctic expeditions of, 55, 71–75, 102, 112–13, 141–42; Balchen and, 123, 139–40; bankruptcy of, 180; Byrd and, 105, 151; Byrd's North Pole flight and, 117, 122–24; death of, 143; media and, 106, 116–17; Owen's hatred for, 239, 262; personality and leadership of, 188–89, 223; in race to North Pole, 71, 106, 111–12, 114–15, 118, 121, 124; in race to South Pole, 141, 184–85, 216, 275; in rivalry between planes *vs.* airships, 127; Scott-Amundsen South Pole Station named for, 461; taking *Norge* to Alaska, 123, 142
Antarctica: aerial rights over, 406; Arctic compared to, 120, 140–41, 274; attraction of, 233, 376, 456; aviation feats in, 309, 458–59; aviation in, *208;* Bull first to set foot on, 183; Byrd naming features in, 218–19, 224, 253, 486n7, 504n9; Byrd's departure from, *214,* 413–14, 458; Byrd's interest in, 216–17, 287, 398, 401; dangers of, 191, 234–35, 269–70, 377; descriptions of, 181, 186, 191–92, 233–34, 346–47, 378, 416; difficulty of transportation in, 190–91, 337; exploration by air in, 189–90, 379–80; explorations of, 181, 277; explorations of coast of, 324–25, 327, 332–33, 380; explorers perishing in, 184, 189; explorers seeking glory *vs.* science in, 188–89; first sightings of, 182; as greatest piece of exploration ahead, 182–83, 192, 215; international claims on, 406–7, 411, 426, 454, 497n2; mapping of, 215, 216, 277, 313–14, 380, 405, 411, 416, 428, 430, 440, 504n9; plant life in, 378; proposed uses of, 426–27, 427; psychological effects of, 186–88, 191, 240, 252–53, 259–62, 352–53; redrawing maps of, 140, 182; regions of, 488n44; role in global weather, 216; scientific stations in, 437, 455; search for land under ice, 324; similarity to other continents, 186; uncertainty of

laws in, 240; U.S. claims on, 313–14, 398, 405, 410–11, 413; U.S. occupation of, 4, 408–9, 412, 459; value of, 410, 426, 497n2; weather governing activity in, 189–91, 240. *See also* Antarctic expeditions; specific expeditions to

Antarctic Associates, 447

Antarctic Development Project. *See* Operation Highjump

Antarctic Expedition, Byrd's First (BAE I). *See* Byrd's First Antarctic Expedition (BAE I)

Antarctic Expedition, Byrd's Second (BAE II). *See* Byrd's Second Antarctic Expedition (BAE II)

Antarctic expeditions: Byrd considering late-life, 401, 405, 442, 447; Byrd's, 3–4, 165, 215, 292, 382–83, 386; Charcot's, 325; commonness of discontent among, 187–88; competition among, 234, 306–12, 322–23, 327; costliness of, 309, 402; dangers of, 4, 219, 246, 325, 337–39; exploration as goal of, 185–86, 349; by German, 407; measures of success of, 219, 276, 285–86, 382; new wave of, 305, 412; rumors of Gould and Balchen planning, 291–92. *See also* specific expeditions

Antarctic Ocean, 185

Antarctic Ocean, The (Owen), 247

Antarctic Peninsula, 439–40, 488n44

Antarctic Treaty (1961), 497n2

Appearance, Byrd's, 8, 23–24, 456; attractiveness of, 170–71; on BAE II, 358–59, 372–73, 375, 384; gauntness of, 451, 456, 462; small size, 13–14

Arctic, 437; Antarctic compared to, 120, 140–41, 274; Byrd in strategic planning for, 3, 432–34, 436; difficulty of navigation in, 132

Arctic expeditions: Amundsen and Ellsworth's, 55, 71–75, 113; aviation's usefulness in, 63, 85, 88, 93, 103–4, 236–37; competition among, 62–64, 66–68, 105, 112–14, 117; dirigibles for, 60–64, 62–64, 66; failures of, 179–80; heavier-than-air craft for, 62–63, 98–100; naval aviation's interest in, 61–64; navy's postwar plans for, 427; Peary's, 61; public interest in, 96, 101;

riskiness of aviation in, 85–90; Wilkins and de Bayser's, 102–3. *See also* Byrd's Arctic expedition; MacMillan Arctic Expedition

Argentina, claims on Antarctica, 406, 426

Armstrong, O. K., 393–94

Army Air Service, 47; naval aviation *vs.*, 60–61, 71, 93–94, 427; plan for round-the-world flight, 60–61

Army and Navy Club, 55

Asia, 421

Astor, Vincent, 105, 109–10, 146

Atwood, Wally, 440

Australia, 405

Auto-Ordnance Company, 53

Aviation: advancing as industry, 103–4, 109, 126–27, 152, 165, 171, 288, 429; aerial photos and, 438, 440; in arms race, 393; army/navy rivalry in, 47–48, 71; bombing by, 47, 98, 393; Byrd's fascination with logistics of, 36, 55; Byrd's rejection of theatrics in, 36–37; Byrd's WWII contributions through, 3; danger of early, 34–37, 40; development during WWI, 33; dirigibles in, 44–45; endurance record in, 155; evening classes on BAE I, 260; feats in, 97, 166, 286, 430; instruments for, 44, 72, 107–18; mobility as American value and, 16; public interest in, 41, 42, 102, 147; in WWI, 39–40. *See also* Aircraft; Naval aviation; specific expeditions

Axel Heiberg glacier, 270–72

Axel Heiberg Island, Canada, 63, 86, 88, 90

Azores, transatlantic flights and, 42–44

Background, Byrd's, 2; attempt to restore family wealth, 16; family history, 8–14; as gentleman, 3; happiness of childhood, 12–15; influence of southern honor in, 17–18; vigorous exercise to build up body, 14; as Virginia gentleman, 17–18

BAE I. *See* Byrd's First Antarctic Expedition (BAE I)

BAE II. *See* Byrd's Second Antarctic Expedition (BAE II)

Baffin Bay, 79

Baffin Island, Canada, 90–91
Baffin Land, 63, 68
Bailey, Clay, 373, 379–80
Baker, Newton D., 303
Balchen, Bernt, 113–15, 117, 151, 157,
    281; accusations about Byrd's North
    Pole flight by, 124–25, 129–30, 134–
    36, 138–40, 477n32; Amundsen and,
    123, 139–40; Antarctic expedition of,
    291–92, 305; on BAE I, 215, 224–25,
    234, 244–46, 248, 251–52, 264; on
    BAE I South Polar flight, 270–76,
    491n42, 492n52; Bennett and, 151,
    194; Byrd countering acclaim for, 309,
    434; on Byrd's competence in naviga-
    tion, 275, 282; on Byrd's leadership,
    251, 281; on Byrd's photographers,
    116–17; Byrd's praise for, 276, 282,
    492n47; Byrd's relations with, 146,
    385, 458–59; on Byrd's return from
    North Pole flight, 122–23; on Byrd's
    transatlantic flight, 156, 158–61, 163,
    170, 482n25; on Ellsworth Antarctic
    expedition, 306–8, 312; in establish-
    ment of Thule Air Force Base (Green-
    land), 434–36, 478n39; feud with
    Byrd over Greenland, 434–35; Gould
    and, 291–92, 458; helping with Byrd's
    North Pole flight, 117–19, 123–24,
    137, 145–46, 307, 476n24; IGY
    Antarctic program and, 454, 458–59;
    Murphy's charges against, 478n39; re-
    lations with Byrd, 128, 139–40, 170,
    251–52, 273–74, 482n25; Ronne's
    Antarctic expedition and, 440–42; skill
    as pilot, 123, 223, 233, 247, 251–52,
    273
Bartlett, Bob, 60, 62, 85
Baruch, Bernard, 444
Bauch, C. E., 62, 64
Bay Fjord, 86. See also Ellesmere Island,
    Canada
Bay of Whales, Antarctica, 185, 406, 428,
    456; BAE I and, 234, 277; BAE II and,
    327, 330, 380–81; flight to Weddell
    Sea from, 306, 309; ice in, 190, 330;
    Little Americas at, 215, 326; studies of,
    277, 380–81
Bay of Whales Harbor Board, 279
Bear of Oakland, for BAE II, 202, 314,

316–17, 319, 330; becoming USS
    Bear, 410; Breyer equipping, 310; in ex-
    ploring of coastline, 332–33; heading
    south, 320–21, 325, 381; trying to get
    through pack ice, 334, 414–15
Bear of Oakland, for Operation High-
    jump, 428
Bear of Oakland, for U.S. government ex-
    pedition to Antarctica, 408, 410, 412,
    414, 416
Beardmore Glacier, 184, 189
Beekman, Governor, 31
Beery, Wallace, 278
Behrendt, John, 376
Beitstad Fjord, 87
Bekkedahl, Cliff, 456–57
Belanger, Dian Olson, 461
Beldock, George J., 445
Bellingshausen, Thadeus, 182
Benazet, Pierre, 399, 401
Bennett, Floyd M., 38, 88; accusations
    about North Pole flight and, 125–26,
    129, 137–38, 140; BAE I and, 215;
    Balchen and, 129, 151, 194; Byrd and,
    72, 96, 110–11, 128; on Byrd's Arctic
    expedition, 107, 110–11, 114–15;
    Byrd's respect for flying by, 84, 155,
    247; death of, 154, 224; flights on
    MacMillan Arctic Expedition, 83–84,
    86–87, 92–93, 476n24; lecture tours
    by, 151, 290; on MacMillan Arctic Ex-
    pedition, 72, 88–89; North Pole flight
    by, 119–24, 138, 145, 477n27; trans-
    atlantic flights and, 151, 153–54
Benson, William, 31, 47
Berkner, Lloyd, 452
Berle, A. A., 448
Berlin, Irving, 253
Biographies, of Byrd: childhood round-
    the-world trip in, 18–21; Murphy's,
    15–16, 20. See also specific titles
Birchall, Fred, 253, 266
Black, George, 262
Black, Richard, 247; on BAE I, 264; on
    BAE II, 343, 361, 380–81; in IGY
    Antarctic program, 454; on U.S. gov-
    ernment expedition to Antarctica, 405–
    6, 408, 412, 416; wanting to honor
    Byrd, 461–62
Black, Van Lear, 150, 258

Blackburn, Quin, 318, 323, 377–80

Blériot, Louis, 164

Bob, Charles V., 218, 281

Boggs, Geographer, 407

Bolling Advance Base. *See* Advance Base

Bolling (ship for BAE I), 225, 250; ice and, 237, 243, 280; not able to return, 236, 243, 280; uses of, 228–30, 234, 236; wintering in New Zealand, 243, 254

Bond, George, 428

"Bonus Army," 292–94, 302

Borchgrevink, C. E., 187

Boris, Parfumeur, 164

Borman Sheep Lined Coat Company, 442–43

Boston: BAE II based at Navy Yard in, 305, 311; Byrd family in, 54, 298

Bowdoin, for MacMillan's Arctic expedition, 70, 75, 77–79, 88

Bowles, Chester, 448

Bowlin, William, 326, 331, 338, 342, 348, 373, 379–80

Bowman, Isaiah, 126, 175, 253, 282

Boyd, Vernon, 341, 360

Boyer, Budd

Boy Scout, Byrd taking to South Pole, 177, 318

Boy Scout with Byrd, A (Siple), 290–91

Bramhall, Ervin, 377

Breckinridge, Henry, 389

Brennan, Mike, 111, 145

Breyer, Katherine Ames Byrd ("Taff") (daughter), 54, 178, 299, 400, 433–34

Breyer, Robert, Jr. (son-in-law), 178, 433–34

Breyer, Robert S. "Bonnie," 178, 278–79, 310, 385, 399, 403

Britain, 50–53, 426, 438

British Antarctic Expedition of 1898–1900, 183, 187

British-Norwegian-Swedish joint Antarctic expedition, 439, 511n15

Britten, Fred, 278

Bronk, Detlev, 452

Brophy, Dick, 234–35; BAE I funds and, 227, 256; Byrd's dissatisfaction with, 232–33, 243–44; as difficult to deal with, 237–38, 254–57; ineffectiveness as second in command, 226–28

Brophy, Mrs., 254–57

Brown, Arthur Whitten, 41, 45, 152

Brown, Gustav, 236, 280

Brown, Michael, 446

Bruno, Harry, 144–45, 151

Buell, Raymond, 399

Bull, H. J., 183

Bumstead, Albert H., 85, 107

Bureau of Aeronautics, 47–51, 56, 67–69. *See also* Naval aviation

Bureau of Navigation, 67

Burke, Arleigh, 460, 462

Bursey, Jack, 235

Burton Island, 429, 438

Business, 396; Byrd's ventures in, 46, 53–54, 69, 442–44; commerce in goals for Antarctic expeditions, 185–86; national influence of, 386, 391

Businessmen: Byrd networking with, 99, 103, 173–75, 178; Byrd's associations with, 282, 386–91, 396–97; Byrd's respect for, 3; funding Antarctic expeditions, 217, 226, 317, 411; funding Arctic expeditions, 62, 64, 99, 146; funding Byrd's organizations, 397–98, 398; supporting Hull's peace through trade plan, 398–99

Butler, Nicholas Murray, 303, 388–89, 393–94, 398–99

Buttinger, Joseph, 449

Byrd, Eleanor Bolling (mother), 10, *193,* 464n2; childhood round-the-world trip and, 18–19; on Dick's adventurousness, 15; marriage of, 11–12; sons' love for, 12–13, 22

Byrd, Evelyn Bolling "Bommie" (daughter), 27, 54, 299, 400, 402

Byrd, Harold (distant relative), 178, 386, 447

Byrd, Harry Flood (brother), 3, 9, 12; BAE I and, 266, 281; BAE II and, 317, 319, 402; boyhood of, 14–15; with brothers, *194;* career of, 16–17, 102, 401; concern about Richard's health, 13–14, 384, 438; defending Dick against fraud charges, 125–26; defending navy's interests, 431–32; honors for Richard and, 149, 277–78, 462; Lindbergh and, 296, 403–4; political stances of, 26, 302–3, 398, 425–26,

431, 450; relationship for mutual advancement with Richard, 149–50, 401; Richard complaining to, 289, 385, 399–400; Richard's competitors and, 128, 440–42; Richard's naval rank and, 57–58, 278; Richard's political activities and, 303, 305; Richard's relationship with, 28, 83; Roosevelt and, 28–29, 58, 401; *Winchester Star* and, 16–17

Byrd, Harry Flood (nephew), 15, 17, 420, 422, 442

Byrd, Helen Ames (daughter), 54

Byrd, Katherine (daughter). *See* Breyer, Katherine Ames Byrd ("Taff") (daughter)

Byrd, Marie Ames (wife), 26–27, 34, *193,* 462; BAE I affairs and, 226–27, 237–38, 264, 276–79, 281, 289–90; BAE II affairs and, 305, 318, 328; communication with Richard, 81, 254, 354; family background of, 54–55; family homes and, 298–99, 400; MacMillan Arctic Expedition and, 69, 75–76, 81; marriage of, *214,* 257–58; power and personality of, 105, 257–59, 450–51; Railey and, 238, 254–59, 289–90, 318; on Richard at Advance Base, 340–41, 349, 355, 357, 359; Richard's leaving for expeditions, 75–76, 146, 225–26, 284, 345; Richard's love for, 28, 92, 355

Byrd, Richard, Jr. "Dickie" (son), 54, 81, 462; BAE I and, 226, 254, 284; relations with father, 299, 340; with U.S. IGY expedition, 456

Byrd, Richard Evelyn: as admiral, *209, 212;* at Advance Base, *206, 207;* with brothers, *194;* with Gould's Geological Party, *200;* with Griffith and Sheridan, *197;* with mother, *193;* in Operation Highjump, *211;* working for Reeves Brothers, *213*

Byrd, Richard Evelyn, II (father), 8, 10; politics of, 11–12, 26; sons and, 12–14, 18–19; *Winchester Star* and, 16–17

Byrd, Tom (brother), 12–14, 17, 58, *194*

Byrd, William (ancestors), 8–9

Byrd, William (grandfather), 10–11, 16

Byrd apples, 58, 178, 259, 328

Byrd Associates, 397–99, 401

Byrd Cloth, for cold-weather clothing, 442–44

Byrd family, 389; in Byrd's background, 8–14; Byrds' neglecting children, 54–55, 102; communication with Richard, 81, 254, 340, 351; effects of lecture tours on, 102, 178–79; homes of, 54, 81, 297, 298, 400; parents' fear for, 296–97; Railey and, 257, 258; Richard leaving for expeditions, 75–76, 146, 225–26, 284, 298–99, 321

"Byrd luck," 4

"Byrd men" (or "Byrd's boys"), 4; falling out by, 170, 241–42, 281–82; nucleus of, 110–11

Byrd's Arctic expedition, 101; finances of, 64–66, 104–6, 126–27, 146, 172. *See also* North Pole, Byrd's flight to

Byrd's Arctic polar expedition: advance base for, 111; contingency plans for, 108–9; crew for, 110–11; departure of, 109–10; finances of, 172; justification for aviation, 109; navigation for, 107–8; problems with ship, 111; race with Amundsen, 111–12

Byrd's First Antarctic Expedition (BAE I), *198,* 434; accomplishments of, 269–70, 276–77, 285; aviation on, 215, 218, 236, 244–47, 250–52, 265–67, 277; awaiting evacuation, 278–83; base sites for, 233–34; books and lectures by members of, 290–91; Brophy and finances of, 227, 244, 256; Byrd's management of morale on, 240–41, 251–52, 269; Byrd's pleasure to have underway, 228–29; camaraderie on, 231–32, 260–62, 264–65, 277–78, 337; crew of, 215–16, 219–23, 229, 232–33, 240–41, 264; debt from, 225, 254, 309; discipline on, 240–41, 260–62, 265, 279; drinking on, 225, 227, 259–60, 264–65, 275–76, 279; effects on Byrd, 246–47, 286–87; finances of, 218–19, 226–27, 253–54, 280–81; flu epidemic, 238–39; fund-raising for, 217, 223–24, 227, 253–54, 277–78; leadership for, 223, 232–33; management of office affairs of, 228, 237–38, 253, 257–59; members recruited for BAE II, 310, 318; missions of, 228, 267–69; morale on, 251, 278–79, 281, 375; planning for, 216–17, 223–25, 236, 251–52, 264, 285; reaching Antarctica, 231; recreation on, 251, 260; return of, 284–85; science on, 215, 266, 268, 269–70; South Polar flight on, 269–76; tensions on, 232, 259–64, 278–79, 282–83, 291; wintering over, 248, 264–66

Byrd's Second Antarctic Expedition (BAE II), *201, 202;* accomplishments of, 379–82; aerial exploration on, 324–27, 379–80; anxious for evacuation, 381; arriving at Bay of Whales, 327; aviation on, 321–22, 324, 326, 329, 331, 373, 375, 379–81, 491n42; camaraderie on, 323, 328, 337; command structure for, 323, 331–32, 335–36, 347–51, 353, 366, 374; crew of, *203,* 310, 318–19, 329–30, 335, 385; departure of, 320; difficulties in moving supplies to base, 329–31; drinking on, 323, 328, 332–33, 336, 382, 488n49; eastern party of, *208;* effects of Byrd's move to Advance Base on, 344, 353, 383; Ellsworth's Antarctic expedition to overlap, 306; expedition staff allowed to overrule officers, 332, 348; finances of, 316–17, 332, 340–41, 354, 357, 386; fund-raising for, 305, 310, 316, 384–86; goals and objectives of, 314–16, 349, 357, 375; leadership of, 345, 373–74; leaving Little America, 381–82; missions on, 346, 373–74; morale on, 324, 351, 375; need for doctor with, 333–34; planning for, 305, 313–14, 321–22, 335; potential disasters on, 335, 339, 377, 491n42; publications based on, 504n4; radio broadcasts from, 324, 327; rescue from Advance Base and, 361–62, *362,* 502n36; return of, 299, 384–86; seen as tool for Byrd's ambition, 344; snow tractors on, *202,* 329, 334, 343, 356–58, 361–62, 364, 366, 369–72, 375–76, 381; tensions on, 129, 323, 328, 331, 336, 348–49, 374, 382. *See also* Advance Base

Camp, Walter, 32, 38
Canada, 39–41, 97
Canby, Henry Seidel, 449
Cannon Fjord, Greenland, 89, 91
Cape Morris Jesup, Greenland, 104, 106–7, 118, 122, 130
Cape Sabine, Greenland, 84, 86–87
Cape Thomas Hubbard, Greenland, 86, 90–91
Carmen Land, Antarctica, 269, 271
Carson, Adam C. ("Kit"), 18–20, 69–70
Case, Senator, 440, 442
CBS, BAE II radio broadcasts on, 324, 327, 328, 351, 357
Chagall, Marc, 448
Chamberlain, Clarence, 153, 155, 157
Chamberlain, Salah, 310
Chantier, USS (for Byrd's Arctic expedition), 112–13, 144–45
Charcot, Jean, 183, 325
Cherne, Leo, 449
Chevy Chase Club, 55
Chile, flight to New Zealand from, 439
Chrysler, Walter, 387, 389
Citoën, André, 329
City of New York (ship for BAE I), *198,* 222, 227, 235, 243, 250, 254, 282; being towed through ice, 229–31; evacuation by, 236, 268, 279–80; overloading of, 224–25
Clark, Grenville, 292
Clark, Leroy, 363, 375
Class, social, 3, 8–9, 54–55
Cletrac (snow machine), 329, 381
Clothing: cold-weather, 76, 109, 115, 342–43, *343,* 442–44; Reeves' Fashion Panorama, 445–46
Coal: in Antarctica, 426; for BAE I, 234; for BAE II, 321; for MacMillan Arctic Expedition, 79–80, 83–84
Coalition Committee, of National Economy League, 302–5
Cohen, Emanuel, 317
Coil, Emory, 52
Cold: The Record of an Antarctic Sledge Journey (Gould), 290–91
Cold war, Arctic defense in, 3, 242, 434–37
Coli, François, 153, 155
Colliers, 160, 169, 171

Coman, Dana, 238–39

Come North with Me (Balchen), 124, 251–52

Commission of Training Camps, 31–32

Communism, Byrd's opposition to, 448–49

Conger, Richard, 457

Congress, U.S., 46, 149, 397, 453; Antarctic expeditions and, 409, 411; Arctic expeditions and, 60–61, 63; "Bonus Army" *vs.*, 292–94; Byrd's influence in, 55, 71, 83, 288, 440–42; on Byrd's naval rank, 56–59, 278; investigating Byrd's pension, 300–301; Ludlow Amendment and, 393–94, 398–99; naval aviation branch and, 47–49; prestige of navy and, 428–29; Ronne's expedition and, 440–42

Continent, new Arctic: Byrd's desire to find, 98, 106, 141–42; in Wilkins and de Bayser's polar expedition plans, 102–3. *See also* Crocker Land, search for

Cook, Frederick, 141, 183, 187, 465n22

Cook, James, 182

Coolidge, Calvin, 56, 301; Arctic expeditions and, 67–69, 144–45; Byrd and, 144–45, 164, 294; naval aviation and, 60–62, 97

Corey, Stevenson, 316, 323, 336, 351–52, 375

Correspondence, Byrd's, 3, 4; from Antarctica, 253–54, 254; quantity of, 173–74, 176, 178–79; with Roosevelt, 178

Courage: Byrd's, 4, 15, 25–26, 92, 97, 165; of Byrd's father, 11; of Marie Byrd, 28; Smith's accusations against Byrd's, 244–47

Cows, on Antarctic expeditions, 324, 381, 468n10

Cox, Edgar, *205,* 332

Cox, Howard, 110

Craven, Thomas P., 47

Crocker Land, search for, 63, 65, 68, 90, 102–3

Crockett, Fred, 264, 269

Crown, John H., 464n6, 466n28

Cruzen, Richard, 414–15, 428–29

Cumming, Hugh, 407–8

Curtiss, Glenn, 37–38, 42

Czegka, Victor, 236, 310–11, 315, 316

Daniels, Josephus, 25–26, 31, 40–41, 48

David, T. Edgeworth, 184

David Livingstone Century Gold Medal, 282

Davies, Frank, 249

Davies, Fred "Taffy," 281

Davis, Dwight F., 164

Davis, John W., 56, 58

Davis, Noel, 152–55

Davis, Robert H., 147–48

Davis Strait, 79, 427

De Bayser, Guy, 102–3

Deep Freeze I, 34, 453, 455, 457

Deep Freeze II, 459

DeGanahl, Joe, 264

De Gerlache de Gomery, Adrien, 183, 186–87

Demas, Pete, 7, 261, 282, 335; on BAE I, 215, 229, 259–60, 264; on BAE II, 331–32, 377; on Byrd's Arctic expedition, 111, 130; in Byrd's rescue, 354–55, 358, 362, 368–73

Democracy: in Byrd's speech on WWII, 418–19; science's effects on, 421

Democratic Party, Byrd's aspirations in, 58

Denby, Edwin, 50, 60–62

Denmark, 79–80

Depression, 1–2; "Bonus Army" of veterans in, 292–94; Byrd blaming "organized minorities" for, 293–94; effects on Byrd, 287, 292; effects on polar expeditions, 316, 318, 402; national influence of business *vs.* politics in, 386, 391

De Steiguer, Rear Admiral, 56–57

Detroit Aviation Society, 102

Dewey, Thomas E., 449

Diem, Ngo Dinh, 450

Diggs, Dudley, 253

DIO: The International Journal of Scientific History (Rawlins), 128

Dirigibles, 44–45; for Arctic expeditions, 60–64, 66; crashes of, 53, 93–94; navy's interest in, 50–53, 60–61, 99; transatlantic flights in, 50–52

Discovery (about BAE II), 385

Discovery Inlet, 233, 382
Disko Island, 78–79
Distinguished Flying Cross, 170
Dog teams, in Antarctic exploration, *201, 204;* tiring earlier than expected, 268–70, 491n35
Dog teams, on BAE I, 217, 225, 263, 280; amount of work by, 235, 243, 267–70; uses of, 244–46, 267–68
Dog teams, on BAE II, 323–24, 344; problems with, 330, 337–38; for rescue missions, 312; on trail missions, 338, 375, 377, 378, 381; transporting supplies by, 329, 331, 334, 338–39, 343
Dolphin (Daniels's yacht), 26, 28
Donovan, William J. "Wild Bill," 449–50
Douglas, Helen Gahagan, 448
Douhet, Giulio, 47
Draper, Morgan, 35–36
Drinking: on BAE I, 225, 227, 259–60, 264–65, 275–76, 279; on BAE II, 323, 328, 332–33, 336, 347–51, 361, 373–74, 382, 488n49; Byrd's, 6, 8, 247, 273–76, 372–73; of Byrd's father, 12
Dufek, George, 414–16, 428, 453–56, 461
Duke, Angier Biddle, 449
Duncan, Jim, 349, 351
Dyer, John, 339, 356, 359, 368

Earhart, Amelia, 179, 226
East Base, for U.S. government expedition, 414, 416–17, 442; Black as commander of, 412; Ronne's expedition using, 438, 440, 511n14
Eastman, Mrs. Lee, 389
Eckner, Hugo, 103
Edsel Ford Ranges, Antarctica, 376, 379–80
Education, Byrd's, 15, 21, 110
Eights Coast, Antarctica, 416, 488n44
Eilefsen, Albert, 377
Eilsen, Ben, 118
Eisenhower, Dwight D., 450
Eklund, Karl, 454
Elephant Island, 185
Ellesmere Island, Canada: in Byrd's Arctic

expedition plans, 64–65; MacMillan Arctic Expedition and, 63, 68, 74, 86–90; MacMillan Arctic Expedition flights over, 83, 85–86, 97
Ellsworth, Lincoln, 2, 127, 174, *195,* 290, 385; Antarctic expedition to overlap BAE II, 305–12, 322–23, 327, 329; Arctic expeditions of, 71–72, 74–75, 102, 111, 114, 124, 141; claims in Antarctica, 406, 497n2; in competing polar expeditions, 71, 111, 309–10; marriage of, 312
Ellsworth, Mary Louise Ulmer, 312
Ellsworth Land, Antarctica, 488n44, 497n2
Emergency Peace Campaign (EPC), 391–94
Endeavor (for Shackleton's Antarctic expedition), 185, 188
Enderle, Gertrude, 179
English, Robert, 320
Etah, Greenland, 64, 74, 81–82, 88, 90–91
Etah Beach, Greenland, *195*
Etah Fjord, 91
Eurasia, fear of postwar unification of, 421–22
Exercise, Byrd's commitment to, 14, 22, 352–53, 372, 490n5
Explorers: adding to human inspiration as well as knowledge, 285; Byrd as, 4–5, 275, 286; in Byrd's family background, 8–9; Byrd's relations with others, 8, 128; as dying profession, 1–2, 5, 179–80, 220; effects on families, 298–99; excitement about, 1–2, 16. *See also* Polar explorers
Explorers Club (NY), 296, 387

Fair Deal, 444
Fashion Panorama, Reeves', 445–46
Faulkner, Charles J. (great-grandfather), 8
Faulkner, Charles James, Jr. (great-uncle), 8
Fear of flying, Byrd's, 271–72, 334
Feury, Jim, 279
Filcher-Ronne Ice Shelf, 438
Finances: Byrd never accused of cheating or profiteering in, 219; Byrd's effectiveness in fund-raising, 99, 226; of explo-

rations, 2–3; fund-raising for Antarctic Associates, 447; of national tour of *Josephine Ford,* 151; for polar expeditions, 126–27, 176, 179–80, 185–86, 217, 402. *See also* specific expeditions

Finances, Byrds': Byrd investing in stock market, 55, 73; expenses of, 442; income from Reeves Brothers, 443–44, 446–47; lack of income, 399–400; Marie and, 54–55, 226–27; sources of income, 172, 174

Fisher, L. P., 226

Flagler Fjord, 87–90

Flemming, Bernard, 366–67

Flood, Henry Delaware (uncle), 8, 12

Flood, Joel W. (grandfather), 8, 16

Floyd Bennett (airplane for BAE I), 272–73, 492n52

Foch, Marshal, 164

Fokker, Tony, 104, 106, 135, 138–39, 491n42; Balchen and, 151, 170; Byrd's transatlantic flight and, 152, 154–58, 170. *See also America; Josephine Ford*

Fonck, Paul-René, 153

Football, Byrd and, 22–23

Ford, Edsel, 3, 171, 396, 397; business banquet for Byrd and, 387, 389; funding Byrd's Antarctic expeditions, 218, 317, 329; funding Byrd's Arctic expeditions, 65–66, 70, 103–5, 146; supporting growth of aviation industry, 104, 109, 126–27, 171; visiting Byrds' home, 298, 305

Ford, Henry, 62, 65, 396

For Deep Freeze I, 457

Fosdick, Harry Emerson, 303

Fosdick, Raymond, 32, 65–67, 253–54, 282

Fountain, Gordon, 319–20

France, 31, 102, 406; *America* in, after transatlantic flight, 159–60, 162–67

Francis, Clarence, 397, 398

Fraud: Byrd's polar flight called, 123–42; Peary accused of, 127

Freeman, Douglas Southall, 11

Freuchen, Peter, 84

Froesch, Charles, 135

Fuel: aircrafts' consumption of, 86, 120, 122; management of, in polar expeditions, 77–78, 88–89, 190, 217, 267,

270, 276; problems on South Polar flight, 271–72; for transatlantic flights, 153, 159

Fund-raising. *See* Finances; specific expeditions

Gender roles, 6, 34

General Foods, 317, 351–52, 357

Geological missions: on BAE I, 267–69, 272, 277; on BAE II, 377–80

Germany. *See* Nazis

Gibbons, Floyd, 258

Gibbons, Herbert Adams, 166–67

Gill, Brendan, 412

Gjertsen, Hjalmar, 325–26, 381

Glass, Carter, 398

Glory: Byrd accused of poaching others', 239–42; Byrd's desire for, 3, 98, 316; as motive for Antarctic expeditions, 185–86, 188–89, 222, 411

Godhavn, Greenland, 79–80

Goerler, Raimond, 59, 127, 130, 132–33, 160

Goldwater, Barry, 128

Goldwyn, Samuel, 449

Gondwanaland, 186

Goodale, Edward, 4, *200,* 251, 269, 279, 456

Goodyear, 64–66

Göring, Hermann, 406

Gould, Laurence, *200,* 277; on BAE I, 247, 252, 260, 264–65, 267; BAE I crash by, 244–48, 491n42; BAE I geological mission of, *200,* 247, 267–69, 272, 277, 377; as BAE I second in command, 232–33, 235, 253, 265, 281; book by, 290–91; Byrd's dissatisfaction with, 243, 268; on Byrd's leadership, 248, 264; in IGY Antarctic program, 441, 452, 454, 458–61; polar expedition by, 291–92, 305; Ronne and, 439–41

Gould Bay, Antarctica, 438–39

Grant, W. T., 40–41

Grayson, Cary, 398

Green, Fitzhugh, 66–67, 70, 169, 171, 175, 402

Green, William, 303

Greenland, 101, 218; Byrd-Balchen feud over, 434–35; Byrd's report on, 3,

432–33, 436–37; ice cap, 63, 83; ice
sheet of, 79, 92–93; MacMillan Arctic
Expedition and, 61, 63, 90–91, 93,
146; Thule Air Force Base, 434–36
Griffith, Raymond, *197*
Grinnell Land, 89
Grosse, Otto, 446
Grosvenor, Gilbert, 64–65, 102, 105; on
Byrd's flight records, 127, 145; Ronne's
article and, 439–40
Gruening, Ernest, 405–6
Guggenheim, Harry, 253
Guggenheim Foundation, 151
Gullion, Major, 97–98
Gymnastics, Byrd in, 22–23

Habe, Hans, 448
Haines, William C., 118–19; on BAE II,
318–19, 326, 330, 342, 374; in BAE II
command structure, 351, 366; Byrd's
relationship with, 282, 323; drunken-
ness, 349, 374; monitoring weather,
277, 326, 374; as polar veteran, 111,
283, 335; rescue from Advance Base
and, 358, 361, 366
Halsey, William, 422
Hammerstein, Oscar, Jr., 449
Hanson, Malcolm, 230, 282; on BAE I,
245, 248–49, 260, 267; on Byrd's first
independent polar expedition, 111
Harriman, H. G., 303
Harrison, Henry, 251, 267, 269, 273, 277
Haskell, Henry, 392, 393–94
Hatch, Alden, 273
Haugland, Vern, 125, 128
Hawkes, Bill, 456
Hays, Will, 324
Health, Byrd's, 451; early injuries and, 8,
22–25, 29, 32; effects of lecture tours
on, 178–79; exhaustion, 226, 321,
437–38, 461; failing, 433–34, 437,
454; fragility of, 22, 32, 457; illness at
Advance Base, 354, 358–60, 363–65,
368, 373; influenza, 41, 226; long-term
effects of illness at Advance Base, 379–
80, 423, 433–34; plane crash injuries
and, 420, 423, 433–34; poor, after
BAE II, 384–86, 391, 402; on U.S.
IGY expedition, 454, 457; writing style
showing decline of, 423, 460

Hearst, William, 236, 265
Hefton, J. W., 46
Hendrickson, Robert, 458
Hermann, John, 317
Heroism, 166; Byrd's celebrity and, 146–
48, 167–68, 170, 287, 386–89; danger
of explorers as anachronism, 179–80;
danger to celebrities, 296–97; public
response to, 170, 220, 423, 483n3
Herrmann, John, 328, 368
Hicks, Frederick C., 47
Hinton, Walter, 38–39, 45
Hitler, Adolf, 418; Antarctica and, 406–7;
U.S. business community and, 387–88,
396, 401
Hobbs, W. H., 103
Hocking, W. E., 110
Hollywood, 3. *See also* Movies
Hoover, Herbert, 398; "Bonus Army" *vs.,*
293, 302; on polar expeditions, 180,
284–85
Horlick, William, 317, 387
Horlick Mountains, Antarctica, 430
Hotson, Fred, 273
Howe, Louis Henry, 65, 301–2, 319
Hoyt, Edwin, 21
Hughes, Charles Evans, 218–19, 397
Hull, Cordell, 392, 395, 398, 408
Hut Point, Antarctica, 183
Hyams, Walter, 257

IBM, 386, 397
Ice bergs, 86, 181, 324, 325
Ice pack, 416; Arctic, 76, 79–81, 120;
around Antarctica, 188, 190, 229–30,
324–25; breaking off barrier, 237, 330;
cracking around Little Americas, 335;
crossing, 329–30, 377, 381; on flight
to North Pole, 120–22; getting ships
through, 182, 228–30, 230–31, 237,
280, 334, 381, 414–15, 455; landing
airplanes on, 88–89, 111, 143; maneuvering ships around, 235, 428; studies
of, 376, 377, 380, 511n15
Ice quality, 74–75, 82, 107, 235, 511n15
Ickes, Harold, 319
Igloodahouny beach, 92
Influenza epidemics, 41, 238–39
Injuries, Byrd's. *See* Health, Byrd's
Innes Taylor, Alan, *204,* 335; on BAE II,

318, 344, 375; in BAE II command structure, 331–32, 362–63, 366, 375; rescue from Advance Base and, 358, 361–63

International Chamber of Commerce (ICC), 396

International Geophysical Year of 1957–1958 (IGY), 376–77, 512n19. *See also* U.S. National Committee, of International Geophysical Year

International Rescue Committee, 448–50, 454

Internationalism: in American peace movement, 392–93; among Byrd's business supporters, 387–89; Byrd's commitment to work for, 390–91; isolationism *vs.*, 393, 417–19; war referendum and, 394, 399

Iron Curtain Refugee Committee (ICRC), 446, 448–50

Irwin, Noble E., 39, 42–45, 47

Isolationism, 393, 417–19

Jacob Ruppert (ship for BAE II), 314, 317, 333, 381; Byrd on, *209*, 321–22, 324–25; dangers of sailing near Antarctica, 325–26; heading south, 320–21, 324; in New Zealand, 349, 351; problems unloading, 330–31

Japan, 388, 420–22, 425–26

Johnson, Alfred W., 75, 300

Johnson, Louis, 313–14, 432

Josephine Ford (airplane), 480n55; Balchen and Bennett taking on national tour, 151; on Byrd's Arctic expedition, 112, 114–17; improvements over earlier planes, 119–20; in Ford Museum, 151; on North Polar flight, 118–19, 121–39, 141, 251–52; problems with, 117–19, 123–24; speed of, on North Polar flight, 120–22, 125–27, 131, 134–40

June, Harold, 335, 375; aerial explorations by, 277, 326, 379–80; on BAE I, 223, 224–25, 260, 277; on BAE I South Polar flight, 270–76, 276; on BAE II, 318, 323, 326, 331, 348, 352; in BAE II command structure, 331–32, 336, 351, 362, 382; Byrd's dissatisfaction with, 233, 385; drinking by, 336,

348–49; rescue attempt from Advance Base and, 361–64; stranded after wreck, 244–46, 248

Kainan Bay, Antarctica, 455–56

Kaplan, Joseph, 451–52, 458

Keefer, Chester, 451

Kellett Company, 317–18

Kellogg, Frank, 164

Kimball, Dan, 432

Kimball, James, 153–54, 156–58

Kohler, Walter, 387, 389

Korean War, 444

Krock, Arthur, 391

La Follette, Robert, 48–49

LaGorce, John, 169, 253, 277, 282

Lait, Jack, 432

Landon, Alf, 391

Landowska, Wanda, 448

Lane, Gertrude, 110

Langley Medal, awarded to Byrd after South Polar flight, 282

Larsen, 225–26; BAE I and, 228, 230–31, 254, 280–81; whaling by, 230–31

Laskey, Jesse, 278

Latty Cove, Byrds' home at, 297–98, 305, 396, 400

Lawrence, David, 103, 106, 174, 218

Leadership, Byrd's: abandoned for own explorations, 332–33, 337, 344; in boyhood exploits, 15; as chafing, 128, 286, 332; changing for BAE II, 322–23; choosing subordinates in, 107, 227–28; concern for men's safety, 85–86, 248; discipline and, 25, 240–41; effectiveness of, 93, 99, 216, 240–41; intolerance of errors in, 4–5; loyalty to *vs.* rebellion against, 260–64; men's response to, 4–5, 30, 242–43, 286, 367, 456–57; "one of the boys" style, 232, 251, 260–62, 322–23; personal musings on, 219, 223, 232; pitching in to help, or not, 229, 236, 271–72, 488n43; praise for Byrd's, 48, 72; respect and praise for subordinates in, 89–90, 146, 159–60, 164, 254, 276, 282, 415; ruthlessness of, 239–40, 329; subordinates' evaluation of, 281, 291

Leahy, William D., 28, 422

Lecture tours, by other polar explorers, 151, 290

Lecture tours, Byrd's, 36; after Antarctic expeditions, 218, 384–86; after Arctic expeditions, 101, 106, 150–51; Byrd planning transatlantic flight while doing, 173–75; effects of, 176–79; income from, 2, 106, 172, 174–76, 218; intensity of schedules, 150, 172–77, 447; limitations in, 101–2; movies in, 101–2, 106; networking on, 174–75, 178; public interest in, 5, 172, 175

Leighton, Bruce, 47

Levine, Charles, 152–53, 155, 157

Lewis, William Mather, 389

Liljequist, Gösta H., 136

Lindbergh, Charles, 155, 262; Byrd and, 1, 5, 296, 403–4; as celebrity, 170, 179, 296–97; isolationists and, 417–18; transatlantic flight by, 41, 152–53, 155–57, 163

Lindsey, Alton A., 4, 361; BAE II science and, 365, 373; on Byrd at Advance Base, 363, 370–71, 488n49

Lippmann, Walter, 303

Litchfield, P. W., 62, 64–66

Little America (Byrd and Murphy), 290–91

Little America I, Antarctic base, 215, 283, 308, 321; buildings of, 236; Byrd's Advance Base and, 7, 341–42, 373; choosing site for, 234–35; construction speed of, 235, 243; fear of ice cracking around, 335; fire at, 339; Gould's geological party returning to, *200*, 277; later expeditions using, 265–66, 306, 311–12, 328–29, 331, 408, 412; life at, 248–53, 259–62, 336–37; missions going out from, 237, 375; missions returning to, 271–72, 346, 367, 373; moving supplies to, 329–30; naming, 234–35; radio broadcasts from, 249, 276–77; radio communication from Advance Base to, 345, 353–55, 358–60; radio tunnel in, *199*

Little America II, *201*, 381; carpenter shop, *205;* construction of, 316, 321, 326, 331; mess hall of, *203;* post office

at, 317; weekly radio broadcasts from, *204,* 317

Little America III (West Base), 414, 416–17

Little America IV, in Operation Highjump, 428–30

Little America V, of U.S. IGY expedition, 456

Liv glacier, Antarctica, 271, 274–75

Loening, Grover, 62–63, 71–72, 86, 93–94, 97–98

Lofgren, Charlie, 232, 264

Longworth, Alice Roosevelt, 56, 57–58

Longworth, Nicholas, 57–58

Loyal Legion, on BAE I, 262–64, 279–80

Ludlow, Louis, 300

Ludlow Amendment, 393–94, 398–99

Ludwig, Maude, 10

MacArthur, Douglas, 293, 425–26

Machines: for BAE I, 267; for BAE II, 329, 334, 337–38, 381; tracked vehicles' usefulness, 376; for U.S. government expedition to Antarctica, 410, 413. *See also* Snowmobiles; Snow tractors

Mackay Radio and Telegraph Company, 317

MacKenzie, G. P., 97

MacLeish, Archibald, 449

MacMillan, Donald: Byrd learning from, 99, 106; Byrd *vs.,* 62–68, 97; Byrd's accusations against, 67, 69; Byrd's flights under, 77–78, 87, 92–93, 97; Byrd's frustration with, 76, 78–79, 91, 93; on establishing advance bases, 86–88; as experienced polar explorer, 61, 81, 91–92; goals in Arctic expeditions, 67–68, 86, 91, 94; on polar flights, 83, 88, 90, 93–94; relationship with Byrd, 69, 73, 94; in rivalry between planes *vs.* airships, 92, 98, 127. *See also* MacMillan Arctic Expedition

MacMillan Arctic Expedition: advance bases for, 86–88, 90–91; aircraft for, 71, 78–79, 93–94; aviation feats in, 84, 97; Byrd commanding Naval Air Unit for, 68–70, 76, 97; Byrd deciding

whether to join, 69–70; Byrd's frustration with, 80–81, 83–84; command
structure of, 69–70, 75, 86, 93–97;
crew of, 215–16; effect on Byrd and
family, 75–76; at Etah, 81, 90–91;
goals for Naval Air Unit of, 90–91;
goals of, 71, 73–74, 76, 90, 94; Mac-
Millan wanting to bail out of, 83–84;
media on, 74, 109; Naval Air Unit
for, 63, 69–73, 76, 83–84, 86–87,
90–91, 97, 474n52; popular enthusiasm for, 75; problems on, 76–81; reports on, 96–97, 474n52; return of,
90–91, 93–97; role of radio on, 81;
ships for, 70, 76–77; timetable for, 82,
86
Magellan, Ferdinand, 182
Magnetism, 84–85, 249
Mail: Byrd carrying on transatlantic flight,
153, 158; at post office at Little Ameri-
ca II, 317, 332
Marguerite Bay, Antarctica, 416, 438
Marie Byrd Land, 237; BAE I explorations
of, 242, 271, 277; BAE II explorations
of, 277, 324, 376, 380
Marines, U.S., 110–11
Mark, Sheldon, 480n55
Markey, Morris, 287–89
Marriage, Byrds', 5, 26–28, 92
Martin, David, 447
Martin, Thomas, 46
Mawson, Douglas, 184
Maxfield, Louis H., 51–52
Mayer, Louis, 317
McBain, Merle, 170–71
McCormick, Bill, 317–18, 322, 334, 338,
374, 503n60
McCormick, Joe, 317–18
McDonald, Eugene F.: Byrd vs., 69, 70,
75, 77–78, 80–82, 84, 95–97; Byrd's
frustration with, 78–79, 93; interest in
radio, 68, 81; MacMillan Arctic Expe-
dition and, 62–63, 67–68; in MacMil-
lan Arctic Expedition command, 61,
80–81, 86
McDonald, Leo, 411
McDonnell, Edwin, 73
McGuinness, Tom, 222
McKercher, Hazel, 305, 401; Byrds' per-

sonal secretary, 227, 298, 402; Byrd's
representatives and, 318, 343
McKinley, Ashley, 241, 262, 291, 349; on
BAE I flights, 242, 277, 492n52; BAE I
South Polar flight and, 270–76; Byrd
and, 242, 251, 385
McLean, Donald, 320
McMurdo Sound, Antarctica, 185, 283,
455–56
McNeil, John, 318, 345, 354
Medal of Freedom, 461–62
Medal of Honor, congressional, 149
Medals and commendations, Byrd's, 26,
145, 149, 170, 174, 282, 389, 461–62
Media: on Arctic expeditions, 74, 116–
17, 119, 144; on BAE I, 165, 218, 223,
238–39, 249, 256, 266, 276–77; on
BAE II, 327–28, 333; ballyhoo for explorers, 179–80; Byrd using, 103–4,
106–7, 109; Byrd's image in, 165–66,
169–70, 287–88; on Byrd's North Polar flight, 123, 126–28; Byrd's relationship with, 126–27, 150, 171, 174, 433;
on Byrd's transatlantic flight, 162–63,
169–70; on competing Antarctic expeditions, 307; competition between
crews covering Amundsen vs. Byrd,
116–17, 123; dirigible crash and, 53;
fickleness of public interest and, 147;
hyping transatlantic flight attempts,
153, 155–56; on IGY Antarctic expedition, 452–53; on MacMillan Arctic
Expedition, 74, 76, 78, 81–82; on Operation Highjump II, 432; on rescue
attempt from Advance Base, 364–65;
selling news rights to, 116–17, 218,
256; U.S. government Antarctic expedition and, 412–14. See also Public
interest
Melville, Frederick C., 227, 231; Byrd's
dissatisfaction with, 232, 243; City of
New York and, 282–83
Metro-Goldwyn-Mayer, 430
Military, 31–32; aviation and, 47–48;
Balchen in, 128, 435; Byrd's career in,
3, 30; Byrd's influence in, 46, 386,
444–45; Byrd's rank in, 53, 55–57; interest in polar expeditions in, 427; opposition to merger of services, 431–32,

435; U.S. IGY expedition and, 453–
55, 460; USAS losing use of equipment
from, 410, 412. *See also* Navy, U.S.
Miller, W. B., 46
Minerals/natural resources, in Antarctica,
216–17, 260, 269, 378, 426
Mingos, Howard, 74, 171–72, 402
Misery Trail, to Little America, 329–31
Mitchell, Billy, 151; on breakup of
Shenandoah dirigible, 93–94; court-
martial of, 97–98; navy aviation *vs.,*
47–49, 71; plan for round-the-world
flight, 60–61
Moe, Torger, 280
Moffett, William, 47; Byrd's relationship
with, 48, 50–51, 54, 62, 99, 259; on
Byrd's *vs.* MacMillan's Arctic expedition
plans, 62–64, 67–68; interest in Arctic
expeditions, 60–61, 64–66; interest in
dirigibles and, 50–53, 60–61, 99;
naval aviation branch and, 49, 61
Molett, William, 139
Mondell, Frank W., 49
Money, as motive for BAE I, 222–23
Montague, Richard, 124–26, 128, 130,
477n32
Moore, R. Walton, 398
Moral rearmament movement, 423–24,
448–49
Morgan, Gil, 348, 351, 363, 377
Morrow, Dwight, 105
Mount Erebus, Antarctica, 456
Mount Grace McKinley, Antarctica, 376,
379–80
Mount Weaver, Antarctica, 378
Movies: about Antarctic expeditions, 186,
386; about BAE I, 218, 250, 287;
about BAE II, 317, 361, 366, 368,
384–85; of BAE I South Polar flight,
274, 276, 430; Byrd using in lectures,
101–2, 106, 172, 443; of Byrd's Arctic
expedition, 106, 115–17; to entertain
BAE II, 324; of U.S. government expedition, 414; of Wilkins's polar expedition, 102
Mulroy, Tom, 115, 215, 261–62, 282
Murphy, Charles J. V., 2, 128, 160, *204,*
219, 333, 465n15; in BAE II command
structure, 351, 366; on Balchen,

478n39; biography of Byrd by, 15–16,
20; on Byrd wintering at Advance Base,
339–40, 343–44, 349; Byrd's relationship with, 314, 328–29; as Byrd's representative while at Advance Base, 343–
44; on Byrd's style, 240, 287; CBS and,
327–28; on explorers as anachronism,
179; ghostwriting for Byrd, 171, 290,
402; as liaison for Byrd at Advance
Base, 341, 353–54, 356, 366; men's
dislike for, 360, 374; Poulter and, 348,
350–51, 366; rescue from Advance
Base and, 356–59, 361–64; weekly
radio broadcasts from BAE II by, 327,
339–40, 351, 364
Murrow, Edward, 450–51
Mustin, Henry C., 47

Nares, George, 182
National Aeronautical Association, 152
National Economy League: Byrd with,
292–96, 300, 305, 316; Roosevelt and,
301–4; seeming hypocrisy of Byrd's position in, 299–300
National Education Association (NEA),
177
National Geographic Magazine, 105; Byrd
not crediting Balchen's help in articles
for, 123–24; Byrd's article on polar aviation in, 98–100; Byrd's articles about
MacMillan Arctic Expedition for, 73,
109; on Byrd's transatlantic flight, 160,
169; rejecting Ronne's article, 439–40
National Geographic Society: Byrd's
Antarctic expeditions and, 218, 282,
317; Byrd's Arctic expedition and, 62,
64–65; Byrd's North Pole flight and,
124, 126–27, 130, 133–34; MacMillan Arctic Expedition and, 61, 68, 76,
79–80, 90–94; scientific work of, 91,
93, 102; working on polar navigation,
84–85, 107
National Geographic Society Special
Medal of Honor, 284
National Geographic Society's Hubbard
Gold Medal, 145
National Science Foundation, 189
National unity, Byrd's goal of, 302–3,
417–19

Nationalism: Byrd and crew said to personify Americans, 163; in competition for polar exploration, 123, 127, 139–40, 146–47

Nature, Byrd's early love for, 15

Naval Academy, 22–24

Naval Aeronautic Station (Pensacola, Florida), 33–37

Naval aviation, 105; in Arctic exploration, 61–64, 93; Army Air Service *vs.*, 60–61, 93, 427; Byrd lobbying for, 46–47, 55, 97; Byrd working to expand, 55, 419–20; transatlantic flights and, 41, 152. *See also* Navy, U.S.: aviation branch of

Navigation, 229, 325; aerial *vs.* land, 133; in Arctic compared to Antarctic, 140–41, 274; around North Pole, 84–85, 107–8; Byrd's errors in, 131–32, 134, 275, 282; in Byrd's flight to North Pole, 120–21, 139; degradation of skill at, 132; difficulty of, 88–89, 132, 140, 160; for MacMillan Arctic Expedition, 72, 80, 84; for South Polar flight, 492n52; for transatlantic flights, 43–46, 158; while ascending Thorne Glacier, 378

Navigation instruments, 140–41; aerial sextant as, 44; earth induction compass as, 108; on flight to North Pole, 119–20, 122, 134–35; sun compass as, 85, 107–8; on transatlantic flights, 153, 159

Navigation reports, for Byrd's flight over North Pole, 127–28, 130, 132–34

Navy, U.S.: air force *vs.*, 435–37; Arctic expeditions and, 427; Army Air Service *vs.*, 71, 97; aviation branch of, 35, 47–50, 62; Byrd advocating for, 57, 420; Byrd as chief polar affairs officer in, 432–33; Byrd's Antarctic expeditions and, 253, 284, 447; Byrd's Arctic expedition and, 105, 110–11; Byrd's assignments in, 24–26, 28; Byrd's influence in, 75, 288, 427; Byrd's North Pole flight and, 124, 130–31, 133–34; Byrd's pension from, 299–301; Byrd's rank in, 55–59, 149, 278; Byrd's relationship with, 63, 75, 103; Byrd's reports to, 78, 81, 124, 130–31, 133–

34, 253, 414, 420–23, 474n52; Byrd's service in, 22, 29, 31–32, 99, 404, 408, 417, 419, 423, 437; considering cold-weather training in Antarctica, 427; dirigibles and, 50–53, 60–61; establishing bases in Greenland, 434; on expected cruising radius of Amphibians, 86; IGY Antarctic program and, 453, 454–55; interest in polar explorations, 60–61; MacMillan Arctic Expedition and, 63, 67–69, 76, 79–80, 90–91, 93–94, 97–98; Medal of Freedom and, 461–62; Operation Highjump and, 427–29, 432; opposition to merger of services, 431–32; Ronne's Antarctic expedition and, 439; Task Force 43 of, 453–54; transatlantic flights and, 38–39, 42–44

Nazis, 448; Antarctica and, 406–7, 411, 426, 507n5; Byrd on, 393, 418; Lindbergh and, 403–4; Watson and, 396–98

Neny Island, Antarctica, 416–17

New Deal, 3, 303, 305, 401, 431, 433

Newfoundland, 94–95

Newsom, Gerald H., 481n60

New York Times, 102, 106–7, 111

New Zealand, 225, 228, 334, 439; BAE I and, 230, 237–38, 253–54, 255, 279; BAE II and, 322–23, 349, 351; claim to Antarctic, 454; other Antarctic expeditions in, 322–23, 414

Ngo Dinh Diem, 3

Nichol, F. L., 397

Nilsen, Captain, 228, 230–31, 254

Nimitz, Chester, 423

Nobile, Umberto, 118, 143

No Foreign War Crusade, 392–93

Nold, A. C., 88–89

Non-Partisan Committee for Peace through Revision of the Neutrality Law, 403

Norge, 102, 112, 118, 123, 142

North Pole: Amundsen and Ellsworth's expedition to, 71, 73–74, 102; difficulty of ascertaining location of, 107–8, 141; dirigible flight to proposed, 60–61; effects on navigation, 84–85, 88–89, 140; MacMillan Arctic Expedition and, 68, 74; not in Byrd's polar expedition plans, 104; race to reach, 16, 118–19, 129–31, 465n22; search for land around, 481n58; Wilkins's plan to take submarine under, 290, 320. *See also* Arctic expeditions

North Pole, Byrd's flight to, 5, 38, 288; Balchen's accusations of fraud in, 124–25, 129, 134–36, 251–52; Balchen's help with, 307, 434, 476n24; in Byrd's Arctic expedition plans, 64–65, 106–7, 122, 218; Byrd's navigation on, 131–34; effects of, 142–43, 146–48, 288; evidence of authenticity of, 139, 140, 142, 481n60; goals of, 109, 141–42; Greenland expedition as preliminary to, 146; personal accounts of, 140; Rawlins's accusations of fraud in, 137–38, 138–39; return from, 122–23, 144–46; Ronne's accusations of fraud in, 129, 136–37; skepticism about, 123–39; timing of, 477n27

North Star (ship for U.S. government expedition to Antarctica), 412, 414, 416

Northcliffe, Viscount (Alfred Harmsworth), 42

Norwalk Tire Company, 46

Norway, 112, 478n39; Balchen's flights to, 435, 458–59; claiming sovereignty in Antarctica, 406–7, 409; whalers from, 280–81

Nova Scotia, 76

Noville, George, 107, 114, 215, 335; on BAE II, 318, 327–28, 348, 385; in BAE II command structure, 331–32, 351; on Byrd's Arctic expedition, 111–12, 115; Poulter using in struggle for command, 348, 350; rescue from Advance Base and, 361, 362; on transatlantic flight, 154, 156, 158, 161, 163, 170

Nungesser, Charles, 153, 155, 164

Nye, Gerald P., 417–18

NY Times: on BAE I, 165, 218, 224, 243, 249–50, 253, 264; Byrd writing Owen's reports to, 239, 242; Haugland's accusations against Byrd in, 125

Oates, Titus, 179, 184, 220

O'Brien, Jack, *200,* 260

Oceans, Poles, and Airmen (Montague), 125

Ochs, Adolf, 259, 331

Odishaw, Hugh, 454–55, 458

Okinawa, Byrd's report on, 422–23

O'Neal, Edward A., 303

Operation Brotherhood, 450

Operation Deepfreeze. *See* Deep Freeze

Operation Highjump (Antarctic Development Project, 1947), 131–32, *211,* 439, 452; aviation on, 428, 430; command structure of, 427–28, 430; Cruzen and, 428–29

Operation Highjump II, 313–14, 431–32, 444

Operation Nanook, 427–28

Operation Tabarin, 426

Organizational skills, Byrd's, 286, 387; promotion and, 288–89; in setting up naval aviation station, 39–40; in South Polar expeditions, 3, 217, 224–25, 281–82

Orteig, Raymond, 49–50, 152

Orteig Prize, Byrd denying interest in, 156, 162

Ortell, Robb, 114

Owen, Russell, 188, 290, 485n2; on BAE I, 218, 230–31, 250; on Byrd, 247, 286; Byrd's opinion of, 232, 261–62, 264, 282; illness of, 238–39, 242; relations with Byrd, 238–39, 242, 250

Pacific Fir (ship for BAE II), 316–17

Pacific Ocean, Byrd's wartime reports on, 421–23

Pacific Quadrant, Antarctica, 215, 218–19, 321, 327, 411

Packard, Arthur, 304

Paine, Stuart, 186, 322–23; on BAE II, 328, 343–44, 367, 375, 377–79; diary of, 329, 331; on expedition mates, 129, 336, 344, 367, 374

Palmer, Nathaniel, 182

Palmer Peninsula, 406

Panama Canal Company, 451

Paramount Pictures, 317, 324, 361, 368, 384–85

Paris: Byrd and crew in, after transatlantic flight, 163, 166–67, *196;* as goal of transatlantic flights, 49–50, 152, 156–57, 159, 161–62; Lindbergh's flight to, 1, 5, 157

Parker, Alton, 115, 138, 233, 277, 282
Passel, Charles, 129, 240–41, 413
Pathé News, 106, 111
Patman, Wright, 301
Patrick, Mason, 98
Peace: American movement for, 391–92;
  Byrd's business supporters for, 388,
  394, 397–98; Byrd's changed position
  on, 398–99; Byrd's commitment to
  work for, 109–10, 388–91, 394–95,
  454; Byrd's disillusionment with movement for, 403, 405; Eleanor Roosevelt's
  No Foreign War Crusade for, 392–93;
  through trade, 398–99
Pearson, Drew, 453
Peary, Robert, 38, 60–61, 141, 223; Arc-
  tic expeditions of, 63–64, 74, 76, 85,
  179–80; arrival at North Pole questioned, 16, 127, 465n22
Peary (ship for MacMillan Arctic Expedition), 70, 75, 94–95; aircraft on, 73,
  82; coal for, 79–80; concerns about,
  76–79; fire on, 77, 89–90; grounding
  off Labrador, 96–97
Pelter, J. A., 339, 368
Penguins, 286, 326, 382, 456
Peninsula base, for U.S. government expedition. *See* East Base
Pensacola, Florida, 33–35
Perce, Earle, 415–16
Perkins, Earl, 319, 348, 374
Pershing, John, 301
Personality, Byrd's, 18, 91, 171; adventurousness of, 15; ambition, 75, 286; bitterness, 117; cautiousness in aviation,
  33, 35, 164, 166; deceitfulness, 18–19,
  67, 125–26; desire for isolation, 345;
  effectiveness for lobbying, 46, 50, 55;
  force of, 14, 240–41, 456–57; growing
  conceit, 287; hucksterism in, 288–89,
  446; impracticality, 344; influence of
  southern honor in, 17–18, 22, 160,
  170; intolerance of errors, 4–5; loyalty
  of, 15, 30, 160, 385; loyalty of, and
  expectation of subordinates', 239, 307,
  309; Markey's summary of, 289, 446;
  maturation through expeditions, 286;
  nobility of, 5; one-upsmanship, 282;
  optimism, 81; patience, 414; praise
  for, 40–41, 48; recklessness in, 22–

23, 37; responses to, 6, 24, 128; self-
  aggrandizement, 50–51, 80; sensitivity
  to criticism, 289; thoroughness of, 14;
  willingness to jump into crises, 54. *See
  also* Courage: Byrd's; Glory: Byrd's desire for; Leadership, Byrd's
Peter I Island, Antarctica, 321
Peterson, Carl O., 366–67, 375–76
Philanthropy, Byrd's interest in, 388,
  447–48
Philippine Sea (ship in Operation Highjump), *211,* 428–29
Philippines, young Byrd in, 20
Philosophy, Byrd's, 109–10, 148, 344,
  414
Photographs: aerial, 112, 438, 440; of
  Antarctic expeditions, 186, 223, 256,
  382; of Arctic expeditions, 101, 112,
  117, 119; of Byrd's transatlantic flight,
  169; from German Antarctic expedi-
  tion, 407. *See also* Media; Movies
Pickett, Clarence, 391
Pitcairn, Harold, 317–18
Plant life, in Antarctica, 378
Polar explorers: Amundsen as, 72–74; in
  Antarctica, 183; Byrd's image as, 287–
  88, 314–15, 402, 416, 430, 456–58;
  desire to find new land mass, 141–42;
  Ellsworth ignored as, 305; MacMillan
  as, 61, 81, 91–92; perishing in Antarctica, 184, 189, 276; Siple as, 191–92;
  traits of, 220–23
Polar Legion Insignia, awarded to Byrd,
  174
Polar sea, MacMillan limiting flights over,
  90–92
Politics: Byrd Associates and, 398–99;
  Byrd dabbling in, 3, 54–57, 314, 417–
  19; Byrd's ambitions in, 58, 292–96; of
  Byrd's business supporters, 387–88,
  398–99; Byrd's connections in, 46, 99;
  in Byrd's family background, 8, 11–12;
  Byrd's influence in, 57, 62, 288, 301–
  4, 401, 423; Byrd's naïveté in, 392,
  395–96, 433; Byrd's tactics in, 58–59;
  national influence of business *vs.,* 386,
  391; over creation of naval aviation
  branch, 47–51; in peace movement,
  392; Roosevelt family split, 56–57; of
  supporters of Iron Curtain Refugee

Committee, 448–49. *See also* Byrd,
Harry Flood (brother)
Pond, James, 150, 172–75, 218, 290
Ponies, Antarctic explorers using, 183–84
Post office, at Little America II, 317, 332
Potaka, Louis H., 334, 339, 361, 375
Poulter, Tom, 325; in BAE II command
structure, 331–32, 335–36, 347–51,
366, 504n72; Byrd at Advance Base and,
342, 349, 354, 356; Byrd's recovery at
Advance Base and, 372–73; dealing with
alcohol problems, 336, 350–51, 361;
rescue attempts from Advance Base and,
206, 354–58, 361–64, 366–70; rescue
of Byrd from Advance Base by, 357–58,
371–73; science on BAE II and, 375,
380–82; snow cruiser designed by, 410;
unpopularity of, 360, 375
Pratt, William, 300
Privacy: Byrd maintaining, 17–18, 21,
172; of Byrd's family, 26–27, 257, 297
Public interest: in Amundsen, 72–74; in
Antarctic expeditions, 177, 218, 307,
401, 413; in Arctic expeditions, 96,
101, 110; in aviation, 147, 166; in BAE
I, 249, 266; in BAE II, 351; in Byrd, 2,
167–68, 169–70, 287, 384–85, 391,
396–97, 443; Byrd using, 226, 295–
96; in Byrd's lecture tours, 172–73,
175; in Byrd's refugee work, 450; in
Byrd's transatlantic flight, 161–63,
169–70; fickleness of, 147; and hunger
for heroism, 147, 166, 170, 179–80; in
South Polar flight, 270; in transatlantic
flights, 152, 153, 156. *See also* Media
Publicity, 178; about BAE I, 233, 249,
287; for Antarctic expeditions, 117,
178; Byrd as showman and, 6, 103,
109, 387, 411–12, 446–47; Byrd over-
doing, 5, 287; for Byrd's Arctic expedition, 16, 106–7; for MacMillan Arctic
Expedition, 73, 81–82, 94, 96–97;
privacy *vs.,* 1, 17–18, 26; for transatlantic flights, 152, 167
Pulitzer, Joseph, 174
Putnam, George Palmer, 106
Putnam's, 218, 290

Quam, Louis, 409
Queen Maud escarpment, Antarctica, 430

Queen Maud Land, British-Norwegian-
Swedish joint expedition to, 439
Queen Maud Mountains, Antarctica: BAE
I and, 267–71; BAE II and, 315–16,
377–78, 380

Radar stations, 436–37
Radford, Arthur, 454–55
Radio, 249; from Advance Base, 340,
345–46, 353–55, 358–60, 366–68,
372; on BAE I, 230, 237, 242, 253,
271–72; on BAE II, 338; broadcasts
from BAE II, 317, 324, 327–28, 339–
40, 351; broadcasts from Little Americas, *204*, 276–77, 288, 331; Byrd asking for Watson to get wave length of,
395–97; Byrd's transatlantic flight and,
153, 162; expanding uses of, 61, 68; on
MacMillan Arctic Expedition, 76, 78,
81–84; on North Pole flight, 119–21;
training on, 78, 260; on U.S. Antarctic
expedition, 415
RAF, 51–53
Railey, Hilton Howell, 282, 491n46; Bro-
phys and, 227, 237–38, 254–57; Byrd
complaining to, 265–66; as Byrd's
business manager, 226–27, 491n46;
Byrds' dissatisfaction with, 289–90,
318; Marie and, 238, 254–59; media
coverage of BAE I and, 250, 258, 264,
276–77; pressing for BAE I evacuation,
280–81; raising money for BAE I, 227,
254, 278–79
Ramey, Roger, 478n39
Ramsey, D. C., 427–28
Rawlins, Dennis: abandoning accusations
of fraud, 138–39; accusations by about
Byrd's polar flight, 126–28, 130, 134–
35, 137–38, 478n37
Rawson, Ken, 362, 375–76, 379–80
Reber, E. E., 72, 83–85, 87, 92
Reckford, Milton A., 300
Reeves, John, 443–46
Reeves Brothers, and Byrd Cloth, *213*,
442–44
Refugees, Byrd's work for, 3, 446, 448–
50, 454
Religion, Byrd's, 149, 245, 247–48, 399
Retreat Camp, 335, 342
Reuter, Ernst, 449

Rhode Island Naval Militia, 30–31

Ritscher, Alfred, 407

Roberts, Brian, 4

Roberts, David, 251–52

Robertson, Ed, 432

Robertson, Reuben B., 455

Robinson, Theodore, 81

Rochefort, Charles, 83

Rocheville, A. C., 89

Rockefeller, David, 253

Rockefeller, John D., Jr., 3, 65, 109, 388; business banquet for Byrd and, 387, 389; Byrd's political activities and, 302, 304–5, 391, 397; relationship with Byrd, 148–49, 266, 305; supporting Byrd's Antarctic expeditions, 218, 317; supporting Byrd's Arctic expeditions, 65–67, 70, 104–6, 109–10, 146

Rockefeller Mountains, Antarctica, *208,* 237, 244–47

Rodgers, Eugene, 225, 245–46, 260, 265

Rodgers, John, 47

Ronne, Edith "Jackie," 320

Ronne, Finn, 126, 129, 453, 479n41; accusations about Byrd's polar flight, 136–37; Antarctic expeditions of, 320, 405–6, 438–42; on BAE II, 318, 330, 332, 377; on Byrd at Advance Base, 362–63, 375, 502n36; Byrd's influence on career of, 438, 479n41, 511n14; dislike for Byrd, 5, 128, 281, 332; International Geophysical Year and, 440–42; setting up Advance Base, 343, 346; withdrawing from group dynamics, 336–37, 381, 504n72

Ronne, Martin, 318

Roos, S. Edward, 332–33

Roosevelt, Eleanor, 448; Byrds' friendship with, 29, 298, 313, 395, 424; hosting reception for BAE I, 284–85; pacifism and, 392–93; Young Men's Democratic Club and, 301–2

Roosevelt, Franklin D., 12, 48, 58, 384, 391; on Antarctica, 313–14, 407, 497n2; Byrd's Arctic expedition and, 65; Byrd's disagreements with, 401, 425; Byrds' friendship with, 3, 28–29, 150, 178, 298, 313, 394–95, 424; Byrd's navy report on postwar planning

and, 422; on Byrd's navy service, 30, 57; Byrd's political activities and, 301, 393–95; Byrd trying to help, 302–4, 417–19; on collective security, 392, 394; commendations for Byrd's transatlantic flight, 45–46; Eleanor's differences from, 392–93; ending friendship with Byrd, 393–95; in family split, 56–57; helping BAE II, 313, 316, 319; hosting reception for BAE I, 284–85; ignoring Watson's request for radio station, 395–97; U.S. Antarctic Service and, 404, 408–9, 413–14

Roosevelt, Teddy, 13

Roosevelt, Theodore, Jr., 56–57, 67

Roosevelt Island, Antarctica, 248

Root, Elihu, 301

Rosendahl, Governor, 79–80

Rosshavet Company, 280

Ross Ice Shelf, 183–84, 216, 355; Advance Base on, 7–8; aerial mapping of, 430; Byrd looking for land under, 277; missions across, 252, 377; Poulter's seismological study of, 381; upheavals of, 327

Ross Sea, 185, 456; BAE I and, 228, 231, 282; connection to Weddell Sea, 266, 269, 376–77, 379–80; ice in, 190, 428–29

Roth, Benny, 237

Round-the-world flight, 60–61, 71

Round-the-world trip, Byrd's childhood, 18–21

Rucker, Joe, 250–51, 279

Ruppert, Jacob, 387, 389

Russell, Richard, 324, 348, 377–79

Ryan, Thomas Fortune, 53–54

Rymill, John, 416

Saetimo Light, 111–12

Saturday Evening Post, articles by Byrd in, 171, 176

Sawyer Bay, 89–90

Scandals, lack of, 5

Scandinavia, 458–59

Schlesinger, Arthur, Jr., 448–49

Schlossbach, Ike, 320, 362–63, 373

Schur, Meinhard "Billy," 72–73, 83–84, 89, 95, 97

Science: as Byrd's motive for transatlantic flight, 156, 162; Byrd's opinions on, 390, 402–3, 421; Byrd's reputation for, 165, 171, 282, 397; Deep Freeze I to establish scientific stations, 455

Science, on Antarctic expeditions, 6, 165, 184–89, 216–17, 224, 376, 438, 511n15

Science, on BAE I, 215, 288; accomplishments in, 229, 258, 269–70, 285; boredom of scientists, 240–41; geology, 260, 267–68

Science, on BAE II: accomplishments of, 365, 378, 381–82; combined with rescue from Advance Base, 361, 363; geological mission led by Quin Blackburn, 377–79; in goals for expedition, 316, 349; Lindsey's Sealarium, 373; measuring elevation of ice, 380; missions for, 375, 377; oceanographic measurements, 332–33; organization of, 332, 375, 377; seismological studies, 380–81; specialists for, 318–19; weather monitoring, 249, 365, 372

Science, on polar expeditions, 288–89, 382–83

Science, on U.S. government expedition to Antarctica, 410, 412

Science, on U.S. IGY expedition, 453–55, 460

"Scientific Work of the Second Byrd Antarctic Expedition, The" (Poulter), 382

Scott, Robert Falcon, 183, 189, 216, 223, 332; death of, 179–80, 184

Scott-Amundsen South Pole Station, 461

Seals, in Antarctica, 456

Secret Land, The (movie), 430

78 Club, 260–61

Shackleton, Ernest, 183–84, 187, 223; Antarctic expedition by, 185, 188, 216, 260; death of, 180, 189

Shenandoah (dirigible), 60–61, 63–64, 93–94

Shenandoah Valley Academy, 21–22

Sheridan, Ann, *197*

Sherman, Forrest, 434

Sherwood, Robert E., 403

Shinn, Conrad "Gus," 429, 461

Ships: dangers of sailing near Antarctica,

185, 188, 325–26, 438; icebreakers for IGY expedition, 452, 453, 455–56; for polar expeditions, 280, 309

Ships, for Arctic expeditions, 102, 112–13

Ships, for BAE I, *198, 202,* 222, 227, 234, 254, 268; maneuvering through ice, 228–30, 243; problems with, 225, 228; selection of, 224–25, 237. *See also Bolling; City of New York*

Ships, for BAE II, 316–17, 330–31, 381; Byrd procuring, 305–6, 310; heading south, 320–21, 325; timetable for, 314, 325, 334. *See also Bear of Oakland; Jacob Ruppert*

Ships, for Byrd's Arctic expedition, 110

Ships, for Hobbs's Arctic expedition, 103

Ships, for MacMillan Arctic Expedition, 76–77, 80–81

Ships, for Operation Highjump, 428–29, 432

Ships, for Ronne's expedition, 438

Ships, for U.S. government expedition to Antarctica, 410, 412

Ships, for U.S. IGY expedition, 452–53, 458

Shirase, Choku, 332

Shirey, Dr., 333, 336, 348

Shropshire, Ralph, 229

Simplicity, Byrd seeking, 385

Sims, William, 31, 301

Siple, Paul, 290–92, 305; Advance Base and, 7–8, 341, 346, 362–63, 375; on BAE I, 177, 262–64, 279–80; on BAE II, *208,* 286, 310–11, 316, 332, 375–76; on Byrd's leadership, 4–5, 323; Byrd's relationship with, 323, 441; command positions of, 332, 412, 459–61; as polar veteran, 191–92, 335; Ronne and, 438, 440, 441; U.S. IGY expedition and, 452, 456, 459–61; with U.S. government expedition to Antarctica, 409, 412, 416

Skinner, Bernie "Rip," 339, 358, 364, 366

Skyward (Byrd), 16, 19, 50–51, 140, 160, 171

Sloan, Alfred P., 387, 389

Smith, Al, 301, 303

Smith, Dean, 222, 247, 285; accusations against Byrd, 241–42, 244–45,

491n46; explorations by, 242, 277; hatred for Byrd, 273–74, 281; on Owen's
illness, 238–39; in rescue of stranded
party, 244–46, 248; South Polar flight
and, 233, 270–76, 273
Smith Sound, 84–85, 90
Smithsonian Institution, Langley Medal
of, 282
Snow, Ash, 415–16
Snowmobiles, 267, 329
Snow tractors, for BAE II, 7, 202, 329,
376–77, 381; leaving supply depots
with, 334, 375–76; problems with,
338, 362; in rescue from Advance Base,
356–58, 361–62, 364, 366, 369–72;
transporting supplies by, 334, 343
Sokolsky, George E., 432
Sondrestrom base (Greenland), 436
Sorenson, Peter, 88, 89, 96
South Georgia Island, 185
South Pacific, Byrd's missions in, 420
South Pole, 141, 184, 216; Amundsen
reaching, 141, 184–85; BAE II and,
378, 492n52; Deep Freeze I to establish
scientific station at, 455; in Operation
Highjump, 430; race to, 182, 184–85,
220, 236, 265–67; U.S. IGY expedition and, 457; U.S. policy on, 398
South Pole, Byrd's flight to, 151, 274,
276, 288, 492n52; geological mission
and, 267, 269; importance to BAE I,
218, 276
South Pole Station (Scott-Amundsen
South Pole Station), 459–61
Soviet Union, 458; Arctic expeditions and,
427, 435–37; Byrd condemning U.S.
policies toward, 425–26; Iron Curtain
Refugee Committee and, 448–50;
postwar planning against, 421, 435–37
Spirit of St. Louis (Lindbergh's plane), 155,
157
Spitsbergen, Norway, 112, 218; Byrd vs.
Amundsen in, 112–15; in Byrd's polar
expedition plans, 104, 106–7, 111–12;
in Byrd's race to North Pole, 118–20,
122–24, 130, 141; in Wilkins and de
Bayser's polar expedition plans, 102–3
Stalin, Josef, 421
Stancliffe, Olin, 375
Stennis, John, 442

Stevenson, Adlai, 448
Stimson, Henry L., 398
Stonington Island, Antarctica, 417
Struggle, 171
Submarines, 290, 320, 428
Sullivan, Walter, 453–54, 485n2
Sulzberger, Arthur Hays, 387, 398
Summers, Wendell "Windy," 18, 131–32,
137, 247, 251
Sun compass, 85, 107, 119, 122, 135, 140
Supplies, for BAE I, 280; Bolling shut-
tling, 230, 234, 243; depots of, 252,
267–68, 270–72; difficulty of moving
into camps, 190–91, 198, 235; offload-
ing, 243, 250; in planning, 217–19,
224–25
Supplies, for BAE II, 323–24, 381; for
Advance Base, 335, 337–39; gathering,
305–6, 316, 321; Ruppert's crew steal-
ing, 349, 351; for trail missions, 338,
344, 375–76, 377; unloading and
transporting of, 316, 329–34, 351
Supplies, for Byrd's Arctic expedition,
108–9, 118, 120
Supplies, for MacMillan Arctic Expedition, 88
Supplies, for transatlantic flight, 153
Supplies, for U.S. government expedition,
412, 414
Svalbard archipelago, 112, 114, 117, 120
Swanson, Claude, 15, 20, 301; Byrd's
naval rank and, 56–57, 278; support
for Byrd, 26, 31, 46, 316
Sweeney, Edward, 439
Symington, W. Stuart, 435

Tapley, Harold, 253, 312, 349
Taylor, David W., 37–38
Taylor, Myron C., 387, 389
Taylor, Seaman, 25
Television, Byrd's appearances on, 447
Thiel Range, Antarctica, 430
Thomas, Lowell, 387
Thomas Watson Escarpment, Antarctica,
504n9
Thorne, Mike, 200, 269
Thorne (now called Scott) Glacier,
Antarctica, 378
Thule Air Force Base (Greenland), 434–
36, 478n39

Thurmond, Strom, 431
Thurston, Harris, 442–43
Thurston Peninsula, Antarctica, 416
Tidewater Oil Company, 317
Tierra del Fuego, 182
Tingloff, Ivor, *205,* 315, 348–49
Towers, John, 41–42, 44, 47
Transatlantic flights, 288; Byrd and crew
    returning from France after, 166–67,
    169–70; Byrd in charge of navigation
    for, 43–46, 72; Byrd's, 26–27, 157–
    63, 169–70, 173–75, *196,* 434; Byrd's
    goal of advancing aviation through,
    103–4, 152; commendations for Byrd's
    role in, 45–46; continued attempts at,
    152–53, 165–66; crashes in attempts
    at, 153–55, 165–66; in dirigibles, 50–
    52; influence on Byrd's reputation,
    164–65, 169–70; Lindbergh's, 156–
    57, 157; navy in race for, 37–38, 38–
    39, 41–45, 42–44, 55; in one hop,
    150–51; public interest in, 155, 161–
    63; races for, 41–42; routes for, 42–44,
    49–50, 155
Trenchard, Hugh, 47
Truman, Harry S., 123–26, 432–33, 444
Tully, J. M., 436
Tunney, Gene, 389

United Nations, 425–27, 458
United States: claims on Antarctica, 313–
    14, 405, 407, 410–11, 413, 497n2;
    military bases in Greenland, 434; Na-
    tional Security Council's interest in
    IGY, 451–52; occupation of Antarctica,
    408–9, 412
University of Virginia, 22
Urbahn, Bess Balchen, 126
U.S. Antarctic Research Program, 458–
    59; of National Science Foundation,
    189
U.S. Antarctic Service (USAS), 414, 427;
    Byrd leading, 404, 413; effects of war
    on, 410, 412, 417; formation of, 408–
    10
U.S. Ellsworth Scientific Station, 129
U.S. government expedition to Antarctica,
    405–11; aviation in, 409, 414–16;
    Byrd's role in, 414, 416–17; command
    structure of, 412, 416, 442; departure

of, 412–13; funding for, 409, 412;
    goals of, 413–14
U.S. IGY Antarctic expedition: Byrd's role
    in, 452–55, 457–59; command struc-
    ture for, 452–53, 455–56, 459–61;
    goals of, 457–60; power struggle over,
    453–55
U.S. National Committee, of Internation-
    al Geophysical Year: Byrd's involvement
    in, 451–52; power struggle over, 454;
    Ronne and, 440–42

Van Allen, James A., 335–36, 512n19
Vandenberg, Hoyt, 435
Van der Veer, Will, 250, 282
Vaughan, Norman, *200;* on BAE I, 234–
    35, 262–64, 268–70; BAE II and, 311,
    315–16; on Byrd's leadership, 241,
    488n43; on transatlantic flight, 160–
    61
Verleger, William, 324–25, 351, 381
Victoria Land, Antarctica, 430
Vietnam, 450
Vinson, Carl, 58–59, 83
Virginia Military Institute, 22
Von der Wall, John H., 375–76
Von Drygalski, Erich, 183
Vyvyan, A. V., 53

Wade, Alton, 319, 375, 412
Waite, Amory H. "Bud," 377, 457; at Ad-
    vance Base, 7–8, 373; in rescue from
    Advance Base, *207,* 354–55, 358,
    366–72
Walden, Arthur, 263, 268
Walgreen Coast, Antarctica, 416
Walker, Jimmy, 144, 170
Wanamaker, John, 148
Wanamaker, Rodman, 3, 37, 135, 148,
    163; *America* and, 151–52, 156; Byrd's
    North Pole flight and, 105, 130, 146;
    Byrd's transatlantic flight and, 151–52,
    154, 157–58, 167, 169; encouraging
    transatlantic flights, 42, 150–51
War, 391; Byrd on, 110, 390; required ref-
    erendum for, 393–94, 398–99
Warner, R. A., 54
Warren, Earl, 448
Watson, Thomas, 3; business banquet for
    Byrd by, 386–91; Byrd Associates and,

397–99; funding Byrd, 317, 394, 400; influence of, 386–87; praise for Nazi Germany, 397–98; wanting international radio station, 395–97

Weather: Advance Base to monitor, 7–8, 314–15, 340, 345, 352, 359, 365, 372, 383; in Antarctica, 186, 188, 189–91, 240, 245–46, 249, 269; Antarctica's role in creating global, 216; on BAE I, 225, 229, 243–44, 248, 252–53, 267, 270, 272–73, 277; on BAE II, 320–22, 324, 326, 366–72, 374, 376, 380; Byrd incapable of monitoring at Advance Base, 355–56, 359–60, 364, 370; for Byrd's North Pole flight, 115, 118–19, 122, 134–39; Byrd's transatlantic service for reporting, 153–54; effects of Arctic light on photo quality, 101; effects on MacMillan Arctic Expedition flights, 83–87, 89, 93; effects on polar aviation, 87, 107–8, 430; effects on polar navigation, 140; extreme coldness in Antarctica, 248, 267, 337, 346–47, 491n35; on MacMillan Arctic Expedition, 90–91, 93; measuring Antarctica's, 186, 249, 273, 277, 374; in Operation Highjump, 430; for transatlantic flights, 156–63; for U.S. government expedition, 414–15

Weddell Sea, 185, 187, 190, 453; connection to Ross Sea, 266, 269, 376–77, 379–80; flights over, 306–7, 309

Weir, Robert R., 132

Werfel, Franz, 448

West, James E., 177

West Antarctic Ice Sheet, 376

West Base. See Little America III (West Base)

Whalen, Grover, 144, 146, 152, 154, 169

Whalers: Byrd asking for BAE I evacuation by, 280–81; Larsen as, 230–31; Nazis and, 406, 426; sailing near Antarctica, 182, 185

Whales, chasing BAE I motorboat, 237

Wheeler, Burton K., 417–18, 425

White, Newton, 51

Whiting, Kenneth, 47

Wickes, Elbert, 175–76

Wickiyup camp, 400, 402

Wiener, Murray, 456

Wilbur, Curtis D., 57, 103, 105; on Byrd's aviation feats, 146, 169; MacMillan Arctic Expedition and, 63, 68–69, 85, 90–91; on search for Amundsen, 73–74

Wilkes, Charles, 182, 405, 408

Wilkins, George Hubert: Antarctic expeditions of, 224, 265–66, 305, 491n42; Antarctic flights of, 224, 234, 236, 272–73; Arctic expeditions of, 102–3, 105, 112, 118; plan to take submarine under North Pole, 290, 320

William Horlick (aircraft for BAE II), 316, 379–80

Williams, Al, 411

Williams, R. Gray, 11

Wilson, Woodrow, 12, 26

Winchell, Walter, 432

Winchester, Virginia, 10, 13–15, 22, 27, 464n6

Winchester Star, 16–17, 19–20, 27, 442

Winsor, Robert and Susan, 297

Wiscasset, Maine, 73, 75, 96–97

With Byrd at the South Pole (movie), 287

Wooster, Stanton, 155

World War I, 3, 29, 42, 388; aviation during, 33, 35, 37, 39–40; "Bonus Army" of veterans of, 292–94, 302; Byrd's military service in, 30; effects of, 219–20; military cutbacks after, 46; naval aviation role after, 41

World War II, 401; awareness of drift toward, 388, 403; Byrd wanting to help Roosevelt against isolationists, 417–19; Byrd's service in, 419, 423; Emergency Peace Campaign in, 391–92; outbreak of, 412; U.S. plans for Antarctica and, 409, 417, 426; war fever in U.S., 391, 393

World's Fair (1939), Admiral Byrd's Penguin Island at, 210, 411–12

World's Work, Byrd's article in, 215

Wrigley, Philip K., 62

Wyatt-Brown, Bertram, 17

Young, Owen, 387, 389, 397

Young, William C., 66

Young Men's Democratic Club, Byrd asked to be honorary chair of, 301–2